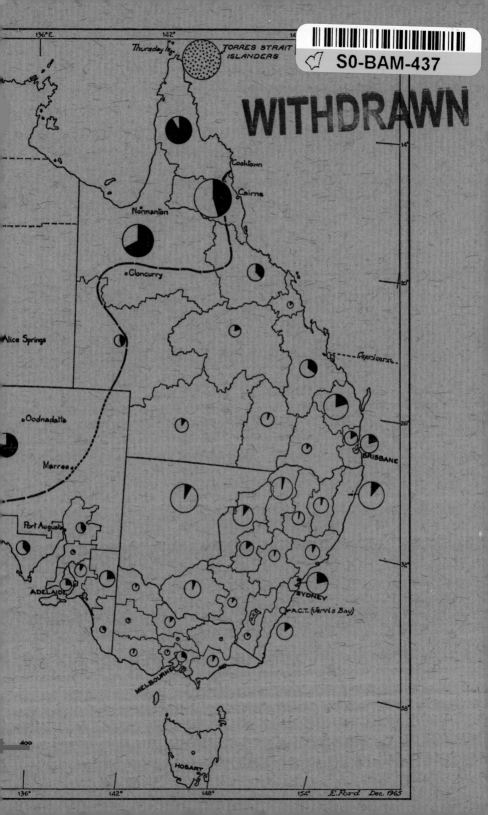

S0-BAM-437

136°E.    142°    148°
Thursday Is.    TORRES STRAIT ISLANDERS

Cooktown
Cairns
Normanton
Cloncurry
Alice Springs
Capricorn.
Oodnadatta
Marree
BRISBANE
Port Augusta
SYDNEY
ADELAIDE
A.C.T. (Jervis Bay)
MELBOURNE
HOBART

400

136°    142°    148°    154°    E. Ford    Dec. 1965

14°
20°
26°
32°
38°

# OUTCASTS
# IN WHITE AUSTRALIA

**Aborigines in Australian Society 6**

A series sponsored by
The Social Science Research Council of Australia

# OUTCASTS
# IN WHITE AUSTRALIA

## ABORIGINAL POLICY
## AND PRACTICE—VOLUME II

*C.D. Rowley*

AUSTRALIAN NATIONAL UNIVERSITY PRESS CANBERRA 1971

# OUTCASTS
# IN WHITE AUSTRALIA

## NOTE ON THE SERIES

The Social Science Research Council of Australia, which was founded in its present form in 1952, is the national organisation of social scientists. Some of its major functions are:

to encourage the advancement of the social sciences in Australia;
to act as a co-ordinating group for the promotion of research and teaching in the social sciences;
to foster research and to subsidise the publication of studies in the social sciences.

To these ends the Council has sponsored a number of major research projects. The first related to the role of women in public and professional life in Australia and was carried out by Mr Norman MacKenzie. His report, together with the associated study of the legal status of women in Australia by Dr Enid Campbell, was published in 1962 in a book, *Women in Australia* (F.W. Cheshire Pty Ltd, Melbourne).

The second major project, carried out by a group of economists, was concerned with the Australian taxation structure and under the authorship of R.I. Downing, H.W. Arndt, A.H. Boxer, and R.L. Mathews, the results were published in 1964 in *Taxation in Australia: Agenda for Reform* (Melbourne University Press, Melbourne).

In 1963 the Council approved its third and most ambitious major project, Aborigines in Australian Society, with the broad objectives of

elucidating the problems arising from contacts between Aborigines and non-Aborigines and formulating policy implications from these;

drawing together existing knowledge in various parts of Australia and undertaking such further original research as can be carried out over a period of three years.

In May 1964, Mr C.D. Rowley, formerly Principal of the Australian School of Pacific Administration in Sydney, was appointed Director of the Project, to work under the general guidance of a Project Committee appointed by the Council. The volumes now being published represent a major research enterprise in which many social scientists collaborated over the length and breadth of Australia.

However, the whole enterprise depended in very large measure on the magnificent support received, from the outset, from the Myer Foundation of Australia and the Sidney Myer Charity Trust. The Council wishes to acknowledge its gratitude for their generosity.

W.D. BORRIE
CANBERRA, 1969

## PREFACE

The concern of this book is with the situation of people of Aboriginal descent (in the main part-Aborigines) in the closely settled areas of Australia; and for this purpose definition must be somewhat arbitrary. I have decided to regard as 'closely settled' those regions of the continent which fall mainly south-east and south-west of the line dividing the endpaper map. The line passes through the census divisions in which those enumerated as *half-caste* are approximately equal in number with those enumerated as *Aboriginal* in the 1961 census.[1] It also approximately separates the areas of sparse pastoral settlement from those which by Australian standards are 'closely settled'. In the sparsely populated regions north of the line, conditions in 1967 were still 'colonial'—typical in many ways of the frontiers with which *The Destruction of Aboriginal Society* is concerned. These conditions are the concern of the third book in this trilogy on Aboriginal Policy and Practice—*The Remote Aborigines*.

Within the vast 'settled' regions there are differences resulting from those past policies and practices of the various State governments on Aboriginal affairs already described. Differences have arisen also from the local variations in ecology, as between, for instance, the environment of a river town and a coastal town in New South Wales, or between south-western Queensland and the environment of the north-eastern coastline, between an area south-west of Port Augusta and an area in the south-east of South Australia, between a town in the centre of the South West Land Division of Western Australia and the environs of towns like Geraldton or Carnarvon.

In the initial stages of this Project my colleague J.P.M. Long and I travelled very widely. Fortunately both of us had had previous experience in Aboriginal affairs, and these travels mainly added to our joint pool of experience. My own experience confirmed my conviction of a basic

[1] This map has been used in previous volumes in the series 'Aborigines in Australian Society'. I wish to acknowledge again that it was drawn by Mr E. Ford from data collated by my colleague J.P.M. Long. Mr Ford also drew the maps reproduced in my other two volumes.

uniformity in social relations. This is, I think, to be expected from the history of settlement and development. The differences between the social facts, broadly considered, correspond with historic phases, so that one seems, as it were, to go back as one approaches and passes our dividing line, from our 'settled' to our 'colonial' regions, into an earlier pattern of race relations.

The differences in State policies have probably had less effect on this pattern than has what was common to all of them. For instance, while it is generally assumed that Tasmania no longer has an Aboriginal 'problem', workers for the Project reported from Cape Barren Island, the home of a very small group of mixed Aboriginal and other descent, a situation and attitudes which could be matched substantially in many other places in the settled regions.[2] The Tasmanian government must have considered that it shared something of a common problem with other governments, because it was represented at the Aboriginal Welfare Conference of 1963, where the assimilation of the islanders was discussed.[3] Here one of the oldest of these residual social situations was presenting a perennial problem to the Tasmanian Department of Social Welfare.[4]

The complexity of the problems facing the research worker, and the enormous dispersal of small groups throughout a continent, has meant that most research effort has been on small areas. The question we had to answer was how, within limited time which was costing money from our limited resources, to choose a few areas which could be managed in the time available, for both descriptive and statistical purposes. For both purposes it was necessary to select.

Should this selection have been of a few widely dispersed small communities? Here the question of costs, in time, effort and money, had to be considered. The background of policy and administration as well as current social and economic facts should, we thought, represent some kind of 'mean' in the range of known current situations.

By the time this book came to be written there was a vast mass of descriptive material and field notes; and of course every small locality was in some way or other unique. For descriptive purposes in Part 2 it seemed best to look for areas which were not remarkable: to avoid, for instance,

[2] Report by P. Wagstaffe, J. Gibson, and J. Manning, based on a visit sponsored by this Project in February 1966: Typescript in SSRC-AP file.
[3] *Aboriginal Welfare: Conference of Commonwealth and State Authorities, Darwin, July 1963: Proceedings and Decisions*, kindly made available (in part) by the Department of Territories.
[4] There was a select Parliamentary Committee to inquire and report in 1948, following prominence of the usual issues in the press during 1947. For a useful article see Heather Meredith, 'Tasmanian Racial Problem—Cape Barren Island', *Honi Soit*, 23 June 1964.

a place like Palm Island, the end of the road for the rigid Queensland policies. It was certain that growing public interest would, before too long, be concentrated on such places. In the end, for reasons of cost and convenience, and because these were areas where the Aborigines were subject to no *known* restrictions special to the area, where in fact the reputation of the towns was that, for Aborigines, they were 'good' ones to live in, I selected my recorded observations on a few unremarkable towns in the mid-west of New South Wales. After having looked at the situations of Aborigines in towns from Cairns to Carnarvon, I believe that in this region they are better off economically and socially than in most rural areas. In parts of Victoria and of the south coast of New South Wales, and in some country towns in South Australia, they seem to have approached a higher degree of acceptance and integration; but one is forever *looking* for people where this has happened, since they may not be thought of as Aboriginal at all.

For rural statistical data on Aboriginal living standards (Part 3) we cast our net wider throughout New South Wales, getting our information in ways which are described below. But here it seemed necessary to find another area where at least some of the possible differences could be brought out. The selection of the Eyre Peninsula of South Australia was a chance one, to the extent that only here was it possible to arrange to have the work done at the right time, under the auspices of the University of Adelaide and the South Australian Department of Aboriginal Affairs.

Also with the sponsorship of universities, it was possible to have metropolitan surveys carried out in Brisbane, Adelaide, and Perth. The results of this work will be published separately—some of it is in this series. Fortunately, Dr Diane Barwick had recently completed a very significant survey of the situation of Aborigines in Melbourne. Her work had spilled over, as it were, into the rural background; and she carried out further work for the Project on the rural areas of that State, with historical background, which in my opinion emphasises the uniformity of the social scene in so far as I was able in the time to study it, both in the literature and 'on the ground'.

If this method of procedure is open to criticism, as it possibly is, I can only say that in order to describe the effects of past policies and practices, having got all the advice from all the sources known to me, I can still think of no better. One advantage of working in New South Wales was that scholars sponsored by the University of Sydney had worked there before. This is, after all, one of the old settled areas. New South Wales first posed a racial problem; and to some extent other policies in the eastern part of the continent were derivative, or reactions, from what was done in the first colony.

The situation of Aboriginal groups in the settled areas has been partly the result of policies to deal with what governments came to regard as a part-Aboriginal 'problem'. It is therefore necessary that we begin this book with a brief account of the emergence of part-Aboriginal social groups and of the policies applied. There have been changes in the laws applicable and in Aboriginal administration since 1967, the cut-off year when the first drafts of these volumes were completed. Some details will thus be out of date in 1971.

C.D. ROWLEY
PORT MORESBY, 1971

# CONTENTS

# TABLES

# THE EMERGENCE OF
I PART-ABORIGINAL COMMUNITIES

1

Today, the descendants of the part-Aborigines have by far the most rapid rate of natural increase of all components of the Australian population; and it is comparable with the highest in the world.[1] Yet it had been easy, back behind the frontiers, to believe that the remnants of Aboriginal society would disappear. Even when predominantly part-Aboriginal groups emerged, they were regarded as no more than vestiges of the old culture and languages, an indication of the passing away of the Aboriginal.

It is suggestive that so little is known of the demography of this section of the population. Even the census figures do not help much, because those of over half-Aboriginal descent have been excluded from censuses, while those thought to be less than *half-caste* (the census term) were counted with the non-Aboriginal population. The figures do offer some indication of relative population densities as between census divisions, but provide little more than a basis for guessing how many people belong to Aboriginal groups. The census categories of *Aboriginal* and *half-caste* could not be so well defined as to offer precise information—another indication that the part-Aboriginal has been regarded by governments as a phenomenon of transition rather than as an end in himself. The 'solution' of the Aboriginal 'problem' would come when he disappeared altogether into a 'white' community without 'coloured' enclaves.

Such a view inhibited the clear emergence of the concept of a separate part-Aboriginal *society* and enhanced the effects of the destruction of

[1] See C.D. Rowley, *The Destruction of Aboriginal Society* (*Aboriginal Policy and Practice*, vol. II), App. B.

Aboriginal society, which prevented the maintenance of more than a fragmentary cultural continuity. The assumption that there was nothing for the part-Aboriginal to inherit from his Aboriginal forebears was true enough of all material assets and rights to material advantage, except for entry to reserves. In a materialist world, his only chance of getting property was from his white ancestors or contemporaries. Thus there was little material point in maintaining careful records. Aboriginal paupers formed ill-defined groups; perhaps they amounted to a separate population, but not to a recognised community.

When a person could escape into more comfortable circumstances he would often do so. But those who were handicapped by appearance and lack of education could not. They remained chiefly in small local groups, without linking organisations other than kinship ties; and they remained politically powerless—so much so that at least until recently government welfare agencies could operate almost without having to give a thought to political questions.

Governments with large 'full-blood' populations tried by means of segregation to limit further part-Aboriginal births. At the same time they came to formulate policies which involved the disappearance of part-Aborigines through miscegenation. Conveniently the 'full-bloods' seemed to be dying out; the part-Aborigines were to be placed in such situations that there would eventually be no traces of them.

Administrative and political decisions could and did correlate culture and 'blood', the degree of Aboriginal 'blood' being used for racial definition. Some legislation made separate categories of *half-caste* or other part-Aborigines, mainly for those whose 'associations' did not already bring them within the Aboriginal category. Most visible part-Aborigines came within the definitions of *Aboriginal*, were treated in the same way— and therefore reacted in the same way—and thus justified continuation of the treatment. In the 1930s some categories were widened (as in Western Australia, with the adoption of the *native* category) to make sure that persons whose poverty and/or recalcitrance were associated with membership of Aboriginal communities shared in the welfare measures. Courts commonly had power to decide on appearance whether a person was legally Aboriginal.

Part-Aborigines, by the time of the 1961 census, outnumbered those classed as *Aboriginal* (over half-Aboriginal descent), in the areas south-east and south-west of the line drawn on the endpaper map.[2] Reference to

---

[2] On the data for this map and their derivation, see ibid., p. 375.

the 'settled areas' in this and later chapters indicates these areas of south-eastern and south-western Australia, not only because of the demographic data but also because they include most of the closely settled country and exclude the sparsely settled pastoral regions.

## GROWTH OF THE PART-ABORIGINAL POPULATION

The earliest legislation of a colony, specifically to establish a pattern of Aboriginal administration, after the frontier had passed on, was the Act to provide for the Protection and Management of the Aboriginal Natives of Victoria, in 1869. It was the first comprehensive law adopted by a colonial parliament to apply to Aborigines; and it so defined the term as to include 'every Aboriginal half-caste or child of a half-caste, such half-caste or child habitually associating or living with Aboriginals'. When in doubt, a justice could decide whether a person was Aboriginal by sighting him; he could make the decision 'in his own view and judgment' (section 8).

By this time, of an estimated 11,500 Aborigines at the time when the first settlers came to take up land at Port Phillip, there remained a known total of 1,834, and of these an unknown proportion were of part-Aboriginal descent. By 1887 the total was down to just over 800, with about 32 per cent classified as 'half-caste'.[3]

By the time of the 1901 census, half-castes outnumbered full-bloods, with 58 per cent of the total of 652. By 1911 the proportion was 69 per cent. By 1921 when the census recorded its lowest total of persons of Aboriginal descent for Victoria, 442 of the total of 586 were recorded as half-caste—about 75 per cent. But for reasons stated elsewhere,[4] there is a tendency of Aborigines to claim full-blood descent at the census; and it is probable that the 53 of the 662 shown in the *Commonwealth Year Book* for 1928 is a clearer indication of the trend. The best indication of the current Victorian population is from the research of Dr Barwick, who in 1963 believed that of some 3,000 Aborigines in the State there might be ten of the full descent.[5]

The figures cannot be taken as more than approximations of the numbers living 'after the manner' of Aborigines. But the pattern repre-

---

[3] The figures were collated from the Radcliffe-Brown estimate (1930) and from the Protection Board Reports by Dr Diane Barwick in A Little More Than Kin: Regional Affinity and Group Identity Among Aboriginal Migrants in Melbourne, Table V.

[4] See *The Destruction of Aboriginal Society*, App. B.

[5] A Little More Than Kin, Table V.

sents almost a completed range of genetic changes: which was, in the event, probably to be completed in Victoria, certainly in Tasmania long before, with the death of the last Aboriginal person of the full descent.

Policy-makers predisposed to equate social conditions with racial origin would see here a 'problem' in the course of working itself out, or of being as it were removed by a curious combination of Divine Providence and the law of the survival of the fittest. All that was required now was to use intensive methods (later referred to as 'social engineering') to change the lives and aspirations of a few hundred part-Aborigines, while the Aborigines went on dying out or having only part-Aboriginal children. But means determine ends; and the few hundred, now increased to a few thousand, have presented a greater political 'problem' in Victoria over the last decade than ever before, because they have learned how to express publicly their reactions to injustices intended to hasten assimilation. The same injustices have probably done more than anything else to strengthen the determination of persons of Aboriginal descent to retain their in-group loyalties and identity.

Similar processes of genetic change have occurred in the wake of each of the frontiers of settlement. It is easier to see them in Tasmania, where the few part-Aborigines who live in the typical 'fringe' or 'reserve' situation (although not legally or even administratively dealt with as presenting an Aboriginal 'problem'), are to be found on Cape Barren Island; or in the small State of Victoria.

In the larger States, especially in Western Australia, which extends over a third of the continent, from the Bight to the Timor Sea and from the Indian Ocean to the central desert regions, such a process, practically completed in the south-west, may be counter-balanced by another, more recent, resurgence of the full-blood population in the northern and central areas. By 1903 there were reported to be 850 known *half-castes* throughout this huge State; and the officer in charge of the Aborigines Department was concerned about such things as the education of the children and the fact that although *half-castes* living with Aborigines were Aboriginal for the purposes of the Aborigines Act 1905, they were not so for the purposes of the liquor legislation; and here too the process of drafting legislation to give more extensive powers of protection and restriction had begun.[6] By 1917 the total of all 'natives' was still not known; but the Annual Report for that year estimated 24,491, of whom at least 1,603 were *half-castes*. A high birthrate in this part-Aboriginal population,

[6] *W.A.P.P.*—Aborigines Department, Reports for Financial Years ending 30 June 1901, 1902, and 1903.

especially in the farming regions and round the towns of the south-west, was offsetting what must have been high mortality in the reported housing and sanitation conditions; already in 1904 there were reported to be over 500 children under sixteen years (something over 50 per cent of the reported total). H.C. Prinsep, the Chief Protector, was advocating legislation to make him their legal guardian so that some kind of schooling could be arranged. (They were generally not allowed into the public state schools.)[7]

No doubt this increase, which by no means matched the total increase of the non-Aboriginal population, allowed prejudice a freer rein, since employment was difficult for these people at most times except during the period of the two world wars. It must have made easy the enforced removal under warrant of both part-Aborigines and the Aborigines in the south-west region, to the settlements at Moore River and Carrolup, and also the 'clearing' of some towns by the removal of unwanted coloured folk into what, in spite of the professed intentions of the government, amounted to concentration camps for every type of 'problem' case.

In 1929 the Annual Report of the Chief Protector in Western Australia noted that the 'increasing half-caste population more than balances the diminishing full-blood people. The half-castes have married among themselves and are in the third and fourth generation'. On the basis of current views of what the Australian population ought to be, there were those who saw dangers in this situation. Thus the *West Australian* in December 1929 commented in an editorial on the half-caste 'problem': 'Half-castes were not greatly in evidence years ago, but they are now in second and third generations particularly in the southern areas of the State.' One of the 'problems' was that a court had ruled that offspring of two *half-caste* parents was not a *half-caste* within the meaning of the Act; this had led to 'defiance of departmental control'. Where such children were females, the *West Australian* said, 'there is danger of aggravating a social blot'. The real worry was of an accelerating increase within what should, by the standards of the new Australian nationalism, be a centre of 'white Australia'. According to A.O. Neville, the Chief Protector, the total had reached 3,000 by 1930.[8] Five years later he reported a total 'native' population of 26,442, of whom 4,245 were *half-castes*. 'Since

---

[7] Prinsep's draft Bill is in his Annual Report for 1904. For many of these references I am indebted to Dr Ruth Fink (now Lātūkefu),who made her notes, taken from the reports and other documents, available to this Project.

[8] Article in *West Australian* (Perth), 18 April 1930.

1915 the character of our work has gradually changed; the half-caste question, then in its infancy, has now assumed formidable proportions.'[9]

The official fuss about a few thousand persons of unsuitable complexion, and the concurrence by the Western Australian government in the prejudice of country town people, which was forcing these persons out of the schools and even out of the towns, is an excellent illustration of how prejudice creates its own special problems. Where there is a special branch of government involved, there will be a tendency for it to magnify its tasks. This is a tendency of any public service department or agency over a period. An Aboriginal affairs department had some of the advantages of the armed forces in that its expressed aim (of getting rid of the Aboriginal 'problem') appealed to prejudices so deep-seated that it was comparatively easy for it to avoid any drastic re-thinking of the need for its work. It probably contributed, in each State, as much to the 'problems' it was ostensibly solving as any other single factor. There is something reminiscent of Lilliputian politics, both in the scale and in the degree of logical absurdity, in the administration of Aboriginal affairs at this time.

The proportion was probably much higher than was appearing in the reports, where Neville, then Chief Protector and later Commissioner of Native Affairs, was reporting in the late 1930s some ten thousand full-bloods 'outside the confines of civilisation'.[10] On counted figures, the proportion of *half-castes* was about one-quarter of the State total by this time. Part of the increase would have come from the more extensive definition of the term *native*, which had been introduced as a general one for the whole population under control in the 1936 Native Administration Act. On the other hand, Neville complained that the enumeration had included persons 'of three-quarter Aboriginal blood' among the 'full-bloods'. Census-takers would, in most cases, have had to make rule of thumb judgments based on skin coloration.

By the time of the 1961 census the numbers recorded were just over 8,000 for both *Aboriginals* and *half-castes*, with an estimate of about 2,000 *Aboriginals* not counted. But by this time the part-Aborigines were one of the most rapidly increasing groups of people anywhere in the world;

[9] *W.A.P.P.*, 1935, vol. 2, no. 22—Annual Report of the Chief Protector of Aborigines . . . .
[10] See, for instance, *W.A.P.P.*, 1938, vol. 1, no. 2—Annual Report of the Commissioner of Native Affairs for the Year ended 30th June, 1937—Population—p. 5. Neville stated that in his opinion the figure was 'too large'. It represented the results of assuming that numbers in the country away from the stations were comparable with those round the stations, an assumption which failed to allow for the factors attracting and forcing the Aboriginal people out of tribal life.

and Aborigines of the full descent were also increasing much more rapidly than the non-Aboriginal population, exclusive of the effects of immigration. Western Australia, with its share of most of the typical Australian historical and geographic situations, may be taken as fairly representing what happened over the continent as a whole. What may have appeared an inevitable historical process of the Aboriginal bowing out before the superior civilisation (from the point of view of any Australian of normal prejudice looking at the southern areas of this State, at Tasmania, or at Victoria, at the beginning of the century) had become some thirty years later in Western Australia (almost as much earlier in Victoria) a different kind of question, with the growth of the part-Aboriginal group (which must on the premises have inherited something of the capacity of the 'superior' race to survive). While the full-bloods continued to dwindle, 'assimilation' could be equated with a process of genetic change in the proper direction. When it became clear later that the Aborigines of over half and of full descent were also increasing, the tendency to see 'assimilation' as a very long process also increased.

Figure 1 represents the rate of decline of those recorded to be of full Aboriginal descent, and the process of racial mixing, in the population considered to be Aboriginal in New South Wales, from 1882 until the

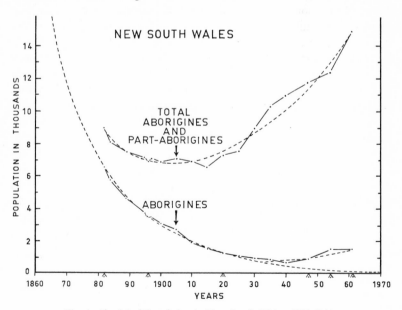

Fig. 1. Aboriginal Population in New South Wales, 1882-1961

1961 census. (The 1966 census established a new base-line for future calculations by introducing new questions.) This graph is based on statistics of those who were easily identifiable as Aboriginal because they were the concern of Aboriginal legislation or administration and subject to special provisions of government, in the period 1882-1961. The year 1882 marked the beginning of an organised government effort to give protection, and the establishment of the Aborigines Protection Board to work with the mission organisations in the Aborigines Protection Association and to provide other relief.

It is interesting to note the early assumptions in the New South Wales Parliament that there would be no need to increase the vote for 1883, for instance, as the Aborigines were decreasing; while the Aborigines Protection Association was showing on its missions at Maloga and Warangesda that the 'half-castes' could be trained to be 'useful members of society'.[11]

There was reference to the need to take the 'near-white' children from their mothers and to 'train' them in institutions. The purposes of the annual vote included aid to the Association, to be spent in accordance with the principles governing other government assistance to charities: in this case the government would grant £2 for every £1 raised by the Association. Though part of this was to temper the hardships of the Aborigines of full descent assumed to be passing away, the discussions exemplified the belief that the part-Aboriginal should be brought into the settler economy.[12] But New South Wales did not develop an explicit theory, from what was implicit, as the basis for an administrative policy relating to the part-Aborigines, even to the extent that Victoria did so, until it adopted and proclaimed a policy of assimilation for all of Aboriginal descent, just before World War II. There was not even a basic Act until 1909.

The 1883 Report of the Protector of Aborigines (who was also the Commissioner of Police) included a census of Aborigines and half-castes listed separately, apparently by the local police officers in each police district, with comments. The comments reveal almost as much about the officers and their attitudes as they do about the local Aborigines and part-Aborigines. There were officers who believed that the part-Aboriginal

[11] See for instance N.S.W.P.D., 1883, First Series, vol. 8, pp. 598-601—speeches by A. Stuart, S.W. Gray, R. Barbour, F.B. Suttor, and W.J. Fergusson.

[12] In the parliamentary discussions from 1883 to the end of the century there was the usual range of attitudes, from the highly prejudiced and inimical to the paternally sympathetic. In the same period the vote rose from £3,600 to over £13,000, partly because of the depression and the droughts of the 1890s.

had inherited the 'worst of both races'. But there were others who had a real respect for both full-blood and half-caste; and many of either classification, in the western districts, were by this time earning equal pay with whites, in skilled work such as fencing and shearing. There was good reason for the belief that the part-Aboriginal could move into the general economy.

The discussions in Parliament in the first couple of decades suggest what the barriers were to be. It is clear that already, where there was close settlement, times were getting harder for members of the Aboriginal group. In the late 1880s the Member for Gwydir pointed out that where they used to be employed as shepherds, they now had to wander in search of a living; that this was getting more difficult with erection of fences and further destruction of the game. The Member from the Bogan area said in the same debate that it would not have been possible to hear such kindly references to Aborigines two or three decades before, because they used to compete with white workers; he assumed that now they did not.[13] Perhaps in most areas there is a memory of better times after the frontier violence had passed on and before the farmers came with fences and activities based on family labour. R. Hausfeld found such memories among the people on the Woodenbong Station in the 1950s; and Jeremy Beckett has written of the traditions perpetuated in the folk songs of the Wilcannia people, of the high-spending, hard-drinking frontier days.

Nor were they likely to be able to compete in a rapidly changing situation. There were references to the education of the children; Members from all parts of the State told of children out of school. Thus the Member for Tamworth claimed in 1889 that of a total of 2,855 of school age (the figure seems to have included those *under* school age) only 323 went to the public schools. They were already in some places being forced out of the schools, as at Yass, though there were occasional approving references to the Aboriginal community.[14]

It is clear from the debates that the group as a whole, including the part-Aborigines, was not wanted in the new towns. The emphasis was on reserves, and on a somewhat limited charity, the administration of which was continually under criticism—of the poverty of a ration which, except in cases where there was reputed to be no game available, did not include meat; of the blanket issue; of the rations actually issued which did not meet the minimum standards—so that on one occasion a Member

---

[13] See *N.S.W.P.D.*, 1887-8, vol. 34, pp. 5877-84.
[14] *N.S.W.P.D.*, 1889, vol. 41, pp. 4347-55. See speeches by Sir Henry Parkes, J. Abbott, and W.S. Dowel.

arrived in the House with a sample of rotten meat from the ration. There is a great need of some social history of this situation.

By the end of the century these people in New South Wales could certainly not have been living in the Aboriginal tradition. Much of the 'wandering' referred to was obviously of the kind which is still maintained —the movement of the seasonal worker after employment. The one could merge into the other without making any particular impression on a sporadically and casually interested government. Thus the growing part-Aboriginal population seems to have remained, as everywhere else, part of the changing Aboriginal society. European descent was not really relevant, except for those who could 'pass'. In this State there was talk, but no consistent attempt (though there were sporadic ones on some of the Aboriginal stations) to push the half-caste off in a direction separate from the full-blood. What mainly happened was a tendency, when it suited the administrator, to deny special assistance to a person who was of 'light caste' (a term which later came much into use). On the other hand, it was probably convenient during the depression years to include all 'castes' in the efforts which were made to remove groups from the town fringes and on to the stations.

There was no effort to handle the 'half-caste problem' in New South Wales as a special sphere of administrative effort. The Aboriginal question was seen rather as one for a limited charity, with the identifiable persons of mixed descent taking the place of the full-bloods. There were those in Parliament who were optimistic that the half-caste would merge into the 'white' population; and those who saw not even this hope for a 'solution'.

After the turn of the century the main effort of the Board was spent on the management of stations and small reserves, on the special apprenticeship system for youths and domestic service for girls, and the usual limited relief, until the late 1930s, when the State adopted its new policy of assimilation. This was proposed as a new policy, and as a departure from an older policy of 'protection'; but the protection had been minimal and sporadic. That there was no separate aim for the half-caste arose from the fact that, unlike Western Australia or Queensland, New South Wales did not contain within its borders a large group of persons of the full Aboriginal descent likely to continue indefinitely as the source of unwanted coloured folk unless special measures were taken to isolate them.

This does not, however, account for the difference between New South Wales and Victorian policy. Perhaps the greater Victorian concern to eliminate persons of light 'caste' from the operation of the legislation was partly due to the smaller numbers involved, so that the problem could appear more easily manageable. But there was also the long history of attempts to manage what seemed a disappearing problem, with a continuity, tenuous at times to be sure, from the days of the Port Phillip Protectorate. This led in Victorian circles to a higher degree of optimism, expressed when governments began to confer on Aboriginal affairs in statements that Victoria no longer had a problem.

When in 1896 Archibald Meston made his report on the Aborigines of Queensland, he was concerned mainly with the more chaotic conditions of the far northern frontier, where the Native Police still operated as the main instrument of government policy. But he was also concerned with the miserable conditions of the part-Aborigines who in a situation almost of *laissez-faire*, except in so far as they partook of the occasional ration and blanket distributions, were beginning to inherit the role of their Aboriginal forebears, especially round the towns of the south-east. He recommended the total exclusion of Aborigines from towns, except those in regulated employment; and more reserves in the south as well as in the mid-north and far north, in addition to the land made available for missions up to that time.[15] The first comprehensive Aboriginal legislation of the following year included in the Aboriginal category the *half-caste* members of Aboriginal families and other *half-castes* who 'habitually' lived or associated with Aborigines; in the context these would have included all of Aboriginal appearance.[16]

The proportion of part-Aborigines in the total 'Aboriginal' population, at the turn of the century, cannot be estimated. The 1901 census indicated 26,670 Aborigines in Queensland—a figure higher than that of any State and some 3,000 higher than that for the Northern Territory. The count must have included many of part-Aboriginal descent; but even allowing for an unusually high proportion for that time, one can only account for the high figure as the result of a very rough guess.[17]

The first Act indicated the obsession with the remaining full-bloods. But the amending Act of 1901 indicated the concern with miscegenation in, for example, the right of a protector to control marriage of female Aborigines, and the prohibition of visitors to Aboriginal camps.[18] By the

---

[15] Meston's Report is discussed in *The Destruction of Aboriginal Society*. It may be found in Q.V. & P. (L.A.), 1896, vol. 4, p. 723.

[16] Aboriginals Protection and Restriction of the Sale of Opium Act 1897, section 4.

[17] Bureau of Census and Statistics, *Commonwealth Year Book* No. 1 (1901-7), p. 145. For an expert comment on this and other figures of 1901 see F. Lancaster Jones, *The Structure and Growth of Australia's Aboriginal Population*.

[18] Q.P.D., 1901, vol. LXVII, and Aboriginals Protection and Restriction of the Sale of Opium Act, 1901, sections 9, 16, 17, and 19.

1930s the Minister in charge of the Bill for the 1934 Act, which made sexual intercourse with an Aboriginal woman an offence, could claim that he was making an honest attempt to deal with the 'evil' of half-caste children born to 'white' men. But in this he was going no further than to express the opinion of J.W. Bleakley, who was an acknowledged expert in these matters and who some years before had been borrowed to advise the Commonwealth on its Aboriginal administration in the Northern Territory. Bleakley, cut off from any contact with cross-cultural administration overseas, and with no more qualification for the task than had Neville in Western Australia (and that both were hard working, well-meaning men, acting in accordance with the popular folklore of their day, one cannot deny), like Neville, stated his policies loudly and often. In his 1929 Report he had written that

policy is to check as far as possible the breeding of half-castes, by firmly discouraging miscegenation. Every effort is made to encourage the marriage of those now with us to people of their own race . . . The cross-breed element provides the most difficult part of the 'Aboriginal' problem, as what they inherit of the superior intelligence and tastes of the whites is generally nullified by the retarding instincts of the blacks.

From the first Act in 1897 there had been provision for exemption of individual *half-castes* from its operation: but 'only a minority can be safely trusted to manage their own affairs'; and in 1929 he had exempted only twenty-nine.[19]

Both Bleakley and Neville later wrote books in which they expounded their ideas at length. In 1961 Bleakley was to say, looking back on his long experience, that 'all mixed-blood races labour under social and temperamental handicaps.' He had the humanity and common sense to realise the environmental and social handicaps; but his final explanation of failure was in the effects of racial mixture.

The most difficult of these handicaps to combat, in the measures to uplift them, is the hereditary Aboriginal temperament. This is often likely to assert itself, even where the person has been brought up in infancy amongst whites or rescued from the degrading atmosphere of camp life. With this type it was not so much a matter of the colour of the skin as the colour of the mind.[20]

It is necessary in fairness to point out here that during Bleakley's administration there was little criticism of these views as basic explanations of the Aboriginal predicament. This was the folklore on which adminis-

---

[19] Q.P.P., 1929, vol. I, p. 1215—Report of the Sub-Department of Aboriginal Affairs.
[20] J.W. Bleakley, *The Aborigines of Australia*, p. 314.

tration and legislation was based; and in this social context Bleakley was outstanding as one who fought for what was then considered an advanced policy for the protection of the Aboriginal people. It was largely because of his work that Queensland was leading the way in expenditure on Aborigines; that even today the settlements are better equipped with housing and facilities than those of any other State; that the special Aboriginal wage system remained far in advance, for instance, of that established by the Commonwealth in the Northern Territory. In some ways he expressed the conscience of his day, in the reaction against the abuse which had led to the beginning of a harsh protective legislation in 1897. There seemed, and may well have been, no other way.

One must also remember that it was during the period of his administration that the new science of psychology, assuming inherent racial differences in intelligence, set out to measure them; and that the general assumption that there are none which can be measured came partly from these efforts. Bleakley was obviously a humane and compassionate man, attempting to apply in all honesty the best policies known to him; with all the resources he had, he tried to remedy as far as possible what seemed mental handicaps by suitable tuition and educational experience. One must remember, too, that the expressions of one historical period have to be understood in their context. His reference to 'the colour of the mind' came from a vast experience of the intractability of the person who has been socialised after one fashion, and who from habit and loyalty to what he has learned to know and respect will resist efforts to change him. Only now are we beginning to learn a little of the complicated processes of social change and of the effects of early socialisation on the individual. And our knowledge is so incomplete that our more 'advanced' views today may well bring the scorn of future scholars who study them out of their social context.

But Aboriginal people were reacting to government policies and pressures then much as they had always done, and do now. Things common to all humanity are more fruitful for the study of government policies than the differences: and most of the attitudes of the Aboriginal minority can be adequately accounted for as likely to have been developed by any minority in similar circumstances. It is therefore worth some thought that Bleakley was in many ways the theoretician of Queensland Aboriginal policy.

By 1935 there were 4,896 known *half-castes* in the State; by this time 65 per cent of all births into this category were officially stated to be of part-Aboriginal parentage on both sides, and an additional 16 per cent were of Aboriginal women and part-Aboriginal fathers.[21] The same situation was currently causing Neville, an administrator of like mind, concern in Western Australia, and worrying Dr C.E. Cook, the Chief Protector in the Northern Territory. As a result, the half-caste 'problem' had a thorough airing at the first conference of Commonwealth and State administrators in 1937. It was becoming clear that part-Aborigines were developing a tendency to marry within the part-Aboriginal group, and, without some special pressures, were likely to increase rather than conveniently disappear into white Australia. This was especially annoying in the light of scientific advice, that in the case of the Aboriginal such disappearance was quite feasible: that the objectionable differences of appearance, assumed so easily to reflect the objectionable 'colour of the mind', could, with the co-operation of those concerned, be 'bred out'.

In the mid-1930s the 'half-caste problem' was of comparable size in Queensland and in Western Australia. By 1946, the annual report of the Native Affairs Sub-Department in Queensland estimated 9,300 *Aboriginals* and 6,480 *half-castes*. In both cases, the same idea that racial origin was a decisive factor in social change had led the administrations into the concept of a double-ended problem, which was to have its effect on the legislation and methods of control. North of the line used in the end-paper map to demarcate the 'settled' from the 'colonial' regions was the predominantly full-blood population. In Queensland, however, the habit developed early of sending 'problem' cases among the part-Aborigines in the settled areas to distant missions in the north. This, plus the somewhat rough-and-ready methods of census-taking among the full-bloods (where the purpose was to *exclude* them from the count) leaves the comparable estimates of *half-castes* and *Aboriginals* open to question. But it is the most reliable count available. In 1961 it indicated that *half-castes* outnumbered *Aboriginals* in Queensland by approximately 11,000 to 8,000.

It would certainly be going too far to assert that this 'problem' sprang only from the minds of government officials and others working in Aboriginal affairs. Racist concepts of causation in social affairs must have deepened the division between Aboriginal society, or what remained of it, and the part-Aboriginal groups. The part-Aboriginal problem of identity, with the consciousness of the non-Aboriginal heritage, would be enough to create difficulties in the way of the two outcast groups making common cause. Where adherence to the Aboriginal Law remained, these

21 Ibid., p. 315.

difficulties, and the relationship of the Law to traditional patterns of marriage, would have been enough to disrupt the handing on of traditions. Many part-Aborigines appear to have been accepted and initiated, but the vast majority would have been looking to the settler economy for opportunity—just as the Aborigines were; so that the real barrier was probably the apparent pointlessness of the indigenous tradition for most of the part-Aboriginal youth.

With the rapid breakdown of Aboriginal patterns of socialisation, the groups in contact would have shared the methods of child-rearing in the fringes and camps, producing a new generation likely to appear barbarous by the standards of either culture. Here was the beginning of the hierarchy of colour which has been noted by anthropologists like Marie Reay and Ruth Fink in country-town Aboriginal groups. For the part-Aboriginal who could not 'pass', and for those whose loyalty to family and group has made attempts to do so appear as treachery, the only possible emotional identity had to be with the Aboriginal tradition. But the wholesale destruction of Aboriginal society meant that this could amount to little more than a stubborn adherence to remembered cultural remnants, supplemented with the folklore of persecution. The economic needs of the part-Aborigines constantly drew them in to the growing points of the settler society in the towns. Here, in the fringe settlements, the tensions arising from their plight have maintained till the present day patterns of behaviour which stimulate prejudice.

South Australian policy was to concentrate government effort on the south-eastern area and, even within this region, mainly on questions arising from the management of the missions, which became government stations, at Point Pearce and Point McLeay. Until very recently, for instance, there was no effective Aboriginal administration in those parts of the State which fall within the 'colonial' regions.

Today with the exception of Gerard mission [wrote Fay Gale, in 1964] there are not a dozen full bloods living within the agricultural belt south of Port Augusta and east of Spencer Gulf. Yet within this same area in 1860, when already full blood numbers had diminished, 11,048 full bloods were receiving rations from five ration depots.[22]

Dr Gale points out that special legislation for an Aboriginal 'problem' began with a law of 1844 relating to half-caste children. The limitation of administrative effort to the closely settled regions, other than in the maintenance of ration depots, at least made possible her important study

[22] Fay Gale, *A Study of Assimilation: Part-Aborigines in South Australia*, p. 41.

of the growth of the part-Aboriginal population of the State, and of the impact of administrative policies up till 1964.[23] The government did not see the Aboriginal 'problem' as a dual one, as happened in Queensland and in Western Australia. A decisive factor may have been the taking over of the Northern Territory by the Commonwealth in 1911, since this event left the South Australian government with only the comparatively sparse full-blood population in the State's desert regions. There was concern, but it seems rather to have been comparable with that in Victoria and New South Wales, where the growth of this new population appeared to defer rather than threaten the hopes of a disappearing Aboriginal question. For instance, carnal knowledge of an Aboriginal woman by other than an *Aborigine* as defined, 'habitual consorting' with her, or the keeping of an Aboriginal mistress did not become an offence until the 1939 Act;[24] and this and other new restrictions probably resulted from the conference of Commonwealth and State officials two years before, at which there was considerable discussion of the 'half-caste problem'.

The steps to segregate part-Aborigines from Aborigines, which were never more than a series of sporadic gestures or an intention, even in Queensland and Western Australia, were not taken. Segregation, mainly on the two large government stations, which followed the first comprehensive Aboriginal legislation in 1911, was for any who fell within the category of *Aboriginal*, which included *half-castes* married to or habitually associating with Aborigines, and *half-caste* children under sixteen years. The term *half-caste* in this connection was a wide one, as it included the child of a *half-caste*.[25]

The attempt seems to have been to segregate and 'train' the whole group in the closely settled areas. 'To add to the trouble', said the Premier in 1910, 'a large half-caste population is growing up.'[26] A Royal Commission of 1913-15 foreshadowed the end of the need for protection (ironically, because of the 'gradual disappearance of the full bloods'). With

the mingling of black and white races, and the great increase in the number of half-castes and quadroons, the problem is now one of assisting and training the native so that he may become a useful member of the community, dependent not upon charity but upon his own efforts.[27]

[23] Ibid.
[24] Aborigines Act, 1934-1939, section 34a.
[25] Aborigines Act, 1911, section 4.
[26] Fay Gale, *A Study of Assimilation*, p. 50—quoting *S.A.P.D.*, 1910, p. 617.
[27] Ibid., p. 107—quoting Royal Commission on Aborigines, 1913. Progress Report, p. 7.

Here was the idea of assimilation, stated so often in the previous century and to become emphasised as an 'answer' after World War II. But, as later, authority, compromising with the resistance of the towns, which were the only places where effective training could be offered, settled for emphasis on the managed reserves, to such a degree that Point Pearce and Point McLeay have possibly had a more lasting influence on Aboriginal attitudes in the closely settled areas of South Australia than have institutions anywhere else. As both have had a century of continuity, as mission stations until 1914 and from then as government stations, one would expect a high degree of institutionalised attitudes to authority among the large proportion of persons of Aboriginal descent who retain the tradition that one or other of these places is 'home'.

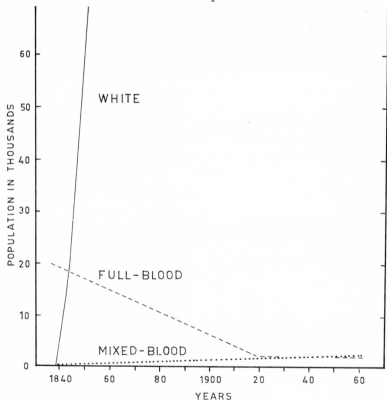

Fig. 2. Relative Population Trends (est.,) South Australia, 1840–1960

*Sources: S.A.P.P.; Commonwealth Year Book,* 1901-58; 1913-15 Royal Commission on Aborigines (S.A.); Reports, Aborigines Protection Board. Redrawn from Fay Gale, *A Study of Assimilation,* by courtesy of the author.

Figure 2, taken from Dr Gale's book, is a useful indication of population trends from the foundation of the State until 1960, although she states that from available records only an estimate is possible. The 1961 census indicated that, of an enumerated total of just under 4,900, over 2,700 were of part-Aboriginal descent. This is almost certainly a considerable underestimate of the total, as are census figures for other States. It is highly probable that the proportion of part-Aborigines is much higher.[28]

It is hard to avoid the conclusion that attitudes to Aborigines, developed in the early frontier contacts, were the prime factor in the development of the present part-Aboriginal minority in the towns and the settled areas. I have tried to account for these attitudes as arising from Western and Christian exclusiveness, enhanced in the conditions of Australian settlement by social distance and misunderstanding and by economic factors.[29] The transfer of these prejudices to all offspring of Aborigines who bore the Aboriginal stigmata has been almost universal and automatic in the past. Had the Aboriginal been well enough equipped for war to establish Aboriginal lands to which he had an acknowledged claim, his descendants of mixed race might have found a sanctuary there. As things happened, they remained in the insecurity of fringe areas where the last of the local full-bloods were dying out, or they were removed with them to the reserves, missions, and managed stations.

POLICIES FOR THE PART-ABORIGINES IN THE SETTLED AREAS

The process of genetic change can to some extent be followed in the extension of the categories of Aboriginal as time passed. At the same time there was ambivalence in popular attitudes, still being echoed in the irritation of many people that persons of largely non-Aboriginal descent should benefit from the special 'hand-outs' to Aborigines: almost as if they formed a specially privileged group. In Victoria this led to the restriction of the category of persons to be assisted, and to the adoption of a policy as early as 1886 that persons of 'light caste' should be forced *off* the reserves, to compete economically and make their way without special assistance. The administrative idea of assimilation, in the last decade (1960s), has involved the notion that families of Aboriginal descent should be pressured *out* from 'segregated' situations; but in practice it tends to be the part-Aboriginal family of 'light caste' which is selected

[28] For a discussion of the shortcomings in figures from past census-taking, see *The Destruction of Aboriginal Society*, App. B.
[29] Ibid.

to move into the house in town. Recent developments in the Lake Tyers situation are a classic example of the way in which thinking in terms of descent, and consequent conflict about the proper place for the half-caste, has operated as an additional cause for insecurity of the Victorian Aboriginal communities.

Where there was special concern with the 'half-caste problem' as a complicating factor in the wider Aboriginal one, governments attempted to interfere in the most intimate areas of human life, especially in attempting to limit miscegenation and to control marriage. While the first might be defended, as it was, as a move to 'protect' Aboriginal women from themselves and from white men, there could be no such defence of the attempts to control marriage—which have probably contributed something to the open disregard of its Western forms by many families in the Aboriginal communities.

The governments which developed and maintained most concern with this matter were those of Queensland and Western Australia.[30] Yet the background of the Queensland legislation suggests that its basis was one of humanitarian concern, that it was a genuine effort at protection. Thus in the 1897 Act, which began the series of comprehensive Acts, 'female *half-castes*' other than those already within the wide *Aboriginal* category, i.e. who were not 'associating' with *Aboriginals*, were accorded protections which the males in similar situations were apparently assumed not to require, and which they shared with women who were legally *Aboriginal*. It was an offence to 'harbour' them in one's home, or employ them except under conditions provided for Aborigines; they could be employed only under written agreements. But all *half-castes* were included with *Aboriginals* in the matter of liquor and opium, with the penalty applying for supply.[31] Against this background it may be possible to account for the precedent set by Queensland in 1901, when it was provided that the marriage of a 'female *Aboriginal*' required the written permission of a 'protector authorised by the Minister' as an extension of protection against men whom the government considered undesirable.[32] (It was the current fashion to blame Chinese settlers for the sale of opium dross to Aborigines and for exploitation of Aboriginal women in the northern areas.)

---

[30] For references to the development of a separate policy for half-castes in Northern Territory see C.D. Rowley, *The Remote Aborigines* (*Aboriginal Policy and Practice*, vol. III).

[31] Aboriginals Protection and Restriction of the Sale of Opium Act, 1897, sections 4, 14, 15, 16, 19, and 20.

[32] Ibid., section 9.

The step is a very clear indication of how protection of a small and inarticulate minority becomes quite harsh discrimination, but it also suggests that there is a connection between Aboriginal welfare legislation and concern for 'white' Australia. In 1939, probably as a result of the 1937 conference of State and Commonwealth officials, marriage of any person classed as *Aboriginal* with any non-Aboriginal was made subject to the permission in writing of the Director of the Sub-Department of Native Affairs; and even a marriage between *Aboriginals* required the permission of a protector (almost always a policeman) or reserve superintendent.[33] The 1934 Act had made what amounted to any request for sexual intercourse between *Aboriginals*, whether the advance was made by the man or the woman, punishable for the *Aboriginal* concerned.[34]

These examples illustrate how in Queensland concern to limit the half-caste problem involved deep interference with the lives of all Aborigines. Even the permission to marry a non-Aboriginal did not free the Aboriginal woman from the controls in the Act. In the case of Dempsey *v.* Rigg, in 1914, it was decided that an *Aboriginal* woman remained such for the purposes of the Act, even though she married a person who was not.[35] When it is remembered that this is but one of many comparable limitations of the rights of Aborigines, which were accumulating up till the end of the 1930s; that they were applied by police officers, whose relations with Aborigines were variable, to say the least, but who were certainly not especially competent as a group in the management of human relations; and that there could be no real control of either the protectors or the superintendents, it is not difficult to account for increasing resentment with increasing sophistication. In Queensland, especially, the administration of the settled regions was based, and remained based, on the assumptions deemed suitable for frontier conditions. This meant, for instance, that the same controlling authority administered a separate wage system for all who were 'under the Act', from the original five shillings weekly under the first legislation up to the special wage system negotiated by the department with the employers and the Australian Workers Union after World War I.[36]

The Western Australian Aborigines Act of 1905, which followed a report by W.E. Roth, the Assistant Protector for Queensland, provided

[33] Aboriginals Preservation and Protection Act of 1939, section 19.
[34] The terms are extraordinarily wide: see, Aborigines Protection and Restriction of the Sale of Opium Acts Amendment Act, 1934, sections 10 and 11.
[35] [1914] St. R. Qd. 245; [1914] Q.W.N. 39; 8 Q.J.P.R. 57, 149—quoted in relation to section 4 of Aboriginals Protection and Restriction of the Sale of Opium Acts, 1897 to 1934.
[36] For details of this system see ch. 4.

by sections 42 and 43 that the marriage of a 'female *Aboriginal*' with any person other than an *Aboriginal* could not be celebrated without the permission in writing of the Chief Protector; made cohabitation of a non-Aboriginal male with an Aboriginal woman an offence; and established the presumption that travelling with an Aboriginal woman was cohabitation. Neville, whose period of control of the Department, first as Chief Protector and after 1936 as Commissioner of Native Affairs, spanned most of the two decades between the world wars, fully shared the concern of his contemporary Bleakley with the 'problem'. He got a good deal of what he wanted in the increased controls of the 1936 Aborigines Act Amendment Act, which gave the Commissioner very wide powers to refuse a marriage, the grounds including disparity in age (an attempt to check the indigenous custom of child marriages with elderly men) and 'any other circumstances which render it inadvisable'. There was a provision for appeal, which would have been largely meaningless. There was also a provision which made an offence the celebration of a marriage without the notice to the Commissioner, or to which he had formerly objected (section 25). Neville had been having some trouble with missionaries, who were on occasions likely to pay more attention to the Christian marriage of their converts than to the breeding program of the Commissioner. The same Act, by section 26, extended the earlier provisions against inter-racial sexual intercourse outside marriage. The execution of this Act was, of course, mainly in the hands of police protectors. It is worth recalling here that many Aborigines living now have been subject to this legislation.

The Chief Secretary, introducing the Act, explained the new term, *native*, as a general definition of all those subject to it, as a means of controlling a situation which had got out of control because of the impossibility of establishing the extent of Aboriginal descent which the earlier definitions had required. The discussions in both Assembly and Council are excellent indications of public attitudes at the time, ranging from a somewhat woolly-minded sympathy to expressed fears of the growing 'half-caste problem'. One Member recommended education in cleanliness and sex for all part-Aboriginal girls. Others wanted to separate the full-bloods from the part-Aborigines. One Member wanted sterilisation of the women. Others suggested that a casual liaison should be overlooked and the full weight of the law be brought against the permanent union.[37]

It is indeed a sobering thought that a debate could be held on this

[37] *W.A.P.D.*, 1936, New Series, vol. 97—L.C.: 22, 29, 30 September, 1, 6, 13, 14 October; and L.A.: ibid., 20 October; vol. 98—L.A.: 3, 10 December

level only three decades ago. But there was also the Member (Hamersley), who claimed that the Bill was aimed at the 'aggrandisement of the Protector and the degrading of half-castes by placing them on a lower scale than before', and who quoted a letter from a part-Aboriginal which stated that though Neville had been Chief Protector for twenty-two years, 'we cannot find one person whose name is on the electoral roll'. This was a reference to the provisions for exemption, of which the Chief Secretary had made much when explaining why the term 'native' had been introduced as such a comprehensive one. The letter also referred to the 'runaway matches' when young people got out of the Moore River Settlement, and to the prosecutions which followed. It claimed that 'quarter-castes' were called 'white' for the purposes of the settlement, but this was to select them for a separate institution in Perth. The darker children were dealt with as half-caste, and remained in the settlement. As this is in accord with the policy which Neville himself was urging and proclaiming, there is no reason to doubt it. Hamersley, the most effective critic of the Bill, told of part-Aborigines who could earn good wages, but whose children were controlled by the Department, which also controlled their wages.[38]

Another letter from a part-Aboriginal read into the debate asked:

Is it that they want to pass a law to say we half-castes, whether we are 90 per cent. white blood, . . . living in a position as good as many white people, are still aborigines, and are still on the same footing as those on the fringe of civilisation? If we are law-abiding and are getting an honest living, are we not British subjects? I think we are entitled to citizenship . . . The plight of the half-caste today is due to this department. They have taken charge of the half-caste aborigines for the last 29 years or so, and what have they done for us? The result is: 'You are a good dog, but keep in your kennel' . . . Now the Chief Protector wants guardianship over all our children, whether born in wedlock or not. Our children are our most sacred rights. We are all married in churches. It seems the . . . Department wants to take charge of all their earnings and to make sure they will be serfs for the State.

Moore, who read this letter, condemned the 'inhuman practice' of taking children from their parents.[39]

The fight for the minds of the children went back to the very beginnings of Aboriginal administration and missionary effort in every State; and in this debate there were enough to defend the means as the only way to give the children 'a chance'. By this time the reputation of Moore

[38] *W.A.P.D.*, 1936, N.S., vol. 97, pp. 973-6—speech by V. Hamersley (East). Legislative Council, 6 October.
[39] Ibid., pp. 977-8—speech by T. Moore (Central). Legislative Council, 6 October.

River, the main government settlement in the south, was such as to maintain a constant insecurity in the part-Aboriginal family.

But the Bill was passed, and the controls on marriage and cohabitation for the *native* were to remain until their repeal in the Act of 1954. The 1936 Act (the Aborigines Act Amendment Act) expressed principles on which the officials of three governments—Western Australia, Queensland, and the Commonwealth in respect of the Northern Territory—could agree at the 1937 conference. As we have seen, South Australia amended its legislation to prevent miscegenation in 1939, but it made no attempt to control marriage. In Queensland, the Act as amended in 1939 remained the basic Act, with power vested in the Department of Native Affairs to control marriage, until proclamation of the Aborigines' and Torres Strait Islanders' Affairs Act of 1965.

The Initial Conference of Commonwealth and State Aboriginal Authorities was held at Canberra in April 1937.[40] It was here that the officials of Western Australia, Queensland, and the Northern Territory developed to its logical (or illogical) conclusions the concept of *two* Aboriginal 'problems'—that of the full-blood and that of the half-caste. Tasmania, of course, had no admitted reason to be represented. H.S. Bailey, Chairman of the Victorian Board for the Protection of Aborigines, spoke as though his 'problem' was practically 'solved', stating that only a few 'full-blooded blacks' and some five hundred 'half-castes' remained.

I came here principally as an onlooker . . . Questions relating to the aborigines affect States like Queensland, South Australia and Western Australia, more than Victoria, and probably New South Wales.[41]

B.S. Harkness, for New South Wales, did not demur. He saw the matter as one mainly of 'assimilating' the ten thousand half-castes; eventual absorption of the thousand or so full-bloods was vaguely implicit. Ignoring the drastic effects of the depression and its administrative consequences on Aboriginal welfare, he stated that the situation in New South Wales had much improved. Though the girls sent out to service resorted to bad habits, it was for the next generation that planning was

---

[40] Commonwealth of Australia, *Aboriginal Welfare*. The document is a summary of the discussion. The conference was organised by the Department of the Interior, and followed a decision made by the Premiers' Conference at Adelaide in 1936. (For the events leading up to this decision and for the Conference's consideration of other matters, see *The Destruction of Aboriginal Society*, ch. 17.) The recommendations are also included. The conference established precedents still followed. The press and voluntary bodies were excluded, so that the expertise of the officials had free play.

[41] Ibid., p. 5.

needed. But A.C. Pettitt, Secretary of the Aborigines Protection Board in New South Wales, stated that the basic problem was the rejection of the part-Aboriginal fringe-dweller, 'on the score of colour alone', and that the pressures brought to bear by the Parents and Citizens' Associations were preventing the children from attending the public schools.

These pressures had been brought over a considerable period, and were common throughout the settled regions of the continent. In that same year of 1937, they were to result in a Minute from the Minister for Education in New South Wales (D.H. Drummond) to his Department, establishing as a principle that where such a request for exclusion was made, and

where a number of aboriginal children are attending the school they should be segregated from the ordinary school pupils and provided with education in a school set apart for the purpose preferably at an aboriginal settlement.[42]

This was, he wrote, a measure 'which lays emphasis, not upon a difference of colour, but upon the natural handicaps of a child [sic] race'—an attitude which led to the assumption that a couple of hours of schooling a day, given by the station manager (who would rarely if ever have the necessary qualification) would be adequate.

M.T. McLean, the Chief Protector for South Australia, had little to say of the Aborigines of the desert areas, since his administration had been almost solely concerned with the two large settlements. The population of Point Pearce, he said, had doubled itself in seventeen years. The answer was absorption, as with the Greek and Italian migrants; but when they were moved out of the settlements they caused 'trouble' in fringe areas which became 'hotbeds of immorality'. At least he saw the dilemma—of institutionalised groups, on the one hand, and of 'trouble' with local government authorities on the other.[43]

Thus the officials of three States saw their problem as one involving part-Aborigines, and in two of them it could be assumed that there would soon be few if any of the full descent. On the matter of what seemed a dual problem, they left most of the discussion to the experts from the Territory, Queensland, and Western Australia. On the recommendations for the full-bloods I have already commented.[44] If detribalised, they should be employed and educated, but kept out of competition with whites; if

[42] N.S.W.P.D., 1943, Second Series, vol. 170, p. 2850—Drummond, reading his own Minute, as Minister for Education, dated 6 August 1937.
[43] Aboriginal Welfare, p. 15.
[44] See The Destruction of Aboriginal Society, ch. 17.

'semi-civilised', kept on small reserves and 'elevated' to the condition of the detribalised; if in the tribal state, established on 'inviolable reserves'.[45] The point here is that there was implicit assumption of inevitable miscegenation; that eventually population would, by the very failure of the measures for making reserves inviolable, become part-Aboriginal.

Neville made this assumption explicit in his statement that the policy of his government was that 'ultimately the natives must be absorbed into the white population of Australia', that this was the objective of the 1936 Act. He quoted the Adelaide Anthropological Board and Dr R. Cilento as authorities that as Aborigines were not 'negroid' there would be no 'atavism'. Half-castes were intermarrying and increasing; they must be taught to read and write and count, know what wages they could get, make agreements with employers: 'that is all that should be necessary'.[46] But to achieve this the government must take charge of the children at the age of six, this being the reason why he had the power to do so, 'no matter whether the mother be legally married or not'. Referring to his power to control marriages, he complained of the missionaries who would not co-operate: 'they allow the half-castes under their control to marry anybody'.[47] Unfortunately, some of the early settlers had had negro servants, and this had produced some breeding problems. He had prosecutions pending against men who had been increasing the 'half-caste problem' by associations with coloured women.

His main difficulty was that he could spend only thirty shillings per head per annum for each half-caste. He made a special plea for Commonwealth financial assistance; the problem was, he stated, solely a financial one. His references to starvation of the full-bloods were part of his argument for help, but they shed some grim light on his confidence that the whole problem of absorption was a manageable one. He had allowed the mothers of the children in his half-caste home to camp half a mile away, and to see the children 'occasionally'. 'At first the mothers tried to entice the children back to the camps, but that difficulty is now being overcome.'[48] One of the Victorian officials stated that such measures would be impossible in his State.

Bleakley described at great length the situation in Queensland fringe settlements, where he said the moral tone of the camps was lower than

[45] *Aboriginal Welfare*, p. 34.
[46] Ibid., pp. 10-11.
[47] Ibid., p. 11.
[48] Ibid., p. 17.

among the 'more primitive classes' of full-bloods, 'as this type of people is usually too sophisticated to be controlled by the native laws and the moral code of the superior race'. Yet they were needed for employment. Education raised the problem of local bodies which objected to Aboriginal children in the schools; and segregated schooling was provided in some areas. His plan was to establish special settlements 'a reasonable distance from the town', and to transfer some families to the large settlements. His experience was illustrated by his description of four sub-categories of half-castes. There were those of mainly Aboriginal 'blood' and wholly Aboriginal character; those 'crossed' with other 'lower types' like Pacific Islanders, Malays, Africans, and the like; those 'crossed' with European or 'higher' Asian types; and the quadroons or octoroons with mainly European 'blood'. The lower types should be so managed as to 'take their part in the development of a self-contained native community'.[49] But the superior type of half-breed, with the necessary intelligence and ambition for the higher civilised life 'should be brought into the white community'. Marriages, he said, had been 'rigidly restricted' for twenty-five years, while 'every encouragement has been given to marriage of crossbreed aboriginals among their own race'. Exemption should be limited to the 'superior types'.

It is worth a note that stated Queensland policy should have been so explicit in assuming an indefinite apartheid arrangement for the 'inferior' half-castes. So far as one can read sense into this muddled nonsense, Bleakley considered Neville too optimistic about absorption of the whole Aboriginal population. The half-caste, as he was likely to be fathered by a 'low type' of white man, could not, he said, 'happily be absorbed'.

Both Bleakley and Neville were kindly and wellmeaning. But they were placed in situations where they had to theorise and act on the common racist assumptions of the Australian folklore; and they had no outside contacts to correct this. The Conference as a whole shared their concern for the 'happiness and welfare of the coloured people'; and expressed its unease by the recommendation that the Commonwealth should seek information on 'racial problems' in America and South Africa.[50] In the meantime, it stated the belief 'that the destiny of the natives of aboriginal origin, but not of the full blood, lies in their ultimate absorption by the people of the Commonwealth and it therefore recommends that all efforts be directed to that end'.[51] This was in the back-

[49] Ibid., p. 8.
[50] Ibid., p. 35.
[51] Ibid., p. 21.

ground to the tightening of legislation in the matter of marriage and associations. Uniform legislation was recommended, as also was the general adoption of the wide definition of *native* used in Western Australia since 1936.

## N.B. TINDALE ASSESSES THE PREREQUISITES FOR ABSORPTION

Australian governments now seemed to be concerned with a program of absorption. A suggestion was made that there should be a survey of the difficulties; and a representative of the University of Adelaide who was present suggested that the University should make a survey to establish whether absorption was possible.[52]

The difficulties were studied by a Harvard-Adelaide Universities' Anthropological Expedition in 1938-9, and its results were published by one of the research workers, Norman B. Tindale, an ethnologist for the South Australian Museum.[53] This was a scientific survey of the possibility of eventual absorption, with recommendations on what was necessary to promote it. Though it was prepared for the advice of the South Australian government, its importance arises largely from the fact that Tindale and Birdsell (a scholar from Harvard who studied the physical data of the mixed-race population) made a wide-ranging comparative study involving different situations in several States.

Tindale pointed out that a great deal of 'passing' had already occurred; that 'passing' depended on the 'near white' appearance of the individual.[54]

Perhaps the most favourable light in which to interpret the recommendations of the 1937 Conference was that the participants had such good reason to assume that popular prejudice against the person of Aboriginal appearance was an unalterable feature of the total situation. Nor can one fairly criticise Tindale for a basic assumption that this was so. Even on the basis of such an assumption his criticism of the State administrations which shared it was at times devastating. Thus he points out the fallacies involved in official records of who were half-caste and who were not, that many and various degrees of racial mixture could be brought together under the term, which must have been true because there were few facilities for proper genealogies. But this, in a couple of sentences, was a logical demolition of the pretensions of some administrations to

---

[52] Ibid., p. 10.
[53] Norman B. Tindale, 'Survey of the Half-caste Problem in South Australia', *Proceedings of the Royal Geographical Society, South Australian Branch*, vol. XLII, November 1941, pp. 66-161.
[54] Ibid., p. 69.

control breeding programs, which justified such practices as the control of marriages.[55]

One finding of the survey was that there was no evidence of a 'marked segregation of characters'—of a grouping of Aboriginal physical and other characteristics which might reappear after several generations of cross-marriages. But the investigators found a tendency for the populations on controlled and segregated settlements to stabilise at a certain level of 'crossing'. This was the result of the history of the community, which on distant mission stations would include the isolation of the girls from the men in the bush, and arrangement of marriages within the mission. Thus the practice of isolation was incompatible with a program of absorption. In these places also the tendency to stability at a certain level of descent was influenced by the very high infant mortality of the children of full descent. Commenting on a diagram indicating a 50 per cent infant mortality among this stabilised section of the Yarrabah people, Tindale wrote that

there are increasing percentages of deaths of children in each succeeding generation . . . seemingly aggravated, if not induced, by poor and probably insufficiently varied diet. Epidemic disease is rife and medical attention is spasmodic, there being no resident doctor in the community of 500. The system of child rearing also requires urgent attention.[56]

At the same station, and sharing the same conditions, he found an 'absence of deaths' recorded for part-Aboriginal children of one 'full-blood' and one non-Aboriginal parent; and he noted that this first generation of part-Aborigines was especially fecund.[57] He suggested that where comparable economic status and education of part-Aborigines resulted in union with whites, their children could be 'absorbed' without much difficulty; that this would be prevented by 'isolation, insufficiency of education and training', which would not, however, prevent it in a future generation.

It may be accepted as a corollary that two successive crossings with 'white' blood, the second accompanied by reasonable living conditions and normal education enables the grandchild of a full-blooded aboriginal woman to take a place in the general community.[58]

It is fair to point out that the pessimism implicit in this finding was a reaction to the hard prejudice which seemed to offer so little hope for a person to be accepted as someone of value irrespective of his appearance.

[55] Ibid.
[56] Ibid., p. 95.
[57] Ibid., pp. 100 *et seq*.
[58] Ibid., p. 115.

Tindale gained the impression of increasing prejudice against the part-Aboriginal, and speculated on the extent to which this was due to American cultural influences.

Half-caste aboriginal informants have on occasions indicated their awareness of this gradually increasing prejudice, which naturally is amplified immediately wherever local policies of segregation are being encouraged or practised . . . The national policy of a 'White Australia' requires there should be as little possible disturbance of the present biological balance . . . The negroid Melanesians . . . were . . . repatriated as soon as this policy made itself felt. The disposal of Australian half-castes cannot be so easily arranged. . . .[59]

Segregation, he wrote, would simply increase the number of mixed-bloods, stabilised at a certain level, who would present a larger 'problem'.

By this time the document which might fairly be regarded as the foundation of the assimilation policy had been issued by the Hon. J. McEwen, as Minister for the Interior, in February 1939.[60] It related only to the Northern Territory, and envisaged 'generations' of change. There was none of the fuss about the increase of part-Aborigines which marked the 1937 Conference; but there were to be different policies for the part-Aboriginal and the Aboriginal. From the standpoint of the 1960s it seems no very progressive statement, with its quoting of authority that the Aboriginal was 'not inferior'—not to the white man, but to the New Guinean—and its assumption that Aborigines on pastoral properties were only marginally useful. But in the background of those not-so-distant times it was epoch-making.

In the first place, it formulated a long-term objective for policy that was other than some kind of social engineering for the disappearance of the race into the white majority, taking the emphasis off miscegenation, although it is not clear just what changes were envisaged for the tribalised full-blood, who was to be left alone and protected while progress was made in advancing the policy with others. The objective was a positive one, envisaging a common citizenship, without postulating genetic changes—

the raising of their status so as to entitle them by right, and by qualifications to the ordinary rights of citizenship and enable and help them to share with us the opportunities that are available in their native land.[61]

[59] Ibid., p. 122.
[60] Northern Territory of Australia: Commonwealth Government's Policy with Respect to Aboriginals: February 1939.
[61] Ibid.

This 'sharing' was for *all* of Aboriginal descent. McEwen seems to have accepted advice from A.P. Elkin, who was the prime mover in New South Wales for an 'assimilation' policy offering equality irrespective of racial characteristics.

Thus the word 'assimilation' was in the air. Sometimes Tindale refers to absorption, sometimes to assimilation. That he was studying race and racial change did not make him a racist. He saw clearly, and emphasised the need for, social, economic, and educational opportunity. His report showed that even granting the assumptions of the racists, segregation would merely increase the 'problem' with which they were concerned. On these grounds he criticised the Queensland government's practice of restraint and segregation, its deep interference with civil liberties; and he saw clearly that what often passed for Aboriginal characteristics were the reactions of a minority to tyranny.

It would seem that gross misunderstandings and abuse are possible ... that the difficulties mixed bloods have in proving victimisation, their frequent inability to receive recognition of the urgency and validity of the reasons for which they break contracts with their employers and misunderstandings of the contract and banking laws, all tend to create an unhappy and unstable people who, undoubtedly, feel that they are being increasingly confined and isolated.[62]

In New South Wales, on the other hand, the infringement of an Aboriginal regulation meant expulsion or exclusion from the government station—even though the family might remain there. He found a one-way flow of 'refugees'—from Queensland to New South Wales, a finding confirmed much later by Dr Malcolm Calley. But the Queensland settlements were far superior to the stations of New South Wales, 'in organisation, educational facilities and degree of support offered'; and he said that in New South Wales teaching was usually done by untrained managers, which was quite true. In Victoria he found that freedom to spend one's money as one wished, even in a hotel, 'acts as a positive inducement towards independence'; that trouble from liquor arose mainly from the thirsty part-Aboriginal New South Welshmen who crossed the border from places like Cumeroogunga. Education was in the hands of State teachers, and 'there seems to be less prejudice against the mixed bloods than elsewhere in Australia'.

He found a teacher-policeman managing the descendants of Tasmanian Aborigines on Cape Barren Island.

He condemned the attempt by the government of Western Australia,

---

[62] Tindale, 'Survey of the Half-caste Problem', p. 126.

with less resources, to follow the Queensland system. After all the emphasis by Neville on the program at Moore River, he did not think much of what he saw there, while outside of this settlement there seemed no effort being made to house either the Aboriginal or part-Aboriginal. Both

tend to live in the bush as nomads, or to erect scrap-iron huts of their own conniving in the vicinity of the small towns. Illiteracy is extremely high, nurture and clothing necessarily poor and adjustment to white life proportionately low.[63]

Naturally enough, in an effort to influence his government, he was tactful about conditions in South Australia. These comments showed a lively awareness of social issues. But his main recommendation for the 'process of physical and social assimilation' for the part-Aboriginal was through 'the simple device of ensuring that a maximum dispersal or spread of the minority group will take place'.[64] He did not say how this should occur; and in the context what he did say was clearly an attack on the policies of segregation. He probably had in mind the two government stations and the missions.

Such a recommendation could offer little hope of solving a *social* issue, however, for it is concerned with genetics more than with social change. In fact, except for references to education it gave no attention to how social change might occur, except in so far as it might result from genetic change. Nor did it take into account the resistances of the people to be dispersed. Their welfare as living individuals is pessimistically written off; concern is for future generations—not really effective motivation of those who have only one life to live, especially if the reward for their sacrifice is for their children more easily to disown them. Within the 'assimilation' concept this totalitarian view of society has not been altogether lost; nor has the readiness of administrators to sacrifice the choices of the living generation for some putative gain by those yet to be born.

Tindale's solution indicates the danger of forming concepts of what may be done in the face of history, for 'how things got this way' is an important part of the problem. After such a clear recognition of the effects of prejudice in producing the social barriers, it is surprising that he was prepared (in some despair, certainly) to throw those on the reserves out of them and to spread them thinly through the 'whites'. As prejudice was increasing, was there any reason to hope that the whites

[63] Ibid., p. 130.
[64] Ibid., p. 119.

would not get rid of them again by pressures on the governments to re-establish the stations and reserves? How was the miscegenation, required to produce what he regarded as essential changes, to occur? Obviously, except in the cases of the lighter skinned who might have a chance of equality, as it had always done: with the girls bearing whiter children, and the men often failing to find wives at all. Nature should be encouraged to take its course; and there is some evasion of the facts as they must occur in personal histories. By leaving the darker people to their fate, in the most hostile and tense situations, he could get to the position where there would be fewer dark ones in the next generation. This also was one of the veiled assumptions which became an integral part of the assimilation concept.

Logical enough in the context, and probably defensible even now if one thinks only in terms of the racial strain and of majority prejudice, this idea of physical dispersal was to be confused for a long time with another 'assimilation' policy which involves the concept of equality irrespective of racial appearance. This was not because of what Tindale wrote but because his pessimism was so well justified by the facts of prejudice that it was widely shared by men of intelligence. (Men of prejudice would tend to think of breeding out a bad 'strain' anyway.) If one takes prejudice as unalterable, it then appears logical to set out to find a way round it; and the only possible way might seem to be so to arrange matters that in the long run there would be no identifiable Aborigines. What Tindale really set out to establish was the logical way to ensure the most rapid 'passing' of the greatest number—and this he did with a cold logic and considerable irony.

### ABSORPTION AND ASSIMILATION

The same conditions were so to influence even many of the best of the officials of the various boards and departments responsible for Aboriginal administration that pressures were brought, in the blessed name of 'assimilation', to move people from their homes on reserves in the attempt to spread them thinly through the majority. Those who thought in the crudest racial terms could comfortably assume that nature would take its course, and the 'problem' solve itself through miscegenation. So the 'practice' of the new policy often involved a resort to older methods, pursued in the name of 'absorption' or simply because a person with 'white blood' should get out into the community and not receive the much stressed 'hand-outs' which Aborigines are alleged to enjoy. Where the whites would not have them, those left on reserves were being 'trained' for 'assimilation'. The same line of thought, based on the pessimistic view that no government ever can or will affront the prejudices of the majority, or of local government areas expressed through their councils, led to the interpretation of effort for assimilation as effort to train the Aboriginal to make him less offensive to the whites. The results have been a marked failure of Australian democracy over the last two decades.

It is hard to assess the impact of the growing part-Aboriginal group on past policies. A 'problem' created in the minds of the policy-makers led to 'solutions' which contributed in important ways to the 'problem'. One is impressed by the inanity of administrative theory, so well illustrated in the attempt to isolate part-Aboriginal from Aboriginal affairs. But it also helps to explain why the conditions round the country towns have changed so little. Part-Aboriginal policy, however, was never a clear entity. For obvious reasons of expense and convenience (of the governments and the non-Aborigines) it was never possible to segregate the two groups; and in all the conditions it would have been about as logical as to separate the short ones from the tall ones. But this particular aspect of a racist tradition has lingered on to confuse the issues raised by the assimilation policy. It is quite possible that carry-over of old methods of management could similarly discredit in the minds of most Aborigines a policy of 'integration'—a word becoming fashionable in its turn. It is not uncommon for public service organisations, with their emphasis on the state of the files, to seek escape from a set of tough dilemmas in such semantic changes, which are cheap and do not bind administrators to anything in particular.

Evidence of press files before the 1937 Conference indicates only sporadic public interest in Aboriginal policy. Over the four preceding years (which were depression years) opinions were expressed mainly on the 'dangers' of the increasing half-caste population, especially in the Northern Territory; the need to protect Aboriginal women from white men; the undesirability of the half-caste remaining to be brought up with full-bloods in the camps and settlements. There were arguments for and against the taking of children from parents, mainly in reference to the Northern Territory and, after 1936, to Western Australia.[65] In this

---

[65] See for instance, *Argus* (Melbourne), 16 January, 4 July 1933, 23 May and 14 December, 1935, 5 December 1936, 21, 22, and 23 April, 7 July, 10 December 1937; *Age* (Melbourne), 31 March 1933, 24 April 1937; *Herald* (Melbourne), 2 June, 19 August 1933, 21, 22, 23, and 28 April 1937.

period also the special mission 'half-caste' settlements were established in the far north of Queensland and the Northern Territory.

An early dissentient from the mainstream of opinion was Professor Wood Jones of Melbourne University, who agreed with the urgency of the 'problem' but stated that it was a social one, involving status for the part-Aboriginal, and not one to be approached as a matter of inter-racial 'breeding out' of physical characteristics.[66] In New South Wales, Elkin was well launched on his campaign for respect, as human beings with access to cultural treasures of their own, for all persons of Aboriginal tradition. In 1935 he pointed out the effects of the depression on those who had come to depend on the cash economy and processed foods:

> In every part of the continent, and not only in the older settled regions, Aborigines, both full-blood and mixed-blood, are to be found who exist solely by virtue of working for white employers or of receiving government or other grants and doles ... We realize that white casual labourers have difficult times during periods of unemployment, but we tend to take for granted that this is not the case with Aborigines.[67]

This is the complete contrast with the views officially dominant, because there is no classification in terms of 'blood'; there is a realisation which is humane in the wider sense, of the fact that all of Aboriginal heritage face the same risks.

Even the so-called McEwen Document envisaged first efforts for the half-caste; and in the first years of the war part-Aboriginal children were being transferred to the missions—to the Catholic Mission on Melville Island, the Methodist Mission on Goulburn Island, and a Church of England Mission on Groote Eylandt, while Bleakley had his special half-caste mission at Purga, just outside Ipswich. In 1941, even the Tasmanian government admitted to a 'half-caste' problem, announcing in October 1941 a plan to train half-castes from Cape Barren Island to work on Tasmanian farms (where there was a war-time labour shortage).[68] To be in the fashion, perhaps, a new station outside Walgett was officially described in September 1941 as a 'model township', for a population which was 'mostly half-caste'.[69]

An interesting development in 1942 was the bringing into the south

---

[66] *Argus* (Melbourne), 14 December 1935.
[67] A.P. Elkin, 'Civilised Aborigines and Native Culture', *Oceania*, vol. 6, no. 2, December 1935, p. 117.
[68] See statement by Robert Cosgrove, Premier of Tasmania, in *Examiner* (Launceston), 7 October 1941.
[69] *A.B.C. Weekly*, 20 September 1941.

of the inmates from half-caste settlements in the Northern Territory, partly because the buildings were required for military purposes, partly for security. One group was taken by the Commonwealth to Balaklava, in South Australia—an action of which the Premier of that State took a 'serious view'; the change of climate was too great, and there were 'many reasons' why these children should have been kept in central Australia.[70] Others were taken from Alice Springs to Mulgoa in New South Wales[71]. Girls from the mission on Melville Island went to Melbourne. Donald Thomson in January 1945 explained the impact of rigid institutionalisation: the missions made it clear to the inmates that they were the unloved of God who must expiate their birthright. He argued for more sympathetic treatment for children taken so early from their parents into this kind of life.[72]

The effects of the war, which drew Aborigines, irrespective of their degrees of descent, into industrial employment and into the cities probably made the kind of program which had been envisaged in absorption of the half-caste even more obviously irrelevant than ever to real situations. When in July 1945 the State President of the Women's Service Guild in Western Australia claimed that the 'breeding out of colour' remained the policy in that State, the Minister for the North-West found it necessary to deny that policy and to claim that it had been to protect *native* women against the white men; while the *West Australian* demanded that the government, still committed to take children from mothers, should give, not only to the half-caste, but to all *natives*, the 'four freedoms'.[73]

After the war, the Administration of the Northern Territory attempted to resume the program of assimilation, with emphasis on the *half-caste*, more or less where it had left off. The Methodist Mission children, now apparently well-liked school children of the Otford area in New South Wales, were to be returned to the new mission at Croker Island; and in 1946 there was criticism of the case of Betty Fisher, who it was claimed had a great future as a singer had she remained in the south.[74] The children were to be returned where they 'belonged', from a situation where they seem to have had no particular hindrances to moving into society, and where they had been sent to 'train' for assimilation. In 1949 the argument

[70] See *Advertiser* (Adelaide), and *News* (Adelaide), 11 April 1942.
[71] *Argus* (Melbourne), 4 June 1942 and 7 March 1944.
[72] *Herald* (Melbourne), 11 January 1945.
[73] *West Australian*, 19, 26, and 27 July and *Daily News* (Perth), 19 and 22 July 1945.
[74] *Women's Weekly* (Sydney), 22 September 1945; *Daily Telegraph* (Sydney), 7 April 1946; *Herald* (Melbourne), 10 April 1946.

was still continuing, with some at least of the Mulgoa children still there, and local people organising to prevent their removal.[75]

Increased press publicity of the 'half-caste problem' after the end of the war probably reflected the fact that chances of employment had brought many of Aboriginal descent into the cities and towns and there seemed to be more of them. This seeming could well have been supported by the fact, for by this time the part-Aborigines were clearly the most rapidly increasing section of the population. A turning point may have been a set of wartime economic factors which probably operated to reduce infant mortality. One obvious factor was the new chance to work for award wages. Much of the publicity after the war resulted from the Aborigines being replaced in employment by ex-servicemen and from the belief of rural employers that the Aboriginal should now resume his proper place as a worker for less than award wages. By this time, the number of full-bloods in the settled areas had become more or less negligible.

A factor which operated in favour of the part-Aboriginal family off the government reserve was that the Commonwealth Child Endowment Act 1941 (No. 8 of 1941) provided for payment to Aborigines who were not nomadic or dependent on the Commonwealth or a State for support. For those in approved 'charitable institutions' amending legislation in the following year (No. 5 of 1942) made possible the same payment in respect of children in institutions maintained by State governments. These measures, and especially perhaps the 1942 amendment, appear to have marked a turning point in Aboriginal welfare, especially for Aboriginal families. The gain was confirmed in the Social Services Consolidation Act of 1947 (No. 26 of 1947).

Although the Commonwealth legislation could at times be selective on grounds of descent, as in the case of the maternity allowance, which at first excluded full-blood mothers (the definition being the usual Commonwealth one of more than half Aboriginal descent, but the administration depending usually on appearance), there was a tendency (since Social Services legislation was not the product of the official experts in Aboriginal affairs) to gear payments to situations rather than to degrees of Aboriginal descent. The Commonwealth Invalid and Old Age Pensioners Act was amended in 1942 to provide for payment to any Aborigines exempted from the special laws. The States at that time did not exempt persons living on reserves; one effect was to increase the movement off reserves and into fringe-dwelling situations, for the habit

[75] See *Daily Telegraph* (Sydney), 31 January, 7 and 14 February 1949; *S.M.H.*, 26 January, 4, 13, and 14 February 1949.

developed in time to 'exempt' persons reaching pensionable age. Finally in 1959 the law was amended to allow for payment of pensions, and for maternity allowances, irrespective of exemption or residence. All had an entitlement except those deemed 'nomadic or primitive' (Social Services Act, section 137A), thus doing away with the confused set of different definitions which had marked earlier legislation.

There still remained in 1967 the matter of payments made to the managements of government or mission settlements, either because of the difficulty involved in individual payments or because the management was treated as a benevolent institution with an ill or ineffective body of inmates. The analogy even extends to the managements of pastoral properties, which have for a long time been handling the age and some other pensions. Such an arrangement would not have been possible for any other group entitled to benefits. Another discrimination is in the restrictions on payment of unemployment and sickness benefits. But discussion of these matters belongs elsewhere.[76] The relevant point here is that the logic of social services, even where the policy seems timidly restrictive, tended to make the division between Aboriginal and half-caste irrelevant. The trend was to make all Australians equally eligible; admittedly, it still had some considerable way to go. Another result was to strengthen the hand of the Commonwealth in Aboriginal affairs generally.

Nonetheless the idea that the half-caste presented a special problem lingered on in the popular and administrative folklore, as it still does. Thus in March 1947 the *Wellington Times* (N.S.W.) reported a conference between a representative of the New South Wales Aborigines Welfare Board, the local Member, the Chamber of Commerce, and someone from the Christian Social Order Movement. The Board officer, arguing for houses in town, used the argument of genetic absorption within 'five generations', but the representative of the town council thought it was better that part-Aborigines should live separately; that otherwise the 'race' would 'degenerate' further.

After the war, nonetheless, there was some hope where before there had seemed none. One significant straw in the wind was the concern, indicated at the annual conference of the State School Teachers' Union of Western Australia in 1946, for the fact that so many part-Aboriginal children were roaming the streets of the towns of the south-west and not attending the schools. The State Department of Education announced its policy that there should be no discrimination in schools.[77] Three years

---

[76] They are dealt with in *The Remote Aborigines*—C.D.R.

[77] *West Australian* (Perth), 28 August 1946.

later the Minister of Education in New South Wales stated that it was policy to enrol Aboriginal children into the public schools; the occasion, however, was a threat by the white inhabitants of a country town to take their children away if this was done.[78] The cynic may see here the continuation of attempts at absorption; the optimist would hope that the motive was to promote equality. By 1950 there were other indications of change, such as the complaints about Aborigines in the capital cities.[79] From now on this was to be an area of increasing importance in Aboriginal affairs, as more people escaped from the old hard patterns of the rural areas. Perhaps it was far easier for the part-Aboriginal to make this change, and to find his children places in the schools, because he was not completely Aboriginal in appearance. The real problem remained, as it still is, the state of mind of the majority of the whites.

[78] *Smith's Weekly* (Sydney), 29 October 1949; and *Daily Telegraph* (Sydney), 9 November 1949.
[79] See for instance article in *Smith's Weekly*, 8 April 1950.

It would be comforting if one could assume that the shape of the
Aboriginal legislation by the beginning of World War II, with all its
restrictions on liberty, was mainly the result of the anxious and paternal
attempts of governments at protection. Certainly a great deal is to be
explained in this way, but there is too much evidence of harsh discriminations in the general law,[1] sometimes prior to the introduction of special
laws on Aboriginal affairs: restrictions and penalties in some cases preceded
the general protective laws.

A definitive study of this process in Western Australia was made
nearly three decades ago by P.M.C. Hasluck. He has described the
stringent and special penalties for Aborigines, in cases where the law
allowed local justices, by 1859, to impose on them floggings and imprisonment up to three years for offences other than major crimes; the extension
of these penalties to half-castes in 1874; the power vested from 1883 in a
local justice sitting alone to award a sentence up to one year—increased
to three years a decade later. The abolition of the special flogging law,
in 1883, was followed by its restoration, under responsible government,
in 1892, without a single dissenting voice in the parliament. By 1893,
writes Hasluck, no Aboriginal could sit on a jury; the range of offences
in his case was wider, the penalties heavier; and he was likely to be tried
by a person interested in his case. *Practice*, he writes, showed even wider
divergence, with accused and witnesses brought in on the neck chain, to
be tried in a manner which provoked his remark that 'the court was a

---

[1] See *The Destruction of Aboriginal Society*.

process by which he was sent to gaol; not a place where he defended himself against an unproved charge'.[2] The State's Attorney-General could say, in 1897, that

Some persons do not understand what is the condition of natives in Australia, for they seem to class them with the natives of South Africa or the natives of India, where the natives are really far more like men than are the natives of this colony.[3]

Hasluck's is the only detailed study of the effect of frontier conditions on Aboriginal legislation. Referring to the 1936 Act and regulations which placed control of children in the hands of an official, controlled movements, allowed for those defined as *native* to be ordered into institutions and confined there, and to be ordered out of towns, and gave even control of marriages into the hands of the official—all, he points out, laws which were fully exercised (they were *additional* to many time-honoured restraints)—he asked prophetically enough 'what possible outcome there can be from a system that confines the native within a legal status that has more in common with that of a born idiot than of any other class of British subject'.[4]

Legislation offers only one indication of the practical restrictions, and of what seem in retrospect the daily tyrannies of officialdom, to which Aborigines at any time were subject. For instance, beyond legislative attempts to control their access to alcohol and to restrict the possession of firearms, and the legislation which prevented Aborigines from giving evidence in court and which provided for special penalties in Western Australia, there was very little *legal* discrimination against Aboriginal British subjects at the time when their annihilation was in full swing. Laws which confined them to particular areas, or excluded them from towns, came later. In Queensland, where the main instrument of 'native administration' up until the 1897 Act was the Native Police, there was no previous Aboriginal legislation except that to control labour on vessels in the pearling industry. In New South Wales, which set the pattern for Queensland, and cut off most of its Native Police and frontier administration along with the State of Queensland in 1859, the first Aborigines Protection Act was passed half a century later, in 1909. Whereas the Queensland legislation has always reflected the harsh conditions of the frontier, that in New South Wales was not introduced until the frontier was only a memory. The South Australian governments cut off the

---

[2] *Black Australians: A Survey of Native Policy in Western Australia 1829-1897.*
[3] Ibid., p. 203.
[4] Ibid., p. 160.

frontier in a different way, and at a later stage, first by handing over the Northern Territory to the Commonwealth and then by practically ignoring the condition of the Aboriginal in its own desert regions.

Some of the earlier laws, passed before the special legislation relating only to Aboriginal affairs, tended to remain. They became part of a body of law relating to Aborigines in some special way, but as incidental to other matters—for example the liquor legislation in some States and the 'police offences' laws. These, together with the common practice of effecting restrictions and exclusions either under regulations or without legal justification (action by local government under health or building regulations, for example, or without any legal support at all, to exclude or discourage Aborigines from town or town services, or the use of police to ensure that Aborigines sat in the poorest seats in the town cinema), make it clear that the acts and regulations governing the activities of the special departments and boards, vesting in them authority over Aborigines, and regulating Aboriginal activities, only partially indicate the situation. But they are adequate explanations of Aboriginal suspicion of government authorities, especially in those of above middle age who have memories of such measures being stringently applied.

By the end of the 1930s the effort at protective and restrictive control had reached a climax which was reflected in the Aboriginal legislation. Much of it was to remain for over two decades. In Queensland a good deal of it was repeated in the Act of 1965.

## THE ABORIGINAL CATEGORIES

In all instances the definitions of persons subject to the laws were in terms of race. A somewhat special case was the Victorian Aborigines Act of 1928, where the definitions of those entitled to the assistance and subject to the control of the Board for the Protection of Aborigines illustrated the history, going back almost to the years of the Protectorate, of the Board's efforts to decide who should have the right to live on its Aboriginal stations and reserves. Up till 1886 all of Aboriginal descent had been encouraged to do so; and

By 1886 more than two-thirds of the Aborigines were settled on the Board's stations, and more than half of these were of partly Caucasoid ancestry. Legislation was then passed to implement the Board's decision to 'merge into the general population all half castes capable of earning their living'. Between 1886 and 1924 this policy of removal was rigidly prosecuted.[5]

[5] Diane Barwick, A Little More Than Kin (1965), p. 99.

The rigid exclusion of persons deemed to be half-caste led to considerable suffering for people who had often established good homes on the reserves. It forms a special part of the Aboriginal folklore in Victoria, where the memory handed down or recalled by the elder people is mainly one of expulsion from their homes and the consequent hardship in an unsympathetic world outside. By this means the Board in time reduced the number of its stations from the original six to one, at Lake Tyers, which has remained the centre of contention. This was the reason why the 1928 Act included as *Aboriginal*, in addition to those of full descent, *half-castes* who lived or associated with an *Aboriginal* (interpreted as one of full descent), *half-caste* children of Aborigines so defined, or unable to earn a living, or who held a special licence from the Board to reside on one of its reserves, and *half-castes* who were thirty-four years of age when the law expelling *half-castes* from reserves was implemented at the beginning of 1887.[6] When it is remembered that this remained the definition in Victoria until 1957, when the 1928 Act was repealed, that the officials of the Board continued to interpret it restrictively, and that its application tended to be decided on personal appearance, it can be seen how this farcically complicated set of definitions could justify arbitrary measures and remain a source of trouble between perhaps the most sophisticated group of persons classed as *Aboriginal* or *half-caste* and officialdom. The term *half-caste*, where the person was not classed as *Aboriginal*, included 'all the other persons whatever of mixed Aboriginal blood'.[7]

Victoria was probably the State in which most attention was given to Aboriginal needs. But this definition, smacking as it does of quite arbitrary official interference, is a good indication of that official readiness to apply doctrinaire measures, intended to solve the Aboriginal 'problem', which ignored the welfare needs of the living. Even the age provision for a *half-caste* would be likely to split families. Dr Barwick has shown how rigidly the Board's members and officers, often going beyond the legislation, insisted on restricting residence on the stations to full-bloods.[8] The expulsion of the lighter skinned, which is what the division of families would mean in practice, could result from quite arbitrary and superficial judgments. Dr Barwick has, for instance, established actual cases in the records where the same person was described at different times, as 'full-blood', 'half-caste', and 'three-quarter-caste'. She has also pointed out how the definition affected the regulations required to manage the Aboriginal

---

[6] Aborigines Act 1928, section 5.
[7] Ibid., section 4.
[8] A Little More Than Kin (1965), pp. 99-100.

stations. Thus a regulation of 1916, which remained applicable to the last station at Lake Tyers, stated that *quadroon, octoroon* and *half-caste* lads of eighteen years could be forced to leave; that only brief visits to the station were subsequently possible, and this at the discretion of the manager; that even such a visit was limited to a maximum of ten days. This remained in force until 1957.[9]

The foregoing may serve to illustrate the mass of regulatory powers which accumulated in the hands of the different authorities in Aboriginal affairs, and which often formed an extension of the basic legislation.

The New South Wales Aboriginal Protection (Amendment) Act of 1936 retained the earlier, somewhat slipshod definition of the 1909 Act— 'any full-blooded or half-caste Aboriginal';[10] and this has probably confirmed administrative habits, by which the Board's officers applied rule-of-thumb methods to assert control or to deny assistance on the basis of personal appearance.

The 1936 legislation was passed while the Board through the police were forcing unemployed Aborigines on to the stations (they were commonly being refused the 'dole'). The difficulty of deciding just who was *Aboriginal* was made easier by the provision which made the 'averment' in a charge or complaint that the person was Aboriginal or even reference to him as *Aboriginal* in such a document 'sufficient evidence of the truth of such averment or reference, unless the contrary is shown to the satisfaction of the Court'. In addition, the court was given power, in doubtful cases, to decide on *sight* whether a person was *Aboriginal*,[11] a power retained in the consolidation of the Act in 1963.

Power of a justice to decide on sight whether a person was Aboriginal had been provided for in the Victorian Bill of 1886, but refused by Parliament,[12] although it had been included in the 1869 Act. This denial of power to lesser courts may have made far greater conformity of the law with justice. But as the decisions had to be made by officials, the result may have been to strengthen their hands in applying the law and regulations. No other State suffered such qualms. Even the phraseology of the 'averment' clause goes back to the Queensland Act of 1897:[13] and it remained in the Queensland law until 1965. Even now in Queensland the Director has power to 'complain' to a court that any person has

---

[9] Ibid., p. 143. The regulation was No. 56 of 1916.
[10] Section 3.
[11] Section 2 (1) (1), which introduced clauses 18A and 18B to the principal Act.
[12] Diane Barwick, A Little More Than Kin (1965), pp. 43–4—quoting *V.P.D.*, vol. 53, 1886, p. 2913.
[13] Aboriginals Protection and Restriction of the Sale of Opium Act 1897, section 26.

'a strain of Aboriginal blood' and should be forced to accept the departmental 'care'; though the matter is now left to the court without the onus on the person subject of the 'complaint' to prove his capacity or his racial origin, the possibilities are hardly in phase with trends in 1965 elsewhere.[14] Similar provisions appeared in the 1905 Act in Western Australia, and are still law.[15] South Australia had provided in 1911 for the statement that a person was *Aboriginal* to be accepted until disproved, and for the justice to decide Aboriginal origin on sight.[16] These provisions disappeared with the repeal of the 1939 Act, in which they had been extended to establish a presumption of age as well as of race; and in 1962 provisions were made for a register of Aborigines.[17]

As efforts at control increased, the official or the court would be continually deciding questions of status which could only be precisely settled if there were genealogies of those concerned. Except in Victoria, where even by the 1930s the government was confidently expecting the disappearance of its comparatively minor 'problem', the definitions were so wide that almost any dark-skinned person might find himself subject to the special laws.

The category of *native* established in Western Australia in 1936 included all of Aboriginal descent above one-fourth. The *quadroon* born after the end of 1936 was freed, along with *quadroons* under twenty-one years who did not live with *natives*.[18] Note how the emphasis in earlier definitions, on Aboriginality by association, remained. There was reason for this, perhaps, where legislation was for groups of people needing help, and which it was inadvisable to disrupt. But when in 1944 it was decided to make special provision for admission of *natives* to 'citizenship rights' (curiously, of Western Australia) the applicant was required to have 'dissolved tribal and native association, except with respect to lineal descendants or native relations of the first degree' for the previous two years.[19] This provision was withdrawn in 1951. But there remained other quite tyrannous provisions, including the one for cancellation of the 'rights'—which operated until 1958.[20] Even children who had passed out of the *native* category with the father passed back into it at twenty-one years; and, until 1958, had to re-apply.

[14] See Aborigines' and Torres Strait Islanders' Affairs Act of 1965, section 20.
[15] Aborigines Act 1905, section 52; Native Welfare Act 1963, section 28.
[16] Aborigines Act 1911, sections 44 and 45.
[17] Aboriginal Affairs Act 1962, section 17.
[18] Aborigines Act Amendment Act 1936, section 2(e).
[19] Natives (Citizenship Rights) Act 1944, section 4(3).
[20] Ibid., with amending Acts No. 44 of 1950, No. 27 of 1951, and No. 58 of 1958.

I recall a well known part-Aboriginal Queenslander, not 'under the Act' and therefore free (at least unless the Director decides that he is within the categories and in need of assistance, when he must face a court) stating that only a 'blood specialist' could decide where the lines of racial division lie in that State: for the Queensland law does not hesitate to call a spade a spade, nor boggle at prescribing degrees of 'blood'. The definitions of 1965 are substantially those of 1939, which included all with a 'preponderance of the blood of Aboriginals', 'half-bloods' declared by a court to require protection, or 'associating with' Aborigines; the child of an Aboriginal mother on a reserve; and, interestingly, any resident of a reserve other than an official or authorised person—so that presumably definition was made easy, simply by retaining the changing population of the reserves within the category.[21]

In its 1939 Act the government of South Australia dispensed with the complications of early categories it had taken over from the 1905 Western Australian Act. It defined all of Aboriginal descent as *Aboriginal*, unless they had been exempted. The provisions for exemption were unrelated to proportions of 'blood', the case depending on 'character and standard of intelligence and development'.[22]

One of the matters which concerned the 1937 Conference of Commonwealth and State officials was this one of conflicting definitions, which with added mobility had begun to make it impossible to retain control of those who were finding their own way out of the places where they were known and were crossing State boundaries. The Conference recommended that the Western Australian category of *native* should be adopted in any future uniform legislation.[23] It also recommended that an Aboriginal who had become 'temporarily resident' in a State other than that in which he was domiciled might be sent home under a discretionary power vested in the Aboriginal authority.[24] That this could so easily be recommended is to be explained by the whole trend of the legislation up till that time to control the location and the movements of those who fell within the categories, or who were assumed by officials or courts on sight to do so.

Theoretically, the provisions for exemption of individuals from the categories formed in Queensland, South Australia and Western Australia a method of giving citizen rights to those whose conduct, with their

---

[21] Aboriginals Preservation and Protection Act of 1939, section 5(2).
[22] Aborigines Act 1934–1939, sections 4 and 11A.
[23] *Aboriginal Welfare*, p. 21.
[24] Ibid., p. 22.

standard of living (and in practice their appearance) had won the approval of authority. In Queensland this power was vested in the Director; but he could exempt a person while still controlling his property and could revoke the exemption at any time.[25] Thus the exempt person was permanently on approval. Moreover, it is clear from the Annual Reports that the power was used with extreme caution and that the numbers exempted could not possibly have matched the increase in the population under control, despite later claims by the government that some 20,000, now claimed to be not 'under the Act', were the descendants of those formerly exempted. The number is extremely doubtful in the first place; and in the second, whatever it really is, is likely to have been due mainly to the failure of the department to achieve its aims in getting under control all those within the legal categories. In Western Australia, which like Queensland had long had provisions for exemption and revocation (without the exempt person being denied control of his property), the 1936 Act provided for appeal to a court, by a person denied exemption.[26] I have referred above to the South Australian provision. In New South Wales, exemption seems to have been envisaged, after the adoption there of an assimilation policy, as a means of legal transition to citizenship; but the provision made in 1943 also provided for revocation of the 'certificate'.[27]

What has been said of Queensland applied to all. Exemption powers exercised by officials within authoritarian systems inevitably increased the scope of those interested in power. Nowhere did the numbers exempted form a stream out of Aboriginal communities. The whole concept was for some vague kind of tuition before equality; and it seems to have been a further affront to ambition in that a mature person was judged by an officialdom which was seldom respected. The 'dog-licence' was prized mainly as a means of access to alcohol. In Victoria, where only the full-bloods were prevented from drinking alcohol, and where the main emphasis was on cutting down the commitments of the Board, there were no provisions for exemption.

### THE RESTRICTIONS ON PERSONAL LIBERTIES

The legal restrictions on personal liberty in the settled areas reached a climax during the great depression which preceded World War II, with

[25] Aboriginals Preservation and Protection Act of 1939, section 5(3).
[26] Aborigines Act Amendment Act 1936, section 34.
[27] Aborigines Protection (Amendment) Act 1943, section 3(b).

effects on Aboriginal attitudes which were to be profound. In these areas the Aboriginal population had become increasingly sophisticated and completely dependent on the cash economy, which suddenly fell into chaos: it seems to have been fully aware of its position in government priorities for relief and assistance.

A.P. Elkin, the real founder in New South Wales of an 'assimilation' policy based on the principle of equality of opportunity, is of the opinion that at this time the Aborigines of that State, long mainly of part-Aboriginal origin, turned decisively away from hope in government, and in upon their own poor resources.

Neville, the Chief Protector in Western Australia, informed H.D. Moseley, who as Royal Commissioner was inquiring into Aboriginal affairs there in 1935, that with the 'increasing indigence' in that State the old Aboriginal ration (which was not at first intended to be more than supplementary to wild game and the produce of the bush, which of course had been greatly reduced in the years of closer settlement) was the 'sole support' of most of them. 'During the last seven years indigence has about doubled but the Department has had to carry on with reduced funds'; and he described how the basic ration of three-quarters of a pound of meat daily to all had by 1930 been reduced to the same amount three times weekly and by 1931 to one and a half pounds per week. 'That is the existing position. As well, there is malnutrition, non-resistance to disease, and insufficient clothing and blankets.'[28]

In 1936 the law in New South Wales allowed an Aboriginal or a person 'apparently having an admixture of Aboriginal blood' to be removed by order of a court to a reserve, where he must remain until the cancellation of the order. (This was at least an improvement on the previous legislation, which allowed persons or groups of persons 'apparently having an admixture of Aboriginal blood in their veins' to be moved by the Board from the vicinity of a town.) It was also an offence to entice or assist him to 'remove from a reserve'.[29] Thus during the depression New South Wales authorities followed the hard practice of what was sometimes referred to in Western Australia as 'clearing the towns'. This correspondence in time of economic disaster with harsh laws is suggestive of majority attitudes. It is almost as though people

[28] See C. Makin, A Socio-Cultural Anthropological Survey of People of Aboriginal descent in the Metropolitan Area of Perth: Section B, Historical Background—quoting A.O. Neville, private papers. This study was undertaken for the SSRC-AP.
[29] Aborigines Protection (Amendment) Act 1936, sections 8A and 8B; Aborigines Protection Act 1909, section 14.

could not bear the sight of Aboriginal misery and mendicancy. And government agencies were doing the best they could, *on the basis of acceptable priorities*, and with the resources they had.

Such limitations on freedom of movement had long been routine in Queensland, and in Western and South Australia. As well as power to remove to a reserve, without reference to a court, the Queensland Director or his officer could keep an Aboriginal there or remove him to any other reserve at will (a power commonly used to remove 'trouble-makers' to the more distant ones); and the Act provided for police arrest as the means of so doing.[30] This remained law until the 1965 Act made reference to a court necessary. By the same means a protector could remove a whole 'camp' away from a town 'to which in his opinion they should not be permitted to have access'.[31] Protectors being police officers, the Aboriginal remained at the mercy of the police. It was also an offence for a non-Aboriginal to enter without a permit or be within five chains of a place where Aborigines were camped: or to 'trespass on' a reserve.[32]

Western Australian law had long provided against non-Aborigines 'frequenting' camps, and had enabled protectors to remove camps from the vicinity of towns and justices to order Aborigines out of town. It provided for the declaration of town areas as 'prohibited areas', and even prevented Aboriginal females from camping near creeks and inlets on the coast at night. It had also enabled compulsory removal to reserves, and had made the reserve a prohibited area for others.[33] The 1936 Act tightened up these provisions. For instance the original Act of 1905 had made it an offence to entice or assist an Aboriginal to leave a reserve; that of 1936 made it also an offence to 'transport or assist' a native who had already 'escaped'.[34]

The 1939 Act of South Australia gave the Board power to remove Aborigines to reserves and keep them there, prevented entry by un-authorised persons, and made it an offence to assist or entice them to escape. It enabled the Board or a protector to remove camps from the vicinity of towns, and to remove individuals for 'loitering' or being improperly clothed. Towns could be proclaimed prohibited areas.[35]

The effect of such provisions on the attitudes of people who had long shared the Australian rural and frontier tradition, and had long lost any

[30] Aboriginals Preservation and Protection Act of 1939, section 22.
[31] Ibid., section 21.
[32] Ibid., sections 30 and 31.
[33] These provisions were in the 1905 Act, and remained in the Amendment Act of 1936. See sections 12-15, 36-41 of the Act of 1905.
[34] Aborigines Act Amendment Act 1936, section 11(c).
[35] Aborigines Act 1934-1939, sections 20-2, 31-3.

operative Aboriginal culture, may be easily imagined. The economic effects must have been catastrophic, since vicinity to town offered the main hope of being 'picked up' by employers for seasonal work. Where the movement was to managed reserves, this coincided with drastic reductions in expenditure on such places, at the very time when their populations were being forcibly increased. For the most part the only 'work' available was the pointless routine of maintaining the institution. The trade unions, in general, were not interested in Aboriginal wages, nor in Aboriginal membership, and seem at least not to have protested at this removal of possible competitors for the employment available. Those who had to go on to the managed stations came under a further restrictive system of control, through regulations aimed mainly at the imposition of discipline, and executed by managers who required no educational qualifications for their appointments.

I have traced elsewhere the background and the development of attitudes inherited from frontier conditions which appeared to justify this kind of legislation.[36] That in the settled areas special limitations on the rights of the person should have been intensified indicates how authority was legislating for the stereotype Aboriginal conceived in early frontier contacts; and also how it was mistaking the disorganised protest of a leaderless and disorganised minority for indications of cultural or genetic traits inherent in Aboriginal personality. In addition to the legal limitations on movement, location, and association (the latter including the attempt to restrict miscegenation), there were special restrictions on personal habits (for instance, drinking laws). Some governments placed control of property in official hands. Some controlled employment under separate laws, establishing separate conditions. Some provided that officials could take over from parents the control of their children. In addition, special laws were eventually introduced for the control of Aboriginal health matters, mainly inspired by the fear of infection and contagion. Prejudice is still commonly defended as maintaining a 'hygiene' and not a 'racial' barrier. Looked at as a whole, all this legislation makes it clear that much of it arose originally from the very real need to save lives in situations which had been out of control. Once such laws are enacted, it is a matter of real difficulty to depart from them, since they both create and maintain social and economic relationships—for instance the habit of dependency, on the one hand, and the advantage to employers of apparently cheap and docile labour, on the other.

[36] See *The Destruction of Aboriginal Society*.

Of all the restraints on personal habits, that which forbade consumption of alcohol was the oldest and the most universal. And as from
the days of first contact alcohol offered the main chance of escape for
frustrated members of a disorganised and repressed community, this
restriction was from the beginning commonly evaded, with open
drunkenness the most common mark of defiance of the police and other
authority. It became so deeply imbedded in the pattern of relationships of
Aborigines with other Australians that the removal of the restrictions
over the last decade or so led to much controversy and to predictions of
dire consequences in each State. Here again Victorian legislation has been
atypical. The Acts from 1869 to 1928 forbade supply to those defined as
*Aboriginal*; but after 1886 this applied only to those of full descent and
others living on the stations. As was common, there were also special
provisions in the State's Licensing Act which forbade the supply of liquor
to an 'Aboriginal native',[37] which allowed discretion to the hotel-keeper
to make his own decision, and led to the usual arguments, with debate on
complete freedom to drink or complete prohibition for all Aborigines,
until the restrictions were repealed in 1957.[38] The arguments in Parliament
and in the press have largely corresponded with those in other States.
They illustrate the widespread belief that Aborigines are congenitally
unable to hold their liquor. In Victoria as elsewhere there are still hotelkeepers who will refuse to serve a person they consider to be Aboriginal;
and the attitudes of police on the matter are still a factor in the actual
exercise of rights. But Victoria was unique in the freedom it offered to the
part-Aboriginal living in the community to drink in the hotel as a matter
of legal right, so that for a long time the part-Aborigines from southern
New South Wales had yet another reason to cross the Murray River.

It seems unnecessary to detail here the provisions of liquor Acts,
licensing Acts, and the special provisions in the Aboriginal legislation
against supply or consumption. Outside of Victoria (and Tasmania) the
effect of them all was that those who fell within the categories could not
be supplied, could not drink, and in some cases were prohibited from
being or working on licensed premises. With the 'pub' as the centre of the
small rural community, such exclusions tended to widen the gulf between
Aborigines and others, and led to the Aboriginal drinking habits which
have been so graphically described by Jeremy Beckett: the 'all-male
drinking groups', excluded from the bar, got their wine (cheap and strong,
quickly consumed and therefore less likely to be confiscated by police

[37] Licensing Act 1928, section 177(a).
[38] The details have been stated by Diane Barwick, A Little More Than Kin (1965), ch. 2.

before consumption) from the back door of the 'pub' and retired with it to the bush—so that an old lady said to him that 'the girls spend all their time looking for a boy and a cigarette, and the boys spend all their time looking for a bottle'. Out in the bush, away from the police, the young 'poddies' learned from their elders the old traditions of the frontier days, in this special Aboriginal adaptation. Aboriginal defiance of authority could coalesce round this universal assertion of equality:

> Aint got no time for dancing, no time for fancy girls,
> They'll just spend your money, slip around with your best pals.
> Aint got no time for taxis, no time for big flash cars,
> But if I've got any money to spend, I'll spend it in the bar.[39]

The effects of this kind of emphasis in family spending added to economic disaster. There has been, it seems, a cycle of causation, with the wage-earner doomed to failure as husband and father, thus adding to his problems in the effort to escape. Another Aboriginal folksong is relevant here:

> Sure he loves the dear silver the family all earn
> And if you don't get it with rage he will burn.
> Sure he swings Ma a little and pops one on me;
> May God keep and protect us, whilst Dad's on the spree.[40]

It seems not too much to say that, for many Aborigines, life became bearable through alcohol; that the momentary defiance of all authority seemed worth the usual aftermath in the local gaol, even when (as was common enough) the drinker had discharged his tensions with an attack on the local policeman and had to take the consequences.

For most people the minor restrictions on conduct cease at the front door of the home. But where Aboriginal homes were on reserves, the laws against drinking extended into the house, as did the regulations against certain conduct on reserves such as gambling, or even harbouring a relative not supposed to be there. The regulations, applicable on managed reserves, under the 1963 Western Australian Act make 'insubordination, indecent or unseemly behaviour, disorderly or immoral conduct, or the use of abusive, threatening or obscene language'[41] offences for which there are penalties.

---

[39] Both quotations are from Jeremy Beckett, A Study of a Mixed-Blood Aboriginal Minority in the Pastoral West of New South Wales, by courtesy of the author. The verse is from the 'Wilcannia Song'.

[40] From Catherine J. Ellis, The History of Music is the History of Mankind. Article contributed to SSRC-AP (typescript, in SSRC-AP file).

[41] Native Welfare Act Regulations 1964, No. 25.

Queensland settlements are managed under regulations where the list of offences could cover just about anything of which a manager could disapprove; and he is provided with his own police force, gaol, and even a dormitory to which he can commit a person without any trial.[42] I mention these regulations as examples only, still operative after relaxations of earlier regulations. Everywhere on managed stations or settlements similar ones were in force. Even where the reserve was not under direct control of the Aboriginal affairs officer, control was vested mainly in the local police. The Aboriginal was probably the only Australian who could be arrested for being drunk in his own bed. General offences like insubordination had to be left to the interpretation of the manager; and as he frequently interfered, even into the details of home management, there was continual 'trouble'. It has also been common to prescribe that Aborigines on managed reserves must, if not employed elsewhere, work on the station tasks at chores which became 'training' with the adoption of the assimilation policy. During the depression such tasks could be unpaid, with refusal of rations as the sanction.

From the time of first settlement the custom had developed of the annual government issue of blankets and clothing to Aborigines deemed to need them, and the need could be very real as the diminution of game decreased the supply of skins, while clearing the land increased the need for shelter. Often, as time passed, the sale of such issues offered a way of acquiring small amounts of cash or goods or alcohol, so that the issues were made for 'the use of' the recipients. Prohibitions against the sale of blankets, clothing, and other items became universal in the legislation, with penalties for the Aborigines, and for others found with these blankets in their possession. The limited issues remained for the obviously needy off the managed reserves. Maintenance of this practice during the depression years, though apparently limited in extent, together with the provision of housing on reserves, provide the main basis for the argument that in the past the Aboriginal has been demoralised by a policy of 'hand-outs'—a curious argument when one remembers that his admission to the general scale of social service benefits began only during the 1940s, and is not even now complete. (In some States particular social service benefits were paid earlier. At least some Aborigines on stations, before the 1939-45 war, received family endowment from the New South Wales government.)

From 1902 the Queensland system of protection, geared as it was to the problems presented by the less sophisticated groups, involved control

[42] Aborigines' and Torres Strait Islanders' Regulations of 1966.

of property; and legislation which stood until 1965 provided that the protector (generally a police officer) should 'undertake the protection and management of the property of all Aboriginals in the district assigned to him', with power to sell or dispose of it, whether real or personal property. The power is now vested in a district officer; but there is now a right of the person affected to apply to a stipendiary magistrate to regain control.[43] Both earlier and current legislation makes the Director the administrator of deceased estates for Aborigines. Prior to 1965 there was no provision for the wishes of the Aboriginal to be taken into account.

Similar provisions introduced in Western Australia in 1905 made the consent of the *Aboriginal* or *half-caste* necessary 'except so far as may be necessary for the due preservation of such property'.[44] But in 1936 the Commissioner received power to decide on how money of a *native* might be spent for his benefit, and to administer deceased estates.[45] By the law of 1963, control of property requires the consent of the 'native'; and the role of the Commissioner in the case of deceased estates is limited to giving information to the Public Trustee where the person has died intestate.[46]

The South Australian Act of 1911 provided for control of property identical with that in the Western Australian Act of 1905; but under the 1939 Act the decision on whether such management was in the *Aboriginal*'s interest became one for a magistrate, not the Board.[47]

The other States did not have comparable provisions, mainly because they were not concerned with the less sophisticated frontier groups. Where the provision was made, there is something ironic in it: claims to real property based on prior occupation had been everywhere ignored. The provisions gave control mainly of cash savings from wages. But they must also have contributed to the general anxiety of those who had managed to make a competence of their own and who feared that they might be brought under administrative control, for the practice of classifying people into categories could mean that anyone with a dark skin in the three States which made such provision might lose control of his possessions.

The provisions, additional to those for child welfare in general, for the Aboriginal authority to take away control of children from parents,

---

[43] Aboriginals Preservation and Protection Act of 1939, section 16; Aborigines' and Torres Strait Islanders' Affairs Act of 1965, sections 27-9.
[44] Aborigines Act 1905, section 33.
[45] Aborigines Act Amendment Act 1936, sections 20 and 21.
[46] Native Welfare Act 1963, sections 23 and 26.
[47] Aborigines Act 1911, section 35; Aborigines Act 1934-1939, section 35.

seem to have been deeply resented. These lent a special and generally feared authority to the local officers responsible for Aboriginal welfare. By the end of the 1930s, the Director in Queensland, the Commissioner in Western Australia, and the Board in South Australia had become the legal guardians of all Aboriginal minors up till the age of twenty-one, superseding the claims of the parents.[48] Such powers could be used in the attempt to apply a special 'half-caste' policy. They were also used to bind children into apprenticeships and other forms of employment, notably to place the young girls into poorly paid domestic work; and to remove them from a home situation considered unsuitable to, variously, general child welfare homes or to special homes maintained by the authority, or by a Christian mission or church for coloured children only, or even to multi-purposed missions or settlements. In Victoria the Board could prescribe under regulation conditions of apprenticeship for part-Aboriginal children or transfer orphans into the care of the Child Welfare Department, a much more reasonable situation.[49] In New South Wales the Board could bind in apprenticeship the child of any Aboriginal, or the *neglected* child of a person 'apparently having an admixture of Aboriginal blood in his veins', acting in this way *in loco parentis*. It also had the general power to maintain institutions for children, under its duty to 'provide for the custody, maintenance, and education of the children of Aborigines'. The parent or other who 'enticed' the child to leave such service or institution was guilty of an offence.[50]

I have myself known Aboriginal parents who believed that some officers have used the threat to 'take' children as a disciplinary measure; in fact, I have been mistaken for an officer of a State administration on the execution of such a mission, and treated accordingly. The changes in the legislation are quite recent, and in some cases partial change only has been effected. The 1966 Queensland laws envisaged the matter of neglected children going to the State Children Department, though regulations may be made (so far as I can learn they have not yet been) for the employment or apprenticeship of the children of 'assisted Aborigines'.[51] As the department may control conditions of employment for 'assisted Aborigines' generally, perhaps the special power is not required. In Western Australia,

[48] See Aboriginals Preservation and Protection Act of 1939, section 18 (Qld); Aborigines Act Amendment Act 1936, section 7 (W.A.); and Aborigines Act 1934-1939, section 10 (S.A.).
[49] Aborigines Act 1928, section 6 (ix) and (x).
[50] Aborigines Protection Act 1909, sections 7(c) and 11-13; Aborigines Protection (Amendment) Act 1936, section 2(e), (f), and (g).
[51] Aborigines' and Torres Strait Islanders' Affairs Act of 1965, section 60(14).

the powers of the Commissioner to act as legal guardian of the children was omitted from the 1963 Act. The power vested in the South Australian Board was discarded in the Act of 1962.

In New South Wales, with the disappearance of the restrictions on drinking, perhaps the main power remaining with the Board over Aborigines living off managed reserves (and the managers are progressively being withdrawn) is that of controlling children committed to its special institutions at Kinchela (for boys) and Cootamundra (for girls). The continued existence of these places (although it seems to be policy to have Child Welfare take over management of all committed children) acts as a stimulus for continued discrimination, since in practice the dark child may be sent to the 'Aboriginal' home, his fair brother to a Child Welfare home. The same homes serve as reception and management centres for the 'wards' of the Board, who may be apprenticed or placed in a foster home.

It seems essential that such vestiges should be removed as soon as possible, with departments of child welfare or the equivalents in each State acting for all children, under common legislation and regulations. Their continued existence is a stimulus to anxieties all too well-founded in the comparatively recent past; and they serve to strengthen prejudice. They can be explained mainly in terms of the long-standing prejudice, which even now is expressed from time to time as the last separate schools for Aboriginal children in the settled areas give way to integrated schooling.

The history of the controls over wages and working conditions in Queensland, South Australia, and Western Australia is directly relevant to current problems of the frontier regions. It will be considered in detail subsequently.[52] These controls, however, are a good example of how laws passed in the first place to deal with pastoral conditions on the frontiers continued to be applied to any persons who were legally Aboriginal, even though the conditions had changed. Queensland offers the most complete example: see Chapter 4.

New South Wales and Victoria had far less obvious problems of 'white management and coloured labour' in the period when this kind of legislation became usual, though problems of exploitation remained. From 1869 until 1957 the Victorian Board had power to issue work certificates, to decide the terms of employment, and to take control of wages. But, according to Dr Barwick, attempts at rigorous enforcement

[52] *The Remote Aborigines* deals with issues current in the sparsely settled northern and central regions. For conditions of employment, see Part III—C.D.R.

were short lived and made mainly by managers of Aboriginal stations. The Board lacked staff to make similar provision for 'wanderers' off the stations. Nonetheless, the legislation remained useful, as it enabled the Board to act in cases of 'blatant exploitation'.[53] From the 1890s the apprenticeship of children was the main activity in this field, but 'few or no half-caste children were ever apprenticed to learn skilled trades'. Boys were wanted mainly for seasonal work, and the girls as domestic labour in Melbourne and the country towns, until

the practice was abandoned during the nineteen-thirties in response to the Aboriginal parents' protests that the girls were often lonely, sometimes ill-treated, and frequently had to return to Lake Tyers to bear illegitimate children.[54]

The New South Wales Act of 1936 had a section which enabled the Board, in cases of ill-treatment by an employer or where a 'reasonable' wage was not paid, to remove the Aboriginal from the employment to a reserve or elsewhere.[55] This also was a power only likely to be exercised in a case of obvious exploitation. As in Victoria, the Aboriginal worker was at the mercy of a labour market in which, in so far as he was identifiable from appearance, he would be handicapped in the search for work; and in so far as the trade unions were (to say the least) not interested in his case (especially during the depression years) and his bargaining position weakened by lack of education and training, and by all the other factors affecting his status, he would be fortunate to achieve award wages or even the basic wage. Even now, the rural Aboriginal tends to find himself engaged in those types of seasonal work where payment may be related to the market price of the product and where there is no effective policing of working conditions and accommodation.

During the depression years it is clear, from reports in the press and from the occasional discussions in the State parliaments when Aboriginal affairs were considered, that there was a concern with Aboriginal health. In this, malnutrition must have been a major factor, but the legislation was as little concerned with nutrition as it was with wage rates. The fear was of contagion and infection; and fear of the spread of venereal diseases was especially marked. South Australia had had provision for a separate system of lock-hospitals and for the segregated treatment of Aborigines within public hospitals since 1911, and for compulsory examinations;

---

[53] Diane Barwick, A Little More Than Kin (1965), p. 148.
[54] Ibid., p. 150.
[55] Aborigines Protection (Amendment) Act, 1936, section 2(l)(i).

and the sections remained in the 1939 Act.[56] In Queensland a protector could order a medical examination, and could order an Aboriginal suffering from a contagious disease to attend for treatment.[57] In Western Australia similar compulsory provisions were made in 1936.[58]

In the same year it was enacted in New South Wales that 'any Aborigine or person apparently having an admixture of Aboriginal blood' could be compulsorily examined and removed for treatment to a public hospital or other institution.[59] In introducing the 1936 Act the Colonial Secretary stressed the 'acute position' arising from what he claimed was widespread Aboriginal infection with gonococcal ophthalmia. Aborigines, he stated, were not so susceptible to blindness from this disease as were whites! A Member of the House who was also a member of the Aborigines Protection Board was even more explicit.

The reason for the urgency of this measure [he said] is because the health of *our own people* is very seriously threatened at the present moment. Either we allow these people to roam far and wide and spread possible disease, or take them from the precincts of the villages and towns where all this wrongdoing happens [*sic*]. In one disease gonococcal ophthalmia smears were taken from the eyes of fifteen aboriginals, and in fourteen cases it was shown that these people were suffering from this very horrible disease.[60] (My italics.)

Only in Victoria (and Tasmania) were such special provisions for the Aboriginal British subject considered unnecessary. The deep insult here, to the sophisticated person, is obvious. Possibly what prevented the erection of separate hospital accommodation on a large scale was the other matter of concern to the non-Aboriginal taxpayer—expense, which ensured that there were not even adequate funds to house or feed the people who had in these later years been moved on to managed stations.

This kind of legislation has to be seen in the context of other laws providing for compulsory movement from the vicinity of towns, for the prevention of miscegenation in some States; of separate laws against prostitution and soliciting, and of those keeping non-Aborigines off reserves. It was not uncommon, in 'colonial' situations, for concern by westerners with the health of 'natives' to begin in this fashion with concern for their own. The tendency to impute to the person of different appearance those characteristics which arouse fear or shame in the pre-

---

[56] Ibid., 1939, sections 25 and 26.
[57] Aboriginals Preservation and Protection Act of 1939, section 20.
[58] Aborigines Act Amendment Act, 1936, section 12.
[59] Aborigines Protection (Amendment) Act 1936, section 2(l)(j); and *N.S.W.P.D.*, 1935-6, Second Series, vol. 149, pp. 4749-50—speech by the Colonial Secretary (18 June).
[60] *N.S.W.P.D.*, 1935-6, Second Series, vol. 149, p. 4844.

judiced group is a well enough known symptom of the mentality which moves towards apartheid situations. It may be fortunate that Australians were at least never ready to face up to the cost of apartheid: or it may be that most governments continued to think in terms of disappearance of the problem group—the Aborigines would die out, the part-Aborigines be absorbed. This health legislation remained on the books until the 1960s; and South Australia still retains provision for compulsory examination and treatment of Aborigines, apart from general health legislation.[61] What is offensive is not the provision for compulsory examination but the special legislation, which if required should surely apply to all who work with Aborigines.

This, then, was the character of the special restrictive law which came to a climax in the 'settled' areas during the great depression of the 1930s. A great deal of the resistance (generally, in the circumstances, passive) by Aborigines to authority, and of their scepticism about any moves by government ostensibly for their benefit, can be explained by reference to it. A full-scale conspectus of this body of law would have included many other matters, like the limits on rights to own dogs, guns, or, if on reserves, live stock. It would show how powers conferred on managers of stations and settlements, both government and mission, either explicitly or implicitly enabled them to prevent the exercise of any customs thought undesirable—explicit in Queensland, where the missionary, for instance, could prevent 'tribal dancing' and other sinful activities; implicit in New South Wales, where a manager could berate the station inmates for wailing at funerals, as not conducive to 'assimilation'. All this will disappear; but it is part of the recent background; and there remain some quite arbitrary limitations on rights, especially in Queensland.

But governments had neither the funds nor often the doctrinaire heartlessness to apply these laws everywhere with equal rigour. There seem to have been many, technically within the categories, who managed to avoid some at least of the limitations on liberty. There must have been many humane departmental officials and local police 'protectors' who followed the rules of common sense. But with the law as it was, every legal Aboriginal *had* to be insecure, if only because there were also many officials who saw their duty as the discharge of the letter of the law and regulations. There is a fairly common kind of generalising which attributes, to persons in this predicament, stresses resulting from 'social change'. This is one of those face-saving generalisations which explain

---

[61] Aboriginal Affairs Act 1962, section 25.

the conduct of a minority in this condition as due to the conflict between the indigenous and the imposed culture. My reason for having in this chapter indicated, in some detail, just what the law three decades ago really was throughout the settled regions, just how recently most of the more repressive features of it have been repealed, is that in itself this is enough to explain conduct arising from insecurity and beliefs about injustice. Present Aboriginal beliefs and attitudes, even were there no other causes, could be adequately accounted for by reference to the rigid controls which reached a climax in the depression years of the 1930s. The same systems of controls have been a factor in maintaining prejudices towards Aborigines.

W hen the closely settled areas were frontiers, and Aboriginal attempts
to live off the land in a rapidly changing environment were being
countered by their extermination or removal, the practice began of
setting aside small areas of land for them to live on. The idea that agriculture is the basis of civilisation has not even yet become completely
obsolete in the administration of Aboriginal affairs. One reason is its
apparent cheapness and the apparent economy in land, in making what
might amount to two or three 'white' living areas provide for the learning
activities and the co-operative or other effort of a couple of hundred
Aboriginal people. The result of such ideas can be seen today in such
places as Cherbourg, in southern Queensland, Lake Tyers in Victoria,
Cumeroogunga or Murrin Bridge in New South Wales, or Point Pearce
and Point McLeay in South Australia. In the late 1920s and the 1930s a
few very large reserves were set aside in what then appeared the most
useless areas of the north and centre of the continent but which now have
become causes of contention as their new value forces a reappraisal.[1]
That the reserves in the settled areas generally fall below two or three
thousand acres in size (and are often very much less), that they have
tended to be on indifferent land, that they have often been in out-of-the-
way locations, and that they share with all other Aboriginal reserves
(except that there has been recently a notable change in South Australia,
which vests all remaining reserves in an Aboriginal Land Trust) the
feature of being Crown lands assigned for the use of the Board or Department responsible for Aboriginal affairs, without any right of tenure

[1] See Rowley, *The Remote Aborigines.*

being vested in the people who live on them, can all be attributed to the relative priorities given in the past to the white settler seeking land and to the Aboriginal group in need of food and shelter. The first reserves tended to be controlled by mission bodies (even today it is common for local reference to be to 'the mission'). But there were also early government stations like those set up under the Port Phillip Protectorate. They originated as places where Aborigines could obtain limited rations when in need, where they left their children, probably because they had to move so much faster after disappearing game, and where the mission schools competed with the adults for the minds of the children. The attempts to establish settled communities were inevitable. In fact, this was the aim of policy from the first.

In South Australia two stations, at Point Pearce and Point McLeay, have been managed continuously for a century or so—first by missionaries and then by government officers. The effort is older in Victoria and New South Wales; both have reserves where persons of Aboriginal descent have lived for comparable periods, but without the same continuity as managed institutions. Every State (even Tasmania with its group on Cape Barren Island) has some out-of-the-way places where Aboriginal people have lived for generations.

It was inevitable that such people should come to regard these places as their own. Much of what has been loosely accepted as 'tribal' loyalty is really the result of common history and experience as inmates of these places, places which in a latter period of unsatisfactory adjustment elsewhere (especially where, as in Victoria, people have a tradition of being forcibly removed from stations which they had come to regard as belonging to them) may be seen in retrospect as the locale of a period of happiness and prosperity, although what we know of the history suggests rather a continual insecurity. There are also quite different beliefs and remembered experiences, of people having been forced *on* to stations and settlements under the kind of legislation discussed earlier, as in the depression years in New South Wales and Western Australia, although this process in New South Wales began back in the 1880s. It had begun long before in Victoria, and had been maintained up till 1886. In Queensland it began even before the legislation in 1897; under the current law it is still possible.

Isolation on the reserves and managed stations, with the conflicting loyalties arising from long residence, have operated as further divisive factors in Aboriginal society, as when two stations have been combined by enforced movement of one group to another place for administrative convenience or other purpose; or as between those who have been determined to live outside reserves at all costs and those who have remained on them. In addition, there is the common belief that the reserve lands in some way belonged to the people who lived there, that they were a grant by Queen Victoria, and that they were often taken from the rightful owners by a mean government. From the history, one would expect the tradition of dispossession to be strongest in Victoria, where it accounts for much of the recent 'trouble' over Lake Tyers. The tradition of forced restriction may be strongest in Queensland and in the south-west of Western Australia, where the opening up of Moore River resulted in the almost immediate scattering of the inmates.

Each of these places has a special history of its own which cannot be outlined here. But those still remaining as managed settlements and stations in Queensland, New South Wales, and Victoria in 1965 (since when the policy in New South Wales has been to remove the managements and to open them up) have been the subject of a special study by J.P.M. Long as part of this Project.[2] Long was impressed by the resemblance of the philosophy of the Aboriginal stations to that which led to measures for 'indoor relief' at the time of the Poor Laws in England; he compared the earlier rationing of the needy, with the annual blanket and occasional clothing, medicines, and other issues, to the Poor Law measures for 'outdoor relief'. This kind of provision certainly reminds one of the measures to feed, clothe, and house the 'poor'. There are, however, additional features. One is the tradition of separate legislation for 'natives'. But in Australia very little of this goes back to the times of colonial administration, to the time before responsible government in the Australian colonies.

To account for the exclusive features of Aboriginal legislation, one has to look for some explanation additional to the traditions of treatment of the unwanted poor and those founded in colonial administration, for the more restrictive of the laws mentioned go somewhat further than either, in some States and in some cases being almost comparable with leper laws. This third element may be the typical reaction of unrestrained 'settler democracies', allowing those to whose interest it was to be rid of Aborigines to get their way at the expense of a diminishing group which was not wanted in the settled areas, either as a source of regular labour or as a market.

[2] Long, *Aboriginal Settlements: A Survey of Institutional Communities in Eastern Australia.* This includes brief appendixes on the missions and stations in South Australia and Northern Territory, and the missions in Western Australia.

The more degraded the general Aboriginal condition, the greater the tendency for those who had been most closely associated with them (especially with the women), and who must maintain a front of respectability, to shun them, to deny them, and to deny former relationships and associations. Prejudice is in part the projection of feelings of guilt on to the stereotype of the victims; and some of the things said in parliamentary debates, not only about Aborigines in general, but about what they were purported to do on the poverty-stricken 'missions', make it hard to account for them in any other way. In the settler democracies of America and Africa, economic motives to remove 'natives' have been very powerful indeed, influencing both the settler who wanted unencumbered land and the worker who wanted to remove competition and to retain high wages. Apartheid, exclusive immigration policies, and isolated settlements for Aborigines spring from the same roots.

Against this background, it was inevitable that what purported to be a protective measure was supported also as a means of removing persons of Aboriginal appearance from the towns and their vicinity. During the depression years the fear of disease probably acted as an additional motive for removal to managed reserves. The amounts spent on these reserves, either departmentally managed or small areas under the eye of a local police protector, were so meagre that they had to be rural ghettos. Moreover, where there was a full-time manager they were treated as multi-purposed institutions; so that while the non-Aboriginal problem case or family might be referred to a specialised source of advice or assistance, the Aboriginal one was likely to be sent to the station or settlement.

We have seen that in the depression years the *unemployed* Aboriginal might be legally sent there. Where there was no real work within the institution, the manager had to invent or create it; and he could refuse rations to those who refused to work. There were special stresses between management and inmates in the Aboriginal 'asylum'.[3] It is worth a note that those who received their schooling on New South Wales Aboriginal stations in the 1930s were taught by managers who were untrained, and for whom the school was one of many chores, taking some two or three hours in a long day. Work either without wages or for a payment which would fluctuate with the amount available in the station budget inevitably conditioned those who worked 'outside', whilst living on the stations, to accept low wages. Thus on a small scale, even in the settled areas, the

[3] See Erving Goffman, *Asylums: Essays on the Social Situation of Mental Patients and Other Inmates.*

station served the purpose of the village or tribal lands in a colony, as a place from which labour could be obtained as required, to which it could be returned when not, and payment for which might make no provision for maintenance of dependants. At the same time there was not the same economic incentive to ensure a minimum level of welfare on the station as existed for the rulers of colonised villages, since economic enterprises, in the settled areas, depended only marginally on station or reserve labour.

## THE NEW SOUTH WALES BACKGROUND

In introducing the State's first Aborigines Protection Act in 1909, the New South Wales Colonial Secretary argued that the needs were for greater control by government of the reserves (which had been managed through local committees) and for control of neglected children. The remarks of another member indicate that the independent-spirited people of Cumeroogunga had been objecting to members of the local committee prying into homes, and had appealed to higher authority. The whole trend was to get Aborigines under control: the Board required power to control the 'camps' as well as to move them. There were references to 'misuse' of blankets and rations. (A whole community might have to live on what was issued to mothers for children and to the sick and old.)[4] The debate marks a turning point away from the Victorian policy of disengagement and reduction of commitments, and by the time of the 1936 Act there were twenty-two managed stations. Even in 1909 there was the problem of those who lived just off a station, defying the authority of managers and local committees.

Back in 1882 the discussion in Parliament had been of the situation on the two missions at Warangesda and Maloga. The 'blacks' were decreasing and the 'half-castes' were being taught in these places to be 'useful members of society', partly on the government grants of £200 and £600 respectively. The attitude at that time had reflected Victorian policies: the assumption was that small amounts needed to be expended as the full-bloods disappeared and their children were absorbed. There was reference to the missions as benevolent institutions; and some talk of taking the 'near-white' children from mothers to participate in the training.[5] Speaking on Supply in 1889, and referring to the stations at Cumeroo-

[4] *N.S.W.P.D.*, 1909, Second Series, vol. 35, p. 2569 (6 October), and vol. 36, pp. 4492 and 4541 (15 December).
[5] Ibid., 1883, First Series, vol. 8, pp. 598-601.

gunga and Brewarrina, a Member posed the dilemma—where a group had settled and seemed to prosper, it was soon 'driven off' by white settlers who wanted the land.[6] And in the long run even where government had originally set aside a sizeable area of good land, what tended to happen (and not only in New South Wales) was that the best land was either leased or sold to non-Aborigines.

In the early years there were attacks in Parliament on the missionaries who administered these stations, and later on the government officials responsible. By the early 1890s the families at Cumeroogunga were pressing for rights to the land they had spent so much labour on improving; but they were never to get them. Where a station or reserve was close to a town, or simply because others wanted the land, there were attacks on the morality of the Aborigines. One Member remarked that the people of Tumut were claiming that the men of the reserve at Brungle were thieves, and the women prostitutes, when 'the fact was the land occupied by the Aboriginals was grudged to them'.[7] If the Aborigines left for reasons of employment, the reserve was likely to be claimed for other purposes. Thus location of a reserve at Nymboida, where there was a manager, but from which most of the people had gone in 1915 to work on railway construction, was queried by the municipalities of Grafton and South Grafton as likely to pollute the water supply.[8] After the 1914-18 war, it sometimes happened that a 'returned soldier' applied for the reserve land and this raised the issue of priority.[9] There was always criticism of the stations: whatever the Board did with its slender resources was wrong from the point of view of those who wanted a particular reserve to be elsewhere.

Conditions at Brewarrina station were generally in dispute, and by the time of the 1936 Act this was still in full spate, though Brewarrina in that year shared its notoriety with the new station at Menindee, whither people had been moved because of water failure in their previous location, at Carowra Tank. They were moved there, however, before proper facilities for water had been established on the new site.[10] Underpaid manager-teachers were, if conscientious, hopelessly overworked; and

[6] Ibid., 1889, First Series, vol. 41, pp. 4347-55, speeches by J. Abbott and W.S. Dowel (22 August).

[7] Ibid., 1892, First Series, vol. 56, pp. 5450-61.

[8] Ibid., 1915-16, Second Series, vol. 59, p. 967 (10 August).

[9] Ibid., 1918, Second Series, vol. 72, pp. 1291-2 and 1343-4 (12 and 17 September).

[10] See *N.S.W.P.D.*, Second Series, vol. 152, pp. 1496 *et seq.* (9 November)—speech by M.A. Davidson, Member for Cobar, and the reply by H.J. Bate, the Member who was also a member of the Aborigines Protection Board.

the funds available to the Board obviously inadequate. There was an obvious bankruptcy of policy or purpose. Even in the matter of education, of which so much was always made in reports and in Parliament, the Board announced its policy, in the 1933 Report, as to establish separate schools 'where the Aboriginal population warrants it, and *where there is objection* to the attendance of the Aboriginals at the public school' (my italics).[11] On the other hand, the first 'treatment room' had been erected at Brewarrina, where there was an outbreak of trachoma; three years later, a similar epidemic at Angledool caused the Board to close the station there and move the inhabitants to Brewarrina.[12] This may have saved the expense of a new room for treatment, and other costs, by reducing the stations from twenty-two to twenty-one, but it was to be a long-standing cause of strife between two groups of inmates under stress. Under stress, too, were the unfortunate members of staff, who were expected to exercise 'reasonable discipline . . . essential to the wellbeing of the Aborigines' on the stations, the Board regretting that those who remained fringe-dwellers off them were suffering from 'lack of requisite disciplinary supervision' which accounted for their 'undesirable conditions'.[13]

Perhaps two or three well-built and carefully managed centres could have been more easily defended. On the other hand the very inefficiency of the operation meant that the attempted controls were continually breaking down: in view of the policy this was not altogether a tragedy for Aborigines. Board policy as stated in the 1935 Report was to assist Aborigines to help themselves on the stations (by providing 'material' while the Aborigines provided the labour); the Board saw its concession that Aborigines might compete in local sports as important in the task of 'graduating the Aboriginal from his former primitive state to the standards of the white man'. By this time, and in pursuit of this kind of objective, it was maintaining forty *separate* schools.[14]

Perhaps this marked the nadir of policy; and anyone who wishes to know just how shocking conditions were should read the evidence given before a Select Committee of the New South Wales Parliament in 1937.[15]

[11] *N.S.W.P.P.* 1934-5, vol. 3, p. 777—Aborigines Protection Board (A.P.B.), Report, 1933, p. 2.
[12] Ibid., 1936-7, vol. 1, p. 1015—A.P.B. Report, 1936.
[13] Ibid., 1935-6, vol. 3, p. 763—A.P.B. Report, 1935.
[14] Ibid., vol. 3, p. 763; and 1936-7, vol. 1, p. 1015—A.P.B. Reports, 1935 and 1936.
[15] Ibid., 1938-40, vol. 7, pp. 609-738—Minutes of Evidence before a Select Committee on the Administration of the Aborigines Protection Board (1937). This Committee lapsed when the parliamentary session terminated. There was no report. Of the nineteen sessions convened, five had lapsed for lack of a quorum.

It sheds valuable light on the role of the stations and reserves. The position was never comparable with Queensland, however, for there the inmate might be kept on a settlement against his will. The power to remove Aborigines from towns or camps thus offered no more than a temporary local solution to obvious distress or disorder. Residents could come and go, though they had to report to the manager; against those who denied his authority the sanction was expulsion from the station, and from their homes there. (This power remained until the managers were withdrawn progressively in the mid-1960s.) It is probable that the Relief Boards' refusal to authorise issue of the 'dole' to Aborigines operated more powerfully to drive the Aborigines into the stations and reserves than did police action in execution of court orders.[16]

Obviously here the situation was chaotic: out of real control by a Protection Board which met for a few hours each month, inadequately staffed, and having to provide for all its stations and reserves on a budget of £45,000 with a call on government stores for clothing and other issues, and about £6,000 for building and repairs.[17]

On all reserves and stations throughout the continent there has always been a notable contrast with the conditions for non-Aborigines in the country towns: yet the logic of the welfare policies was for conditions which at least offered a minimum of comfort and the safeguarding of health. Any planning for economic progress was hopeless from the start, since all genuine growing points were occupied by towns or townships. The reserve was the 'anti-town', the place to which the unwanted were consigned. But it had to be close enough to serve town needs as required— for labour, even for sexual adventures.

The evidence indicates how much must have depended on the efforts of underpaid and often devoted managers and their wives, who often worked long hours in nursing the sick and caring for children. But, as tends to happen in cases of 'broken-backed' administration, the head office was out of touch with the local managers, and instructions were so vague that some stations did not even have copies of the regulations under which they had to operate. As usual in such situations, the unforgivable official sin was inadequate reporting and accounting.

Housing conditions were such that one manager reported two and three families to each house of four rooms. The galvanised iron huts in the western area could be very cold or very hot. There were references to the difficulties of getting the inmates to wash themselves in the rivers

---

[16] Ibid.: evidence by Mrs C. Kelly, 7 December 1937.
[17] Ibid.: evidence by the Secretary of the Board, 26 November 1937.

in winter. Managers were forced to demand varying hours of work from men otherwise unemployed, in return for the rations: this settled down to a routine of two days weekly in return for rations only. Work without incentive always creates trouble for management. The evidence indicates that some managers did not know the procedures for getting additional rations for able-bodied men in the period when there was no local seasonal work. Managers and their wives gave evidence of malnutrition, of the breakdown of hygiene measures which were initially primitive, and which they attempted to enforce by punitive means; of the lack of regular visits by health officers, of the presence of tuberculosis, venereal disease, diseases of the eye, the effects of whooping cough epidemics on the children, and lack of facilities to isolate infectious disease on the station; of the objections by townsfolk to admission of station people to the local hospitals. 'Camp dwellings', shacks built from scrap, often supplemented the houses built by the Board.

Through the evidence it is easy to see the tensions between management and inmates. There is reference to outbreaks of violence, to addiction to methylated spirits, to the defiance of authority attempting to use unpaid labour to supplement the rations by gardening—which could only succeed where a manager skilled in personal relations was in charge.

One new note sounded in the evidence, with the Aboriginal voice being heard. Especially interesting is the evidence of W. Ferguson, the Organising Secretary of the Aborigines Progressive Association, a body which had begun to exert political pressure, and the very existence of which as an articulate group owed a good deal to Ferguson himself. We still await biographies of men like this who were pioneering the effort to develop an Aboriginal leadership and organisation of the inarticulate remnants of Aboriginal society.[18] He was active at Dubbo when the inquiry began, and an article by him in the local press, stating that Aboriginal evidence was not wanted by the Select Committee, had led to his being called.

We have all the best learned men and women in the world [he said] opposing our claim for freedom, for we have learned by past experience that the scholars and students will recommend that the race be preserved for scientific purposes.[19]

This was essentially a cry for an identity which would involve equality with whites as members of the 'white' Australia, not of the hypothetical

[18] A biography of Ferguson is being written by Mr J. Horner, of the Aboriginal-Australian Fellowship, Sydney.
[19] N.S.W.P.P., 1938-40, vol. 7, p. 661—Minutes of Evidence of Select Committee.

'Aboriginal' universe. The background was the growing agitation and concern about the conditions of the full-bloods on the now far-distant frontiers of economic development.[20]

Men like Ferguson, and Jack Patton of Cumeroogunga, shared the philosophy of the rural Labor movement. Ferguson referred to his own background, as a man expelled from a station, and he attacked the autocratic power of managers and the Board's attempts to get work done by paying under-award wages. He was interested in equality, and not in some special Aboriginal identity, and was proud of his non-Aboriginal descent. His evidence can be contrasted with that of M.M. Morley, Secretary of the Association for the Protection of Native Races, who spoke of the need for anthropological knowledge on the part of some at least of the Board members. Ferguson's distrust of anthropological knowledge as the basis for future policies has been maintained by many of the part-Aboriginal spokesmen since his day. There is, I believe, a feeling that some anthropologists emphasise Aboriginal *differences*, while they themselves are interested in Aboriginal *equality*. His case for equality as the solution of the 'problem' included arguments for the right to live on reserves without management (which the government was to concede three decades later), the same rights as non-Aborigines when unemployed, the same social service benefits, and the same educational opportunities.

Evidence was given by another Aboriginal labourer who had worked for award wages. He blamed the Board for the fact that he had been refused municipal relief work in Cowra. Another complained that he had cleared, fenced, and lived on reserve land for thirty years, only to see it leased to a non-Aboriginal—a complaint which could have been made by the working population of Cumeroogunga, where by this time 2,000 acres formerly used by Aboriginal farmers, and cleared by their labour, was under lease to a single 'white' farmer.[21]

The situation could hardly have been more likely to promote discord and tensions between management and inmates. The manager acted *in loco parentis* in such matters as the indenturing of young girls as domestic workers. He tended to be blamed for the low wages (they started on as little as one shilling and sixpence pocket-money and two shillings in a trust account weekly) and for what happened to them in service, for they were almost completely defenceless in a society which would attribute their pregnancies to some special *Aboriginal* drive. A boy in the

[20] See *The Remote Aborigines*.
[21] *N.S.W.P.P.*, 1938-40, vol. 7—Minutes of Evidence of Select Committee: evidence by Davis, 26 November; Grant, 7 December.

fourth year of apprenticeship received £5 4s. per quarter. The members of the Committee considered this sweated labour; it was less than payment to children apprenticed by the Child Welfare Department at the time, but it is only fair to say that this too could have been similarly designated. The manager might spend a great deal of time, as many did, taking the sick to the local doctor, looking for employment for the men, trying honestly to be an effective schoolteacher, organising work to improve housing and other conditions. But even if he was thinking only of people and their needs, rather than of his own status and place in his department, he was inevitably the target for all the enmity towards the distant and hated 'Board'.

Nor should the efforts of the Board be entirely discounted. There were some stations on which the schools were taught by trained teachers. The policy was that when a man worked off the station he should receive a fair wage, and the best managers would insist where they could on the relevant award wage. (Others, in effect, acted as agents of employers, arranging a useful cheap labour pool.) Water reticulation was being installed at the rate which funds would allow. The Board handled child endowment money (then paid by the State) and tried to ensure that it went towards supplementary food for the children by paying it in the form of orders. (The police who handled off-station payments often did this.) This, however, was the one regular source of cash; and where it was not paid in cash there was another reason for complaint. An order placed the recipient at the mercy of the local storekeeper; the Aboriginal point of view was that if he received cash he could order clothing and the like from city stores. Part of the tension arose from the obsolete view that people who have wanted money all their lives and have had very little of it can be 'taught' to use it wisely by control of their expenditure, and that such skills can be taught in this kind of multi-purposed institution. Ferguson, asked why Aborigines should refuse to work hard for their rations and issues without cash, replied that 'it is bad for anyone to have to work for his food. Why, even the government gave the dole without requiring white unemployed to work.'[22]

The year 1937 had also been marked by the conference of the State officials with the Commonwealth, and the Board, in its 1938 Report, stated that it had asked for funds to appoint more teachers on the stations, so that standards could be raised, in order to assist 'lighter caste' Aborigines to merge into the general population. It estimated the problem population as 805 of full descent, and 9,610 of mixed descent, with about two-thirds

[22] Ibid.: evidence by Ferguson, 2 December 1937.

of the total on the twenty-one stations and some fifty other reserves. The Report was critical of governments in the past for lack of support or interest: it pointed out that after five meetings where attendance of members had failed to produce a quorum, the Select Committee had lapsed without reporting. It claimed to have arranged for inspections and reports by the Department of Health, and for more treatment centres attended by trained nurses.[23]

Interim results of a health survey were published in the 1939 Report. They indicated no evidence of marked malnutrition or tuberculosis, but that trachoma and tooth decay were very common. The report emphasised the need for funds to improve separate schooling and housing. The economic situation of those on the stations was critical, with no less than 46 per cent of an average number of over 800 able-bodied men living on rations, for which the Board expected two days work per week. Commonwealth old age pensions were restricted to those without the 'preponderance' of Aboriginal 'blood' which made a person an Aboriginal for Commonwealth purposes.

An inquiry by the Public Service Board into the administration by the Board was in progress; and there is a new attitude evident in this Report, with new though woolly ideas of 'assimilation' in the air.

Until prejudices on the part of the white community have been overcome and the Aborigines themselves have been taught and led to take their place side by side with their white brothers, the complete assimilation of these people will not be achieved.

The emphasis was to be on tuition; and naturally enough the Board saw this as occurring on the stations and reserves, since these were its main assets. Therefore it was concerned about those who reacted stubbornly against removal under the Act to the stations, and instanced a case of twelve families moved from Texas, on the Queensland border, to the Boggabilla Station.[24] Thus, as the war roused the nation out of economic depression, and the Aboriginal worker found himself in demand, a new policy was taking shape.

In August 1938 the Public Service Board, having taken over the investigation left incomplete by the Select Committee, had reported.[25] There is a common sense and humanity in this Report which contrasts with the spirit of the report of the joint conference in 1937 of Common-

[23] Ibid., 1941, vol. 1, pp. 1151-3—A.P.B. Report, 1938.
[24] Ibid., pp. 1155-61—A.P.B. Report, 1939.
[25] Ibid., 1938-40, vol. 7, pp. 741-86—Aborigines Protection Report and Recommendations of the Public Service Board of New South Wales 1940—dated 16 August 1938.

wealth and State officials. It recommended that the Protection Board make an immediate survey with a view to increased assistance; that it embark on education and training programs to facilitate absorption into the *economic and social life* (my italics) of the community, which was an aim very different from that of making the genetic disappearance of the people of 'light caste' easier. The difference, however, was seen as arising from a situation which had come to resemble that in Victoria. Those under control were now, said the Report, mainly of 'half-caste or less'; and the 'best opinion' was that administration should be such as to promote economic and social *assimilation* (my italics). The 'best opinion' referred to was mainly that of A.P. Elkin. The key to the future, the Report stated, lay in education and training, and these in turn required adequate supervision and control by qualified persons.

One could perhaps criticise, as in an economic and political vacuum, the assumptions implicit here, that equality should be deferred until the Aboriginal was 'ready' for it. This concept of 'readiness', in the case of colonial peoples, was to indicate the confidence that it is in the interests of the subject peoples to wait for equality until they have been properly taught. But this was not a vacuum; it was in the wake of the most drastic economic depression, and at a time when prejudice of townsfolk against Aborigines was very high—so high that it could seem that the Aborigines' only hope lay in learning to conform, so as not to arouse further opposition. The belief in racial differences seemed even to scientists far more justified than it now does. It is worth stressing again that the emphasis was on social and economic assimilation; that this document does not have, for instance, that degree of pessimism in which white prejudice was rated so highly that the only hope for equality lay in physical absorption. Nor is it just to criticise the Report of the Public Service Board on semantic grounds. The term 'assimilation' at that time did not have in Australia the associations it now has. If the term 'integration' had then been used, there would probably now be a tendency for those who disagreed with subsequent policies under that name to talk of 'assimilation'.

A new approach must be judged in the context of the time. This report was concerned with a series of practical problems arising from a long history. There was no effective Aboriginal leadership with which to deal; even now, it is only being evolved. The idea of 'community development' as a method of government was to evolve mainly from re-thinking by colonising governments as the war indicated the need for new policies. In the light of what was believed about Aboriginal irresponsibility, the problem was seen as one for the development of welfare and education services as then conceived. The abdication of controls could well seem to be abdication of responsibility. The comparison of the reserve and station was with other institutions for the handicapped, not with the towns as economic and social centres which must have their own economic and social viability. It was as unthinkable to open them up as it would then have been to open the mental asylums. It is to the credit of those who made this report that the handicaps were seen as educational, and that prejudice was also seen as a prime cause of the Aboriginal predicament.

This is not the place to trace the development of the assimilation policy. It is worth commenting, nonetheless, that its expression in this document had a more *humane* ring than had been enunciated anywhere else except in Victoria. It was possibly because persons who were as much 'white' as Aboriginal did not seem to present the same problem in absorption, which could now be assumed not to require special administrative measures; and perhaps, too, because New South Wales and Victoria had now so few full-bloods. Even then, however, there is a way in which the objective as stated went beyond the physical details of personality. The idea of disappearance of racial differences was not lost, but the emphasis was on social and economic assimilation as a step to be reached as soon as possible, with no exclusion on grounds of appearance. Such reports are always compromises, so that inevitably the idea of physical absorption remained as part of the assimilation concept or associated with it, either as part of the process or as eventual result.

The emphasis on training and education *before* equality of rights remained within official interpretations of the policy. This was to throw special emphasis, in turn, on the places where the training was to be done. Of the present Aboriginal communities in New South Wales, the older people will remember very well (and will have handed on their memories to the young) the hard life on stations during the depression years. And many of the young will remember the efforts to process their age group into a state where they would be ready to be accepted by the whites—to be 'assimilated'; they will remember, too, the constant interferences in the details of family and personal life which marked the stations, from the adoption of the policy until this kind of effort, by the withdrawal of managers, was implicitly admitted to be useless. The station was conceived as a training institution in a way in which it had not been earlier; the old chores might have to be performed, but they were now justified with the new jargon of assimilation. It was assumed that Aborigines were in a condition to require remedial treatment, but the goal was an eventual equality.

In retrospect one can see the inevitable resentments which came from attempts at the more efficient management of groups on reserves, through exhortation and other pressures, to make the Aborigines fit for closer association with the whites. But there were important recommendations for improvements, on the basis of the status quo. The government was asked for increased funds for housing; to allow for the rationing of children in addition to payments of Child Endowment; for rations comparable with those issued to other unemployed; and for better medical and dental services. Aborigines should be trained for maintenance work and for nursing services on the stations, to prepare them for work in the general community. The schooling should take children beyond current standards, which were said to be those of eight-year-olds in the public school system. The first requirement was for teachers, and even where a station had one officer, he should be chosen first for his teaching skill. The government should no longer give way to the local hostility which forced Aboriginal children out of the public schools, and public education to this end should be through local committees and churches. Payments of Social Service benefits should be in cash; and the staff should assist in home-making. Cash payments and such incentives as leasing station lands to individuals should be used as incentives to work. Girls should be trained in home management and dressmaking. For all these ends stations should be extended and properly planned. The assets of the indirectly managed reserves, of which fifty were then occupied, should be used to better effect.

For these objectives trained staff was necessary. Positions on stations had not carried the rights of membership of the public service; it was recommended that all should be public servants and that their fitness for the work should be reviewed. A qualified Chief Inspector, who should be the executive officer of the Board, should be appointed; and there should be a cadet training system for staff recruitment.

The main hindrances were said to be white antipathy, and a general 'apathy' of station residents. Nowadays we know more about apathy as a defence, as an alternative, for persons under stress, to aggression or excessive co-operation with institutional management.

Ferguson, before the Select Committee, had made what amounted to *political* demands for legal equality and full rights. The Board's report summed up the current restrictions on rights—that Aborigines could not vote or drink liquor, did not receive maternity allowances, old age and invalid pensions if more than half 'caste'; could not get relief work if living on a station; received child endowment in the form of orders rather than cash; and were subject to other restrictions under the Act and regulations. It was argued that restrictions could not be generally removed without 'harmful' effects, this perhaps foreshadowing the 1943 provisions for exemption. Thus the emphasis in the new policy was on managed welfare. The idea of government negotiating with pressure groups was of course not new, as the history of the trade union movement indicates: perhaps it requires effective organisation of the groups, so that even now the idea may seem revolutionary in Aboriginal affairs. The removal of the special legal restrictions, and the withdrawal of the station managers, was to be deferred in New South Wales until after amendments to the Act in 1963.

The Report of the Public Service Board was followed by amendments to the Act, in 1940 and 1943.[26] The first marked the new emphasis in policy by replacing the Protection Board by the new Aborigines Welfare Board, of nine members, including the Secretary of the Chief Secretary's Department as Chairman, with four officials from relevant departments, one 'expert in sociology and/or anthropology', and two to be nominated by the Minister. The 1943 amendment was something of an administrative break-through, providing for two additional members—a 'full-blooded Aborigine' and the other 'either a full-blooded Aborigine or a person apparently having an admixture of Aboriginal blood', both to be elected by postal vote of Aborigines.[27]

But none of the previous controls were relaxed and, particularly over children who became wards of the Board and Aborigines in employment, the legal controls were tightened. From 1936, for instance, the Board could decide to receive wages from an employer when this appeared in the 'best interests' of the employee. The 1940 amendment enabled such a decision to be made in the interests of the Aboriginal's wife or children. If the wage was 'unreasonable' or employment conditions unfair, or the employment seemed to the Board likely to impair the employee's 'moral or physical well-being', the employment could be terminated and the Board remove the Aboriginal 'to such reserve, home or other place as it may direct'.[28] Perhaps the continuation of old restrictions, and their extension in a few instances, would have had far more effect on Aboriginal attitudes than the new provisions for Aboriginal representation, and than

[26] Aborigines Protection (Amendment) Act, 1940, and Aborigines Protection (Amendment) Act, 1943.

[27] See Aborigines Protection Act 1909-1963: Regulations 25-37.

[28] Aborigines Protection (Amendment) Act, 1940, section 3(f), amending section 13C; and section 13B (1943).

that for exemption certificates[29] (which anyway were subject to cancellation, and were wanted mainly as giving the right to drink, and to retain control of one's children).

Histories of the beginnings of Aboriginal protest in the settled areas remain to be written. The voice of W. Ferguson before the Select Committee expressed the sophisticated demand for equality, and in political terms. In January 1938 he and J.T. Patten, another part-Aboriginal, from Cumeroogunga, had celebrated the 150th anniversary celebrations of the 'foundation' of Australia by hiring a hall in Sydney for a 'Day of Mourning and Protest', with a conference of Aborigines and a deputation to the Prime Minister. In the following March had appeared the first publication of the Aborigines Protection Association, the *Australian Abo Call*. The demands were for full citizen rights, better education, and full equality of opportunity with other citizens.[30]

This kind of political movement, by no means limited to New South Wales, was for equality in the growing points and economic centres—in the towns and cities where equal opportunity could be found. Its implications were the exact antithesis of current thinking in terms of welfare on reserves, by governments and by those who saw the problem as one of managed welfare. Even now the two points of view have not really met. In the meantime, government remained vulnerable to the country town pressures to keep Aborigines out of town—until they were 'ready'. To confront local and central government, strong Aboriginal organisation, of a kind not yet achieved, was essential. This was a sub-group which was to remain disorganised, partly because there were no areas of activity within which an emergent leadership, legitimate in Aboriginal eyes, could emerge. This situation was to remain at the core of the problem from then till now; and in this connection it is worth repeating that the legislative restrictions on rights remained until 1963 in New South Wales. By that time the Progressive Association, for instance, had lapsed; it was re-constituted in 1963.

To some extent, these protests received publicity because of the current national interest in revelations of what had been happening on the distant frontiers. People like Michael Sawtell and Mary Gilmore were present at the foundation meeting of the Association; and Sawtell had assisted in its organisation. The Sydney press was publishing correspondence which referred to the period of frontier massacres in New South Wales,

[29] Ibid., section 3(b) 1943, amending section 18 (section 18C).
[30] See *S.M.H.*, 4 March 1938, and *Argus* (Melbourne), 29 March 1938.

with the usual replies from those who resented such references to the pioneer tradition.[31]

This carryover from the frontier history was to remain till this day a continual source of intellectual confusion, and to offer in Aboriginal affairs a continual opportunity for breast-beating: for the frontier problems remained current on the national scale. In turn, this fact made it harder to see the potential of the sophisticated Australians of Aboriginal descent in the older settled areas. It made their problems difficult to isolate so long as they had to be identified by welfare staff, and very much more so in States which had the frontier problems to deal with as well. The way out of the dilemma may have been organisation to negotiate with Aboriginal groups; to throw on to them the responsibility of determining what they wanted; and to take a firm hand with local government to ensure that they were located where their needs could be satisfied by their own effort. The main concession in this direction was Aboriginal representation on the Board, which was initially demanded by the Aborigines Progressive Association.

A 'manifesto' of the Association, in January 1938, is perhaps the most bitter of all Aboriginal protests.

You took our land by force . . . You have almost exterminated our people, but there are enough of us remaining to expose the humbug of your claim . . . to be civilised, progressive and humane . . . We do not wish to be regarded with sentimental sympathy like koala bears as exhibits . . . [nor] studied as scientific or anthropological curiosities . . . We ask you to teach our people to live in the modern age, as modern citizens. Why do you deliberately keep us backward? Is it merely to give yourselves the pleasure of feeling superior? Give our children the same chances as your own and they will do as well as white children.

Intermarriage had no 'ill effects'.

We ask you to be proud of the Australian Aborigines . . . that we are a naturally backward and low race is a scientific lie . . . At worst we are no more dirty, lazy, stupid, criminal or immoral, than white people. Also your slanders against our race are moral lies, told to throw all the blame for our troubles on to us.[32]

Here was the identification with the full-bloods on whose conditions in the frontier regions most attention at that time was focused.[33] Elkin, as Professor of Anthropology and Chairman of the Association for the Protection of Native Races, had been pressing for reforms and a new

[31] See *S.M.H.*, 5, 7, 9-11, and 14 March 1938.
[32] *Argus* (Melbourne), 13 January 1938. I am indebted to Mr J. Horner, biographer of W. Ferguson, for this reference.
[33] See *The Destruction of Aboriginal Society*, chs. 16, 17.

policy for both the State and Commonwealth: and for the Northern Territory this involved use of reserves for general educational purposes. Thus the frontier situations deeply affected thinking in the closely settled areas. At the same time there was a linking of Aboriginal spokesmen from Victoria with those of New South Wales. In April 1938 a Committee on Aboriginal Citizenship Rights began to agitate in Sydney. Events in the Northern Territory fused with indignation in Sydney; Judge Wells in Darwin was attacked along with the Protection Board in Sydney. But there was confusion in policy aims. The C.A.C.R. wanted reserves for 'full-bloods' and full rights for part-Aborigines. Some conservative Aboriginal spokesmen, like David Unaipon of South Australia, rejected the move behind the manifesto as 'political', to this extent agreeing with governments that this was a welfare problem only.[34]

The Communist Party was active in Aboriginal affairs; and this tended to discredit 'political' demands in the eyes of those who believed the matter was essentially one of welfare. The *Australian Abo Call* issued six numbers in 1938, publishing correspondence from all over the continent; but the C.A.C.R. appears to have rejected J. Patten, the editor, over the Cumeroogunga 'strike' of February 1939. Thus the confused debate carried over, and more or less petered out in the war years. The core of the problem was illustrated by a 'strike' of parents in Collarenebri against the proposal to admit twenty Aboriginal children to the school in February 1940;[35] by references in the press to crowding into the special Aboriginal wards in hospitals;[36] and by government deferment to local opinion on such issues. A former Minister for Education in 1943, explaining in the House his decision that 'where aboriginal children occur in any marked number it would be desirable in their own interest that they should be excluded from the ordinary public school and suitable provision for their education made', could argue that the measure was not a 'racial' one because the schools did not exclude 'races of colour other than white, whose mental and physical attributes, though different' were 'nowise inferior to those of the white race'. It was 'the nomadic nature of the aboriginal' which made him and his children different. Therefore the children 'of marked aboriginal characteristics' ought to be excluded,

not because they are an offence to the white people or to white children, but that in their own interests they might receive a suitable training under conditions which are conducive to their highest welfare.[37]

[34] *Argus* (Melbourne), 13 January 1938.
[35] *Daily Telegraph* (Sydney), 2 February 1940.          [36] *S.M.H.*, 9 February 1943.
[37] *N.S.W.P.D.*, 1943, Second Series, vol. 170, pp. 2850-2—debate on Aborigines Protection (Amendment) Act, 1943.

The trend, then, was to make the reserve and especially the managed station the basic instrument of policy. But the war gave such a fillip to the sagging economy that in 1944 the Board reported that over 90 per cent of the able-bodied men on the stations had been continuously employed, mainly in local rural occupations, for the preceding three years.[38] There had been a rise in such employment from 64 per cent in 1940 to 79 per cent in June 1941 and 82 per cent in June 1942.[39] Aborigines were getting award wages. After 1943, the Board had greater powers to construct station buildings, but of course there were wartime shortages of materials and skills; and the situation where the majority lived on the stations and reserves was never to be reached. In 1941, for instance, there were under 4,908 on stations and reserves, and 5,708 acknowledged to be 'nomadic' or living in 'camps'.[40]

Aborigines were being called up for civil construction work. The growing optimism and humanity in the official attitudes is indicated by a protest in the 1942 report against the rejection of a high proportion of those who had enlisted. The wartime reports are critical, at least by implication, of the readiness of the Education Department to give way to local prejudices of parents. References to white prejudice come to balance those to the drinking and gambling of Aborigines on wartime wages.

The earlier objectives of housing most Aborigines on reserves were progressively relegated. In 1940 there was a reference to the common complaints from local government bodies about the fringe-dwellings; the view expressed was that the councils should prevent as far as possible the growth of fringe settlements (then still called 'camps', as the philosophy that this was a stage in movement into membership of the town had not been fully developed), until the people could all be accommodated on the reserves.[41] This was reminiscent of Poor Law administration, with local authorities passing on the poor to other areas. There was pressure for funds for housing and training facilities. The station becomes more definitely conceived as a training institution; and the 1944 report stressed the need of training for 'citizenship', lifting the status of the Aboriginal woman and of the Aboriginal worker. But the wartime experience of earning off reserves was making the policy aims impossible.

While this more or less rural view of the Aboriginal question was retained, more Aborigines than ever before were working in industrial

[38] N.S.W. Aborigines Welfare Board (A.W.B.) Report, 1944.
[39] Ibid., 1942.
[40] N.S.W.P.P., 1941-2, vol. 1, pp. 1169-76—A.W.B. Report, 1941.
[41] Ibid.—A.W.B. Report, 1940, pp. 1163-7.

types of employment; and urbanisation into Sydney (and all Australian capital cities) was stimulated as never before. This must have had a profound effect on Aboriginal sophistication. Like the other wartime changes, it was a development out of phase with a policy which saw communities living under control on stations as being 'trained' to enter the wider community. Yet the stations and reserves were essential as offering at least some secure places for those who did not choose to take their risks in the unfriendly vicinity of the towns or to try to remove themselves from the eye of authority into the capital city or large industrial town.

By 1945 the total on stations and reserves had declined by 11 per cent; and as the population figures suggest that the war years were years of considerable growth, there would have been a greater decline in the proportion on reserves.[42] A very high proportion of those on unmanaged reserves were in receipt of rations—perhaps many of them the less efficient and the demoralised—for the report remarked that there was more movement into employment from the managed stations. By 1951 the reserve and station population was again just under 5,000. It was to approach 6,000 in 1961, and was much the same when this Project commenced.

More recently there has been a decline in management effort, reflected in the transition from station to unmanaged reserve. To judge from its published comments, the Board had come to acknowledge at last the illogic of the separate reserve, but without perhaps appreciating the extent to which that separation had been the result of policy measures influenced by prejudice in the country towns.

It is neither natural nor logical to expect the State to maintain aborigines living together in artificial groups on the principle that the State owes them such an existence, especially those in whom aboriginal blood is in the minority.[43]

The bitter words of the 1938 manifesto, that 'your slanders against our race are moral lies, told to throw all the blame for our troubles on to us' may still have some point, for in 1964 the Board reported that

the greatest task of all facing the Board is to change the attitudes of the Aborigines and their thinking towards helping themselves rather than leaving it to the Board and voluntary associations for the solution of their problems.[44]

[42] Ibid., 1945-6, vol. 2, p. 803—A.W.B. Report, 1945.
[43] Ibid., 1961-2, vol. 1, no. 90, p. 11—A.W.B. Report, 1961.
[44] Ibid., 1965, no. 9, p. 10—A.W.B. Report, 1964.

The report was concerned here with the real problem of Aboriginal dependency, but surely this in turn is a response to the total situation, which certainly includes attitudes *to* Aborigines. These attitudes, in turn, offer the basic explanation for there being a 'problem' marked by 'Aborigines living together in artificial groups'.

The emphasis on managed stations probably received support from the Commonwealth-backed policy of assimilation as demonstrated in the Northern Territory, especially after the Northern Territory Welfare Ordinance of 1953, which emphasised control of the Aboriginal *ward*. The frontier retained its profound influence on official thinking. What made less impact was the other fact, that under the Welfare Ordinance *only* the Aboriginal of the full descent was to be subject to special restrictions; simultaneously, part-Aborigines were freed of legal restrictions. At the same time, it should be remembered that the dwellers on the New South Wales stations could move away at will; that economic and social pressures, not legal restrictions, kept them there. For many urbanised families, and many who lived near the towns where they could hope for employment, the old reserve was still 'home'. For many the association with these places offered the one refuge when needed. There was also the widespread belief that these places belonged in a special way to those who were born on them. When the Aborigines Progressive Association was re-formed in 1963, one of the demands was for Aboriginal ownership of all reserves. There are considerable variations in the histories of the States in this respect, but there remain sound psychological reasons for meeting such claims, as the government of South Australia has recognised, as well as economic reasons. It seems reasonable that what has been devoted for a long time to the needs of Aborigines should continue to be so devoted; and such measures form at least one modest way in which persons of Aboriginal descent may be conceded small property rights.

To attempt a full history of reserve and station policies even in the closely settled areas, which form the background to present attitudes, would involve a complete work in itself. The Aboriginal predicament has for a long time been illustrated and epitomised on the reserve, where the full implications of policies and priorities can be seen by the occasional visitor. This must have been one of the reasons for using the permit system to exclude the awkward visitor. Even during the war, there was a good deal of publicity about conditions; and naturally this made the best news where the conditions were worst, in the north and centre of the continent. Thus, once again, the situation in distant frontier areas added bitterness to the debates on conditions in the south, which were bad enough to require no such impetus.

In New South Wales the comparatively early commitment to the aim of social and economic assimilation for all Aborigines in the State was a positive policy, even though, as some reports of the Board indicate, assimilation tended to be confused with ideas of physical absorption. For this positive thinking most of the credit must go to Elkin, who had advised Wallace Wurth, Chairman of the Public Service Board. He formed the link between Commonwealth and New South Wales policymaking: and was advising the Hon. J. McEwen, Minister for the Interior, about the same time. Had the Board withdrawn its managers over a period three decades before it did, or had it been able to pay and train them better, there may have been less bitterness in the memories of life on the managed station, though of course there were always good managers and bad ones.

In the mid-1960s, when this Project began, the situations were still basically those of the controlled institution, in which some managers saw their responsibility as involving interference in matters of personal liberty as part of processing for assimilation; and they suffered from the inevitable reactions. But if the restrictive legislation which supported such interference was made necessary by the responsibility of having to control these places, the reserves were also made necessary by the legislation which placed special restrictions on citizen rights. They were also necessary as places of refuge from local discrimination. One instance may suffice. As late as 1948 there were people in Yass who objected to the location of a reserve on the town boundaries. It would prevent extension of the 'residential area, perturb those who had to walk past it to visit the cemetery, and stimulate undesirable migration of Aboriginals to town where the ratepayers had invested money'.[45] Yass recognised its responsibility to Aborigines; but it should be discharged several miles away, as in the cases of Tumut and Cowra.

So long as governments defer to such opinion, there is not a great deal which small departments and boards with low priorities can do.

Life on the stations gave a special savour to the breach of rules which appeared unjust to the inmates, since they did not apply elsewhere. But even without a manager to supervise, living on reserves breeds a species of micro-politics which is unique, with the various well-meaning outsiders, the police, the local government officials, officers of the Board

---

[45] *Tribune Courier* (Yass), 25 March 1948.

and others involved in various ways interacting with and being used by the residents. Perhaps there is something like this in all small communities. The difference is that where a single government body is held generally responsible, all the problems come to it in the end. But here the official gets involved as a father-figure and often as a participant in disputes; he may be tempted to use power in ways never intended in the legislation, or to exceed his proper authority.[46]

I have given some detail on the impact of past policy in New South Wales mainly because the best way to indicate conditions resulting first from the depression and then from the war is to look more closely at the record in at least one State. Perhaps it is worth reiterating that the conditions affecting New South Wales affected the whole country; that Aborigines everywhere were in great economic difficulties; and that this had been a factor in 'trouble' outside the settled areas where there was starvation, especially in the centre of the continent. This was the background to re-thinking in New South Wales by a few influential people. The ideas of social and economic equality expounded by Elkin in that decade were to be diluted by a good deal of the racist assumptions of the folklore in their application, despite his membership of the Board. But he is probably correct in regarding this time as a turning point in Aboriginal affairs.

### THE STATIONS AND RESERVES IN VICTORIA

The history of the managed reserve in Victoria goes back to the time of the Port Phillip Protectorate. After responsible government there was no systematic rounding up of the 'wandering Aboriginals' to confine them on controlled stations and small reserves, as was to happen in Queensland, for a time in Western Australia and, during the depression years, occasionally in New South Wales. There has been bitter contention in Victoria for over eighty years, but it goes back to the moves, beginning in the Act of 1886, to force *off* reserves those who were regarded as half-castes, and therefore competent to earn their own livings elsewhere. Small numbers were always involved, in the aftermath of the initial destruction of the tribes by disease and in frontier incidents. The researches of Dr Diane Barwick are now disclosing the acute tragedies of literate and modestly prosperous families of part-Aboriginal folk which were

---

[46] In 1958 there was an interesting study of a housing settlement on the outskirts of Perth, entitled Cooraradale, by John Wilson, which illustrated these points.

divided after 1886: the 'lighter castes' to be sent out and kept out of what had been their homes; the others either following or accepting their lot. In the face of attitudes in the country towns, this meant continual insecurity for a people not wanted anywhere, who must live as fringe-dwellers and seasonal workers. Dr Barwick has established this accent on dispersal as the foundation of policy from 1886 until the latest dispute centred round the Lake Tyers Station.

In New South Wales social and economic pressure was to force Aborigines away from the towns and into reserves and stations, but where the station was established on land which offered a chance of economic development, there were other pressures to move the Aborigines else-where. This was in accord with experience which began much earlier in Victoria, where the method of protection proposed by a Select Committee in 1860 remained basic policy in spite of reduction of the commitment after 1886. The proposal was that

In order to make permanent provision for the maintenance and management of the Aboriginal population, a sufficient quantity of land be set aside in different districts, to be held in trust by a Board of Trustees resident in the particular district, in connection with a Central Board to be appointed from residents in Melbourne, under whose control any expenditure incurred on account of the Aboriginal inhabitants shall be defrayed.[47]

These local committees were likely to become really involved, to an extent which did not happen in New South Wales. When reading the detailed accounts of local station politics, as described by Dr Barwick, one is impressed with this difference. Perhaps, in spite of all that was to happen when the move began to expel the part-Aborigines from the stations in 1886, the Victorian people of Aboriginal descent benefited from this kind of political experience. In New South Wales the local committees were allowed to become defunct after the 1909 Act. In the period of extending the stations, which occurred when the best land had already been taken up, there was less likelihood of getting good land or of interaction between station residents and others in the locality.

When the stations were set up in Victoria they were sometimes carefully selected with a view to farming and other activities. The result was that there were strong local pressures to acquire the land and remove the stations. This had happened with some very early mission stations, a good example being the Coranderrk Station. Over the ten years prior

[47] *V.P.P.*, 1859-60, vol. 2, no. 19—Report from the Select Committee upon Protection of the Aborigines.

to the 1886 Act, Aborigines there were involved in a somewhat hopeless but courageous and temporarily effective fight to protect their interests in land which they had developed.

Between 1875 and 1885 [writes Dr Barwick] the protests of residents of Coranderrk Aboriginal Station against the policy decisions of the Board for the Protection of the Aborigines caused a stir in the press and Parliament without parallel during the century that the Board administered Aboriginal affairs.[48]

When one reads the details of a most sophisticated and determined use by Aborigines of political pressures, involving members of parliament and of the Board, managers of the station, and Aboriginal spokesmen, one obtains some sense of the injustice involved in the subsequent policy of dispersal, on the simple doctrinaire grounds that part-Aborigines should be forced to make their own way without the right of access to what had been their homes. Perhaps one result of such deliberate disintegration of social groups, and separation of families from family assets, is that possibly fewer Aborigines in Victoria could play such roles in defence of their interests, even now, than at that time. In Victoria, especially, one can see the effects of a consistent policy of dispersal, which makes the social controls which Aboriginal groups recognise impossible to operate, which separates the potential leaders from followers, and renders the politics of decisionmaking irrelevant because nothing may be left for any but individual decisions.

Before 1886 there were signs of a social re-integration on the stations, with the station acting as the home for those who went out to employment on the surrounding properties. Victorian policy was comparatively humane and was being applied rather less restrictively than it was later. As Dr Barwick points out, the Aboriginal inhabitants of a station had citizen rights. The managers prior to 1886 had to persuade the residents to accept the rules. She tells how in the 1870s Coranderrk Aborigines frequently sued each other, and sometimes the residents on a station sued the manager. The vice-chairman of the Board said in 1881 that

We have no legal authority over them at all. If we had legal authority we should not have any trouble with them on the stations, but when you tell them to do anything they can please themselves whether they do it.[49]

But from 1887 onwards, rules were introduced for managers to apply on stations. Although many of these were not supported by legislation, they

[48] Diane Barwick, seminar paper entitled Rebellion at Coranderrk.
[49] Diane Barwick, A Little More Than Kin (1965), ch. 2, p. 145.

were applied in their various forms until 1957, when Charles McLean, in a special report to the Victorian government, pointed out that the current regulations for discipline and control could not legally be applied to anyone on the last remaining station at Lake Tyers.[50] Some of the rules were never published; but a regulation operating from 1890 till 1957 required obedience to the manager; and the able-bodied must work or be expelled. These infringements on 'rights' applied to the very few living on stations: they amounted to little more than institutional rules.

Those off stations were subject to less restriction than in New South Wales, and considerably less than in other States—the result, it seems, of the good sense of Parliament at critical periods rather than from any enlightened policy on the part of the Board, which appears to have been a curious collection of people who met only occasionally up till its re-constitution in 1957.[51] It then managed to arouse the anger of Victorian Aborigines with its attempt at more definite methods of dispersal in the name of assimilation.

Organised protest by Aborigines was an indication that they had long been accustomed and able in Victoria to say what they wished. While there is a closer approach to 'professional' protest by Aborigines there than elsewhere, they have been especially provoked by the rigidity of a government still thinking in the terms of a century earlier and of the policies of absorption of the half-castes which were current in the 1930s. This required more definite control of those on the Board's one station at Lake Tyers—not to keep them in, but to disperse them. By regulations in 1958, a resident's permit was necessary, but it was subject to cancellation. Residents must obey the manager, who could impose a fine. If able-bodied, they must work as directed by the manager; refrain from bad language, gambling, being drunk, or owning firearms, intoxicants, poisons or explosives without permission. This, with a stated program of building houses dispersed through wide areas, was well calculated to stir up the whole set of issues associated with Aboriginal reserves, with Lake Tyers in the 1950s and 1960s as the crux of the issue, as Coranderrk had been eight decades earlier.

Victorian fringe settlements are as unpleasant as any anywhere; and they are scattered far and wide through the State. But one result of having in a sense liquidated its *admitted* commitment, to the full-bloods and the reserves, was a reluctance on the part of the Victorian Government to

[50] Ibid.—quoting *V.P.P.*, 1956-8, vol. 2, no. 18—Report on the Operation of the Aborigines Act 1928 and the Regulations and Orders Made Thereunder.
[51] Aborigines Act 1957 (no. 6086), section 3.

admit that any 'problem' remained. It had always pushed for 'assimilation'; and at the time of the depression the official view was that the 'problem' was on the verge of solution, though the scattered fringe-dwelling settlements must have been as bad as their counterparts in New South Wales. Those off reserves and out of control of the Board were regarded as already established in the community; and unless they were full-bloods they had no claim on the State. So the Chairman of the Board told the Commonwealth-States conference of 1937 that his State's problems were 'not acute'.

I came here [he said] principally as an onlooker . . . Questions relating to the aborigines affect States like Queensland, South Australia and Western Australia more than Victoria, and probably New South Wales.[52]

Victoria was not represented at the next conference in 1948, and the Premier declined the invitation to that of 1951 on the ground that in his State 'the problem of the Aborigines had [virtually] disappeared' and because he felt that 'Commonwealth intervention is hardly warranted'.[53] He had much to learn about the tenacity with which human groups adhere to their separate identity; and of the inevitability of this reaction on the part of a small minority facing high prejudice.

Though it also reflects the small numbers of Aborigines involved, the facts that managed stations at no time numbered more than six, and that there were over the whole history perhaps a dozen other reserves, reflect again a rigidity in the Victorian policy. The fact that Aborigines dependent on casual and seasonal work would be forced to establish dwellings of some kind at convenient points for securing it meant that fringe-dwelling areas like those in New South Wales developed. A greater flexibility might have led to demarcation of some of these areas as reserves. That this was not done often involved additional insecurity, as those who lack any form of tenure are more vulnerable to town authorities who want to force them to go elsewhere.

Since 1917, the only station has been at Lake Tyers. The station at Framlingham, which became a reserve only, in that year, has, like Lake Tyers, had a most interesting history, illustrating especially the strong ties of communities to places regarded as their own. Re-thinking in Victoria and a new look at 'assimilation' did not occur until the 1950s, and these two places have been at the centre of bitter argument in Aboriginal affairs until now.

[52] *Aboriginal Welfare*, p. 5.
[53] Commonwealth of Australia: Department of Territories, File 55/857: Australian Council of Native Welfare: Record of First Meeting, 3 and 4 September, 1951.

## SOUTH AUSTRALIAN POLICY ON RESERVES AND STATIONS IN THE SETTLED AREAS

Something of the pressures which made the managed station almost inevitable, so long as the Aboriginal was not wanted within the town, is suggested by the establishment of the Davenport Station in the mid-1960s right on the outskirts of Port Augusta; and by the development of a large station at the old Lutheran mission location at Koonibba, a few miles west of Ceduna. Reserves may be set aside with a notion that they will be used by Aborigines, either for living areas (as is so in most States) or for agriculture; or they may be established for the use of a mission or government department in its work of sustaining, protecting, and training a considerable number. By 1860 there were forty-two reserves of the first kind in South Australia, mostly between the Murray and the Gulf of St Vincent, varying in size from 52 to 240 acres. Of these no less than thirty-six had already been leased to non-Aborigines. One comparatively large reserve of over 5,000 acres had been established for the Poonindie Mission, the forerunner of the later controlled stations. By 1913, ninety-seven had been declared, but sixty-four of them had been 'sold or leased to whites'.[54]

If an uncontrolled reserve is conveniently situated for employment or offers some kind of subsistence, it will be inhabited. Many of the first South Australian reserves were set up under the Waste Lands Act of 1842, but the chance of an Aboriginal making use of farming land was then small indeed, although Aborigines could live on some of them where this was possible without capital or agricultural skills. Fay Gale points out that although a Royal Commission in 1913 recommended training for membership of the general community, in fact from then until World War II the policy was one of segregation, ostensibly from the evils of drink and immorality in the towns.

As we have seen, the Act of 1911 gave the Chief Protector adequate powers, as he could have a person moved to the reserve and kept there; for South Australian legislation was essentially of the 'frontier' type, like that of Queensland and Western Australia.

The Aborigines Department took over direct control of the old Point McLeay and Point Pearce Missions in 1914. There were also two Lutheran missions at Koonibba and Killalpininna at that time, but they remained in mission hands. Fay Gale says that in reading the evidence before the

---

[54] See Fay Gale, *A Study of Assimilation: Part-Aborigines in South Australia*, pp. 154, 155.

Royal Commission of 1913, 'it is difficult to realise that it is a discussion of the situation in 1913-15 and not of the present day'; and she refers, for example, to complaints that land at Point Pearce in 1913 had been leased to outsiders and not farmed by the inmates—which was also a common complaint in 1960.[55] On each of the two major government stations, by the 1960s, there was a century of institutionalised living in the background;[56] and although one effect of the new impetus from yet another burst of enthusiasm for assimilation was active rebuilding and other efforts to make the best of what was there, the background over-shadowed both. They had always been centres from which the men went out to work as required; and, like reserves everywhere, they were refuges for people with special problems other than that of being Aboriginal.

The tradition was also the result of closer settlement, which made it impossible for Aborigines to live outside except in some relationship with the town or a particular rural enterprise. Where they were not wanted in the towns, and where the employing enterprise offered only seasonal employment, they came or were sent to the stations. Where other justifications were lacking, the common one was the need to keep them away from the *temptations* of the town. Fay Gale has quoted the words of the Premier introducing the 1911 Act as setting the program for a 'tight policy of segregation', which was to be maintained until World War II. Aborigines were to be kept

away from the towns, and where and when such was found expedient— . . . for their own benefit . . . to live in certain localities, and on special reservations [where there would be] safeguards which would keep them away from the bad influences which now follow from their being scattered throughout the country and townships. For one thing, they would be prevented to a great extent from getting intoxicating drinks, and from the gross immorality . . . now prevalent in certain parts of the State.[57]

No effective steps were taken to expel Aborigines from the locations where they had been long established. The trend was rather for Christian missions to take over management of established settlements; and even this had to wait for a resurgence of missionary effort. Thus in 1925 the Australian Aborigines Mission took over management of the old camp at Swan Reach, on the Murray, where there was a typical fringe shanty town, from which the children were not permitted to attend the town

[55] Ibid., p. 108.
[56] See Judy Inglis, 'One Hundred Years at Point McLeay, South Australia', *Mankind*, 1962, vol. 5, no. 2, pp. 503-7.
[57] *S.A.P.D.*, 28 September 1910—quoted in Fay Gale, *A Study of Assimilation*, p. 109.

school a mile away. In 1945 the mission (now the United Aborigines Mission) moved to Gerard, but left some of its clientele behind on the old site. Gerard was purchased for a government station as part of the assimilation program in the 1960s. In 1965 the missionary was still there, while the effort to produce a self-supporting open town at Gerard was in the hands of a local committee and the government. There was a similar situation at Davenport Station, just outside Port Augusta, with a new government station being built beside the old Umeewarra Mission, which had been established on the sandhills outside the town in 1937.

That missions should be active within the closely settled areas so late, and that their work there should have continued until the 1960s, partly illustrates the extent to which conditions further out, in the harsh desert regions, set the general standards. Conditions deemed suitable for Aborigines there were acceptable everywhere. The missionary is perhaps especially conditioned to accept the worst poverty: and although Daisy Bates was not one, her heroic efforts over sixteen years at Ooldea from 1919 had established a model of self-sacrifice which could have had its effect within the closely settled areas. The conditions faced for so long by the government officers at Point McLeay and Point Pearce, as well as those faced by the mission in the vicinity of farms and townships, were essentially produced by the exclusiveness of the whites and the absence of organised leadership among the Aborigines. Writing in the early 1960s of both stations and missions in the closely settled areas, Fay Gale described them as slums marked by overcrowding, lack of privacy, unemployment and under-employment, and the lack of individual incentives.

There is the all pervading atmosphere of apathy and hopelessness. The future seems to offer these people nothing. They lack initiative. Ruled by white officers they have no voice in the planning of affairs and therefore exhibit little interest in the activity of the station.[58]

The weight of this past was obvious even on a brief visit to stations at Point McLeay and Point Pearce in 1965, when the new government effort was being revealed in new construction. Beside the old stone houses were the new brick ones being erected. Pieces of old farm machinery, long rusted into disuse, contrasted with new machine sheds being built. But the old tensions remained between management and inmates; and one had the feeling that the established pattern of life was going to be difficult to change. With the amount of land available for

[58] Ibid., p. 167.

the employment of the men in the maintenance and farming work, there had obviously long been a choice between keeping the most obsolete, labour-biased methods, in order to provide more work (which can hardly be reconciled with ideas of 'training'), or using modern methods and ceasing to pretend that those who could not get work outside might be employed under some station scheme.

Even the proportion of the labour used to make repairs for damage caused by what the management sees as idle irresponsibility does not make up the difference between a token and a real labour demand. One of the results of new policies then being applied was that the more ambitious families had been moving out; but the rapid population increase could leave a 'hard core'. Even the complete re-equipment of these places, with a view to their acceptance as townships and open villages later on by the local government authorities, was probably not so essential as withdrawal of the management from the situations of control, so that at last they would cease to be institutions.

To this end, the decision in 1966 to vest all reserves in the Aboriginal Lands Trust for the first time recognised Reserve Councils representing those hitherto in the situation of inmates as having a right to decide the future of a reserve. In 1967 amending legislation provided that regulations should establish these Councils in such a manner that they would have the legal powers to admit or reject visitors to the reserve.[59] But the chances of better housing, and the special ties arising from a century of attachment to the two main stations, were creating a problem, since even the Aboriginal Affairs Act of 1962, framed as the basis for the new assimilation policy, gave to the Minister power to refuse entry to an Aboriginal —a move to restrain those who now wanted to return. The Minister could also (Section 20) declare an Aboriginal to be a 'trainee' if he had 'consented to enter or remain within an institution'; in such case the trainee must remain and complete his training to the satisfaction of the Minister.

### SETTLEMENTS AND RESERVES IN WESTERN AUSTRALIA

While the Roth Report of 1905 seems to have provided impetus for some real effort in the north and west of the State, the drift in the closely settled areas of the south-west was towards a lowering of Aboriginal status and welfare. In 1910 the government resumed twenty-eight

[59] Aboriginal Lands Trust Act, 1966, section 16, and Aboriginal Affairs Act Amendment Act, 1966-1967, section 3.

pastoral leaseholds between Wyndham and Halls Creek to set up the reserves and cattle stations intended to contain and train Aborigines and so to prevent the cattle killings which were a basic cause of 'trouble'. It also took positive steps to combat leprosy and other diseases.[60]

In the south-west of the State, however, this was a period of closer land settlement. Biskup gives evidence of the efforts by the Chief Protector to have blocks in each Agricultural Area reserved for Aboriginal selectors—a suggestion which was rejected in 1908.[61] He says that the power under the Land Act to grant or lease areas up to 200 acres was actually used, with a few Aboriginal settlers doing well. There were seven so established in 1906. Others were established under the general conditions for selection of blocks and Biskup says that round Busselton, Newcastle, and Quairading at that time Aborigines held some of the best lands. Apparently the poor harvest of 1912 and the drought of 1914-15 ruined most of them. Lack of access to loan funds was a factor. Another was the tug of kinship ties. Biskup quotes a Lands Department file noting how the successful Aboriginal farmer attracted his relatives to the farm to share his wealth.[62] This is always a critical factor where a kinship-oriented society is making its way into a cash economy. Duty to kindred prevents the accumulation of capital, so that there is no cushion against the inevitable setbacks in farming or business.

In any event, these seem to have been exceptions: for most, and for the usual reasons, there was only itinerant rural work for the men and domestic employment for the women. The place to get such employment was the town; and by 1900 Prinsep, head of the Aborigines Department, had drafted a Bill which would have given him power to remove them from the towns.[63] This of course involved removal to reserves. Power to make such removals was established in the Aborigines Act of 1905 (sections 12-14) on the model of the Queensland legislation. As in Queensland, the managed settlements, whatever else they were purported to be, became multi-purposed institutions where every kind of problem case might be sent—the syphilitic, the illegitimate child, the widow with dependent children, the unemployed, the unwanted or anti-social adults, the rebellious girls.

In addition, in the closely settled parts of the State, the power to expel

[60] See P. Biskup, Native Administration and Welfare in Western Australia 1897-1954, p. 122.
[61] Ibid., p. 145.
[62] Ibid., pp. 146-7.
[63] C. Makin, A Socio-Cultural Anthropological Survey—quoting Aborigines Department file 830/00. The draft is discussed and outlined in the Report of the Aborigines Department for 1901.

Aborigines from the towns meant that inevitably there would be shanty camps just outside the limits. The justification for the expulsions was, as usual, to remove the Aboriginal from temptation: as though prostitution were an individual act, and drinking alcohol peculiar to him. In his 1901 Report, Prinsep stated that he had drafted his Bill 'to prevent natives from hovering anywhere within the outskirts of white settlements or towns', and the beginning of the 'town reserve' at a distance from the town boundary is foreshadowed. 'They could then be made to remain at such a distance from the settlement that it would not be worth their while to loiter there, nor worth while the whites to seek their distant camps.'[64]

Eight or nine miles seems to have been the usual distance. In his 1902 Report Prinsep describes the Welshpool Reserve, nine miles out of Guildford. This set the pattern for decades. Of note is the complete disregard of the needs of employment: of the man who had to be at the town to be 'picked up' for seasonal work, and of the employer seeking workers. This was also in accord with the pressure from trade unions, protecting the interest of the white worker. Though the 1905 Act made it illegal to remove an Aboriginal who was already employed, this was not adequate protection for the seasonal worker. Perhaps the Western Australian and the Queensland legislation made the most explicit of all concessions to the prejudices and fears of the townsfolk. There were second thoughts, as in the Report of the Chief Protector for 1907, where he showed reluctance to declare prohibited areas, because

if natives are driven from centres where they can pick up some sort of sustenance by occasional jobs of work, they will find themselves on the large runs where they are not wanted either and dogs are poisoned.

Moreover, the Aboriginal worker might be required; so that at Carnarvon he would not 'proceed too fast as ... it might tend to harass trade in the district'.[65] But in 1908 police were directed to enforce provisions against Aborigines loitering in towns.

The plight of the Aborigines in the settled areas seems not to have been seen clearly, but overshadowed (as in Queensland) by the frontier conditions. The myth was well established that the 'native' was incapable of sustained work, and an incurable nomad. Like other such myths this could operate as a self-fulfilling prophecy, as lack of employment brought undernutrition with consequent effects on performance. In spite of Roth's recommendations, the 1905 Act, indicating the obsession with the frontier, made no provision for a minimum wage.

[64] Ibid.
[65] W.A. Report of Chief Protector 1907—extracted by Dr Ruth Fink.

In 1912 the *West Australian* reported that the State Executive of the Australian Labor Party had recommended the abolition of Aboriginal employment except by the government, in order to offset the effect on union members of cheap station labour; the recommendation was that all employment should be on large reserves managed by the government.[66] It was obvious enough that *full* employment on reserves would require very large reserves and that any realistic attempt to provide for these would meet overwhelming opposition. Wherever there have been reserves there has arisen the problem that a few are employed, while the others either must be idle or be kept 'busy' on pointless institutional tasks.

Yet it is hard to blame governments when the New South Wales section of the Australian Association for the Advancement of Science, in 1913, could recommend only training in 'simple mechanical arts' on the reserves as offering a solution.[67]

Commenting on the resolution of the A.L.P., one Bill Harris, a part-Aboriginal, wrote that

they might just as well ask for the imprisonment of all the Aborigines, for that is about what it would amount to. Why take from the Aborigines the right to work for their own living? . . . So long as they are paid a fair wage and let it be one of the protector's duties to see that they are fairly dealt with.[68]

In the pastoral areas where Aborigines were not allowed guns, they had to have dogs to hunt; but the pastoralists killed the dogs to protect the stock. Even Harris could see no solution other than small reserves. This was no solution because water, not living space, is the basis for life in most of Australia; and where there was a water supply there was white settlement.

The Annual Report of 1914 indicated that the town reserves were the sites of considerable 'trouble', with apparently unemployed Aborigines expressing their resentment. The government had approved the idea of 'native settlements' in the south-west, and the site for the first one was to be sixteen miles out of Katanning. It was to be a multi-purposed institution: an answer to all the problems and a means of removing these problems from the sight of townsmen.

Socially outcasted [*sic*] from European races, their presence cannot be absorbed by the community, and they must stand alone to work out their own salvation. Inherit-

[66] *West Australian* (Perth), 19 September 1912—extracted by Dr Ruth Fink.
[67] Reported in *West Australian* (Perth), 9 January 1913.
[68] *Sunday Times*, 6 April 1913.

ing the nomadic instincts of the native race, they, under present conditions, roam about the country making a precarious living, and speaking generally fall upon the government's support in their old age. Serious consideration must . . . be given to this problem and while there is yet time other suitable unoccupied portions of this State . . . should be reserved for their future use.[69]

As well as providing a means of handling geriatric problems of the part-Aboriginal who had inherited deplorable nomadic instincts, these settlements would provide employment, trade training, and schooling for the children.

The kind of pressure which was coming from the towns is nicely indicated by a letter to the *West Australian* in May 1912 from 'A Father' of Katanning.

Australia boasts of her White Australia policy, and rightly so. In Katanning we are faced with a serious problem. At our local state school we have no less than sixteen pure black and half-caste children . . . There is an enrolment of seventy children so it is impossible for the teachers to keep these Aboriginals away from the others . . . We must keep our children free from possible contamination . . . The welfare of our little White Australians is of far greater importance to us than the possible hardship inflicted on, I trust, a very small minority of our citizens . . . Keep the children of the different races separate and the trouble will die out.

Removal of Aboriginal children from State schools had been going on since 1905 and possibly earlier, not as a matter of educational policy but in a series of surrenders to local pressures where these were strong enough, and even where no alternative schooling was available. In this the Western Australian situation may be compared with that in New South Wales. At Quairading in 1915 the Progress Association, having used pressure to have the Aboriginal children expelled from the local school, was demanding that the government should provide another school for them. The responsible Minister condemned their insincerity, and stated that

if it is the general desire of every little town in the farming districts to have a State school for natives, as well as for white children, then it is up to the people of those towns to pay for it.[70]

The school situation was a symptom of the general town situation and of the refusal of local government bodies to share common services. That central government did not override such prejudice or objections arising from cultural differences was the central fact which made inevitable the attempt to provide the services separately, at 'suitable' places

---

[69] Annual Report of Aborigines Department 1914, pp. 1-2.
[70] Correspondence in *West Australian* (Perth), 15 May 1915.

which no one else wanted for the most part. Where Queensland was at least prepared to devote comparatively large sums to develop reserves, Western Australia seems to have had neither the resources nor the will, especially for those in the south-west where the problems were less spectacular.

Carrolup was founded, on the site out of Katanning, in 1915, the first year of Neville's Chief Protectorate; and the following year saw the beginning of Moore River settlement near the rural township of Mogumber. Employment was easier to get in the war years, and money wages were being paid. But pressure to remove Aborigines from the vicinity of towns was maintained; and the establishment at Carrolup was directly related to the pressure coming from Katanning. The announced purpose of Carrolup was to be a home for the old and ill, an institution for 'waifs and strays', and to provide schooling. Girls were still in canvas dormitories a year later; the older ones ran away and when recovered had to be kept in close custody; but according to the Chief Protector's Report for 1918, 'the natives appear to be happy and contented'.

The end of the war reduced the chances of employment. Both settlements were being established: with about ten thousand acres Moore River was very well located, on excellent land which had been resumed. The 1919 Report described the introduction of a new system whereby the police removed the Aborigines to the settlements under warrant—a system designed for rapid execution of the power under the Act, and for avoiding delays which would have occurred had justice been a matter of any concern. (The Aboriginal who refused to obey an order to move would then have had to be prosecuted.) This warrant system, of doubtful legality, remained in force until 1948. But in his 1919 Report Neville, having described the settlements as a 'sociological experiment' with inmates including drunkards, prostitutes, and criminals (in addition to the 'waifs and strays' referred to earlier), expressed his satisfaction that 'the reserve and settlement system is the only true solution of the native question'. He wrote also of how Aboriginal 'prejudice' against confinement gave way to contentment when they 'realise what the Department is trying to do for their welfare and happiness'. In fact the settlements must have been typical of most Aboriginal institutions, with inmates seething with resentment; and this conjecture is supported by their subsequent history.

There was a garment industry at Carrolup, which saved the government money in the annual distribution of clothing to the needy. The beginning of an apartheid economy on the model of the Queensland settlement system was optimistically forecast in statements that the settlements would soon be self-supporting. But in 1922 Carrolup was closed down and the inmates were taken to Moore River, which now became the centre of the Aboriginal garment industry.

By 1926, as a result of the merger and of regular removals from the towns under warrant, Moore River had 300 inmates. Bill Harris was still a spokesman for the part-Aborigines of the south, and at the end of that year he wrote that

Mogumber (Moore River) is a mixed settlement where native men and women are forced to live along with murderers and other offenders from all parts of this State. Six of them were made police ... to terrorize the others and keep them in the compound. The place has also gaol cells. ...[71]

(The old gaol still stands, and a grim hole it is still.) The resemblance to the Queensland system, with the manager appointing 'police' who wear uniforms, the gaol, the making of escape a criminal offence—in fact, the whole arrangement under which it became the equivalent of a crime to have Aboriginal appearance, since it led to involuntary incarceration, is reminiscent of the Queensland system.

We have already looked at the effects of the great depression which now began. Neville was trying to get funds for another settlement, especially for the unemployed youth,[72] but in the same year the expenditure on rations at Moore River was reduced. The government was now spending somewhere round £13 per head per annum there. In 1932 ten men and eighteen girls escaped; Neville was worried that the penalty was six months gaol, and had a prohibited area declared round the settlement to prevent outsiders 'enticing' inmates to get out. Sixteen of the young girls who had escaped gave birth when they were brought back.[73]

With the depression at its worst, the Town Clerk of Northam wrote to the Chief Protector in December 1932 complaining of the skin diseases allegedly suffered by Aborigines on the outskirts, and attached a letter from the local medical officer stating that the camp lacked water, had crude sanitary arrangements, that there was a menace to the health of Northam. He recommended that water be laid on for treatment, and that 'natives' be 'moved from the Northam district to a more suitable area'. Neville decided to remove the whole 'camp' population to Moore River, for *quarantine there*, which was a nice example of priorities in Aboriginal health. There is no doubt that town pressures led directly to this decision.

[71] *Sunday Times*, 14 November 1926.
[72] Annual Report of Chief Protector, 1931.
[73] Ibid., 1932.

The result was that no less than forty-one adults and forty-nine children were removed under warrant by the police. For good measure some families *not* camped on the offending town reserve were included. The instructions showed little regard for private property. 'No dogs, conveyances, live stock or other property inconvenient to transfer will be taken with the party.' But for those taken by train, there were to be provided 'three large buckets of tea. The party will be under escort and will not be permitted on the platform'. But arrangements were also made to take the horses and buggies by road.[74] According to the *Northam Advertiser*, some who were employed on a farm near the town were included with their families, because the police were rationing the families.[75]

When the party finally arrived, the matron there found three children and one woman affected with skin disorder.[76] There was of course 'trouble' at Moore River with the newcomers, and some described as 'ringleaders' were released at the end of the quarantine period only on a signed undertaking to keep away from Northam. Those who came back established a 'camp' three miles out of town, and even their journeys into town to buy supplies were the subject of renewed complaints by mid-1933.

These events, and some similar issues at Wagin, where there had been complaints about the Aboriginal 'camp', were part of the background to the Moseley Royal Commission. Evidence before that Commission was by no means all one-sided, including some by Aborigines and some from persons like Mrs M.M. Bennett, who was deeply concerned with the failure to meet basic needs. She advocated the setting aside of a 'real living area' in each district, with proper housing, water supply and sanitation, and she stressed basic human needs for family and community life, food, and education. When she remarked to the Commissioner 'I am trying to look at them simply as human beings', the reply was 'We all regard them as human beings. However, humanity is not all on one level plane. You want natives to have things they would not appreciate.'[77]

---

[74] The correspondence on which this paragraph was based was copied from the Departmental file by Dr Ruth Fink, who made it available to the SSRC-AP.

[75] 18 January 1933—extracted by Dr Ruth Fink.

[76] Superintendent of Moore River to Chief Protector, 18 January 1933—extracted from file by Dr Ruth Fink.

[77] Evidence by Mrs M.M. Bennett, reported in *West Australian* (Perth), 20 and 21 March 1934. The Report of the Royal Commissioner Appointed to Investigate, Report, and Advise upon Matters in Relation to the Conditions and Treatment of Aborigines, January 1935, does not include this evidence.

Moseley reported that the 'camps' should be as far from the towns as practicable and that Aborigines should be allowed into town only under a permit system, for reasons of health (non-Aboriginal, of course), mendicancy, access to liquor, and the like. But he condemned Moore River as a 'woeful spectacle'. There was a 'compound' for the education and protection of children, and a 'camp' for indigents. As for the first, he condemned verminous dormitories and bough-shed-type classrooms, and the lack of utensils, so that children ate with their fingers. No vegetables were grown there, and there was shortage of meat, fruit, and eggs. The place of detention should be pulled down. There was lack of security, and the girls from the dormitory visited the 'camp'. The camp should be removed. His recommendations included one for settlements devoted to the care and training of children. Neville's 1935 Annual Report commented that it was unfortunate that the Commissioner had made his visit when things were not 'normal' and it admitted that more facilities were required—as illustration: the small children were being taught in the open air by an Aboriginal monitor. An immediate response to the visit was to enclose the girls' dormitory with wire mesh and to place bars on the windows.

The next few years did bring better physical conditions, and there was even a kindergarten by 1937. But a 'Special Representative' of the *West Australian*, while admitting the improvements, pointed out that the old camp was still there 'rusty iron, torn bags, shabby men, rheumy crones with spindly children on visits'. He also condemned the attempt to meet in one institution so many different needs:

creche, orphanage, relief depot, old men's home, old women's home, home for discharged prisoners, home for expatriated savages, for unmarried mothers, for incurables, lost dogs' home and a school for boys and girls.[78]

The annual reports show that the removals by warrant continued; and that up till the outbreak of the war persons continued to be prosecuted for escaping. The Report for 1940, the year of Neville's retirement, indicated that the cost of food and staff for Moore River was £9 per inmate per annum. It had again been decided to grow some food on the farm.

The same Report mentioned the re-opening of Carrolup. The policy was to remove there 'indolent natives and children . . . thereby clearing the towns and districts of the worst types . . .', which was having 'a wholesome effect as quite a number of natives secured work to escape removal'.

[78] *West Australian* (Perth), 3 August 1937—extracted by Dr Fink.

But although Carrolup was being 'planned' to cater for 500 persons, and Moore River for an increase, wartime employment, along with the extension of social service benefits by the Commonwealth, together brought about an upward trend in economic conditions. The proneness of resentful people to defy authority, and to spend the additional earnings in ways disapproved by the whites, meant that the warrant system continued to be used as a sanction—even as a labour sanction—against 'idleness and casualness', natural enough reactions against employers who were now suffering from wartime labour shortages.[79] The paying of social service benefits direct to those not on settlements provided impetus, to those who were entitled to them, to leave. As elsewhere, there was resentment from the darker people who were judged to be more than *half-caste* and so *not* entitled to assistance. The irrelevance of the ruling was seen where darker families had living conditions more in accordance with non-Aboriginal norms than *half-castes*. In 1943, although 159 persons were incarcerated under warrant, there were only 232 people, and a total of 26 adult males, on the two settlements.[80]

At the end of 1943 the Commonwealth Commission on Post-War Housing was hearing evidence in the State. It indicated that by this time, in spite of what had been happening, there were families established in country town and metropolitan housing. The prospect of housing assistance of course raised questions of where the houses should be built, as well as the awkward question of when a house is really wanted in the process of change from nomadism. Generally, the response to both questions has everywhere been conservative: money has been spent on 'transitional' housing and on housing *away* from the towns. But the new ideas of assimilation, though at this stage related to that of the *half-caste*, resulted in an estimate of some 276 houses required for 'natives', of which only thirty were wanted at Moore River.

The question of housing marked the beginning of a change in the situation as between local and central government throughout the closely settled areas. As, especially in the years after the war, Aboriginal families began to move into the towns and the capital cities, the complaints were about depreciation of real estate values, and hygiene, where before they had been about immorality and hygiene. At least this had a more modern ring. Increased economic opportunity of the war years was to make inevitable the withering away of the controlled stations and settlements. (Although they have been maintained with strong government support

[79] See Annual Report, Commissioner of Native Affairs, 1942.
[80] Ibid., 1943.

in Queensland, economic and political logic could quickly change the policy.) Those who found homes elsewhere often kept them; in the post-war climate of opinion it was more difficult to impose new pressures. War-time building restrictions had made it impossible to keep abreast of a rapidly growing part-Aboriginal population; a new effort on the scale which seemed to be required was made only for the 'full-bloods' of the Northern Territory.

Conditions at Carrolup and Mogumber became a political issue towards the end of 1944. In both the population had risen, and in 1944 the settlement schools had been closed, it seems for lack of teachers. The criticism came from the Opposition in the House, from mission bodies, from local clergymen, and, most significantly, from some former employees such as teachers and nurses who had worked there. Matters for criticism were apparent lack of any real policy, the absence of education facilities, inadequate provision for health, and especially the treatment of children—the use of an ineffective dormitory system to incarcerate children at night, the failure to incarcerate them effectively, the use of the punitive cell, association with former criminals, corporal punishment, and the general living conditions.[81] What is most significant perhaps is the scale of the protest and the publicity it received, since whatever the conditions were at that time, clearly they must have been much worse earlier. Some of the protests were linked with demands for Commonwealth control of the whole program. The first protest seems to have come from the Anglican Synod of the State, later supported by the National Missionary Council. The very effort to improve conditions had resulted in recruitment of teachers and trained nurses, who would naturally look at an old situation with professional eyes. Thus after this explosion of publicity had waned, former members of the staff at Moore River were complaining about the practice of bringing up children in such a social environment.[82] It has happened elsewhere in Aboriginal affairs that an impetus to change an old system comes from within the responsible service, in itself an indication of the lack of Aboriginal organisation and leadership. Even the government defence of these places was mainly by stating the staff deficiencies of the war years. One result of the protests was that teachers of the Education Department took over the settlement schools from the beginning of 1945.

[81] See *West Australian* (Perth), for 8 August, 10 and 15 September, 26, 24-28, October, 3, 8-11, 16-18, 23, and 30 November, 2 and 20 December 1944; *Daily News* (Perth), 10 and 14 September 1944.
[82] *West Australian* (Perth), 21 July 1945.

The Annual Report for 1945 mentioned the movement into Perth and into country towns, and other effects of higher employment and payment of social service benefits. The Education Department was resisting the few requests now being made for removal or exclusion of Aboriginal children. Furthermore, Aborigines were now becoming more important as a market, as the Commissioner of Native Affairs noted in his 1945 Report:

It can also be said that segregation . . . in respect to towns are a negation of business acumen, since the wage spending power of the natives is now upwards of half a million a year in Western Australia . . . It should be an offence to advocate racial discrimination . . . so far as our detribalised natives are concerned.

Yet both settlements seem to have been maintained in much the same way until the appointment, in August 1948, of Stanley Guise Middleton, a senior officer of the old Papuan administration then serving in that of Papua-New Guinea. His scheme for division of the State into districts was approved; and his appointment of District Officers, several of them from Papua-New Guinea, marked the death knell of the settlements. He was the first officer in such an appointment in any State to attempt to see the problem as a whole, and as a fluid situation. Assimilation, which was becoming the popular term for progressive change, meant more to him than the eventual results of miscegenation; and in his very first Report he attacked the predominant attitudes of white townsfolk. What he found in the south of the State, no less than in the north, was typical of a plural society, with the races associating mainly for economic purposes.

Generally speaking, interest in the native is manifested only from the economic point of view. He is welcomed at harvest, mustering, shearing, and similar agricultural and pastoral times of need, or when he or she has wages or child endowment money to spend in the towns, but is expected to get back to the reserve or camp as soon as possible after the job is completed or the money spent, and stay out of sight, and presumably out of mind, until again required. Little, if any, thought is ever given to the terrible effect this attitude is having upon the minds and outlook of the natives themselves towards the white community generally.

He agreed with a statement by Bateman that if

the native were clean, tidy and reliable, and lived under conditions similar to our own, the prejudice would be largely broken down . . . [But, he wrote] I . . . cannot as yet see how this can be achieved under circumstances which require so far as the average person and local authority is concerned, that natives shall be kept in settlements and on reserves sited on land that has very little, if any, value, and is not required for development by whites, or at best on privately-owned building blocks located in swamps, on stony ridges, or in juxtaposition to sanitary dumps and rubbish tips, which is the only land, generally speaking, that local authorities are prepared to sell and natives able to purchase. A very positive and firm policy will be laid down and plans submitted with a view to combating this unjust treatment of the people whom this department is charged to protect.[83]

By the end of 1951 Carrolup was being transformed into a 'farm school' for boys, with the girls transferred to the care of missions. The last report of V. H. Sully, the superintendent Middleton had placed in charge, appears to justify the criticisms so often made. 'The whole place was in a shocking condition. There was no administration or supervision of staff. In fact, the dormitories were enough to make anyone sick.'[84] The boys of school age went to mission schools (now taught by Education Department teachers), and the Marribank Farm School was for boys over school leaving age. This was the beginning of a new policy, to involve local employers in a committee and to use the missions for specialist purposes. The 1951 Report described the handing over of the Moore River Settlement to the Methodist Overseas Mission, the missionary-superintendent of which, the Reverend E.A. Clarke, like several of Middleton's officers, had had Papuan experience. In a discussion in 1965 he told the writer that when he got there fourteen years before he found only four bed-ridden old men and a few children; the others had fled as soon as the government had relinquished control, some of them as far away as the eastern goldfields towns.

I have given this somewhat detailed account of policy on reserves in Western Australia because the issues are posed perhaps more starkly there than elsewhere. Middleton's action was essential in order to clear the way for any real chance of integration. One consequence was, of course, to deny for the Government and for his own department an easy recourse of removal to a settlement when a local problem occurred, and the rapidly increasing population made the problems of health, housing, and education more obvious, and heightened the contrast between conditions in the towns and those on the town reserves and in other fringe-dwelling areas. On the other hand, his success in getting his way may not have been so speedy had the Western Australian government been in a position previously to commit considerable capital to the development of the settlements, as was the case in Queensland.

[83] W.A.P.P., 1951, vol. 2, no. 10, p. 7—Annual Report of the Commissioner of Native Affairs, 1949, citing W.A.P.P., 1948, vol. 2, no. 19—F.E.A. Bateman, Report on Survey of Native Affairs.
[84] W.A.P.P., 1951, vol. 2—Annual Report of the Commissioner of Native Affairs, 1950, p. 19.

In Western Australia, as elsewhere, the spending by Aborigines since the early war years had created new vested interests in their freedom to enter towns, although it took time to have the law on prohibited areas withdrawn. But the enthusiastic local policeman who required permits for shopping or attendance at the cinema from those on the town reserve was now likely to find some opposition from businessmen whose pockets were being affected. All over the closely settled areas of Australia, by 1950, small local bodies interested in Aboriginal welfare were appearing. The background was such that they seldom found any effective local Aboriginal leadership to deal with—a problem which still remains.

Since 1897 Queensland has committed far more capital and effort to the development of its Aboriginal settlements than has any other State. This has been (and still is) part of an integrated policy that requires detailed treatment to allow the various aspects to emerge from the complex whole. From 1897 until at least 1965 the practices and the basic legislation formed a consistent and interlocked system; and the attempt was much more consistently made than elsewhere to see that it operated uniformly throughout the State. Queensland had a strong influence on policies and practices in South Australia and Western Australia, States which had similar concern with Aborigines still considered to live under tribal conditions; and when the Commonwealth began to look for expert advice in the Northern Territory, it looked to Queensland. Consistency within the system meant that there was a consistent attempt to deal with all people within the legislative categories ('under the Act') everywhere within the limits of the State: in effect, what seemed necessary in Cape York was assumed to be necessary in the southern areas.

Consistency must break down unless the policy is given high priority: yet Aboriginal policy has consistently had low priority wherever economic matters are to be considered. This has meant a continued yielding of principle to expediency. Thus when the people of the old mission of Mapoon were wanted out of the way of bauxite mining and exploration, many of them were offered freedom from controls. In effect, suddenly they could be officially 'assimilated'. To be really efficient, the policy required much higher expenditure than was ever available. Lack of funds and staff meant that a substantial part of the group falling within the categories was only sporadically brought effectively within the system. If they were nuisances, they might find themselves taken to a settlement. If they were skilful, they might avoid police protectors whose duty it was to hold their wages.

Queensland legislation was mainly a cumulative effort to apply the principles established by Meston in 1897. A study of the Acts and Regulations from 1897 until the consolidation of 1939 indicates a consistent attempt to block the loopholes and to improve the system. Within its limits, as in the setting of uniform wages for Aborigines and in the efforts to police them, to control earnings, to provide a safe home base from which the men went out to work, there was a well-meaning and persistent effort. The Queensland government led the way in expenditure on settlements, with the result that Aborigines there were better housed, even if more rigidly controlled, than they were under any other government. The system is most conveniently examined by reference to the consolidation of the Acts and Regulations which was compiled in 1955.[1]

In 1939 the Chief Protector became the Director of Native Affairs. His full-time field staff consisted only of the superintendents of the government settlements and their staffs, which grew as the effort at controlled improvement on these places increased. From the beginning of this system until the Aborigines' and Torres Strait Islanders' Act of 1965 was implemented, the Director's main efforts were in the management of settlements, in the controls which could be exercised through the system of police protectors, who controlled the 'country reserves', and in the system of labour contracts (which involved holding the worker's bank book and controlling his expenditure), and in supervision of the efforts of those missionaries who under the legislation were appointed to posts as superintendents of mission settlements and exercised the powers of the government superintendents.[2] The Acts gave very wide power of control to the Director, and through him to his officers, both full-time and part-time; and his action or omission to act was 'deemed to be a lawful act or omission until the contrary is proved'.[3]

---

[1] The main Acts were those of 1897, 1901, 1928, and 1934, which were consolidated in 1939. In 1946 the 1939 Act with minor amendments was issued as The Aboriginals Preservation and Protection Act of 1946. Regulations were consolidated in The Aboriginals Regulations of 1945. The 1946 Act and the 1945 Regulations were issued together, probably as a handbook, in 1956, as The Aboriginals Preservation and Protection Acts 1939 to 1946, and Regulations Thereunder, with an Index (Government Printer, Brisbane, 1956).
[2] Aboriginals Preservation and Protection Acts, 1939 to 1946, sections 8 and 9.
[3] Ibid., section 7(c).

## LEGISLATION ON SETTLEMENTS AND RESERVES, TO 1965

The reserves and settlements (which were the reserves under control of government or mission superintendents) form the king-pin of the system, so it is logical to deal first with the legislation relating to them. It should be stated here, however, that by no means all those who fell within the categories of Aboriginal were established on reserves or settlements. In the closely settled areas of the State, there were four government settlements: at Cherbourg, adjacent to the town of Murgon, at Woorabinda south-west of Rockhampton and south-east of Emerald, at Yarrabah some miles out of Cairns, and on Palm Island, an island in the Barrier Reef chain off the coast due east of Ingham, with the same relation to Townsville as Yarrabah had to Cairns. In the area of Cape York and the Gulf were a number of mission settlements on extensive reserves.[4]

The country reserves were widely scattered, tending to be established, in the New South Wales fashion, where there were already fringe-dwelling groups dependent on seasonal and casual employment in the surrounding areas. Most were in the northern and western areas, tending to group between the pastoral and closely settled regions of the State—nine in the vicinity of Cairns—but they were strung out from Birdsville to the Gulf. Most are situated conveniently to a town and to the former office of the police protector,[5] so that the main difference from the unauthorised fringe settlement was that those who lived there could be ordered to leave or to remain, and were under the supervision of the protector.

The superintendent or protector was responsible for 'welfare and discipline'; and the Aboriginal must obey 'all lawful orders'. Any order related to 'habits of orderliness or cleanliness' was a lawful one. 'Dancing or other native practices' required his written permission, but must cease at midnight. Otherwise such practices were an offence. The officer could prohibit 'any game, whether played with cards or otherwise', take over any articles or money used in a 'prohibited game', and dispose of them at his discretion. No Aboriginal could leave the reserve without his permission, which was also necessary to keep any livestock on a reserve. An Aboriginal must deliver to him any of his possessions 'likely to be the subject or cause of a disturbance of the harmony, good order, or discipline of the reserve'. Medical inspections were compulsory.

---

[4] See *The Destruction of Aboriginal Society*, ch. 4.
[5] By the Act of 1965 police were replaced as protectors by court officials, but in many cases the policeman may be the court official.

Threatening or abusive language, or intoxication, were special offences on a reserve, as was 'any act subversive of good order or discipline'. Any firearm could be seized, whether held under permit from the officer or not.

Every Aboriginal on a reserve could be ordered to work for thirty-two hours weekly, without remuneration, on the 'development or maintenance' of the reserve. Corporal punishment could be inflicted on those under sixteen years, but required the permission of the Director. The Aboriginal Court (which in practice on settlements was, until the 1965 Act, the superintendent sitting as a magistrate) could confine a child in the settlement dormitory until he reached the age of sixteen years. Entry by Aborigines to a reserve required permission or a removal order from somewhere else. Once there, the regulations provided that an Aboriginal should not 'leave or escape' without permission, 'or, except in the course of his duty, proof whereof shall lie with the defendant'. He could be ordered by a protector or superintendent to remain in a 'specified part' of the reserve (which could include a dormitory, so that no sentence by the Aboriginal Court was necessary). With the approval of the Director, a protector or superintendent could order all mail to or from the inmates to be delivered to him, and he could peruse it; and the writer or recipient who tried to avoid this was guilty of an offence. The officer could confiscate and destroy what he considered obscene.[6]

Entry to reserves by a non-Aboriginal was very rigidly controlled, requiring both permission and conduct while there 'to the satisfaction of the protector or superintendent'. A condition of entry was that his person and belongings could be searched at any time. He could be expelled by order of the same officer.[7]

The settlement offered a dumping ground for unwanted persons or for those deemed to be in need of 'protection'. The power to remove Aborigines from any 'camp', 'within or near the limits of any township or place to which in his opinion they should not have access' was vested in the protector.[8] Any Aboriginal other than one married to a non-Aboriginal (to whom the Act did not apply) or the 'half-blood' child of such a person could 'be removed from any district to a reserve and kept there for such time as may be ordered by the Director', who could also remove an Aboriginal from one reserve to another.[9]

[6] Aboriginals Regulations of 1945, Regulations 17 to 32.
[7] Ibid., Regulations 33 and 34.
[8] Aboriginals Preservation and Protection Act of 1939, section 21.
[9] Ibid., section 22.

These powers were used for disciplinary purposes. A troublemaker on one reserve would often find himself removed to another. Palm Island seems to have been suitable for additional punishments, as when a person, having served a short court sentence, might be removed there. Escape from Palm Island was almost impossible. When on a settlement, the Aboriginal was subject to a degree of official authority which has never applied to persons in Australia outside of gaols and asylums. Thus *any* act on a reserve which the officer considered injurious to health or a 'menace to peace and good order' could be prohibited. Needless to say, possession of liquor (or opium) was an offence.[10]

The Act provided for regulations to establish Aboriginal Courts on reserves, with both criminal and civil jurisdiction, limiting the penalties in the former case to £1 or sentences of three weeks.[11] These civil courts could exercise jurisdiction, for offences which if committed 'outside' would go to the magistrates' courts, so long as the sum involved did not exceed £50 ($100) and both parties were Aborigines, as well as cases involving breaches of the regulations. The court was appointed by the Director and could be a protector or superintendent sitting alone. On the settlements it was composed of the superintendent with a clerk of the court appointed by him from his staff.[12] Thus the Director discharged some functions usually belonging to the institutions for justice, though he might have no more legal knowledge than his 'courts'. The superintendent would have had no legal training. The appointments were either of missionaries or men who were expected to make the government settlements as close to economically self-contained institutions as possible. It was inevitable, therefore, that these courts carried on into the 1960s the earlier frontier traditions of kangaroo courts for Aborigines. Their nature and functioning were indicated by Dr C.M. Tatz in 1963.[13] The superintendent, under the Regulations, could deal with almost any action of which he disapproved, as an offence. There was provision for visiting justices; but the court records were apparently such that these visits could be little more than formalities. Fines went to the Aborigines Welfare Fund maintained by the Department.[14] Representation by counsel required permission of the court.[15] The recourse on

---

[10] Ibid., sections 23, 24.
[11] Ibid., section 12(3).
[12] Aboriginals Regulations of 1945, Regulation 35.
[13] 'Queensland's Aborigines: Natural Justice and the Rule of Law', *Australian Quarterly*, vol. 5, no. 3, September 1963, pp. 33–49.
[14] Aboriginals Regulations of 1945, Regulation 36.
[15] Regulation 38(2).

appeal, which would mean risking the wrath of the superintendent later, was to the visiting justice.[16]

The superintendent appointed his own police; and one of the special features of the Queensland settlements has been the sight of the Aboriginal police in the uniforms of the Queensland police force. Perhaps this carried on in a new context the traditions of the Native Police. As the superintendent arranged pay and promotions, there is some logical ground for comparing their position with that of 'trusties', especially as he could also dismiss or demote them. They had powers of arrest for breach of the regulations or on the direction of the superintendent.[17] To make the system complete, there was also the settlement gaol, with the gaoler appointed by the superintendent.[18] Sentences could be served there, up to the limit of three weeks; but the practice seems to have allowed for two consecutive sentences to be served in the settlement gaol. Prisoners could be employed as directed by the superintendent.

It is interesting that such powers were also vested in mission settlement superintendents. A somewhat unusual feature of the Queensland Christian mission was the mission gaol.

### CONTROLLED EMPLOYMENT

From the commencement of the special legislation in 1897, no person could employ an Aboriginal without the permission of a protector. (All superintendents on government settlements were protectors; in later years, at least, some mission superintendents were not.) A separate system of the type long used for 'native labour' in British colonies was established, with an individual contract of employment setting the conditions and wages in accordance with separate standards laid down in the regulations. The Aboriginal was 'signed on', and the contract endorsed by the protector. The limit to the 'agreement' term was twelve months, probably because most women and children were expected to remain on the reserve or settlement. The protector could direct the employer to pay to him 'the whole or any portion' of the wage. He could cancel agreements or inquire into complaints; but if he considered the employee to be at fault, he could order him to go back to work. There were penalties for breach of agreement by either party, one of which was 'inciting to desert'.[19]

[16] Regulations 40–4.
[17] Regulation 52.
[18] Section 51.
[19] Aboriginals Preservation and Protection Act of 1939, section 14 as amended in 1946.

Thus the employee had no legal redress for any breach of agreement, nor could any worker 'under the Act' learn to make his own bargain with an employer, or to manage his own money and affairs.

How could such a 'colonial' system of employment have flourished in Queensland up till now (for the new legislation of 1965 did not depart basically from it)? Part of the answer is to be found in Queensland preoccupation with what had been the worst frontier conditions and the reaction of its politicians and administrators to them, after 1897. But history may provide another reason, for Queensland had had special experience—in the Pacific Island labour trade for the first sugar plantations. The first legislation to control this trade was drawn up in the same department of government which was concerning itself with the drafting of legislation to protect Aborigines recruited for employment at sea.

Here it is worth referring back to the debate in the Queensland Parliament on the Native Labourers' Protection Bill of 1884. This was introduced 'to prevent improper employment of Aboriginal natives of Australia and New Guinea on ships in Queensland waters', for the masters were accused of using the same methods of recruiting as were common round the coasts of New Guinea—seizing not only the men, but young girls to entice and keep them aboard.[20] It is interesting that a considerable part of the 1939 Act was devoted to the regulation of employment on vessels.[21]

The responsibility, first of the Chief Protector and subsequently of the Director, for the control and welfare of the Torres Strait Islanders has had a good deal to do with this maritime flavour of the legislation. Moreover, responsibility for the Islanders, whose moves into employment from villages in the Strait offer a clear analogy with the system of migrant labour in New Guinea, must have tended to set standards for the employment of Aborigines out from reserves and settlements. The contract system was established for both. But it came into Queensland as an obsolete pattern, adapted to somewhat old-fashioned colonial administration—obsolete, that is, in reference to the labour conditions applying generally in the Australian community. In this framework of administration the settlement may be seen as analogous to the Pacific Island village: the men, in general, go out to work; women do also, into domestic employment. They are afforded the protections not of the general labour laws but of the individual contract. The origins of the

[20] *Q.P.D.*, 1884, vol. 43, pp. 183–92—debate on Native Labourers' Protection Bill. This was passed, but with penalties which rendered it innocuous for the recruiters and employers.
[21] Section 15.

individual contract go back through colonial labour laws to the old Master and Servant laws and to the efforts made to give legality to the colonial 'contract', after slavery became illegal, by adapting the apprenticeship system to the circumstances—a system which had the advantages of justifying low wages and of firmly binding the employee.

The regulations limited the age of the contract-maker to sixteen, except with special permission, though for other Australians there can be no contract with a minor.[22] Food and accommodation were regulated; and a comparison of what was 'suitable' for Aborigines with what the Queensland Station Hands' Award provided is an object lesson in discrimination, even in the 1960s.[23] There is not much point in giving details, for the simple reason that, except for the sporadic efforts of part-time police protectors, and the local knowledge of superintendents, contracts could not be policed: until 1966, the only full-time field staff of the Department was that of the settlements, and the conditions for Aboriginal workers did not concern any other department. Conditions varied, of course: as in the Northern Territory and Western Australia, they ranged in the outlying areas from good to shocking, as they did even within the time of the surveys made for this Project.

At least working hours were those set in the Station Hands' Award, but only one week's holiday was provided for. The cash wage was well below the award for non-Aborigines and was supplemented by a ration scale, as on a tropical plantation in New Guinea. (The 'white' worker received 'keep' as set out in the award.) If the employee did have his family with him (this was not obligatory on the employer), they also received rations; but the employer could demand twelve hours free work from the Aboriginal employee's wife in return, in 'domestic or other duties suitable for a female'.[24] (Not even in Papua or New Guinea was there such a provision.) The employer paid to the employee only that part of the wage which the protector did not require. He had to keep a record of what he had paid; but there was no provision that this record should also be kept, or even seen, by the employee.[25] The employer forwarded the record to the protector; and the opportunities for some fiddling were obvious: human nature being what it is, the cases of illiterates especially must have offered opportunities for a nice arrangement.

Until bank books began to be issued to Aborigines 'under the Act' in

[22] Aboriginals Regulations of 1945, Regulation 57(3).
[23] Regulations 59-65.
[24] Regulations 68-71.
[25] Regulation 73.

1966, they were held by the superintendent or protector. All wages, other than the 'pocket money' paid direct by the employer, were paid to the protector, who maintained the bank books. Money credited in these went into a trust fund with the Commonwealth Bank, with the Director as trustee. The Director could withdraw money for payment of a 'just debt'. He could delegate his authority to the protectors and superintendents, to operate on individual accounts, with the safeguard that a withdrawal over £10 ($20) must be reported and that only he could authorise one over £20.[26] Thus even to spend his own money, the Aboriginal required permission of a protector.

This system dated back to the time when bank officers were far away, though there are still parts of Queensland where there could be difficulties in proper administration of this quite obsolete legislation. It offered a real temptation to the protector. Especially in dealing with illiterates, but also in dealing with others who were so completely at the mercy of any whim he might have in interpretation of his legal powers, there were, to say the least, responsibilities which no public servant could have in dealing with non-Aborigines. It is as though the banker keeps the account without any copy to the customer. The Queensland police are, from what one can see travelling round the State, an impressive body of men. But every organisation has its weak links. The arrangement offered a permanent opportunity, at least, for Aboriginal suspicion.

This system of employment, in later years, has been used mainly for work in the pastoral industry, where, along with that in the pearling industry, the lower Aboriginal wage continued to apply. But it had this relation to the settled areas of the State—that from each of the four settlements, and from many of the country reserves, men were continuing to go out into employment under this legislation.

The Aboriginal wage was subject to income taxation. In addition, there were, until 1965, contributions made compulsorily from *gross* earnings to the Welfare Fund, for their own welfare and relief. These deductions were assessed and made by the protectors and superintendents. Single men and women, and those without dependants paid 5 per cent; married persons and others with dependants, $2\frac{1}{2}$ per cent. Aborigines received savings bank rates of interest. Additional proceeds from investment seem to have been paid into the Welfare Fund, along with the proceeds of the trade stores operated by the Department on the settlements, proceeds from the sale of produce from settlements and reserves, and fines.[27]

[26] Regulations 11-13.
[27] Regulations 6-9.

## OTHER LEGISLATION

By law, the officers managed all property, both real and personal, with power to dispose of it.[28] The Director was the legal guardian of all minors, who for this purpose (though not for signing labour contracts) meant those under twenty-one. He, through protectors, controlled all marriages 'with any person other than an Aboriginal'.[29] Carnal knowledge of Aboriginal women was an offence, except in marriage, for any but an Aboriginal.[30] An almost incredible provision was that if a person were charged under the Queensland Criminal Code with carnal knowledge of an Aboriginal girl under the statutory age of consent, 'it is a defence to a charge of any of the offences defined . . . to prove that such girl had developed a state of puberty . . . '.[31] The reasons go back into frontier conditions, when the Aboriginal group offered access to the women in the process of adaptation; and into the impossibility of determining ages. But this provision was completely incongruous with the laws against miscegenation and an outstanding example of the injustice which may arise from the retention of obsolete frontier-oriented laws, even within the closely settled areas.

On the credit side, the 1945 Regulations provided for elected councils on reserves and settlements where the Director had approved them. But the Director could declare a candidate ineligible 'for any reason whatsoever'. No legal powers vested in a council, perhaps for the simple reason that those of the protector or superintendent left nothing much to be decided. In fact, the Regulations stated that a council

shall not have any jurisdiction over the Aboriginal police, Aboriginal workers while so employed, or any person, matter or thing, unless such jurisdiction has been allocated to it in writing by the Director or superintendent.[32]

This provision was probably an attempt to bring Aboriginal administration into greater conformity with that in the Torres Strait Islands. Here there had been village councils, wielding real authority, from 1907. They were necessary partly because, as there was no challenge to the Islanders' control of the land or village resources other than labour, it had been necessary to delegate authority. Thus did Queensland, as a colonial power, forestall for over forty years the efforts of the Commonwealth in New Guinea to develop local democracy.

[28] Aboriginals Preservation and Protection Act of 1939, section 16.
[29] Ibid., section 19.
[30] Ibid., section 29.
[31] Ibid., section 36(3).
[32] Aboriginals Regulations of 1945, Regulation 49(5).

## BACKGROUND TO THE LEGISLATION

The system in Queensland obviously owes a good deal to the traditions handed down from early mission efforts; and to be fair, it represents a long-held view of what is good for Aborigines. The settlements inherited from early missions the dormitory system, under which children or others, whose activities it was necessary in their own assumed interests to restrain, might be kept from the influence of parents and others. It could be, and was, used for punitive purposes.

As with the stations in other States, the settlement was a multi-purposed institution. The generally well-meant but ill-informed effort which went into it can be compared with that made by the Commonwealth in the Northern Territory since the 1939-45 war. Such a long sustained effort in the one direction illustrates a determined paternalism and something of the strong influences of tradition in the public service of Queensland. It also illustrates again the dominance of the interests of the pastoral industry, for which the reserves and settlements have provided under contract an important and dependable source of cheap labour. The good intentions professed were supported by all the conditions round the country towns which Queensland shared with the other States. Here was a way of getting trouble-makers, poverty stricken people whose condition disturbed good citizens, and other unwanted persons out of the way. How many were actually removed to the settlements it is impossible to say. J.P.M. Long, who has made an intensive study of the annual reports, has estimated that from 1911, the first year when figures were given, until 1940, at least 5,762 were so removed. Over a thousand of these were removed during the depression years 1934-8.[33] The first spate of removals occurred earlier, from 1897; and it would be interesting to see the population figures for the years when the conditions must have been as bad as on stations and settlements in other States. After studying the population figures for Cherbourg, Woorabinda, Palm Island, and Yarrabah since the 1939-45 war, Long found that by 1965 there had been a total increase of about 11 per cent to just under 4,000.[34] As natural increase has to be taken into account, so too must allowance be made for the permanent absence of a large proportion of the adult men. The trend was somewhat inconsistent with acceptance of an 'assimilation' aim; but the 1957 and 1958 Reports of the Department of Native Affairs spoke of the need to 'create confidence' and of government resisting pressures

[33] *Aboriginal Settlements*, p. 96.
[34] Ibid.

towards 'an impetuous forcing of people to change their environment while they are unwilling to accept the responsibility of full citizenship'. But no figures for removals since the war were made available.

Perhaps the confirmation and development of the system established by Meston owes most to the determination and good intentions of Bleakley, whose views the Queensland government supported. This is illustrated by his statement at the 1937 conference of Commonwealth and State Officers, that the Aborigines Protection Society, which had been pressing the Australian government to promote development for Aborigines on reserves, had probably obtained its inspiration from the Queensland system.[35] His vision included self-supporting communities engaged in agriculture and fishing on the mission settlements of the far north. But here too they became economic adjuncts to the pastoral industry.

His description of the conditions in the pastoral areas indicates that with the resources he had, and with the recognised system of government priorities, settlements could seem major welfare projects. Even so, the employers of the males were still refusing to maintain dependants. 'Even where relief can be given, issues of flour, rice, tea, sugar and beef offal are inadequate substitutes for the native game and fruits.' Yet 'native labour' was 'an important asset of the Commonwealth' and should be preserved.[36]

Bleakley was far too humane to think even mainly in economic terms. The whole logic of welfare, as then conceived, and as then seemed possible, forced him to think in terms of central points where services—for health, rationing and clothing, education of children, housing and employment—could be centralised or created. It was he who had begun, after World War I, a wage system far in advance of what existed in other States with frontier conditions. What was logical for the most needy groups had to be adapted, within the resources available (and he was supported with these to a greater extent than under any other government at that time), for all, including those in the most closely settled areas.

To the 1937 conference he described the conditions of fringe-dwellers round the towns. On the one hand, the fringe-dwellers were required for local labour: the men on the surrounding stations and for clearing work on the farms, and the women as domestics. Thus he faced difficulties in removing them or their dependants. On the other hand, the women were bearing more problem children of 'mixed breed'; and there is no need to repeat his views on this matter. Then, the children were sometimes

---

[35] *Aboriginal Welfare*, p. 7.
[36] Ibid., p. 8.

not wanted in the schools (though from the evidence available there seems to have been more tolerance among Queensland country folk than in either New South Wales or Western Australia). His compromise was to work towards the establishment of 'villages' a reasonable distance from town; and it is interesting to see how similar circumstances produced something parallel with the 'town reserves' of Western Australia. Already, he said, he had had to establish some separate schools. He hoped to supply water and sanitation services. Where this could not be done, there was the transfer to a 'suitable' settlement.[37] (He was sometimes prone to this circular argument, bringing him back to his starting point; he had already stated why many could *not* be removed to settlements.) But these out-of-town 'villages' were no more than the country reserves, under the supervision of the police protectors, within the legislation we have described. They formalised the relationship of fringe-dweller to police far more definitely than in any other State, giving the police the control, as protectors, of the bank accounts, as well as all the power vested in the Regulations. Though by Australian standards the Queensland government was generous in its appropriations, it was not generous enough to provide on the country reserves the level of housing and other facilities which came in time on the settlements. (It is necessary to indicate here that in praising housing on the settlements, my comparison is with other *Aboriginal* housing.) A country reserve was and is often a rural slum.

A good example of what could happen in the end was the fate of the special settlement for 'superior half-castes' of which Bleakley made much in 1937. This was at Purga, out of Ipswich, where an 'industrial colony' was begun for them by moving away all 'full-bloods'.[38] The Premier outlined what was still a 'plan' in 1939; but it was by then to be a rural village supplying some labour to local farmers. The people there were 'healthy and contented'.[39] In the following year the whole project was handed over to the Salvation Army.[40] By the end of the war years, all the Salvation Army had there was a small children's home, with ten inmates; it was closed in 1948, and the children who had not been placed in 'situations' were to be sent off to settlements.[41] Nonetheless a fringe settlement was still there in 1958, and it became news with a murder and

---

[37] Ibid.
[38] There is an interesting non-official account of this in the *Argus* (Melbourne), 2 April 1937.
[39] *Courier-Mail* (Brisbane), 10 June 1939.
[40] *Age* (Melbourne), 16 November 1940.
[41] D.N.A. Reports for 1945, 1946, 1947, and 1948.

professions of terror from others who now lived there, and who claimed that they were outnumbered two to one by the hundred or so Aborigines. The Aborigines still carried water from the same muddy dam; the Shire Council was still wondering what to do; the Health Department was still expressing concern.[42] In fact things were much the same as when Bleakley had had the 'full-bloods' removed twenty years before: the usual rubbish tip, the hessian latrines, the shanties, and the overcrowding.

Such is the difference between the imagined future and the real result, when effort is directed within a policy based on false assumptions as to the things which determine conduct, and as to how social change may occur.

In 1958 and even later, such a problem might still be settled by removal to a settlement. This is why the uncontrolled settlement is still less conspicuous in Queensland than in New South Wales; and why mobility is probably higher, as people continue, in ways they have learned, to evade their police protectors.

A good example of the use of the settlement as a way out of a problem occurred in 1960, when the conditions of a fringe group living at Acacia Ridge were discussed in Parliament. The Minister for Native Affairs indicated that as these people were not 'under the Act'—i.e. not of full descent—they could not be removed to a settlement; if it could be shown that any of them were, his Director would deal with them. As they were still there in the following year, and their plight being stated by the Opposition, and the subject of pressure from voluntary bodies, the Minister offered to accept in Cherbourg Settlement those who were removed, to make way for *Housing Commission* homes. Some of their homes were eventually demolished—and the agitation attributed to the Communists.[43] To be fair, two families were placed in the first Housing Commission homes, and more have since found homes there.

There was not always such concern about degrees of descent. The records must be such that these people must have had a clearly established exclusion from the racial categories which could decide their destinies. There is no need to repeat here the reasons why appearance is likely to be thus decisive. But the point which ought to be made is that the Queensland government has never had within its system of control all those who identify as Aboriginal. By 1965 the claim was that there were no less than 22,000 not 'under the Act'—a claim which seems ill founded, and

---

[42] *Sunday Mail* (Brisbane), 31 August 1958.
[43] See *Courier-Mail* (Brisbane), 8 September, 13 November 1960, 28 March, 1 and 10 April 1961; *Sunday Truth*, 9 March 1961; and *Sunday Mail*, 19 March and 9 April 1961.

which was based on a guess in one of the annual reports, with an annual allowance for natural increase. Even in the minds of those affected, there is uncertainty: doubts about status may be one of the main reasons for escape into the City of Brisbane.

The popular folklore in Queensland includes many stories by rural non-Aborigines of the process of rounding up of the Aborigines, over a long period. This was carried out by police as a routine chore. There is no need to describe again what has been involved in such removals. What happened in Western Australia in the process of 'clearing the towns', over a few years, has been long inbuilt into the Queensland practice—so deeply that there is a strong remainder of the earlier methods provided for in the 1965 Act. Yet much of the certainty and confidence of the government that it leads the way in progressive policies seems to remain. In April 1965 the Minister responsible repeated the claim that over 20,000 'Aboriginals and part-Aboriginals' were living as 'ordinary citizens' (which simply meant that either they did not come within the definitions or had successfully avoided the government's welfare activities) and enjoying the 'same rights and wages'; he denied that the 1965 Act conflicted with the Universal Declaration of Human Rights: 'Rather than being discriminated against, Aboriginals are getting many privileges. For example, the State is paying for eighty-seven of them from remote areas to board at secondary schools.'[44]

### THE LEGISLATIVE CHANGES OF 1965-6

According to the 1961 census no less than 40 per cent of Queensland Aborigines were locked away in this system of settlements and controlled contract employment; and by 1965 over 4,000 persons, some 30 per cent of those in the settled areas, were living on the four large settlements.[45] The extent of commitment was probably a factor affecting the new legislation of 1965 and the Regulations of the following year. The changes followed the report in 1964 of a Special Committee, of officials and academics, with one member of Aboriginal descent, and a Member of Parliament as chairman, which had recommended repeal of the Act and Regulations.[46]

This report is a curious document, because it is so much against the trends elsewhere. On the whole it would retain the system of tight control, though subject to appeals to the courts, which do not mean much to people

---

[44] *Courier-Mail* (Brisbane), 19 April 1965.
[45] Long, *Aboriginal Settlements*, p. 91.
[46] *Report of Special Committee enquiring into Legislation for the Promotion of the Well-Being of Aborigines and Torres Strait Islanders in Queensland 1964.*

who do not know their rights. A nice irony is in the Preamble, where the Universal Declaration of Human Rights is quoted to the effect that 'all human beings are born free and equal in dignity and rights'. Access to liquor was recommended (though not on reserves for three years); voting rights (with the majority suggesting the possibility of a Special Roll and an Aboriginal member); withdrawal of the Director's right to control marriage, and of the discriminatory provision as to the age of consent in carnal knowledge cases.[47] Aborigines should be admitted to the Station Hands Award wage—but the 'slow worker' provisions should be relaxed in their cases. 'Equality in dignity and rights' should not be rushed, it seemed. As for the compulsory payment of earnings into a bank account, 'for a period [unspecified] it would be prudent to retain trusteeship in the case of those ... whose level of social and economic understanding warrants it'.

The new legislation did bring to an end many of the most discriminatory provisions, but it retained the emphasis on the settlement; and those 'under the Act' can still be directed to go to one.[48] The Director of Aboriginal and Torres Strait Islanders Affairs for the first year after the passing of the Act could 'declare' any person 'having a strain of Aboriginal blood' to be an 'assisted Aborigine'. Since then this has been a matter for a court. An interesting analogy is with the neglected child, who may be 'charged' with being one; any person in Queensland may be *charged* with 'having a strain of Aboriginal, or as the case may be, Island blood', and with being in need of 'care under this Act'. If the charge is upheld, his children under seventeen years also lose their freedom, and are 'declared'. The person with this suspect 'blood' runs a special risk in Queensland since the law was liberalised: if he is charged with an offence 'whether or not such person was convicted of the offence with which he was charged' the magistrate may order that he be provided with this special 'care', which is obviously a useful way of dealing with Aboriginal trouble-makers.[49]

Among other reforms the 'settlement' has become the 'community', and the superintendent has become the manager. Not only may an Aboriginal be legally directed to live on the community establishment;[50] he may have his property taken over and managed by the Department, and

[47] For Director's powers, see Aboriginals Preservation and Protection Acts, section 36(3).
[48] This legislation came into operation in April 1966. It consists of An Act to Promote the Well-being and Progressive Development of the Aboriginal Inhabitants of the State and of the Torres Strait Islanders: No. 27 of 1965; and The Aborigines' and Torres Strait Islanders' Regulations of 1966.
[49] Aborigines' and Torres Strait Islanders' Affairs Act 1965, sections 20 and 21.
[50] Ibid., section 34.

be incarcerated by the manager in a 'dormitory' (since it would be against human rights to call his cell a gaol), if the special Aboriginal Court has not already sentenced him to the Aboriginal Community gaol. (The manager is also the gaoler.) He may be sent to the dormitory for an 'offence against discipline' or if he 'leaves or escapes or attempts to leave or escape, from such reserve or community', for immorality, breach of the hygiene rules, or failure to obey an instruction by a member of the community staff. This, *without reference to a court*. If he is kept in the dormitory for over six months, the manager must report the circumstances to the *Director*.[51] Thus it is still true that in Queensland one can be incarcerated either for crime or for being Aboriginal.

The new Act came into operation, with the Regulations, in April 1966. Off the 'communities', as on them, the reforms in terminology have been more impressive than those in practice. Instead of the old police protectors there are District Officers who are Clerks of the Court; but in the outlying rural areas, where this is a key appointment, the local policeman is also the Clerk of the Court. To be fair, where there is a separate Clerk, the new practice is to be preferred. Whoever the official is, however, he still has control of the bank accounts. There are as before provisions for compulsory saving, which have always offered special temptations for isolated officers, since there have always been substantial sums involved. The 'Agreement' binding employer and employee is optional for the District Officer to decide—not for the Aboriginal worker.[52]

Perhaps the new nomenclature foreshadows other changes. The 1966 Regulations have formally established Aboriginal Councils for each community and mission reserve, vesting them with powers of the local government type, as well as very wide additional ones, to make by-laws for the 'peace, comfort, health, moral safety, convenience, food supply, housing and welfare' of the members, and for the planning and development of the reserve. At least here is some scope for initiative, in a body which is at least in part representative. The Council has its own chairman, who, if he is determined, can take an issue beyond the manager. Under the former legislation, the councils were merely to 'confer and consider with the protector or superintendent matters affecting the welfare of the inhabitants'; and the superintendent was chairman.[53] But here again there has been no reckless transfer of power. Of the four 'assisted Aborigines' on a Council, two only are elected. The other two are appointed by the

---

[51] Ibid., section 70.
[52] Aborigines' and Torres Strait Islanders' Regulations of 1966, section 71.
[53] Aboriginals Regulations of 1945, Regulation 45.

Director, who may remove *any* councillor from office. As a further precaution against radical changes, the manager may suspend any council resolution or order, though the chairman may 'institute a reference' to a magistrate if he wishes to challenge such a decision—thereby risking consignment to the community dormitory. Any by-law is ineffective until approved by the Director.

The other area for break-through to democracy is that of the Aboriginal Courts. In part this may have been a result of the exposé by Dr Colin Tatz,[54] which had revealed a quite extraordinary situation (but without arousing much comment): the regulations themselves, it seems, could not be challenged even where they appeared to go beyond the powers in the Act:

Regulations made or purporting to be made under this Act shall . . . have the same force and effect as if they were enacted in this Act . . . and shall not be questioned in any proceedings whatever.

Even more astounding were the details, published by Tatz, of decisions by superintendents in their magisterial roles. One suspects that they were the more spectacular; but they drive home the point of Dogberry promoted to the Bench, while still in control of the police and the gaol. Court 'records' consisted mainly of the charge and sentence and presented a most extraordinary picture of what the superintendents thought the law was. The hard choice between complete submission to stupid authority or punishment, often quite arbitrary, is revealed in the glimpses given by Tatz—but never again revealed, though never refuted: one was of the man who received fourteen days for failure to produce a stool on demand, and for wilfully destroying the bottle supplied; the other, of a man fined two shillings for attempted bribery of a policeman.

The new legislation marks the end of the kangaroo courts. But on communities there remains a separate court system, though only for breaches of the regulations. A court is either constituted by two Aboriginal Justices of the Peace or, where there are less than two, the council may function as the court. In effect this is a transfer into the Aboriginal community of the council-and-court system of long standing in the Torres Strait Islands. But the manager retains all his executive powers and, as officer in charge of the community's police, may ensure that offences more serious than those against the regulations are taken to the ordinary courts. The Aboriginal Courts may fine up to $20 and may settle civil disputes

[54] 'Queensland's Aborigines: Natural Justice and the Rule of Law', *Australian Quarterly*, 1963, vol. 5, no. 3, pp. 33-49. The quotation is from Aborigines Preservation and Protection Acts, 1939 to 1946.

involving up to $200. The change would have been more impressive had they been directly linked by appeal to the general court system. The first appeal is to the District Officer, however; only in the case of further appeal does the issue go to the visiting Justice. Thus the executive authority substantially controls the courts.

Probably the best side of Queensland cross-cultural administration has been that of the Island courts and councils. There they could operate as a means of adjustment because the traditional social organisation and means of production remained. What will they become in the very different circumstances of the Aboriginal communities? The manager is still the gaoler; yet the need for a gaol at all is not clear, since as far as one can see from the regulations, the Aboriginal Court's powers are limited to fining. Are these gaols for the separate and special convenience of all 'assisted Aborigines'? Or could the gaol also serve as the 'dormitory' to which the 'assisted Aboriginal' may be consigned by the manager for a breach of discipline?

The offences against discipline are spelt out: failure to obey a lawful instruction by the manager or any of his officers; idleness or careless work; behaving in an 'offensive threatening, insolent, insulting, disorderly, obscene or indecent manner'; destruction of property; and, finally, conduct which 'in any other way offends against discipline or good order'.[55] No age limit is set; so apparently this is for adults. Nor is there a time limit as in the case of a sentence; unless the person is discharged sooner, his detention after six months must be reported to the Director 'and thereafter at regular six-monthly intervals during such detention'.[56]

Probably the tone of the 'communities' will be set by the continuation of the Aboriginal police. As before, these are appointed by the manager; they have the same powers of arrest as before, but more masters, since members of the council may also instruct them. Where the Director orders an assisted Aboriginal to be 'transferred' to a reserve (from another reserve or from anywhere else), the Aboriginal police may be used. They therefore constitute a special police force under the control of the Director, not, as before, limited in their functions to the settlement. The manager may still appoint, promote, or dismiss them. They have no status in the State police: there is no provision for their training. If the manager can order persons arrested, they have to be held until the court meets; perhaps this explains the continued need for the gaol. In this whole context, the relationship of the Aboriginal police to the manager is central to the

[55] Aborigines' and Torres Strait Islanders' Regulations of 1966, Regulation 70(1) and (2).
[56] Regulation 70(7).

administration of the new communities; it cannot be otherwise. And the communities must remain central to the whole Aboriginal situation in Queensland because of their size, because of the power of the Director to commit any assisted Aboriginal to them, and because of his power to declare, and of his right to approach a court to declare, any person to be in need of assistance.

There are many humane and sensible protectors among the police; and many hard-working and well-meaning officers on the staff of the community settlements. There are many who can feel sure that their work is worth while as an end in itself—the women who teach good house-keeping, the nurses and others who spend the best years of their lives in these poor surroundings, with poor equipment and the continual frustrations of working for and with people who are conforming to the pattern of all such situations, and those concerned with education. The tragedy is that sacrifice and goodwill cannot in themselves promote changes, except in individuals. There is no hope of *social* change leading to a general betterment of Aboriginal conditions in any system of this kind: for one thing which we have learned over the last few decades is that imposed programs, either in institutions or outside them and irrespective of how laudable the intentions may be, are self-defeating. There is, if we look at such programs from the administrative point of view, no guarantee of common aims as between the governors and the governed. Where, in special circumstances, as in the case of a volunteer army, perhaps, there is such common purpose and a consensus, there are fewer problems, though they may still arise.

We may also consider the nature of institutions of the closed type, and the tendency of the inmates to make their 'secondary adjustments', using its facilities for their own ends, not the purposes of the administration. Here also we can study the reactions of people who are under stress, and with a strong belief that they have been treated unjustly—a feeling which must grow stronger with each generation of experience and with education.

Even where considerable equipment and effort is devoted to training for outside employment, the results appear meagre. I have not heard of an Aboriginal training centre of this type anywhere which has ever sent out a flow of workers properly trained for any trade or industry and equipped with certified qualifications which are recognised in a particular trade. This, in spite of very considerable expenditure on training for employment, is not an indictment of Aboriginal ability or the quality of the instructors (though these have been too often persons with no qualifications) but of the ineffectiveness of the controlled settlement as preparation to live and work 'outside'. Even where men go out to work from these places, as so many have been doing for so long, they do not, in this way, get decisive experience of handling their own affairs. In Queensland this criticism is especially relevant, since the expenditure of the worker's own money is something he may not be allowed to decide.

Officers of this administration have defended the 'system' on the grounds that the practice is better than the law; that it is necessary to have laws of this kind, but that the kind-hearted officer uses his discretion in enforcing them. Nothing, of course, could be more damning, since such a defence is the admission that the officers are not really bound by the law; and discretion may operate both ways. This simply strengthens the evidence that executive power predominates. Many other features of this legislation indicate that Queensland policy in 1967 remained much the same as it had been in 1897, and it must prove an embarrassment to the Commonwealth. One can only account for the fact that it has not attracted the attention of the International Commission of Jurists by assuming that Australian lawyers have not yet much interest in legislation for Aborigines.

# JOURNEY
# WITHOUT COMPASS

Most Australian country dwellers know from the outside the places where the Dark People live in separate communities. Some are, as it were, inmates of special institutions maintained for them, as though they require some kind of separate treatment. Some groups are in unobtrusive clusters of poor huts, which are convenient for getting casual work or for being picked up by a local employer. Or the place may be convenient for social reasons, such as access to the main street of the town, but at the same time not highly visible to the townsmen. Others may live in the town, sometimes in small groups of houses all built to a uniform pattern, but sometimes in houses they have secured for themselves.

They may live on an Aboriginal station or on the lowest land inside the river bend, which no one else will use for building, or on a flat liable to flooding, which is to be found sometimes in the midst of a double-ended town. In Western Australia, they often live just out of town on the 'camping reserve'. They may be newly installed in new homes recently erected in town (sometimes after heated resistance by the town council) as one of the recent moves for 'assimilation'. In all these situations, one's first contacts are likely to be frustrating.

Looking back on early efforts, I can endorse the remarks of others, that the Aboriginal shows ingenuity in avoiding other Australians. Over the long period of discrimination, he had had to establish a whole range of defences. Ordinary family privacy may be a recently established luxury. The housewife will keep you at the door; she is 'just cleaning up'. The men will not be there, and especially if you are not known and have an appointment. Many of them are away from home for long periods, as one would expect where the proportion of seasonal work is high and where most of the work is rural labouring. But even where one has the entrée to the family group sitting down together (if this is possible), one has to counter the ingrained suspicions and fears of just about every mature person there. 'What', one feels they are thinking, 'is this one really after?' Any attempt to get information tends to be frustrated, not so much because people cannot be bothered, but because of their worry that here is another attempt to harass and disrupt a recently established harmony or a privacy long and carefully guarded in a hostile world. One has memories of worried, hushed conferences of the women in the background when the man indicates some readiness to talk.

In many areas there has been a long sequence of very good reasons for this worry and suspicion. There have been pressures from health and building inspectors of the municipality or shire council; from the police; from officers of the welfare authority; from the Child Welfare officer in matters of truancy or of reports which may lead to the taking away and institutionalising of the children. More recently there has been the sometimes patronising interference of the organisations which are everywhere springing up, as a late indication that other Australians have the conditions of these folk on their consciences.

One of Dr Barwick's non-Aboriginal informants complained that they 'slipped through his fingers like sand'. In fact they had to do this for a long time to survive; then, to avoid incarceration in institutions; then, having failed, as many of them did, to establish security on the missions, stations and settlements, they had to develop ways of using for their *own* purposes the resources supplied by government for *its* purposes, in what Goffman calls 'secondary adjustments'.[1] This meant that they had to develop techniques of avoiding head-on conflict with white men as far as possible. In its extreme and most tragic form, this may still be seen in the joking relationship which a part-Aboriginal may establish with a non-Aboriginal stranger, even at the expense of derogatory references to his wife as 'this old gin', and of debasing himself by playing the clown. This also is defence, involving complete personal capitulation in lieu of something worse, such as the same situation of capitulation in grim earnest. Better to joke about it, and get the tension-release of laughter. For the most sensitive, volatile, and intelligent of the Aborigines have for generations been coming up against the most crass and stupid and ignorant white men in the rural areas (as well as intelligent and per-

[1] Goffman, *Asylums: Essays on the Social Situation of Mental Patients and Other Inmates.*

ceptive ones). Colour prejudice places *all* Aborigines at the mercy of prejudiced non-Aborigines: for some Aborigines in such cases, life *has* to be a joke to be bearable at all.

WESTERN TOWN

As our Project office was established in New South Wales it was natural enough to make the first contacts through the New South Wales Aborigines Welfare Board. This in turn meant that early contacts would include those with people living on Welfare Board stations. It happened that the first interviews were at Yerangoo Aboriginal Station, across the South West River from Western Town,[2] just about in, but apparently not quite of, the town: for instance, the station had a phone number, but the telephone book gave no address for it. The name Yerangoo Station, though it appeared on the sign at the gate, was not in the book—just the entry 'Aboriginal Station'. Recent changes in legislation and regulations had left to the station manager discretion to admit or refuse visitors, as the sign at the gate now indicated.[3] Like other Aboriginal stations, Yerangoo had the manager's dwelling and office well situated to control the entry of vehicles; but otherwise (from all outward appearances) Western Town could have been a satellite village. I had passed part-Aboriginal children walking over the bridge to school as I drove out in the early morning. The houses looked comparable with many in the town across the river. There was a playground with swings, slippery slide, and other equipment.

The manager seemed competent and humane. Yet, no matter what his personal qualities, his role involved paternal control among people who had developed to varying degrees the 'dependent personality'. I had just begun to talk to him when a girl of about twenty years came running to him with a finger cut on a tin. He, as the multi-purpose father figure, either dressed it or had it dressed (I forget which); later that same day I saw her with hard withdrawn set face, walking along the main street of the town. He told me of the children who ran to him to avoid parental punishment; of the wives who came with complaints against their husbands.

The other side of the situation was suggested by a talk we both had with an age pensioner in his house. The pensioner claimed that a previous

---

[2] Because real persons would otherwise be hurt, I must in this case use fictitious names—C.D.R.
[3] In early 1966 both the title and the role were disappearing; managers were being removed from direct supervision of stations, and becoming 'welfare officers'.

manager was wont to establish and maintain his authority, to those who challenged it, by threats to have their children taken from them. Later experience indicated just how easy this would be for the unscrupulous manager determined to get control of a situation (which has long been difficult enough in all conscience). Aboriginal Welfare officers in 1964 worked closely with Child Welfare officers not only in New South Wales but in the other States too. In each State administration, the Aboriginal Welfare authority is naturally assumed to have some special knowledge of the circumstances of Aborigines. The tradition of taking away the children goes right back to the beginning of the interaction between white and black: to the determined efforts of the first missionaries who in desperation tried to break the handing on of 'heathen' traditions from old to young by locking the young away from the elders. In New South Wales and other States the fear of losing one's children was real. Protest is one factor, in a situation of multiple causation, which leads people to live recklessly; they are, therefore, all the more likely to provide real reasons for the taking of the children to institutions. On the one hand, parental demoralisation often makes it impossible for authorities to leave the children; on the other, old fears of such action help to produce despair and demoralisation.

The background is in a context of excessive drinking and violence, which some managers had to deal with, as I found later, by constant recourse to police assistance. This one did not need it. The same suggestive tradition of violence is to be seen in the interest of Aboriginal men in the boxing ring, one of the few places where an Aboriginal lad can 'belt the daylights' out of a white man and be praised for it.

The manager introduced me to some of the people in houses which he regarded as well kept. Theoretically this was the worst possible way to meet people, but they seemed to like him and to suffer me politely. They were obviously not well-to-do, but they had their share of possessions, arranged with obvious house-pride in some cases. Especially was this so in some of the 'lounges': spic and span but obsolete furniture stood on polished linoleum; objets d'art including sea-shells and china pieces had stood long behind glass, and in one home there was the polished belt which indicated that here had dwelt, or here was the repository of, the reigning welterweight champion of the State—a nice reminder of the background of easy violence when the men are 'on it' (i.e. 'the drink'). I remembered that as a boy I had seen my first boxing match in this town; that the local champion came from the 'camp', which in those days had been a conglomeration of hovels right on the river bank.

These families were certainly not pent up here by government authority. In New South Wales, Victoria, and South Australia, most of the tension about Aboriginal rights to live where they wish has for a long time arisen the other way—from the fear that they will be uprooted, either for some misdemeanour by the household head or for policy purposes. There had been no controlled government stations in Western Australia for over a decade.

From Woodenbong to Wallaga Lake, from Bourke Reserve to La Perouse, New South Wales Aborigines on stations and other reserves believed that they were living on land which had been given to them (generally by Queen Victoria) in recompense for the loss of everything else in Australia; and the belief was at the root of the refusal, so widely characteristic, to pay the small rents demanded by the Welfare Board. Here the rents were from five to fifteen shillings per week; but in 1964 very few were paying them. Yet this was not an old community of in-bred families running to seed. It was part of a wider community including families living in Condobolin, Griffith, Cowra, Darlington Point, Yass, Brungle, Coonabarabran, and Dubbo, with a good deal of travelling for economic purposes by the men, and by whole families when suitable seasonal work, like the fruit picking at Young, was available. Journeys to and from Sydney, for medical treatment or other reasons, were common-place. The young boxer I remembered was now a little old grandfather down on the reserve at Griffith, with his son and grandchildren. The old couple with whom we spent most of an afternoon had come to settle down there from Condobolin. A hundred miles or so is nothing to travel for a religious revival or for a funeral. It would be interesting but difficult to establish how far the present circuits of visiting and work-seeking adhere to much older migratory routes inherited from the Aboriginal tradition. Now the routes and the times seem to be dictated by the demands of the cash economy, which has little known relationship to that which preceded it.

I had seen the children going into town to school. Over seventy of them were enrolled there, and there were over twenty under school age. The manager told me that many had been going to school without lunches or lunch money. As the distance is at least two miles, it was not surprising to hear that some of them had been in trouble at school for stealing food. He was arranging for the Welfare Board to supply the cost of bread, and persuading the station welfare club to assist from its funds. This was not a problem of poverty in the sense of families not having enough money for bread. Although there is a problem of *management* of money, this does not account adequately for mothers who send children off to school with not enough to eat. Obviously there are complex reasons for this kind of demoralisation or indifference or neglect. The story certainly fitted the pattern of alcoholic exuberance and violence. I saw the high school headmaster. He knew nothing of the lunch situation, but spoke in terms which were already familiar, of 'poor application' and 'bad family conditions' which went with poor achievement, especially in secondary work. One teacher in his enthusiasm sent for two part-Aboriginal girls to see me; they stood in mute agony while he patronised them and dissected their family backgrounds, the spirited one giving out clear signs of hatred. One can only guess at the effect of well-intentioned patronage, coming just as the child discovers (at the time of puberty) that she is no longer included in the old peer groups from the primary school.

Much of the talk about assimilation has been of the training of the young to be different from their parents. It is worth remembering that Aborigines have been going freely into New South Wales secondary schools only with the generation which has grown up since World War II; that before that war the station manager acted as part-time teacher and that the opportunity was for some four years of primary education only, with an adapted syllabus, within the capacity of the manager and the assumed capacity of the children. Others, off the stations, no doubt made their own way into the schools. But positive pressures to improve schooling have been developed mainly over the last decade, with the awakening of official consciences and awareness. The first reform was to put the Education Department teacher into the station school and have the full course there. The next, not yet complete, had been the integration of the station school with that of the town, so that there are as few 'Aboriginal' schools as possible. But this, so long as prejudice is strong, makes more likely the tragedy of the child rejected by his peers at the time of the first life transition.

Schooling is *par excellence* an area of activity where multiple causation of 'failure' is clear. Aboriginal parents, in Western Town as elsewhere, believe that there is no point in children attending school after the legal 'leaving' age of fifteen years. There tend to be fewer influences in the home for academic ambition than in non-Aboriginal groups, though clearly there are white families where books and other stimuli are just as rare, and as completely disregarded, and where the 'culture of poverty' is as well exemplified. A very brilliant and ambitious child with some luck and much courage might well overcome all this, and some are doing it. But then the question must continually arise of whether the result is worth the effort and worth losing companionship in the one group where the child is fully accepted—for the Aboriginal group will often condemn him for presumptive 'flashness'.

Most success stories of Aborigines are of bitter struggles to be regarded as honest and sober folk; of battles to meet the ethnocentric criticisms from the Australian middle class; to be regarded as 'respectable' in spite of one's skin coloration. I remember that when I attended in 1960 a conference at the University of New England, on the Aboriginal question, a part-Aboriginal lady there was being held up as the example of what her people could do. She was a member of the Country Women's Association. She had a house in town. Her family was accepted by the neighbours. Her husband was in regular work. The next time I saw her was in 1964. Her husband had given up the struggle for acceptance, taken to drink, and left his job; she had given up her house in town and retreated to the station from which she had come years before. Perhaps the members of the C.W.A. had the feeling that they had done their best, but that the struggle to be 'like us' (i.e. 'assimilated') had been too much. We have to be patient; it all takes time.

Only an unusually determined person can spend a whole lifetime trying hard for acceptance by people whose unthinking insult he fears; and it can be a lonely road through the dull regions of the stolid Australian middle classes. There is always the temptation of the volatile, exciting, unconventional Aboriginal group—and the solace of its 'I told you so' about the white man. But not many, especially among the womenfolk, do get the chance to make the break from the Aboriginal group. On Yerangoo Station the fact was brought home to me by a young girl of about fifteen years, who had just left school on the insistence of her parents. There was no real obstacle to prevent her from continuing. In one of the less organised homes, with her mother ill, she sat alone and lost in the high school uniform. Her family was about to go to Young for the fruit picking, and she would go with them. The manager told me that hers was the sixth such case in the short time that he had been there; that the other five girls who had gone away for seasonal work had all come back pregnant. After all, this is what the average middle-class Australian expects of Aboriginal girls: and Aboriginal conduct is the perfect example of the potency of the self-fulfilling prophecy.

Before I left I had a look round Western Town. Especially at night, there are Aborigines in places where they would not have been four decades ago. In one of the restaurants, for instance, there were part-Aboriginal girls dressed in exaggerated teenage clothes, with extreme upswept hair-dos (then the height of fashion, or a fashion just going out), playing the juke box, laughing through rotten teeth, the obvious neglect of minds and bodies at their tender years (I would guess sixteen or seventeen years for the three of them at the most) making dreadful and pathetic contrast with what might have been and with what probably would have been had they not been damned with membership of the Aboriginal group. The advocates of assimilation as a 'solution' of this problem of rigid race relations would see significance in the fact that the girls were in town at all, and especially in a restaurant with some money to spend. They were certainly likely to produce children whiter than themselves. They were further into the town than they used to be, no doubt *because* they now had some money to spend.

Another change since my boyhood there was in the location of the station. The camp I remembered used to be on the river bank opposite the town. It was a flat area subject to flooding, which probably explains why it was left for 'the Blacks' in the first place. The station is now on higher ground behind, though the flat is still part of the reserve. It is good lucerne growing land, but it is not farmed by anyone at the station. The share farmer who had the use of it provided a half share of the profit to the station social club. Here again, in this use of the one economic asset besides labour and the women, there is something wrong; and one suspects, at least, that what is wrong has something to do with mothers sending children to school without food and taking children from school at fifteen; with the undertones of violence; and with the ever-present paternalist control. Here was the final result of a long social history.

As our work developed we had a good deal to do with the Western Town community, with groups both on and off the station. It proved profitable to probe in some little depth into a situation like this where there has been recently no special publicity about conditions, nor news of special local discontent. It was no better, no worse, than so many other situations. It had its share, for instance, of grandmother-dominated families, with the woman in her fifties or sixties doggedly holding the family together with limited resources, while the second generation moved periodically after seasonal work and left children in her care. This was an anchoring arrangement for the family, often a last resort against disintegration into the homes of Child Welfare or those of the Welfare Board at Cootamundra (girls) and Kinchela (boys). It was also an influence for conservatism and for adherence to attitudes which have been held for a long time by most part-Aborigines, since it means that the older and therefore the most conservative generation of the women have much to do with the socialisation of the children.

The incidence of broken homes on the station proved in a survey made in December 1965 to be very high indeed,[4] since over 57 per cent of all the children living there were in female-dominated families without fathers; but this was probably due mainly to policy of the Welfare Board in giving preference in station housing to deserted wives. Stories of broken homes included wives going away with other men and leaving their children with husband, or *de facto*, or mother. Careful probing also showed up here what was missed in more rapid inquiries of the kind we generally had to make—of illnesses so much taken for granted that they are not reported in the single interview; of the high proportion of persons living on age and invalid pensions without other known income. Then there were the cases of menfolk in gaol; menfolk crippled in accidents and waiting for compensation; of a young lad from here, shot in the head while trying to break into a kiosk in Sydney. A young girl had smashed the interior walls of her home, and was at the time in a mental home; her brother was in Kinchela. The head of another family, in his thirties, had had three years with a boxing troupe and had killed a man in a street fight but had been acquitted; he was now living on an invalid pension with wife and two children to support. A young boxer living with a seventeen-year-old girl in another home was waiting to join up with a boxing troupe; I later met this man while he was serving a sentence in Dubbo gaol for hitting a policeman; he has since repeated the offence.

Some of the women had sisters who had 'married white', and an elderly woman had a daughter who had done so and was living in Sydney. One of the most efficient families depended on the good name the menfolk had for droving. They had a boy of sixteen and a girl of thirteen in high school, but there were problems as the father was away on the road for eight months out of the twelve. The mother said she would 'like' to move from the station because of the drinking and fighting, but apparently this was not a serious intention. Perhaps little chance appeared of finding elsewhere accommodation comparable with the very comfortable and cheap house the family already had.

Five to ten children were usual, sometimes where the husband had deserted the mother. In one such case a seventeen-year-old girl had a *de facto* relationship which helped with the budget. Marriage is expensive, and divorce even more so. Therefore it is not surprising that a depressed group has worked out its own standards, approximating those of persons in similar conditions in this country and in others.

[4] Long, *Aboriginal Settlements*, p. 165.

Where the father of a part-Aboriginal child is a white man with a family and wife of his own, it seems usual and characteristic that the mother takes no court action: she will not 'put him in'. One man with a good Irish name was back from a couple of weeks in Bathurst gaol for breach of Regulation 11 under the Aborigines Protection Act, which forbade being drunk on the reserve. He was under forty, received an invalid pension because he suffered from high blood pressure, was unemployed, and did not at the time receive unemployment benefits. He had an elder brother in even worse case who had been a boxer and was now described as both 'punch-drunk' and an alcoholic. Pensions, including deserted wives' pensions, were prominent as a source of income.[5]

There were at least four other families in or near the town; a later survey discovered one of these living in a shack on the side of the old Aboriginal station. On Yerangoo Station in 1965 there were twenty-two houses, all occupied, and we subsequently located three families living in houses elsewhere, and one in a railway worker's tent. In due course we were able to interview a sample of eleven households, the selection as fairly as possible representing each situation. We found an average of 7·27 persons resident in these. In the 1961 census the average for houses in non-metropolitan towns like Western Town was 3·59 persons; while the corresponding rural figure was 3·73, and the average for all dwellings in the State 3·5.[6]

Others, of course, have established themselves in much smaller communities round about. In one of these, Gongola (also a fictitious name), about forty miles from Western Town, there was in 1964 a small reserve with only one house on it. In New South Wales, reserves tended to be demarcated where Aboriginal families established themselves for purposes of convenience or employment or where they were descended from people who had 'always' lived there. Gongola was a village of about 400 persons. The reserve 'supervisor' was, in the tradition of this State, the local policeman. He estimated a total of twenty persons of recognised Aboriginal origin in and about the village; there were definitely eight adults, but he was not sure of the number of children.

Here too were cases generally similar to those found at Western Town. The success story was of a man who had had hydatids, whose wife had

[5] Family details quoted here were established by Mrs Janice Monk, an Australian graduate working for a higher degree from the University of Illinois and also as a member of this Project team. Mrs Monk used the questionnaire developed for this Project. Her survey work was completed in 1965.

[6] Census of the Commonwealth of Australia, 30th June 1961, vol. 1, part IV, Table No. 4.

left him, some of whose children had died, and then others had been taken (three of them were 'put to the State'), who had been in gaol. Now, however, he had a job in the local gristing mill (where lucerne is processed). His wife was back with him, and so were two of his children. He was, one of my informants told me, now a 'good coon'; and the fact that the phrase could be so easily and unthinkingly used was significant. In the local estimation, this for an Aboriginal was success. This is one of the reasons for the comparative lack of belief in economic progress and social mobility among Aborigines: they have, in the main, ups and downs within narrowly prescribed limits, from which they escape by being very able individuals indeed, or by ceasing in some way to be known as Aboriginal. Only rarely do they have *careers*, marked, as careers commonly are in an egalitarian society, by a general upward mobility in social life and by increase of wealth with increasing years. The rarity of such cases illustrates either very high discrimination or very poor levels of ability. The general Australian view of Australia cannot admit the first, and so the popular folklore relates failure with Aboriginal descent.

Another Aboriginal, an invalid pensioner, was employed at the hotel; another (who I was told was very dark of skin) was an alcoholic. But of the three Housing Commission homes, two were said to be occupied by part-Aboriginal families.

My talk with the policeman was interrupted by the entry of a part-Aboriginal lad with reddish hair and freckles, in response to a message from the police station. He had bought one truck from a dealer in Cowra which soon broke down and he had traded it in on another. But work was difficult to get and money in short supply. This lad was barely literate, and had not been reading his notices from the Department of Transport about the need to return expired number plates. Letters from the police station had been similarly ignored, until the constable had word passed round the town; and here he was, anxiously wondering 'what was wrong now'. He now revealed that the second vehicle had been repossessed by the dealer and that, in a final defiant gesture, he had picked up the expired number plates and thrown them into the back as it was driven away.

One wonders whether Public Service clerical work ever catches up with cases like this. In this one, a kindly and reasonable police constable probably straightened out the lines of communication between the part-Aboriginal citizen and the machinery of the State. At the same time one could see all the possibilities for officials interested in using authority, and the extent to which this minority, almost by definition educationally handicapped because of its special history, must depend on official good will and patience. One race-prejudiced junior member of the Public Service of State or Commonwealth, or even local government, in Employment Office, Housing Commission, or health office of the town council, can effectively block any inarticulate Aborginal citizen from the services to which he is entitled. Where the position at the office counter is occupied by a person with racist views, the part-Aboriginal may well be kept waiting at the end of the queue or his file be kept at the bottom of the pile; or he may be the victim of prejudiced judgments as to rights or suitability for access to particular public services or facilities. That a good deal of this has occurred in the past is suggested by the reluctance common among Aboriginal people to take the initiative with government agencies.

Another explanation is that so many lack the basic civic education which all citizens are assumed to possess. Some public servants responsible are uncertain of the exact responsibilities of the Aboriginal Welfare authority of the State. This can lead to a refusal, perhaps in good faith, of a service to which the applicant is entitled, because of a misconception— for instance a belief that the proper provider of *all* services is the special Aboriginal Welfare authority.

### GRIFFITH, N.S.W., 1964-5

Within the visiting circle of the Western Town people is the big Riverina town of Griffith. Here in 1964-5 there were sixteen homes occupied on the Three Ways Reserve, just on the fringe of the town. Later we located a further nineteen homes distributed among three camp sites within the town boundaries—at the council camp ground, at the Hill Camp, and at Frogs Hollow, which, as the name might suggest, shares a swamp drainage area with the Three Ways Reserve.[7] As at Western Town, the small houses were somewhat crowded by the standards applicable to New South Wales citizens generally, with an average of 6·8 persons in the ten we selected as constituting a fair sample for interview. But pressure of persons on rooms, compared with the averages in the 1961 Census, indicated an even wider divergence from the general rural and country town norms for accommodation.

There is no Aboriginal station here, but we were able to form first impressions of the situation through the Griffith Aborigines Assimilation Organisation, which had been active for some five years. Its Annual

[7] Mrs Janice Monk did this work also.

Report for 1963-4 indicated that it had been meeting each month in the Community Hall on the reserve, from which an average of ten or so of the adults attended. The Organisation had been making representations to the Aborigines Welfare Board, apparently with some success, for improvements to the reserve, such as overflowing sullage trenches and the need for fly wire on the houses. It had affiliated with the Australian-Aboriginal Fellowship, a New South Wales organisation, and with the Federal Council for Aboriginal Advancement, to whose annual meeting at Canberra it had sponsored five Aboriginal and three other representatives. One result of these contacts had been some re-thinking by the Organisation of the semantics of Aboriginal affairs. The Report stated that following the conference at Canberra it was realised that it is 'wrong to insist on Aborigines abandoning their heritage by the cultural suicide of assimilation'; and the proposal was to change the title of the Organisation by substituting 'Advancement' for 'Assimilation'.

As well as managing the hall on the reserve, the Organisation had tried to improve school attendance by the children there; had established reading sessions in the hall; had approached and assisted the Save the Children Fund to establish a pre-school centre in the hall before the end of 1964. But the 'sand' had been 'slipping' through their fingers also. Attempts to get school leavers into local employment had come to nothing. When the Organisation offered special references to boys who would ask for them, only one had. A visitor had talked vaguely of co-operatives for the unemployed—for 'cleaning cars and windows, laundry work, keeping goats, or weaving cumibungi mats'. But it was still the pattern of seasonal farm work for the part-Aborigines; and one can guess from other experience the realistic pessimism with which they had listened to these schemes.

Besides employment, the other vital area for integration into the economy and polity of the community is housing, not so much perhaps even for comfort or for health as for security: security for the growing child, and for his schooling and other education; security for the worker's family, without which there must always be stress and nagging worry. The Board had been asked to build three houses in town and two more on the reserve, since those living on Frogs Hollow camping ground had been threatened with eviction. The Organisation had failed to get either telephone or mail delivery on to the reserve. Here the question arises of what level of service is 'suitable' for persons of Aboriginal descent. There would also be other reasons, such as the fear of vandalism, for failure to provide such common services as a telephone; while the absence of house numbering may have made delivery of the mail difficult. But these problems are not insuperable.

The Organisation had worked mainly for the visible forty or so adults and the hundred or so children on the reserve. But, in addition to the sixteen reserve households, we found a further nineteen scattered over the camp sites in 1965, and four established in houses in the town area. One family (of a railway worker) was living in a tent. Of two interviewed in the town area, one was in an old home on a two-acre farming lot on the outskirts, the other in a temporary self-built house on a town building block. All kinds of shanties were found on the camping sites, from houses occupier-built of timber and industrial scrap to one dwelling made up of a utility truck with a tent and occupier-contrived pan latrine. To judge from the numbers of those in households where people were interviewed, there were more living under these conditions than on the reserve. Griffith was one of the more convenient centres for those dependent on seasonal farm work, so immediate economic necessity had dictated the housing conditions.

Fringe housing, as it is euphemistically called by people knowledgeable in matters relating to Aborigines, tends to be occupier-built of the scrap which lies about the town rubbish tip. But it may be that the durable iron has been used in many houses; that a few sheets have served the same family in earlier locations. Those who look for anthropological explanations will see in this a development from the wurlie; but it is the last resort in accommodation for very desperate family situations as soon as the worker is committed to static employment anywhere. Once he has standards of comfort, it is uncomfortable; once he has to face with his family the health risks of town living, it is a health risk for all of them because of its lack of running water, and often of effective waste-disposal arrangements. We saw a great deal of this kind of housing all the way from Queensland to Western Australia. A young Australian scholar with American experience worked during 1965 in Cowra, Griffith, and Deniliquin, none of which had been a centre of agitation featured, like some others, in the national press, nor had it caught the attention of Student Action for Aborigines or other groups publicising bad conditions. She said the poorest shacks of Negroes in Mississippi were tradesmen built, or seemed to be; that the houses of the part-Aborigines were, as far as she knew, unique. In fact, this is not so, as anyone who has looked around the great cities of Asia knows; or, if one wishes to see it in the Australian context again, it can be found here and there in the un-authorised settlements of Port Moresby. The significant point is that, in a very wealthy country, housing for 'coloured' people, even in towns to which there has been no great migration, includes a high proportion of shanties erected by the occupants from second-hand iron and other less durable industrial scrap; and that all over the continent people who live in country towns still take this situation as a matter of course.

The families so housed included a considerable number of children under school leaving age—for instance the five shanties, off the Reserve, which were visited in 1965 had twenty-four between them. Any assessment of achievements at school should be informed with this background of what the study conditions at home, and the conditioning, had to be. For the very young child, socialisation must have lacked much of the range of stimuli which give to the children of the more well-to-do the advantages of early familiarity with the tools of Western intellectual endeavour. Here there could not even be that small degree of security for the kind of personal development which success in the national economic life and familiarity with the national culture demands; here the first impulses of a genius might turn sour and come to nothing.

This is admittedly a commonplace of human wastage, and characteristic of poverty generally. But the fact that so many Aboriginal people live under these conditions cannot be irrelevant to Aboriginal lack of success in most of the sophisticated areas of activity. In 1965, for instance, the first part-Aboriginal student was working in the final year of a degree course; his graduation at the end of that year made his effort something of a *tour de force*, even though he was in many ways atypical in his experience.

The existence of this kind of poverty, whether among part-Aborigines or others, is an interesting comment on the whole system of social services in Australia. In this context the relevant body is the New South Wales Housing Commission, which no doubt performs its difficult functions well. But people in seasonal work and on the move are not good at paying rent, irrespective of the attitude to payment of rent which has become part of the pattern of resistance of those conditioned by life on reserves and stations. Probably those who could invest in a Housing Commission home would see that the rent is paid; in fact, there seems no evidence that they are less competent in so doing than non-Aborigines as a group. But a Commission which does nothing special for Aborigines will not have a great number of them on its books. They will be kept out by lack of the initial finance required, and possibly by the provisions limiting the numbers of persons who may dwell in a Commission home until it is the property of the occupier. Moreover, any organisation is as effective as its least efficient officer in the chain of contact with the public; and any housing authority must face the problem of its local officer in whose mind the part-Aboriginal stereotype is a bad risk. Thus an Aboriginal's application may be left, in some cases at least, at the bottom of the pile, so as to avoid a 'problem'; or he may be advised that since the Welfare Board is the relevant housing authority in his case, he must apply to the Board for help.

In New South Wales, the Aboriginal Welfare Board house was generally of recognisably poorer quality, and smaller, than the basic Housing Commission house. There had not, up till 1965, been any arrangement by which the Welfare Board could supply housing at housing authority standards and design as there had been in Western Australia in recent years. This situation is sometimes defended as a 'learning' one: small houses for large families may be called 'transitional', the implication being that a family has to learn how to live in a little house before it can be trusted with a big one. The real reasons include limits on finance and ideas as to what is suitable for part-Aboriginal families. In fact, among the local experts in social change, learning to sweep out the houses regularly in the manner of the middle-class housewife had been commonly accepted as 'training' for 'assimilation'.

On stations like Yalangoo, and on reserves like the Three Ways, the reserve is 'vested in' the Board.[8] This means that the land is Crown land and goes back to the Lands Department for reallocation when the Board no longer requires it. The Aboriginal group has no legally established interest in either land or buildings, which also belong to the Board. (This situation has been common throughout Australia, although recently legislation has been introduced in South Australia to vest control of reserve lands in a special Trust representing Aboriginal groups.) A permit from the Board was in 1964-5 necessary for anyone but its representatives or the police to enter or remain on a reserve; an amendment had left discretion to the local manager or other representative of the Board. (It is only fair to mention here that the Board by 1967 had withdrawn most of the managers.) Thus there is some reason for regarding the station as an institution comparable with (say) a hospital, and the inhabitants as inmates. Certainly the situations reveal the tensions characteristic of the inmate-management relationship.

Another institutional characteristic was that whatever management decided to do or approve tended to be justified in terms of the purposes for which the institution existed. Thus, if the Aboriginal worked on the

[8] Aborigines Protection Act, 1909-1963, section 8(1).

station or reserve, this tended to be called 'training' conducive to assimilation. If he worked somewhere else, that helped assimilation also. Drunkenness, strangely enough in Australian circumstances, tended to be frowned upon as contrary to the assimilation policy. The manager had power to expel persons who frustrated his discharge of the Board's policy. Substantially, of course, the station was the same *kind* of institution as it was long ago when the policy was to civilise and Christianise the dying remnants of the Aboriginal race.

Throughout Australia, great numbers of persons of Aboriginal descent were institutionalised without their consent. Others were forced by economic circumstances to seek shelter in institutions of this kind, since so little of the resources of the Aborigines had been left for them, and since even those of mixed descent tended to be classified with their Aboriginal parents. This institutional background, which meant that in practice generations of Aborigines and part-Aborigines in some areas have been dependent on the whims of managers or supervisors, with the vaguest directives or notions of policy, has made its contribution to current part-Aboriginal attitudes.

The police were responsible to the Board for proper supervision of the Griffith reserve. This raised issues which had concerned the Organisation. The houses on the reserve being government property, and the police having rights of supervision vested in them, the situation of the part-Aboriginal as a tenant was at the least doubtful. One fairly common cause of resentment against the police has been the assumed right of the latter to walk without warrant into any house on a reserve. The Organisation had just assisted those living on the reserve to take such a case to the court. The story was that an Aboriginal had been taken out of his 'own' house by police who then charged him with drunkenness. From the point of view of the police this seemed to be well-established routine: drunkenness on a reserve or station, irrespective of conditions, was an offence under the regulations.[9]

What was unusual in Aboriginal affairs was not that a man was allegedly pulled out of bed in his house to be charged with drunkenness, but that a group of non-Aboriginal townsfolk should have taken the matter to a local lawyer, who was looking into the legal aspects of the matter. A few people were beginning to look at the shacks and the conditions of part-Aborigines with a new interest. The part-Aborigines in towns where this was happening seemed as inarticulate and as elusive for personal contacts as ever, as inward-looking a group as one would

[9] Ibid., Regulation 11.

find anywhere. The protests came mainly from the interested organisations of non-Aborigines, sometimes with a (generally inarticulate and uncomfortable) part-Aboriginal member or two. In this town, the first impetus is reported to have come from a Dutch migrant. One can imagine how shocked he must have been at the contrast of the shacks of Frogs Hollow with the kind of housing he had been used to in Holland. At Armidale, in northern New South Wales, it seems that an American lady induced 'town and gown' to look again at the scenes around the local rubbish tip with which so many of us have been familiar since childhood.

Another influence may well be the growing contrast of the conditions of the part-Aboriginal group with those in an affluent society; possibly, more generous impulses have begun to carry over into action only when people can easily afford them. Young people are better off, and also better educated. There is more concern about racial discrimination, which may in part stem from higher education, in part and perhaps indirectly from international pressures, which is affecting long-established attitudes on racial matters—on immigration policy, the colonial tie with New Guinea, and on the Aboriginal minority. Australians have begun to travel, especially the young.

All this is very recent; so it is not surprising that few part-Aborigines are either trusting or ready to change ingrained patterns of protest and conduct. In any case the new deal offered locally so far tends to be a doubtful one. In Griffith, for instance, the failure to find permanent jobs for part-Aborigines was acknowledged by the Organisation. Permanent employment and effective housing go together for a poor family. Without the first, the second is just about impossible, since it involves either regular rent or payments at regular intervals to purchase, in a location within range of employment. The causal relationship, as usual in social affairs, is a multiple one; without the established home, it is difficult for a worker to become well enough known, educated, and trusted to find permanent employment.

This is not the whole explanation of the common pattern of unreliability in employment, of which we heard so much everywhere, from Weipa to Gnowangerup, from Broome to Bega. Important among many other factors seems to be a profound and realistic disbelief by Aborigines in the possibility of change. This is, *par excellence*, the case of a community under stress reacting in accordance with well-established patterns of belief about white men and their promises. When a choice has to be made between an employer's convenience and some social or family matter, the pull of the in-group tends to be the stronger: off go the workers en masse to an important funeral, often without notice to the employer. The non-Aboriginal does not do this kind of thing so often, according to reports; one guesses that the reason is that he cannot afford to do so, because he is not, like the part-Aboriginal member of the town fringe group, certain of the support of his kindred through adversity.

Another factor goes right back to the early contacts between the races from which this minority has sprung. The nomadic pattern of life was essential, and it often suited the employers (and still does on the pastoral properties of parts of northern Australia) to get rid of their employees at certain times of the year in the 'walkabout'. The walkabout is one of the main features of the Aboriginal and part-Aboriginal stereotype today. Many employers and others concerned with Aboriginal administration *expect* unexplained absenteeism or absenteeism without notice. Here again is an example of multiple causation. The employer tends to reject Aborigines for permanent employment; it is no accident that a high proportion of the permanent jobs they do hold are in government agencies like railway departments and main roads boards. So many Aborigines are forced to look for seasonal and other temporary work: few have the chance to develop more settled working habits unless they move to the large cities.

Employers of seasonal work for which there are no policed awards tend to look for part-Aboriginal labour. To a large extent the pattern of Aboriginal mobility is based on such opportunities. Thus, people from Cowra, Griffith, and Western Town tend to go to Young for the fruit picking. This, like the bean and pea picking on the south coast of New South Wales, offers something of an annual holiday as well as an important source of income. Yet even seasonal work movements have been restricted, because employers prefer other employees where they have to pay the same money. It is also very difficult for an Aboriginal family to move beyond the circle of relatives and friends, since Aborigines are not welcome in most hotels, nor can they afford them. Being the last to be 'put on' and the first to be 'put off', they have to face higher risks of missing employment. Possessing for the most part low literacy skills, they have no effective means of making definite arrangements in advance; and the stereotype tends to operate against them where they try to operate through official or other agencies. So they tend to fit into the local interstices, as it were, of the national pattern of seasonal work, in occupations to which the caravan dwellers and public servants on paid holiday and the married women paying off their houses do not travel. Janice Monk found that in Cowra in 1965 the caravan dwellers were hired for picking asparagus (part-Aborigines were reported to be too slow at this); women from town picked the beans; Aborigines were hired for the tomatoes. In the Young area, others generally picked the cherries; Aborigines picked the prunes. From Griffith as from Cowra some men went shearing and droving; and into temporary farm employment in the surrounding irrigation area.

Griffith was in 1964-5 an important centre for such migrations. That farmers would justify the allocation of the more menial and less well-paid work to the Aboriginal was not surprising. The conduct of the migratory groups, the tensions between them and the police and local authorities, reinforced the stereotype of the feckless Aboriginal. Aborigines were expected to be unreliable and many of them continued to be so. But Janice Monk, a very careful observer who spent months looking into these situations in Cowra, Griffith, and Deniliquin in 1965, found that there were several families established in homes (in Deniliquin especially) in permanent employment, and maintaining their families well.

Such families face another kind of problem if they live in the town itself and are visibly of part-Aboriginal descent, since they must live in the perpetual expectation of deliberate or unthinking insult. In addition, there is the pressure of the neighbours for them not to entertain their less presentable relatives; pressure of the health and other authorities not to 'overcrowd' the house. Thus there is a constant dilemma in the choice of whom to affront—relatives or neighbours?

Aboriginal unreliability was stressed by schoolteachers in Griffith and Leeton. Well-meaning teachers devote great efforts to getting Aboriginal children ready for examinations considered important by employers and educators. But children who turn fifteen (the legal leaving age) tend to leave school at once, and without notice. Few non-Aborigines seem to have seen in this action (in which the parents are the decisive agents) a form of protest and an assertion of independence which, unlike truancy, can be made safely and within the law. Another reason is the parental scepticism referred to earlier. Many Aborigines do not believe promises that school success leads to ecomonic success. This reaction also is typical of the 'culture of poverty', whether Aboriginal or otherwise. Minds have to be opened to real possibilities of something better. It does not appear that the main reason for leaving school at the leaving age is economic. In many cases observed, the child continued to do no work, sometimes for months, and this of course led to other problems. The scepticism of the parent has been too often reinforced by the school experience of the child.

Very often puberty has brought him rejection by his age-mates and companions through earlier years and the primary school. The attitudes of the children in both cases, Aboriginal and non-Aboriginal, reflect those of the home and of the adults.

## DENILIQUIN

It was the winter of 1964 when we made the first contact with the situation in Deniliquin, a cold and windy time for the shanty-dwellers on the wrong side of the river. Here too there was an active group of citizens determined to do something about Aboriginal affairs; it seemed a small one, but determined. Formerly there had been a station at Moonacullah, some twenty miles or so out of town; it became a 'reserve' only after 1954, and disappears from the list of reserves after the Board's 1961-2 Report. The people remaining had apparently been judged ready for 'assimilation', and were now established in thirteen new-looking homes, all together in one area on the outskirts of the town. The two acres on which this Welfare Board housing stands had recently been gazetted as an Aboriginal Reserve. We found eight other families living elsewhere in town. Five families in 1965 lived in the shacks on the river bank site known as the North Reserve. (There were eight or nine at least in July 1964.) Numbers per dwelling were higher here than those in Griffith: we studied in 1965 a cross-sample of nine dwellings, the average number of whose occupants was 7·44.

Every new contact in every new town, as we developed the scope of our inquiries, shed new light on part-Aboriginal relations with the town communities, with the municipal authorities, the police, and the Board. The situations were not remarkable for their variety; but each new experience highlighted different aspects of the same complex problems: and checking back to situations earlier studied generally indicated that what to us looked like new situations had existed in those places also. One of these was Aboriginal attitudes to the payment of rents for homes on reserves and stations. From reports, the group from Moonacullah, in the Welfare Board homes assessed at £49 per annum rentals, had continued the tradition. The local welfare organisation was concerned that the tenants could find cash for television sets, but not for rent. Janice Monk looked into this when she got to know these people in 1965. It appeared that most of the television sets were on hire purchase from one of those firms which operated on a national scale and has now brought catastrophe to the shareholders; local firms refused to sell on hire purchase to

Aborigines. She also found that of thirteen houses occupied by the people from Moonacullah, seven of the breadwinners had permanent employment, some with the Irrigation Commission, others at the local brickworks.

The Moonacullah station people had originally belonged mainly to the group of part-Aborigines who lived along the banks of the Murray River towards the end of the nineteenth century. The ties were still strong; and some of the townsfolk in 1964 told how the new houses were often crowded out with visitors from Robinvale and other Murray River towns. Deniliquin is situated on the pastoral country of the plains; and there is a good deal of employment on a seasonal basis available, except in drought years, which brought special hardship to places like this during the period of the survey. Managers would depend on getting men known to them in certain work like burr-cutting or shearing. But even the shearers generally worked within a limited range, which limited also the period of this employment to three months of the year. A few of the girls went out to domestic work on stations. The pattern was again of movement for employment within a limited area where the employee was known and where he had relatives to provide accommodation.

In 1965 Janice Monk learned of an exceptional case of a man who went as far afield as South Australia, exploiting his special skills with 'mulesing' sheep and picking fruit. But he had no really firm basis for his venture. His car was old and 'blew up': this clipped his wings. We found a similar case on the south coast of New South Wales of a man who had a truck of his own and who moved from the north coast of New South Wales to Victoria following seasonal employment. But when we met him some weeks later, he had had to sell the vehicle, and move into the station at Wallaga Lake.

There is a further reason why few part-Aborigines are members of the seasonal work crews who follow the work from the sugar seasons of northern Queensland to hop picking in Tasmania. This kind of life requires either special skill and no dependants or some capital in the form of a home where the family can be left in security or a caravan where they can live if they accompany the breadwinner. The Aboriginal seldom manages to amass this basic and reliable capital equipment. Those who venture far afield without it are likely to fail through breakdown of vehicles or some trouble at home. In the Deniliquin case the man had applied for a Housing Commission house and was reported to have been rejected because of rubbish accumulated around the shack in which he was living. This was probably partly due to his long absences from home.

Here again is an example of multiple causation. He could not invest in a Housing Commission home because he was not in town long enough to tidy up the one he had. But without such an investment he could not maintain his efforts to better his economic situation by travelling further afield.

The Deniliquin Welfare Committee in 1964 was taking special interest in what it considered serious health risks to people living on the North Reserve. The President, who had been a nurse, had written to the Department of Health at the beginning of that year that

We have seen small children, eighteen months and two years, suffering with infected fly-blown ears. Mangy dogs, lice-ridden children, are all part and parcel of the fringe area along the north bank of the Edward River, where the majority of these folk live.[10] No sanitary service is provided by the Council either.

A test of forty children with the Mantoux technique had given 'a number' of positive results, according to this informant. It was, she said, very doubtful if more than a small proportion had had protective inoculations against whooping cough, polio, and diphtheria.

The river bank reserve here resembles those used for Aboriginal housing in several other towns of western New South Wales in that it is on the inside of the river bend, and therefore on the low bank, which is most subject to flooding. At the time of my own visit in 1964 there were at least eight shacks there, all built of the usual old iron, scrap materials, and rough timber. The President and Secretary of the Welfare Committee assured me that there were some large families of children in these houses; that the population was then increasing. I had no chance of checking this at the time; figures of persons per house for the sample of the town as a whole in 1965 were, as we have seen, higher than those in Griffith.

We were to see a number of these scattered river slums. Like the others, this one had suffered considerably from the floods of the late 1950s. It seems that in Deniliquin part-Aborigines still depended to some small extent on the river bank ecology for subsistence, for the position is somewhat more complex than that of outcasts forced to live on the 'wrong side' of the river. In these circumstances they have generally been pressured inexorably into the lowest-lying land; but proximity to the river has been essential for water as well as for some fish and small game. Ruth Fink has shown how important was the part played in part-Aboriginal diets by kangaroo, wild pig, and fish, and traditional Aboriginal foods, on the mission at Brewarrina in the 1950s.[11] Since that

[10] Janice Monk recorded only five houses there in 1965—C.D.R.
[11] Social Stratification: A Sequel to the Assimilation Process in a Part-Aboriginal Community.

time much has happened to make matters worse for the river-bank slum-dweller. Myxomatosis has largely killed off the rabbit; part-Aboriginal population increases and other factors like closer settlement and increased town populations have helped to decrease the fish available. Probably nutrition standards have declined, but proper nutritional evidence for this does not exist. That some dependence on game at Deniliquin remained was suggested by the statement by one of my informants that those who had to move from the river in floods could not live on their earnings while away from it. On the other hand, the whites were alleged to have had first preference for blankets and other issues of flood relief. For three years running there had been floods, and tents were supplied by the Civil Defence organisation of the State government; conditions of the Aborigines were reported to be 'shocking'. What must have been more drastic in effect than loss of the river-bank supplement to the food supply was the loss of income, by people who had always lived hand to mouth, caused by the floods. Children, I was told, went without food, and one woman died.

The plight of feckless inhabitants of the river bank seemed to have stimulated only limited local concern. As they did not pay rates they had no claim to town services. In 1964 I was informed that there was no water supply, garbage disposal service, or sanitary service for the houses in this area. This is a typical and complex problem, where certain categories of persons are not accepted, for racial or some other reason, as full members of the town society. The duty of the municipality to provide basic services for safe living has to end somewhere. It is always likely in such circumstances that members of the outcast group (or, if the situation is a colonial one, as in New Guinea for instance, the 'native' group) will establish themselves just outside the serviced area, and develop a shanty town under the noses of the authorities. The authorities, for health reasons or for the appearance of the town, will try to be rid of the shacks, even if they are just outside their jurisdiction. The part-Aborigines of the river bank had to live where they had access to employment: so they had to be available in town. This site offered them easy access; and each day one could see several of them walking across the bridge and into the main street.

The alleged attitude of the local council was that if people would live over the river in these conditions they could stew in their own juice. Yet these were mainly people originally from Moonacullah, like those settled in town. They had left the station years before to make their own way; now the less enterprising families were established in the town. The aesthetics of this kind of settlement tend to be confused with health and welfare. Commonly council officers will worry about the *unsightliness* of this kind of accommodation and use health and other regulations to have it removed. As they want to get rid of it, their attempts to do so will be justified as far as possible in terms of national and State policies. That they had backing in this from the Board is suggested by the statement in the Board's Annual Report for 1961-2.

Although it is contrary to the Board's policy of assimilation to erect further homes on Stations or Reserves and have additional areas set aside as Reserves for Aborigines, this action has been forced on it in many instances because of unsanitary conditions under which Aborigines are found to be residing and the fact that many are as yet unready for town housing. This position often arises when Aborigines congregate in a particular area and are allowed to set up an unauthorised encampment, which is generally located on a Travelling Stock Route or Town Common. Failure by local authorities to take early action under the provisions of the Public Health and Local Government Acts results in such encampments expanding in size and population to a point where a serious menace to health is created.[12]

One may well wonder whose health is under consideration here, since the action commonly taken under this legislation, if it is taken at all, is to pull down dwellings which do not meet the minimum requirements. The Aboriginal family has to have shelter somewhere, and will take what remains of the materials and build the same kind of shelter somewhere else. I am not suggesting that there were easy answers for Board or municipal council. But the finance and works potential available to the Board for the provision of special housing were far too small even to house those whose dwellings were in danger of being destroyed (and often were) by local government decision, let alone to pull down more dwellings, no matter how decrepit. The Aboriginal suffers like other poverty-stricken groups from the national housing crisis. That he is not alone is clear enough, but his present accommodation, in about one-third of cases in New South Wales country towns, is a point of special vulnerability and anxiety.

The problem of Aboriginal housing is especially hard to define, because of assumptions that families in dire circumstances are in some phase of learning how to use houses: that they 'are as yet unready for town housing'. As one looks further into the centre of the continent, for instance at places across the Darling River, or at 'unauthorised encampments' off the Aboriginal reserve at Bourke, one may find apparent justification for the assumption that the collection of small, iron, one-room shacks in

[12] *N.S.W.P.P.*, 1962-4, vol. 1, no. 108—A.W.B. Report, 1962, p. 3.

which some family groups live (along with the shade of the neighbouring trees) is some kind of transition shelter, an adaptation of the wurlie. But it is also surely significant that no other shelter is available for these people. It is easy to justify their lot superficially by comparing it with that of the non-Aboriginal shearer or other pastoral worker camped on the bank of the Darling—or, for that matter, on the bank of the Gascoigne at Carnarvon. But the non-Aboriginal will be more likely to have resources elsewhere; he may still be as poor as the Aboriginal people nearby but, other things being equal, he has greater economic potential, if only because he has no special barrier of prejudice to overcome. He is also more likely to be effective in taking the action necessary to get help when needed from the State. Thus, though those on the Yerangoo Station appeared to receive the Social Service benefits to which they were entitled, through the efforts of the manager, those at Griffith and Deniliquin often did not. Janice Monk noted that people get the forms to apply for various benefits, pensions, and coverage from medical benefit schemes, but that somehow the operation is seldom completed unless there is a sympathetic and patient official available.

Sometimes a busy but helpful police officer will go beyond the call of duty in this way, but tension between Aboriginal groups and the police is common. One lady in Deniliquin told how she had herself taken cases to the police as the agents of the welfare services; that the Aborigines concerned would not have gone willingly to the police station. She also said that the police themselves wanted a welfare worker appointed locally.

What effect Aboriginal-police tension has on Aboriginal security in any one of a hundred variable situations is difficult to guess. There is little doubt that it does exist. At a conference of Aboriginal representatives from all over the State, held in Sydney in 1965, allegations of police bullying were one of the main items for discussion; while representatives from Queensland added their experiences of alleged similar happenings there. In Deniliquin one heard allegations not unusual in western towns— of Aborigines charged and gaoled for minor offences which would not lead to action in other cases. For their part, police often face a hostile silence which makes it difficult to solve the occasional serious crime within the part-Aboriginal community. Other authorities may be similarly frustrated, as when a child from one river-bank reserve, terribly disfigured in a mysterious fire, was deposited by some unknown person in the town hospital: neck and shoulder fused, and one eye missing, she was even discharged back to the river-bank group, on the easy official assumption that 'her own people' would look after her—which again illustrates the gap between 'camp' and town and the elusiveness of the Aboriginal, developed as defence against all officialdom.

Fire as well as floods are a high risk in these dwellings, and create special economic risks for people who have developed no habit of covering their possessions with insurance. Even where the cash value of what they have to insure is low, it represents a minimum requirement without which the family has no security at all. No statistics of fires were kept during our survey; but in the area where I personally spent most time in 1965, two of the forty-four households interviewed had their homes destroyed by fire in that same year; and in each case one life was lost.

It may well seem that these towns of the south-west of New South Wales would have the reputation of being 'hard' or 'bad' towns among the Dark People, but from what indications we could get, the reverse is true. At all three major centres and at Western Town they informed us that their town was 'a good place to live'. The most successful are those who can get a house in town and regular work. That comparatively few have done so may illustrate social strains involved in cutting themselves off from their fellows who want them and going to live among those who openly do not or who express patronising and conditional approval.

In the pastoral industry in 'colonial' Australia out beyond the closely settled areas, those who fell within the legal definition of Aboriginal in 1964-5 were legally paid lower wages than the award rate for non-Aborigines. This was not so in New South Wales; especially in the western regions of the State one heard stories that lower wages are in fact paid by many employers. The most one can assert is that an unscrupulous employer can in fact do this because many Aborigines will not know what they are entitled to or, if they do, will not have the knowledge or the confidence to protect their economic interests. There are some kinds of employment where the living conditions are either difficult to inspect or may be disregarded because union workers are not employed. The legal provisions for certain minimum accommodation requirements can be evaded more easily if the employer uses Aboriginal labour. Only recently have some trade unions shown any interest in having Aboriginal members. Seasonal work like fruit picking, bean and pea picking, potato digging, or corn husking offers opportunity for the small operator without much capital to get by with Aboriginal labour. As the Aboriginal so often lacks any irreplaceable skills, may suffer from poor nutrition, and tends to have a large family to support, he will have small bargaining power on his own account. A group of Aborigines is largely defenceless economically, as it lacks 'hitting power' through strike action. Even where the farmer or other employer employs no other labour, Aborigines cannot improve conditions by industrial action alone, because they are so easily replaceable. An exception would be where a farmer has depended on an Aboriginal group for so long that others do not offer; but it is doubtful whether confidence in any leadership offering would lead to a successful strike, unless a large trade union took up the issues. I was assured that many persons who employ Aborigines around Deniliquin pay less than the award, and I found one case where a man cutting wood was paid £9 per week; but it was impossible to check on these stories or even on the number of hours worked in the one known case, or the amount of wood cut.

If discrimination at Deniliquin appeared more obvious in some respects, such as the obvious neglect of the river-bank people, than what could be seen in Griffith, it was less so in others. Janice Monk found part-Aboriginal members in town churches there in 1965, but not in either Griffith or Cowra. At Cowra, the Catholic diocese had been bounded by the river which cut it off from the station for a long time, and the only service to Catholics there had been from Koorawatha. This had changed by 1965, and the priest from Cowra celebrated Mass on the station. But no Catholic from the station went to church in town while Janice Monk was there, although she was informed that once a year an Aboriginal was invited to speak in the Baptist church. On the station the established Christian organisation was the Aborigines Inland Mission. Jehovah's Witnesses had a base in one house. The Aborigines Inland Mission, an organisation which depends on enthusiasm and the emotional experience of conversion rather than intellectual training, is one of the most important Christian organisations with predominantly Aboriginal membership. It maintains a centre at Singleton where young persons, generally in their late teens, are trained for its mission work. This and the United Aborigines Mission have had a long history of work on Aboriginal reserves, and their efforts have extended well beyond New South Wales. There was a non-Aboriginal pastor of the A.I.M. living in a mission house close to the Three Ways Reserve at Griffith and conducting services there in 1965; and another in Deniliquin who held services in his own house.

There is competition these days for part-Aboriginal souls. Among the fundamentalist sects especially there has been a proliferation. One interesting experience for anyone who is old enough to have read of the Four Square Gospel of Aimee Semple McPherson in Los Angeles, or who may have seen the old Temple of the Angelus (in something of a decline these days), is to hear the Four Square Gospel preached by a part-Aboriginal on the river banks of western New South Wales. From

Deniliquin an active Salvation Army captain had departed for Sydney not long before I was there; he had, among other achievements, established a brass band with all-Aboriginal membership, which played for some town functions as well as at religious services. Both Methodists and Baptists in Deniliquin included Aboriginal families in their congregations.

A few townsfolk were concerned about the health and diet of children in the large families. The choices offering were often grim enough: either the child, often without an effective father, ran the considerable risks to which the poverty of the family exposed him or faced the bleak future of growing up in an institution. This, if he happened to appear to the local Aboriginal Welfare Officer to have 'Aboriginal features' and a dark skin, might be the infant welfare centre at Bomaderry, to be followed by a boyhood at Kinchela, near Kempsey. (Girls would be sent to the Cootamundra home for girls.) If he were cosmetically fortunate, he would grow up with non-Aboriginal children in homes maintained by the Department of Child Welfare. Part-Aboriginal attitudes today illustrate partly the high rate of institutionalisation in the past. This is another example of the operation of multiple causation.

More positive approaches had been grasped at by thoughtful local people. The Health Department was reported to be considering a centre staffed by a properly trained health worker; the local people concerned wanted a trained welfare worker as well. In fact the need might better be met by a trained multi-purpose worker, with the emphasis on education leading people to look at their own problems in the light of what is possible, making known the facilities already available and the proper way to make use of them. This type of worker is rare in Australia but there seems to be little hope of linking the Aboriginal *communities* with the nation without efforts in this direction. The point is that Aborigines have to become prime movers before their conditions generally may be improved. But this requires new incentives and new kinds of organisation in these fringe-dwelling groups.

## DARETON AND BALRANALD

In the area where the Darling joins the Murray, the settlement at Dareton had a reputation among Aboriginal people from Melbourne to Deniliquin as an unpleasant place to live. Here in 1964 a research worker from the University of Melbourne found some 140 part-Aborigines, the majority of whom were camped at the rubbish tip a couple of miles from town.

The main improvement to their conditions since the previous year was that this part of the tip

was no longer used for refuse. The humpies are made of flattened kerosene tins and rags. There is a similar camp at Fletcher's Lake ... The council has repeatedly threatened to bulldoze unoccupied humpies in both these camps. There are sometimes as many as ten children and two adults in a single humpy. Only one item of furniture, an old iron bedstead, and a few battered suitcases were seen during my visits. Food consists mainly of Johnny cakes, tea and soft drinks. Sometimes a few of the men went kangaroo shooting. With the closure of the Wentworth freezing works, this has unfortunately declined, but they occasionally go after kangarooes and rabbits to get some meat. A few people are allowed to use [fruit] pickers' huts in the off-season, and their living conditions are incomparably better.[13]

Two families only had tradesman-built houses (at Curlwa); significantly, the male breadwinners of both had permanent employment in the fruit industry. The rest dug ditches when the work offered, and picked grapes in the season. School attendance was poor, alcoholism prevalent, illegitimate children commonly offspring of teenage girls. This all increased the prejudice in Dareton, where some shops refused to serve Aborigines (they had the good reason that they might not be paid); whites were served first in others as a matter of course. Religious contact was maintained by the Aborigines Inland Mission lay preacher from Mildura. Efforts to help had been made by Mildura and Merbein people. Some of the Methodists were working in 1964 for resettlement of this group in Victoria. There was, needless to say, less enthusiasm from the police or the local government authority of Mildura.

Conditions in Dareton had been publicised in the Melbourne as well as in the Mildura press in 1957. The settlement of people there had been the result of a drift, from places as far-flung as Murrin Bridge, Lake Cargelligo Ivanhoe, Broken Hill Wilcannia, Hillston, and Condobolin,[14] probably, an indication of the attractions of seasonal work in the fruit picking industry. The interested people in Mildura, organised into the Sunraysia Aboriginals Welfare Group, criticised the New South Wales Board for its alleged neglect of the people there; after three years of agitation it apparently succeeded in getting the New South Wales authorities to set aside thirteen acres for a reserve in 1960.[15] By the middle of the following year the Save the Children Fund had money to contribute to the erection

---

[13] L.A. Hercus, Notes on people of Aboriginal descent living at Balranald, N.S.W. and at Dareton (Coomealla) N.S.W. (typescript). SSRC-AP file.
[14] Diane Barwick, A Little More Than Kin (1965), p. 386 quoting press references.
[15] Ibid.

of a welfare centre at Dareton. But the situation was still much the same at the end of 1965. Councillors of the Shire of Wentworth were under pressure from citizens to do away with the 'camp', for the usual aesthetic reasons. The Council wanted the State government to resettle the families there somewhere else. The Aborigines Welfare Board lacked resources to supply housing. A reporter from Sydney found in October 1965 two families who had been living in what he called a 'Hell's Acre of Crazy Huts' for ten years and more. Aborigines told him that they would like to have their homes near the river, so that they would not have to cart water from neighbouring fruit properties in buckets.[16]

In case this is thought to be characteristic only of a place so out-of-the-way as Dareton, we found on this survey conditions much the same, in places quite close to major town centres: for instance, families were living like this, and carting water from the river in plastic buckets, at Murrays Flat, within a few miles of Bega, earlier in the same year.

Each situation seen had a historical context of its own, which is the most neglected though often a very important part of the local and regional history. The story of Dareton-Wentworth-Mildura race relations is one example of hundreds throughout the two States concerned, in fact throughout the whole continent.

Between Deniliquin and Dareton, and out on the flat plain between Hay and Robinvale, is the pastoral town of Balranald, where a hundred or so part-Aborigines have worked most of their lives in the pastoral industry, as seasonal workers. In 1964 there were at least two families in the town itself. Some families are out on the stations, on one of which a further twenty lived permanently and had sheds, huts, and caravans; and on the mission in 1964 there were six of the usual poor shacks. The figures given by the Welfare Board for 1963-4 showed thirty-one persons dwelling here; Mrs Hercus, whose description of Dareton I have just quoted, stated that the shacks were 'over-populated'. One had just been burned down. For water the reserve depended on a pump and the good-will of an Italian horticulturist; sometimes there was none. Even the children were reported to drink methylated spirits: there had been 170 charges, mainly for drunkenness, during 1963.

The small and typical part-Aboriginal fringe settlement has a history established in the records over eighty years at least, during which Balranald has been one of the focal points in a pattern of migrations dictated by the demands of seasonal work. Perhaps this movement has

[16] Dooley Harrison in the *Daily Mirror* (Sydney), 27 October 1965.

been a factor making for continued separateness from the non-Aboriginal society of Balranald. The reserve is where it is because it offers access to water and to work in the pastoral industry. Over the last two decades there had been fruit picking within travelling distance, which for an Aboriginal family tends to coincide with the area where there are relatives. It is also risky to go far from a place where there is certain food, shelter, and water, when one is likely to be 'last on and first off'. There is thus a tendency to limit the search for employment to within a day or so of travel from the base 'camp'.[17]

I can confirm the impression given by Mrs Hercus of a hard local overt prejudice, reflected in the astonishment that one should show any interest in, or have any business to do with, the 'niggers from around here'.[18] People blinded by prejudice cannot believe that there can be serious interest in and a desire to know the objects of their prejudice. (It is obviously dangerous to make judgments on overtly expressed attitudes; experience suggests that often people of genuine kindliness will speak in this way.)

But the situation has often passed beyond the point where an individual response to Aboriginal need has much impact on the recipients. Pity and charity merely emphasise the pattern of relationships. There is obvious foundation for the stories of apparent ingratitude, where well-meaning folk go to great trouble for Aborigines only to be 'let down' at the moment of decision without explanation. In every State one finds the rigid local patterns of discrimination on the one hand and on the other the accompanying absence of expressions of appreciation for the efforts of those who try to assist. Equally as common is the suspicion of would-be Aboriginal leaders ('Who does he think he is? A white man?'). Hard-working officials in the State departments responsible for Aboriginal welfare are often the objects of bitter satire—as well as the recourse of the satirist when he is in trouble. The Aboriginal group everywhere is reputedly impervious to exhortation and to all advice given 'for their own good'. So far is this the case that in our movements through these situations throughout the country we have grown accustomed to speculations, especially on the part of those whose full-time employment involves daily wrestling with these problems, as to the obvious apparent limits to Aboriginal intelligence. By even the better educated officials, the question has been raised of mental processes of a different kind from those of the person of European descent. The answer to this kind of

---

[17] See Appendix, 'Balranald Reserve, New South Wales', p. 177.
[18] Hercus, Notes on people of Aboriginal descent . . .

speculation is that nothing in the pattern of attitudes and action cannot be explained by the original clash of two completely different cultural traditions, especially by the circumstances, by the subsequent history of race relations in Australia, and by the impact of government policies.

There are good reasons for the Aboriginal groups' avoidance of co-operation, but the place to look for them is not among hypotheses which cannot be proven (such as the commonly assumed, but long discredited, relationship between race and intelligence). The anthropologist, who knows better than this, will naturally tend to explain part-Aboriginal attitudes and actions in terms of a continuing Aboriginal tradition. It would be strange, in all the circumstances of long rejection by members of non-Aboriginal society, if there were not living elements of Aboriginal culture even in Redfern and Fitzroy. But the more we learn about the history of government policies, and of what has happened to part-Aboriginal communities over the last century, the more closely do Aboriginal attitudes conform to those of rejected racial minorities in other Western countries.

We have been handicapped by the long neglect of the Aboriginal in Australian history; but enough is now known for us to question what may have been an overemphasis by anthropologists on the effect of transmission of cultural elements. One might mention here such examples as the tendency for part-Aborigines to migrate within well-established limits. As indicated above, there are very good economic reasons for the traditional limited pattern of seasonal movement, which coincides with the employment offering. As for apparent indifference to immediate economic advantage, this can be accounted for otherwise than by survival of the gathering and hunting tradition: for instance, by lack of opportunity, and by a profound scepticism when white men seem to offer it. Another example is the high proportion of mother- and grandmother-dominated households. This the anthropologist might well ascribe to the existence in the area concerned of a matrilineal tradition inherited from Aboriginal ancestors; and he may well be correct as far as he goes. He may point out that in Aboriginal society things pertaining to the flesh were assumed to come to the individual from the mother and through her; that things of the spirit came through the father, whose responsibility it was to maintain the sacred ties with the country and the ancestral spirits; that when these ties were disrupted, or the belief in them lost or rendered impossible, the father lost much of his significance. The argument is subtle enough, and worthy of respect. But it is also true that mother- and grandmother-dominated families characterise other deprived groups. In the poor communities of Jamaica, for instance, Edith Clarke found the pattern of grandmother- and mother-controlled families, without fathers or with fathers absent;[19] the daughters living in marriage or concubinage where marriage is too expensive and too risky; the same poor housing, with the males off looking for seasonal work, and involved in sequences of sexual unions, while mothers and grandmothers tended to maintain the children. The main difference is that the poor Jamaican is a peasant with at least some land, a place to live and build without too much worry about the building inspector or the health inspector. The part-Aboriginal family often lacks the security of the poorest peasant.

Late in 1965 the Moynihan Report on the condition of the Negro family in the United States was drawing attention to the economic and other factors which caused a high incidence of fatherless families, and the effects thereof in terms of delinquency and health.[20] It seems, therefore, logical to conclude that historical and economic causes arising from contact have had positive effects; that the incidence of mother- and grandmother-controlled households, with father dead, absent, or not regarded as a member of the household for other reasons, may be part of a continuum and therefore a cultural survival, but that this is not as significant as the *causes* for its survival; and that this kind of family would have developed in any human group subject to the same pressures and policies and to the same degrees of prejudice and discrimination.

Among the causes of this kind of matriduxy are the historical ones from the first frontiers, when the women were of value in the white man's world as sexual partners, while most of the men were not required as workers. Another is that the men, for reasons which so far we have only mentioned in passing, tend to lose status because they are ineffective in the role of breadwinner and provider. This may lead to despair and to alcoholism, which in turn increases the inefficiency of the adult male. The model often set for the boys is not such as to produce in them ambition or hope; they assume that life holds the same lot for them.[21]

---

[19] *My Mother Who Fathered Me.*
[20] Office of Planning and Research, United States Department of Labor, *The Negro Family—The Case for National Action* (Moynihan Report).
[21] This is by no means meant to be criticism of the anthropologists, who after all pioneered the whole field. Because the historians and economists left the Aboriginal largely out of the picture of Australian development, the anthropologists had to work within the limits of their own discipline. But this does not justify the totally 'anthropological' explanation of a situation to the exclusion of history and of hard economic fact. I cannot accept the following, for instance, as adequate explanation of the high mobility of part-Aborigines: 'Nomadism is evident in the way the part-Aborigines have been inclined to be on the move a great deal, going from town to town to see the agricultural shows. It is also seen in their interest in

## OLD CUMEROOGUNGA

The special history of part-Aboriginal people in the Murray River region has involved, from the time of separation of the State of Victoria, a small margin of choice for them: if they considered one State authority to be oppressive, they could always cross the river. Fortunately, this area has been included in Diane Barwick's studies of the social and historical backgrounds of people of Aboriginal descent who visit Melbourne.[22]

The Murray River appears to have been more densely populated than most other riverine areas at the time of first contact. One result was that in the early 1880s the Aboriginal groups on the New South Wales side were large enough to have located there the first State-sponsored institutions for Aborigines since the end of colonial administration.

We cannot here do justice to the long history of the Cumeroogunga Reserve. But this oldest, and in its heyday by far the biggest and most important, of the New South Wales Aboriginal stations epitomises the efforts of the State government, on the one hand, and frustration and avoidance by Aborigines, on the other. The result of decades of government policy and control there was, in the end, to scatter the offspring of the Cumeroogunga community. Some escaped, as it were 'across Jordan', and established themselves in Victoria. Probably hundreds of others are scattered along the river banks and in the fringe settlements of the southwest of New South Wales; and as Diane Barwick has shown, the descendants of Cumeroogunga people are prominent in the Melbourne Aboriginal community. That this is a story of failure is indicated clearly enough in the social and economic disabilities of these people on both sides of the border.

Developed from the Maloga mission, and later from one controlled by the government-sponsored Aborigines Protection Association, Cumeroogunga, on the New South Wales bank opposite Barmah, became the showplace of the Aborigines Protection Board for almost a quarter of a century before 1915. It was a base from which the men went out to seasonal work on neighbouring properties; where they worked when

---

seasonal work. Moreover, they quickly sense when there is likely to be good food-gathering conditions . . . in some town. Indeed, in one northern town so many were attracted that the Government had to provide a new reserve with new houses on it.' (Quoted in *Public Health*, published by the N.S.W. Public Health Association, June 1965, p. 6.) Surely it is more meaningful to say that Aborigines go after seasonal work from hard necessity? And that they are so short of housing that there was a 'housing rush' when the word got around that some were to be provided?

[22] A Little More Than Kin (1965), ch. iv.

such employment was not available; and where some of them had control and use of farming land on which they grew wheat and raised stock for their own profit. Here a whole village was erected and maintained by Aboriginal labour. The sixty buildings of 1915 included church and school. Men and boys were trained there in carpentry and farm work, and known for skills in house and boat building.[23] There were forty-six cottages laid out in three streets; water was reticulated to each from large storage tanks; and 'in 1908, when the station population reached its peak of 394, a hot-air engine was installed to pump water from the river'.[24] For twenty years, this supply maintained cottage gardens as well as the station orchard and vegetable garden.

By World War II, most of this was a memory. By 1923, two-thirds of the reserve had been leased; by the end of a further five years most of the stock was sold; farm machinery was taken to other stations or worn out; the water supply system had broken down in the late 1920s and was never repaired. Of the situation in 1937 Diane Barwick writes:

Only the dark people remembered that Cumeroogunga had once had facilities equal to those of the great pastoral stations of the Riverina and had been the home of a stable, contented and prosperous community. Half the residents now lived in bag huts, for twenty-one cottages had been pulled down when the occupants went away to work—in order to discourage them from returning to the station.[25]

Contentment and stability may here be comparative; certainly a look at the pictures of the people of Cumeroogunga (or for that matter pictures remaining of groups from other reserves like that at Dubbo, in the early part of the century) suggest that here was a community which thought well of itself, and was by no means a congregation of paupers. But there was always trouble with management. It seems to me erroneous to underestimate this indication of the tensions between inmates and staff typical of institutional situations. Yet things did become much worse as the result of the changes which occurred; and Dr Barwick has provided a most telling documented study of what happened there.

There was always pressure from local interests for the land which the station occupied; and this seems to have increased when the improvements carried out by the Aboriginal workers were completed. This pressure was largely decisive. Doctrinaire policies, resulting in pressures on some who were less visibly Aboriginal to leave the station, necessarily split families and forced many of them to go elsewhere, for the emphasis in application

[23] Ibid., p. 423.
[24] Ibid., p. 424.
[25] Ibid.

(as it has largely remained to this day in matters where some distinction is to be based on the alleged amount of 'Aboriginal blood') must have been applied to get those who looked less like Aborigines to leave. Thus parents who wanted to keep their children together would often have to give up their homes. Such policies followed the example set by Victoria. Aboriginal communities were first established and then disintegrated for the same combination of doctrinaire reasons and non-Aboriginal economic pressures. It was policy that part-Aborigines should get out into the community and in practice the stations were for the people of *apparent* Aboriginal origin.

At Cumeroogunga as on other reserves there was no legal vesting of the assets in the Aboriginal group. The Aboriginal farmers had worked the land on the basis of a permissive occupancy not established in the law, and so always likely to be revoked in a change of administrative policy. One wonders how different the outcome might have been had the historical circumstances produced recognised rights in the land which could be protected by lawyers.

The turning point here was the 1909 Aborigines Protection Act, which provided that 'the Board may remove from a reserve any Aboriginal who . . . in the opinion of the Board, should be earning a living away from such reserve'. This enabled the Board to act on the assumption that able-bodied men, and all others of less than half Aboriginal descent, should leave the reserves for wage employment. Forty farm blocks which had been cleared by the occupants were taken back by the Board from 1907.

Resentment of forced removals and expulsions strengthened the Cumeroogunga people's belief that the 'government Board' had unjustly deprived them of land which 'Queen Victoria' had 'given' for their perpetual use. The denial of title to, and the final resumption of, some forty farm blocks laboriously hand cleared by men who believed the land would 'belong to' their families was a lasting grievance to the people of Cumeroogunga. The reminiscences of the block-holders and other members of this pioneer generation (many of them were still alive in the nineteen-fifties) kept their several thousand descendants wistfully aware that the reserve had once been a model farm, that the land long leased to white farmers for grazing stock had once produced as much as twelve bags of wheat to the acre, and that in the 'great days' of the 'old people' barges had called regularly at the Cumeroogunga landing to load wheat, oats, maize, hay, wool and hides for shipment down the Murray to market at Echuca. The legends naturally enough gloss over the bad years when flood, droughts and plagues devastated the crops, but the contemporary produce accounts confirm the accuracy of much of this oral history.[26]

One of the reasons for the short-lived success of these Aborigines appears to have been the availability of educational facilities at least

[26] Ibid., pp. 433-4.

comparable with what was available for the non-Aboriginal community in the region. The schoolteacher who went to the station from the original mission at Maloga, one Thomas James, was an Indian from Mauritius. Though he was later employed by the New South Wales Department of Public Instruction, he remained with the same community all his working life and until he retired in 1921. His influence went far beyond the school; he married into the group, his descendants remain prominent among them. His son participated in 1929 in the first conference called by the Commonwealth Government on Aboriginal affairs. Here must have been one of the few cases where, perhaps from the accident that a coloured man would not be in demand for other schools, a consistent if limited educational development was available; where the school remained a centre for adults as well as the children; where there was sound primary instruction without the teacher being committed to breaking the traditions which bound the group together. Possibly this was one of the factors which made a conglomeration of people from different tribal traditions into one community.

For Cumeroogunga was not, nor were any of the stations in the 'settled' areas, formed by a coming together of an Aboriginal 'tribe' or other group on to part of its own 'country'. While this might be so for a few of the original inmates, essentially all these establishments were formed by collecting remnants remaining after the disastrous period of frontier contacts. When the missionary, the Reverend Daniel Matthews, after 1874 had brought the first mission group together at Maloga, he attracted the nucleus from the surrounding pastoral stations. This of course aroused the resistance of those who were losing cheap labour. This nucleus was from the Joti Jota and Pangerang tribes of the Murray River, but others came from much farther afield, for until 1880 Maloga was the only institution offering shelter in New South Wales (the earlier missions having all failed). People were brought there from as far away as the Bogan River. Thirteen Queensland Aborigines found in Sydney were sent there; and in 1881 Matthews took over thirty from Maitland and the Sydney wharves. There were also recruits from some of the Victorian stations as these were closed down, or as those not considered to be Aboriginal were sent out. One of the best-known families in the Cumeroogunga tradition is descended not only from the mainland Aboriginal but also from the original Tasmanians.[27]

[27] See Tindale, 'Growth of a People: Formation and Development of a Hybrid Aboriginal and White Stock on the Islands of Bass Strait, Tasmania, 1815-1849', *Records of the Queen Victoria Museum, Launceston* (N.S.), no. 2, p. 21.

Most Aboriginal groups in the closely settled areas have comparable beginnings. Most 'Aboriginal' ties, at least throughout eastern Australia, which are so often and easily assumed to be 'tribal', are essentially common traditions of an institutionalised sub-group, united to some extent by these memories, and in some kind of opposition to the prejudice and discrimination of other Australians. The first missions and stations were established by gathering remnants, left in the aftermath of the frontier episodes, into convenient areas for control and protection.

The old grievances about Cumeroogunga were well aflame when I made contact with those who remained there in 1964. People still living there remembered the forcible removal of children in 1919 by the inspector from the Board with police assistance—an action taken, apparently, to place the young people in institutions and apprenticeships, to keep down the population of people with lighter skins on the reserve, and to break the traditions which were assumed to be the basic cause of why so many part-Aborigines continued to be born. Some of the children who were taken away, and others who watched this removal, are among the spokesmen and leaders of the Melbourne Aboriginal community today, and their memories of this experiment in assimilation have given them an abiding distaste for official efforts to 'take our children away from their own people and try to make them "pass" and turn against us'.[28] There is no Aboriginal administration which has not practised forced removal of persons from one place to another, on general policy grounds and not on the grounds merely of parental neglect or the delinquency of the persons removed; this background is part of the part-Aboriginal and Aboriginal folklore.

Our first acquaintance at Cumeroogunga was an elderly descendant of the family of part-Tasmanian origin; he was a product of James's school, and his family ties extended from Shepparton to Deniliquin and along both sides of the Murray. The most notable dispersal had occurred on 4 February 1939, when John Patton, who with Ferguson of Dubbo was attempting to organise Aboriginal opinion in New South Wales in the late 1930s, apparently provided the stimulus for all but four families to cross the Murray into Victoria and establish a camp at Barmah, on the opposite bank.[29]

[28] A Little More Than Kin (1965), p. 461.
[29] For accounts of this episode, which seems to have been something of a turning point in Aboriginal affairs, see *S.M.H.*, 6, 8, 9, and 27 February and 4 March 1939; *Argus* (Melbourne), 8, 9, 11, and 14 February, 1 March, and 29 April 1939; the *Age* (Melbourne), 7, 10 March and 12 April 1939; and the *Herald* (Melbourne), 16 and 21 February, 11 March, 18 May, 24 July, and 11 October 1939. The manager of the station stated that the reason was fear that

In 1964 the main preoccupation of the Aborigines dwelling on this reserve was to have the opportunity to restore some of the prosperity which was reputedly there before 1915. There was still the link with the Aborigines Advancement League of Victoria, which had provided some help in the period of the 1939 'strike'; the purpose was now to have some of their former lands made available for mixed farming on a community basis, pressure for which had been exerted for several years. In its 1963 Report the Aborigines Welfare Board (p. 12) referred to advice received from the Department of Agriculture, that the area did not offer much hope for co-operative agriculture, and stated that the capital expenditure required would not be warranted. But by the middle of 1964 the Board had approved the establishment of the scheme proposed by the Victorian Aboriginal Advancement League 'subject to certain safeguards'.

This somewhat reticent statement omitted the fact that the Cumeroogunga families had been resisting pressures to disperse, and that the Victorian Aboriginal Advancement League had gone into the attack with a delegation to the Chief Secretary of New South Wales.[30] The

children would be taken. Douglas Nicholls, then a leading footballer in Melbourne, said that people thought it better to qualify for the dole than to subsist on rations issued by the New South Wales Welfare Board. J. Patton and W. Cooper both stated that the value of the ration at New South Wales stations was three shillings and sixpence per day, with half that for a child. The group appears to have returned after six weeks camping in bough and bag shelters, but in mid-May over seventy of them went across to Barmah again where their very bad living conditions were subject to comment for a long time afterwards. They seem to have been able to hold out partly because of help from the Aborigines Advancement League in Melbourne. As late as October, Patton was arguing with the Victorian Minister for Labour and Sustenance that these former Cumeroogunga people should qualify for Victorian assistance when needed, since they worked for some months of each year in the fruit picking activities of the State and paid income tax on their earnings. The group at Barmah probably changed a good deal but was still there at the end of 1942 (see *Herald* (Melbourne) for 14 December 1942). By the end of the war, Barmah part-Aborigines formed just another of the Victorian fringe groups.

Patton was a part-Aboriginal with obvious ability. On Australia Day in January 1939 he and Ferguson had organised a Day of Mourning and Protest throughout New South Wales and a gathering at the Australia Hall in Sydney. On 31 January 1938, he had led a deputation from Cumeroogunga to Canberra which interviewed the Prime Minister, J.A. Lyons, and J. McEwen, Minister for the Interior, asking for Commonwealth control of Aboriginal affairs, under a Ministry of Aboriginal Affairs (Diane Barwick, A Little More Than Kin (1964), p. 172—quoting *Argus* (Melbourne), 1 February 1938).

In March 1939, after the 'strike' at Cumeroogunga, he was tried for 'incitement' of the inmates to quit the station, and placed under bond. His actions were possible because he was an official of the Aborigines Progress Association; possibly he was able to visit all stations in this capacity. In April he addressed students at the University of Melbourne.

It is suggestive, at least, of a progressive deterioration of morale, that leaders of this quality have been so very rare since his day. For the airing of the whole matter in the New South Wales Parliament, see *N.S.W.P.D.*, 1938, vol. 156, pp. 1425-2784 (31 August-18 November).
[30] In February 1963; referred to in 1963 report of the Aboriginal-Australian Fellowship.

reserve families still considered themselves to be a wronged group, deprived of lands specifically set aside for them.

This view was partly justified when the Crown Solicitor stated that there had been no legal justification for the earlier leases of sections of the reserve to non-Aborigines (which suggests that very often an Aboriginal group may be more in need of legal advice than of the exhortations of officials or the ministrations of welfare workers). The Aboriginal representative on the Board included in a list of grievances the fact that this land had been leased to 'white growers of tobacco and small crops'.[31] A press statement in March 1964 indicated that the Board had agreed to the use of 1,700 acres of the reserve for a farming project, to be controlled by the League.[32] A requirement by the Board was that the League should provide capital of £5,000 ($10,000) for the project. The League was planning for the appointment of a manager and the formation of a company with Aboriginal shareholders, to whom this amount should be advanced as a loan.[33] But in April 1965 it was reported to the annual meeting of the Federal Council for Aboriginal Advancement that no agreement had yet been finalised, the secretary of that organisation stating that the Board had requested the League to indemnify it for 'any action taken against the Board relative to the Reserve'.[34] The Board's concern seems to have been related only to responsibility for any staff employed rather than to possible action by current leaseholders. By April 1965 the League had raised £1,200 and had set aside £3,000 as a loan to Cummeragunja Pty Ltd.

That such a tangle of negotiations between one State welfare authority and voluntary bodies of two States, and one on the national level, should have proved necessary to get a very small co-operative project launched was possibly due to the fact that the ties of this community are with Melbourne rather than Sydney. The current members of the Board and its staff can hardly be blamed for circumstances which arise from the long history of Aboriginal affairs policy. But the case may serve to illustrate the degree of complexity which lies ahead in Aboriginal affairs, if governments move for the creation of Aboriginal property rights in the long-settled rural areas. There is little doubt that this is one of the issues around which the resentments of Aboriginal groups coalesce.

[31] James Morgan, Report to the Aborigines of New South Wales, 27 October 1964.
[32] *Courier-Mail* (Brisbane), 28 March 1964; *Smoke Signals*, vol. 3, no. 2, June 1964, p. 25.
[33] See *Sunday Sun Guardian*, and *Daily Mercury* (Illawarra), both 10 July 1964.
[34] Statement by S. Davey, Secretary, in agenda and reports, Federal Council for Aboriginal Advancement, 8th Annual Conference, p. 12.

In June 1964 this was the main topic of my conversation with the men on the reserve. Mr Briggs, an elderly man to whom others referred one, stated that the fourteen families who remained 'had been battling for this'; that they wanted security for their homes and a future there for the young people. The reserve had fallen into a general and obvious decay. The sergeant of police at Moama, who had taken a real interest in its rehabilitation, had been advocating that piped water be laid on to the houses and that a pump be installed. It was reported that Works had the water situation in hand and that one of the local Apex Clubs was donating a pump, so that by community and government effort there was the hope that the amenities of the 1920s might be restored. Lavatories had to be rebuilt, and the Board had arranged for electricity to be taken to the site; but the houses were in such poor condition that there was at this time doubt as to whether house lighting would have to wait for the new houses. Those on the reserve had definite ideas of what they wanted and what they considered their rights to be. It was understandable that they should be somewhat vague as to the details of negotiations; but at least the League had had discussions with some of them in Melbourne.

This story raises a basic question of causation in Aboriginal affairs. Diane Barwick points out that almost every Report of the Board up to 1915 indicated successful operations at Cumeroogunga.[35] What happened after that? Was the 'failure' simply due to something lacking in the Aboriginal people, an explanation which would be in accord with common prejudices?[36] It may be worth noting that the Board, prior to the 1909 Act (still in 1967 the basis of current legislation) lacked any definite statutory powers of control; that it operated stations largely through the help of local committees; that its members were Members of Parliament and private citizens, except for the chairman, who was the Inspector General of Police. In 1916 it was reconstituted to give an overwhelming majority of government officials. The trend from then onwards was for its powers of control to increase; and the urge to promote public service efficiency could be satisfied by the appointment of inspectors to ensure control from the centre. About the same time, the right of Aboriginal farmers to farm lands on the reserve as their own was withdrawn. The government had always been concerned that persons who could qualify as non-Aboriginal should be citizens in the general community; what in the early years of the century was a somewhat crude

---

[35] A Little More Than Kin (1965), p. 437.
[36] For later official and non-official statements attributing 'failure' to Aboriginal shortcomings, see ibid., p. 425.

concept of absorption of the half-caste and those of 'lighter caste' became at the end of the 1930s the assimilation policy, without any radically different approach in the practice of the Board's officers.

That there was a great deal of 'trouble' at the station after 1916 can be adequately explained by the growing institutionalisation of the situation. Increasing interference from managers, in matters like removal of children; the loss of individual enterprises with the end of individual landholding; the effects after World War I of closer settlement, which reduced the opportunities for seasonal work on pastoral properties off the reserve, and which tended to restrict the men to the station; the demoralising effects of the arrangements for rationing without work available during the depression of the 1930s—all are factors which helped to produce the protest of 1939.

To my mind, however, the central fact is that of a group of people with nowhere else to go, who are in the situation of inmates of a multi-purposed institution which for lack of funds and meaningful policy, and in the absence of trained staff, is not efficient even to preside over social changes. The reactions of these people are those of groups under stress anywhere. If from their many origins there are indeed some cultural predispositions, as there may well be, it is not necessary to postulate these as the *cause* of Aboriginal actions and attitudes; these may be adequately accounted for by historical and economic factors and by social factors arising from the relationship of the group with government and with non-Aboriginal society.[37]

It is of the essence of prejudice that members of a distinguishable group, the object of prejudice, are assumed to have certain characteristics; that *all* members of the group have them. Aborigines are assumed to be un-reliable, feckless, and unstable; prejudice need look no further than this for explanation. Such views were officially given in 1938 as the cause of failure. That the patterns of Aboriginal behaviour are so often in such direct contrast with those of middle-class rural Australian *mores*, at least as professed, is an excellent example of the self-fulfilling prophecy. When so many arrangements are made for the control of irresponsible people, and so many people 'know' that they must not be given responsibility, there follows the temptation to discharge the allotted role, and consider-able difficulty in reacting in any other way.

The sympathetic sergeant of police at Moama mentioned a few cases. One man refused consistently to pay his rent of seven shillings and sixpence a week, although he earned good wages. He also refused

[37] Dr Barwick's study of these circumstances is definitive and convincing: ibid., ch. iv.

to pay for a driving licence, and then refused to pay the fine for
not having one; he also refused to register a vehicle; and for all this
also refused to give an explanation to the perplexed authorities. He
had been fined because his children were not attending school; there
were several fines for two shillings and sixpence, with £1 costs (so
low, no doubt, because of the stereotype of Aboriginal poverty); the
warrant for each two shillings and sixpence fine was costing six shillings.
He was a competent shearer, and a heavy drinker; in one recent bout
he had apparently damaged the latrine of the Welfare Board house
in which he lived; probably on the complaint of the health inspector
the Board had to ensure that this was attended to. In addition the Board
had to do something about his fence, which was falling down. Surely
a case like this indicates intelligent protest, whether justified or not?
And whether it is justified or not, it seems more logical to look for
causes why the situation might produce such reactions from any group
of people rather than to try to account for them through alleged special
attributes of Aborigines.

No doubt if the co-operative at Cumeroogunga fails—and a co-
operative operation of this kind is most difficult and sophisticated—
reasons will be found in the Aboriginal character. Seventeen hundred
acres is not a very good start for a venture for fourteen families, especially
against so demoralising a background. Very competent leadership indeed
will be necessary—and very good luck, if the standard of success is to be
solely economic; nor is $10,000 a great deal of capital, in view of the high
costs of farming machinery.

Finally, would there be serious consideration of a plan to establish a
co-operative for fourteen non-Aboriginal families on no more than
1,700 acres? Is not the situation again loaded for failure?

### DARLINGTON POINT

Of the missions, which became the three first stations in New South Wales,
two were in the southern area. The other was at Warangesda, three miles
from the site of Darlington Point, on the south bank of the Murrumbidgee
west of Narrandera. This station offered one of the success stories in the
1890s and the early part of this century. A visitor in 1913 wrote of the
wheat and the 800 sheep there, even though by this time policy had been
to provide mainly for the old and the indigent.[38] The station here was
maintained until 1920, forty years after J.B. Gribble established the mission;

[38] W.K. Harris, *Outback in Australia or Three Australian Overlanders.*

some of the families went to Cumeroogunga, others to Moona Cullah; but some remained. Of approximately 800 persons in the police area in 1964, those who were of part-Aboriginal descent were said to form a high proportion: just how high there was no way of knowing.[39] But here there was said to be an integrated community. There was no special reason for many of them to think of themselves as Aboriginal except that some had recognisably Aboriginal features. It was said to be against local tradition to mention such things, yet there will be no real equality until they can be a matter for some pride. Some people of part-Aboriginal descent have land of their own. Others work for the Water Conservation and the Irrigation Commission, the timber mill, the cotton gin, and the Shire Council. One of the problems for local authority was that of unemployed relatives who moved into the area; another was that some of Aboriginal descent exhibited high prejudice against others whose homes and habits conformed to the Aboriginal stereotype.

For those who publicly acknowledged their Aboriginal origins, there was still a reserve which was under the supervision of the local policeman.

The situation at Darlington Point indicated a further complexity, for it suggested that the research worker seeking contact with Aborigines over a wide region would find easily enough the groups which identify as such, but only a long and patient effort in one area would indicate all of those who remember that they are of part-Aboriginal descent. Those with whom we were making contact formed, as it were, the unsubmerged part of the iceberg; but considerable numbers of others had 'passed' or were 'passing' out of Aboriginal society.

While this Project was being carried through, there was another being carried on by the School of Public Health and Tropical Medicine from Sydney University, in an area which cannot be disclosed. Patient research in this limited area, involving the making of contact through Aboriginal informants, disclosed a much more affluent segment of the part-Aboriginal group. It was characterised by higher incomes, better housing, and a much higher proportion of non-Aboriginal spouses than we had found in the same area. The research also found a high correlation between non-Aboriginal *appearance* and success in establishing families in the towns, independently of the Welfare Board.[40] Dr F. Lancaster Jones, in work

---

[39] The Aborigines Welfare Board took an unofficial census in 1965. The estimate for persons of part-Aboriginal descent at Darlington Point was round 400, of whom fifty were estimated to be half-caste—a category still in use by the officers of the Board in 1966.

[40] This research is directed by Dr R.H. Black, Professor of Tropical Medicine. I am indebted to him, and to Mr R. Hausfeld, Senior Lecturer in Anthropology, School of Public Health and Tropical Medicine, for permission to use this information.

undertaken for this Project, found a high rate of disappearance (he called it 'statistical passing') when he compared census returns of 1961 with those of 1954, the age group in which this was especially marked being of persons between twelve and twenty-one years in 1961.[41] One might hazard a guess that this disappearance from the group ready to declare themselves Aboriginal or 'half-caste' in the census was occurring mainly among those cosmetically favoured by absence of Aboriginal features and skin coloration.

'Passing' is not 'integration' or 'assimilation'. Rather is it indicative of a degree of race prejudice against a 'coloured' minority. Those who are lucky enough not to have inherited the badge of inferiority will often take the opportunity to escape; those not so lucky have little chance of establishing that equality in social contact with other Australians which is the somewhat vaguely defined goal of the assimilation policy.

[41] *The Structure and Growth of Australia's Aboriginal Population*, pp. 27-31.

## APPENDIX

*Balranald Reserve, New South Wales*

As Dr Diane Barwick was working on the whole area from which Aborigines look to Melbourne rather than Sydney, I asked her for a note on this settlement at Balranald. The story is so typical of the sheep-carrying areas right across the continent that it seemed worth while including it here *in toto*:

*Balranald Reserve, New South Wales.* The earliest census of and official report on Aborigines in the Balranald district was made by local police in the winter of 1882, at the request of the recently-appointed Protector of the Aborigines. The police enumerated 98 fullbloods and eight half castes, of whom only eight were 'children' under the age of twenty years. Of the adults, 45 were forty years of age or older. The police declared that no government aid was needed, as some natives were employed on sheep stations and others lived by hunting and fishing.

The detailed police censuses, published in the annual reports of the Aborigines Protection Board, list nearly ninety Aborigines, all but eight of them fullbloods, from 1889 to 1891, but the average number between 1892 and 1899 was less than thirty and from 1900 to 1905 less than twenty.

The Board insisted, as a declared policy from the beginning, that able-bodied natives, both fullblood and half caste, must support themselves, and most of the Aborigines of the Balranald district continued to work and camp on Yanga, Canally and Paika Stations. The New South Wales government had begun distributing blankets annually during the eighteen-sixties, but it was not until 1891 that six aged natives were issued supplies of flour, tea and sugar, together with some clothing.

On October 1, 1892 a reserve of 142½ acres, located approximately two miles from the town of Balranald, was set aside for the use of Aborigines, and huts were erected there for the use of the 'old and infirm'. Some fencing materials were supplied in subsequent years, and materials for additional huts were supplied in 1906. The reserve was unsuitable for farming and was intended only as a campsite. Police issued rations of flour, tea and sugar, occasionally some meat and, very rarely, some clothing to a handful of residents who were unable to support themselves, and gave half-rations to their dependent children. The numbers given aid over the twenty-four year period for which figures are available averaged only seven adults and 2·6 children and the average annual expenditure was £58.

The Aboriginal population of this district appears to have grown after 1906, although the census totals fluctuated erratically from year to year. Only seven fullbloods, mostly aged men, were enumerated after 1909, but a steady increase in the number of half castes—apparently young couples with children—doubled the Aboriginal population to a total of 45 by 1914. It is impossible to say whether these half castes were newcomers to the district or were local people counted for the first time, perhaps because they had actually settled on the Balranald reserve. There is no corresponding decrease in the numbers at nearby centres: Euston, Oxley,

Maude, Hay, Moulamein or Barham, and the numbers in the Deniliquin district also show a steady increase at this time. But more than a hundred Aborigines left Cumeroogunga Station between 1908 and 1915 and it is likely that several families known to have resided at the Balranald reserve during the nineteen-twenties and nineteen-thirties had actually moved from Cumeroogunga before or during the war years.

The Board's reports from 1916 to 1939 give no information about Aborigines in the Balranald district, but the Public Service Board's 1938 report noted that there were 109 Aborigines living on the Balranald reserve. When Aborigines Inland Mission workers first visited from Moonah Cullah Station in 1929 they found only two families living on the reserve but reported that sizeable numbers were working and living on Canally Station, some sixteen miles away. The Moonah Cullah missionary spent several months at Balranald in 1932, and other workers visited for a month in 1935, but a resident missionary was not appointed by the Aborigines Inland Mission until May 1937. Until Miss Ayling retired about 1958 detailed comments about activities here, and the names of many Aboriginal residents, were published in the two journals issued monthly by the Aborigines Inland Mission. Thus, although the Aborigines Welfare Board reports after 1940 gave no information other than population figures, the history of this small community may be fairly adequately reconstructed from these notes, together with the relatively complete genealogies compiled for most of the Aboriginal families of this region.

Only a small number of those Aborigines who have lived and worked in the vicinity of Balranald since the nineteen-thirties are descended solely from the original local tribal groups. Employment opportunities on the large pastoral stations of this region attracted Aboriginal workers from distant areas, and the unsupervised reserve at Balranald was for many of them a conveniently central winter camp from which they could not be evicted at the whim of town or shire councils. Some of the families who settled at Balranald after the first world war belonged to branches of cognatic stocks (notably Coombs, Edwards and Pike) which had migrated from Ebenezer Aboriginal Station to the Lake Boga-Swan Hill district of Victoria between 1886 and 1910, moving from there into New South Wales, probably via the unauthorised camp at Barham, during the 'twenties and 'thirties. Others came from Cumeroogunga and Moonah Cullah Aboriginal Stations. Some of these families (notably the Briggs, Morgans, and Hamiltons) had come originally from Cooranderrk. Families from these two stations settled in sizeable camps at Moulamein and Barham during the two decades after the first war, migrating from there to pastoral stations for seasonal employment. During the nineteen-forties there was also a southward migration from the Menindee district. The Aboriginal population of this locality had declined from 54 fullbloods in 1889 to 21 persons in 1915, and only a handful were given occasional supplies of food from 1900 onwards. But in September 1933 the two hundred residents of Carowra Tank Station [this reserve, notified in 1907, was made a supervised station in 1927] had suddenly to be transferred, as a result of the failure of the water supply, from their home on the drought-stricken plains north of Ivanhoe. A new reserve of 1,000 acres, a portion of the Albemarle pastoral station, was set aside for them on the Darling River, six miles from the town of Menindee, and a new station was built. But there was little work for them there and by 1939 the Aborigines Protection Board had already decided to close the Menindee Aboriginal Station as soon as a better site could be found. Some wanderers from this station came to the Mildura-Wentworth-Dareton area during the late nineteen-thirties, and their success in obtaining well-paid seasonal work in the rapidly-expanding orchards and vineyards encouraged further migration during the 'forties. At the fruit-growing centres on the Murray and Murrumbidgee rivers, and on the pastoral stations, the northerners camped with families from Balranald and Moulamein, and some of the immigrants began to winter over at the Balranald reserve, eventually settling more or less permanently in the Balranald district. The Menindee Aboriginal Station was closed in April 1949, when those willing to move were resettled at the new Murrin Bridge Station near Lake Cargelligo, two hundred miles to the east, but a number of former residents remained in the vicinity of Menindee. Those who had settled in the south became linked by marriage to Balranald families. The Aborigines Inland Mission maintained resident missionaries at Carowra Tank in 1908-09 and again from 1922 to 1933, and subsequently at the Menindee Station from 1934 to 1949, but their role in acquainting the Menindee and Balranald populations and stimulating this southward migration was probably slight.

As the population of the Balranald reserve grew the Aboriginal occupants erected their own tents and temporary shelters to supplement the few small huts erected by the Board before 1907. It was not until 1938 that the Board supplied roofing iron and other materials for additional dwellings. The reports of the Aborigines Welfare Board do not mention any subsequent assistance, but Miss Ayling's report to the Aborigines Inland Mission in April 1945 announced that the Board had supplied materials for fencing the reserve boundary and the cottage allotments, and contemplated providing a piped water supply from the river, a quarter mile away.

The Board continued to give occasional supplies of food to a few aged and indigent Aborigines until 1948. Before 1913 no Aboriginal child in this district had received any education, as the families were usually camped on pastoral stations more than ten miles from any school, but the Board's reports from 1913 to 1915 noted that one or two children were now being educated privately. Some time later Aboriginal children were admitted to the State school at Balranald, two miles from the reserve, but were suddenly excluded about 1935, presumably because the parents of white children had complained. Former residents of the reserve recall that the local Roman Catholic priest opposed the ban and offered to educate the children without cost at the parochial school, but the Board declined this suggestion, proceeding instead to erect a school on the reserve. An elderly woman teacher was appointed by the Education Department in August 1936, but the school was not apparently maintained for very many years. Aboriginal children were once more admitted to State schools in New South Wales during the nineteen-fifties, but as most Aboriginal families in this district migrated annually to pastoral stations or to the fruit-growing centres for seasonal work, many children had only intermittent schooling and many of the young adults of today are functionally illiterate.

The censuses made annually in June show that there were more than a hundred Aborigines at the Balranald reserve at the beginning of the second world war and half that number after 1942. There were little more than thirty residents during the winters of the late nineteen-forties, and an average of fifty during the winters of the nineteen-fifties. But there was considerable seasonal fluctuation: less than fifty were enumerated in June 1950 and June 1951, yet the missionary (who lived in the town and regularly visited the reserve) reported in December 1950 that 31 adults and 36 children were living on the reserve and another 16 adults and 26 children were living in and around the town of Balranald.

Miss Ayling noted that this population was exceptionally mobile; she had commented repeatedly during the nineteen-forties that most or all of the reserve residents had gone away to Mildura or Swan Hill to camp during the summer picking seasons. The expansion of the fruit-growing centres on the Murray with extensive irrigation created new employment opportunities for the Aborigines of the Balranald district. From the eighteen-nineties until the second world war local employment in the vicinity of the reserve was limited to trapping rabbits, chopping wood, charcoal-burning, shearing, droving and doing general station work. This was still the pattern for much of the year in 1950, but the development of a local tomato-growing industry, as well as peas and beans, attracted Aboriginal workers to the Balranald district in December and January. As soon as this finished the families dispersed to the fruit and vine-growing centres on the Murray, often not returning until late April. Since 1947 a fruit-growing industry has developed on soldier settlement blocks at Robinvale, and during the nineteen-fifties more and more Balranald Aborigines began to seek seasonal work here rather than at the more distant centres on the Murray.

Miss Ayling had reported in 1943 that several families had recently been able to rent small cottages in the town of Balranald, but satisfactory town housing continued to be scarce and too expensive for families who could not be sure of finding regular year-round work in the district. More and more began to winter over in temporary accommodation in and near Robinvale but the Victorian government provided no assistance until 1960, when some eighty Aborigines, most of them sometime residents of the Balranald reserve, were rehoused in twelve staging cottages at the Manatunga settlement on the edge of town.

The number of residents of the Balranald reserve rose to 70 in June 1963, but declined again to 41 in June 1964. During 1964 the New South Wales Aborigines Welfare Board began investigating the possibility of rehousing the reserve residents, and in 1965 let tenders for the construction of six cottages in Balranald, at a total cost of £14,000. The Superintendent of Aborigines Welfare (personal communication, November 20, 1964) has stated that the Balranald reserve will probably be returned to the Lands Department 'in the near future'.

# SOME PROBLEMS
# OF IDENTITY AND STATUS

I had no discussion with Aboriginal leaders or organisations about their place in community or town, though not for want of effort. Aborigines would talk about individual grievances, but there was no discussion of an Aboriginal *cause*. Nor, as far as I could learn, was there any Aboriginal initiative to promote a cause, even at the municipal level. Voluntary bodies in some places were attempting to promote welfare and even defend civil rights, but it was clear that their efforts were being frustrated by lack of any leadership recognised as legitimate within the local Aboriginal group (or groups) and by lack of any organised body of Aborigines with which they could deal and on which they could depend. When they made arrangements, they were 'let down'. Elsewhere I have offered some explanation of why this should be so.[1] My argument is that Aboriginal society originally lacked a multi-purposed or hierarchical leadership; that the nature of white settlement, and of the methods of administration which developed later, left nothing which an emergent leadership could be profitably concerned with; and that authoritarian control, imposed without any confrontation of Aboriginal group by government authority, and without either negotiation or agreement between the opposed interests, discouraged the emergence of spokesmen who might in time have been recognised as leaders within Aboriginal and part-Aboriginal communities. Today these small groups often continue in a state of chaotic anarchy, which may even affect the family; so it is often the mother who holds it together. While government attempts to deal with individuals *only*, while individuals remain resentful and regard

[1] See *The Destruction of Aboriginal Society*.

it as representing the whites who refuse equality, there are two possibilities. One is that Aboriginal society remains disorganised; but the other, inevitable perhaps if new policies are not found, is of dissident anti-governmental organisation. In this direction lies even the possibility of organised violence. 'Black Power' would have seemed just as impossible a few years ago in the United States.

Aborigines certainly have a cause which is worth common effort and sacrifice. In the long run, only their own efforts will enable them to enjoy their full legal rights. In our look at south-western New South Wales, we found some of the issues which call for determined and united action. An obvious one is the common location of Aboriginal housing, with the frequent lack of municipal services. There is often a clear political conflict between Aboriginal interests and the views of the local government authority, ready to demolish dwellings on aesthetic grounds without waiting for other housing to be supplied or obtained. There is a not unusual local government view that the 'problem' should be 'solved' somewhere else, in another town, leading to use of council regulations to demolish fringe dwellings. This surely provides grounds for strong representations by Aborigines to the central government. The potential clash between central and local government may not be very promising as an issue to be legally exploited, since the local member is likely to press for the interests of the municipality. Nonetheless, it offers a chance for Aboriginal leadership to get local issues into national and State politics.

So far, such efforts had come almost entirely from the interested voluntary bodies. These bodies cannot provide a continuing leadership, but they can play an important part in its emergence, in some national strategy to promote such an objective. I can see little hope of Aboriginal leaders and followers playing an effective political role except through the development of new Aboriginal institutions with which governments are prepared to deal. Before developing the argument it seems desirable to describe other situations.

It has been usual for 'Aboriginal' research to be concerned almost exclusively with Aborigines. This, I believe, has resulted in a too heavy emphasis on Aboriginal culture as a limiting factor, and in turn it has encouraged the schoolmasterly efforts of officials to 'change' the Aboriginal. This approach, involving the study of a *part* to the neglect of the *whole*, involves the risk of taking effect for cause. Except for the special circum- stance of lack of leadership (which could also be matched, even among some Amerindian groups) the part-Aboriginal of the 'settled' areas is reacting very much as depressed racial minorities in other western industrial communities have done. The suspicious hostility, discharge of tensions in alcoholism and personal violence, the reactions of aggression, of withdrawal into 'apathy', and even of occasional excessive co-operation with authority ('crawling to the boss'), suggest not Aboriginal differences but the fact of their common humanity. Their needs are those common to other Australians. Their aspirations are restricted, not by the limits of need, but by the limits on their hopes. That they proclaim a difference, and attempt to found it in a special and different heritage of their own, proves only that they are subject to the same social laws as the rest of the human race. Denied a common Australian identity, they seek an Aboriginal one. Their ignorance and confusion is a condemnation of the rest of us; and our governments reflect the popular prejudice when they look for the causes in the Aboriginal mind and character.

There is an obvious difference of status, but this arises from majority attitudes. In south-western New South Wales in 1964-5 there was no corresponding *group* of 'poor whites' occupying similar types of accommodation, although there must have been non-Aboriginal families on lower cash incomes than many Aboriginal families. Aboriginal groups were probably no worse off in *per capita* income than certain classes of non-Aborigines, particularly age pensioners, deserted wives, and their dependants. But the Aboriginal group included a high proportion of both. In some areas the pensioner may be the wealthy member of the extended family group. (This has been commonly so in the remoter pastoral areas of Australia.) And when an Aboriginal obtains a regular income in this way, he will often spend it in ways not generally approved. The Aboriginal more often follows the 'improvident' frontier tradition of the Australian bush than do non-Aboriginal pensioners and other poor people. An elderly Aboriginal lady on a reserve, expecting her first pension payment, had arranged to celebrate. Her grandson was ready, on stand-by, to 'go a message'—the jargon for going into town to get flagons of wine from the hotel. At least twenty people were assembled on the day; the flagons duly arrived. Next morning, I drove to town one of her relatives, with eighteen empty flagons for re-sale at the hotel. I mention this case because it is not uncommon and because the lack of reverence for cash is more common among Aborigines than others.

We found some Aboriginal families in good accommodation; some men in permanent employment. But the man in permanent employment, with a house in town, had apparently achieved the limit of possible success. In some cases these men had already begun to sever their ties with the Aboriginal group. The only indication we had, in this area, of a *group* of people of Aboriginal descent established as owners of property or otherwise as men of some substance was at Darlington Point; but even if this 'substance' was more than hearsay, they were apparently unwilling to be considered Aboriginal.

Thus difficulties of identity and definition include that of how to regard such people, who have some Aboriginal ancestry and have either forgotten it or wish to do so or have no particular reason to be highly conscious of it. Yet there may be places where people are accepted without 'passing', in the sense of denying completely their Aboriginal origins. Prejudice is probably not *everywhere* unyielding. The most promising situations appear to occur in very small communities, where Aborigines and others have come to know one another, and where there are no significant economic differences. Even there, Aborigines may have to reject the improvident group in the 'camp' for economic reasons, since a family cannot amass capital so long as it remains vulnerable to demands from a wide circle of relatives and others interested in immediate consumption. Those with a genuine concern for their children often see the best future for them away from the drunkenness and violence common in the fringe-dwelling communities. Nor should one underestimate the effect of efforts by the Aborigines Inland Mission, the United Aborigines Mission, and other church or mission bodies, in the rejection of 'improvident' standards.

For a long time part-Aboriginal families have had access, under handicaps of varying degrees, to the main sources of Australian culture which, even when it is denied, is their main heritage. While the only 'success' possible generally involves cutting ties with 'demoralising' influences of the riverside camp, the process of doing so is difficult: for economic reasons, for the lack of alternative accommodation, because of white prejudice, and finally because of condemnation by the 'improvident' part-Aborigines, who regard such an attempt as a kind of treachery.

The family established in town may thus suffer a double social handicap. If the parents are determined to be 'respectable' they must contend not only with the prejudice of non-Aborigines but also with the condemnation of those from whose traditions and demands they are trying to free themselves.[2] Sometimes such people cling desperately to the only known

[2] Dr Ruth Fink has described very well just such a situation in the New South Wales town of Brewarrina in Social Stratification—A Sequel to the Assimilation Process in a Part-Aboriginal Community. See also her 'The Caste Barrier—An Obstacle to the Assimilation of Part-Aborigines in the North-West of New South Wales', *Oceania*, vol. 28, no. 2, 1957.

solace, to a puritanic Christianity which rejects the attractions of the material world.

Where such a process has been going on for a long time, there may be a number of part-Aboriginal families in the country town fully integrated into its economy and respected by the more enlightened non-Aborigines. This group may ignore even close relatives from the reserve and the river bank. Small-town barriers may still restrict them to low status over a generation or longer. Intermarriage with whites may bring higher status to a later generation (which is not much comfort to this one). Perhaps this bleak prospect for the ambitious innovators stimulates the current movement into the metropolis, where economic opportunities are better and there is less likelihood of close interest by neighbours.

It would be a gross overstatement to claim that the country town in the 'settled' areas exhibits all the features of the plural society, where people in the different racial groups tend to adapt their attitudes to those in other groups in terms of what is traditional in their own, where each group tries to make use of the other for economic purposes, while avoiding intimate social relations: for there is no longer a separate Aboriginal tradition, except of protest and avoidance. Yet the known part-Aboriginal *evolué* is in such a small minority that attitudes to himself and his family will tend to depend a good deal on who are his neighbours, what kind of people dominate the town council, and his own and his wife's social skills. It is probably more difficult for the family to get full acceptance now than it was late in the last century. The number of part-Aborigines of substance apparently formed a higher proportion of the rural work force seven or eight decades ago than they do now. They seem still to have retained status of superior accomplishment in the bush,[3] working as station hands, teamsters, and in other rural tasks. In both New South Wales and Victoria, from the period of first establishment of the Aboriginal stations, there was a view that these were basically for full-bloods; that the part-Aboriginal should be out in the community keeping himself like anyone else. This feeling justified the fragmentation of the station communities, by pressures to expel the half-castes, who at the turn of the century seem to have been able to claim the prevailing wages.

In the rural work force the tradition of part-Aborigines is much older. It was the Aboriginal who taught the first of what Russel Ward calls the 'nomad tribe' (the itinerant pastoral workers) to adapt European techniques of land use to the bush. Unfortunately, Dr Ward has not examined

[3] There is an interesting discussion of the point in Jeremy Beckett, A Study of a Mixed-blood Aboriginal Minority in the Pastoral West of New South Wales.

the contribution of the Aboriginal to the formation of Australian rural traditions, which is a pity, as I can think of no one more competent to do so. Jeremy Beckett has made the point that Aboriginal fringe-dwelling *mores* today are very similar to those of the nomadic casual workers of the latter part of the nineteenth century and the early years of this one.[4] In a very telling article, he points out that one of the songs of Dougie Young, a part-Aboriginal who still works in Wilcannia, indicates identification with the full-blooded Aboriginal, but also 'this time in a curiously nineteenth-century context'. The refrain placed in the mouth of George, an old full-blood, goes like this:

> I'm tall, dark and lean, and every place I've been
> The white man calls me Jack.
> It's no crime, I'm not ashamed I was born with my skin so black,
> But when it comes to riding rough horses
> Or working cattle, I'm mixing with the best,
> In the land where the crow flies backwards,
> And the pelican builds his nest.

The joke about the crow flying backwards to keep the dust out of his eyes is as old-fashioned as Aboriginal English . . . and the pride in 'riding rough horses' belongs to the time of George's youth. Here we have the idealized Aboriginal, a 'smart horse-man' living away from town and trouble in a simple society where he has a recognized place. The uncomfortable truth is that such cattle stations have receded almost as far as old George's ceremonies, which are only a few degrees more anachronistic than good horsemanship.[5]

Although now this kind of society is far back in time in the south-west, something like it may be found in a long journey in space, in the lives of the part-Aboriginal and Aboriginal stockmen of 'colonial' Australia. But modern systems of communication have done a great deal to destroy this world where the Aboriginal could establish some kind of equality, even superiority, on the job; since one effect of radio and air communication has been the ease with which people and ideas can move; since Australian culture is more and more dominated by metropolitan values, the demands of the world cash economy, and control by distant businessmen who tend to accept the stereotype of the feckless Aboriginal. Superiority in the bush is being destroyed as the special bush skills are replaced by closer settlement, fences, and mechanisation.

In a small museum at Dubbo there are photographs of the part-

---

[4] Ibid.; also 'Aborigines, Alcohol and Assimilation', in Marie Reay (ed.), *Aborigines Now*.
[5] Beckett, 'The Land where the Crow Flies Backwards', *Quadrant*, vol. 36, no. 4, July-August 1965, p. 43.

Aboriginal community of the Talbragar Reserve as it used to be. Here were men and women of some substance, the women in the full dresses of the Victorian era, and the men, with their solid-looking watch chains over portly waists, also obviously well enough housed to look after good clothes and well enough fed to have this air of prosperity. One would look far to find as many part-Aborigines from any one community as well dressed today.

What happened in the seven or eight decades since those days? For complex reasons there seems to have been an increase of prejudice. Economic reasons include the development of closer settlement: as white families moved into smaller areas, there was less of the old pastoral work. Sheep stations offered less of the kind of work for which the part-Aboriginal was noted. Racist views flourished as Aboriginal living standards declined; these in turn made opportunities for employment more difficult. Along with this development were those of the responsible administrative authorities. Aboriginal administration became more centralised, and more doctrinaire. Protective legislation increased in volume and effects; and the more protection, the more discrimination. Living conditions on the river banks became more difficult. The old pastoral economy with its often easy paternalism gave way to more urgent concern with profits; it was less likely that employers would take any risk of employing part-Aborigines.

By the time of the great depression in the 1930s, there was no effective public opinion in New South Wales to ensure that the unemployed Aboriginal got even the dole; he might have a place on an Aboriginal station where he worked for rations only.

Even in schooling there were similar changes. From about 1895, dark children tended to be excluded from the public schools. When teachers were later appointed for Aboriginal reserves, it was assumed that they need not be trained, for when station managers were appointed, one of their duties (without any training) was to teach for a couple of hours a day in the schools. This of course had results which seemed to justify the use of a special limited syllabus. In turn, this meant that schooling was meaningless for most.

Whatever the causes, identification of which must await more studies by social historians, one of the results was an impression on part-Aboriginal minds (by the 1950s there were very few of the full-blood Aborigines left in New South Wales and Victoria) of *meanness* by government; of much fuss about the expenditure of small amounts; of needless interference by officials in the lives of Aborigines; and of general contempt and rejection by the town communities. A.P. Elkin recalls that he had hopes in the early 1930s that within a few decades there would be no real 'problem' community; but he considers that the treatment of part-Aborigines during the depression years ended these hopes; that the people 'turned away' from the whites and in upon themselves.[6]

The depression, which left such an indelible impression on the politics of the Australian Labor movement, may well have expedited the process of rejection, in a circular and complex downward spiral of causation. At the height of it, unemployed non-Aboriginal men were being forced to live in camps in order to receive the 'dole', as were some miners. But the prejudice implicit in the whole previous history came to the fore in the case of the Dark People then. Their common attitudes today probably owe a lot to what happened then. This impression is based on many conversations with older men, who bitterly remember having to work on Aboriginal stations for poor rations without wages.

Since the 1890s, the extension of protective legislation had gone together with development of a special section of the public service to handle Aboriginal affairs. It was staffed by men with no training whatever. They often had ability and good intentions; many had neither. This, with special legislation, the increased use of police officers to police such restrictions as those on the use of alcohol, or against non-Aborigines visiting reserves, all tended to heighten tension, widen the gulf with non-Aboriginal townsmen, and lower the comparative status of the part-Aboriginal. No return to Aboriginal traditional life was possible, either culturally or physically. Farmers erected fences and excluded part-Aboriginal trespassers; game decreased. The Dark People had nowhere to go, apart from their reserves (where an increasingly institutional atmosphere was developing), but to the river bank which no one else claimed, where they could get water, and where they could wait for whatever seasonal work became available, while the women eked out their earnings at times with prostitution and domestic employment. This, again, lowered the status of the group in the eyes of the respectable townsfolk. Even in the 1960s it was sometimes difficult to visit Aboriginal homes without having explained to police officers that one was not there for doubtful purposes.[7]

As the full-bloods died out, the Dark People took their place in the popular folklore and in official thinking. The administrative efforts to isolate part-Aboriginal women from sexual approaches by non-Aboriginal

[6] Personal communication, 1965.

[7] The statement is based on personal experience.

men meant more controls. Although there were always considerable numbers who were living away from the multi-purposed institutions, the definitions of Aboriginal were wide enough to include a substantial proportion of the Dark People. Anyone with Aboriginal 'blood' might be regarded as a person not fit to drink, and be especially likely to have his children taken from him. In some States Aborigines could legally be taken to Aboriginal stations against their wills. However people got there, these institutions tended to set the tone of relationships with representatives of government. The Dark People, in their increasingly wretched conditions, which formed an increasing contrast with those in town as white Australians grew richer, seemed to give some support to the old fiction of racism—that the true 'native', in his pristine state, is to be admired and that the 'half-caste' inherits the 'worst of both races'. This old myth is still professed belief by some persons with administrative responsibility for Aborigines. I have heard it from their own lips, and in more States than one. The prejudice which was formerly discharged against the Aboriginal now had to find a new target, in the dark Australians.

While part-Aborigines do not live in a closed caste, they are somewhat more than a *class* of poor Australians, as is evidenced by the pronunciations of governments, town councils, officials, and white Australians generally, and by the common assumption that upward mobility for the Aboriginal involves his giving up, as it were, his Aboriginality. He wins condescending approval if he achieves the limited goal of permanent employment. Those who have gone further are still so few as to form the subject of comment and publicity.

In the total picture of Australian politics the Aboriginal had hardly been heard by 1964. Aboriginal spokesmen were rare, for reasons already suggested, although the national, State, and local organisations interested in Aboriginal welfare were becoming more widely vocal.

This does not mean that the Aboriginal is not a political person; rather, his politics are about things somewhat different from those of Australia as a whole. In this south-western region, we found certain relationships which are of first importance to members of an Aboriginal group. For dwellers on stations there was the relationship with its manager; for all dwellers on reserves, and for most mothers, there was the relationship with the Welfare Board. Some are tenants in Board houses; others will have children who are wards of the Board; and most will have something to hope or fear from actions or recommendations of the Area Welfare Officer. In their relations with the distant Board and with its local representatives, there is the carry-over from the background of institutions, of the camp situations, where they were under authoritarian management. In this respect Aboriginal politics are the politics of the asylum, hospital, camp, or other authoritarian institution: of inmates against the management.

Here are the dependent personalities; and some among those off the controlled reserve revealed the symptoms of the long-term inmate trying the world 'outside'. The housing shortage led sometimes to attempts to get back 'inside', back on to the station. The habit of playing the institutional roles, of attempting on the 'outside' to go on acting as if one were 'inside' avoiding and defying the 'boss' results in political and social chaos. Institutional conditioning explains in part the habit of living for the moment. There is no need to save or to think of the future, nor is there any point in so doing, since the institution will continue to provide at the same minimal level for one's satisfactions, no matter what the individual does. This background conditioning involves a situation where officials and Aborigines both use the jargon of the institution. Officials must justify all that is done by management as part of the 'cure' or of other *raisons d'être* of the institution, whatever it may be. More recently, in the institutions for Aborigines, this has been the jargon of assimilation. This conditions inmates and those who still think like inmates to a pattern of double-talk. There must be cynical discounting of all appeals to logic or self-interest among any people who have suffered from this over long periods. Where many have formed their in-group associations and *mores* under such circumstances, their attitudes will remain and be reinforced by discrimination 'outside', where officials may use, or are assumed to use, the same kind of double-talk.

Aborigines have suffered such discrimination everywhere. Those who make their own way, and establish themselves on river banks or beside water taps in the outer suburb of a big town, near an orchard in the Riverina, beside the racecourse at Nowra, by the back gate of a compassionate farmer at Bega, have been conditioned for years to threats, exhortations, and appeals, from the police, from health inspectors, building inspectors, from welfare officers and others. Boards, departments, police, inspectors, truancy officers, and the rest must be deceived, cajoled, dodged, evaded. This is the essence of part-Aboriginal politics.

So far there has been little opportunity to become involved in either national or state political matters, and little interest in doing so. Of the debates about Aboriginal affairs, becoming more frequent, and over the last few years more logical and tolerant, few Aborigines ever hear. There is little evidence of participant interest in national affairs.

I remember that some matter related to World War II came up in conversation with a group of Aboriginal men. They ignored the issue as of no account; 'that', said an elderly man to me 'was nothing to do with us'. There is no wide belief in the efficacy of pressure applied through Parliament. When the New South Wales Joint Parliamentary Committee in 1966 visited one reserve, which one would expect to be in the forefront of Aboriginal sophistication, most of the people were 'away'. In fact, they were watching from a distance while the long train of expensive state cars drove through the gates. This avoidance of involvement in issues which are directly affecting them is based on long experience which has taught them a profound disbelief in the honesty and reliability of authority. At the same time they have not yet learned how to question or challenge that authority.

In the United States in 1959, the political tone was quite different from that which marked Aboriginal affairs. There was a great deal of discontent, and plenty of protest. The debates on Indian affairs went on at State and federal levels: Indian authors and leaders were active in both, on the reserves, and in conferences with representatives of the Bureau of Indian Affairs. (How many conferences have there been over ten years in Australia between official government welfare organisations and the Aborigines?) Indian councils were amalgamating to get more political hitting power. By contrast, Australian part-Aboriginal groups were behaving like escaped inmates.

In no area covered in this Project could one avoid being impressed by statements and actions symptomatic of insecurity. On stations, settlements, and missions, in 'colonial' and 'settled' Australia, there were questions. What is to become of us? the dwelling? the reserve? What is the government (or Board, or council, or police officer, or manager, or welfare officer, or inspector of health, truancy, buildings, etc.) doing about . . .?

Dr Barwick has well illustrated why this should be so, in the story of the hundred years of debate and uncertainty about the 'future' of Lake Condah; from the story of the other Victorian station at Coranderrk; and from the quite recent years of uncertainty for the few families remaining at Lake Tyers. New South Wales, South Australia, and Western Australia also have this background of communities long established in circumstances where nothing was ever to be taken for granted—for there was no fixed tenure; and where eventually for doctrine, or for reasons of expense, communities were fragmented. At other times, in Queensland and Western Australia, Aborigines were collected by police action and were incarcerated. The legislative history, especially in matters which affected status and rights consequent on status, illustrates similar proneness to arbitrary decisions without warning or consultation. But all this has been only the background to situations where local decisions have been made affecting local groups, in which much depended on the character and beliefs of officials with effective power over Aborigines.

This heritage of uncertainty springs from the period of the first contacts with white men. Before that time, the whole country, and the spirit beings assumed to inhabit it, constituted certainty and security: the spiritual certainty of the Dreaming. When the land seemed to fail them, in drought or flood, this too was part of a universe where all was satisfactorily explained and accounted for. Nothing which the white man brought replaced this. Those part-Aborigines who inherited only what the 'whites' left for the 'blacks' have remained ever since at the mercy of what seem arbitrary decisions. The only escape has been by fading away out of part-Aboriginal society. The fringe-dweller is at the end of a very long road, along which there have been few fixed points, little in the way of certain hope and promise.[8]

In 1964, discriminations in the law were passing. In Victoria there were a few regulations for the managerial control of Lake Tyers, the one remaining station. In New South Wales the Board retained power to control reserves and stations and to remove occupants therefrom without reference to the court. In neither State (with these exceptions) was there an effective restrictive category of 'Aboriginal'. Nor was there in Tasmania, which still included one tiny community, on Cape Barren Island, where the families were identified socially, but not legally or even administratively,

[8] It is interesting that over a hundred years ago Aborigines of the Murray area were beginning to be articulate in their own defence and knowledgeable in the method of getting their grievances heard at the level of State politics. Diane Barwick, A Little More Than Kin(1965), p. 393, quotes from a letter from a Victorian Local Guardian in 1860: 'Since the Murray has been navigated by steamers, the natives have found it scarcely possible to catch fish, heretofore their chief means of support. A native of the Moira tribe, who rode up the Murray with me . . . informed me of the intention of himself and five other aborigines to proceed as a deputation to His Excellency the Governor to request him to impose a tax of £10 on each steamer passing up and down the Murray, to be expended in supplying food to the natives in lieu of the fish which had been driven away.'

Two decades later forty-two men from the Maloga mission signed a petition to the Governor of New South Wales; but this was probably prepared by the officers of the Aborigines Protection Association. The petition pointed out that white settlers had occupied 'all the land within our tribal boundaries'; claimed that with the training they had had they could support themselves if land were available for them; and stated their desire 'of settling down to more orderly habits of industry, that we may form homes for our families'. (Diane Barwick, A Little More Than Kin (1965), p. 404—quoting from news clippings in Mitchell Library.)

A century later the Aborigines of Yirrkala were petitioning the Commonwealth Parliament for recognition of the right of occupation.

as Aboriginal. South Australia had its two special categories—that of Aboriginal, and that of Person of Aboriginal Blood—with special legislation applying. Western Australia had its category of Native, carefully defined in terms of racial origin. In the new Queensland Act of May 1965, the definition of an Aboriginal showed the same detailed attention to the proportion of 'Aboriginal blood'.

In South Australia and Western Australia in the mid-1960s rights were being extended, partly on an area basis, in such matters as access to alcohol. Queensland retained its tight control: regulations to allow drinking and voting were expected. In the Northern Territory, out in 'colonial' Australia, part-Aborigines had been legally freed from control and the effects of protective-restrictive legislation since 1953; and the Welfare Ordinance of that year had used considerable semantic ingenuity to ensure that most, if not all, of Aboriginal descent only should fall within the special provisions of the Ordinance for 'wards', a term nicely suggestive of their inmate status. In 1964 the wards were legally set free, though the Director of Welfare retained power to control the institutions where most of them live; and the low wage established in the Wards' Employment Ordinance continued to apply to those working in the pastoral industry.

Thus under the various Aboriginal jurisdictions (each of which goes its own way) the laws on which Aboriginal rights depend had been changing. Most of these changes had occurred within the preceding decade or so. Sometimes, for administrative convenience of the authority concerned, regulations have lagged behind the statutes, especially where managers have still to control institutions for Aborigines only. Still further behind lagged the attitudes of officials concerned with Aborigines, even of those who were not especially so concerned, but whose responsibility it is to interpret priorities for services. Equality of civil status, or near equality, might bring more Aborigines into the bar of the hotel (where a few years ago they had to swallow quickly illegal 'plonk' on the woodheap). But there had been no noticeable increase of the numbers in hotel accommodation. Economic and social facts remained unchanged. The degree of anxiety produced in two of the most sensitive areas for the poor remained—anxiety about security of the home, and about employment. Although the Aboriginal group offered some alternative satisfactions, it could not offer security in these vital areas.

Perhaps the most striking evidence of the tensions caused, and that best attested, was of the very high incidence of heavy drinking among the men. This was so universally the case that we collected some statistics on the matter, which will be referred to later. Part-Aboriginal *per capita* incomes are, from the evidence, a good deal higher than those of Asian slum-dwellers. Though the Aboriginal group lacks the wealthy *élite* which marks American Negro society, many Aborigines earn as much as other members of the non-Aboriginal Australian working class. There was a high degree of dependence on social service payments. Many people did not get what they were entitled to, partly because they had not applied in the way required, or lacked information. But the part-Aboriginal is not in an economic situation as hopeless as millions of Indian villagers. His danger of dying of starvation is minimal. Perhaps he resembles the American Negro because he has the sophisticated range of needs which only social acceptance and economic stability can satisfy. He is suspended in Australian society, in the 'settled' areas; there is no life for him outside it. Yet he faces continuous danger of rejection and insult from non-Aboriginal members of that society. His anxiety results not from real fears of starving to death. Men without hope do not have to suffer from anxiety. The fear is of loss of his home or his children; of the time he must wait for the next job; of what authority will do to affect him.

In most cases he shares the general Australian materialism, the respect for men with plenty of money. Among Aborigines one finds admiration for the 'big spender', the successful worker who is ready to 'blow his cheque' and 'shout' for his mates.[9] There is often a hard sardonic humour. No group anywhere can be quicker to see through humbug, or more pointedly ironic, at least among themselves or with a trusted confidant, in their comments on it. Perhaps it is these qualities which have made the part-Aboriginal so often a popular member of the fettlers' or road-building gang. But even such acceptance is generally only partial; he returns to an insecure family situation, and is likely to have to put his work into second place because of urgent matters relating to accommodation or the needs of family and relatives.

So the part-Aboriginal in settled Australia shares the dream of the Australian worker. The dream of economic success is always *possible* of achievement. But in most cases, for reasons directly or indirectly related to prejudice, success eludes him. For the women, life is likely to be more frustrating. Very few have skills to enable them to rise out of occasional domestic or other lowly employment. Nor does marriage offer the security which other women can confidently expect. The move into town or even to the metropolis may increase the awareness of prejudice and discrimination, especially as the women are so often still assumed to be fair game for non-Aboriginal sexual adventurers.

[9] See Beckett, 'Aborigines, Alcohol and Assimilation', pp. 38-47.

The problem of identity is psychologically basic for the part-Aboriginal in 'settled' Australia, as it is for the American Negro. He is inextricably in, but is constantly reminded that he is not a welcome member of, general Australian society. The sub-culture of the camp and reserve may offer substitute satisfactions, but these form a kind of mirror reversal of the standards of that world where ambition might be satisfied. He faces social pressures which, unless he is of unusual determination and ability, drive him continually back to this obsolescent underworld, where people live in a kind of caricature of the way in which the pastoral workers of the bush lived half a century ago.

DUBBO AND WELLINGTON, 1964-1965

Neither Dubbo nor Wellington has either a well-known Aboriginal community or any special reputation for discrimination; and both would probably be described by the Aborigines who live there as 'good towns'. What was seen in both is useful in filling out the picture I am attempting to give with details from actual situations; and if these are better than most in the continent as a whole, this may be all to the good at a time when Aboriginal affairs are becoming increasingly the excuse for emotional breast-beating.

When I called at the home of one old man in Dubbo, the door was opened by a young woman who made the usual worried inquiry—was anything wrong? Old Jack Smith refused to come out until he had put on a coat and tie;[1] he then accompanied me to the Talbragar Reserve. He had been born there nearly eighty years before; he told me that the modest little house in town was gained when he had won a big prize in the state lottery. He also told the story which one heard in different versions about almost every old established reserve—that it had been made over to the Dark People by Queen Victoria; and that eighteen acres of it had been specially granted to his grandfather. There were the usual details of litigation, leading up to the usual denouement of the story—that someone else unjustly got the land. This kind of story is common, I think, among old men of his generation, white or dark; this old man spoke with the accent,

[1] I do not use real names, as I have no permission to do so—C.D.R.

and mainly in the context, one remembered from one's elder country relatives long ago. He had nothing against the local police; but swore horribly about the 'Board'.

The reserve is about five miles from the centre of town. Taxis charged twelve shillings and sixpence each way, so that unless people came in in their own transport, or in the school bus, a shopping or other visit cost twenty-five shillings. The link though the school bus seemed the only obvious recognition of the reserve as part of Dubbo, where there were old shacks of the worst type; they seemed to be located in the lowest part of the area inside the junction of the Macquarie and Talbragar rivers. It was winter and there were wood fires in the shacks, but no lights. In one dark room was an old lady said to have lain ill there for many years. A very old man was lying convalescent in the weak sun outside another house. Nearby, there were eight young men standing round a quite useful-looking car, talking; another eight or nine boys and young men sat on a woodheap playing cards. There had recently been rain; the soil seemed spongy and water-logged. Women battled with brooms in and round the shacks; the usual interminable washing was going on. It seemed a place mainly for the unemployed and the old, and their children and grandchildren. The conditions for housekeeping and general living made an almost incredible contrast with the prosperous town conditions a few miles away.

Old Jack took me into each house and introduced me. I was told of the big flood in 1955 when some of the shacks were washed away and people had to be rescued; people said that they had 'petitioned' for the right to remove their houses on to a higher part of what they claimed as originally reserve land. But they were opposed, they said, by the Pastures Protection Board, a local government body which in each of these centres where there are saleyards has to provide a suitable area for the yards and for agistment of stock hard by them. Here in 1964 there were three sales each week. The Aborigines believed that theirs was a priority *after* the need for saleyards and sheep waiting for the sales had been met; that both had been provided for at their expense by cutting down the reserve area from forty-two to eighteen acres; and that the result was to leave them the most low-lying of this river-bank area.

This was the remnant of the community which had appeared so different in the old photographs kept by a local resident with an interest in the history of the town. The thousands of artefacts which are still easily collected by those interested in this area indicated that Dubbo had been an important camping area for Aborigines before the white man came there. The community of the Dark People seems also to have flourished for a time;

Dubbo was still a centre of religious activity for the part-Aborigines, and in 1964 both the Aborigines Inland Mission and the 'Brethren' were paying special attention to their needs. I was informed that every few months there was a big religious gathering here of one or other of the various sects which cater especially for Aboriginals.

Dubbo is a centre for Aboriginal administration, with an Area Welfare Officer.

Dark People from the area to the north and west came here for hospitalisation—from Gulargambone, which possibly has the worst living conditions, on its reserve, of this part of the north-west, close to rubbish tip and night soil treatment plant; from Coonabarabran, Warren, Narromine, Coonamble, Gilgandra, Balladoran, and Peak Hill. One Welfare Officer, no matter how capable, with a typist to serve him and the Child Welfare Officer, could hardly keep abreast of the personal problems which found their way from all this region to his office, let alone keep *au fait* with what was happening on the scattered reserves. Men with permanent employment in town came to him with problems: requests for housing loans from the Board; that he try to locate an errant daughter; for assistance in finding employment for children; on matters relating to schooling, to pensions, and to medical assistance. One person regarded as a 'success', as he held a position of some responsibility in the railway yards, a married man with four children, was waiting there one morning before the office opened. It had been 29 degrees that morning at seven o'clock; he was dressed in singlet, thin jacket and jeans. He had no interest in local religious movements or in Aboriginal 'affairs', although one of his uncles had been a leader recognised throughout the State in his day; he had the permanent job, and his only obsession now was to get his own home, with a loan from the Board.

Because Dubbo has a centre—the Aborigines Welfare Board Hostel— where hospital out-patients can live, Aborigines come there from outside the area. The hostel had been erected about 1958 with financial assistance from the wharf labourers of Sydney and labour from the local Apex Club. Aboriginal informants claimed that some local interests had opposed the establishment of a large centre in town for fear that it would become a centre for drinking and prostitution. One reason for it, they claimed, was that hotels, at least until recently, would not accept Aborigines. Aborigines also said that these days the hotels would not refuse Aboriginal boarders, partly following the action of one determined Aboriginal woman who had gone to the police station when refused. Curiously, a hotel which barred Aborigines from the 'lounge' still had a large Aboriginal clientele in the public bar, partly, it was said, because that was where Aborigines had got their supplies when it was illegal to sell to them.

In Dubbo the protests of 1938-9 are still remembered. Mrs Pearl Gibbs, a former member of the Board and now manager of the hostel, has full records of the activities of William Ferguson and Jack Patton; Dubbo, she says, and not Sydney or Cumeroogunga, was the place where the movement began, and the main centre of agitation. Press clippings suggest that this town was in fact a centre for meetings of Aboriginal folk just prior to World War II.[2] This also suggests an earlier stage in the process of part-Aboriginal urbanisation, when there was more opportunity for Aboriginal opinion to coalesce in a large country town like this than in the metropolis.

The metropolitan ties of southern towns like Griffith and Deniliquin are with Melbourne; from this region they are with Sydney. One of the most telling factors in current social changes affecting the part-Aborigines as well as the rural community generally is the rapid increase in spatial mobility. By Australian standards there has been a spectacular extension of good bitumen roads; with fast cars making easy transport possible, so that one may drive these days quite comfortably from Sydney to Bourke in a day. The Board still provides free rail transport for Aborigines in need who have to go to Sydney for specialist treatment for themselves or their children. But there is a great deal of movement, from towns in this area, into and out of Sydney, generally by road. Aborigines who have the poorest housing may have cars these days; and it seems quite easy for those who do not to find someone who will take them.

The incentives are those which take the young or the ambitious from the rest of the town community: election for change and the appeal of the great metropolis for people who have grown up in an urban-oriented society. For Aborigines, there is the tug of the city, the hope of employment, excitement, and undefined change, which tend to be increased in the background of country town monotony. There may also be the special hope of escape from the hard pattern of prejudice and discrimination, where one is well known, into the anonymity of the metropolis. In the Dubbo-Gulargambone-Coonabarabran area, certain addresses in Sydney kept cropping up in conversation as places where a man down on his luck, or new in the city, could always find a welcome and a bed, if only on the floor—addresses in Redfern, Toongabbie, Parramatta, Marylands, Stanmore.

The movement is not one way: the number of those coming back seems to be significant, though not offsetting the movement into the city.

[2] I was able briefly to examine this collection, which remains in the possession of Mrs Gibbs.

A typical case came to the office of the Area Welfare Officer in 1964. The man had obtained employment on the basic wage in Sydney. He had five children, and expected to establish himself on the basis of a permanent wage, plus child endowment. But he found himself paying £6 ($12) weekly rent for one room only; fares and other high living costs soon drove him back again. He had no house to come to, and found accommodation on the Nanimah Reserve at Wellington.

This is a time of incipient urbanisation, it seems, for Aborigines in the east of Australia, and indeed from all parts of 'settled' Australia. To some extent this represents the attempt to escape from the long-established discriminations of reserves and country towns; to some extent it may result from population increases. There is an ingrained tradition of movement, which must arise from the lifetime of following seasonal employment. Those who talk about the walkabout have at least this justification: what they explain as something instinctive may be more convincingly explained as the tradition of the group and lifelong habit, since work and food could be gained only by constant movement. Urbanisation is an important aspect of the redistribution of a population, especially in Australia where the 'urbanisation index' is over 57 per cent. But whereas it is easy for others to move and re-establish themselves in the city, it is more difficult for Aborigines. The handicaps are mainly the breadwinners' large families, the fact that they are predominantly rent payers, the high rents in the cities, and the almost universally low skills, along with the prejudice of employers, who hesitate to employ persons from a group with a reputation for in-built unreliability.

Moving to the city is not a matter of carefully planned movement out from a safe rural or country town to the city, since the basis for planning is not there. It is often a gamble on the chance of finding a job in the new location. There is little to lose because assets—housing and other family capital—in the area of origin tend to be slight. People have little to lose because they have little. Closer settlement, mechanisation, labour-saving devices, and the effects of the 1964-5 drought were all playing a part in stimulating Aboriginal movement to the metropolis, where research has indicated the desperate search for suitable accommodation within the range of low wages and big families.

Economic factors not only attract but push the Aboriginal family out of the old rural setting into the city; keep it mobile in the city; and then often force it back to the rural area of origin. To some extent this movement is determined by the pattern of communications, but there are some curious blanks in the picture, which call for more research. In New South Wales, for instance, there are two interesting cities which should, but apparently do not, attract large numbers of Aborigines—Wollongong and Newcastle.

In any process of re-settlement, permanent residence in a new area will occur when the total satisfaction there outweigh those in the area of origin. Until this is the case, people will be drawn back to where they came from. Among the Aborigines, as Dr Barwick has shown, the reasons for return are as likely to be social as economic. She found that people returned to the country towns from Melbourne, in the early 1960s, for compelling social reasons, sometimes at the expense of their permanent employment. This may also be happening in the case of those who move in and out of Sydney. It would be a mistake, however, to reach any conclusion without looking more closely at the number who may take an occasional holiday out of the city, but who have established their homes and families there.

Perhaps this process of re-location could be accelerated as one aspect of a national plan to assist those Aborigines who desire it or who opt for it. These are the people in any society who are in the forefront of social change. Metropolitan social influences, with greater emphasis on impersonal exchange of services for cash, offer more hope of logical race relations than can be found in the hard old traditional structure of the Australian country town. Nor should too much emphasis be placed on the tendency of new-comers from the country to go 'home' again; for the return may be part of a process of re-settlement, which in all societies with marked kinship orientation develops out of a series of visits. The visits to town grow longer, and the stage may be reached where the new location is the 'home'. Visiting may continue; but the pattern is qualitatively different in that the newly urbanised person thinks of himself as living and working in the city, and going to the country for his holidays and for important social occasions.

Part-Aboriginal movements have thus two main polarities. There is the movement after seasonal work, generally within a limited area, because of the dependence on relatives and friends for accommodation, and the economic risk of going too far afield after uncertain temporary employment. Then there are the movements between the rural area and the metropolis which may offer better hopes of permanent employment. It is little wonder, then, that in each region and in every State there was the greatest uncertainty in statements by welfare authorities and police when they were asked for part-Aboriginal numbers in various locations; and that it sometimes happened that one went to a reputedly large group, to find a few deserted shacks; or to a reputedly small one, to find a large group. This kind of movement, with flimsy resources, increases the general insecurity.

Another cause of casualty from the family and the work force is the gaol sentence, often earned with some enthusiasm and taken lightly. Such, for instance, was the case with two brothers with whom contact was made in Dubbo gaol. One was a painter, the other a plumber and general builder, mainly on farm and station properties. Both were from Coonabarabran; both begged me not to mention to their grandmother where they were. There was something both pathetic and innocent in their concern for 'granny'. Both had been very handsome; one still was; the other had become somewhat battered. The reason for this was clear enough from the offences which had brought them there, and of which they spoke frankly. They are two of six brothers; all have had their spells in gaol; and in all cases, they said cheerfully, the main reason is drink. They had been living and working at Gulargambone. They claimed that they were not allowed to drink in the hotel there in spite of the recent amendment to the law; that the 'publican' blamed the police, the police the 'publican'; they had the traditional wine party in the bush, had a fight with the police, and here they were. This is the kind of circumstance which is likely to interrupt permanent employment. These men were married, with families; the employer of one of them was supplying meat and some money to his wife and children.

If one looks at this from the point of view of the school child, it is clear that school performance will often be affected by movement and by sudden catastrophe. The catastrophe will often be the result of the apparently irresponsible conduct of the father; and this in turn is related to the higher status of the mother. The temptation of an opportunity to discharge tensions in this way will suddenly prove too much for men who are generally sober and dependable. I can recall the case of one such, a man who had moved into a very poor shack (it was, in fact, a disused cowbail, with the room for the separator at one end) because it was all he could get to be near enough to town so that his older children could go to high school. He was working long hours for low wages at farm labouring to make sure he kept his job and he had managed to put two girls into neat high school uniforms and have them established in their classes. But one morning when we went to see his wife, all was in chaos. There had obviously been one of those uproarious drinking bouts in the locality the night before; someone had put his truck out of order by pulling out all the engine wiring; he was stumbling around it red-eyed and sick, late for work already, his girls unable to get to school. They had probably not had any sleep; the school bus had gone. The truck took most of the day to fix; and it was the only means he had of getting to his work on a farm some miles away. This is typical of the breakdowns which occur where there is so little security and so much worry and tension.

Children from the reserve were going mainly to Dubbo Central Public School in 1964. Those whose families had settled in town were mainly at the North Dubbo Public School; according to the headmaster about 70 of the 350 children were part-Aboriginal. He told a story often heard, of homes without stimuli or interest; but stated that in this respect Aboriginal children compared with those of other families living on a labourer's wage. The Area Welfare Officer stated that one effect of intelligence testing, at the time of passing on to secondary work, was to break the association of most Aboriginal children with others, since the Aborigines were badly handicapped in tests emphasising verbal ability. They found themselves in the special classes for the children deemed less intelligent; this in turn led to loss of interest. Add to this the rejection by age-mates at puberty in many cases; the lack of interest at home; often poor nutrition and lack of study facilities. It is not surprising that most leave school the day they are fifteen, even if the sequel is a long wait for employment.

On the other hand the attendance of seventy or so children at this school would, on the average number we established of 2·56 children of school age in families of this central western area, suggest that from twenty-five to thirty families were in 1964-5 established in houses in town. Seven of nine families interviewed in Dubbo were in houses on town building blocks; the average number of persons in these nine households was 6·33, again indicating considerable overcrowding by rural and country town standards. While this pressure on accommodation probably operates against school performance, the availability of light at night and other services may well offset this. Possibly the greatest barrier is in the indirect effect of prejudice and the parental attitudes which are to a considerable extent the result of prejudice.

When the first contact was made with the Aboriginal reserve at Wellington, it was over 130 years from the establishment of the first mission to the Aboriginal at Fort Wellington. The Nanimah Reserve is about five miles from the centre of the town, but it is approached through a perfect example of the rural slum, of part-Aboriginal squatters on the 'town common', a magnificent site beside the Macquarie River. Two or three old shacks on the reserve suggest that accommodation here had been much the same as on the common until recently; but the row of new tradesman-built five-room houses, giving a street-like effect, and matched by the equivalent row of closets behind, indicated that whatever policy might be, here in effect was a rebuilt part-Aboriginal village. There was also a partly built hall, which had been donated, we were told, by the Wellington Lions' Club.

On the town common in November 1964 about forty adults with sixty-seven children were living in fourteen dwellings, with an additional three empty ones, a symptom of the high mobility of this population. Those absent were probably in temporary or seasonal employment elsewhere. Thirteen dwellings were of scrap iron, the more or less traditional 'tin shacks'. There was another hut of timber; two were of timber and iron. Three of the men there were invalid pensioners; two were war pensioners; one man and one woman were age pensioners; there was at least one deserted wife and two deserted *de facto* wives; one man was 'on compo'[3] (workers' compensation). There were two reasonably comfortable houses, one of which was occupied by a couple of invalid pensioners, the other by a non-Aboriginal, who was described as a contractor and was married to a part-Aboriginal. Of about sixty-seven children, many had no visible trace of their Aboriginal ancestry.

There was no water or sanitation service provided by the town council or the Board for these people. An Aborigines Welfare Officer with whom I discussed their parlous situation considered that they 'chose' to live here in order to avoid 'responsibility'. While there is a good deal of evidence to indicate that groups of this kind behave in ways which affront the local middle-class *mores*, it is hard to see that they had much alternative as to where they might live, since the housing situation in this part of the State meant that *someone* has to live in these conditions, and to live *somewhere* where the local health and building regulations can be ignored.

Council action to pull down these houses, without positive provision somewhere, simply means that there will be more shacks elsewhere—and as conveniently situated as possible for access to employment and relatives.

Conditions round Wellington were the subject of a short survey by the student organisation Abschol in 1965.[4] The organisation looked in vain here for Aboriginal employees in shops or in the limited small industry offering; they report that none was found. This probably reflects a general shortage of employment of this kind. What is interesting is that when jobs with some small regularity and status are few, Aborigines will not get them; the statement in defence that 'we have not enough employment for whites' is not uncommon. The main local employment for Aborigines, it was said, was on market gardens, where they were alleged to be underpaid,

[3] Australian slang for workers' compensation.
[4] Reported to the annual meeting of the Federal Council for the Advancement of Aborigines and Torres Strait Islanders in 1966.

£10 ($20.00) being stated as the usual weekly wage. Whether this is true or not, there seemed to have been no union inspection of this work, probably because it is paid as seasonal work for which no fixed award has been established. This is one of the reasons why such work is left for the Aboriginal worker and his family. Here, as in other parts of New South Wales and Victoria, whole families go in the season on to farms to dig potatoes, a task which takes the children from school. Young people who hope for award wages tend to move to Sydney to try their luck.

The range of accommodation for Aborigines round this town is comparable with that in and around Dubbo; later examination of a sample of thirteen homes showed that the average number of occupants was about the same—6·31.

The teacher on the reserve was impressive and devoted; the children seemed happy enough. The teacher said that their capacities were of the range one would expect among any group of children; but in performance they were on the average at least one grade lower. One reason he gave was that indifference at home meant that setting homework was pointless. In five years he had not heard one expression of interest in school work by a parent. Before his time, he said, it was the tradition for the child who reached sixth class to sit out the remaining years of schooling there. He had begun the placement of such children in the high school in town. But they still 'left' automatically at fifteen years; their parents expected this. The Lions' Club had provided a scholarship to get a girl to high school in Bathurst, because there was a hostel there. The reason for providing it in such a way that the girl must live away from home was stated to be the fear that otherwise she would probably have her studies interrupted by pregnancy.

Such a belief, and any justification there might have been for it, illustrate not only the outcast situation of the people on the reserve and the common nearby. Where such expectations are held, they tend to operate as self-fulfilling prophecies, since a young girl about whom such beliefs are held will attract the attention of sexual adventurers. Because women and girls on reserves have been considered fair game for a long time—in Wellington, from the accounts of the first mission, one could fairly guess for 130 years —the caution of the Lions' Club and its educational advisers was well grounded in experience.

The location of this school in 1964 suggested that the townspeople did not really want Aboriginal children in the Wellington schools. The teacher carefully explained that the location of the school at Nanimah was not an example of segregation, but purely 'geographic'. To be fair, since this visit was made, many of these separate schools, just outside towns, have been closed, and school buses provided (as at the time in Dubbo) to take the children into the town school. What we saw there, then, is a reminder of how recently schooling was segregated for many Aboriginal children; and what the teacher said about the children who 'sat out' the remainder of their schooling in the top class, a reminder of the fact that this had been the usual thing for a long time. Little wonder, then, that so few Aborigines have made a success of schooling.

The situation is very common where a reserve has a squatter settlement hard by, or in some other place conveniently located perhaps for employers to pick up temporary workers, or simply as offering somewhere to build a shack which is not highly visible and therefore likely to be pulled down by a council for aesthetic reasons. Those who live on the reserve often regard as beneath them those who live in the shanties on town common or Crown land without permission. They may consider themselves more steady and respectable. But often those on the common or Crown land are there because they refuse to live under control of the Board or its local representative, who may be a police officer or, where there is a teacher in charge of a reserve school, the teacher-supervisor. They are often envious of the better housing on the reserve. At the same time they look down on the occupants, and look upon themselves as people with some spirit and independence.

Each of these towns has a special Aboriginal dimension of its history which is unique. For instance, there is a story of interest and obvious significance which has led from the hopes of the mission at Fort Wellington in 1830 to the sorry dead-end in Nanimah in 1965. Equally neglected has been the Aboriginal dimension to the contemporary human geography of the Australian country town. There is significance, of human relationships, in the *site* generally occupied by the Aboriginal reserve, and part of the town common where Aborigines might be allowed to build their shacks.

I mentioned this point to the Director of Civil Defence for New South Wales in 1964, saying that from my own observation of these locations they seemed the most likely to be flooded. He stated that this had proved to be the case. In the big floods of 1956, his organisation had had to supply tents for evacuated residents of Bourke, Brewarrina, Collarenebri, Walgett, and Condobolin. The greater proportion of the families to be provided with this emergency accommodation was Aboriginal: no less than 100 at Brewarrina in the February, when fifty-one tents and six marquees were supplied also to Collarenebri, and all for Aboriginal families. Tents were sent for Aborigines to Condobolin no less than eight times between March 1956 and October 1964. Moama and Narrandera had to be supplied with Aboriginal emergency shelter in the middle of 1956. Euabalong was supplied with twenty-five tents in August 1960, and Deniliquin, in three floods in 1958, with twenty-eight, in 1960 with fifty, and in 1964 with fifty-five. That the town services are not planned to cater for the fringe-dwellers was nicely indicated in May 1961, when the town of Armidale was supplied with tents and palliasses to deal with a sudden outbreak of illness on the reserve. The Director had proposed to municipalities and shires that they should have their own emergency supplies of tents.[5] Would such a proposal have been necessary if a substantial number of non-Aborigines had been in similar insecurity?

Aboriginal fringe settlements do not develop where they do by accident. Some western towns have none: at Parkes, for instance, there are three or four families, but so well integrated into the town that few people there think of them as 'different'. One of the factors involved in the growth of fringe-dwellings is the chance of employment: as a convenient place for being 'picked up' by employers looking for seasonal workers (to pick beans and peas, say, at places like Reedy Swamp Road, or Murrays Flat out of Bega): or the group of shanty houses at Enngonia, west of the Darling and due north of Bourke (where the need is for station workers). Or the spot may be strategically located in relation to the route followed year after year in following the sequence of seasonal work, like Yass. (It is interesting that there is a reserve at Yass, so close to the A.C.T., but not within the A.C.T. itself.) There may be special reasons, such as administrative or local government discouragement in the past, for the absence of fringe-dwellers. Aborigines may dwell on a reserve, in self-built housing or in Board houses, or there may be no reserve where it is convenient for them to live.

Beside some towns, as at Wellington, there are both reserve and 'squatter' settlements. In the background there is sometimes a history of dispute with the Board or its representative, leading to movement off the reserve. Another reason for the squatter settlement may be limited facilities on the reserve. People may have moved just across its boundaries to have more freedom, especially as the rules of the stations and reserves made gambling or drinking there offences under the Protection Act and Regulations. When age and invalid pensions were first extended to persons falling within the State definition of Aboriginal, they could not be paid to persons living on government stations; those qualified for them by age or illness

---

[5] Letter of 21 October 1964 from Major-General I.N. Dougherty, Director of Civil Defence for New South Wales (SSRC-AP file).

often moved off, and others, also dependent on the pension or for other reason, followed.

A squatter settlement may increase, or begin, because word has gone out of increased employment or housing opportunities, especially if the town concerned gets the reputation of a 'good' town, where the council is sympathetic and the police reasonable. One example of this, in recent years, has been Armidale, where, partly as the result of publicised local effort, a group of new houses was provided on a site where Aborigines had been camping around the tip, and the area was developed. But here a large fringe was avoided by administrative discouragement. An example of the second case is Condobolin, where new economic developments have attracted new settlers. The attitude of the Area Welfare Officer, the Commonwealth Employment Officer, the town council, the local police (who are responsible for the issue of rations until an unemployed worker becomes eligible for unemployment benefits), are all likely to affect the location of a family on the look-out for house and work. But the predominant reasons are somewhere to live, work, and have access to water, the last being the reason for the high number of riverside dwellings inhabited by people who cannot get homes in town or serviced by piped water.

All this means that there is a subsidiary economy, as well as polity, which forms the daily world of the rural Aboriginal; for what we have been noting in western New South Wales is repeated throughout 'settled' Australia. The inhabitants of this world are more or less at the mercy of officialdom in a way that other Australians are not; and officialdom is a factor determining where they may live. Yet there is a high proportion of families with permanent domicile in or beside a town. This is a moving population but not a wandering one. Statistics quoted later will show that over 65 per cent of rural householders had been living in or beside the same town for ten years or more, though only 22 per cent had occupied the same dwelling for that period. Seclusion from the road is an advantage, since shacks visible from passing cars tend to be the subject of complaint to building and health authorities. An excellent example of a settlement conditioned by these requirements can be found, if one wants to look for it, right in the low-lying land between one south coast town and a small suburb (out of consideration for one's Aboriginal friends, it is not fair to give the location here). The council obviously knows about it, and so do the police; but trees hide the iron houses from the busy road fifty yards or so away. In another part of the south coast, close to one of the large towns, a farmer tried to house his Aboriginal seasonal workers by purchasing old buses from Sydney and having them equipped for accommodation. Although this would have meant improved facilities, his scheme was rejected by the shire council because the resultant dwellings would have been 'visible from the road'.

Government policy, and the attempts by station managers to promote 'assimilation' and good housekeeping by limiting the numbers in Aboriginal station housing, and in Board housing elsewhere, has not been accompanied by a building program likely to overtake the increased demand as the Aboriginal population increases. The size of Aboriginal families indicated in 1964-5 that in the next generation the fringe-dwellers would increase considerably, unless there is a very great increase of housing available. Another trend of course is to get away from the fringe and migrate to the capital, so that some streets of some suburbs form the urban equivalent of the country town fringe area. It might well be that the provision of housing in the city will in the long run make the greatest contribution to the solution of the fringe problem, since there are many social forces directing the young and ambitious to the city. Alternatively, it could be argued that the solution of problems arising from the apparently rapid urbanisation of Aborigines is to get them established in country towns where work is available. Obviously, planning for new housing in *all* areas where economic development is occurring has to be integrated with planning for the inclusion of the Aboriginal into the community and economy of Australian citizenship, with government ignoring local racist prejudice and the usual fears about real estate values.

One of the most interesting examples of the philosophy that all is well, that the Aboriginal is really struggling to be like the whites, and that his squalor indicates his innate handicaps, with careful tuition offering the best hope for him, is that which looks at the town fringe as a 'learning' situation —a stage where the family learns housekeeping before moving into town. The fringe settlement is the disgrace of Australia, with many of the dangers of the workers' slums in African and Asian colonial towns, a place where the family is less likely to learn than to disintegrate completely. Integration into the economy can only come from the kind of government effort which has never yet been made. The spokesmen for Aboriginal rights and the Aborigines themselves are quite right when they select two key requirements—full access to permanent employment, and access to housing that is equal in fact as well as in theory. If this is a matter of millions now, it will be a matter of many more millions two decades from now. The question is already too serious and urgent for central governments to be swayed by the interests and protests of local government authorities which oppose Aboriginal movements into town.

Aboriginal rural and country town housing in 1964-5 posed an interim and a long-range problem. There was urgent need for immediate action to alleviate the situation of families in the worst shacks, which we found to constitute over a third of the total. Then there was a long-range problem of good permanent housing, 'long-range' only in the sense that immediate construction of enough proper houses was obviously impossible.

It is important not to confuse movement to and from seasonal work with a permanent wandering, and not to think of the Aboriginal as on some kind of permanent walkabout. One good reason why a family will accompany the breadwinner to a temporary place of employment, at the cost of the schooling for the children and even worse accommodation than at the place of domicile, is that the dweller in a squatting settlement has no control of the site or the dwelling, so that greater security for the family may be one reason for the family movement. Another, of course, is that work by the children supplements the family income. But the statistics we gathered suggest that these movements are limited and that the family will return to the place where the breadwinner is known, to where he has 'always' lived. The probability is that access to a safe dwelling will prove one important step in family stability, with effects on the education of children and on the tensions and anxieties of parents.

The problem is not simply one of supplying the house or temporary improvements to the shack. It is too easy here to fall into the fallacy of mistaking one part of a complex social problem for the whole. Emergency housing, where there are children, should certainly be supplied whatever the cost. It is clear that there is a danger of settling for the 'transitional' housing to which some Aborigines and many of their friends have been objecting: this must only be offered as a guaranteed interim measure, as the first stage of planned re-housing. No family in this country should be constrained to live in a hovel. Obviously also, there has to be a clear understanding of responsibilities on both sides—government and Aboriginal family. There has to be an agreed program, within which the Aboriginal family accepting an interim improvement to its housing situation (and making a fair contribution towards it) has also the chance of acquiring a permanent home on a site which is convenient. This involves confrontation, of a kind which has seldom occurred, between central government and Aborigines. It will be extremely difficult to organise this kind of discussion until there are local Aboriginal organisations with which governments can deal. It is idle to argue that the Aboriginal can make his application 'like anybody else' so long as most Aborigines believe that they will be discriminated against, and so long as these beliefs continue to be verified by local government, official, and general social discrimination. This is why I believe that the Aboriginal hand must be strengthened by encouragement of corporate bodies at the local, grass-roots level, with provision of government assistance, and with a readiness by central government to hear their requests and to entrust to them responsibility to handle government subsidies and loans for purposes on which both 'Aboriginal company' and government are agreed. Only within such organisations may a leadership and a following develop. Without leadership recognised by the group, there can be no agreement on priorities as between families and projects. For the basic need of the Aboriginal in these situations is not for gifts but for increased opportunity to help himself; and for the strength which comes from combined action to confront the local authority and to win the respect which a majority will be constrained to give to any minority which shows that it is not to be dismissed and disregarded.

The town, not the squatting settlement or the reserve out of town, is the growing point and the focus of economic opportunity. Social integration may be more *obviously* difficult when most Aboriginal families move into town. But clearly, until they do, and others are forced to interact with them, the processes of integration will not commence. On this point central government has to overrule any objections by local government, which should obviously not be heard on such a matter as that of what racial category of Australian citizens may live in town.

Here too is the place for solution of many of the social problems which have been coming as it were to a head in the metropolitan areas. Preference to live in a metropolitan slum may not be so often made if there is a new approach to the situation in and round the country town.

## CONDOBOLIN, 1964-1965

In the mid-1960s, while this survey was in progress, 'freedom rides' organised by Student Action for Aborigines had begun to direct national attention to towns where discrimination was reputed to be more obvious, probably because of the comparatively high proportions of the part-Aboriginal populations. In 1965 Moree had by far the largest Aboriginal station in the State, with over 400 residents; but there were estimated to be more in the other Moree locations, including the much-publicised Top Camp on the Inverell Road.[6] Walgett, also in the north-west, may have had the biggest Aboriginal community in the State, with a possible 600 persons of whom just under 150 were located on the station. The oldest

[6] Long, *Aboriginal Settlements*, pp. 68-72.

institution for Aborigines in New South Wales was the Aboriginal station
at Brewarrina, which was about to be closed down after eight decades.
By early 1966 the families from here and from other river-bank humpies
were to be moved or allowed to move into thirty new houses in what
amounted to a 'conspicuously segregated Aboriginal residential area'.[7]

In this north-western region the social climate was not well suited for
calm assessment during 1964-5. Although it was reputed to have the worst
part-Aboriginal living conditions in New South Wales, the continued
presence of large numbers over long periods indicated that employment
opportunities existed there. As for prejudice and discrimination, the
conditions already described in less publicised towns were quite comparable with those in the north-west. These situations attracted less
publicity, where only a few families were involved. Their dwellings were
often seen only by the persistent inquirer. But the proportions of those
living in some kind of 'social ghetto', and of those living in the town,
would probably be no greater in Moree or Walgett than in towns like
Wellington, or Cowra, or other country towns with no particular
reputation for racial discrimination. In the north-western towns some at
least among the Aborigines were prepared to settle for the current
situation as being the best they could hope for. Things were much the
same everywhere: to stir up emotions only caused 'trouble' and it is
understandable that some Aborigines in the north-west resented the
activities of the 'freedom riders'.

There was little of recorded discrimination at Condobolin. The only
press story we could find was of the refusal of Condobolin Rugby players,
back in 1929, to play against the Boomerang club, from the 'mission'
(reserve); with the result that so many other towns sent offers to play the
Boomerangs that in June 1929 they were 'booked' for seven weeks ahead.
The Mayor of Condobolin had pointed out that the critics had no
knowledge of the facts; that the Condobolin players had not refused to
play against Aborigines, but only against those from the 'mission'; that it
was insulting for critics to assume the presence of a 'colour line' in
Condobolin; that no area in the State had a better record in this respect
(which could well have been true); that tuberculosis was 'prevalent' on
the reserve; and the refusal was a matter of health.[8]

The incident, trivial and long forgotten, remains typical in two
respects. First, there is the readiness of townsmen who consider that they
have no racial 'problems' to deplore the situation in towns with a

[7] Ibid., p. 78.
[8] S.M.H., 20 and 28 June and 3 July 1929.

reputation for discrimination. Second, there is the universal tendency to claim that what avoidance of the Aboriginal group is admitted results from the needs of health. The 'hygiene barrier' has long been part of the jargon, without necessarily implying an active concern with the *reasons* for poor hygiene and for absence of facilities for cleanliness and health. The great increase in standards of material comfort in country-town Australia has made it easier than ever for the townsman (like his American counterpart) to confuse cleanliness with rectitude (Godliness being old-fashioned): to alter the order in the old maxim about cleanliness and Godliness; and to transfer, in the established manner of prejudice, feelings which bear the connotation of uncleanness, disease, and immorality from himself and his family to the group which the 'white Australian' assumes bears the mark of inherent inferiority. Thus does the Aboriginal, like the Negro, serve for white men as the sacrificial victim—not, in this country today, with his life, but only with his happiness and chance of success. So that more of the whites may feel at ease, the Aboriginal must give up hope; he must see his own opportunities and those of his children restricted to what the whites consider Aboriginal talents to justify; he must get used to the fact that his wife will be insulted, that his daughter will be the object of sexual experiment by those who would fear to make advances elsewhere. Otherwise, as the laws restricting his rights are withdrawn, he may consider himself a free man. If he cannot stand this situation in one town, he may try his luck in another, where the same things will happen; or go to the city, where his chance of changing his status will correlate with the prominence of his stigmata—the shape of his features and the colour of his skin.

From Condobolin westward Aborigines seem to have made the usual forced adjustment to the pastoral station, and to have remained in this state of paternal rule until about the turn of the century. But by 1898, when the railway was extended to Condobolin,[9] closer settlement had made the town a centre for wheat as well as wool production. In the purely pastoral days no doubt it had been a convenient point for wandering workers, Aboriginal and others, to be picked up for employment. The next three decades saw the construction of weirs; and then in 1935 the Wyangala Dam, on the Lachlan. The wheat industry was boosted partly by research commenced in 1910. The mid-1960s was a period of rapid

[9] As well as visiting this town we were fortunate enough to have a study of Condobolin (along with one of Aborigines in part of the metropolis) undertaken by Robyn R. Iredale, a geography honours student, who was undertaking a thesis for the degree of Bachelor of Arts at the University of Sydney, in 1965. A copy of her thesis (The Enigma of Assimilation: The Position of the Part-Aboriginal in N.S.W.) is held in the records of this Project.

growth, with new strains of wheat available which withstand dry conditions, and the conversion of about half a million acres from grazing to farming. There was also American investment in cotton growing. In 1965 the town had over 3,000 residents.[10]

The present reserve, of sixteen acres in South Condobolin, was established in 1900. In the following year there were twenty-eight full-bloods and nineteen half-castes recorded for the area. Nine 2-room houses were built by the Board in 1910.[11] It was always possible for police or other officials administering reserves to move away persons who were regarded as bad influences (as it still is).[12] Persons so removed from the reserve tended to remain nearby, in areas convenient to employment and to relatives. Robyn Iredale says that the present Murie settlement, a group of shacks off the reserve, commenced after 1939.[13] Possibly another reason was the former requirement that Aborigines could not receive pensions while living on reserves: by moving a small distance they became eligible. That the reserve population had increased during the depression is practically certain. This seems to have happened on most reserves. Because the police had doubts about the claims of Aborigines to the dole, they could only get rations by moving on to a reserve. But the Murie camp remained small, and in 1948 is said to have had only two tin shacks. In the following year, however, there were eleven.[14]

The Murie was formerly part of a stock route (a common type of fringe site, since the stock route near the town generally has water); it was then controlled by the local Pastures Protection Board. The council had, years before, obtained a lease and divided it into some twenty half-acre and quarter-acre lots, for which rates were set; Robyn Iredale found not only that the Aborigines there did not pay, but that they did not even know what the rates payable were.[15] The Town Clerk told her that 'attempts had been made to legalise settlement on the Murie for many years'. Action by council officers to prevent extension of squatting there does not have to be explained solely in terms of prejudice. Part-Aborigines on the Murie would refuse to pay as a matter of principle. When council officials know that some men living under these circumstances are earning wages as high as some taxpayers, they feel naturally enough that some

[10] Ibid., pp. 56-9.
[11] Ibid., p. 61.
[12] See N.S.W. Aborigines Protection Act 1909-1963, section 8. Note that 1967 is the cut-off year for these three volumes.
[13] The Enigma of Assimilation, p. 62.
[14] Ibid.
[15] Ibid., p. 82.

action to control the situation is necessary. But the background of history and the whole context of race relations is such that each of these issues, at least from the Aboriginal point of view, becomes primarily a racial matter. What may be a matter of principle at the level of council decision may appear arbitrary discrimination at the level of eviction and destruction of an occupied house.

'It is interesting to note', writes Robyn Iredale, who spent some time there and examined the parish maps, 'that both the Reserve and the Murie were located on the lowest land surrounding the town, i.e., on the flat south of the river.' So whilst the town danger level for Condobolin provided that homes and property were above flood level, W.A. Bayley reports that in 1950, 1951, 1952, and 1956

the floods spread across the flat south of the river, covering the Murie and Aboriginal Mission and the people were moved to the Condobolin school and to the hospital hill for shelter. That this location was more than coincidental is supported by information on the low elevation and flooding of many other Aboriginal Reserves and Stations. That is, the latter were established on plots of land that at the time were of little use for any other purpose.[16]

There have been at least six floods since, big enough to require the removal of Aborigines. A local historian states that from 1944 the reserve became a matter for council concern and that during the fifteen years up to 1965, welfare of part-Aborigines had been given 'considerable attention'.[17]

As far as I can gather, [writes Robyn Iredale] this was mainly in the form of gifts of books to the school library; special Education Week celebrations at the school; an annual Aborigines' Day at one of the churches and vague proposals at council meetings to improve housing. For example, 'a proposal to build homes for Aborigines in Melrose Road in 1949 was opposed as aldermen questioned the moral training of the Aborigines, whom, it was felt, it might not be advisable to place among the people at that stage'.[18]

According to her, the council began to relax this tender care for the rate-payers about 1958, since when sixteen part-Aboriginal families moved

[16] *Down the Lachlan Years Ago* (Condobolin Municipal Council, 1965)—quoted ibid., pp. 64-5.
[17] Ibid., p. 65.
[18] The Enigma of Assimilation, p. 65—Quoting Bayley, *Down the Lachlan*. The school referred to was on the reserve, and thereby segregated. The attitude of Condobolin aldermen in 1949 seems to remain basically that of the Australian community as a whole: there is anxious concern in a general way for a solution, provided that this does not involve cost or inconvenience. But this is no more than our own local version of a phenomenon illustrated internationally by the attitude of the western to the poor nation-states. It also illustrates that the Aboriginal is not unthinkingly accepted as an Australian, although the ancestry which is in question may have been established in the country some 40,000 years.

into houses in town.[19] This was perhaps in part due to the activities of a Condobolin Assimilation Committee.

Perhaps this change of local climate had the usual effect in attracting more Aborigines. In July 1964 there were 348. Of these, the 'teacher-superintendent' of the reserve stated that only 68 per cent had been there continuously for the previous year; of the remainder, 27 per cent were 'transients', who would be people hoping to get houses and jobs; and only 4 per cent were classified as 'visitors'.[20] People from both the Murie and the reserve had moved into town houses, and 'many families, though they never gave this as their reason, have come to Condobolin over the last 12 months or so, in the hope of getting a Mission or a Murie house'. The council had been trying to discourage this influx. When a similar thing happened at Armidale, the Board had prevented gross overcrowding of new houses on the reserve by placing an officer in the town. But these people in Condobolin had been attracted by hope, not of a new house but of a reserve house or hovel on the Murie. There were other attractions, of course, including the prospects of employment. The part-Aboriginal population of the town had increased to over 10 per cent of the total. Some were camping in the caravan park; so the council limited the length of a camping stay there. With tents going up on the Murie, it was threatening in 1965 to bulldoze Murie houses when the residents moved out; but families there were 'doubling up' in the houses, with the new-comers ready to take over from their hosts. Robyn Iredale mentions the case of one family which built a new house on the Murie, and hoped to retain it, as the breadwinner had found employment.[21]

I first went out to visit people on the Murie in the midst of a very cold spell in July 1964, and saw there a very clear indication that the council was prepared to go further than destroying empty shacks. A woman with five children had, with her eldest son (she told me) bought £12 worth of timber off-cuts and erected a 'house' with an earthen floor. When I saw it, it was flat along the ground. That the house had been knocked down by the police and health authorities I was able to confirm; they had used a truck to do this. As the house could have been no worse than others on the Murie, this was clearly an attempt to contain the settlement there. The police could have been acting as representatives of the Board, or of their own department in the interests of law and order. That the six dwellers in this home had now moved into the detached 'laundry' of a Murie shack indicated that the action had not advanced the cause of health.

---

[19] The Enigma of Assimilation, p. 66.
[20] Ibid., pp. 66-7.                    [21] Ibid., pp. 67-8.

Inquiries only led one further into a whole tangle of causation. The occupant claimed that her house had been built on land leased by people who had given her permissive occupancy; that she had bought an older house on the site, had it knocked down, and built her own; that she still had to pay water and sewerage rates. I was later informed by a Condobolin clergyman that she was by no means the helpless widow; that she was a known criminal, etc. She appeared to me a determined and able person; and one could see her making the most of any chance coming her way to get shelter for her family. But no matter what she had done, here was being inflicted a hardship hardly necessary in a 'good' town in well-to-do Australia in mid-winter. One could hardly but be moved by the pathetic £12 worth of timber off-cuts, broken in the mud, with the few scraps of old iron. Five children and a woman had had the roof pulled from over their heads, as it were, on an issue of policy.

Here in the midst of Australian prosperity is a situation directly comparable with the fringe of the colonial town of the plural society, where the whites cannot bear too close a view of the slums of the 'natives' and where houses may be destroyed on aesthetic grounds, leaving families with nothing at all. Slum housing, where Aborigines are concerned, is often dealt with as a barrier to 'assimilation'; as a menace to health. The houseless person who shivers in the bush or in someone else's laundry is not such an obvious danger to health; if a family is dispersed elsewhere, at least the obvious barrier to local 'assimilation' is diminished.

The situation was made even more intriguing by the presence on the Murie, in another shack built of the same materials, of a part-Aboriginal missionary, from the International Church of the Four Square Gospel, founded by Aimee Semple McPherson several decades ago, in Los Angeles, and established (originally as the Elim Four Square Gospel) in Australia after her visit in the early 1920s. He was passionately protesting on behalf of the family, and expected himself to be the next victim of the health officer or the police. He had an obvious cause, and had defiantly completed his house *after* the demolition of the other: he was now waiting for his martyrdom.

I was informed later, by a spokesman for his Church, that he got it, just as the woman had. But I remember him well, because he was a brave man in many ways. He had no chance of making a widely known public stand; but he was doing what he could. He came from the far north coast of the State, where the Pentecostal movement in which his Church believes flourishes among the Aborigines. He had been refused entry to the reserve. At that time the refusal must have come from the central office of the Board. Its problem was that of any institution vested with extensive authority over a group of people living under institutional conditions. The Aborigines Inland Mission, already established for many years on the reserve, is not a pentecostal church movement, so that his admission to the reserve could have caused 'trouble', and he was being opposed by the town clergy. Possibly, in the aftermath of a recent Revivalist movement on the reserve, there seemed good reason to avoid such 'trouble'.

But one cannot help pondering on the degree to which this man's position as a nuisance to all kinds of established authority made it easier to condemn and demolish his house, which he claimed also to have erected as his church. I gather from the spokesman of the Four Square Gospel[22] that he has now given up mission work and has returned to rural labouring. His Church, according to this informant, made fruitless representations and protests to the Aborigines Welfare Board, after the demolitions, on his and the woman's behalf. But he was, in his hour of defiance of all authority, with a real cause, a good example of what can happen if a member of an Aboriginal group finds the reinforcement of a dedicated group membership. It was possible for him, perhaps, only in the sphere of religion. He was the only genuine Aboriginal rebel I had met.

That this story would never have been told but for a chance meeting may remind us how much of what happens in the Aboriginal fringe is forgotten by the local communities and the officials. They do not have to remember, for the discouraged or dispossessed Aboriginal drifts elsewhere, or manages to adjust somewhere. His bitter memories ensure that the difficulties facing the administrators with whom he has to deal will remain; and these difficulties in turn are seen as due to typically 'Aboriginal' traits of unreliability and ingratitude, which harden local government attitudes so as to reproduce such situations.

This brief contact with the missionary may serve to introduce a new dimension of part-Aboriginal life. Symptomatic of the status situation is the adherence of large numbers of Christians of Aboriginal descent to religious bodies which make their appeal especially, though not necessarily exclusively, to those of Aboriginal descent. Malcolm Calley and R.G. Hausfeld some years ago described the place of the Assemblies of God among part-Aborigines of the north coast of New South Wales.[23]

[22] Pastor A.E. Banton of Wentworthville, Sydney.
[23] See Malcolm J.C. Calley, 'Race relations on the North Coast of New South Wales', *Oceania*, March 1957, vol. 27, no. 3: Hausfeld's description of the Pentecostal movement at Woodenbong is in his unpublished M.A. thesis of June 1960, Aspects of Aboriginal Station Management, ch. xiv.

This body, and the Church of the Elim, which adhere to the Pentecostal beliefs, had pastors in contact with Aborigines in western New South Wales in 1964. There were Assemblies of God extending from northern New South Wales along the coasts of Queensland at least as far north as Townsville; and J.R. Beckett, in 1963, described the active community of this faith in the Torres Strait Islands.[24]

More active in this western area of New South Wales, from the limited observations we were able to make, was the Aborigines Inland Mission, an old-established body with a training centre at Singleton and a long background of effort among Aboriginal people in all parts of the Commonwealth. The Singleton Bible Training Institute provides a 2-year diploma course for men and women who may enter on signing a 'statement of doctrine'. Those who complete this course, of Bible learning with some subsidiary training, such as English literacy where necessary, may either return home or elect for a further year, which qualifies them for missionary or pastoral work. The Institute also prepares adherents of other churches, and works very closely with the United Aborigines Mission. The latter is regarded as a sister church, and is associated in the production of texts at a printing works established on the reserve at La Perouse.

By agreement with the U.A.M., the A.I.M. does not now operate directly in Western Australia or South Australia, but it does in other States and the Northern Territory. When the A.I.M. was first established in 1905, it was to carry out mission work for other Protestant sects. This was the organisation which established the original Moonah Cullah mission out of Deniliquin. Half a century has seen its emergence as a church in its own right, providing for Fundamentalist worship by Aborigines. The A.I.M. view is that discouragement has been faced by Aborigines attending other churches and that Aboriginal people prefer their separate types of worship.[25] This organisation maintains several churches on stations and reserves; and there was one on the reserve at Condobolin, which had been there since about 1918.

The awakened consciences in Condobolin, and the coming to the town of ministers of other religions who genuinely wished to include Aborigines in their congregations, had led to some interesting tensions in 1964. The Singleton Institute does not give formal training in music, but the young people include several interested in the guitar. Mr. Caddy, a spokesman for the A.I.M., informed me that Aboriginal people prefer 'swinging' tunes

[24] Politics in the Torres Strait Islands.
[25] Information provided by W.R. Caddy, Editor of *A.I.M.*, the journal of the organisation.

for their hymn singing and that they tend towards emotional services. It is not, I think, unfair to assume that this faith puts more emphasis on the emotional process of conversion than upon academic instruction in doctrine, except, of course, for the basic Bible studies. He himself volunteered the comparison with Negro churches in the United States.

Prior to December 1962 there had been a series of Revivalist meetings on the reserve. After one vacation all the children in the school told the teacher there that they had 'turned Christian' in the holidays; and in that year there had been a great deal of activity with house meetings, Christian 'teenager' evenings, Bible study meetings, and the like. The inhabitants were divided on the proposal to instal a television set in the new hall at the end of 1962, some stating that 'TV and dancing' were sins. Eventually the hall was equipped with television by the decision of the people; whether or not with the agreement of the A.I.M. I cannot say.

The reserve people generally described themselves as Church of England, Catholics, or Methodists. By 1964 Church of England and Catholic clergymen were trying to attract the people into their churches in town; and there was discussion of whether a separate centre of A.I.M. worship for the Aborigines who were moving into town houses should be established in town in addition to the A.I.M. centre on the reserve.

The gap between Fundamentalists and those Christians who place more emphasis on education and precise doctrine does not need to be expanded here. The interesting point is that this had become involved with the wider question of the relations of the Aboriginal group with the other people in Condobolin. The idea that the Aborigines needed a separate church of their own when they moved into town—an idea that its opponents who discussed it with me admitted to be held by most Aborigines—was being opposed as contrary to 'assimilation'; the A.I.M. accused of being 'segregationist'. This of course raised a fundamental issue of choice and of rights. Here again was the common assumption that the Aboriginal must conform in his personal choices to the assumptions of what the white majority do. It was schooling before rights, perhaps, in another context. Perhaps religion has been the one area in which Aborigines outside those constrained to live on missions have had unrestricted freedom. They would certainly resent any pressures which seemed to come from the town 'establishment' against their own church. And as for the arguments about assimilation, or integration, it seemed that a group which had depended for consolation on its separate organisations would continue to need them, especially those whose lives are being drastically re-ordered by the movement into town housing.

The sixteen acres of reserve, situated in a swampy bend of the Lachlan, do not appear to have been whittled down since they were first gazetted in 1901.[26] The reserve had been excised from a permanent common on the Condobolin 'Run'. Perhaps this bend in the river had long been occupied by Aborigines, who had adapted here to the station economy.

One of the problems of the Board (and it is common to every State), is the resistance of the local government organisation. Aldermen tend to be vulnerable to pressures from various real estate interests, especially those of the home owners, who will so often object to the idea of having an Aboriginal family next door. These objections are based sometimes on observed behaviour of the most visible groups around the streets of the town, sometimes on mere prejudice and hearsay, generally on fears that entry of the Aboriginal family to the street will cause the value of property there to fall, that the visits of members of the camp community will bring into the neighbourhood the alleged or real violence and drunkenness of the reserve, and so on. These objections tempt central government to settle for an 'assimilation' policy, which involves delay until Aborigines are 'ready' for town life about which they presumably learn on the reserve. They also make it difficult for the best intentioned local government to yield to pressures by the central authority to establish Aboriginal families in town.

Yet Condobolin was changing in 1964-5. From east to west of the continent, there can be found towns where the State government authority has had to compromise, where failure to get blocks for Aboriginal housing in town led to the purchase of land just outside it. One such purchase, at Boona Road, is on the side of town opposite to the reserve and well back from the river. But it is well out of town. (One finds many identical situations and finds them in several States. There is, for instance, a practically identical situation at Gnowangerup, in southern Western Australia.) This may be better sited than the reserve and the fringe area for health, flooding, and the like, but the location both symptomises and tends to perpetuate social segregation. The Boona Road area was also a reserve, of thirty-nine acres; and the Board in 1959 had erected four houses there, apparently beginning a program which was not continued because it became possible in the meantime to purchase town housing lots. Twelve were purchased, in lots of three and four together, perhaps for reasons of costs, perhaps for companionship for the future occupants, but these groupings were spread through the town on both sides of the railway line.

[26] Robyn Iredale, The Enigma of Assimilation, p. 61, and reproduction of Lands Department Survey Map of South Condobolin.

By 1964 twelve families had been selected by the Board to move into these houses. The Condobolin Assimilation of Aborigines Committee, which had been formed a few years before, seems to have played a big role in the change of attitudes which made this possible without the central government overriding the local government.

By the end of 1965 eight households from the reserve and three from the Murie had been relocated in town. The Condobolin Council was planning to relocate families from the Murie, hoping that they would be established on the reserve; but things had not gone that way. Only two of the fourteen Murie families had proved willing to live on the 'mission' (reserve). Placing a family in other accommodation did not mean that a house would be vacant, because families had been 'doubling up' on the Murie. In some cases families who had been waiting in bush shanties hard by moved into Murie houses. Yet all the houses were occupied, since people from other areas came to live at the reserve.[27]

The figures for all Condobolin given in Robyn Iredale's census of July 1965, of 348 residents in fifty-eight dwellings, indicate that the result had been to reduce average numbers per dwelling to six—below the norm for Aborigines in rural New South Wales of just over seven persons. What it was before the moves would be hard to guess, as some of the families had apparently come from elsewhere into Condobolin housing.

Other evidence, given later, indicates that, contrary to some popular belief, as more space becomes available, part-Aborigines do not crowd in irrespective of family ties; that where a family gets more space in the dwelling, the trend is to spread out in it and become more comfortable. In a few cases children who have lived elsewhere are now able to be with their parents, and some families formerly unable to have elderly people with them now do so. It is common for all members of a 3-generation family to share the same dwelling, almost irrespective of the number of rooms and the space available.

Robyn Iredale's figures indicate that conditions on the reserve and the Murie were probably as bad as ever. There were 97 people in twelve houses on the reserve, and 105 in fourteen dwellings on the Murie, giving respective averages of eight, and over seven, persons. Murie people had refused the better housing, washing, and bathing facilities on the reserve because they resented most of the town houses being allocated to 'mission' people. If their houses on the mission were not good enough for the mission people 'we certainly aren't going to live in them'; and they maintained that if they did go there the Board would forget its promise

[27] Ibid., p. 75.

to build eight more houses—that they were 'tired of living on Welfare Board promises'.[28]

This kind of stress *within* the part-Aboriginal population had been noted by anthropologists long before. What might appear on the national scale as no more than social and political trivia affecting a few families in a small country town are repeated so often and so widely that cumulatively they may pose much which is central to the dilemmas in Aboriginal affairs throughout 'settled' Australia. Aboriginal politics remain mainly the micro-politics of local government areas. Fortunately, New South Wales is the one State where this kind of situation has been studied by anthropologists, though sporadically, over a couple of decades. Using Condobolin as our starting point, we can use their work to deepen our understanding.

[28] Ibid., p. 76.

During World War II Dr Marie Reay studied part-Aboriginal society in Walgett and Moree (in the latter, with Grace Sitlington). She saw Walgett in 1944, when the demand for labour had enabled Aborigines to demand equality in wages for seasonal work like shearing and cutting scrub, 'but they are given grudgingly, and the permanent employees are less fortunate'. Although it was illegal to supply liquor to persons of Aboriginal status in those days, employers did so to attract workers. Dr Reay drew a picture of the 'caste barrier' in a country town. Those whites who lived beside part-Aborigines on permissive occupancy of Crown land, and even those who mixed socially with them, she said, tended to be regarded as Aborigines. 'This is an unshakeable belief and applies not only to these whites but also to the immediate neighbours of aboriginal families living geographically within the general community.'[1]

A direct effect of discrimination by the whole community was that of the Aboriginal 'against himself'. John Howard Griffin, writing of the American Negro, describes 'his contempt for the blackness that he associates with his suffering; his willingness to sabotage his [fellows] because they are part of the blackness he has found so painful'.[2]

It is impossible, surely, for anyone who has not been on the other side of the 'caste barrier' to realise what it means to have grown up in a racial minority which the majority have *automatically* assumed, not only in popular opinion but also in the law-making processes, to be inferior;

[1] Marie Reay, 'A Half-caste Aboriginal Community in North-western New South Wales' [Walgett], *Oceania*, vol. 15, no. 4, June 1945, p. 296.
[2] *Black Like Me*, pp. 53-4.

which may still be so regarded in much administrative practice; and where membership of the overwhelming majority is denied, even where the denial comes from a comparatively friendly source.[3] By working amongst Aboriginal people one may gain some idea of what this means, for one may be classified as Aboriginal by association. This helps one to understand the pressures which push the coloured person into the Aboriginal sub-group, and the daily price which must be paid if he cuts himself off from it.

Dr Reay wrote, of Walgett in 1944, that even those whom the townsfolk in general regarded as Aboriginal, but who were not, considered that Aborigines could not possibly be allowed access to alcohol. (They were making a good thing of supplying them illegally.) Most whites in town, she found, did not know the Aborigines. They saw them in town mainly when they were brawling and drunken, assumed that they were 'unclean' in all senses of the term, and places of amusement were segregated. Of the background of employment in the pastoral industry she wrote that 'Thrashing was a common practice in this district until about thirty years ago'.[4]

Even more valuable background to the current situation is given in the study of Moree by Dr Reay and Grace Sitlington, published some years after the end of the war.[5] They described a hierarchy of 'classes' in Moree *Aboriginal* society, with upward mobility depending on the virtues of cleanliness, saving, industry, and regard for material possessions. There was 'social climbing' not so very different from the non-Aboriginal patterns in town. But the attitudes of the highest 'class' to the lowest illustrated the twisting and deep wounding of personality and self-esteem resulting from the 'caste barrier'. Members of the upper 'class' regarded the families in the worst shacks beside the town rubbish tip as 'a disgrace to the town', echoing the words of white people. 'This', wrote the observers, 'is because they are aware that most white people classify all mixed-bloods as "blacks", and fail to distinguish between the various classes of mixed-blood society.'[6] This was 'the final shame ... being "classed as black", being outcastes to the total [white] community'. Theirs was a desperate hope to cut themselves off, somehow to ignore the barrier. 'By adopting opinions which are generally held by white people,

[3] For the story of a white American who had his skin blackened and moved in Negro society, see Griffin, *Black Like Me*.
[4] 'A Half-caste Aboriginal Community', p. 299.
[5] 'Class and Status in a Mixed-blood Community (Moree, New South Wales)', *Oceania*, vol. 18, no. 3, March 1948, pp. 179-207.
[6] Ibid., p. 185.

they minimize the social distance between themselves and the general white community and enlarge the gulf between themselves and the lower class.'[7]

No great changes have occurred since 1948. For the part-Aboriginal in southern Australia, only 'white' society offers opportunity of constructive change. He has no separate future as a social being. If his children are not established in that society he has it on his conscience that he has left them nothing. A Negro said to Howard Griffin that

when he looks at his children and his home, he feels the guilt of not having given them something better. His only salvation is not to give a damn finally, or else he will fall into despair. In despair a man's sense of virtue is dulled. He no longer cares. He will do anything to escape it—steal or commit acts of violence—or perhaps try to lose himself in sensuality. . . .[8]

The upper 'class' was the result of desperate efforts to find a niche in town society.

Their rejection of Aborigines who seemed to them to typify the stereotype which society would not accept was taught to their children. At that time, the school bus for Aborigines was used not to bring the reserve children in to the town school *but to take the town Aborigines out to the reserve school.* Town children were instructed by parents to avoid personal contacts with reserve children; to make sure that their cups and combs were not used by them. The term 'dirty' was applied much as the prejudiced whites used it, to indicate 'unclean, diseased'. These same more ambitious people tried to prepare their children for what was *possible* for them in a prejudiced society by limiting their aspirations to types of employment which whites would allow. They were trying also to train them in how to 'get along' without incurring the risks which might come from offending white people—especially the risk of derision.

To recognise the uselessness of all this effort would be unbearable; and yet it has remained generally true that full acceptance into the 'white' society depends on disappearance of the signs of Aboriginal origin. As symptomatic of deep distress as the striving to keep within call of the white Joneses is the readiness often reported of part-Aboriginal girls to look for non-Aboriginal husbands; for the sake of their children, they will 'get the white blood'.

Only by ignoring the existence of the 'caste barrier' could one regard this 'upper class' as on some sort of ladder leading 'upwards' into white society. People in this group can seldom go further, and the main limiting

[7] Ibid., p. 195.
[8] *Black Like Me*, p. 109.

factor is skin coloration and the shape of facial bones. Most studies of such situations tend to be brief; the position at any one time may be that of a series of families arranged in a hierarchy of classes. But it is unlikely that more than a minority of families which at any time form an Aboriginal *élite* actually remain permanently the 'good' families. Even if parents are sufficiently tough-minded to go through with a life of accepting prejudice, and projecting it upon their less fortunate relatives and fellow Aborigines, it is less likely that their children will be.

To say this is to question all the effort which has been expended by welfare officers and others in selecting and preparing Aboriginal families to move from fringes and reserves into country towns. Much of this effort has gone to ensure that their conduct will be inoffensive to white neighbours; *Aboriginal* adjustment is naturally emphasised by an administrative body concerned mainly with Aborigines. It is simply assumed that somehow or other they will be stabilised by acceptance into the town society. Yet this can come only with changes in the attitudes of the non-Aboriginal townsmen. The 'barrier' has to be breached. This requires, surely, Aboriginal organisation for united pressures, and for united action to obtain equal rights. So long as the 'barrier' remains unbreached there will remain a process of potential Aboriginal *élites* turning back into the life of the groups from which they have tried in vain to dissociate themselves. This may be more likely to happen where the move into town has been the result of arrangements made by government authorities, and the way made apparently smooth and easy. To suffer both white prejudice and the hostility of the part-Aboriginal group takes courage and endurance of no mean order, and a definite purpose. What does appear to happen is that a few families eventually establish themselves; they live lives largely within a small elect group. This may be regarded as part of the general process of moving into more sophisticated areas of the cash economy and society: the establishment, as a kind of residue of those who eventually stay, over those who try to change from the fringe and give up, of a part-Aboriginal nucleus, which eventually attracts others. But in the meantime the Aboriginal population rapidly increases, at such a rate that the residual population may increase.

The position may change over the next generation as increased opportunities for formal education offer the first hope of Aborigines with professional and technical skills. What happens when the first part-Aboriginal medical graduate puts up his plate in a country town? The nearest approach to Aboriginal professionalism in 1965 was that of the pastor of a religious sect which caters mainly for Aborigines. But technical and professional training may offer more than acquisition of wealth and property by Aboriginal businessmen. The importance of high skills can hardly be overrated, because they offer hope of putting Aborigines into positions where they begin to interact with people in the higher ranks of society. An Aboriginal doctor in the country town and hospital will throw the social hierarchy into a nice confusion, present a dilemma to the real estate man; above all, place the issue squarely before the opinion-makers, and in a fashion which makes it impossible to postpone decisions by vague talk about 'assimilation'.

When Dr Reay and Miss Sitlington looked at Moree, Aborigines of the highest 'class' formed a very small group of the total Aboriginal population. Although overtly they had cut adrift from the other Aborigines and were wont to talk pathetic nonsense about 'good families', they mingled with the reserve people for gambling and other social purposes at the weekend. All itinerant Aborigines were at that time sent to the reserve, and one purpose of visits by 'good' families would have been to look for suitable spouses for daughters. Sport, dancing, and funerals brought all Aborigines together. Thus it was the fringe or reserve group which provided wider social contacts. In view of the lasting effects of socialisation in early childhood, it is not surprising that a family which at one time is held up as an example of 'assimilation' may later be found 'back where they started'. Many whites will see this as the 'failure' of less well-endowed persons to 'meet our standards'. When the back-sliders agree, as they often will, they accept the overwhelming evidence of their own inferiority. The scale on which this may happen when there is a special push given by government policy was in 1965 being illustrated by the recent attempts to set up families from Lake Tyers in Victorian country towns.

The process is a more valid indicator of change where the decision has been made by the parents themselves. Such attempted urbanisation is happening on a small scale in country towns all over Australia, and on the large scale (in terms of Aboriginal population) in each capital city. The 'caste barrier' is probably less effective in the great cities, especially for those of light coloration. Human relationships there can be much less personal, and far more of the symbols of social acceptance can in the last resort be bought for cash. Whether the family stays in the metropolis will depend to a higher degree on economic success than where the movement has been into the small country town. It is therefore not surprising that over the last decade there has been increased movement into the capital cities.

Some have justified the 'fringe' as a situation intermediate between the government station and the house in town, seeing a whole process of 'assimilation' in terms of a one-way geographical-social shift. But this is to ignore a very long history of fringe-dwelling, which began when the first tribal remnants were forced or attracted into the economic growing points. Their exclusion from town society has been accompanied by long sophistication in the cash economy. That they have not had much money to spend does not mean that they have not been strongly attracted by material advantage. It is misleading to assume that the part-Aboriginal fringe-dwellers of today are in the cross-cultural learning situation of the first tribal Aborigines who gave up nomadism and sat down round the new points of settlement and began looking into the Australian version of the cash economy and the European world. The fringe-dweller, even in the most remote parts of Australia, does not have to learn to appreciate the material advantages he sees in the town. His background in southern Australia is *not* tribal. The most remote situation from which he might come is from some out-of-the-way government station or settlement; and in so far as this background contributes to his attitudes, these are the attitudes of the institutions.

If the fringe were really part of a great scheme, rather than a sure indication of the breakdown of any effective policy, there would be an extension there of municipal services. It could not be, as it so often is, a slum which has been in the same place for a long time. The fringe is clearly a place where people live because they must. They depend on the town for the services available for employment, and to be near relatives and friends. It is a symbol of frustration, not 'progress', if only because the housing is generally worse than that on the government stations.

People have sometimes come to live in fringe areas because they refuse to accept the discipline of the government station. Sometimes they have been ordered off the station and have had nowhere else to go. The fringe-dweller is not, as the theorists of progression might argue, a simple-minded person anxious to learn through imitation of the people in town. There is much evidence to show that he will react the other way.

Here we are involved in questions of multiple causation, further complicated, as in all human affairs, by the inevitability of multiple and varied responses to the same causes. The Aboriginal family lives in the fringe area partly because there is not enough cash and credit at its disposal to pay for the house in town. At the same time the lack of any chance of investment in real property leads members to dissipate earnings; and saving may seem pointless. Therefore the house remains out of reach.

While some will escape from this dead end situation by a successful move on to a town block, and cut the ties with the fringe-dwellers, others will turn inwards to the activities of the group on the fringe for solace and recreation. Yet others will try their luck elsewhere. Thus the argument that the fringe is a stage in developmental civilisation is a fallacy which flows from thinking in terms of locations, arranged in order of increasing attractiveness from the theorist's point of view. The hard fact is that material success requires money; that men live and raise their families where they can get it most effectively (often where they are known personally to one or more employers). Also involved is a good deal of movement by men without their families, a factor in the breakdown of parental unions. Permanent marriage requires permanent foundations; permanent foundations for a life together of man and wife are expensive. One had the impression, reinforced from other sources, that among part-Aborigines formal marriage ceremonies are relatively unimportant. But there is a good deal of movement with families also, especially in the limited cycles of seasonal work, where the children may supplement parental earnings by assisting in fruit picking and comparable work.

A balm to local and municipal consciences is the popular myth of the walkabout. It is easy to look at the fringe-dwellers as a group of gypsies, here today and gone tomorrow, and for the town council to withhold essential services. In our survey of these situations, as statistics presented below will show, we found evidence of high rates of movement as between dwellings, no less than 25 per cent having changed dwellings in the preceding three months. On the other hand, over two-thirds of the families had been domiciled in the same neighbourhood, i.e. in or round the same town or reserve, *for at least ten years*. It is, clearly, possible for people to live in and round the one town for a long time without attaining the security and stability which it is tempting to assume results from long residence. Since children growing up in Aboriginal homes have the same basic needs for assurance and apparent permanence as others, it is likely that impermanence of the place of abode adds to other causes for lack of confidence. The impermanence of housing is added to the impermanence of father's employment.

Against this background, the fringe settlement hardly seems to be fairly assessed as offering 'preparation' for life in town. To all the uncertainty we could add the effects of these lower standards of housing, the difference in police practices of law enforcement and in what the council requires for health and building practice, the difference of public utilities and services.[9] Jean Lagassé, writing of fringe-dwelling Métis in Manitoba, points out that fringe-dwellers are removed from the social pressures to maintain standards of 'economic, social and moral behaviour' which they tend to maintain in the 'white' town; that public opinion *expects* what are lower standards by its own, and condones them in the fringe as necessary evils. 'People surrounded by inefficiency and disorder' lose hope in their own possibilities: 'in order to find some happiness, the fringe dweller must develop a philosophy of life suitable to his condition ... and the search for happiness in more easily attainable goals'. Finally, the fringe makes it harder, not easier, to establish families in town, since those in town assume that this is the way all members of the fringe-dwelling group live. 'Their concept of what a Métis home looks like is taken from the fringe settlements.'[10]

Admitting that fringe settlements do serve the purpose of 'an asylum midway between the two cultures', Lagassé argues that they can be defended only as better than *distant* isolation. In the Australian settled areas, where there are no comparable vestiges of indigenous culture, they seem equally indefensible. The attempt to disperse them on a piecemeal basis, by sporadic application of local government regulations, merely adds to their worst features of instability. The fringe area has to be established in the minds of townsmen *as part of the town* and part of the responsibility shared by Commonwealth, State, and local government.

There is an interesting sequence of observations, by Marie Reay and Ruth Fink, of the town of Brewarrina. Dr Reay worked there in 1945. Twelve years later she mentioned those who dwelt in 'shacks and humpies in a riverbank camp' across the Barwon from the town, saying that it was made up then of people who had left the Aboriginal station. They had other reasons, going back, says Dr Reay, to early tribal differences, to reject the company of people on the 'Mission' (reserve), but the move to the outskirts of the town was an act of defiance of the white management also.

Most of the riverbank people, having found their taste of 'Mission' life to be not without its bitter flavour, were triumphant at having got away from the 'Mission' when local white opinion, as they judged it, wanted 'the blacks' to be 'classed out nine miles'. Their move to town was, inevitably, no simple expression of incompatibilities and conflict, but also a deliberate rejection of differential treatment.[11]

[9] For this convenient listing of some characteristics of the 'fringe' I am indebted to Jean Lagassé, *The People of Indian Ancestry in Manitoba*, vol. 1, pp. 69-70.
[10] Ibid.
[11] Marie Reay, 'Behavioural Responses to Discrimination. A Supplementary Note', *Oceania*, vol. 28, no. 2, December 1957, p. 111.

This was part of a comment on Dr Fink's discussion, in 1957, of the 'caste barrier' in the same town, a discussion which further develops the point that stresses within the part-Aboriginal sub-group are produced by the discrimination of whites. The term 'caste' was deliberately used to indicate 'a group of people assigned opportunities on the basis of criteria over which they have no control'.[12] The 'establishment' of Brewarrina at the time, she says, maintained rigid exclusion of those with the visible signs of Aboriginal origin—skin colour and features—from social recognition and economic advancement. In Dr Fink's time there, twenty-five part-Aboriginal families, who had established themselves in town, had been trying to cut the ties with people on the station. Their social activities imitated those of the whites. They had a further incentive to deny their relatives on the reserve (often brothers and sisters, whose skin and features offered them no hope of acceptance by the whites), in the certificate of exemption, which gave all the rights of a citizen, but which has since lost its appeal because the right to drink has been extended to all.

Dr Fink described a 'middle' group, more recently moved from the mission into town, sending their children to the town school and beginning to cut the ties with mission society. This perversion of values, and ordering of society on the basis of colour, which tends to split even the nuclear family, indicates how unthinking prejudice may have the gravest consequences. What James Baldwin has called the 'innocence' of the townsfolk's comfortable assumption about colour had produced an Aboriginal surrender. 'For a woman to gain status', wrote Dr Fink 'she must either be light in colour or marry a white man.'[13] She analysed the composition of twenty-five households who regarded themselves as superior; in 48 per cent of the cases, the foundation of a claim to status was marriage to a non-Aboriginal (44 per cent white husband; 4 per cent white wife). But in another 8 per cent of cases the claim was based on marriage of a daughter to a white man. A further 32 per cent had lightly coloured skins. In only 12 per cent of cases was the main basis to claims of high status the ownership of property; it is interesting that in these cases the shade of coloration did not seem to be so important.[14]

This kind of intermarriage, which eventually produces children who are not objects of discrimination, was about all that the concept of assimilation amounted to for most governments until the end of the

[12] Ruth A. Fink, 'The Caste Barrier—An Obstacle to the Assimilation of Part-Aborigines in North-West New South Wales', *Oceania*, vol. 28, no. 2, December 1957, p. 100.
[13] Social Stratification: A Sequel to the Assimilation Process in a Part-Aboriginal Community.
[14] Ibid., Table 1, ch. 4.

1930s and, as practised by Aboriginal administrations, for long afterwards. Aboriginality was the kind of original sin which must be bred out; 'colour' was the sin of the father which would be visited upon the children. Dr Fink showed how the superior 'class' was at the mercy of prejudiced whites and how its assumptions of superiority were based on criteria which were not accepted by the darker and poorer folk on the station who had no chance of 'passing'. Within Aboriginal society, then, this was hardly a 'class', because in judging its members, other Aborigines used the standards of the camp and the reserve. It lacked any kind of social legitimacy and acceptance—either by other Aborigines or by the town as a whole. This kind of striving to 'pass' which leads to preoccupation with skin coloration was the subject of a comment by a very dark Negro to John Howard Griffin, that

... we're old Uncle Toms to our people no matter how much education or morals we've got. No, you have to be almost a mulatto, have your hair conked and all slicked out like a Valentino ... [The white man] *utilizes* this knowledge to flatter some of us, tells us we're above our people, not like most Negroes. We're so stupid we fall for it and work against our own. ... [15]

Even in Aboriginal administration in 1964-5 there were officers still using the service jargon to refer, when describing the Aboriginal population of a country town, to so many of 'high caste' and to so many of 'low' or 'light' caste ('caste' being used in the sense of skin coloration as indicative of degree of Aboriginal ancestry). In practice decisions on rights could be made on this basis. I have heard this kind of reference made in a statement by a government Aboriginal welfare organisation to Aborigines; it arises from non-Aboriginal 'innocence'. Officials will still carefully select the girls with the lighter skins for positions as waitresses in hotels and cafes. Acceptance by Aborigines is, in the main, adaptation to a fact of life. Gunnar Myrdal wrote, in words which can be directly applied to the Aboriginal situation, that 'The American order of color caste has even more directly stamped the Negro class system by including relative whiteness as one of the main factors determining status within the Negro community'.[16]

The whites who maintain the 'caste barrier' tend to explain Aborigines' behaviour as something inherent in the old culture; the more ignorant, as something of a deficiency in the Aborigines' mental equipment. Yet the excesses of drinking, gambling, occasional violence, the instability of the family, the educational backwardness, narrowness of interests, the

[15] *Black Like Me*, p. 43.
[16] *An American Dilemma*, pp. 695-6.

ignorance, and the bursts of defiant alcoholic exuberance, have not as much to do with any known features of Aboriginal culture as with the culture of the bush and the frontier (as Jeremy Beckett has pointed out). Second or third generation part-Aboriginal English (i.e. English which is learned in the part-Aboriginal home where the old vernacular is no longer known, or has left only the occasional patois expression) is of the broadest bush (white or black) Australian, as are the mannerisms and gestures which accompany it. If one might be allowed to adapt to this situation the words of Myrdal about Negro culture in the United States, 'In practically all its divergences [Australian part-Aboriginal] culture is not something independent of general [Australian] culture. It is a distorted development, or a pathological condition, of the general [Australian] culture.'[17] There is something pathological in the 'upper class' Aborigines' bitter rejection of the others; not, one guesses, so much an imitation of the whites' efforts to develop and hold prestige, as to escape derision which meets any degree of conformity to the stereotype of Jacky the blackfellow, Jacky in Aboriginal lore being the equivalent of Uncle Tom in the American Negro tradition.

Dr Fink says that Aborigines remaining on the mission, in reaction against prejudice, tended to live out the part which was expected of them by the prejudiced whites and by their relatives in town. Moreover, there was no incentive to change from the patterns of behaviour which Beckett ascribes to the period when most workers in this part of the country, white or black, formed part of the 'nomad tribe' of hard drinkers. Those of darker complexion remained out of town. Though dark girls might hope to 'marry white', the reverse was rare. This also must have contributed to a state of mind among the men which made drinking and fighting something more than acting out a role.

Saving, and investment in homes and furniture, were part of the status striving by the upper 'class'. This was all to little avail, since the only whites to mix with them were those related by marriage. Out on the mission, men ran the gauntlet of the police to drink alcohol which was then illegal for them; they had to pay more for it; it was, says Dr Fink, a 'symbol of defiance' and a protest. Gambling was also frequent. In the decade or so since, there has developed no widely held concept like the 'negritude' of Africa south of the Sahara or the racism in reverse of the Black Moslems. But the emergence of Aboriginal intellectuals could produce similar ideologies. In the improvident group an educated but frustrated Aboriginal leader may one day find his support, with the

[17] Ibid., p. 928.

Aborigines in the upper 'class' trying to play the role of the Negro moderates.

Improvidence was part of the values of the itinerant workers who first set the patterns of conduct along the frontier. This was the way in which their non-Aboriginal forebears for the most part had dealt with money; and in setting themselves against the careful ethic of saving and 'getting ahead' they were expressing something from the remains of an Aboriginal heritage. Here also was the protest and contempt of the hard-drinking, hard-working frontiersman against the careful clerks and merchants of the town and the greedy 'publican' who was on the receiving side of the bar when the 'gun' shearer called on all present to help him drink out his cheque. They also saw the officials, especially the officers of the law, as the bushrangers' friends saw them: mainly among part-Aborigines today one can find those old attitudes to the police.

How much of the folklore of the bush is of Aboriginal origin? How much of this anarchic view of the world came, not from the early European migrant, but from the society which his coming had thrown into a state of anarchy?

In 1964, a decade after Dr Fink had studied Brewarrina, I was assured by a non-Aboriginal at Condobolin who was active in Aboriginal welfare work that there was no 'colour bar' in town, only a tendency of whites to generalisations, that Aborigines were 'dirty', that they lived in hovels, that they do not wash, etc. There is plenty of evidence that Aboriginal people know that whites think and talk of them in this way; and among other reactions is

an aggressive assertion of low-status; it seems to say 'Look at me—I'm coloured and I'm dirty, drunken, lazy, irresponsible, like they all say—that's my privilege, because I'm coloured—I can do as I like, because that's what they expect of me anyway'.[18]

In 1965 Robyn Iredale found in Condobolin the 'two class system described by Ruth Fink for Brewarrina, and that presented by Marie Reay for Moree, Walgett and Bourke';[19] but the 'upper' class in town, anxiously attentive to home making, thrift, sobriety, and the other middle class values, were not accepted in 'white' homes, except, she says, for some who 'passed for whites'. There were nine of these 'upper class' families, of whom five had made their own way and were not dependent on assistance from the Board. All considered themselves superior to those on the mission (reserve) and the Murie; they 'emphasise their own

[18] Ruth A. Fink, 'The Caste Barrier', *Oceania*, vol. 28, no. 2, December 1957, p. 103.
[19] The Enigma of Assimilation, p. 76.

superiority and justify this in terms of their vastly improved standard of living'. They were wont to criticise both mission and Murie standards of housekeeping, and habits of neighbourly borrowing. Miss Iredale found more co-operation, mutual aid, and in-group solidarity on the mission, and less emphasis on economic independence, which was not surprising, as the Welfare Board, for instance, paid for waste disposal and water. Because their conduct was less obviously an affront to middle class *mores* than that of the Murie group, she regarded them as occupying a position in the Aboriginal social hierarchy midway between the town group and the group on the Murie. Murie people thought of themselves as independent, and as superior to those on the reserve in this respect. But they made no effort to pay rates and felt free to fulfil the roles of the 'different' Aboriginal, with the emphasis on drinking, gambling, and other assertions of the 'freedom' which in their eyes distinguishes them from the subservient group on the mission.

The parallels here with the observations of Dr Reay and Miss Sitlington, and of Dr Fink, do not have to be overemphasised. If these are 'classes' they are such on the very small scale of Aboriginal micro-politics, and exist on a most uncertain basis. Rather do these divisions illustrate how resentment may be discharged within the group itself. Disunity results from attempts to adjust to overwhelming social forces. There is not a reasonable degree of social autonomy, nor sufficient control of property, nor economic opportunity, to make such autonomy possible except as a basis for future dissidence. Some basic autonomy is essential if they are to make compromises and adjustments to the town as a whole. Present disunity cannot endure indefinitely; and education may hasten the process of Aboriginal unity in an Aboriginal cause.

Dr Reay referred, in 1949, to a 'pathological condition of disequilibrium' reflected in two sets of relationships.[20] The first is that with white Australian society; rejection by that society *as a whole* has meant that Aborigines cannot easily pursue goals in common with others. I have already referred to the man who impatiently remarked that World War II 'was nothing to do with us'. The second set of relationships she defines is *within* Aboriginal society, where there is continuous conflict between the in-group values and those of the Australian community as a whole. Some of her illustrations here are still most relevant. A belief in education clashes with the value of the child's earnings in seasonal work; ambition to 'make a home' and 'get on' clashes with the demands of sharing and

[20] 'Native Thought in Rural New South Wales', *Oceania*, vol. 20, no. 2, December 1949, p. 112.

kinship; European sexual *mores* with those of the Aboriginal group (where they may conform quite strictly to the old Aboriginal *mores*, so far as these remain possible and can have meaning).

I do not think that anyone has posed the dilemma of the Australian fringe-dweller quite so well:

> The strongest integrative force is the consciousness of the very factor that determines disharmony—common membership in a rejected minority ... Resentment of government interference and of local forms of discrimination is fused with an historical resentment of the white man's usurpation of their land ... The mixed-bloods value European goals, but if they direct their lives consistently towards them they must disperse ... and be slowly and painfully absorbed ... as individuals. The 'drifting' and 'shiftlessness' which observers deplore ... can only be overcome if they cut themselves adrift from the coloured community, where the casual borrowing and sharing and the emphasis on gambling make these qualities inevitable. They look forward to a future which promises loss of identity, but delay this future by clinging to their identity to give themselves some measure of solidarity and security.[21]

The Aboriginal who asserts that he is 'as good as the next man' has often been regarded as a 'trouble-maker', for he upsets this adjustment.

Dr Fink has written of a part-Aboriginal in permanent employment in a town in Western Australia which she does not name, but which I guess to be Mullewa (and after this lapse of time, the guess surely can harm nobody, especially in view of the likelihood that the case has long been forgotten by the whites). He began to make such pronouncements, and to protest against the far from unusual discriminations of the town. Public opinion, which had approved and accepted him in his role as a 'good' Aboriginal, now turned against him; he lost his permanent job, began to drink more heavily, and soon was playing the role of the feckless Aboriginal.[22] No doubt the innocent folk of Mullewa reflected that the compulsive drive to go walkabout had undermined his efforts; that the half-caste inherits the worst 'blood' of both racial groups; that time must be given for such morally and intellectually limited personalities to 'evolve'.

Dr Malcolm Calley, in the late 1950s, found that Aborigines on the far north coast of New South Wales divided whites into two categories—'those who are "good to" and those who are "not good to" Aborigines'. But being 'good' in this context meant only

> a willingness to suspend the cruder aspects of segregation [which] the Aborigine accepts ... as a boon, as a graceful surrendering of rightful privileges. Very few claim

---

[21] Ibid., pp. 117-18.
[22] *The Changing Status and Cultural Identity of Western Australian Aborigines. A Field Study of Aborigines in the Murchison District, Western Australia, 1955-1957.*

such treatment as a right, and the few who do are considered 'bad types' by the white community, and sometimes suspected of 'Communist sympathies'.

Proper behaviour, with whites, was 'keeping out of trouble', he says; and only one family was noted for the fact that its male members regularly 'got into trouble', for an attitude expressed by one of the young men when he told Calley that 'my brothers know how to talk to white people, they do not talk up to them like the other people round here do'.[23]

Resentment against the New South Wales freedom riders was due to the same anxiety about questioning a *status quo* in which 'everyone is happy'. Nor should one discount the arguments that some part-Aborigines were resentful of having a situation disturbed in what they regard perhaps as a 'good town' where there is at least employment, and little tyranny or interference so long as the coloured people 'know their place'. They feared that the whites would take a harder attitude when the 'freedom riders' had gone: the opening up of the baths, of admission to the saloon bar or to the higher cost seats in the cinema show are not as important to them as their chance of getting, through local public servants, the social service benefits to which they are entitled, nor as the attitudes to them of the police or (especially) of employers, and the chance to work in types of employment where there is no effective supervision of working conditions and wages by trade unions. Especially they had to consider the attitude of the municipal or shire council, which can use health and building regulations to make it impossible for them to keep their dwellings, where they have access to employment, water and other necessities, where they are known to police and the Employment Officer. The first may issue them with rations for the first couple of weeks out of work, and they must depend on the Employment Officer for unemployment benefits.

The best argument for freedom riding by young people is that any small gains in bringing Aborigines into closer contact with others gives them the chance to interact. Housing, sport, use of public facilities are already theirs by *legal* right; if in some cases prejudice becomes more overt, some non-Aborigines may learn by having to appraise the situation for the first time. The proliferation throughout the nation of local bodies to promote Aboriginal welfare is an indication that much of this is going on; although one has to admit that such bodies are often ineffectual, they have played important roles in some towns. That the university students of at least one State have gained this first-hand contact with the country

---

[23] Malcolm J.C. Calley, Bandjalang Social Organisation.

town Aboriginal group is of some real importance. Let us hope there is a great deal more freedom riding; and much more rocking the boat!

If the Aboriginal does not openly rebel, he might conceivably hide his attitudes, except for the expression of them which is possible in the small Aboriginal group. Covert resentment is no less consuming for being hidden from its objects under the mask of 'apathy'. Outward apathy and inward tension can easily enough go together. The actions of such persons in this kind of stress, especially the males who do not have the outlets available to the women in their child-bearing and raising, will conform to the *mores* which the group professes, for they are cut off from the stimuli which could give them a deeper understanding of their situation and of the concept of an Aboriginal cause. They lack the education necessary to articulate their case in terms which may enforce the attention of the opinion-forming national leadership. They have to accept the general view of themselves as the truth; but they protest by taking to extremes the action expected of them. When the intellect is entrapped in the racist illusion, there is no hope that life can hold anything better.

Men under such circumstances make the best of what they have. Jeremy Beckett has stressed the attractions of the free life without responsibility, especially to the men; they are freed because they are fulfilling a role assigned to them by society and are able to follow every momentary whim. This in turn creates conditions of insecurity and enmity within the Aboriginal group. Disorder is expected on the fringe settlement, which attracts disorderly persons looking for a suitable environment. Here they will come to get women, to drink to excess, to fight with friends and enemies; and here with them will come the white hangers-on who are always ready to capitalise on the poverty and misery of others. The man who has his family in a house which he does not own has little chance of dealing with aggressive drunken people and others having a 'party' on what should be his front lawn: he will have no right to order such persons off his land, as he does not own it. He may try to get a house in town so that his children 'have a chance', and grow up away from this disorder.

Such a man will often be attracted by a Christian sect which stresses in its teaching that there is little of value in this world: that he is 'being tried'. He may, from his own experience, accept the dominant view on colour, since the disorder from which he tries to escape is created by coloured people. His resentment will be diverted to these Aborigines as secondary objects. By them, he is considered 'too flash' to acknowledge his proper obligations. His conformity is considered to be 'crawling' to the whites. There is deep resentment when he denies his own kin. The great interest in kinship helps to ensure that his reputed preference for his own advancement over duty to kindred is widely known.

The local part-Aboriginal group lacks effective social controls, even to support a member against the whites. The power to deal with the nuisance or the criminal has been taken over by the instruments of the State. As the group is thereby saved from the most serious threats, and as in the main its members have little to lose, resentment can find some expression in the support of *any* rebel against authority, at no special risk. The choices open, therefore, are to put up with the drunken nuisance around the 'camp' or to be criticised by other Aborigines.

# PART-ABORIGINAL
# RELIGIOUS EXPERIENCE

Part of the complex of micro-politics in and round Condobolin was a degree of religious non-conformity by Aborigines. Religion is conspicuously the area of freedom in the secular state. This Aboriginal non-conformity suggests a tendency to look towards institutions of their own or in which authority may be exercised by persons with dark skins. That Aborigines should adhere in large numbers, in so far as they adhere at all, to sects of the Fundamentalist type is also suggestive of a need for escape from the conditions of the material world. The comparison, by a spokesman of the A.I.M., of his church with those which flourish among the American Negro communities was suggestive in this respect. Equally so is the tendency to religious exclusiveness and the wish for a church of their own, as an institution apart from those of the whites. Of the Pentecostal movement on the north coast of New South Wales, Calley wrote that 'There is no doubt that the feeling of worth that membership in this movement confers is in part a reaction against the inferior status assigned to them by the whites'.[1] It is tacitly accepted, he says, that 'though the whites have all the good things of this life the Aborigine can expect to be compensated in the next'; like Lazarus, he 'will look down from Heaven and exult in the torments of the damned'. The first shall be last and the last, first; the Aboriginal 'is the most beloved of God'.

Christian sects which encourage their adherents in glossolalia and other physical symptoms of ecstasy may have something in common with the cult movements of Melanesia. Both tend to be found where power to

[1] Malcolm J.C. Calley, 'Race Relations on the North Coast of New South Wales', *Oceania*, vol. 27, no. 3, March 1957, p. 205.

control has been held by an apparently unsympathetic authority which is not regarded as sharing the values of the group. The activity of cult or sect rectifies the balance and restores, if only in imagination, a relationship considered proper. In parts of Australia so affected, as well as in New Guinea, the balance to be restored is that between white men and coloured.

'On the far north coast [of N.S.W.]', writes Calley, 'as elsewhere in Australia, all secular power and authority is in the hands of white men (station managers, welfare officers, policemen and employers) ...'.[2] Moreover, the sect as an institution provides in its regular meetings and activities an area for leadership where the white man does not operate, or at least only through the occasional missionary.

Religion provides the only avenue to leadership among the Bandjalang. Within the Pentecostal sect an Aborigine can achieve status and authority and make decisions without reference to white outsiders. Over his religious life the administration can exercise only very limited control ... From this position of strength the religious leader, or even the rank-and-file sect member, may feel himself able to do what Aborigines never do. In a dispute with the [Aboriginal] 'Station' manager the Pentecostal man can count on the support of other pentecostals, who see him ... as being persecuted for the sake of Christ [and] ... the manager as a minion of Satan, and pray loudly and openly that the devil be cast out of him.[3]

Pentecostalism seems bound to spread more widely if Aboriginal aspirations rise and the gulf between their living and educational standards and those of non-Aboriginals remains. At Condobolin, members of the more widely accepted ministries were well aware of its extending influence. By 1964-5 the movement was winning Aboriginal converts out through Armidale, Guyra, Tingha, and across the north-west of the State. Their activities had, as in Condobolin, aroused the attention, perhaps the effort, of the sects which are considered more orthodox in the general community. One Catholic father had been working intensively among Aborigines in this north-west area; the Ministers Fraternal in Armidale had been stimulated.

One elderly lady, living on a reserve close to a north coast town, made a significant comment, which may help to account for this. She claimed that other religious organisations catering especially for the Aborigines 'cut people off' from non-Aboriginal Christians, that they tended to think of separate Aboriginal churches, but that in the Assemblies of God, non-Aboriginal ministers and Aborigines were equal. She had an especially

[2] Malcolm J.C. Calley, 'Pentecostalism among the Bandjalang', in Marie Reay (ed.), *Aborigines Now*, p. 56.
[3] Ibid.

poignant problem of identity. Her mother had been a servant in the home of her father, who was already married with children; the father acknowledged her in spite of his family and town opinion, and maintained her. But she had never found acceptance in town. She said that although she had had to come to live on the reserve she could not accept the interests of the people there as her own. She had found acceptance by non-Aboriginal persons, with a recognition of human equality, she said, only in multi-racial worship and fellowship of the Assemblies of God. What else, she asked, had the person in her situation to turn to, except alcohol? When she turned in desperation to God, and sought identity in the supernatural realm, she experienced, in common with non-Aboriginal fellow-worshippers, the emotional release of speaking in tongues, and the 'supernatural baptism without water'.

Dr Calley described how the Pentecostalists of the far north coast reconciled what remains of Aboriginal belief with Christianity. From time immemorial Christian missionaries have dealt with the pre-Christian hierarchy of gods and spirits as evil and representatives of the devil. The Aboriginal Pentecostalism he describes[4] resembles the Melanesian cult in identifying the traditional creative and other deities with members of the Christian hierarchy. R.G. Hausfeld found at Woodenbong Station that adherents of the station Pentecostal church included some elements of Aboriginal tradition in the beliefs professed, reconciling Aboriginal with Christian creation myths.[5]

This reinterpretation of the Christian myth so as to assert the value of the Aboriginal heritage, and the attempt, in a limited way, to reject 'white' modes of conduct, is the limited reaction of a powerless and tiny minority. The European heritage has been too well established, and the discouragement in attempts to adhere to Aboriginal ways of too long standing and too complete for attempts to change the world with new ritual. All that remains is to work for a special place in heaven, and to find places of honour in the overwhelming mythology of the white man, for those Aboriginal spirit figures that are remembered. Where the old culture has been hopelessly lost, this reinterpretation in terms of Aboriginal myths cannot happen; but other changes can, including adherence to sects which are obviously in disfavour of most of the whites. Something analogous to the emotional extremes of some Negro sects could be in the process of developing. It is perhaps ironical that the descendants of people who resisted the Christianising process for so long should be revealing

[4] Ibid., p. 52.
[5] Aspects of Aboriginal Station Management.

interest, to the extent that they do, mainly in sects which are least in favour among the middle class whites who provide the models for the 'assimilation' policy.

Hausfeld describes the ban on 'worldly pleasure' for the faithful—drinking, gambling, smoking, films, secular songs, organised sport, and other activities were banned. Aboriginal songs and corroboree dances were not. A breach of the ban was 'backsliding'. This type of Revivalist movement is of course by no means limited to Aboriginal groups. What is significant is that *separatist* Aboriginal Christianity seems generally to take this form. Among those who were 'saved' on the Condobolin Reserve, the most publicised sins included 'the drink', 'smoking', 'going to the pictures', 'the dance', etc. A breach of the ban was 'backsliding'. 'I used to be a Christian, but I took to the dance.' ('Sinful' dancing seems to be the secular dancing of the 'whites'.)

This tendency to seek a new area of freedom in religion practised in their own way, and uniting people over wide areas, for what amount to festive occasions was subject of comments by Dr Ruth Fink, who described religious occasions at Brewarrina in 1954. Those who were not 'Christians' by the standards of the group (then those of the Aboriginal Inland Mission in this area) went to the rodeo; the Christians went to the 'convention', where both Aboriginal and non-Aboriginal preachers were heard in a large bough shelter specially built, with groups attending from Quambone, Gulargambone, and Bourke. A decade later, there were similar observances, with the same emphasis on emotional 'conversion', and against those sins which may offend the middle class of an Australian country town, and which restrict saving and 'getting on'—

drinking, gambling, wasting money, and swearing. The lesser sins, equally forbidden for a Christian, are dancing, singing popular songs [popular tunes for hymns are a different matter.—C.D.R.] going to the picture show or to entertainments such as boxing, rodeo, or football. Any dark person who drinks or gambles is not a Christian; likewise any white man, even if he be a clergyman, is not considered a Christian if he plays cards. [6]

Perhaps the observances of the Aboriginal Inland Mission represent an older and more conforming system of religious belief than those of the Assemblies of God. There are no statistics of church affiliation by Aborigines, but it is probable that church-going people are in a considerable minority, one that could easily be increased by increasing social distance between Aboriginal and the general society, especially if there is no rapid progress in education. In the meantime, the breach between

[6] Social Stratification: A Sequel to the Assimilation Process in a Part-Aboriginal Community.

those 'saved' and others may form yet another cause of tension, and may become a factor in the micro-politics of Aboriginal society.

There is of course nothing special to the Aboriginal in this. Where frustration has been widespread because of the gap between aspirations and the conditions of life, at all times of great stress in history men have sought for the quick transitions to a better world, or for a 'way' to change this one and have heaven on earth; and sought it, in desperation, in the realm of imagination. James Baldwin has expressed the effects of social crisis on one young Negro boy, and the escape through conversion.

The summer wore on, and things got worse. I became more guilty and frightened, and kept all this bottled up inside me, and naturally, inescapably, one night, when this woman had finished preaching, everything came roaring, screaming, crying out, and I fell to the ground before the altar . . . with no transition, no sensation of falling, I was on my back, with the lights beating down into my face and all the vertical saints above me . . . it was as though I were yelling up to Heaven and Heaven would not hear me . . . utter disaster was my portion. Yes, it does mean something—something unspeakable—to be born, in a white country, an Anglo-Teutonic, antisexual country, black. You very soon, without knowing it, give up all hope of communion . . . The universe, which is not merely the stars and the moon and the planets, flowers, grass, and trees, but *other people*, has evolved no terms for your existence, has made no room for you, and if love will not swing wide the gates, no other power will or can. And if one despairs—as who has not?—of human love, God's love alone is left. But God—and I felt this even then, so long ago, on that tremendous floor, unwillingly—is white. And if His love was so great, and if He loved all His children, why were we, the blacks, cast down so far? . . . Over me, to bring me 'through', the saints sang and rejoiced and prayed. And in the morning, when they raised me, they told me I was 'saved'.[7]

That the question as to God's mysterious ways and purpose had occurred to the Aborigines was indicated by a short statement I heard in 1965, from an elderly Aboriginal man from the north coast of the State. The occasion was a conference of Aboriginal people from all over the State, held in Sydney. The old man, dignified and well-dressed, called for 'a glass' (spectacles), read a text from the Bible, and then went on to explain that the Aborigines had sprung from three brothers, all descended from Abraham, who had sailed into Clarence Heads in a sailing ship; and that Abraham would return in this generation to the same place. 'All this affliction', he stated, 'is for our experience and to test us.'[8]

[7] James Baldwin, *The Fire Next Time* (London: Michael Joseph Ltd; New York: Dial Press. Copyright © 1962, 1963 by James Baldwin), pp. 33-4. Reproduced by the courtesy of the author and the publishers.
[8] Speech given at 1965 conference organised by Australian Aboriginal Fellowship, Building Workers' Industrial Union rooms, Sydney.

I do not wish to imply at all that the attention he got was any more than politeness to an elderly man, especially as the delegates were a sophisticated and quite impressive group of Australians, well aware of the need for political action. But the facts remain that Aboriginal Christianity is an important dimension of Aboriginal life; that Aborigines are poor and lack education; and that the emotional religious sect, which sets out to create a whole acceptable environment of activity and belief, serves the same purpose for them as it does for others who are poor and deprived. It is also true that some of these sects, at least in some areas, attract mainly Aboriginal adherents. The idea of black skin as a 'trial' inflicted by God I have found among Aborigines I know personally, especially those who have determinedly established themselves among the whites—and whose lives involve daily reminders of their racial origin. There was an account in the journal *Zaire* years ago, by a new missionary to the Congo, who found that his flock had long accepted their descent from Ham, and the colour of their skins as a special punishment passed on, a mark put upon them by God. When he insisted that this was not the case, they were even more deeply disturbed. 'Why, then, has he inflicted upon us these black skins?'

The concern among non-Aborigines at Condobolin with what had been happening in the realm of Aboriginal religion may have been in part due to the novelty of such active exercises in this part of Australia, since according to Dr Beckett, who has worked for years in western New South Wales, there has been little general concern with religion since the decline of true Aboriginal culture.[9] Yet the process of evangelisation can be very rapid; and the presence of a Four Square Pentecostal part-Aboriginal missionary on the Murie in 1964 may foreshadow bigger things. With ministers of more orthodox churches proclaiming the truth of speaking in tongues, resistance from the divided religious establishments could be undermined. Verging on this western region is a long-established Four Square church in Narromine; both this and the Assemblies of God are in Orange; and the latter in both Parkes and Peak Hill; there have been missions from one or other to several centres west to Wilcannia. It is an interesting point that the Four Square missionary on the Murie in 1964 had come originally from among the Bandjalang of the far north coast.

[9] See 'Kinship, Mobility and Community among Part-Aborigines in Rural Australia', *International Journal of Comparative Sociology*, March 1965.

The difficulties arising from attempts to establish more Aborigines in town houses have for some years been preoccupying authority in every State and have been a cause of controversy all over 'settled' Australia. Aldermen who represent the local government wards concerned are likely to avoid this by opposing change.[1] For example, in the Victorian town of Drouin, in 1958, a non-Aboriginal couple brought into town, and established temporarily on a block they owned, an Aboriginal family which had been living on the bank of a creek eight miles from town. The press reported that residents in the street were divided. Some 'didn't mind' but two property owners did so, sufficiently to have their names used. 'Many householders' were said to be considering protest against the scheme of the Buchanans, who owned the land and subsequently sold it to the Welfare Board which was negotiating with the Housing Commission. 'We definitely don't want Aborigines here', said one who was reported as an 'ex-serviceman'. 'Most of us paid big money for our land and houses and they would not be worth a cracker if Aborigines moved into the street.'[2] But move in they did, with some others; and two years later the same street was being quoted in the press as an example of neighbourly relations between Aboriginal and other families. 'I want my grandson to grow up like a white child . . . For the first time in their lives

---

[1] For a good example of this aldermanic attitude, even in the City of Sydney, see *S.M.H.*, 25 June 1966. The City Council had refused to allow the Foundation for Aboriginal Affairs to use Redfern, Waterloo, and Alexandria town halls for dances, 'following complaints by residents of rowdy scenes outside'. The Foundation pointed out fairly enough that noise in the streets was a matter for police action with the individuals concerned.

[2] *Advertiser* (Adelaide), 24 September 1958; *Herald* (Melbourne), 25 September 1958.

he and my younger children have a future', said one woman who had come there from the riverside shacks at Mooroopna. The neighbours (the same family whose head had led the protests two years earlier) 'could not be kinder'.[3] There is no indication in the later report of what had happened to real estate values in the street.

Also in 1958, the Wade Shire Council had a problem at Griffith, which involved a tenancy in the Kenna Avenue residential area. The building inspector advised the council that the prospective tenant had been 'especially selected' by the Aborigines Welfare Board and held a 'citizenship card', i.e. had been exempted from the special laws then applying to Aborigines. A councillor (who, one might guess, represented the ward in which Kenna Avenue is located) objected that 'my concern is the congregation of these people. You know what Aborigines are. You could count the best part of a dozen of them in front of the Hotel Griffith tonight.' The building inspector stated that the Board had 'made it clear' to the family concerned that 'no congregating would be allowed and drunken orgies strictly forbidden'. A nicer illustration of the level of discussion, and the conformity of the prejudice to the text books on the subject, could hardly be found. The council decided to defer its decision on whether an Aboriginal family could live in Kenna Avenue. The shire president's suggestion that a house should be built for the family on the Aboriginal reserve illustrates a politician's desire to avoid awkward issues.[4]

Jean Lagassé tells how, an Indian family having placed a deposit on some land for housing in a Canadian town, the citizens brought pressure to bear on the seller, who refunded the deposit. The research worker who reported the case was told by a leading citizen, 'We do not have any Indian problems in town because we know how to deal with them'.[5] This view extends far beyond Australian country towns, for this is precisely the argument for White Australia. Canadian municipal authorities have at least a selfish economic reason for it—that an increase of poor people may involve increase of *local* taxation for social services. This is not so in Australia. Yet what happens in the microcosm of the country town illustrates the essential aspects of the great Australian racist mirage: that we can avoid racial 'troubles' by externalising them. The councillors of an Australian municipality who believe this are essentially *en rapport* with national policy, so often expressed as 'We do not have a [colour] problem, because we know how to deal with it'.

[3] *Herald* (Melbourne), 12 December 1960.
[4] *Age* (Melbourne), 9 October 1958.
[5] *The People of Indian Ancestry in Manitoba*, vol. 1, p. 167.

The result of such refusal to see the whole of an issue and of concentration on a part of it is to postpone and possibly intensify future 'trouble'. For the nation, foreign affairs acquire all the additional tensions of racism. For the town, deferment of equality and integration of housing mean increased costs and other difficulties for the future, to which the current United States inter-racial tensions have obvious relevance.

Here we have a national prejudice operating on national and on local scale; but it is one and the same thing. Nor, in a country where the government is chosen by popular election, is it surprising that so few politicians will openly affront popular prejudices. To a considerable degree a politician has to pay lip service to popular illusions to get and to hold his position, even where he does not share them. There are two main types of prejudice relevant in the cases where Aboriginal families are rejected from a town or a street.

The prejudiced personality, as defined by Allport and others, exhibits a form of emotional instability; he *has* to have some people to despise because he needs to feel superior, to 'belong' in a recognised hierarchy of worth and status, to conform as well as to belong. He suffers from a form of mental illness; and when he comes to deal with Aboriginal people he is not likely to be influenced by logic. It has often happened that such a person occupies a position (such as Town Clerk) where he can vitally influence the situation, misrepresent the facts to councillors, or use their ignorance of the situation in other ways to meet his own needs. One such person may often provide the leadership in cases of discrimination.

But ignorance about Aborigines, or any other group, may be the less secure ground for prejudice in many cases. We all to some extent believe what has come down to us through the folklore; and many of us have neither reason nor stimulus to question such assumptions. For instance, I have often been asked by well educated persons whether Aborigines have the mental capacity of others; the questioners had never applied what they know very well about human intelligence to this special case. Where prejudice is based on this kind of ignorance, the best chance of allaying it is through neighbourly contact—although prejudice may be so definite that this may simply increase it. It applies both ways: many Aborigines assume that *all* whites are overbearing and untrustworthy.

Yet there have been occasions when reception of Aborigines in town has been almost enthusiastic. Thus when the Victorian Board was building eight homes at Orbost, in 1961, a special committee was formed to assist the Aborigines, who had come from Lake Tyers Station, to adjust.[6] But

[6] *Age* (Melbourne), 17 November 1961.

the families who went there were stated to have been 'selected'; it is possible that later developments might indicate resentment for having been 'forced' to leave Lake Tyers.

Nearly every town which is convenient for seasonal workers to live and spend their money in will at least have a fringe settlement. Yet in one of the 'best' areas in all Australia we found in 1965 an important country town where Aborigines spent their money but where they could not find housing. Wallaga Lake, an Aboriginal station, was situated far enough away to keep them out of town—and out of regular employment. There was an interesting situation in 1965, in that Aborigines lived in shanty dwellings in Mumbulla Shire (which surrounds the Municipality of Bega) but spent their money in Bega. It was not surprising that the shire wanted Aboriginal housing established in town, as it faced all the health and other problems of shanty dwellings which the town of Bega was avoiding. Sporadic and seasonal work was to be found on the vegetable farms round Bega: on and round these farms Aborigines lived wherever the farmers would allow them. The worst shanties seen were at Murrays Flat and Reedy Swamp Road, though within a small area the conditions varied greatly. Before blaming the farmer for the conditions on his farm, it is only fair to remember that he always has the alternative of sending the family away; that in most cases checked he was not charging rent, although some farmers were refusing, according to the Aboriginal tenants, to allow men to work elsewhere, *even though it was the off-season for picking, and he had no regular work for them.*

One man who had nine children, his wife, and her father in a shed, said: 'You have to do the pickin' to live 'ere. We used to have a house under the mountain out there, but the floods cut us off and the road was no good.' In this particular case, the man was allowed to work elsewhere in the off-season and had taken a job with a 'battler' on a farm out near his former home. His reason for moving was that he had six children of school age and some of them qualified for high school; all were going to school in Bega. The shed was actually a cow-bail with one enclosed dairy room when we first saw it. Soon afterwards it had been enclosed; but for the first bitter months of winter the wind had howled through this family on their cold concrete floor. The enclosing had been done by the farmer, probably at his own expense. Even the furniture had been left at the other house.

The farmer pointed out that housing is a government responsibility; that he supplied the iron for the cow bail, and had done what he could. It may have been compassion, or it may have been an investment, to let the large family stay there, at the cost of criticism from the health inspector and others; the children, their mother said, picked beans 'in the holidays'.

Nearby was a large family of bean pickers in the off-season. Here the home was dominated by the typical indestructible Aboriginal grandmother, with two daughters, one resident son-in-law, and thirteen children; all go picking in the season, including the old lady, but her task these days was to mind the young children. The roof was of holed iron, the walls inside of cardboard, mostly covered with old iron outside; two of the six 'rooms' had wooden floors, There was a kerosene refrigerator, which one of the farmers told me he can get these days from the sale of 'trade-ins' in Nowra for four or five dollars. No light or water was laid on; the 'girls' carried the bath water, I was told, from the creek two hundred yards across a paddock. Washing was done at the creek, to which clothes, buckets, and tubs were carried.

In a small shed close by, of about 150 square feet, without internal divisions, was a woman with three children; her husband was working elsewhere. A large open shed, also nearby, was occupied by a young couple and their baby and five other people, including an age pensioner and his wife; all were related. Half the shed had been floored roughly by the use of round timbers as cross beams; the other half was bare earth. On the bare ground was a fire, over which cooking was done in a drum. Outside, when we first went there, the young couple played with their baby on some canvas on the grass; as we went over, I saw one of the children in the cow bail being smacked by the devoted mother for licking spilt food from the old concrete floor; in both cases there was real devotion to the children. The old pensioner said: 'I had just moved into a house at Tilba Tilba. The health inspector came and moved us out.' The young man said: 'We were in a house at Beauty Point. Councillor —— came with the health inspector and we had to move. So we came here.'

With me was a part-Aboriginal friend who had spent his boyhood in the Boys' Home for Aboriginals at Kinchela, near Kempsey; the young father in this wretched shed had been there with him, and a grim background it must have been in some ways. They exchanged reminiscences— of how they had looked at the world going by along the road outside, and longed to be out there; but now, said the young man, he looked back at those years 'as a good, safe time'. Here there could be no security or privacy; to organise a bath would be a major task, involving the carrying of water, probably from the creek, and then heating it over the open fire.

These dwellings were very close to the old farm house, a good solid brick building of about 1,200 square feet, which the owner had left probably years before to live in Bega. Here a lady of part-Aboriginal descent lived with her Polish husband; they had cleaned up the rooms, restored the roof and painted it, and were able to use part of the water storage capacity of the tanks. It was interesting that this family should have the one livable home in this cluster. One of the other old ladies, not wishing, I guessed, to be impolite to me, said that the white head of the house 'must have crawled to the boss'; but she told my companion that he got it 'because he's a white man', although 'he's only a pea picker like the rest of us'.

'Poor buggers' said another old lady 'has a lot to put up with round here.' One of them had been trying for a house in town, as she and her husband did not drink and others here all did, especially 'in the season' (one could hardly wonder why); but, she said, 'they have just knocked down five beautiful houses in town'. Had the Bega municipal council been condemning and destroying houses to keep out Aborigines? No one could say.

For all these people one latrine was visible. Electric power came to the spot, but was connected only to the large weatherproof shed which housed the farm machinery—one more indication of priorities.

Rather better conditions were to be seen on other farms, mainly because the buildings used were more weatherproof, and some of them were tradesman-built. Four adults and six children lived in three rooms amounting to about six hundred square feet; they carted most of the water four hundred yards from the river in the plastic buckets which have somewhat lightened the toil of many Aboriginal women round Bega. Drinking water came from a tank without a tap; the woman said that complaints to the owner had had no result over two years. But a tap does not cost very much and they had been living there rent free; had they been conditioned in the long tradition of institutions to the assumption that the landlord or the 'boss' always looks to the state of accommodation? In the meantime, so long as there was water in the tank, her 'girls' she said, had had to clamber up the side of the tank and dip out water for drinking with the bucket! In a tent, thirty yards away, lived another daughter and her husband, with three children.

A similar house a short distance away on the same farm had for a long time had a gutter from which the water overshot the tank; and the tank was full of holes. The 'boss' had promised to patch it, but did nothing. (Nor did the householder.) Three adults and four children depended on water carried from the creek. Firewood had also become scarce; in the absence of vehicles, it had to be carried for some distance. Even in the season, some of the farmers refuse to supply it—and then become annoyed when the pickers stop early in the afternoon to get wood and water for the night.

One of the farms supplied timber off-cuts for firewood; and here the tiny overcrowded houses were comparatively well built and roofed with iron without holes. These were the 'good houses' (for Aborigines) of which the farmer was proud. In one of them (of about 150 square feet and all one room), lived a young couple with a child; fireplace, used for cooking, lounge chair, table, bed, were all there. Here another 'graduate' from Kinchela lived on unemployment relief and social service benefits like Child Endowment, from February to October. None of the farmers round here, he said, would let their Aboriginal tenants work elsewhere. While this was not true completely, it seemed true in his case. If he went to work elsewhere he must give up the 'house'; unless he could get work within travelling distance of home, he must leave his wife and baby here, in housing at the mercy of the farmer, and among the demoralised 'drunks' on pension days.

People at Murrays Flat said that Reedy Swamp Road was even worse; and perhaps it had been during the picking season. All that remained when we went there were some iron shacks between the edge of the road and the fence; a few others, with the occasional tent, were in the bush behind it. At one of these places there was a celebration in progress, with flagons of wine being consumed. A handsome young woman with wild hair and decayed teeth mistook me for a Welfare Officer, accused me of having been responsible for having one of her children taken by the Child Welfare authorities, and struck me. The egalitarianism of such a group was indicated by the reluctance of even her husband to restrain her. In the background, one of the small children ate dry bread (a loaf arrived with two more flagons); and the washing hung drying on the wire fence.

In the paddock behind, among high gumtrees, a full-time employee of the Mumbulla Shire lived with wife and family, on the property of a farmer who 'will not shift us'. Like so many others they heard all the rumours of houses becoming available; he believed that the 'Board' wanted to put all the proposed ten houses together; the Mumbulla Shire, he said, wanted to scatter them. He was an intelligent man, with a realistic assessment of the predicament he shared with the others there. He was no sentimentalist, and even argued that what was happening to Aborigines was largely their own fault. Bega was a good town, he said, where the hospital was not segregated.

Farmer-employers are of all kinds. One we met told us that when the

Government Medical Officer had objected to the conditions on his farm, he replied that he would 'kick them all out' and had heard no more. When he wanted them he would take a truck and 'pick them up'. He spoke in terms of sound animal husbandry: of dry accommodation, water laid on, baths, beds, and refrigerators supplied cheaply secondhand from the Bega sales; said that he did his best for them. (A check with Aborigines showed that he did in fact have the best accommodation round Murrays Flat.) He made much of the 'immorality' of Aborigines and their disregard of the marriage ceremony; he would like the chance of getting into the witness box to tell what he knew about them. This was the typical love-hate relationship of the colonial plantation manager who expresses contempt for the 'native', but can talk about little else. If the Department of Labour and Industry were to 'get on to' him again, he would 'clear the lot'.

An interesting local arrangement is that the farmer in the harvest season arranges to buy the food and other supplies, necessary where the women also are in the fields, perhaps; this is insisted on in many cases on the grounds that otherwise the workers will 'drink it all' and be unfit for work. Aborigines claim that the farmer will have an 'arrangement' with a shopkeeper; that they are victims of overcharging. This man referred repeatedly to the 'dirty' Aborigines and claimed that he compelled the women to wash clothes and person.

A more perceptive neighbour made the remark that Aborigines actually came to believe that they are bodily offensive; that this might operate in a cycle of causation, and that care of the person seems pointless; that squalor is the final state of self-condemnation. It was all too complex; but perhaps it was too easy to make such speculations about people most of whom have to carry water from a creek.

Other shanty places had apparently been surpassed by the one at Stoney Creek or Angledale, four miles or so north of Bega, which in late 1964 was making headlines. One of the attractions of this place was as a useful picking-up spot for local farmers. Another was the water which could be got from Stoney Creek. The third was the availability of the building material of the desperate—the tins, cardboard packing, old car bodies, etc. from a nearby tip. This tip had been the scene of an accidental death which focused the attention of the *Canberra Times* on conditions of living which had passed almost unnoticed for the previous five years; the press photographs of the shanties, exteriors, and interiors could be at Murrays Flat; in fact one old pensioner who lived there had had to move from Stoney Creek.

Another facet of the situation was tension between the two local governments. According to an officer of Mumbulla Shire in 1965, there were no Aboriginal families housed in the Municipality of Bega; they simply shopped there, and on pension days one saw the women dressed in good clothes and going off there for the day's shopping and gossip. In the summer season they camped there, along the river on a town reserve from which the council usually tried to move them; but they had to get water somewhere, and their labour is still necessary for the vegetable growers. The men drank there and had the occasional brawl in the streets. Young people from different parts of the district may even court there, since it is mainly in the town streets that they can meet, but this must be under the suspicious eyes of the police. In the afternoons the women sit in front of the post office in the sun. But they all seem to live in Mumbulla Shire. This is a nice example of how economics and social life make the town as necessary for the Aboriginal as for anyone else. No Aboriginal to whom I spoke complained about the police or the people of Bega; but Bega had no Aboriginal community, only Aboriginal business.

The Stoney Creek shanties were on a stock route, and the area was controlled by the Eden Pastures Protection Board. In August 1964 a Bega man applied to the Protection Board for a lease of the site and was reported in the press as proposing to evict the Aborigines if he got it. The village of Angledale, close by, also comes into the story, the president of its Progress Association describing the settlement as a 'menace'. Aborigines 'terrorise passing motorists', carry on 'petty pilfering', and are considered 'generally undesirable'.[7] The Bega man, it was reported, had the support of Bega people; but one of the ostensible reasons was that Aborigines should be moved 'for their own good'; they had been living 'in humpies roofed with tin, getting their water from the creek, and using blackberry bushes for toilets'. A Bega clergyman claimed that the Ministers' Fraternal had tried three years before to get land for a reserve, had had plans for homes drawn up, and was approaching the local service clubs to build them; that the Aborigines Welfare Board had taken the matter out of their hands; that the ministers would have acted as local trustees for the reserve.[8]

The *Canberra Times* urged the New South Wales Government to embark on a five year plan to 'abolish all . . . camps and reserves, whether official or unofficial';[9] and launched on a full-scale campaign with

[7] *Canberra Times*, 26 August 1964.
[8] Ibid., 27 August 1964.
[9] Ibid.

descriptions of the very bad conditions at the Creek, no better nor worse than so many other places.[10] Some at least of these families had come from Wallaga Lake. Their reasons seem to have been dislike of the paternal management and the sound economic one that the seasonal worker has to be available for the convenience of the employer; otherwise someone else who is there gets the job.

The press articles led to action. In September it was announced that five families had 'decided' to go to Wallaga Lake, after what was described as 'a day of intense activity'. Officers of the Aborigines Welfare Board, and members and officers of the Mumbulla Shire went together to Stoney Creek, inspected the huts, and, as the press account says, 'discussed the alternatives' with the people. 'The Aborigines squatted under the trees by the side of the creek and conferred before deciding to move.' The reporter wrote that they moved so that their children could go to school—an interesting reason, since Wallaga Lake is farther from any school than is Stoney Creek. One cannot but doubt what the 'alternatives' were, since the shire president announced at once that he had arranged for demolition of houses 'and the cleaning of the camp site' as soon as the occupants had moved. He had had to get permission from the Pastures Protection Board for this, but thought it necessary to reassure good clean folk in Bega and Angledale that their eyes would no longer be offended. '"All signs of occupation must be removed", he said.'[11]

Bega Municipality, having no Aborigines in town, formed a nice microcosm of the Commonwealth enjoying its absence of racial strife because the cause was excluded, to be retained in Mumbulla Shire. At the end of the year the shire resolved that a proposal by the Welfare Board to erect housing on the south Bega common be postponed, as 'not in the best interests of these unfortunate people'. Their segregation just outside Bega would increase their handicaps, as

it has been proved that segregation encourages idleness ... deepens their sense of inferiority ... and when occurring at the fringe of a town like Bega makes them less socially acceptable so tending to stifle the naturally charitable inclinations of the local citizens.[12]

But the shire also wanted Wallaga Lake closed, so that Aboriginal children would be nearer to schools, and a conference with Commonwealth and State authorities to work out a plan. The shire's official description of the circumstances is worth quoting:

[10] Ibid., 28 August, 1, 3, and 10 September 1964.
[11] Ibid., 3 September 1964.
[12] Mumbulla Shire—statement of 15 December 1964 (roneo-circular letter).

These people tend to congregate in small fringe communities living in torn tents and shanties constructed of rusted iron, flattened out biscuit tins and packing case timber ... with earth floors. The structures often house up to eight persons and are located on small crop holdings, public road reserves, or river banks, in the vicinity of garbage dumps ... in close proximity to Bega. The encampments lack elementary toilet and ablution facilities ... and endanger the health of the public at large ... The Aboriginal children generally do not receive formal schooling [which is probably correct only during their stay during the picking season—C.D.R.] and their lack of training in basic hygiene perpetuates the undesirable traits of their parents and elders ... Generally speaking the Aborigine is *socially unacceptable*.[13]

The diffidence of the shire in stating what should be done about housing was, I discovered, due to the need not to trespass on the preserve, as it were, of the Bega Municipality; integration into the town was what it was hinting at, and possibly one reason for pressing for the conference with Commonwealth and State representatives. In fact, I was informed by the Shire Clerk that 'full integration like New Zealand is the Council's express view'. The council, he said, had been one of the movers in having the separate school at Wallaga Lake discontinued; there were the usual stories of the headmaster who sent children back to their homes because they had head infestations.

The conference did not happen. The affair of Stoney Creek was soon forgotten by all but the Aborigines concerned, once the humpies were knocked down and the people removed. We met one man who had been there, and who moved to Murrays Flat rather than go back to Wallaga Lake; his story was that some who had been away working had not only homes but clothing and other possessions bulldozed into the ground; that the cars (referred to in the press accounts as wrecks) had also been demolished, although they were in use. There was still special local activity by health authorities in 1965. A pensioner at Murrays Flat had been evicted from his shanty because of complaints of his children's head-lice by a schoolmaster; and the local health officer did not know where he had gone—'probably back to the Angledale tip'.

The Bega Council was pressing, it seemed, for control of the land which was being considered for resumption for the Welfare Board houses; as one of its officials said, aldermen wanted the Aborigines to have the security of being in a community group, 'not scattered through the town' (which probably extends a whole two or three miles along the main road!). What the members of the town council really wanted, obviously, was something like the *status quo*; they would settle for a fringe settlement.

[13] Mumbulla Shire, roneoed statement (undated). My italics—C.D.R.

The only move made by the State government had been participation in action agreed with representatives of local government. Like other Aboriginal welfare authorities, the Board's priorities were such that it must negotiate with local councils. In an interesting comment during the parliamentary debate on amendments to the New South Wales Aborigines Protection Act, in 1963, a Member who was also on the Board said that there were plans to build thirteen houses in Lismore but that whenever the Board tried to get the building program started, the local council would move to stop it, by proclaiming a 'green belt' or by other means.[14] The local Member, with his electorate probably in mind, demanded improvements out at Cubawee, the reserve near Lismore. (This was essentially the attitude of Bega representatives—that Aborigines needed togetherness, but not in the streets of Bega.) Those of Cubawee, he said, had been there for a long time; it was a 'tribal area'. It was wrong to build houses for them anywhere else, unless in an 'industrial area' (which of course Lismore was not), since people who have houses also have to have jobs.[15]

This avoidance of responsibility is possible because of the political insignificance of Aboriginal groups. Seldom will the town council say 'We will not have more Aborigines in town because we don't want them'. The objections are generally based on either the need for Aborigines to be trained in some way first or on the need for some other arrangement which is for their own good. Where, as in Western Australia, the government has been erecting 'transitional houses' which differ from the standard of the State Housing Commission, it has been easy for councils to insist on the government meeting this standard. The case is not so convincing when one looks at other houses in town, which are often of poorer standard than the 'transitional' houses. But the local council will know well enough that the government of that State has not the funds for many Housing Commission houses for Aborigines. The Goomalling Shire, for instance, in 1964 threatened to resign as a body if their Member, the Minister for Native Affairs, did not scrap plans to build transitional houses in Goomalling.[16] In an editorial on Housing for Natives on 5 June 1965, the *West Australian* stated that 'erection of homes on terms acceptable to local authorities has been the biggest barrier to progress'.

In 1962, the moderate effort by the Queensland government to build homes in country towns came up against similar opposition from local

14 *N.S.W.P.D.*, 1963, Third Series, vol. 44, pp. 3183-200, vol. 45, pp. 3278 *et seq.*
15 Ibid.
16 *West Australian* (Perth), 28 April 1964.

councils, supported, it was stated in the press, by local citizens who had vacant lots next door. The towns of Kingaroy and Wandai had been chosen by the government as places to start a scheme which was to be extended to Cairns, Mareeba, Mossman, Hervey Bay, Clermont, Mitchell, Cunnamulla, and St George. 'Some members' of the Kingaroy Council were reported to oppose the move; and one councillor said that 'the Government is only using Kingaroy as a guinea pig for this scheme'.[17] There should, he said, have been more preparation of the Aborigines and more consultation with the council. He was not against helping the Aboriginal, and neither was the council; but the homes would be 'well away from' water mains and power lines and there might be costs involved for the council.[18]

In mid-1965, the Aborigines Welfare Board of Victoria was well advanced with its plan to settle some thirty Aborigines, some from Lake Tyers and some who had been dispersed from there through Gippsland, on a site near Morwell—near, but not in, though the Board was applying to have the four and a half acres re-zoned from rural to residential land. The Morwell Shire Council protested, even though the site was already serviced with sewerage, power, and water. But the Victorian Aboriginal Congress also protested, partly because the Aborigines concerned were said not to wish to move from their current homes,[19] and partly on the grounds that the government was 'building a new camp'. Morwell Council did not want them at all, even on the 'fringe'; while the Aboriginal spokesmen, led by Pastor Nicholls, said in effect that if the houses were not to be in town, the people would be better off where they were.

A South Australian example shows that this is a problem which all State governments face. Port Augusta occupies a very special place in the human geography of Aboriginal affairs, for this is the point of attraction for Aborigines from north, east, and west—not only part-Aborigines and full-bloods from our 'settled' Australia, but those from the pastoral stations beyond, and from the Musgrave Ranges and the opal fields. It was also a convenient place to bring those in need of health services or other assistance. But the building up of housing and other facilities there brought local resistance in 1964. However, the Member for the area in the legislature declared in Parliament that there was a colour bar 'right out in the open'. The Minister for Aboriginal Affairs was equally out-spoken, declaring the policy of his department to be 'to house Aborigines

[17] *Courier-Mail* (Brisbane), 17 November 1962.
[18] Ibid., 17 and 24 November 1962.
[19] *Age* (Melbourne), 22 June and 12 July 1965.

in any country town in which the Aborigines desired to live and in which there were employment possibilities'.[20]

The attitude of local government to the Aboriginal group is always a matter of first importance for that group. The main interests of the group have to be in local affairs, for the range of employment and of their social contacts will be mainly within the areas of one or two local government councils. They cannot obtain costs of removal to other areas from an employer department, bank, or firm. Those who move after seasonal work must generally go as single men, except for long established movements into employment which is an Aboriginal monopoly. They will fear that houses may be condemned, or that permissive occupancy of council-controlled lands may be withdrawn. Personalities, like the mayor, the health inspector, the building inspector, will be of interest and importance. The Aboriginal has little chance of influencing the attitudes of these officials.

All this points up the need for active association of local with central government in programs to establish Aboriginal families in towns. The case for steps to strengthen Aboriginal confidence and organisation, and for assisting them to live where they want to live, is clear. Subsidies to local government may well be involved. But so long as councils are allowed to retain the illusion that they may drive Aborigines away somewhere else, and so long as respectable people can assume that there are other places where 'they will be looked after', the present chivvying of would-be Aboriginal settlers will go on, while their numbers, and the size of the problem, increase more rapidly than effective housing.

In the meantime, there are new movements in the country towns and a new questioning by non-Aboriginal people as to why things are as they are. Long ingrained, unthinking habits in local institutions—the hospital, the police station, the shire or municipal council, the pastures protection board, the chamber of commerce or progress association (which is likely in the most wretched of small villages to resist the purchase of land for Aboriginal housing)—are beginning to come under the scrutiny of small active groups with a new interest in the Aboriginal. So are attitudes in all these, even in some of the churches, where for a long time attendance of Aborigines has been almost unthinkable, along with those of doctors, teachers, and public officials. Though these groups have little Aboriginal support, and cannot substitute for Aborignal pressure groups, they do indicate change in the social climate. But central government must begin to govern in this matter. Local government can hardly continue to receive

20 *Advertiser* (Adelaide), 30 September 1964.

its tacit consent for claims to control the kind of people who live in its area. On such an issue of human rights it has to be overruled. But it also has to be subsidised; and one way of doing both is through government support of Aboriginal organisations. A real *rapport* between central government and Aborigines is essential.

In July 1966, for instance, the Narrabri Municipal Council (supported by that august body, the West Narrabri Progress Association) was opposing the establishment of a housing settlement 'near the main north-western rail and road approaches to the town', because Aborigines living there 'would create a poor impression on visitors'. The site had been suggested by the Narrabri Pastures Protection Board, so that it would be out of town. The Deputy Mayor stated that 'the site could be seen by every train and road passenger moving along the trunk road towards Narrabri'. Too long has the Aboriginal been left to the mercy of these politicians of the parish pumps, from Narrabri to Gnowangerup.

To some extent the past treatment of the Aboriginal may be explained by the nature of the local government body. So long as this was represent-ative of the ratepayers only, without representing those citizens who do not pay rates directly (but may well be contributing substantially to council funds indirectly, as through the purchases they make locally, or through what they may pay for council services), local government tended to be obsessed, especially in rural and country town areas, with the level of the rates. The change to adult franchise in New South Wales has not yet had much impact on this attitude, partly for lack of interest in local government. There remains a petty meanness in council decisions, a conservatism in the tradition that money from rates goes to minor construction only, and a belief among townsfolk that the job of local government is to operate on the lowest possible budget.

A real concern to have the Aboriginal integrated into the business of the country town, then, would include him, with the other poor and the non-ratepayers, into the electorate. It seems essential in Queensland to consider the local government franchise in this connection. It might also go further, and make it possible for an Aboriginal company or association to have special representation on the council; not to vote but to act as a spokesman for a special interest. This could go far to provide a local forum and to make a rallying point for the very many non-Aborigines who wish to help. An Aboriginal voice in local public affairs, even without vote, could serve to influence local public opinion on the whole range of discriminating practice, and to present the Aboriginal view on conflicts of long standing with various authorities, departments, and private interests: for instance, that between Aboriginal groups and the State police, which forms a notable source of tension from one end of this continent to the other. At present, the vital issue of a place in town for Aborigines is discussed between council and a local voluntary body. Obviously the interests involved should be represented within the council.

The maladjustment described is one within *Australian society as a whole*. Too easily is it assumed, especially in the context of an assimilation policy, that the 'solution' is to be found in assisting the Aboriginal to adjust, for the basic problem in 'settled' Australia is the old and obvious one of white prejudice. Governments which operate in their international relationships on the basis of such prejudices have, equally obviously, tended to avoid a head-on clash with this deep-rooted sentiment, or what is assumed by cautious politicians to be such. Caution can mean that the government may realise the problem but be unwilling to take the risk of statesmanship and affront what is assumed to be public opinion. As a result, it may settle for a program to house-train the Aboriginal family; to prepare it for 'acceptance' by prejudiced whites. There are pious hopes that in time 'education' will alter attitudes of the majority.

In its crudest form this maladjustment involves physical fears and repulsion, mainly produced by the white Australian imagination. These feelings are typically expressed in the defence that one is not racially prejudiced but that one does believe in a 'hygiene barrier'—statements which I have heard from one end of the continent to the other.

It was easy enough to find recorded examples, if one went to the press reports; and these often indicated the complex motivation of people who claimed to have opposed discrimination. There were also examples of the use of a 'hygiene barrier' by public authorities, to avoid awkward situations. In 1965 a newspaper reported on Bourke, where there was no 'colour discrimination' in schools, hospitals, or in the Returned Soldiers' Club. The report made much of the fact that both races used the same labour ward. Significant was the assumption that this was something of a break-through. The matron also reserved the right to reject a 'dirty' Aboriginal from a ward and to put him on the verandah; could she have similarly rejected a non-Aboriginal, instead of having him washed?[21]

At the time of the student demonstrations in some of the more notorious towns, little attention was paid to the hospitals, partly no doubt because the situation is changing, but perhaps also because it is almost impossible to know what the essential situation is. One of the most deep-

[21] Anne Goldie, 'Harmony in Black & White—There's No Colour Bar in Bourke', *Woman's Day*, 12 April 1965, p. 12.

rooted suspicions of danger from too intimate a personal contact with colour relates to illness, and especially to birth. Within an ostensibly integrated institution, like the local hospital, all kinds of arrangements to allay such fears are possible; for instance, in the same ward, special beds may be used. I have direct personal knowledge of a statement by a child welfare nurse that she always publicly disinfected her centre after visits by Aborigines, to reassure the majority of her clients.

A New South Wales Minister for Health found it necessary on at least two occasions in the 1960s to threaten that hospitals which practised racial discrimination would lose the government subsidy. Three decades earlier, the New South Wales Parliament was debating a Bill for compulsory treatment of gonococcal ophthalmia among Aborigines. The Aboriginal Welfare Board was to be responsible. The Minister introducing this measure said that unless the Board could have special powers, there would be a threat to whites; that whites might suffer blindness. He also assumed that the Aboriginal was in some way less severely affected: that the disease was for him not so serious. The association of a feared disease with colour was clear enough. The Member for Cobar suggested that treatment should be given in special hospitals.[22] He may have heard of the 'lock' hospitals of Western Australia.

How far had deep-rooted prejudice and fear changed over three decades? Overtly at least, in some places like Bourke, a good deal; though it was still necessary to proclaim absence of prejudice. But the threats by the Minister for Health suggested that there could be many kinds of evasion and reassurances to fear. Sometimes there has been open defiance. When in 1961 the Minister (W.F. Sheehan) announced the Labor government's intention to ban segregation in all public hospitals, he told the press that he had already asked that segregation be ended at the Moree District Hospital. The Chairman of the hospital board replied that any order by the government would be ignored, and that all other board members would support him; that any attempt to alter the current situation would 'lead to trouble'. The Mayor thought that the whites would not object to *sharing wards* (my italics) provided that the Aborigines selected were 'good types'. There was an average number of fifty non-Aborigines and twenty Aborigines in the hospital; the Aborigines did not want to be near the whites, so why force them to be?[23]

In 1965 the same Minister was making the same kind of threat; and one can see clearly enough the limits to what legislation or executive

[22] *N.S.W.P.D.*, 1936, Second Series, vol. 149, p. 4750.
[23] *Age* (Melbourne), 12 May 1961.

action can achieve in such cases. (Yet, what it *can* achieve, by setting
public standards, is very important indeed.) The Leader of the Country
Party pointed out that the withdrawal of subsidies would result in
patients having to suffer for the discrimination practised by the hospital
board. Sheehan's principle was clear: that there should be no segregation
except for medical reasons.[24] Yet in an institution which exists for
medical treatment, anything that is done can be defended as necessary
for medical reasons.

The Minister referred to the effect of segregation on international
opinion. It was interesting therefore that the delegates to the Aboriginal
Welfare Conference of 1963 had reported to their Ministers that while
the treatment and medical attention in the Northern Territory was

identical for all races ... it has been the usual practice to provide separate ward
accommodation for Aborigines and non-Aborigines, solely because this has been the
continuing wish of both groups ... It is a firm policy ... to progressively eliminate
all hospital segregation.[25]

The situation at the hospital in Bourke was probably as favourable
for Aborigines as any in the country towns, since in other respects Bourke
has earned its reputation as a 'good town'. According to the president of
the shire council, issues involving the 'hygiene barrier' came to the fore
when his council was planning to build a swimming pool. The people
who argued that 'We must have a policy' were often concerned how best
to exclude Aborigines from using it. But the council rejected this, on the
ground that such restrictions were 'just asking for trouble', that the pool
had to be for all to use.

The tangled consequences of discrimination in such matters were
illustrated at Kempsey, where before the days of the first freedom rides,
the municipal council had a by-law excluding Aborigines from the baths.
This dated from January 1949. No Aborigines, under this decision, could
enter the baths except those who were students at the high school; and
even they could enter only with the school swimming party. The council
established the rule when it specifically refused a request to *allow*
Aboriginal children to swim in a carnival; which seems to indicate that
there had already been a ban in practice, which aldermen now tried to
back with some logic. According to the press report, the council view

[24] *S.M.H.*, 6 March 1965. Part-Aborigines at this time were legally non-Aboriginal, but
whether in fact they were hospitalised in 'white' or 'Aboriginal' wards I do not know.
[25] Aboriginal Welfare Conference of Commonwealth and State Authorities, Darwin, July
1963; Proceedings and Decisions, p. 21.

was that it could not allow the children in without allowing the adults, and a town medical practitioner was reported as stating that Aborigines in the baths would be a danger to public health. The Aborigines Welfare Board at the time had accused the council of discrimination and stated its intention of referring the issue to the Department of Local Government. That Department was reported as stating that it had no power to direct the municipality in the matter.[26]

One result was that Aboriginal students who went swimming with school parties would leave the water with the others to be counted by the teacher; the other children would return to the water, but the Aborigines were required to leave the baths. A young married woman living with her husband and baby in an upturned iron tank at Green Hills told me this in 1964, without prompting; I was asking only of her memories of school days, and this was her most vivid one.

This was the situation up until the visit by the freedom riders. The press in May 1965 announced that the Kempsey Council had withdrawn the ban, on grounds that the 'health and hygiene of Aboriginals' had improved in recent years. Reading this I wondered whether hygiene could ever have been less effective than it must have been in the conditions of Green Hills in mid-1964; but the council needed to save face. The Government Medical Officer assured the public that hookworm and roundworm could not be transmitted through the baths.[27]

The most deep-rooted fears are not really to be allayed by scientific evidence about health; they are not based on logic, but on the magic of the folklore. Their existence is one of the main arguments for positive legislation of the South Australian type, but preferably giving the injured party a right to civil action.[28] A government which is not prepared to go as far as this can, I believe, fairly be accused of not being sufficiently concerned about Aboriginal equality to risk any considerable loss of votes for it. Yet without precise rights expressed in positive laws, there is no way in which Aborigines can press legally for equality. For instance, from the little we have seen of the difficulty of defining exactly what does happen in a particular institution like a hospital, there is clear need for definite statements of principle, which can be applied through the courts if necessary. Without such legislation central government has no really precise grounds on which to take action against local governments which practise discrimination. Its absence suggests that, for

[26] *Sunday Telegraph* (Sydney), 14 August 1949, and *Daily Telegraph* (Sydney), 15 August 1949.
[27] *S.M.H.*, 5 May 1965.
[28] For discussion of this South Australian legislation, see pp. 413-14.

political and other reasons, central government so far, and with the exception of South Australia, is not prepared to take such action.

The association of 'colour' with uncleanness, like the alleged basis for the colour hierarchy to which we have already referred, may easily overwhelm Aborigines who are ignorant of the complexities which have produced their condition. A poignant experience is to witness a part-Aboriginal proclaiming his own uncleanness as something with which he was born. This sometimes happens in drink; but the belief may also be revealed under special stress. I have personally heard a man attribute a permanent uncleanness to himself and declare that there was no point in effort to change, as he was 'only a blackfellow'. There is a kind of self-hate which may express itself in extravagant action, as well as in absence of care, or of grooming, for the person. On one occasion, with two other members of our team, we met a young man just out of gaol. He had come to one of the typical large grandmother-dominated households to claim his wife, who was one of the daughters, and to see his children. But his wife had taken another man. His reaction was to break a bottle and to cut his arm to a depth estimated by the medical member of the team to be at least half an inch, and through a very dirty woollen jacket at that. Basically the same reason explains language which is shocking by the standards of Australian society in general (or at least used to be).

The final collapse of morale is in the belief that one is a member of a worthless group, and individually worthless; that what one does is of no account.

# AN ISOLATED
## ABORIGINAL STATION

The reserve beside the country town, whether it be managed station or not, will commit the inhabitants eventually to membership of the town, to dispersal, or to a more or less perpetual existence on the fringe of general society. But there are other situations where the legacy of the period of institutionalising the Aboriginal population is the problem of isolated groups under some degree of institutional control. The only station of the Australian Capital Territory, at Wreck Bay, was possibly the most hopeful and attractive example of such an isolated community in the mid-1960s, when arrangements were made with the government of New South Wales, which had previously administered it, to vacate it so that the policy of the Commonwealth Department of the Interior could be applied there. This was to make Wreck Bay an open village. There were two New South Wales stations on the coast of New South Wales which are similarly isolated, at Roseby Park and Wallaga Lake, and two on the north coast, at Tabulam and Woodenbong.

Such problems could be seen more forcibly in 'colonial' Australia, on the missions of north Queensland, the Northern Territory, and the far north of Western Australia, and on the government settlements of the Northern Territory. They could (and still can) be seen also on Queensland government settlements within 'settled' Australia, especially the very big one on Palm Island, and at the isolated community at Woorabinda. Victoria still had its isolated Lake Tyers, in spite of official efforts to liquidate it as a liability; South Australia its two stations of very long standing indeed at Point Pearce and Point McLeay, as well as a comparatively new one at Gerard and one also at Davenport.

In the western area of New South Wales, about half way between
Euabalong and Lake Cargelligo, Murrin Bridge was the most recent of
these monuments in the State to the long sustained effort to 'civilise' the
persons of Aboriginal descent within multi-purposed institutions. It is
a reminder of the gulf between policy and practice, since its construction
was completed as late as 1949, some eight years after the Aborigines
Welfare Board had, in its first report, outlined the steps it proposed to
take towards 'assimilation'.[1] Had the New South Wales government been
considering the matter first in 1949, this station would probably never
have been built, or at least built on the present site, so far from any town.
But plans for what was to be a 'model Aboriginal settlement' were
sufficiently advanced by June 1945 for the Chief Secretary to make a
public announcement: there was to be accommodation for 300, with
(separate) church, school, recreation facilities, and the 950 acres would
provide for agricultural development.[2] It seems to have been 'opened'
officially in April 1949, when the Sydney press reported that there was a
settlement of forty-two homes erected along one street, with hospital,
electricity supply, and pumping plant to supply water from the Lachlan.
Aborigines could earn fifteen to seventeen shillings weekly for work on
the property, said the report; the men already were earning £6 to £8 per
week for work on surrounding farms and stations.[3]

Fifteen years later, not an acre had been cropped. One reason was
probably that most men were employed elsewhere, on station and farming
work to which they and their fathers had long been committed. Other
reasons are those which applied to all reserves and stations. Partly these
are matters of the resources available, including land and other capital,
and partly of the inmates' lack of incentive, itself a reflection of the social
relations of the institution or other reserve structure. Such areas of land,
at the time when Cumeroogunga was being established, would certainly
have been cropped and developed. That so little of such areas has been
used for farming may be due to the kind of land available in many, but
not all, cases; and one would guess that some of the land at Murrin Bridge
is useful river flat country. The whole area might have the potential of
one good farm, and there have always been from 250 to 300 people living
there. The employment available on the station is mainly on maintenance
of a living area from which the men have to go out to earn their livings,
since management has been geared to family welfare rather than agricultural development.

[1] N.S.W.P.P., 1941-2, vol. 1, pp. 1169-76—A.W.B. Report, 1941.
[2] Sun (Sydney), 15 June 1945.                    [3] Daily Telegraph (Sydney), 6 April 1949.

The location of Murrin Bridge illustrates the practice of establishing Aboriginal groups for the convenience of administrators and local townships—well out of sight, but as conveniently as possible for the type of employment in which they were proving useful. Its isolation also shows how established means of dealing with a 'problem' may be continued, irrespective of pronouncements on new policy and aims: for 'assimilation' had been the aim and the policy for just about a decade before the completion of the station; and if this meant anything, it meant attempts at closer association between Aboriginal and non-Aboriginal society. The policy was politically possible, perhaps, only as a long-term objective, and the building of this kind of station tended to be justified as providing for the 'training' (in citizenship, etc.) necessary before Aborigines could be helped to set up houses in town. The same kind of argument was used elsewhere, as in the Northern Territory, where in the 1950s the big settlements for the full-blood *wards* were either established or further developed, at considerable cost, well away from towns for the most part, and justified as training centres.

In New South Wales, station residence was not legally compulsory, though it may have been economically so. Where housing and other help was available, there Aborigines, especially those who had been conditioned to life in institutions, would go. That an isolated station should be commenced in the last year of the war may be explained partly by the emphasis placed on agricultural development of stations in the first statement of the Board on its assimilation policy. Agriculture would be good for health, would be a means of teaching a useful occupation (in the case of Murrin Bridge, to a labour force which had had to live by rural employment!), while the gardens by the homes on the new stations and reserves would develop pride in them and a desire for improvements.[4] Possibly no one in authority remembered the earlier steps to disperse 'lighter castes' from Aboriginal stations, but that the Aborigines would remember what had happened on the other western stations seems to have been ignored.

Partly Murrin Bridge was the answer to a practical problem, of containment of the Aboriginal population which had been largely displaced by the extension of settlement westwards which had followed the building of the Condobolin-Broken Hill railway. A station at Carowra Tank had had to be abandoned when the water failed in 1934, and the Aborigines moved from there to Menindee on the Darling.[5] By

[4] *N.S.W.P.P.*, 1941-2, vol. 1, pp. 1169-76—A.W.B. Report, 1941.
[5] There is a useful summary of the background of Murrin Bridge in Beckett, A Study of a Mixed-blood Aboriginal Minority in the Pastoral West of New South Wales.

1938 John Kinchela, of the Aborigines Progressive Association, was writing to the press about bad conditions there, with tuberculosis allegedly rife, malnutrition through inadequate rations, bad water, and the like.[6] Shortly before there had been references to six deaths there in six weeks, and an official admission that although it was not known that the site was an old burial ground, human bodies had been found in the sandhills there.[7]

What was new in the 1930s was the expression of concern, not the conditions or the deaths. The kind of thinking which led to the establishment of Murrin Bridge may be illustrated by a comment of the Board in the 1940 Report: that a new site had been acquired for the Menindee group, with better employment opportunities, and areas to grow vegetables; that Aboriginal camps near town posed special problems and the people preferred sordid conditions there to 'improvements' farther away.[8] At that time the plan was removal to a new site in the Walgett area, but the eventual selection was of isolated Murrin Bridge.

The acreage set aside for Murrin Bridge was about the same as that of the former station on the Darling; only Brewarrina and Cumeroogunga at the time had more. The purpose of stations was the care of Aborigines 'who need the Board's care and protection, or who prefer community life'; families had to meet their own needs, except that the aged and ill would be cared for and rationed.[9] Yet families who refused to meet their own needs were not being pressed to leave. The Board was in the position of any authority which has maintained for a long time a system of institutionalised in-door relief. A Commonwealth-States Conference in February 1948 had agreed that Aboriginal authorities should use reserves for positive aims; that there should be 'training' for local employment, and development of the resources on the reserve for the benefit of Aborigines. But there was no precise definition of the 'training', nor reference to what kinds of resources might be there. Aboriginal welfare still had a low priority: in the 1948-9 financial year, for instance, the Board's recurring expenditure was just under £69,000, or around £15 per person resident on reserves and stations.[10] Capital expenditure amounted to another £60,000. Even by 1963-4, when population on reserves and stations had increased by some 26 per cent, and overall expenditure was over £73 per head as against about £30 overall in

[6] *S.M.H.*, 17 December 1938.
[7] *Labor Daily*, 23 September 1938.
[8] *N.S.W.P.P.*, 1941-2, vol. 1, pp. 1163-7—A.W.B. Report, 1940.
[9] *N.S.W.P.P.*, 1948-50, vol. 3, p. 841—A.W.B. Report, 1948, p. 8.
[10] Ibid., pp. 8-10.

1947-8, the difference could probably be more than accounted for by inflation. As the management was untrained and poorly paid, it is not surprising that there had been no spectacular progress at Murrin Bridge by 1964.

That the picture then should be such a perfect example of the institutional management-inmate syndrome may be better understood from Dr Beckett's studies of social disintegration in this whole western region.[11] After the first assertion of the invaders' power, with depopulation from the usual causes, there seems to have been the kind of adjustment already described round the pastoral homesteads. Perhaps the first Aboriginal stations in this place did save the remnants, because they made it more difficult for people who had so little left to live for to rush into a kind of mass suicide. I think that one can go back to these events, and see in this first contact period something of the recklessness of life and health which is partly a frontier tradition but much more a legacy of the time of greatest despair when, as Elkin would say, the Dreaming was lost: it was impossible to 'return to the mat', and there was no place of equality in white society.[12] Some idea of what this means is indicated by Beckett's population figures for 1883 and 1915, in the 'far west' of the State (roughly, the area west of a line drawn through Brewarrina and Condobolin). The decline was from over one thousand to 375. But the main decline, in which whole tribes had disappeared, was before the Protector took the 1883 figure.[13]

Probably by 1883 the first adaptation (which Elkin calls 'intelligent parasitism') was passing or gone, since this depended on a precarious balance of forces allowing the Aborigines to live in their own society, and adapt according to the rules of that society, while at the same time making the gestures of obedience and working as required on the stations. The station established at Carowra Tank in 1926 was for pauperised remnants, who had had a 'camp' there.

Beckett says that by the time of World War I those in the camp at Carowra Tank had begun to 'marry wrong', though as late as the early 1930s old 'clever men' there were still trying to enforce 'the rule'. By 1957, when he was there, a few old men were using sorcery for their own

---

[11] See A Study of a Mixed-blood Aboriginal Minority, pp. 54 et seq.; and 'Kinship, Mobility and Community among Part-Aborigines in Rural Australia', International Journal of Comparative Sociology, vol. 6, no. 1, March 1965, p. 11.
[12] The reference here is to A.P. Elkin's 'Reaction and Interaction: A Food Gathering People and European Settlement in Australia', American Anthropologist, vol. 53, no. 2, April-June 1951.
[13] See Beckett, 'Kinship, Mobility and Community', p. 12. The figures came from Protector of Aborigines (1883) and the Aborigines Protection Board (1915).

ends, and no longer for social ends.[14] The adjustment to the pastoral economy had been progressively disturbed by the breaking up of large holdings and closer settlement by holders who had no place or employment for Aborigines. To the failure of water at Carowra Tank and the movement of the station to Menindee one must add the context of the great depression of the 1930s. Some part-Aborigines seem to have received the 'dole',[15] but most seem to have had to move to government stations for relief of a less substantial kind. The law, as we have seen, provided that Aborigines camped near a reserve or township could be removed; and during the depression police seem to have acted to force Aborigines back on to the stations. There was no need to prosecute through the courts; the result could be achieved by knocking down the houses. This law was withdrawn in 1963,[16] but the same kind of action against Aborigines camped on town commons has continued until now, under the local government health or building regulations.

This, then, was part of the background of the people moved into what was to be a model institution at Murrin Bridge. On the other hand, the war had meant shortage of rural labour, and better opportunities and rewards, for Aboriginal farm and station workers.

In 1964, unthinking white men in Lake Cargelligo and in Euabalong still referred to this group in terms of the usual stereotype. For instance, a casual inquiry of a garage hand in Lake Cargelligo was rewarded with the news that 'the nigs' there had 'just got new houses' (this had occurred sixteen years before) and that they were now smashing up the floors for firewood.

The picture of human behaviour painted by a harassed but efficient and humane station manager (who was quite aware that his position was more or less hopeless) was characteristic of the English workhouse or debtors' prison in a Dickens novel. This was of a brawling pauperism, marked by the not uncommon highly developed skills in playing on the weaknesses of management and using the institution for inmate purposes. Perhaps these could be summed up as the determination to live for the moment, and the throwing of responsibility as far as possible on to the management, even for the maintenance of dependants in some cases where the man was earning good wages. At this time men were employed anything up to a hundred miles from the station, coming home for the

---

[14] Beckett, A Study of a Mixed-blood Aboriginal Minority, p. 56.
[15] Ibid., p. 54.
[16] The relevant section of the Aborigines Protection Act was section 14, which was repealed by Act No. 7 of 1963.

occasional weekend. Few sent money home, although those who came home would bring it; the manager sometimes had to use police to approach men in other areas to get them to send money to wives. Child endowment money often served to keep those at home. Malnutrition, in the view of management, had affected the children; this manager had got funds for a midday meal at the school (on the station) and supplied vitamins. In the meantime the men were spending a great deal of their earnings on liquor; some would refuse work, after a spell away, and live from day to day on what their wives got from child endowment.

The descriptions of brawling drunkenness and fornication were at least in keeping with the general appearance of the thirty-two houses; and they were by no means contradicted by the descriptions of observers in a position to be more detached. When Beckett spent some time there in 1957 there were some 250 people in thirty-four houses, which indicates heavy overcrowding by the standards of the general community. Of all the households, he says that only those of the three 'handymen' employed by the station paid rent, and that one very prosperous household head received a demand for eight years of arrears.[17] This appears to be insistence on rights which people believe they have. It is essentially the same kind of defiance which results in the smashing of houses, especially the windows, many of which were broken still in 1964, partly no doubt in defiance of the managerial inspection of the houses. The manager, continually replacing window panes, fully realised the ridiculousness of his situation. But women and children had to be sheltered. So the child may become a kind of hostage. Just as management may improperly use the child as a control over the parent, so the parent may use his own child, in this institutionalised world, deliberately to embarrass authority. There is something of this, I think, in parental discouragement of interest in schooling.

According to Beckett, the opposition to authority in 1957 was covert. People paid the price of outward obedience and respect, as in using the term 'boss' and 'missus' to the white station staff, although the term 'mate' was used between Aboriginal and non-Aboriginal men in the world 'outside'. Possibly the Board staff here modelled their conduct on that of others 'in charge of' Aborigines, as on the pastoral properties. Of the inhabitants over twenty years of age, 85 per cent had lived most of their lives on Aboriginal stations; a consequence was that the dominant

[17] Beckett, A Study of a Mixed-blood Aboriginal Minority, ch. 4. On another station, where rents were fifteen shillings (2-bedroom house) and seventeen shillings and sixpence (3-bedroom house), I saw the rent book which indicated *average* arrears of approximately 300 weeks' rent.

impressions about white Australians among women and children were based on experience of 'mission' staff.

In short, here was a range of *inmate* attitudes to the institution; with inmates making their 'secondary adjustments' to use its resources for their own purposes, willing to bear with the handicaps of isolation and of being managed in return for housing which was in practice mostly free, for social services which could be got here without trouble, for running water, for sanitation, and for generally 'being looked after'. This is what Erving Goffman has called a 'self alienating moral servitude' in reference to inmates in asylums, which may be for different purposes, but basically perhaps not different in kind, since in both, management is assumed to possess the expertise required to change human behaviour. Such an institution can exist within general democratic society 'by invoking the great tradition of the expert servicing relation', and the inmates 'can find themselves crushed by the weight of a service ideal *that eases life for the rest of us*'.[18] It is indeed hard to account for the continued existence of an institution like Murrin Bridge on grounds which leave out of account the motive of easing life for 'the rest of us'. This is not to argue that the way out of such a commitment is easy.

When two American students, Paul Shinoff and Burt Rodgers, went there in late 1964 the social situation seems to have been little changed: 'Few families pay their rent, and street fights are a regular occurrence.'[19] There was, however, a Progress Association of six elected residents, to whom the manager gave credit for each improvement of conditions obtained; it had low status among the group described as 'anti-manager'. The picture of conduct and aspirations confirms that of Beckett in 1957.

While there are exceptions, most homes are uncared for, property is handled casually. Both children and adults are discouraged from bettering themselves or the community. Men . . . make little effort to lift themselves above the subsistence level . . . They know that . . . their family . . . will always have . . . food and shelter . . . Even when a man has extra money, he will still conform to the basic social patterns of poverty.

Only 'farm and labouring' jobs were sought, not clerical or sales positions. The boys aspired to be drovers or fencers and admired the hard drinking of the men.[20]

18 *Asylums*, p. 386. My italics.
19 Selected Attitudes of Murrin Bridge Aborigines (typescript), p. 19. This study by two American students in sociology was by arrangement with the Aborigines Welfare Board and the Department of Adult Education, University of Sydney, in 1964.
20 Ibid., pp. 25-6. As a prelude to their study, they quote this sentence from the essay of a 14-year-old schoolboy: 'In the future when I leave school I am hoping to fence on big farms and stations and to move about.'

The girls wanted to get away to towns or the city, and many had done so, but not the boys. The observers noted a lack of individual initiative, and a conformity to the code of the hard-drinking bush worker earlier described by Beckett. One comment they make tells a great deal. They say that they will not discuss drunkenness, but leave the matter to the experts; that when a fight occurred they were passive onlookers. 'There were several ways in which our life was different. We did not get drunk, we went away for two weekends, and we went into town on three occasions for dinner.'[21]

In a country where the cash economy dominates so completely, no matter what the cultural explanations for such conduct may be, a progressive survival demands some minimum of order in basic economic matters, even within the family—for instance in transfer of funds from 'breadwinner' to family through the mother and the provision of regular meals (since other activities, like school attendance, have to be ordered by the clock). Management's guess was that no more than three of the thirty-six households had regular meal schedules. Men entitled to unemployment benefits would fail to apply at the office (I suspect, because this would involve recognition of the manager's paternal role). The management would bring pressure to bear for the sake of the children; in the meantime families would survive by borrowing from others. It was the manager's view that the rare attempts by non-Aborigines in the nearest towns to be friendly were rapidly discouraged by the immediate reaction of some Aborigines to 'put the nips in'. This aggressive readiness to affront the white man's respect for the dollar and to transfer to the white manager (or to any other, as a part-Aboriginal who held the task for a while found) intimate family responsibilities is exactly in accord with descriptions of similar situations on managed Indian reservations in North America by Margaret Mead, the Hanks, and others. It indicates in the words of the Hanks a 'social syndrome of malsatisfaction'.[22]

It can of course be argued that the views of a manager concerned with assimilation will be culture biased. Yet the argument loses force when one asks what the non-European culture concerned really is in these cases; whether it is really, in any significant difference from the dominant one, anything more than a mirror-reverse of the values which authority has represented for so long. For what remains of the old tradition, and for

[21] Ibid., p. 6.
[22] L.M. and J.R. Hanks, *Tribe Under Trust: a Study of the Blackfoot Reserve of Alberta*, p. 176; see also Margaret Mead, *The Changing Culture of an Indian Tribe*, p. 71; and C.D. Rowley, 'Aborigines and other Australians', *Oceania*, vol. 32, no. 4, June 1962, p. 260.

what people consider important—such for instance as the frontier tradition of mateship, where it occurs, or pride in Aboriginal origins and skills, where anything of this is left—there must, in any democratic and 'developmental' system of administration, be respect and assistance. But the overt attitudes here promised nothing to be grasped by authority as a starting point for building of community spirit. Reintegration has to come, in these situations of apparent hopelessness, *from within the group*; in response rather to objective opportunity, firmly presented and certain, than to any exhortation or 'education' program; to the kind of offer which includes the hope of gaining strength to stand up to and oppose non-Aboriginal society, by democratic and legal, but also by effective, means.

Other causes of tension were exacerbated by isolation and over-crowding. The manager had been pressing in vain for a public telephone; and part of the reason for isolation of a quite obsolete kind was the fact that the only way to ring out was to do so through the office phone. The Post Office would agree to put a phone into a store but not to establish a public booth, perhaps because of fear of wanton damage. But no business-man in town was interested in the proposed store, especially as people had to buy in town anyway, perhaps because of the low priority given to Aboriginal needs. Potential storekeepers on the station may have seen the problem of refusing credit—and perhaps the greater one of giving it—so that although two men had been to the co-operative training centre at Tranby (in Sydney), nobody on the station would take charge of a store.

Until 1964, there had never been a daily bus service to the nearest town, Lake Cargelligo. The bus ran out from town only for the cinema nights. In 1964, however, the station 3-ton flat-bed truck went to town twice daily, to take the secondary schoolchildren to and from school. Yet this was the first year, in all the history of the station, in which such attendance had been possible. When the manager had first moved for it, the education authorities had suggested an extra class at the station primary school. There had been previous experiments with correspondence courses. It is an interesting comment on the situation of unofficially segregated schooling that a school bus had been running for a long time for twenty-five miles, from another direction, into Lake Cargelligo, while the children of Murrin Bridge had been repeating sixth class, waiting for their fifteenth birthdays so that they could legally leave. Times were changing; the manager had gained permission to use the truck for the children, and in 1964 ten were completing the first year of secondary work.

This isolation had resulted in some children reaching the school leaving age without seeing a town as large as Lake Cargelligo (pop.

*c.* 1,000). Socialisation had been what was available in segregated schooling and the demoralised families. The bus fares and cinema prices together had amounted to ten shillings or more. As there was no shop at the station, these children had missed the learning experiences of buying sweets, as well as of 'going to the pictures'; they had learned to read to little purpose where there were few books. According to Shinoff and Rodgers, in 1964 'there were books visible in three homes (out of 32), magazines in 12, and a newspaper in one'.[23]

Segregated schooling leaves results which take a long time to eradicate. Of the children then attending Lake Cargelligo High School, the same observers wrote that

their older siblings were forced to sit through the sixth grade 2 or 3 times before they reached the age of 15 ... Since they were wasting their time, the children automatically dropped out at 15 ... Those who are from 15 to 25 are the young men most looked up to by the school age boys. These men are the ones who sat through the sixth grade 3 times. Their feelings towards their school and towards education in general may be easily imagined.[24]

Perhaps one reason for the continuation of the station school is that it had accommodation and facilities for 100 children. The Department of Education, as a matter of policy, was abandoning schools of this type; but the existence of what amounts to a sizeable village might well make it necessary for some time to isolate the education of the younger children there. Even for the high school children of 1964, transport facilities offered far less status or comfort than those considered adequate for other children. One can imagine what would have happened had white children been involved. But the objections of the parents at Murrin Bridge were covert; it was the manager who was left to work very hard, as he was doing, for a school bus service. 'Most parents objected to their children going into the school in the station truck. It is a windy, bumpy road and in winter, it is extremely cold.'

Yet isolation had its compensations. The manager remarked on the great skill of these children in fishing and hunting in the bush. Paul Shinoff wrote that

they live in a world of kangaroos, emus and ring-necked geese. The boys one afternoon casually showed us the five different types of ants that they found in the area. They explained the different eating and nesting habits. In the morning before school, they go down to the river and check their fish nets. They can spot a rabbit at a distance where we could barely make out the burrow it was sitting on.[25]

[23] Selected Attitudes of Murrin Bridge Aborigines, p. 22.
[24] Ibid., p. 31.
[25] Ibid., p. 40.

How much of this interest and expertise is culturally determined; and how much a matter of making the most of the environment?

'Overcrowding' is of course comparative. Of the thirty-two houses, four were of three rooms only, with verandas; there were fifteen with two bedrooms; and thirteen with three. Shinoff calculated that there were 7·7 persons per house and that in some there could not be enough 'conventional sleeping space', commenting also on the makeshift furniture.[26] But having seen these battered homes with the rows of latrines behind, in the traditional Australian rural style, I would estimate them to offer comparative comfort, by the standards available to part-Aboriginal groups. The higher figure of persons per house has to be offset by the fact that among these houses there are no shanties of one or two rooms of the type so common in a fringe area. Yet overcrowding in these comparatively good conditions was such as to exacerbate tensions. There was a code of the bush here, but no leadership with acknowledged responsibility; little control of children; and the manager attributed the perpetual squabbling, which inevitably brought the contending parties to him, partly to the crowded housing conditions. Young married people had to live with parents; drunkenness caused the usual disputes; young children were growing up in these conditions of long standing. Obviously people would compare their conditions with those enjoyed by the station staff; and those with experience of towns and cities would know that most people are much more comfortable. Aborigines in this kind of situation react just like anybody else. At the root of discontent there must also be this factor of *comparatively* poor accommodation for persons of their race and judged suitable for them. Their reactions will correspond with those of camp-dwellers and inmates of institutions in all similar situations.

Part of the remedy seemed in 1967 to be through the Welfare authorities' abdication of power. Managers were being withdrawn in 1965-6 from these stations. There would be many people, especially older ones, who would wish to live on at Murrin Bridge; and no doubt they will do so.

[26] Ibid., p. 22.

To go out towards the centre of the continent from these mid-western towns is like going back in time. As one approaches the approximate boundaries between our 'settled' and 'colonial' regions, discrimination is more obvious, crude, and open; and resentment less restrained. In a sense, too, going into a station like Murrin Bridge was like going out to the Darling: one experienced the same kinds of social tensions.

In 1964 the Aborigines at Murrin Bridge were still maintaining contacts with those of their relatives who had remained on the banks of the Darling. The main concentration of these was at Wilcannia, a hundred miles or so northwards along the river from the old station site at Menindee. This is an area of dry grasslands, stocked mainly with sheep. Casual and contract work on the sheep stations has given Aborigines a foothold in the pastoral industry. In 1957 Jeremy Beckett found that round 70 per cent of Aboriginal workers went out into this work, from Murrin Bridge, Euabalong, and Wilcannia.[1] His perceptive studies of the Aborigines at Wilcannia need no embellishment, and it is doubtful whether attitudes of Aborigines or non-Aborigines there had changed very much since 1957. A new economic factor was the annual movement from Wilcannia down the Darling for the grape and fruit harvests of the Murray, beginning at Mildura and working eastwards. It is highly probable that the Wilcannia Song has been heard far and wide along the Murray, and even into the Murrumbidgee Irrigation Area, in the picking season. Beckett has caught some of the wild exuberance of part-Aboriginal adherence to the traditions of the frontier, and his work is a useful corrective and reminder that life in the part-Aboriginal group

[1] A Study of a Mixed-blood Aboriginal Minority, p. 30 and Table IX.

has its times of climax and high excitement[2] and that resistance to the middle-class ethic is not always covert.

Herbert Simms, a part-Aboriginal well known throughout New South Wales, who was working with this Project in 1965, independently confirmed this view. He wrote in his field notes of the reports he heard of the fights which still occur when men from the shacks in the 'Mallee', an area of Crown land on the same side of the river as Wilcannia, cross over on to the reserve and become involved in a party.

Often times it is a case where the police come and take them in for being found drunk on the reserve, fetching a fine or a time in gaol ... This town would be the worst I have found for Aborigines to sit around the streets and hotel corners; it is very noticeable. Many of the men will approach a person coming to the town for either cigarettes or money for a drink.

Good money is earned by some, he writes, but is spent in drink either in the hotel or 'in the supply of flagons or bottles of wine taken out to the Mallee area and drunk'. Something of the defiant commitment to the old frontier drinking traditions are expressed by the Aboriginal folk-singer, Dougie Young, whom Herbert Simms found in 1965 in permanent employment for the council as a driver:

> They say it's a crime drinking beer and wine,
> Will lead a good man astray,
> But when it comes to grog I'm a fair-dinkum hog
> I suppose I was born that way.

> But I'll drink and roam till the cows come home,
> If it will give my poor heart ease,
> I don't care who knows, I work for my dough
> And I'll spend it as I please.[3]

High consumption of alcohol is not necessarily limited to the Aborigines. From a brief experience of one Sunday afternoon, I would be inclined to compare Wilcannia with a typical town in 'colonial' Australia in this respect. This was in May 1964; my wife and I had booked into a hotel where most of the Aboriginal drinking occurs, and I remember being rapidly recognised as a stranger before I had reached the door by a half

---

[2] See 'Aborigines Make Music', *Quadrant*, Spring 1958, pp. 32–42; 'The Land Where the Crow Flies Backwards', *Quadrant*, July-August 1965, p. 38; and 'Aborigines, Alcohol and Assimilation', in Marie Reay (ed.) *Aborigines Now*, p. 32. For an interesting comment by Beckett on the work of Dougie Young, see 'Aboriginal Balladeer', *The Australian*, 3 July 1965.

[3] Beckett, 'The Land Where the Crow Flies Backwards', *Quadrant*, July-August 1965, p. 42—quoting Dougie Young.

drunk part-Aboriginal lad who was alert enough to thrust out his hand for money. In the bar Aborigines and others were drinking, including two or three non-Aboriginal women with their men, and some young part-Aboriginal girls with their boys. The hallways and the front lounge and office were strewn with papers, leaves, gravel, and one or two broken glasses. Obviously the police were not restricting Sunday trading at this hotel. It is interesting that this should be the case, since the police in that same year seem to have been vigilant in patrolling the reserve and the Mallee. Beckett, who stayed on the reserve, writes that the police would drive past several times a day looking for 'drunks', and would shine their lights on to the houses at night. 'The local Aborigines', he wrote, 'are used to this and take it so much for granted that drinkers often make no attempt to hide.'[4]

My impression was that the whites drinking on this afternoon in the bar were not representative of the townspeople as a whole; that possibly they belonged to an 'improvident' minority. Beckett says that the only white people with whom Aborigines had intimacy of any sort were the police.

With the remaining townspeople there is a relation of avoidance, modified only sufficiently to permit the transfer of goods across counters. My association with the Aborigines rarely brought me into contact with whites. Two of the three hotels will have no dealings with Aborigines at all; the third . . . earning the reputation for being a 'blood house'. . . .[5]

That the whites in the bar were not representative was brought home to us next day, when one man with whom I had business showed clearly his doubts as to my probity after a night spent in this hotel; while another, who managed a garage, expressed his shocked concern to my wife for our 'mistake'. Yet one could see here in this bar something of the atmosphere in which the frontier unions of Aborigines and others were established, and I noted especially the real concern of an old white Australian bushman who courteously escorted his very dark female companion. The indications were that the racial groups associated for economic but not, with this kind of limited exception, for social purposes; and that in economic affairs the white man is always the employer.

In this Darling River area and to the north-west of the river, housing is probably as poor as anywhere in the State. There could be as many as three hundred Aborigines round Wilcannia. Herbert Simms, with assistance from the local police, could locate only one family in the town

[4] Ibid., p. 41.
[5] Ibid.

itself. There were fourteen houses, in two rows, on the reserve, and all other accommodation seemed to be on the Mallee, although Beckett refers to groups of shanties along the river banks. It is very difficult to obtain a fair sample of households in such a situation, and we could only do our best to ensure that our results were not unfairly weighted towards the worst. A selection of four homes on the reserve, the only one in town, and six from the Mallee gave an average household group of $7 \cdot 9$, which is very high indeed considering the nature of some of the shanties and the fact that one of the households had only two persons (with five visitors who were not counted). The better homes are probably those on the reserve, in spite of their battered condition. Fibro shower-latrine units at the back of the houses seemed especially battered, and hardly of much use for privacy. The glass from broken bottles of countless celebrations shone in the dust before, between, and behind the houses. At the time I was there the supervisor was a citizen employed in one of the shops. He had the task because he had always been interested in helping Aborigines, he told me. He stated that the usual thing is to break the bottles, and then to complain about feet being cut on the glass. This was consistent with other stories heard from the whites—of feckless workers, reckless extravagance, alcohol, and inconsiderate noise. For instance, I was told that the Mallee people, lacking sufficient 'nap' for warmth on the winter nights, are wont to stroll singing through the town to the reserve, hoping for a party there. In a small town of about one thousand people, this is likely to keep good citizens awake in their beds.[6] Obviously the Aborigines know this very well.

The Aboriginal community seems to have increased here during the war. It was a convenient place for getting pastoral employment, and some appear to have come here after having been removed from Broken Hill by the police. By 1948 the accommodation was bad enough to lead to controversy in the Sydney and Broken Hill press. The Reverend Mr Brooks of Wilcannia wrote of the scandalous conditions, where a man could lie for a week ill in a tent on the reserve, and ten or twelve people live in a one-roomed hut of iron.[7] This kind of hut may still be seen north-west of the Darling, and may represent the worst housing situation of all, since people live in stabilised conditions but lack all but the barest minimum of provision. It is comforting to trace the one-room iron shanty back to the wurly, to look on its use as indicative of a 'transitional'

[6] According to the 1961 census there were 839 people in the town, and 144 on the Aboriginal reserve.
[7] *S.M.H.*, 29 June 1948.

situation. But these people are not living as nomads, nor have they the skills of their tribal ancestors. They require proper housing and sanitation. It is common to see a household group living in two or three of these one-roomed iron shacks at a place like Enngonia, for instance, so placed as to make the most of any shade available. It could be defended as a carrying on of the old ways, were the *location* somewhere in the bush and the family living by hunting. But the men are either station workers or waiting for work (or avoiding it and trying to live on social services, or simply unable to work); the children and the women have the needs of all other Australians who live on processed foods. They depend on purchases like all but perhaps two or three hundred nomads in the whole of this continent. They can obtain essential food and clothing only by purchase (or charity), and are as much in need as anyone for safe places to store them. Because of the poverty of their diet they are perhaps even more in need than most of proper sanitation, clean water, and effective shelter.

In reply to the Reverend Mr Brooks, in 1948 Michael Sawtell, of the Aborigines Welfare Board, said that Aborigines were not willing to help themselves, that there was nothing to prevent them from improving their lot but that they preferred to live in the manner which had so shocked Brooks.[8] An interesting indication of the change in attitudes among opinion makers was the spate of letters in reply; people were beginning to question the old argument that 'civilisation destroys' the Aboriginal. There was discussion of the need for education, training, and housing.[9]

At that time most of the shanties were placed on the beautiful banks of the river opposite the town. At the request of the council, the City of Broken Hill sent its chief health inspector to advise. He agreed with Brooks's statements, wondered why no local social or religious workers had hitherto been interested, and replied to local demands that the reserve should be closed and the Aborigines moved by pointing out that this would not deal with the problem, except in so far as it would remove the threat of disease from the white townspeople. The men living there were employed on surrounding pastoral properties, were willing and able to pay off houses. The inspector had apparently inspected Menindee Aboriginal Station 'some years ago'; at Wilcannia the current situation was worse than it had been there. Conditions of the latrines on the reserve were such that disease was likely to spread through the town. The towns-people had managed to get separate ones provided for Aboriginal children

[8] *S.M.H.*, 1 July 1948.
[9] *S.M.H.*, 3 July 1948.

at the public school.[10] Some two years later, apparently on representations by the Member for Cobar as well as the Board, the government was planning to build twelve, possibly fourteen houses. The main question was where: the government architect was questioning the reserve site, because of flood danger; the Board was thinking of placing the homes on the town side of the river where the services already were.[11]

This, in retrospect, appears to have been one of those locally decisive moments: placing the houses across the river with access to services would mean placing them *in* the small township. It is at this point that housing schemes seem to have gone awry in the past. One can hardly with justice criticise the caution of a Board with low priorities in its approach to the local council. One can, however, deplore the priority given to Aboriginal welfare, while recognising the part likely to be played in the negotiations by local members anxious not to offend the voters in their electorates by forcing them to accept Aborigines as neighbours. This sensitivity of the State governments, and of the Northern Territory Administration, to local non-Aboriginal opinion, or to some spokesman's view of what that opinion will be has played an important part in this kind of situation, and may explain why the Country Party has generally lagged behind the forefront of changing opinion in Aboriginal affairs. The Board, said the press, would have to consult all sections of the community before the site for the houses could be decided.[12]

In the event, the fourteen houses were built across the river from the town. The result of this decision could well be more decisive for the future of the town and of both groups than any degree of cultural difference which may be argued to justify such a decision. Except for the one family we found, only the shanties of the Mallee are on the 'white' side of the river, and the good folk of Wilcannia, seeing Aborigines mainly when they are shopping, drinking, or waiting in town, may have the stereotype picture of an Aboriginal confirmed, since they do not see Aborigines as neighbours. In the main, the contacts which occur out of the sphere of employment are incidental, tension-laden, and involuntary, which according to the findings of Simpson and Yinger may increase prejudice.[13] Yet there are white men in town who do work of the same type as many Aborigines, who are as well educated, and no better. The pleasant contacts of a family with a new neighbour should, in at least

---

[10] *Barrier Daily Truth* (Broken Hill), 2 July 1948.
[11] Ibid., 4 December 1950.
[12] Ibid.
[13] Racial and Cultural Minorities: An Analysis of Prejudice and Discrimination.

some cases, have tended to reduce prejudice; while the same result could be expected to follow from any important activities in common for the town or the street. But two communities remain at Wilcannia, so that when a scholar like Jeremy Beckett visits his Aboriginal friends there, he is an object of suspicion; and I found myself socially discredited for having spent a night in the hotel patronised by Aborigines.

This is one of the most important questions affecting attitudes to Aborigines, and it goes as directly to the root of inter-racial tensions here as it does in the United States. In a country where money is so important, one of the main arguments and beliefs of the townsmen who resist the establishment of an Aboriginal family in their own town, or especially next door in their own street, is that they will lose money because of the fall in real estate values. I do not think any research has been done in this country to examine the truth of such assumptions. But Fred Case and Lynn Clark, in the United States, found that

the entrance of non-whites into an all-white neighbourhood may or may not cause a decline in property values. If prices . . . are above average, vacancies are few, and the owners refuse to be panicked into sacrificing values, prices will remain firm. If some owners do panic and sell below the established market, all property values in the neighbourhood will tend to drop. But prices will soon rise again and become firm if the demand on the part of non-white families continues.

If prices have begun to fall before Negroes move in, and the situation is an urban one, where they occupy big old houses which they have not the resources to maintain, prices will probably continue to fall.[14]

Deutsch and Collins found that in integrated housing there was more neighbourly contact and interaction between Negroes and whites, with more whites holding some Negroes in esteem, than in a situation of segregated housing.[15] Wilner, Walkley and Cook, after further inquiries, added a qualification, 'provided that the contact is not marked by competition for limited goods or by strong social disapproval of inter-group friendliness'.[16] If there is a situation where the whites are excluding the others from equality, the new association 'is burdened with increased guilt'; the 'relevance of racial origin is extended to a wide range of situations'. Social climate is all-important, says Leo Kuper, one of a group of workers who examined the situation with the support of a very big

[14] 'Property and Race', in John H. Denton (ed.), *Race and Property*.
[15] M. Deutsch and M.C.E. Collins, *Inter-racial housing: a psychological evaluation of a social experiment*.
[16] D.M. Wilner, *et al.*, *Human Relations in Inter-Racial Housing*—quoted by Leo Kuper, 'Sociological Aspects of Housing Discrimination', in John H. Denton (ed.), *Race and Property*.

American group of hard-headed realtors. Discussing integrated housing in a single project, he writes that

the inter-racial integrated housing projects use the relationship between prejudice and discrimination to reduce prejudice. They create a *non-discriminatory situation*, in which the direct experience of contact *on a basis of equality* . . . may help to undermine the hostile stereotypes and to reduce prejudice.[17]

The italics here are mine, and the point is clear. It is less possible to reduce prejudice, even if the objects of it are established as neighbours, if they are in inferior accommodation. Equality has to be there from the start; the more ways in which Aborigines in town are clearly equal, the more possibility there is of decreasing prejudice (provided that the social climate, in the sense of some willingness to consider equality, is favourable). Obvious discrimination, such as the poorer type house for the Aboriginal, confirms prejudice. Prejudice as to what is suitable for Aboriginal needs has justified cheap and poor housing in the past, even in towns. Clearly, then, what might have turned the tide in Wilcannia was not only a decision by the government, in the face of local opposition, to house Aborigines in town, but to provide a standard of house at least comparable with those already there.

[17] Kuper, 'Sociological Aspects of Housing Discrimination', pp. 132, 133.

As one moves westward in New South Wales, or for that matter towards the boundary of our 'settled' regions in any State, the conditions tend to merge into those of the 'colonial' areas. Along and west of the Darling, or in areas where it is possible to get at artesian water without great expense, and where pastoral employment or the produce of a small market garden and a few sheep can make up the additional income required to supplement such lonely occupations as kangaroo hunting, goat mustering, and prospecting, one finds the occasional Aboriginal family established in circumstances which remind one of the frontier conditions as they used to be. Out 'back-o'-Bourke' there is a curious sense of going back in time, even though every working activity these days is geared to the prices on the world markets. Aborigines are trying to live the free life of the bush in a rapidly changing economy. Out here, rigid controls of the Northern Territory type have not been imposed on them: and they have been, at least legally, entitled to award wages— once they came south of the Queensland border.

A house of iron over a bush timber frame can be very comfortable, sometimes with a brushwood awning for coolness in summer, and with great chimney and fireplace for the winter. In many cases the whole house, garden, and surroundings show the neatness of the capable bush-man: at the same time, should the need arise, the basic materials (galvanised iron, stove, and furniture) are easily transported by truck. Possibly few such occupiers have approached the Western Lands Commission for proper tenancy rights, but such an alternative to town dwelling should be encouraged in this western region, where occupation or employment offers away from town. A watered location is likely to be suitable for a village, but bores are expensive, and safe waterholes in rivers pre-empted by long-established pastoral occupation. The pastoralists' homestead will often be at the only water point for a hundred miles, so that other sites for workers' dwellings require sinking of bores. They may, by arrangement with the pastoral manager, build near the homestead water supply, but they have no permanence of tenure, since the leasehold conditions commonly prevent the taking up of land for such purpose within a mile of the station homestead.

### ONE OF THE OLD PASTORAL STATION COMMUNITIES

This was the situation of Aborigines living near the homestead of W——Station, out north and west of the Darling. There must have been Aborigines here since the station was taken up. In December 1964 there were about 130, of whom 77 were children. There had never been an Aboriginal reserve there. The Aborigines had combined with the whites from a small village close by some years before to build a school and teacher's residence. There were now two teachers.

Here I met the intelligent, able, and quite illiterate Tom X——, the type of Aboriginal frontiersman who reminds one of the white and coloured ones in *Such is Life*. He could not afford to move to Brewarrina, unless a 'proper house' in town were to become available; if that happened, he could range further looking for work. He claimed skills in a wide range of pastoral activities, and in timber milling. He knew where he could borrow a disused mill, where the best timber was, and where the demand was likely to come from. He claimed that he could dismantle the machinery, and that he had enough spare parts of his own to build a second mill.

'What', I asked him, 'is your usual occupation?'

'My occupation is everything: shearing, horse-breaking, sawmilling, tank-sinking. I do a bit of welding. I do just about everything except carpentering.' But he lacked capital.

One could see thirteen of the reasons why, for his wife and twelve children shared the iron and timber house and the bough shelter facing west. If he got the mill he was working for, he could build himself a good timber house, he said, for about £800 ($1,600). However, the station owner could disallow any settlement within a mile of the homestead. That was one reason why the dozen or so houses were all built of second-hand iron (with old nail holes) over bush timber. Yet they differed from those on the reserve in Bourke in greater neatness and workmanship, and on one had the impression that the men here were a competent lot with their hands. Their dwellings provided efficient shelter, without any security for possessions. Bough shelters made for cool sitting in the shade. The beds were wire frames standing on oil drums, with mattresses and covers. There was no depressing heap of rubbish, no old rags tramped into the soil around the homes, nor rusty tins, broken bottles, and the like.

A previous manager had tried to drive them away by preventing them from using the taps at the shearing shed. But they had sunk wells in the bed of the river, rolling water up in drums to the homes (quite a common way for Aborigines to get their water in this region). This was in the constituency of a Labor Premier, and one wondered what would have happened if this group had been non-Aboriginal. I would guess that the small area which now remained of the old W—— Station would have been subdivided for 'closer' settlement.

These Aboriginal folk were a potential asset to the business of the region. One hawker brought fruit and vegetables all the way from Dirranbandi. A woman brought dresses from her frock shop in Sydney once a year. The men earned well (except in bad seasons) and they spent their money locally.

X was one of five brothers, all hard working and all able to earn well. He and two others were trade union members. One brother was shearing regularly his two hundred sheep a day, had a rented house in Cunnamulla, and a car. But, said X, 'he is no better off than me'; obvious reasons included ignorance of investment procedures, lack of caution in saving cash, and difficulty in getting enough at any one time to invest. I was somewhat impressed with X's explanation of the problem of getting a house on land of one's own, and of the importance of this as the foundation of modest prosperity.

What we're really driving after is a bit of land to build on. We don't need any help from the government if we could only get the bit of ground to start off. At least we could cut our own timber. There is a bit of mill work, and if I can get enough ground to put me mill on, it would be something very important to us. We live all our lives around here, and . . . it is time we got into something like that where we would have something very important to us . . . something to show for our money . . . If we could get a bit of land we can build our own place on which we can call our own.

(He made the point at some length that, without the chance of acquiring real property, he was no better off than a man who did not work at all. What was implicit in the remark was that such a man would have to be fed by somebody; that he himself must spend the money he saved to keep the man who did not work.)

We work all the year round here and we don't know whether we are supposed to stop on this bit of land that we are camped on just at the moment. And another thing that brings us all back to the one level here, that we have nothing to put our investment into. We just work here and spend our money as we get it. We got nothing here we can put it into; a house or anything to occupy the wife or families ... We just got to camp in a humpy, the same as anybody else. So if we work night and day, it doesn't make us feel any better than the man who doesn't work.

(Here I said that what he called a humpy was well built and comfortable, though better suited to three than fourteen persons; that the workmanship was clearly such as to suggest that he could have built much more attractively and comfortably.)

Well, if you build a house that is worth anything ... we might be shifted any time. We don't know how we stand. I know this is private property, and we can't build anything that's worth while.

(What would he do, I asked, if he could get a home lease from the Commission for Western Lands? These are available very cheaply, and subject to certain improvement conditions.)

Yes, if I could get the lease I would be very much obliged. There would be four other fellows besides me here, my four brothers. That we have been after for quite a while. So if we can get this lease it will be something for us to go on with ... I would say about three or four acres, I suppose, to grow a bit of vegetables and a few fruit trees or something like that. And a water supply ... I'd have some place privately to keep me tools and me machinery and that under, and to stack me timber.

(When one is tempted to say that Aborigines on the common or reserve are indifferent about the nature of their shanties, we might well remember the point made earlier about lack of any security of tenure; and this further one of the difficulty of maintaining one's tools of trade and few treasured possessions might be pondered over by those who assume that Aborigines do not store them because they do not place a value on material things. Would he, I asked, run a few sheep?)

Yes, that is another point here. While we are out working we often bring home two, three sheep. And we could even buy our own half a dozen or dozen sheep and bring them home and put them in a little paddock and keep for killers.

(From experience elsewhere, as when the government of Puerto Rico forced the owners of large properties to sell land over a certain area and gave the *campesinos* enough land to have a garden and a few animals, the results could be more far reaching, for this allowed the *campesinos* to refuse the worst paid employment. No longer were they compelled to work for whatever they could get, without the chance of bargaining. Some Aborigines do seem to be exploited by payment at less than award rates; the security of home, garden and a few sheep could operate against this, and also enable the contract fencer or other worker to refuse any unfair offers. Would such a stake in land and home, I asked, make his wife and family feel any more settled and secure than now?)

Well, I mean, they would have more things to occupy their mind. They would feel more at home . . . that a man was working and trying to better them. But the way we are now . . . I suppose they feel the same as I do. I mean we work all the year round and we haven't got nothing to show . . . But the way we are now, I mean, we can't say it's my camp or their camp. The boss will come along and say 'Youse'll have to shift to some other place'. Well, that's the finish.[1]

He made another point about absence of any rights to the site of one's home and land; that if, as often happened, men from other places brought hard liquor out here to drink, he had no right to order them away from the vicinity of his home. This has some bearing on reluctance on the part of some workers to work far away from home; if their dwellings are on reserves or common land, they often have good reason.

One or two of the men had been interested in life insurance, as a means of safeguarding families and to establish credit for housing. The Area Welfare Officer had supported them in this; but when one of the local insurance agents had expressed willingness to insure them, his head office had refused.

X had come here from Dirranbandi, in Queensland, with two of his brothers, all bringing families with them—and probably the iron for the houses. Other areas of origin for people in this area included St George, Cunnamulla, and Thargomindah. They claimed that they had a better chance of the award wage in New South Wales. They were not, they said, legally 'under the Act' in Queensland, but they claimed that they were likely to be treated as if they were—directed to a place of employment at the Aboriginal wage, under threat of a charge of vagrancy.

X did not hold any higher opinion of the police south of the border; they 'treat every blackfellow alike'. He had, he said, taken one of his children into Brewarrina just before the relaxation of the drinking restrictions on Aborigines. His brother had been caught drinking there two weeks before and X, on this occasion, was mistaken for him, arrested, charged with vagrancy, and spent some hours in the lock-up before the police recognised their mistake.

He and the other Queenslanders at W—— lived at one end of the

[1] This interview was tape recorded by me and a record is in the SSRC-AP file—C.D.R.

small cluster of homes; at the other lived the old station families. Tensions, typically discharged against secondary objects, kept the groups apart. The Queenslanders were all Catholics; the others, adherents of the Aborigines Inland Mission. Until the newcomers arrived, I was told, station workers among the Aborigines had always eaten the meal provided outside the mess-room. X, handed his plate by the cook at the door on his first day, had refused to eat it outside, went in, and waited. The cook, nonplussed at this departure from old tradition, had refused to serve him. 'Don't blame me; it's always been like this.' X told the manager that if he was good enough to work with whites and get the same wages, he was good enough to eat with them. The manager told the cook to serve him in the mess-room. But, said X, some of the others who had always eaten under the tree outside refused to go inside; they preferred to eat outside by themselves.

The basic question was that of land tenure for home sites. Since the station has depended for so long on Aboriginal labour in the past, there would seem to be no great hardship in excision from the lease (or if necessary, purchase from the freehold) of living areas—not for yet another reserve, but for purchase by occupants. There is good argument here for helping them to win strength by incorporation: for negotiation with the station manager, with the Welfare Officer, police, and others whose decisions are of vital importance. Some such measures could give the people a chance to learn to work together, irrespective of religion or area of origin, for the common good; to establish the credit of members with business firms and others, like insurance companies, with guarantees; to take responsibility for payment of rents, of instalments on homes; or, as one might anticipate in this kind of area, to give guarantees for the purchase on credit of the sheet iron needed for immediate extensions to houses, which would be a matter of priority as soon as tenure is established. Common action could be taken by the new 'legal person' to exclude from property vested in its members or itself the unwanted 'drunks'. In this way people might learn to make their own approaches to officialdom with confidence, and especially to protect themselves without official interference.

At W—— the social order was demonstrated at the annual school prize-giving. The whites, pastoralists and others, were kindly and pleasant to all. They showed great kindness to the Aboriginal children, who made up most of the school membership. Aboriginal and other parents were there. But the groups did not mix, except in conversation. The whites, when the time came to sit, occupied the two front rows of seats, in the shade of the school. The Aboriginal parents sat in other shade to the rear; they moved closer when the children sang carols. All had the same soft drinks and cakes in the school basement. The Aborigines and all the children then departed; the cartons of beer appeared, and the party, as far as the whites were concerned, really began. Perhaps this was the homestead tradition of the Christmas party for the hired help, who knew the proper time to depart. It might also have illustrated habits long formed while Aborigines could not legally be offered liquor.

These people were really kind, and the Aborigines obviously enjoyed the whole thing. The President of the Parents and Citizens told me that the Aborigines were 'very happy' with the houses they had; that they were gradually improving them; that they would have no chance of looking after 'real' houses. The educated ones would sweep the dirt floors neatly; but the 'scrubbies' slept in their clothes, never washed the dishes, copulated in front of the children. (How, one wondered, could he know such a thing?) Station labour was not as efficient as it used to be. It had not occurred to him that there was less learning on the job, or training of any kind, than there used to be; that these days the smaller stations wanted efficient single men for short terms only. A very old pensioner on the reserve at Bourke had made the point to me that he had been trained for the various station tasks but that, these days, the cost of a worker was much higher. For instance, an extra employee in these days of mechanisation means purchase of an extra truck to make full use of him. It is much cheaper, as the pastoralists in the Northern Territory have claimed, to employ fully literate jackeroos, whose wages are not a matter for concern, than Aborigines at award wages.

### ENNGONIA—BACK O'BOURKE

A remote concentration of Aboriginal pastoral workers in this north-western region was at Enngonia, some seventy miles or so almost due north of Bourke along the road to Cunnamulla. The village had a police station, a store, and one or two houses of reasonable quality, to judge from the outside, and at the time of my visit seventeen family groups housed in shacks as bad as the worst that one gets used to expecting, in terms of overcrowding and facilities. Severe drought meant severe unemployment at W—— and here; perhaps, too, it accounted for the drift from Queensland. Several families here maintained their ties with people at Cunnamulla.

This village depended on water from a single bore, so that without another bore there could be no separate fringe settlement for the Aboriginal majority. Social integration had thus been favoured by isolation and by circumstances; but an unfavourable circumstance was that Aborigines formed the majority group. Incredibly, in 1964, sixteen new houses being built for the Aborigines Welfare Board were located half a mile from the centre of town where Aborigines then lived, on the site of an old reserve.

Such a decision, so similar to that made at Wilcannia over a decade earlier, could only have been the result of local social pressures and the sensitivity of politicians to them, especially as it involved the cost of another bore. One wondered if the arguments about the value of the real estate had been used in this barren spot, where the substitute for gaiety of flowers was the glitter of broken bottles and the various metals of imperishable industrial scrap-tins, old wire, wrecked kitchenware, and the like, which shone with the glass, industrial blossoms in the dust. The Aborigines had located their shacks conveniently to where possible employers could find them as required; half a mile, some of them said, could mean a real difference in earnings. Nor were they sure that they could keep up rent payments to the Board. These are certainly low enough, but fifteen or seventeen shillings could mean something for a seasonal worker with eight or nine children in time of drought. If they moved, and failed to get station work, they would have the problem of arrears in rent. If they did not (this was said to me only on condition that names were not used), they could be forced to move their present homes, or have them bulldozed.

I was there in December. One could imagine what the bitter winds of winter could mean here; imagine the trials of Aboriginal mothers at night, who wrap their babies in hot rags, heated from time to time before the fire. Perhaps in good times there would be fewer families gathered here at the pick-up point for casual work. The policeman remarked that the white inhabitants were anxious to see the end of their shacks.

There was a population of about 600 in the whole police district, of whom some 160 or so were identified as Aboriginal; of some 300 offences in the district in the previous year leading to charges, about 250 were said (by the policeman) to have been committed by Aborigines. Out on the pastoral stations, in these days of closer settlement, the employer required not the family but the individual worker for a short term; it does not pay to provide family accommodation. Villages like this, then, within easy distance of the properties, are essential for the industry to the extent that it depends on casual work.

In some cases, two or more separate one-roomed shacks formed a single dwelling. This way of using iron over bush timbers saves construction problems and allows most use to be made of small areas of shade. It also allows for the separation of adults from children for privacy, where only a few sheets of iron are owned. Water had to be rolled in oil drums from the bore—for several hundreds of yards in some cases. An old woman and her grand-daughter, whom I saw doing this, told me this was usual for them.

I met one family living in two of these separate one-roomed shacks, both with dirt floors, and one with a large fireplace which served for cooking and for warmth in winter. Here lived a man, his *de facto* wife, and eight children. Part of the accommodation was a double bed under a tree. Bed, tree, and rooms were fenced in with a rather pathetic attempt at garden; the furniture was mainly broken beds, boxes, and oil drums. The eldest boy had just topped his first-year class in a secondary boarding school hundreds of miles to the east; his success was being spoken about among the Aborigines in Bourke, and, I was told, as far afield as Nyngan, for he had beaten several sons of local pastoralists.

The breadwinner had a utility truck, but work was scarce; he would get three weeks or two weeks at a time; no more. He could do nothing but wait right here for the next employer to come looking for him. To the uninformed, the sight of this father of eight playing with his baby son on the bed under the tree would be one more proof of Aboriginal fecklessness.

In one cluster of four separate one-roomed structures was a family of householder, wife, twelve children, and two step-children. The eldest was twenty-three and all the children had grown up on this barren town common. In the shade of a pepper tree sat the wife and four other women, enjoying a game of cards. They said that their menfolk were away at work but that twelve men in the village were out of work. (The drought became much more serious later.) There was talk of the new houses. Two men who were there said they would have been willing to 'go short' to pay the rent if they had been built 'in the street', but they objected to the segregation. Moreover the new houses would require furniture, but this required more work. At that time in mid-December both men were hoping for work to have some cash for Christmas; otherwise there would be nothing before the New Year. If, they said, a man gets into debt for a few weeks in rent, he must earn 'double' to catch up. The other alternative was to go to Bourke; but they were not known to employers there. For some a sheet of iron is a matter for careful investment. Others, when they do have money (or credit), will spend it all in one drinking bout. Both are very human reactions of men who know the anxiety of poverty.

On the way out to this area from the east, I had driven past the great wealth of the 1964 wheat harvest. Long lines of the big bulk-wheat trucks waited at the railway stations and sidings—up to ninety of them in one or two places. This was wheat for China, and storage was all-important. Plastic sheeting was being laid on the ground, and hundreds of sheets of galvanised iron, the basic building material of inland Australia, were being used, propped up as walls, to protect the grain. Here was a recognised national emergency, with export income involved. I thought of this at Enngonia; and again when I met an age pensioner on the reserve at Bourke, who was setting aside an amount from each pension payment, buying a sheet of iron as he could afford it (taking the risk that it would be stolen by someone in need, since he had no safe storage). His purpose was to have a roof without holes, so that he might apply with some hope to have his grandchild brought home to him from the Child Welfare Home. It was a revealing illustration of priorities in Australian society, prompting a thought on the nature of equality. Any Aboriginal with a wheat crop had the same right as anyone else to have it protected by the iron walls at the railway station; or if he were a stock owner on his own land, he had the same right as others to be subsidised for the sinking of bores.

Aboriginal poverty lacks any tradition, even knowledge, of the basic techniques of investment. Aborigines have assimilated the philosophy of the 'improvident' seasonal worker that imbues the periphery of the industrial world with which most of them have had contact. The attitude is reinforced by inexperience in possessing real property. When the young shearer comes home with his cheque, prestige comes from big spending. But there is something more: it is giving, free, generous, without accounting, complete; and what he can give for a while to others in the group is a good time, a temporary escape, a few hours of real manhood, equality in the bar, and 'fun round here'.

The promotion of new values must depend to some extent on raising the level of enjoyment of daily life for the whole family, to offer something more than work, gossip, and sex. When the bright young lad came home to Enngonia, his father was lying on the bed under the tree knowing that his only chance of work was to stay there. Women sit all day in the shade, with minimum household tasks. For the numerous children when out of school there is very little indeed; their wanderings through the bush on learning expeditions are limited to the dusty environs of the camp. There was a tennis court in the midst of the shacks at Enngonia; I asked one of the men if he had ever played tennis. 'They wouldn't have us', he said; and went on to tell me that he had played cricket as a boy at school; but this was his only experience of organised sport. We have already noted the propensity for boxing, which is an outlet for the individual with the required physique. In many country areas Aborigines are distinguished as footballers.

I remember meeting, during this survey, a man whom I had admired when as a young man I had played with and against him at Rugby League, the universal game of the New South Wales country areas. I had not known him at all as an Aboriginal, because he came from another town; and he is only 'Aboriginal' now because he has always belonged to the Aboriginal group. It gave me something of a shock to see him in 1965, sitting on the floor of his humpy, fat and elderly, making boomerangs for sale. When his football days were over, he had mixed little outside the Aboriginal group.

Such groups seem to need purpose, and social integration with other Aborigines and with the townsfolk as a whole. Places like Enngonia need, as do the fringes of country towns throughout the country, the integration which can come only through common pursuit of something of their own, involving better living standards in material life. One reason why one thinks of incorporated bodies is that even if the task of promoting them fails in nearly every case for a long time, such effort does not have to be justified by administrative success. By the standards of the democracy which Australians profess, it provides experience which is *an end in itself*. We can be sure now of one thing—that there can be no constructive social change promoted by government action which does not begin with the learning experience of people associating to talk out their problems and to set their objectives for action.

## THE SAME PATTERN IN A VERY 'GOOD' TOWN—BOURKE 1964

An important centre for Aborigines in this part of the State is the reserve at Bourke, a non-municipal town which at the 1961 census had a population of over three thousand, with almost another thousand spread out along the winding banks of the Darling River. In stating the poor conditions on the Aboriginal reserve, one has to admit that there are many others living in comparable conditions of very temporary housing on the riverine flats. In December 1964, when I first went there, the first serious effects of the great drought which was to continue at least into the middle of 1966 were being felt in the pastoral industry; and among the shack-dwellers off the reserve were said to be many pastoral workers other than Aborigines. The difference in the situations of Aborigines and others in such circumstances are more real than obvious. It is more probable that for the non-Aboriginal worker these are temporary quarters; and there is no prejudice to be faced and overcome if he moves to change his circumstances.

But it did seem that, by the standards Aborigines are constrained to use, Bourke is a 'good' town. There were Aboriginal women working in the shops and hotels—not, as is so usual, as maids only, but serving in the bar; and there were always considerable numbers in the streets, which was not surprising since the main reserve is quite close to the centre of the town—perhaps another significant fact, since there are other less convenient locations which could have been used. This quite significant difference in attitude, at least as expressed in the use of services and institutions, could be ascribed to the carrying on of some of the conditions of the frontier days, were it not for the fact that there seem to be such dramatic differences from the situation at Wilcannia, which may be even closer than Bourke to frontier conditions.

At that time there were said (by the Board's local staff) to be about 400 persons of known Aboriginal descent, and in addition there were people of probable Aboriginal ancestry whom the Welfare Officer would not dream of approaching in his official capacity. They did not need him, and in any case, he believed, they would have resented the reminder of their origin. This is the state of mind and of affairs which appears to be accepted as a reasonable outcome of an 'assimilation' policy. But surely such determined attempts to forget one's origins are symptomatic of mental stress and of what almost universal prejudice can lead us to. The much vaunted 'integration' surely means nothing if the objects of prejudice feel that they must 'pass', deny their relatives, to be accepted as equals; and what looks like sycophancy and treachery to other Aborigines will hardly stimulate a readiness to accept such people as models.

Once again, there was the range of situations—official reserve, unauthorised fringe, a group of dwellings in town, and others established in town by their own efforts. The official reserve at the time of my visit was the site for at least twenty-eight shacks, and so far as I could see these were all occupied. They were all obviously built by the occupants, mainly of the inevitable galvanised iron sheets nailed over rough bush timbers. I spent some time visiting in four of them; and in each case the floor was packed earth. One had linoleum laid on this. It was one of the most effective houses, with good iron in the roof. The head of the house was an age pensioner; his household consisted of his wife, his daughter with her two very young children, an obviously pregnant grand-daughter of fifteen years, another grand-daughter of the same age, in from

Wanaaring, and a lad of six. There were four rooms, without kitchen or bathroom; for cooking the inside fireplace, for bathing (I was told) the round tub in which the daughter was up to her elbows in the never-ending washing which women undertake in these conditions in the battle to keep their children clean. Two of the rooms were bedrooms. There was no water laid on; no electric or other power or heat from the town supply; and, I noticed, no books. There were two double beds and a cot, some kerosene lamps, and a kerosene refrigerator. There were serviceable seats for six persons, including a stool and an oil drum. There was the usual bench outside along one wall, with the tub being used for laundry.

It was midsummer and the iron was hot. The man was from a Queensland pastoral station originally, the lady from Cumeroogunga. The families of either or both were likely to come here. On this occasion there were ten adult and at least eight child visitors, but they had brought their own bedding and were camped in the somewhat limited shade. They had come for one of those occasions when the Aboriginal folk are accustomed to show their solidarity and acknowledge the ties of kinship; there had been quite a large funeral, and I was there in the aftermath of it all. The funeral was the outcome of an earlier celebration, when the young men, in a state of some excitement, had been throwing each other into the Darling River; one of them had failed to surface, and his funeral had just been celebrated.

I discussed with the old man his attitude to accommodation. Was he satisfied with what he had? No; he needed another room at least. Why did he not build it? 'Iron', he said, 'is thirty shillings a sheet. I have some money in the bank, but one has to keep that for emergencies.' He told me of an old lady living on the reserve who had to have another room, built of iron without the holes which second-hand iron has, so that she could, as it were, get her grandchildren out of pawn, for they would remain in the Child Welfare home until she could satisfy officials that she had proper accommodation. She had asked this man to get some iron and to cut bush timber for her; but he was too old for that work, while the kind of iron which she or he could afford would not satisfy the authorities. Would some of the young men lounging after the funeral get the timber? Apparently not.

He introduced me to the age pensioner I have already mentioned, with grandchildren in the custody of Child Welfare. This old 'battler' had erected the frame of the special room required, and was buying the iron, one sheet at a time as he could afford it, nailing it on as he got it to prevent theft. Breakdown in the nuclear family, with the grandparents attempting to meet the needs of grandchildren, was found in yet another house. An elderly widow had her sister, sister's husband, and five of the grandchildren of both sisters in a dwelling of two iron rooms, with a partly open bough shelter attached, where she sat on one of the several beds resting on oil drums and talked to me. She too hoped to get grandchildren back with her, but was waiting for her male relatives to build a better home for her on a better site, on the other side of the reserve.

According to the Reports of the Board, this was the year of highest population on the Bourke reserve, with 168 people residing there.[2] The lowest number recorded since the war had been fifteen. The trend was to increase, probably reflecting mechanisation and closer settlement, and, more recently, drought. In a situation of changing techniques, the drought could well break the habits of employment and expedite labour-saving technical change.

There was a high proportion of aged pensioners on the reserve. My elderly informant, secure on his pension, had something of the air of one who has achieved a well-earned competence. In addition to his age pension, and his wife's invalid pension, the only other income coming into his house at that time was £1 ($2) per week child endowment for the daughter, plus what she referred to as 'a few bob now and then' which the father of one of her children sent her. The pension, intended as relief, looks so much like opulence that there is something in the claims of the prejudiced that the Dark People will plan and scheme to get pensions as soon as they can. Most significant here, but a point often missed, is the level of aspirations involved and the realistic acceptance of what is possible if one is Aboriginal.

The complete dreariness of existence on the reserve was utterly depressing; it was a real fringe in this respect. Little wonder if 'fun' when it happens includes outlet for violence. Bourke was a 'good' town but no member of this family was also a member of any community organisation there.

Water from the river had been supplied to the reserve for some years; but only in 1964 had it been brought into taps—up till four months before my visit it had, according to my informant, cost five shillings a drum to get it from the main watering point 'down at the pump', though one could make one's own arrangements for getting it. It would be somewhat pointless to have the water reticulated into houses of this temporary nature so it had been brought to several taps in the open air, one tap serving five or six houses. In a city of south-east Asia, such provision of

[2] *N.S.W.P.P.*, 1965, no. 9—A.W.B. Report, 1963-4, p. 13.

water may be regarded as a major public health measure; but it seemed somewhat out of phase in Australia. To save carrying, however, long lengths of plastic hose were being used on the taps. There were no communal laundries or bathrooms; but there were a number of new two-seater pan-system latrines, covered by iron structures on concrete bases, and serviced twice a week by the council, which also collects the garbage twice weekly. At the minimum, here was recognition that public health is one and indivisible where the fringe is so close to town.

Even closer to the town was the unauthorised settlement of eight or ten houses on the 'Old Pound', where the shacks were even more temporary; and there was no sign of the usual services at all. The site was in from the road and behind the stockyards. It seemed to be a transit camp for people who refused to stay on a reserve, for the usual reasons; while those on the reserve, referring to this site, say that people should not be allowed to live under such conditions. Yet I met here a man as impressively self-confident and independent as X, of W——. He was living in a tent with some of his ten children, perhaps all of them, as makeshift beds surrounded it. His wife was ill in the hospital; and they were waiting for her there. The family came from Wanaaring, where he had completed four rooms of his house and erected the frames for four others. So far he had not been able to amass enough capital to buy all the iron at once. He hoped to negotiate a deal for some good second-hand iron at ten shillings a sheet. His house when completed would have a dining room and kitchen and six bedrooms.

I asked whether there was any point in a scheme to subsidise or under-write the purchase of materials with provision for repayment. He thought so, as the enterprising man with a family of this size (all, he claimed, with healthy appetites) is unable to accumulate enough capital to get the iron and the land required for building.

One could not but be impressed with the obvious health and apparent happiness of the children who were there, including a girl of fourteen years or so who was cooking the family meal efficiently over an open fire. The father wanted to stay in the bush; from his point of view, Bourke was a large town. A number of his relatives had died there; he said there was always more illness in town; and from what I had seen I could not question it. Meat was cheaper in the bush.

Again, I thought of the possibilities of an Aboriginal company, as purchaser and supplier of iron and other building materials which people want, or perhaps a co-operative, a savings-loans society or association, with government backing to guarantee credit.

Yet this perhaps too unqualified picture of poverty is by no means the whole story, even of the situations of those who live in the special Aboriginal slums. The stories one hears constantly of the reckless expenditure of earnings may be often exaggerated, but there is no doubt that they are often true. Some men who live in hovels of this kind can earn their hundred dollars or more a week as shearers, and are likely to have nothing from time to time. One man without enough money in his pocket to ring Dubbo, where he was well known to a taxi driver, came to the Welfare Office in Bourke to borrow it. He was able to hire the taxi to go to a shearing shed in Queensland (at a cost of over £100) because the driver knew that he would be paid eventually. Part of the explanation is the 'inmate' outlook, and the dependent personality. People believe that it is the special task of the Board and its officers to look after them. The other belief that they have been wrongfully deprived of the country's wealth justifies the acceptance from the Board's officers of whatever they can get, as well as demands made on the spur of the moment. While I was in Bourke, a mother from Wanaaring (about 100 miles away) rang the Board's office; her child was ill and the ambulance could not come. A Welfare Officer went out by car. When she arrived she found that the mother, without thinking further of the 'Board', had hired a taxi and passed her on the road.

Herbert Simms, investigating conditions in homes east of Bourke, found that it was common practice in one small town for the householder on the reserve to ring up the one store which gave credit, order a packet of cigarettes, and ask the storekeeper to 'get Joe to bring them out'. Joe was the taxi-driver. Perhaps an Aboriginal corporate body might provide avenues for investment in things of higher appeal than the whims of the moment and make possible the amassing of material, social, and cultural assets. The opportunity at once involves responsibility. For those who are already self-confident and responsible, it provides increased opportunity and the chance for leadership.

# ABORIGINAL LIVING STANDARDS
III       AND THE MOVE TO THE CITIES

In 1965, household surveys, using interviews, were undertaken in non-metropolitan areas in two States—New South Wales and South Australia. In the New South Wales survey we attempted to cover the State as a whole, outside Sydney. For reasons of time, costs, and mobility of the population, no sampling of dwellings throughout the State was attempted. The method of selection was first to ascertain, within an area centred in a country town, the number of houses occupied by Aborigines. These were classified according to tenure under which the land on which they stood was held. As nearly as possible, one-third of dwellings in each category were then chosen for interview. Where there were two or three dwellings in a small township we selected one for interview. We also attempted so to select that the dwellings were fairly representative within each of our five divisions of the State. Attention was also paid to overall numbers, so far as they could be established, living in the different land-tenure situations within the State. Care was taken to avoid country towns which had recently been centres of demonstrations, partly to avoid the suspicion with which our inquiries might have been met but mainly because we preferred to risk understatement rather than exaggeration.*

We could not know accurately either the size or distribution of the population. It is possible that we overstated the proportion of families established on town building blocks and that, in making the selection, isolated homes in the bush were overlooked. We also tried to represent fairly in the selection all non-metropolitan areas of the State. For this purpose we divided it into five regions: North Coast, South Coast, South

* An earlier version of this chapter was read to ANZAAS in 1965, and published in *Quadrant*.—C.D.R.

West (Cowra to Deniliquin), West (Wellington to Wilcannia), and North West (Dubbo-Collarenebri). In the last-named of these regions we avoided Moree (where the counted population averaged 10·5 persons per dwelling) and Walgett (where the average was 8·4 persons) for the purposes of this particular survey.

The final selection of dwellings, classified according to land tenure, was as follows:

| Land Tenure | No. of Dwellings |
|---|---|
| Aboriginal Welfare Board station | 31 |
| Aboriginal Welfare Board reserve | 45 |
| Crown land or town common | 45 |
| Town building block | 27 |
| Other privately owned land | 30 |
| Other situations | 5 |
| Total | 183 |

The South Australian survey was arranged through Dr Fay Gale, of the Department of Geography, University of Adelaide, who was given help by Professor R.G. Brown, Department of Social Studies, and with co-operation and assistance of the South Australian Department of Aboriginal Affairs. It was centred mainly on Port Lincoln, Whyalla, and Port Augusta, with interviews also in smaller centres of the hinterland—Coomunga, out from Port Lincoln; Iron Knob; and station towns along the railway line from Port Augusta to Marree. Interviewing was carried out by students of the Department of Social Studies, using the same questionnaire as that used in New South Wales. The dwellings were selected for them by Dr Gale; and they had preparatory work for the task in the University's Departments of Social Studies and of Geography, as well as assistance from the social workers employed in this area by the State Department of Aboriginal Affairs.

The selection of areas for survey work depended largely on where assistance of this kind was available, but there was good reason for selecting the Eyre Peninsula and some hinterland townships tied by rail or road to the main centres there, because the results shed some light on the effects on Aboriginal living standards of urbanisation in a newly industrialised region. The students were able to interview twenty-four non-Aboriginal families living next door or adjacent to Aborigines interviewed: the number is obviously too small for any conclusions to be drawn. A total of sixty-two questionnaires were successfully completed by interviewing Aboriginal householders, whose dwellings may be classified on the same basis as the New South Wales selection.

| Land Tenure | No. of Dwellings |
|---|---|
| Department of Aboriginal Affairs station | 5 |
| Department of Aboriginal Affairs reserve | 4 |
| Crown land or town common | 2 |
| Town building block | 42 |
| Other privately owned land | 8 |
| Tenure not recorded | 1 |
| Total | 62 |

In each case, data were obtained on the dwelling and its facilities and on the occupying household. Data were also obtained on individual family members and visitors. In the New South Wales households, 1,283 persons were included, and in those selected in the Eyre Peninsula, 400. In this chapter we are concerned mainly with the living conditions of the families interviewed.

The populations in both States were increasing very rapidly. Over 53 per cent in both groups were children under fifteen years of age, and 75 per cent of the total in each group were under thirty years of age. Rural and country town patterns of racial discrimination appear to operate as one factor promoting increased urbanisation. There is, however, some marriage into the Aboriginal group. The 183 families in New South Wales included ten male and two female non-Aboriginal spouses; and the sixty-two families in the Eyre Peninsula, nine male and one female spouse.[1]

The households were maintained almost exclusively from seasonal and labouring work and from social service payments. Seasonal work involves a high degree of movement, but within a pattern limited by resources, for the man who is likely to be 'last on and first off' the job cannot afford to risk as much as others on the chance of distant employment. Seasonal work over long distances also requires capital equipment, like caravans, if the worker is concerned with the security of his family, especially if he does not hold any title to the land on which his house stands, so that the family may be at the mercy of chance intruders. The

[1] Robyn R. Iredale—The Enigma of Assimilation—found that the higher wages were earned by non-Aboriginal males who had married into these groups—one in an urban area of Sydney and one in a N.S.W. country town.

Aboriginal has been excluded from hotel accommodation in many places; he may have to depend on relatives when he moves after work, and his movements be limited accordingly.

In this type of economic and social poverty, effect often looks like cause: the situation is one of *multiple* causation. A worker who must take seasonal work may be offered nothing else, because of the assumption that he will inevitably have the urge to 'go walkabout'. The typical country town situation constitutes, from the Aboriginal point of view, what L.M. and J.R. Hanks have called a 'social syndrome of mal-satisfactions',[2] and a 'push' factor, as it were, out of non-metropolitan Australia into the other world of the metropolis, where the demands of the cash economy may prevail over long-standing race prejudice. Hopes for change may attract Aborigines into towns where new industrial development offers new kinds of opportunities. Some of the differences between the situations in country town and rural New South Wales and those in the Eyre Peninsula probably arise in part from acceptance of such opportunities, since forty-two of the sixty-two families co-operating in the Eyre Peninsula survey were living on town building blocks.

Most of the families we met suffered deprivations; and their outlook illustrated the 'culture of poverty'. Of the non-school population over school age in New South Wales, age at leaving school could not be established in over 25 per cent of cases, which may in itself be significant. But of the remainder, 52·5 per cent had left school under fifteen years of age, and 42·8 per cent between fifteen and seventeen. Only 1·6 per cent had been in school at seventeen; 3 per cent were stated never to have attended school. There was no information for 32 per cent of the Eyre Peninsula people; of the remainder just under 32 per cent were stated not to have attended school; 44 per cent had left school under fifteen years of age, and the other 24 per cent left school between fifteen and seventeen. As for confident hopes that new opportunities will rapidly change this situation, only 13·4 per cent of the New South Wales 15-19 age group were in school; 7·7 per cent had left between twelve and fifteen: 71·8 per cent had left at fifteen, or between fifteen and seventeen years; no information could be obtained in the other 7 per cent of cases. In the Eyre Peninsula group the numbers were too small to have much signifi-cance; but the fact that only 13 per cent of the 15-19 age group were still at school may help to confirm the New South Wales figure.

We set out to establish the standards of formal education of those not in school. For 29·5 per cent of New South Wales persons, and 24·5 per

[2] *Tribe Under Trust: A Study of the Blackfoot Reserve in Alberta*, p. 176.

cent in the Eyre Peninsula, this information could not be established.
Attainments of the *remainder* are as set out in Table 1.

**Table 1:** *School Attainments*

|  | N.S.W. | Eyre Peninsula |
|---|---|---|
|  | % | % |
| Incomplete primary schooling | 35·2 | 49·6 |
| Primary only | 35·5 | 36·0 |
| Secondary, below Intermediate | 27·2 | 10·8 |
| Intermediate | 2·0 | 3·6 |
| Leaving Certificate | Nil | Nil |
| Any tertiary or technical course or qualification | Nil | Nil |
| Total | 99·9 | 100·0 |

Note that these figures relate to those out of school and above school
leaving age. But such a situation forms in itself a strong handicap, although
only one amongst others, on the efforts of those in school.

The extremely high proportion of Aboriginal school leavers at fifteen
years or so, all over Australia, has been the subject of much recent
comment. The level of education of the adults confirms and limits the
level of aspiration. The Aboriginal dwelling and its level of facilities may
emphasise the effect of prejudice of the other children at school and the
frequent enough assertions by Aboriginal kindred about the necessity of
limiting the aspirations of children in a society marked by colour prejudice.
Puberty of the school child often arrives with the shock of exclusion from
the group of age-mates known through the early years of schooling.

On the basis of statistics of the 'age-grade distribution' of all pupils in
New South Wales schools in August 1965, we found that in the 393 cases
where data were available, 21·4 per cent of the children were placed in
classes below what would be the average for age; those above the class
expected were negligible in number. On the basis of similar information
for South Australia, figures were 31 per cent for those below expected
achievements, and 1·5 per cent for those above. Such a situation goes with
homes which lack facilities for early intellectual stimulus relevant to a
literate culture and in which parents have little interest in such facilities.
One indication may be the presence of books in the dwelling, exclusive
of school texts and weekly magazines. The situation established is shown
in Table 2.

In the New South Wales group, under 15 per cent of males and under
6 per cent of females over twenty years of age had bank accounts of any

kind. For 10 per cent of males and 11 per cent of females in this adult group we had no information; but we did establish that 75 per cent of the men and 83 per cent of the women did not have them. Those women who

**Table 2:** *Books in Dwellings*

|                                   | Per Cent of Dwellings | | | |
| --------------------------------- | ------------- | ----------- | --------------- | ----------------- |
|                                   | Not Known     | No Books    | 1 to 10 Books   | Over 10 Books     |
| New South Wales                   | 26·8          | 66·6        | 2·7             | 3·7               |
| Eyre Peninsula                    | 6·4           | 64·4        | 16·1            | 12·8              |
| Eyre Peninsula— non-Aboriginal*   | 4·2           | 20·8        | 29·2            | 45·7              |

* Information on the small non-Aboriginal selection of 24 dwellings is, of course, suggestive only.

do have them seem to use them mainly for the receipt of child endowment and other social service benefits. Of the Eyre Peninsula group, 49 per cent of the men and 28 per cent of the women had bank accounts; there was no information for 6 per cent of men and 10 per cent of women. Of the New South Wales group, 25·6 per cent were covered by medical benefits; and 6 per cent of cases were not known or recorded. Yet the risk of hospitalisation, for instance, was fairly high, as 16·8 per cent of this population had been in hospital during the previous year. Once again, the Eyre Peninsula group figures suggest a higher sophistication, more guidance, or better opportunity: 59·7 per cent of this group were covered by medical benefits; details were not established for 9·7 per cent. The risks appeared to be about the same as in New South Wales, as hospital admissions in the previous year were recorded for 15·6 per cent of this population. (Pregnancies formed the highest single reason for admission in both groups.) In New South Wales 21·4 per cent and in the Eyre Peninsula 44·1 per cent of adults over twenty read current newspapers. (No information on use of the daily press was available in 16 per cent and 9·5 per cent respectively of the adults.)

Those people interviewed exhibit the symptoms of groups under stress. The non-Aboriginal caller is often met with suspicion, and there is the sound of worried inquiries in the background: 'what is wrong now?' Statistics of Aboriginal crime collected for the Project by police authorities in four States, and dealt with in a subsequent chapter, confirm the existence of a tense and anxious community.

It seems fitting to raise here the question of causation, especially in the light of popular and some other assumptions that Aborigines live as they do because they are Aboriginal. There is a common assumption of *uni-linear* causation, which explains the Aboriginal predicament in housing and dependence on seasonal work as culturally determined from a nomadic past.

The milieu and technology of Aboriginal nomadism have, however, long been irrelevant to the situation of part-Aboriginal fringe-dwellers, whose basic needs are those of other Australians. There is enough evidence of the demand for reasonable accommodation to confirm this. Alcoholism, 'reckless' expenditure, neglect of children, deliberate affronts to Australian middle-class morality, a campaign against officialdom, gambling, refusal to pay rents, are all to be expected of a frustrated caste group which has been the object of race prejudice, subjected to special legislation and to paternal control by officials, and conditioned within special institutions to make its own secondary adjustments in order to pursue as far as possible its own defiant purposes.

The importance of this institutional background in the case of the men may be indicated in Tables 3 and 4.

**Table 3:** *Institutional Background—Aboriginal Males over Fifteen Years*

| Type of Institutional Experience | N.S.W. % | Eyre Peninsula % |
| --- | --- | --- |
| Not known | 19·7 | 12·3 |
| Aboriginal station (multi-purposed) | 31·0 | 17·8 |
| Aboriginal station, and Aboriginal welfare 'home' | 1·8 | 5·5 |
| Aboriginal welfare 'home' (only) | 0·7 | Nil |
| No institutional experience stated | 46·7 | 64·4 |

**Table 4:** *Years Spent in Institutions (Multi-purposed and Specialised)—Aboriginal Males over Fifteen Years*

| Period | N.S.W. % | Eyre Peninsula % |
| --- | --- | --- |
| Not known | 29·6 | 19·2 |
| Under 4 years | 1·9 | 5·4 |
| 4-8 years | 1·8 | 2·8 |
| Over 8 years | 20·1 | 8·2 |
| Has not lived in institution | 46·7 | 64·4 |

Note that if we disregard the cases in which questions on institutionalisation were not answered, some 34 per cent of the New South Wales group had had institutional backgrounds, and about 29 per cent had lived for eight years or longer in an Aboriginal institution.

The part-Aboriginal component is increasing more rapidly than any other (excluding immigrants) in the Australian population. It is probably one of the most rapidly increasing groups in the world. It is potentially an asset of great value to the Australian community. Economically, it is significant as a source of labour and as a consuming group, especially as it is a youthful community—younger for instance than the much publicised population of Singapore. But there is some risk that within affluent Australian society the social gap between Aborigines and other Australians will increase. It is already so wide, north of the demarcation lines illustrated in the endpaper map, that there seemed some justice in referring to the northern regions in this context as 'colonial' Australia. The danger is that the long-term adjustment in the northern and central regions will be of the type which has set limits on the potential of the part-Aborigines in the south. There may be some risk, if the economic and social gap between the prejudiced group and the objects of prejudice is seen as coinciding with the gap between the wealthy and the poor nations of the world. The sooner steps are taken to promote economic and other equality, the cheaper this will be, since this is a population which can double its numbers in two decades. Leonard Broom, the American sociologist recently in Australia, referred to Aborigines in the south of the continent as the 'unnecessary minority'—unnecessary because their minority status rests mainly upon majority prejudice.

HOMES AND PEOPLE

'Overcrowding' is a comparative term, but the evidence indicates that Aboriginal families have on the average almost twice as many persons per dwelling, and almost three times the number of persons per room, as other Australians, irrespective of size and construction of dwellings and rooms. A comparison of both groups taken together, and with the 1961 census figures, is shown in Table 5.

**Table 5:** *Dwellings and People*

|                      | Aboriginal % | All Australia* % |
|----------------------|--------------|------------------|
| Rooms per dwelling   | 3·90†        | 5·16‡            |
| Persons per dwelling | 6·87         | 3·55             |

* Excluding full-blood Aborigines.
† Excluding known bathrooms.
‡ Excluding bathrooms, etc.

In New South Wales we found an average of 7·04 persons per dwelling, and in the Eyre Peninsula 6·48. (The small group of non-Aborigines living adjacent averaged 4·4.) In both States, the non-metropolitan and rural average for persons per house in the 1961 census was round 3·7.[3]

Visitors are not included in these figures. Of the New South Wales dwellings, 22 per cent had visitors at the time of interview, the numbers ranging from one to seven. The mean number of visitors in these dwellings was two. High urbanisation and the attraction to employment opportunities in Port Augusta and Whyalla probably help to account for the fact that 34 per cent of the Eyre Peninsula homes had visitors, and that the average number for the homes visited was nearer three than two. (But only two of the twenty-four non-Aboriginal families had visitors.) Persons looking for employment, taking holidays, participating in family occasions, these depend on friends and relatives for accommodation. The reasons include the economic need to keep in touch, as well as the social need to be present on such occasions as funerals; comparative cheapness, since hospitality is reciprocated; and the difficulty faced by Aborigines in many places in finding hotel and other accommodation. At the same time the duty of hospitality may tend to prevent the accumulation of capital for investment in domestic comfort and security, education, etc. The result is a cushion against poverty, at the expense of the ambitious individual. The problem is not, of course, peculiar to Aborigines, but is a part of wider patterns of poverty, and especially marked in the processes of urbanisation of indigenous people in colonial towns, and of indigenous minorities in metropolitan cities.

In 1961, the all-Australian census figure for persons per room in all types of dwellings was 0·69, which was also the New South Wales figure for rural housing. But our selected Aboriginal dwellings in that State averaged 1·63 persons per room (exclusive of visitors). The *range* was from an average of 1·92 for the dwellings on Crown land or town common, where the occupiers could have no tenure rights (except for a few cases where a railway hut is built on Crown land) and the proportion of self-built shacks is high, down to 1·18 for dwellings on town building blocks. But in getting these figures we counted all enclosed rooms, bathrooms, kitchens, semi-enclosed sleep-outs, etc. The census figure, of course, excludes bathrooms, laundries, pantries, etc.; but what can be done where one room may serve as all three? For the Eyre Peninsula the best comparison may be the 'other urban' census figure for South Australia, of 0·72 per room. That the Aboriginal figure was only 1·28 may be the result of recent urban and

[3] 1961 census, vol. 1, part IV, Table 4, and vol 4, part IV, Table 4.

industrial development (since forty-two of the sixty-two families were in the expanding towns), and of South Australian investment in cheap housing.

Table 6 indicates the pressure of persons on accommodation.

**Table 6:** *Persons and Rooms*

|  | N.S.W. % | Eyre Peninsula % |
|---|---|---|
| One person per room or less | 13·5 | 30·3 |
| Two persons, and over one per room | 45·9 | 40·5 |
| Three persons, and over two per room | 28·6 | 20·8 |
| Four persons, and over three per room | 7·2 | 3·8 |
| Over four persons per room | 3·7 | 4·6 |
| Not recorded | 0·9 | Nil |

### ABORIGINES, RENTS, AND HOME OWNERSHIP

As recent publicity in New South Wales suggests, the Aboriginal is not likely to be exploited as a rent-payer. In the non-metropolitan areas, he is not a high consumer of real estate services, nor a conformist in his patterns of expenditure on housing. His attitude to rent is, I think, part of the carry-over of inmate attitudes to officialdom and the institution. It is frequently and quaintly described officially as the result of a past policy of 'hand-outs'— an interesting illustration of how easily prejudice will seize on those aspects of the past which fit the argument. It is profitable to study just what, in the past, was 'handed out' to this pampered group and how!

There is, of course, the difficulty of getting houses to rent in a country largely occupied by home-owners and purchasers, and in the face of prejudice. There are problems of meeting regular rent payments. It should be remembered that the shacks on the Aboriginal stations in New South Wales have only recently been replaced by the present dwellings; that where this has not happened, no rent is charged; that in these institutions, rent payments are comparatively recent; and that they conflict with a very common Aboriginal belief that the reserve lands were a compensatory payment.

In rural New South Wales, the census of 1961 indicated that 67 per cent of all homes were owned or being purchased by occupiers. We found that just round 9 per cent of the Aboriginal dwellings were in this category, with the occupant owning or purchasing the house and the land on which it stands. Yet no less than 35 per cent of householders stated that they 'owned' their dwellings. What the additional 26 per cent 'own' (probably not in strict legality, since the owner of the land owns the building) are the component parts of the dwellings—the second-hand iron, the furniture and equipment; but not the land. Just under 37 per cent of all dwellings of the New South Wales group were shacks built by occupiers or other persons without building skills. This indicates partly the need felt to avoid rent payment, and partly the unavailability of houses which families on uncertain incomes can afford.

In spite of efforts to avoid rents, 41·5 per cent were in dwellings for which rent was required—18 per cent in dwellings rented at what appeared to be an approach to economic rates, and 23 per cent paying (or owing) the nominal rates required by the Aborigines Welfare Board—then, for instance, seventeen shillings and sixpence per week for a reasonable 3-bedroom house. (In 1961, 23 per cent of Australian occupiers paid rents; in New South Wales country towns, 27·3 per cent.) Another 11·7 per cent were living rent free in Board houses, either because of the state of these dwellings or because occupiers were old or ill or widows. 13·7 per cent paid rents to private landlords: 1·6 per cent to the Housing Commission; and nearly double that proportion, 2·7 per cent, were in homes provided by an employing public authority. The fact that employing authorities provided more dwellings than the Housing Commission suggests that the Aboriginal, for financial and other reasons, is at the end of the queue for public housing in non-metropolitan New South Wales, as for other services. One of the reasons could be that Aboriginal claims are so often dealt with, in all parts of Australia, as matters for the separate Aboriginal welfare authority: 3·8 per cent were purchasing homes, but the weekly payment rates suggested that most were purchasing through the special Welfare Board scheme. Of the employing public authorities in all States, the railways are the most important, offering the egalitarianism of the fettlers' gangs, and often a home for reasonable rental as well.

But, at the price generally of quite shocking accommodation, over 56 per cent were living rent free in some way or other, and another 29 per cent paid rents of the token kind to which institutionalised populations (soldiers, asylum dwellers, and Aborigines) have been conditioned: in these cases, under two dollars per week. All but six of the fifty-three householders paying nominal rents lived on Aboriginal stations or reserves, so that their houses can be assumed to be government-owned. Of the dwellings in the country towns, on town building blocks, we found that two-thirds were rented; most of the remainder were occupant-owned or being purchased.

In the Eyre Peninsula, 53 per cent of the dwellings were rented—17·7 per cent from private landlords, 8 per cent from the Housing Commission, 6·4 per cent from the railway or other employing public authority, and the remainder from the Department of Aboriginal Affairs. This means that 32 per cent were paying rents under conditions applicable generally—a significant difference from the situation in New South Wales, probably arising from the higher industrial-urban nature of the Eyre Peninsula dwellings.

The difference suggests that when the Aboriginal gets involved and committed in the cash economy, as a fuller participant and consumer, with more regular wages, his past conditioning becomes less relevant. He has to get on to the treadmill with the rest of us, keep up his hire purchase payments, pay his rent, and lose himself more in the impersonal urban mass. He has, even then, not attained the same degree of ownership as other South Australians. The 'other urban' (country town) figure for South Australian rent-payers in 1961 was 24·8 per cent; as in New South Wales, the high proportion of rented dwellings marks the failure of the Aboriginal householder to satisfy the need he shares with others, to 'own his own house'. His attitude to rent-paying, conditioned by his belief in his rights to land and by his institutional background, is a factor which in turn conditions public and private landlords against him—another illustration of complex multiple causation.

The gap between need and conventional ownership is filled partly by renting but largely by self-help, with the land and materials available; the results include the shacks on town commons, Crown land, or private land situated conveniently for employment and supplies—the so-called settlement.

To some extent this is a general problem of poverty, since in a time of housing crisis someone has to live like this. What is significant here is that such a high proportion of Aborigines do so. Prejudice has combined with poverty to place them at the end of both the housing and the employment queues.

In the Eyre Peninsula there was a similar but smaller gap between dwellings *said* to be 'owned' and those on land actually owned by the occupant. The claims for ownership covered 29 per cent of homes and 20 per cent were on land owned by the householder. An additional 6 per cent were being purchased. This 26 per cent of house and land owned or being bought may be compared with the 9 per cent in the rural areas of New South Wales; and one may fairly attribute some of the difference to the challenge and opportunity of recent industrial growth.

The 26 per cent is still, to be sure, a long way from the 59 per cent of homes owned in 'other urban' areas of South Australia. But the difference from the New South Wales figure has important implications for those parts of Australia where an Aboriginal work force is already available on the sites of new mining and industrial developments.

Yet the householder-built shack formed over 24 per cent of the Eyre Peninsula group. Perhaps we could guess that something between this figure and that of 36·6 per cent (the New South Wales proportion) is typical of 'settled' Australia as a whole. It may be worth a passing note that housing is obviously far worse in that part of Australia which falls to the north of our boundary lines, and that metropolitan housing has been recognised as a most urgent Aboriginal 'problem' in metropolitan areas.

The scrap of which the shacks are built differs little from the building materials used on Aboriginal stations until comparatively recently, even in New South Wales.[4] The ways of the part-Aboriginal population have, as Jeremy Beckett has shown, been formed to some extent in the frontier experiences; and the change from 'stringy bark and raw-hide' to iron for Aborigines had begun back in the 1880s,[5] though as late as the depression years there were still bark huts for them in the western areas of the State.[6]

In case it may seem that only small families are living in these shacks, these 36·6 per cent of dwellings in New South Wales were occupied by 35·7 per cent of the population; the South Australian 24·2 per cent of shack dwellings were occupied by 28·3 per cent of the people. To what extent is this a general problem of poverty? This kind of accommodation is returned in the census under the heading of 'Shed, Hut, etc.,' which for the nation as a whole formed 1·5 per cent of dwellings in 1961, and were occupied by 1·2 per cent of the total population living in private accommodation. If we take the census 'rural' figures only (the highest), the proportions were 4·2 per cent of the population living in 2·7 per cent of the dwellings. There could be no clearer indication that this situation is not *only* a result of the general housing shortage, but the effect of history and current attitudes, in a cycle and culture of poverty special to the

---

[4] See, for instance, reference to the 'iron and timber houses' in evidence before the Select Committee on the Administration of the Aborigines Protection Board in 1937, *N.S.W.P.P.*, 1938-9-40, vol. 7, pp. 609-738.

[5] In 1883 the Police Protector to the Aborigines in New South Wales wrote that 'Bark being scarce, iron huts would improve their conditions', Report to Protector to the Aborigines 1883, pp. 10-27 (appendix).

[6] *N.S.W.P.D.*, 1937-8, Second Series, vol. 152, pp. 1496-517—statement by G.E. Ardill, Member for Yass, in debate on Aborigines Protection Board.

Aboriginal. In drawing the line between the shanty and the tradesman-built house we included any safe and well built construction in the latter category; to make the point clearer, fuller details of the shacks are given below.

What the figures so far given suggest is that between one-quarter and one-third of the non-metropolitan Aboriginal families face health risks from the lack of drainage, plumbing, water, and other services; that their children lack light and space for education; that the shanty offers little security for possessions or persons, especially where the householder has no control of the land; that there is a lack of storage for food and clothing. In ninety of the New South Wales homes, on Crown land, town common, or uncontrolled reserve, there could be no fatherly authority to order intruders away from the door: in them lived 210 children, the girls often considered fair game for the town drunks, so that violence is part of the scene. Moreover, where there is a fringe area, the police are generally alert to what happens there; and this supervision is a further cause of 'trouble' and resentment.

The evidence is that the kind of housing needed and wanted is that common to other Australians. Where, as in the New South Wales group, just under 12 per cent use two structures or more as one house, or share a large dwelling, this is from necessity as much a 'temporary' measure as when they live in a tent (as some families do) or a car body (as do some single men). The South Australian group were experiencing the other aspect of the housing crisis, where the Aboriginal lives in the metropolis: 6 per cent were living in single rooms (five families), and a total of 25 per cent otherwise than in separate single dwellings.

The stereotype Aboriginal of the Australian folklore cannot gain anything by acquiring a larger house: he will merely fill up the additional space with his friends and relatives. This belief is stated to justify opposition by the non-Aboriginal home owner to the movement of an Aboriginal family into his street. He fears for a fall in the value of his property and the crowds of Aborigines who will follow the newcomers to the street; and he helps to bring pressure on the council and the local Member to safe-guard his investment.

We decided to examine this assumption. Houses were classified according to estimates of space into three categories—under 600 square feet, 600-1,200 square feet, and over 1,200 square feet. Then the number of people in each type of house was averaged. As Table 7 shows, the Aboriginal family, like any other family, is a unit which will overcome obstacles in order to live together, irrespective of the size of the dwelling

it occupies. This conclusion is borne out by the high degree of correspondence between the proportion of the total number of houses in each
category and the proportion of the total population living in each category
of house. For the Aboriginal, a house is a house; if he is lucky enough to
be able to get a bigger one, his family does not invite the neighbours or
relatives to share it with them (except where they have no other place),
but spreads out for more comfort.

**Table 7:** *Relation of Population to Dwelling Space—N.S.W.*

|  | Dwellings % | Population % |
| --- | --- | --- |
| Over 1,200 sq. ft | 8·2 | 8·9 |
| 600 to 1,200 sq. ft | 59·0 | 61·2 |
| Under 600 sq. ft | 32·8 | 30·4 |

Of the dwellings under 600 square feet nearly half were on the town
common or Crown land—dwellings of squatters without security of
tenure—and another third were on Aboriginal reserves. About one-sixth
were on private property, mainly on farming or other lands at the edge
of the town.

The Eyre Peninsula figures are too small for the location of the small
shacks to have much meaning, but the relation of housing space to numbers
of persons in the dwelling (Table 8) confirms the conclusion just drawn.

**Table 8:** *Relation of Population to Dwelling Space—
Eyre Peninsula*

|  | Dwellings % | Population % |
| --- | --- | --- |
| Over 1,200 sq. ft | 1·6 | 2·0 |
| 600 to 1,200 sq. ft | 74·2 | 77·8 |
| Under 600 sq. ft | 24·2 | 20·0 |

Where the house has far too little space, beds will be found outside under
a tree and used for sitting as well as sleeping: 9 per cent of dwellings in
New South Wales had outside beds.

### HOUSING, HEALTH, AND FACILITIES FOR CLEANLINESS

#### WATER

The position with respect to water supplies in the New South Wales
dwellings is shown in Table 9.

**Table 9:** *Water Supply, N.S.W.*

| Source of Supply | Population % |
|---|---|
| Piped water | 56·5 |
| Effective rain tanks | 4·0 |
| Tap within 50 yards | 13·2 |
| Tap over 50 yards | 13·2 |
| Tank supplemented from creek, river, or dam | 3·5 |
| Creek, river, or dam only | 8·3 |

The proportion without safe water plus those who must carry it amounted to about 38 per cent of the people, which corresponded roughly to the proportion living in shanty buildings. Carrying water is a common chore for the women in these cases, though the washing may be taken to the water. It has to be carried, however, for personal washing, washing of utensils, and sometimes for drinking. The pollution of streams at the towns must add to the health risks. The plastic bucket has constituted an important technical advance in these situations (as in New Guinea, and Central and South America).

Of the Eyre Peninsula dwellings, 21 per cent depended on a tap elsewhere: in none of them was there any recorded indication of dependence on natural water.

## BATHING AND SANITATION

**Table 10:** *Bathing Facilities*

| | Persons | |
|---|---|---|
| | N.S.W. % | Eyre Peninsula % |
| Not recorded | 1·8 | Nil |
| Bathroom in dwelling | 51·4 | 69·3 |
| Communal bathroom | 4·8 | 2·3 |
| No bathroom— portable tub only | 37·3 | 21·5 |
| Other means used | 4·1 | Nil |
| No apparent facilities | 0·8 | 7·0 |

The 'other means' refers, *inter alia*, to the use of the river or other natural water.

It may be noted from Table 11 that 16·3 per cent of persons in the New South Wales group (5·3 per cent in the Eyre Peninsula) were servicing their own pan systems and that another 5 per cent in New South Wales were being accorded the standards of the Australian public convenience, as they depended on a communal (but serviced) pan system. Where the householder services his own system, or digs a pit latrine, much depends on his efficiency and on his control of who uses the service. If his dwelling is on Crown land or town common he does not have such control. Council or Welfare Board sanitary services were available to 62 per cent of the New South Wales dwellings.

**Table 11:** *Sanitation*

| | Persons | |
| --- | --- | --- |
| | N.S.W. | Eyre Peninsula |
| Type of Provision | % | % |
| Sewered W.C. for dwelling | 15·9 | 49·5 |
| Sewered W.C. communal | Nil | 2·9 |
| Pan system serviced by authority | 41·2 | 0·5 |
| Pan system householder serviced | 16·3 | 5·3 |
| Pan system serviced but communal | 5·0 | Nil |
| Pit latrine for dwelling | 21·3 | 33·3 |
| Other | 0·2 | 5·0 |
| No apparent facility | 0·2 | 2·9 |
| Not recorded | Nil | 1·0 |

GARBAGE DISPOSAL

Table 12 states the position observed for both groups.

**Table 12:** *Garbage Disposal Services*

| | Persons Involved | |
| --- | --- | --- |
| | N.S.W. | Eyre Peninsula |
| Disposal | % | % |
| Not recorded | 7·7 | 8·5 |
| Regular service | 51·0 | 57·8 |
| No regular service | 41·3 | 33·7 |

Public health is not conveniently divisible along racial lines, but refusal to extend the service to the fringe areas may be justified by statements that Aborigines will not pay rates; that they are on land where they have no right to be; that they should be 'looked after' by the 'proper' authority. Here is part of the explanation of the state of many Aboriginal dwelling sites, where rags, paper, and tins have been tramped into the ground; where old beds, broken bottles and other industrial scrap may glitter in the sunlight. Such a setting is often explained in terms of the past nomadic culture: the nomad left his waste and the sun did the rest. A more viable comparison may be with the state of frontier townships seven or eight decades ago. The basic reason is that the Aborigines affected are not accepted as suitable persons to whom town services should be extended. They are 'here today, gone tomorrow'. Yet we found, in the New South Wales group for instance, that no less than 85 per cent of these household heads had been in their present localities for over three years and 65·6 per cent for over ten years.

## HOUSEHOLDER'S RIGHTS ON THE HOMESITE

The Englishman's home may be his castle, but only a minority of Aboriginal householders have effective control of the sites of their dwellings. The state of many sites, already referred to, operates to confirm local prejudice: the place is 'like a blacks' camp' and may be referred to as such. Officials responsible for reserves, and others on whose land Aborigines dwell, may complain, but they do not stop to think that here there is neither a recognised leadership nor a demarcated area of tenant-type responsibility and rights. In the New South Wales group it was found that 40 per cent of the dwelling sites were sufficiently littered to call for a comment by interviewers (40·4 per cent of the dwellings had no regular garbage disposal service). But when one considers that only 57 per cent were fenced, and therefore it would be hard to consider the household head responsible, it seems fair to assume that, with the opportunity, the Aboriginal will maintain his front and back yards much like other Australians. It is also relevant that a significantly high proportion of Aboriginal families were found to have female heads without spouses. Yet 40 per cent of the New South Wales group had planted lawns, 34 per cent gardens of some kind, and 19 per cent had fruit trees, even though a high proportion of the men are in seasonal work and labouring away from home. In the Eyre Peninsula, the 21 per cent reported as in littered surroundings were markedly less than the 30·6 per cent of dwellings without regular garbage service. However, 27 per cent were unfenced.

Even if he lives on a reserve, the Aboriginal has only limited control of his home or the site. It has been common for police to exercise a right of entry to houses, even to arrest Aborigines at home for being 'drunk on a reserve'. Lack of control also renders the occupant helpless against the less responsible of the other Aborigines: cyclical causation operates here, and it is quite common to find these small communities split into factions. A dilemma is posed by this tendency. In spite of the factionalism on the reserve or common, economic reasons plus racial prejudice dictate that a family live in this area: the dwelling must be where the work is. But at the same time it is often sited as far from other members of the Aboriginal group as it is possible to get, without being either too conspicuous from the road or too far from the town. Another reason, however, is the terrain: if one must live in the area liable to flooding, one looks for the highest ground, subject again to being inconspicuous to the police and the health and building inspectors. In the New South Wales group, no less than 30·6 per cent of the dwellings were over fifty yards from any other; 13 per cent of the people lived over one hundred yards from any other family. In the more urban Eyre Peninsula group, only three of the sixty-two dwellings were over fifty yards from neighbours; in fact, all three were over five hundred yards from neighbours—obviously in country areas.

### CONSTRUCTION OF DWELLINGS

The only comparison we can get with general Australian standards and materials is with the census figures for walls of dwellings.[7] The 1961 census figures include those for dwellings with walls of 'calico, canvas and hessian' and for an 'other' category which excludes the conventional brick, stone, concrete, wood, iron, and fibro cement. The total of these two amounts to 1·7 per cent of all houses, in the rural areas of Australia as a whole, which of course includes the far north and desert regions, while most of the New South Wales group were in country town and fringe areas. Yet over 31 per cent had walls of typical town dump material—scrap metal, timber off-cuts, canvas, hessian, cardboard, and the like; 7·6 per cent had walls of galvanised iron in any kind of condition, and this was comparable with the national figure of 5·3 per cent, so that in this respect at least the Aboriginal dwelling is typical of a range of outback dwellings. According to the census, 4 per cent of walls in South Australia are of iron, and only 0·5 per cent of scrap. The figures for Eyre Peninsula Aborigines were 25·8 and 14·5 per cent respectively.

There are no census figures with which to compare other details of construction, but some of these details are set out in Table 13.

Our interviewers were asked to attempt a rating of each dwelling. They were asked to try to ignore the factors of aesthetics and permanence and, taking into account numbers, sex, and ages of the occupants, to

[7] 1961 census, vol. 8, part 2, Table 11, pp. 26-7.

**Table 13:** *Construction of Dwellings*

|  | N.S.W.<br>% | Eyre<br>Peninsula<br>% |
|---|---|---|
| Glassed windows | 61 | 88 |
| Walls lined or partially lined | 58 | 71 |
| Floors of sawn timber on frames, or concrete, etc. | 78 | 92 |
| Earth or makeshift floors (such as timber off-cuts<br>   or lino on earth) | 22 | 8 |
| Roofs of scrap | 27 | 13 |

consider how far the dwelling met each of ten listed needs. For its functional efficiency in each of the ten requirements, marks were to be awarded out of ten—five if barely satisfactory, ten if the function was well discharged. This was of course subjective assessment; but it was an attempt to check against assessment on non-functional grounds. The ten functions were:

> living space per person
> sleeping space, with reference to privacy and ventilation
> shelter
> storage of possessions, with reference to space and security
> cooking facilities
> storage of food, with reference to hygiene, preservation, avoidance of
>    contamination
> washing facilities, for persons, and clothes
> waste disposal, with reference to sanitation, garbage disposal
> heating and temperature control
> lighting

Sixty-seven of the New South Wales dwellings were not assessed in this way, for various reasons. Those which were, were visited by a very careful and conscientious research assistant of part-Aboriginal descent who had ease of access to the homes. The Eyre Peninsula assessment was made by university students. The results, a functional rating that takes overcrowding and the state of general facilities into account, are set out in Table 14.

**Table 14:** *Functional Assessment of Dwellings*

| Points<br>Range: 0-100 | N.S.W.<br>% | Eyre<br>Peninsula<br>% |
|---|---|---|
| 0-25 | 7 | 3 |
| 26-50 | 62 | 26 |
| 51-75 | 27 | 55 |
| 76-100 | 4 | 16 |

Partly in order to see whether a significant correlation might be established between housing and health, a 'housing scale' was worked out for each individual. Points were allocated for bathing facilities, water supply, sanitation, garbage disposal, and the type of construction (materials used for walls, roof, and floors, along with points for size and maintenance). Ratings for both populations in accordance with the resultant scale, with a maximum of 50 points, are set out in Table 15.

**Table 15:** *Populations Rated in Terms of a Housing Scale*

| Points | N.S.W. % | Eyre Peninsula % |
|---|---|---|
| 0-10 | 11·7 (13·2) | 1·3 (2·5) |
| 11-20 | 18·6 (19·4) | 18·5 (18·0) |
| 21-30 | 16·4 (17·3) | 11·3 (13·0) |
| 31-40 | 14·7 (12·8) | 19·5 (16·0) |
| Over 40 | 37·7 (36·4) | 49·5 (51·0) |
| Not recorded | 0·9 (0·9) | Nil |

The percentage in parentheses indicates the proportion, in each rating, of all children under fifteen years. Understandably, the larger families tend to rate lower on the scale. These housing standards form a special handicap for the child.

### INSIDE THE HOUSES

Privacy, like overcrowding, is a comparative term. It may be as much a matter of family and social conventions and sanctions as of space and furniture. But without either effective leadership and management or the maintenance of deeply ingrained avoidance conventions, privacy for married couples would be almost impossible in many of these homes; and there would be little chance of a 'room of her own' for the unmarried woman or girl.

Other evidence suggests that the Aboriginal family is passing through a stage of weak controls, and that the household head does not often provide firm control.

The most common situation throughout Australia as a whole is that of the five-room private dwelling, occupied by an average of 3·7 persons. This means that privacy can be arranged where necessary, since rooms can be used for different purposes as required. But in Aboriginal dwellings the problem seemed somewhat different, the arrangements for privacy generally difficult. It was also clear that floors and items of furniture other than beds often had to be used for sleeping. Table 16 is the result of an attempt to estimate the relation of persons to sleeping accommodation, not in terms of bedrooms but of places in a bed or equivalent. We would, for instance, count a double or three-quarter bed as two places, a single bed as one place. A sofa or 'lounge' would be counted as one bed place.

**Table 16:** *Sleeping Places and Persons*

|  | N.S.W. % | Eyre Peninsula % |
|---|---|---|
| Not recorded | 5·5 | 3·2 |
| Dwellings with excess of persons over sleeping places | 51·4 | 30·5 |
| Dwellings with sleeping place for each person | 13·7 | 40·3 |
| Dwellings with 'spare' sleeping accommodation | 28·9 | 25·8 |

In the New South Wales group, 8·7 per cent had twice as many persons as places to sleep (except floors). This situation is an indicator of the obsolescence of the Aboriginal situation in 1966; and it is no answer to reply that a small proportion of non-Aboriginal families are equally ill equipped for comfort or security of the person. A result of these conditions must be a high incidence of contagious and infectious diseases: the difficulty of isolating the sick adds to the higher incidence likely in a social situation where a greater number of contacts between persons arises from the larger families.

As for comfort, we found that in New South Wales 40 per cent had not enough chairs for the family members, and the figure was the same in the Eyre Peninsula (where *none* of the small group of non-Aboriginal families next door or adjacent were in this situation). In New South Wales 24 per cent, in Eyre Peninsula 17 per cent, were wholly or partly dependent on makeshift items like oil drums; 7 per cent in New South Wales and 5 per cent in the Eyre Peninsula had no conventional seats at all. This may not add one iota to discomfort, but it illustrates the fact that the Aboriginal household is often only a marginal consumer of commodities catering for comfort or prestige.

One indicator that things may be changing was the presence of refrigerators in over 70 per cent of the homes in both States. Only one in four in New South Wales, and one in five in the Eyre Peninsula, had neither refrigerator nor ice-chest. Yet even the old fashioned meat safe may be found, keeping company with the flat irons heating on the old fashioned wood-burning stove. Radio sets were also common: 69 per cent of homes in both groups had them. The point might be borne in mind in the planning of community education programs. It is also suggestive of the vulnerability of sensitive persons to programs expressive of prejudice, especially those of the type which perpetuate the Australian myth of the 'comic savage'.

A serious lack in shanty dwellings is of secure storage, for documents, family treasures, clothing and the like. People have their finery and are proud of it, but it must be difficult to maintain, especially for mothers of large families. This may be one reason why many Aboriginal women are eternally working. We found that maintenance was fair to good where the house was reasonably functional; one cannot 'maintain' a pile of rubbish, but a high proportion of these women 'battlers' seem to be always trying to do so, even to sweeping the dust round the shacks.

The tradition of the Christian poor is to mend and make their clothes; and of the Christian rich to do the same for the unoffending and helpless heathen. This habit meant that the sewing machine was a necessity in the poorer and middle-class home. It was interesting to find that only 19 per cent of Aboriginal homes in New South Wales, and 22 per cent in the Eyre Peninsula, had them. (The small non-Aboriginal group had them in twenty-two of the twenty-four dwellings.) But this fits impressions of an 'improvident' pattern of consumption. Cheap clothing might be bought, worn, and thrown away rather than mended. Food was often bought as required and consumed immediately. One reason might be the absence of safe storage, another the impractibility of the whole family sitting at table for a meal together. Statistics cannot really indicate the bareness of homes without cupboards, wardrobes, or pantries: or the impression of men going out to work in winter clad in thin shirts and trousers without woollen underwear or coats. It fits in with living for the moment, with the reckless expenditure, with the high proportion of addiction to alcohol; with protest, hopelessness in the face of prejudice, and with the maintenance of the frontier traditions where they are no longer relevant, partly because of the absence of any other.

### WASHING AND COOKING

Only 51·4 per cent in the New South Wales group of dwellings had laundries. Half the laundries, however, had washing machines, while 2·7 per cent of dwellings had washing machines without laundries. In the Eyre Peninsula 72 per cent had laundries, washing machines, or both. In New South Wales, for 2·2 per cent there were communal laundries. Over 40 per cent had nothing but the tub at the dwelling (used by 37 per cent of the women over fifteen years). Washing at river or creek is still necessary for those in 2·7 per cent of homes. In the Eyre Peninsula nearly 5 per cent used communal laundries, 21 per cent the tub or dish, under 2 per cent the river.

Cooking facilities show a similar obsolescence. Only 54 per cent in New South Wales had separate kitchens, and only 11·5 per cent had electric, gas, or oil stoves in them. The rest of the stoves were old-fashioned wood-burners, and another 21 per cent of dwellings had wood-burners without a separate kitchen. Seventeen per cent of the women have to cook on the open fireplace inside, and 2 per cent to cook outside. In the Eyre Peninsula group, 87 per cent had kitchens, with other than wood stoves in 12·9 per cent of cases; 78·8 per cent had wood-burning stoves, a few of them without kitchen. Under 5 per cent of women had to cook on an open fireplace. Unfortunately there is no basis in the census for comparison; but those figures suggest poverty of aspiration as well as economic poverty and the conservative traditions of the women who seem to be forever working.

## LIGHT, POWER AND HEATING

Of the New South Wales dwellings, 57 per cent had electricity, but over 40 per cent were without either gas or electricity. For light over 34 per cent depended on oil lamps, and 6 per cent on candles. Fire risk as well as inconvenience was high. In the Eyre Peninsula 21 per cent had to depend on oil lamps or candles, with no visible facilities at the time of interview in 4·8 per cent of cases. Here again is the obsolescence which goes with the shack and the life of a pioneer frontiersman in seasonal work. Lamps and candles may be effective enough, but hardly in these crowded dwellings. Two of those in our New South Wales survey are known to have been burned down with loss of life within twelve months. The obsolescence is indicated by the fact that, in 1961, 96·8 per cent of Australian dwellings had electricity or gas, and in the rural community 81·7 per cent. This is closely approached by the Eyre Peninsula, mainly *urban* group, with 74 per cent. Most dwellings in both groups where heating is required depend on the wood fire: the picture of the family round the fire at night was the only one which aroused this observer's envy.

## THE HOUSEHOLD

Several anthropologists have noted the role of the women in keeping together the part-Aboriginal family and in maintaining the home, and we found many evidences of matri-focused authority. The dominant elderly woman who 'battles' to keep a home for dependent daughters and grandchildren on social service benefits (especially her pension) is not perhaps as common as often assumed, but she is in many ways the most impressive figure in the household. She is commonly the acknowledged holder of authority over the extended family beyond the household. Generally conservative, what she conserves is the tradition of hospitality and sharing. 'You couldn't send them away without a feed.' By the anthropologist, her position may be traced back to the Aboriginal culture, and the effects on it of the loss of the spiritual role of the man; to the fact that what is material in man came through the woman, and that only the material remains. But her situation, and that of the younger woman who will also tend to conserve the frontier traditions, are also directly relevant to the current economic and social circumstances of Aboriginal society.

One of the frustrating facts for the working male is his comparative failure as earner and provider. Where he does succeed, this is often away from home. He often enjoys security neither at home nor on the job, while at the same time he has a large family to maintain. Prejudice is such that to get out of this situation he must establish a special reputation with the white middle class of the town for steady sobriety (which generally means turning his back on the group, and denying their claims to sharing); he then needs what he can earn to furnish his new house and so placate the neighbours. If he 'succeeds' he often faces a grim kind of life, where his associates are others in the same predicament. Success, as the whites define it for him, not being attractive, and other goals not being clear for him, he will tend to fall in with the tradition of heavy spending and hard drinking which he has inherited and which is the main kind of defiance of authority available to him, with the effect that he may become even less effective as a provider. One of the apparently weaker links in the family is that between spouses: this is common in any society where the men have to travel a good deal after low-status employment.

Aborigines may be less concerned than other Australians about the formalities of marriage. We did not inquire into this at all; but spouses differently named were quite common. What happens when a marriage breaks up does not disperse the family. The mother stays with the children, or takes them to her mother. When she forms another alliance, the children are treated as belonging to both spouses.

It was a common experience to hear men in their thirties refer to 'my aunty', 'my granny'; and even for an elderly man, if she is still alive the source of authority and the judge of right and wrong may still be 'mum'. The study of Melbourne Aborigines by Dr Diane Barwick has developed the significance of this matri-focused authority.[8]

In an attempt to delineate the structure of the household group, we recorded the relationship of each member with the household head. The results are set out in Table 17.

**Table 17:** *Relationship to Household Head*

| Relationship | N.S.W. % | Eyre Peninsula % |
|---|---|---|
| Household head | 14·0 | 13·8 |
| Spouse of household head | 11·2 | 11·8 |
| Parent or parent-in-law of household head | 0·7 | 0·8 |
| Offspring of household head or spouse | 56·2 | 45·4 |
| Grandchild or great-grandchild of either spouse | 12·0 | 12·6 |
| Nephew or niece of either spouse | 2·1 | 4·4 |
| Other relative | 2·0 | 8·5 |
| Spouse of offspring of nephew or niece | 1·0 | 2·1 |
| Adopted | 0·2 | 0·3 |
| Not related by blood or marriage or adoption | 0·5 | 0·5 |

One guesses that this shows certain differences from the general Australian household pattern. In New South Wales 81 per cent, in the Eyre Peninsula 71 per cent, were household heads, spouses, and their children. But in both groups grandchildren made up 12 per cent of the average household. Looking at this another way, we can estimate this as indicating the proportion of three-generation family groups. Urbanisation will inevitably tend to increase the proportion of nuclear families: we may even find Aboriginal matriarchs, in time, in old peoples' homes. But, in the present state of Aboriginal *mores*, such evidence of assimilation would be unthinkable.

The difference between the groups is mainly the higher proportion of nephew-nieces and other close relatives in the Eyre Peninsula group. This may be the result of location of most of the dwellings in the developing centres of industry. The trend probably goes further in the metropolitan areas. Table 17 also indicates again the significance of the family and kinship; only one person in two hundred is not a relative.

A matri-focused authority was perhaps less significant than the economic and other handicaps faced by households where the main decisions have to be made by a woman as household head. In a male-

[8] A Little More Than Kin, Table XIX, p. 312.

dominated society and economy, where the household often faces insecurity of tenure, and where the dwelling itself may have to be built and maintained by self-help, a high proportion of female household heads will be significant. In New South Wales, 20·8 per cent of households had female heads, and 21·2 per cent of all persons were in families where a woman was managing without help of a spouse. The corresponding percentages in the Eyre Peninsula were 21 and 22·5.

The much publicised Moynihan Report, of the United States Department of Labor, claimed that in 1962 over 23 per cent of Negro families were effectively fatherless and under female control.[9] The report stated that in the 1950 census 18 per cent of non-white families and 9 per cent white families were female-managed; that by 1960 the Negro figure had become 21 per cent with the white families still at 9 per cent. Perhaps the comparison of this Negro figure with that of the groups we studied is suggestive. From the short published version of the Moynihan Report it is not possible to ascertain the sources of the 1962 statistics. Nor is it possible to trace any comparable trend in the Aboriginal case, so far as I can ascertain, from census sources. Certainly the proportion of persons in female-managed families in our groups is higher than the proportion of such families. For instance, the proportion of persons living in dwellings with female household heads, in New South Wales, was over 24 per cent; over 23 per cent of children of school age were in this situation.

It is difficult to get a comparable figure for the community as a whole. If we take all dwellings in the census, there are 15·99 per cent with females in charge,[10] but the United States calculation would hardly be based on *all* dwellings. If we take from the 1961 census figures for household heads of *private houses* those 'never married' (to delete as far as possible single persons living alone), we get a figure of 12·5 per cent.[11] This may provide a fairer comparison. (Does it mean that the Australian family is less stable than the American?) If we take Australian female household heads who were separated, widowed or divorced, as a percentage of the total household heads, the result is 13·1 per cent.[12]

However the situation compares with that of other Australians (and it seems that the difference is significant), that of Aboriginal families is comparable with what has been the object of special concern (and some controversy) in the United States, where it was part of an established

[9] *The Negro Family: The Case for National Action*, p. 9.
[10] 1961 census, vol. 8, part II, Table 28, p. 52.
[11] Ibid., Table 29, p. 53.
[12] Ibid., Table 29, p. 55.

pattern which included a rise in the 'non-white' crime rates in spite of a movement out of economic recession. Is the Aboriginal crime rate increasing also?

What is significant for this study is that over a fifth of Aboriginal children are living in incomplete family situations. To this should be added the effect of what appears to be impermanence in Aboriginal marital ties, though this too may not be very different from the total Australian situation. It is, however, especially characteristic of families anywhere who are poor, and where the men depend on seasonal employment. A high proportion of seasonal and other temporary employment means that a high proportion of the children must be effectively fatherless at some time in their lives. Thus the matri-focused family is part of a cycle of poverty; and this must further handicap large families on low incomes. It cannot be argued that female control weakens family ties, but in these circumstances the family is likely to be less successful, in an advanced cash econony, in securing an adequate income.

Edith Clarke has described a somewhat similar situation in Jamaica,[13] of the men in itinerant seasonal work, with the family mother- and grandmother-oriented. Yet in Jamaica the very poor family is likely to have an acre or two of its own, on which married or concubinal daughters may build and live. The Aboriginal mother running a family can seldom be secure: when she is, it tends to be through the charity of the Board or Department. Of those in New South Wales, only 30 per cent were on Aboriginal stations or on town building blocks (which might involve being accommodated in Board housing). The others were living in fringe situations. Nor were they facing less responsibility than couples in the management of children, of whom there was an average of 4·3 in each female-managed dwelling, and 4·4 in others. They cannot put small savings towards security in a dwelling: the shack of iron and scrap marks the difference from the Jamaican situation. As in Jamaica, their children live a great deal in the open air, playing round the houses. But here there is often no confining and protecting yard, no recognised family plot with a fence, from which the intruder may be excluded. Any stranger has the right to be on the common or Crown land.

## MOBILITY

Mobility in seasonal and labouring work creates the impression of mobility of the home base. The materials of about a third of the dwellings

[13] *My Mother Who Fathered Me.*

in New South Wales, and less in the Eyre Peninsula, certainly are such as to make for a rapid removal if necessary, after demolition, or if the family is moved to the place where work is available. But in New South Wales we found that over 85 per cent of householders had been living in their present localities, for instance in or beside the same town (or on the same Aboriginal station) for over three years; and over 65 per cent had been there for ten years or over. This was consistent with a process of urbanisation, as those who had gone to the metropolis or industrial centre would not be included. Periods spent in particular dwellings tend to be considerably lower: only 47 per cent had been in the same dwelling for three years, and 22 per cent for ten years. No less than 23 per cent had 'moved house' within one year, and 35 per cent within two years.

The Eyre Peninsula figures showed a difference which was probably the result of including newly expanded industrial towns: 58 per cent had been in the same town or locality for three years, 29 per cent for ten years. Another factor has been the marked influx into Port Augusta in recent years of Aborigines from out beyond our boundary for 'settled' Australia.

The matter for thought here is that many householders who have been over ten years in or beside a town may not be within the community which receives its services; they 'should not be there'. For them, not local government but the central government should 'do something'.

## A POLITICAL PROBLEM

I return to the fact that one-third of these people are children of school age; and that over half are under school leaving age. No less than 23 per cent are in the 0-4 age group. The effects of overcrowding, insecurity, inadequate equipment, causing and resulting from breakdown in household organisation and family management, must by their effects on early socialisation and schooling and aspirations tend towards repeating this situation, on a larger scale, in the next generation. And the household is only one aspect of the problem. Employment and incomes present a situation which is just as depressing.

The situation is very complex indeed. Its solution will not be approached through education and training, housing schemes, health measures, the end of all discriminatory legislation, outlawing of discrimination and the like, unless a creative effort can be made to produce leadership, and the chance is offered for the leadership to operate. Most of the creative decision-making can come only from the Aborigines. How to enable a poor and depressed group to decide what it wants, and to operate within the law to get it, is the main challenge which faces this nation inside and outside Australia, for the problem is basically the same in 'colonial' Australia and in New Guinea. The same kinds of skill are required in schemes to assist communities in Asia who are passing through critical phases of social change. These are also the kinds of skill in which Australia is notably deficient.

The core of the Aboriginal situation is political in the wider sense. Basically the Aboriginal needs, by his own effort but within an administrative framework which makes this possible, freedom to decide with other Aborigines what he wants, and taxpayers' assistance to get it. Above all he requires the kind of organisation which will give him hitting power to advance his interests in legal-liberal society.

This chapter is concerned with employment in country towns and other rural areas; with the kinds of employment which are still widely considered as the norm and as suitable for Aborigines. So long as these groups remained rural based, they were likely to continue as the holders of the less skilled and rewarding positions, with a high proportion of unemployment by Australian standards. The move into the metropolis or, as in the case of those in the Eyre Peninsula, into extending industrial towns, was one way of breaking out of the old pattern. But the figures already quoted for educational attainments indicated that leaving school at fifteen years was still the norm. No matter what the educational effort, it will take perhaps a decade or more to bring any marked changes in the kinds of employment.

### THE MEN AND BOYS OVER FIFTEEN YEARS

Current occupations of the men in both areas are set out in Table 18.

The high unemployment figures for New South Wales marked the effect of the drought and the fact that Aboriginal workers were those most likely to be dismissed. For Australia, an unemployment figure of 20 per cent was high indeed. It was also nearly eight times as high as in the Eyre Peninsula, where most of the households were in developing industrial centres and where the unemployment rate was little above what would be regarded as serious for the Australian work force as a whole.

In New South Wales just over 56 per cent of the males over fifteen years were effectively in the work force at the time of the survey in 1965.

**Table 18:** *Current Occupations—Aboriginal Males over Fifteen Years*

| Type of Occupation | N.S.W. % | Eyre Peninsula % |
|---|---|---|
| General labour, including unskilled seasonal, construction, maintenance, agricultural and pastoral; and factory or mill hand, wharf labourer | 46·0 | 46·6 |
| Semi-skilled construction, maintenance, mechanical; semi-skilled agricultural or pastoral; foreman ganger supervisor; clerical; sales; fishing; taxi, bus or truck driver; other transport | 10·2 | 19·2 |
| Qualified tradesman | 0·4 | 4·1 |
| Managerial position (agricultural, pastoral, commercial, factory) | Nil | 4·1 |
| White collar public service | Nil | Nil |
| Hotel employee | Nil | Nil |
| Pensioner, or still at school | 19·3 | 16·4 |
| Unemployed | 20·1 | 2·7 |
| Not known | 4·0 | 6·8 |

Only 1·5 per cent received the age pension. If we deduct this and the 4·7 per cent of those over fifteen years who were in school from the 19·3 per cent of those recorded as 'pensioner or at school', this leaves 13 per cent neither unemployed nor on age pensions. Without putting too much emphasis on the accuracy of the answers to the questionnaire, this does suggest a very high proportion of men dependent on invalid pensions. But the most important factor it establishes is that nearly half the work force in each State was employed in unskilled labour; and of those known to have had any employment at all, over 80 per cent in New South Wales and 63 per cent in the Eyre Peninsula were so employed. In New South Wales, some 18 per cent were in what we somewhat generously described as semi-skilled occupations, and under 1 per cent were in skilled employment; 26 per cent of the Eyre Peninsula group were semi-skilled by the same standards, but here no less than 11 per cent were either skilled (i.e. qualified) tradesmen or in managerial positions of some kind. The association of higher skills with urbanisation into industrial centres is clear.

That the New South Wales figures gave a somewhat atypical impression of the more usual situation, and that the movement out of the general labourer situation in the Eyre Peninsula was comparatively recent, is suggested by the figures indicating the nature of previous employment in each case. For the purposes of Table 19 those who were currently

**Table 19:** *Previous Employment—Aboriginal Males over Fifteen Years*

| Type of Occupation | N.S.W. % | Eyre Peninsula % |
|---|---|---|
| General labourer* | 62·2 | 54·7 |
| Semi-skilled* | 14·2 | 11·0 |
| Qualified tradesman | 0·7 | Nil |
| Managerial position* | Nil | 2·7 |
| White collar public service | Nil | Nil |
| Other | 0·7 | Nil |
| Not known | 10·2 | 19·2 |
| At school | 4·7 | 1·4 |
| No previous employment | 7·3 | 9·6 |

* Defined in Table 18.

unemployed as well as those in employment were asked to state their previous employment. The New South Wales answers suggest that the drought had reduced the proportion in semi-skilled employment, but the figure has to be treated with caution: the lower proportion may be due to movement of those who had been accustomed to higher wages into the Sydney area. In fact most of the movement indicated was between unskilled categories which are not separately shown in Table 19. Another fact not indicated was that all factory workers in the Eyre Peninsula group who recorded previous employment had been employed in rural areas— mainly on general labouring, unskilled construction, and maintenance. The previous employment in New South Wales had been in unskilled rural occupations, in more than four cases out of every five. Something of the obsolescence of the 'Aboriginal' sector of the economy is suggested by the fact that the 1966 census revealed under 9 per cent of the male work force in rural industries. Note that not one of either group had ever been employed as a white collar public servant. On the other hand, public authorities were easily the most important employers. As Table 20 shows, by juxtaposing past and current employment, this trend is comparatively recent. Partly this seems to have been the result of government policies. The fact that by 1965 over 41 per cent of *all* males over fifteen years in the Eyre Peninsula group were in public employment of some kind must be due to policy. The New South Wales figures show the effect of drought, of mechanisation in agriculture and the pastoral industry, and probably of government policy, most commonly implemented by employment of Aborigines in government-owned railways.

The casual and seasonal nature of employment, and perhaps an unusually high mobility in and out of positions classed as permanent,

**Table 20:** *Previous and Current Employers—Aboriginal Males over Fifteen Years*

| Employer | N.S.W. Previous | Current | Eyre Peninsula Previous | Current |
|---|---|---|---|---|
| Government or public authority | 10·2 | 17·2 | 13·7 | 41·1 |
| Agricultural enterprise | 23·0 | 10·6 | 12·3 | 5·5 |
| Pastoral enterprise | 12·8 | 6·2 | 15·1 | Nil |
| Retail enterprise | 0·7 | 1·1 | Nil | Nil |
| Construction firm or contractor | 5·1 | 4·7 | 2·7 | 1·4 |
| Manufacturer | 10·2 | 10·6 | 12·3 | 19·2 |
| Garage or workshop | 1·5 | 1·5 | Nil | Nil |
| Mining | 0·4 | 0·4 | 5·5 | Nil |
| Self-employed | 4·7 | 3·3 | 6·8 | 5·5 |
| Other | 2·9 | 0·7 | 1·4 | |
| Not known | 14·2 | 4·4 | 17·8 | 8·2 |
| Not previously employed | 14·3 | | 12·3 | |
| Currently at school or pensioner | | 19·3 | | 16·4 |
| Currently unemployed | | 20·1 | | 2·7 |

marked the New South Wales rural workers especially. Of those in employment, and in whose cases the relevant details were established, 60 per cent had been in their current situations for less than a year. The corresponding percentage in the Eyre Peninsula was 39: though the total in whose cases the relevant facts were known was only 74, one would expect a higher proportion of permanent employment in the large towns where most of them lived.

The unemployment figures indicated in Tables 18 and 19 were extremely high in New South Wales when compared with the overall national figures, since governments have been committed to 'full employment' policies. A better understanding may be gained if we consider the 20 per cent of Aboriginal male workers in the drought year of 1965 (remembering that drought conditions became more severe later) in the light of what was happening to the unskilled manual worker. By July 1967 the Commonwealth Employment Service had an average of 10·3 registered applicants for each unfilled vacancy in this type of work.[1]

Among the unskilled manual workers, rural Aborigines would be in the most difficult position. At the time of this survey, we had difficulty in establishing the period of current unemployment, a difficulty which is easy enough to account for where workers may at any time obtain casual

[1] K. Farrell, Some Problems of Aboriginal Employment in Relation to Education.

work for a few days or at any time find themselves unemployed. In the Eyre Peninsula, where we obtained answers in about half the cases of unemployed men, none had been out of work for longer than two months. But in New South Wales, where also just on half the number gave the period of unemployment, no less than 2·9 per cent of all male workers had been without work for over six months.

Table 21 is based on questions asking for all details of skills and experience *claimed*; these factors are therefore more likely to be overstated than understated.

**Table 21:** *Skills and Experience—Aboriginal Males over Fifteen Years*

| Skills and Experience | N.S.W. % | Eyre Peninsula % |
|---|---|---|
| Trade, technical, commercial, with supervisory experience | 0·4 | 1·4 |
| Professionally qualified | Nil | Nil |
| Trade qualifications without supervisory experience | 0·7 | 2·7 |
| No formal qualifications—has specialised employment experience | 27·4 | 30·1 |
| No qualifications or recognised skills or special experience claimed | 58·1 | 56·2 |
| Other experience relative to employment | 1·1 | Nil |
| At school | 4·4 | 1·4 |
| Not known | 8·0 | 8·2 |

The conformity here between the two groups is so close as to confirm other impressions that the main difference between them is due to recent access by the Eyre Peninsula men to employment in towns where there is new industry. The proportion of lads over school leaving age still at school is lower, in fact, in this group than in rural New South Wales. But even if all those who had remained at school attain high qualifications, the immediate effect will be small. In Australia, the changes in methods of production have profound though delayed effects on the patterns of education; but most of these pass the Aboriginal youth by; he is simply not integrated into the education system. Those who work hard to get Aboriginal children to succeed in school, with homework centres, preschool centres and the like, are certainly looking in the right direction. But this situation is one beyond facilities, services, and administration. Without the basic *political* solution which offers hope by making possible an Aboriginal leadership, with a degree of autonomy for decision-making, I believe that all these efforts will come to little, except in individual cases. A political initiative from government, leading to consultation and negotiation, is required to produce motivation for change. If this is to happen, and the problem of motivation is about to be solved, this in turn will enable such efforts to be rewarded by the results which they merit.

Table 22 sets out the results of the inquiry into post-primary education and training of the male work force.

**Table 22:** *Post-primary Education and Training—Aboriginal Males over Fifteen Years*

| Level of Education and Training | N.S.W. % | Eyre Peninsula % |
|---|---|---|
| Primary school only | 58·4 | 72·6 |
| Post-primary, but did not reach Intermediate or equivalent | 20·4 | 6·8 |
| Intermediate certificate or equivalent | 1·5 | Nil |
| Leaving certificate or equivalent | Nil | Nil |
| Secondary school plus apprenticeship | 0·4 | 5·5 |
| Apprenticeship, no secondary schooling | Nil | Nil |
| Technical college | 0·4 | Nil |
| Professional, agricultural, accountancy or commercial training, with or without qualifications | Nil | Nil |
| Any other training | 0·4 | Nil |
| At school | 4·4 | 1·4 |
| Not known | 14·2 | 12·3 |

There were no 'failed' professional or technical trainees: Aborigines simply did not undertake such courses. Of the men in Eyre Peninsula, 26 per cent, and of those in rural New South Wales, 31 per cent, stated that they had worked mainly with other Aborigines, statements which support the other indications of livings earned on the fringes of the national economy. Those who so replied in New South Wales were employed almost exclusively as labourers and seasonal workers, and in unskilled pastoral and agricultural work. The same trend could be seen in the Eyre Peninsula, but the numbers were too small to be significant.

The attempt to obtain some indication of incomes was not really successful. The only way to make this attempt was to ask questions as carefully phrased as possible. We asked for an average of weekly wages received over the preceding three months, and also for income from pensions, sickness benefits, unemployment benefits, and from any other sources, for the same period. Periods of unemployment during the three months apparently led to confusion: this likelihood is strengthened by the fact that about 9 per cent in New South Wales and about 14 per cent in the Eyre Peninsula, known to be employed, stated that they were un-employed. Another difficulty was the high proportion of answers in which one or more of the possible items had not been recorded. For that and more obvious reasons, the figures in Tables 23 and 24 can be no more than suggestive.

**Table 23:** *Average Weekly Wage over Three Months—Aboriginal Males over Fifteen Years*

| Average Wage | N.S.W. % | Eyre Peninsula % |
|---|---|---|
| Nil— | | |
|    unemployed | 29·2 | 16·4 |
|    at school | 4·4 | 1·4 |
| $1 to $29 | 8·4 | 2·8 |
| $30 to $34 | 8·4 | 13·7 |
| $35 to $39 | 12·0 | 13·7 |
| $40 to $44 | 13·1 | 16·4 |
| $45 and above | 13·5 | 17·9 |
| Not known | 10·9 | 17·8 |

Even if we disregard the figures for unemployment given here, substitute those given in earlier tables, and go so far as to assume that all unemployed received the unemployment benefit, there was a sub-stantial number of workers who received less than the basic wage level, here approximately indicated by the $30-$34 range. On the other hand, we faced the problem, typical of situations which exist as it were beyond the limits of the statistical norms, that these workers include a large proportion of those in the 15-19 age group. Of the 23 per cent of males over fifteen in this group, only 4·4 per cent were in school. The gearing of wages to age affected average wage levels, as well as average earnings, including unemployment and other relief measures.

This is not poverty by Asian standards; nor is this poverty shared by Aborigines alone. As a reminder of this fact, Table 24 includes comparable figures for the small group of non-Aborigines who lived in the same areas in the Eyre Peninsula. It gives the best indication we could get of the range of incomes for male workers.

This statement of average weekly income was attempted in less than four cases of every five. If we take $30-$34 as indicating the level of the basic wage, approximately 27 per cent in New South Wales and 18 per cent in the Eyre Peninsula were averaging less than this in income from all sources; this was to be expected from the unemployment figures. No

**Table 24:** *Average Weekly Income from all Sources—Aboriginal Males over Fifteen Years*

| Weekly Incomes | N.S.W. % | Eyre Peninsula Aboriginal % | Non-Aboriginal % |
|---|---|---|---|
| Nil—at school | 4·4 | 1·4 | Nil |
| $1 to $9 | 4·0 | Nil | Nil |
| $10 to $14 | 13·1 | 13·7 | 10·7 |
| $15 to $19 | 2·9 | 1·4 | Nil |
| $20 to $24 | 4·4 | 1·4 | 3·6 |
| $25 to $29 | 2·9 | 1·4 | 3·6 |
| $30 to $34 | 8·4 | 13·7 | Nil |
| $35 to $39 | 11·7 | 13·7 | 7·1 |
| $40 to $44 | 13·5 | 15·1 | 7·1 |
| $45 to $49 | 4·0 | 4·1 | 3·6 |
| $50 to $54 | 2·9 | 5·5 | 7·1 |
| $55 to $59 | 0·7 | Nil | 3·6 |
| $60 and over | 4·7 | 6·9 | 28·5 |
| Details from all sources incomplete, or uncertain | 22·3 | 21·9 | 25·0 |

contemporary figures were available from the census. The incomes of the small non-Aboriginal group included in Table 24 suggests that those who live next door to Aboriginal families will have equivalent numbers of male workers on incomes less than the basic wage; but they also suggest that a definitely higher proportion will receive well above the basic wage. The figures included pensions as well as wages; and about 6 per cent had income from other sources, of which the main one appeared to be Workers' Compensation.

As will be seen from Table 25, the most common source other than wages is not from the unemployment and sickness benefits payable to workers who have been employed, but from invalid and age pensions. In New South Wales there was a notable gap between the 20 per cent stated to be unemployed at the time of the survey and the 7 per cent who received unemployment benefits. An attempt was also made to establish what real property or cash reserves were held. The information gained confirmed other evidence that these workers are almost solely dependent on wages and pensions.

It appears that the greater likelihood of unemployment, and the high number of dependants per worker, are more important causes of poverty than special wage rates; that while the Aboriginal, even in the area where he seems to have greater social mobility than in any other non-metropolitan area, the south coast of New South Wales, is likely to supply all the seasonal work for types of employment which pay on market rates

**Table 25:** *Pensions and Other Income—Aboriginal Males over Fifteen Years*

| Income | Nil % | Pension or benefit or income stated to be rec'd % | At school % | Not known % |
|---|---|---|---|---|
| N.S.W. | | | | |
| Unemployment and sickness benefit | 79·9 | 7·0 | 4·4 | 8·8 |
| Invalid/age pension | 77·0 | 13·9 | 4·4 | 4·7 |
| Repatriation pension | 93·0 | 1·2 | 4·4 | 1·5 |
| Other than wages or pensions* | 86·8 | 1·5 | 4·4 | 7·3 |
| Eyre Peninsula | | | | |
| Unemployment and sickness benefit | 86·3 | 2·8 | 1·4 | 9·6 |
| Invalid/age pension | 76·7 | 16·5 | 1·4 | 5·5 |
| Repatriation pension | 95·9 | 1·4 | 1·4 | 1·4 |
| Other than wages and pensions* | 87·6 | 1·4 | 1·4 | 9·6 |

\* Includes Workers' Compensation.

rather than a minimum wage, his wages in the settled regions are generally those fixed by law for all in the same work. I admit his comparative defencelessness against the unscrupulous employer; but there are good economic reasons for employing men who are not consumed by a sense of unfair treatment.

The Aboriginal worker will tend to be 'last on and first off' the job, so he can take less risks. He will tend to have a higher number of dependants. In the New South Wales group, for instance, over 53 per cent of all males over fifteen years out of school had dependants under fifteen years; no less than 31 per cent had from four to ten dependent children (under fifteen), and over 10 per cent had one or more dependants in the 15-19 age group. The corresponding percentages for the Eyre Peninsula were 60, 28, and 3.

In an economy where hire purchase plays an increasing part in distribution, the Aboriginal, perhaps because he is regarded as a poor risk, makes minimal use of this as a cushion against the effects of fluctuation in earnings. In Table 27 I have included the hire purchase commitments of males over fifteen years in the small non-Aboriginal group living beside the Aboriginal families in the Eyre Peninsula. The figures must be treated with caution because of the large proportion of cases in which the situation was unknown. Hire purchase facilities could probably be more easily extended to organised Aboriginal groups, with some degree of responsible

**Table 26:** *Ownership of Property—Aboriginal Males over Fifteen Years*

| Property | Not known % | Claims ownership % | States does not own % | At school where relevant % |
|---|---|---|---|---|
| Motor vehicle | | | | |
| N.S.W. | 6·2 | 22·2 | 68·2 | 4·4 |
| Eyre Peninsula | 6·8 | 30·1 | 61·6 | 1·4 |
| House | | | | |
| N.S.W. | 3·3 | 6·6 | 90·1 | — |
| Eyre Peninsula | 8·2 | 11·0 | 80·8 | — |
| Other real estate | | | | |
| N.S.W. | 5·1 | 1·5 | 93·4 | — |
| Eyre Peninsula | * | * | * | — |
| Shares in company | | | | |
| N.S.W. | 5·5 | Nil | 94·5 | — |
| Eyre Peninsula | 8·2 | 1·4 | 90·4 | — |
| Tools of trade | | | | |
| N.S.W. | 5·8 | 1·1 | 88·7 | 4·4 |
| Eyre Peninsula | 8·2 | 12·3 | 78·1 | 1·4 |
| Livestock—100 or more | | | | |
| N.S.W. | 5·5 | Nil | 94·5 | — |
| Eyre Peninsula | 8·2 | 2·7 | 89·0 | — |
| Other property | | | | |
| $50-$200 | | | | |
| N.S.W. | 6·2 | 3·6 | — | — |
| Eyre Peninsula | 9·6 | 9·6 | — | — |
| $201-$600 | | | | |
| N.S.W. | 6·2 | 3·6 | — | — |
| Eyre Peninsula | 9·6 | 6·8 | — | — |
| $601-$1,000 | | | | |
| N.S.W. | 6·2 | 0·7 | — | — |
| Eyre Peninsula | 9·6 | 9·6 | — | — |
| $1,000 + | | | | |
| N.S.W. | 6·2 | 0·4 | — | — |
| Eyre Peninsula | 9·6 | 4·1 | — | — |

* Questionnaire not successful—'House' and 'Real Estate' answers identical—C.D.R.

**Table 27:** *Hire Purchase—Aboriginal Males over Fifteen Years*

| | N.S.W. % | Eyre Peninsula Aboriginal % | Non-Aboriginal % |
|---|---|---|---|
| Not known | 26·6 | 11·0 | 14·3 |
| Under $10 per month | 4·0 | 4·1 | 3·6 |
| $10 to $20 per month | 4·4 | 10·9 | 10·7 |
| $20 to $30 per month | 2·2 | Nil | Nil |
| $30 to $40 per month | 1·8 | 4·1 | 21·4 |
| Over $40 per month | 2·6 | 8·2 | 10·7 |
| At school | 4·4 | 1·4 | 7·1 |
| No hire purchase payments | 54·0 | 60·3 | 32·1 |

leadership, and especially if such groups could be guaranteed by government financed banking operations. The case for associations obtaining credit, for savings and loan societies, is as clear as for so many other particular measures—for special education measures, steps to improve housing, and the like. But all require an organised group to deal with; and without such a group with an acknowledged internal authority structure, there can be little consistent motivation to carry through consistent plans into action.

It is probably a truism that those who most need insurance policies are least likely to have them, and the Aboriginal worker illustrates the cycle of poverty in this respect. Once again, the results of a survey can be offered only as suggestive: in the background which I think has been established, they are probably enough to make the point. As a further comment, figures for the male non-Aboriginal group in the Eyre Peninsula are also included in Table 28.

**Table 28:** *Insurance Policies Held by Aboriginal (and some non-Aboriginal) Males over Fifteen Years*

| | | Eyre Peninsula | |
| Insurance Situation | N.S.W. % | Aboriginal % | Non-Aboriginal % |
| --- | --- | --- | --- |
| Not known | 10·6 | 12·3 | Nil |
| Both life and property insured | 3·3 | 2·7 | 42·9 |
| Either life or property insured | 10·6 | 28·8 | 14·2 |
| Neither life nor property insured | 75·5 | 56·2 | 42·9 |

Once again, there seems to be a relationship between the high degree of urbanisation of the Eyre Peninsula group and higher levels of financial security for the worker. Yet the worker and his dependants generally have other economic defences. These are to be found in the ties of kinship and in the morality of sharing, which have perforce been continued from both the Aboriginal tradition and that of the earlier communities of the Australian frontier and adapted to current conditions.

The Aboriginal worker is not predominantly active in formal organisations, although he may have to learn the techniques of formal organisation to improve his social and economic standing. Table 29 illustrates the situation. There are no comparable figures for the community as a whole; again, as suggestive only, the small non-Aboriginal neighbour group from the Eyre Peninsula is included.

Probably most Aborigines who join trade unions do so for the same reason as others—because they must, to gain the employment they need, or to hold what they have. For 11 per cent of the Aboriginal men we

**Table 29:** *Membership of Clubs and Organisations—Aboriginal (and some other) Males over Fifteen Years*

| Type of Organisation | N.S.W. % | Eyre Peninsula Aboriginal % | Non-Aboriginal % |
|---|---|---|---|
| Not known | 7·3 | 11·0 | 3·6 |
| Aboriginal, or predominantly Aboriginal, membership | 1·5 | 1·4 | Nil |
| Aboriginal organisation plus community or other | 1·1 | Nil | Nil |
| Community organisation only | 5·5 | 15·1 | 32·1 |
| Not a member | 80·3 | 71·2 | 57·1 |
| At school | 4·4 | 1·4 | 7·1 |

were unable to establish whether or not they were trade union members. In New South Wales, the proportion of Aboriginal males over fifteen years, excluding the 'unknown' cases, who were union members was 24·5 per cent. In the Eyre Peninsula, it was 43·8 per cent. Probably the higher figure in the Eyre Peninsula reflected the stricter policing of union policies in industrial situations, and the greater awareness which comes from industrial employment. The New South Wales situation is probably a carryover from the earlier lack of interest by rural trade unions in the Aboriginal worker; it reflects the uncertainties of seasonal work, the difficulties of organising it, and possibly the social gap between the Aboriginal and other workers in the traditionally oriented society of farm and sheep stations. Only 14 per cent of the unemployed in New South Wales were union members, mainly seasonal workers for whom it was difficult for unions to police awards, and who are far more dependent on being known by particular employers than on membership of unions.

### THE WOMEN AND GIRLS OVER FIFTEEN YEARS

By 1961, 20·38 per cent of the *total* female population of Australia had been mobilised from the household to the work force.[2] The proportion of females over fifteen years in the work force was just under 30 per cent, and of those engaged in home duties, approximately 55 per cent.[3] These figures obviously do not account for all women in these age groups—

[2] Commonwealth Bureau of Census and Statistics, 30 June 1961, vol. VIII, Australia: Statistician's Report, p. 293: Occupational Statistics of Females: Numbers and Percentage Distribution, 30th June, 1961.

[3] Calculated from 1961 Census—Occupations of the Population of Australian States and Territories.

others would be at school, or persons about whom the facts were unknown, or engaged neither in the work force nor home duties, for a variety of reasons.

The main significance of Table 30 is in the small percentage known to be in paid employment. The fact that the women in the small non-Aboriginal group in the Eyre Peninsula included the smallest proportion in wage employment, and that all three figures were round half the Australian figure calculated for the age group, may indicate how low incomes and large families restrict the activities of women irrespective of race. Here is another segment of the cycle of poverty as it affects the Aboriginal household. In Table 30 the 308 Aboriginal women from New South Wales and the 99 from the Eyre Peninsula may be regarded as a fair sample. The 29 non-Aboriginal women are obviously not a fair sample of non-Aboriginal women from poorer families.

**Table 30:** *Current Employment—Aboriginal (and some other) Women over Fifteen Years*

| Type of Employment | N.S.W.*<br>% | Eyre Peninsula<br>Aboriginal†<br>% | Non-Aboriginal‡<br>% |
|---|---|---|---|
| Not known | 4·5 | 3·0 | 0 |
| Home duties (own dwelling) | 60·1 | 73·7 | 69·0 |
| Wage employment | 14·9 | 16·2 | 13·8 |
| Self-employed (own business) | 1·0 | 0 | 6·9 |
| No apparent employment, at home or elsewhere | 12·7 | 1·0 | 0 |
| Stated never employed | 1·3 | 0 | 0 |
| At school, or pensioner | 5·5 | 6·1 | 10·3 |

\* N = 308.    † N = 99.    ‡ N = 29.

An additional 2 per cent of Aboriginal women (and 7 per cent of the small non-Aboriginal group) were in part-time employment. Full-time domestic employment was easily the most common form of full-time employment for Aboriginal women—6·5 per cent of those over fifteen years in New South Wales, and 9·1 per cent of those in the Eyre Peninsula. These figures represent about 44 per cent and 56 per cent respectively of women in the work force. The percentage of female employees engaged as paid domestic workers for Australia as a whole was 7·36 in 1961. This confirms the obsolescence of the economic position of Aboriginal families. Next in importance in New South Wales was outdoor agricultural employment, and in the Eyre Peninsula, sales and clerical work. Agricultural work accounted for 21 per cent of female employment for wages in New South Wales, which may be compared with the national percentage of 0·74 per cent. Clerical, typing, and sales work made up over 34 per cent of paid employment in Australia in 1961. In rural New South Wales, only 6·6 per cent of the Aboriginal women were so employed: the barriers of prejudice and lack of education and training, which made such ambitions often difficult, were matters of comment in the press by 1965. The proportion among the Eyre Peninsula group was over 12 per cent of the work force, a further reflection of the effects of urbanisation.[4]

Table 31 sets out what could be gathered of the post-primary school training or qualifications of Aboriginal women over fifteen years: once again, with the small group from neighbouring non-Aboriginal families in the Eyre Peninsula included for comparison.

**Table 31:** *Post-primary Training or Qualifications—Aboriginal (and some other) Women over Fifteen Years*

|  | N.S.W. % | Eyre Peninsula Aboriginal % | Non-Aboriginal % |
|---|---|---|---|
| Not known | 12·7 | 19·2 | 17·2 |
| Nil | 79·5 | 76·8 | 62·1 |
| Nurse |  |  |  |
|   qualified | 0·6 ⎤ | Nil ⎤ | Nil ⎤ |
|   not qualified | 0·3 | Nil | Nil |
| Domestic |  |  |  |
|   qualified | Nil | Nil | Nil |
|   not qualified | Nil ⎬2·5 | Nil ⎬2·00 | Nil ⎬13·7 |
| Technical |  |  |  |
|   qualified | Nil | 1·0 | 6·9 |
|   not qualified | 0·6 | Nil | 3·4 |
| Any other training or quals. | 1·0 ⎦ | 1·0 ⎦ | 3·4 ⎦ |
| School child or pensioner | 5·2 | 2·0 | 6·9 |

Table 32 relates stated levels of average earnings by Aboriginal women over a 3-month period to the proportions which claimed such level of earning. Its main relevance is that it suggests that no more than 3 per cent of all Aboriginal women in either group could be regarded as self-supporting in terms applicable to the community at large. A high degree of accuracy cannot of course be claimed: indeed replies to separate questions about the same general theme are often at variance.

In New South Wales, the figure for average earnings had very

---

[4] The further figures relating to Aborigines are taken from tabulations from the SSRC-AP survey. For those on the occupations of Australian females in general, see Statistician's Report 1961, pp. 274-5: Occupations of Females, Australia, 30th June, 1961.

probably been affected by the drought. At least 9·7 per cent (over 11 per cent did not make the information available) of women who were not pensioners, employed in home duties, or at school (under 2 per cent of all women over fifteen years) were stated to have received unemployment or sickness benefit for part or the whole of the previous three months.

**Table 32:** *Weekly Wage Earnings Averaged over Previous Three Months—Aboriginal Women over Fifteen Years*

| Average Weekly Wage | N.S.W. % | Eyre Peninsula % |
|---|---|---|
| Not known | 5·8 | 4·0 |
| Nil—not employed for wages or at school | 79·2 | 80·8 |
| Under $5 | 2·9 | Nil |
| $5 to $9 | 4·9 | Nil |
| $10 to $14 | 1·3 | 5·1 |
| $15 to $19 | 1·3 | 3·0 |
| $20 to $24 | 1·3 | 4·0 |
| $25 to $35 | 3·2 | 2·0 |
| Over $35 | Nil | 1·0 |

A partial explanation of this situation is that in the 15-19 age group, on the somewhat limited evidence we had, the Aboriginal girl is more likely than others to commence having children. Census figures indicated that just under 7 per cent of all Australian women in that age group were married, although this would not include all who were living with spouses.[5] Women in this age group numbered only sixty-nine in our New South Wales families and fifteen in the Eyre Peninsula. Of the total, twelve, or over 14 per cent, were married or otherwise living with a spouse. This of course is the age when youth is socialised into employment in the national cash economy (and into the national political system, at least to the extent that he or she becomes conscious of having economic interests). Early part-Aboriginal marriage, and the very high value placed on children, are factors in the demographic situation already described.

From observation, I had the impression of a large proportion of stable unions where the male spouse regards the children of an earlier union as his own—as something of a bonus, in fact. Nor is there any particular stigma attached to the illegitimacy of the child, either for the mother or the child. Girls who have babies remain at home; they marry or form firm unions in due course. I had no statistical basis for these impressions; but

[5] Commonwealth Census, 1961: Bulletin No. 31, Table 18.

often man and spouse used different surnames. Often the information was freely volunteered, by couples who placed no importance on legal marriage. It would be interesting to know how far this attitude has been a response to attempts by some governments to control marriage. A kind of early trial marriage, followed by a firm union, seems common; and the union may be with a new spouse. Divorce is an expensive procedure and seems not to be considered necessary. As it is commonly thought necessary by non-Aborigines who change sexual partners, comparisons of sexual *mores* would be difficult, even if the statistics on marriage and divorce were available.

Early sexual experience may be rather effect than cause of the absence from the regular work force of the very young Aboriginal woman. By the time she is thirty, she is, on our figures, about as likely to be or to have been married as the non-Aboriginal woman. The proportion of widows, divorcées, or women separated from spouses, in our New South Wales Aboriginal families, was 14·2 per cent. The national average in the 1961 census was 14·5 per cent.[6] What happens in the 15-19 age group is especially likely to determine the whole pattern of a woman's life. If she is of part-Aboriginal descent she is especially vulnerable, for social reasons already stated.

In later years, her chances of integration into the work force probably diminish. In New South Wales we found that 41·5 per cent of Aboriginal women over fifteen years had over *four* children. The figure for those in the Eyre Peninsula was 37·3 per cent, and for the small non-Aboriginal group, 24 per cent. The details are set out in Table 33.

Mothers with living children in the small non-Aboriginal group averaged 2·96 children, which compares fairly closely with the national average of 2·80, given in the 1961 Statistician's Report for *all* issue, dead or living, of Australian mothers.[7] But the comparable figures for the Aboriginal mothers were 4·9 for New South Wales and 4·5 for the Eyre Peninsula. The difference would probably be emphasised if the figures for live-born children who had died were taken into account: 23 per cent of New South Wales Aboriginal mothers and 24 per cent of those in the Eyre Peninsula had lost one or more of their children through death; the figure for the non-Aboriginal mothers in the Eyre Peninsula (which I stress again can only be suggestive) was 10 per cent. Each case, involving

[6] These figures raise questions about the emphasis in the previous chapter on the female-dominated *family* in Aboriginal society. But I can do no more than state that we took our evidence from the people most carefully; that we actually counted and checked the categories; and that our New South Wales sample seems adequate.

[7] Commonwealth Bureau of Census and Statistics: 1961 Census, Statistician's Report, p. 382.

**Table 33:** *Surviving Offspring—Aboriginal Women over Fifteen Years*

| Surviving Children No. | N.S.W. % | Eyre Peninsula Aboriginal % | Non-Aboriginal % |
|---|---|---|---|
| 0 | 26·0 | 21·2 | 17·2 |
| 1 | 7·5 | 9·1 | 20·7 |
| 2 | 8·8 | 14·1 | 17·2 |
| 3 | 5·2 | 6·1 | 13·8 |
| 4 | 6·5 | 11·1 | Nil |
| 5 | 10·7 | 10·1 | 6·9 |
| 6 | 7·1 | 10·1 | 10·3 |
| 7 | 7·5 | 7·1 | 3·4 |
| 8 | 6·5 | 4·0 | Nil |
| 9 | 3·6 | 3·0 | Nil |
| 10 | 3·2 | 3·0 | Nil |
| 11 | 2·3 | Nil | 3·4 |
| 12 | 0·6 | Nil | Nil |
| Not known | 4·5 | 1·0 | 6·9 |

pregnancy and another responsibility during the life of the child, had operated as a further tie to domesticity. In addition, 14 per cent of the New South Wales mothers had foster children.

All this conforms with the general argument of obsolescence of the Aboriginal family when examined in the hard logic of the national economy. The women who keep the homes together in so many cases can have had little other economic experience. Their constant preoccupation with domestic details in the kind of homes we have described is reminiscent of how women lived in poor families a generation or two ago. Such lives may be heroic and satisfying, but they ensure that the woman remains a hard core of part-Aboriginal conservatism. As so often she is the main socialising personality for the children, these attitudes are handed on. That the children are increasing, now that few in this country need starve, in spite of conditions apparently conducive to ill health, seems to indicate considerable efficiency in the mother's (and grandmother's) role.

Yet part of the requirement for equal economic and social participation is experience somewhat wider than the eternal 'battling' round poor homes. To live in 1965 like characters in a Henry Lawson story of a poor selector's family, to adhere basically to his simple faith in mateship and sharing, with small Aboriginal groups, is to make the best of being cut off from a real participation and effective citizenship.

W here there are no political institutions through which the protests of an entrapped indigenous minority, or of a colonised majority, may be effectively formulated and expressed, it is reasonable to look for the results of frustration in the crime records. These may indicate protest or a mental and emotional instability, if they differ from the average for the country. To some extent, and in 1964-5 this remained true in Aboriginal affairs, they will be indicative of special laws applying to the minority. Both the proportion of offences to the size of population and the kinds of offences which are most common, especially where they differ from the majority norms, may be significant. The difficulty is that as a rule the government statistical services do not separate offences by Aborigines from those by others. The exception has been Western Australia, where the annual Statistical Registers have given separate figures for Aboriginal convictions at magistrates' courts, and for committals from those courts to higher courts. When the research for this Project was being undertaken, it proved possible to secure the co-operation of the Commissioner of Police, who supplied figures which were being arranged for publication. The result is that we had access to figures for the years ending in June of 1962, 1963, and 1964.[1]

Here, however, we come up against a typical dilemma of statistics, very common in the field of Aboriginal affairs. Was the Commissioner of Police returning figures for *natives* under the Western Australian legislation,

---

[1] Commonwealth Bureau of Census and Statistics, Statistical Register of Western Australia, 1962, Part VIII—Law and Crime. Figures for the two succeeding years were made available by the Commissioner of Police, who had them ready for publication.

or for *Aborigines* in accordance with the Commonwealth practice of treating as Aborigines (as distinct from half-castes) those with a 'preponderance' of Aboriginal descent? The evidence of the statistics themselves, the range of offences, and the proportion of Aboriginal offences to the total returned for the State make it clear that the figures refer to *natives* under the Western Australian legislation. This is confirmed from what one can learn by inquiries from the Commonwealth Bureau of Census and Statistics. But the use of the Commonwealth term *Aborigine* is a nice additional reminder of the cause of this type of problem—that, until recently, reliability in statistics on Aboriginal affairs did not receive high priority. We are safe enough in using these, however, since, if the figures are for full-blood *Aborigines* only, they are obviously an understatement of the situation.

On the 1961 census figures, *Aboriginals* and *half-castes* formed 2·8 per cent of the population of Western Australia. But Aboriginal convictions at magistrates' courts, and committals to higher courts, represented 8·87 per cent of the total in the years ended June 1962 and June 1963, and 11·32 per cent in the following year—figures which average out to just under 10 per cent over the 3-year period. Even if we allow for a heavy under-enumeration on *Aboriginals* in the census, here is a clear enough indication of differences from the norms of the majority and of the population of the State as a whole.

A comparison of the relative proportions of various types of offences leading to conviction or committal is instructive; these are set out in Table 34 below.

**Table 34:** *Types of Offence, Leading to Conviction or Committal, for the Years ending June 1962-4, in Western Australia*

|  | Aboriginal offences* | | | Offences by persons other than Aborigines* | | |
|---|---|---|---|---|---|---|
|  | 1962 | 1963 | 1964 | 1962 | 1963 | 1964 |
| Against the person | 2·96 | 2·9 | 2·8 | 1·2 | 1·1 | 1·2 |
| Against property and currency | 10·4 | 10·1 | 10·2 | 13·3 | 14·8 | 13·5 |
| Drunkenness and other offences against good order | 61·3 | 61·8 | 67·6 | 14·9 | 13·4 | 13·0 |
| Offences under the Native Welfare Act | 14·3 | 12·3 | 5·8 | Not significant | | |
| Traffic offences | Not significant | | | 54·0 | 55·4 | 55·8 |
| Other | 11·0 | 13·0 | 13·4 | 16·7 | 15·3 | 16·5 |

* % of totals for each group.

Offences for drunkenness and offences against order were consistently over 60 per cent of the total for Aborigines, as against a proportion which in the community exclusive of Aborigines was consistently under 15 per cent, or one-quarter of the Aboriginal percentage. If we look at this as a health matter, the difference constitutes some evidence of mental ill health, to be dealt with by tackling the root causes. Alcoholism of Aborigines has been long recognised as a 'problem', but attributed to some special weakness in Aboriginal personality. Almost certainly it is an effect of the special social condition and economic predicament of the Aboriginal, and in part of long-standing frustration and resentment. The figures understate the predominance of offences of this kind, since round about half the offences under the Native Welfare Act were for the receiving and supply of liquor, involving persons who under the special laws could not legally receive or be supplied. The 'other' offences also include breaches of the liquor licensing laws.

The increase in offences linked with drunkenness in 1964 corresponds with a decrease in prosecutions under the Native Welfare Act. The new Act, which received assent at the end of 1963 and was in operation for the second half of the report year, may have been one reason for the change, as it involved a general relaxation of restrictions.

For the Aboriginal, drunkenness and disorderly conduct, as interpreted by the law, play a part resembling that of traffic offences for others. Arrests and charges arising from the use of alcohol are probably, for the Aboriginal, a matter of no more concern than charges for traffic offences for other Australians. While the Aboriginal is driven to destroy himself, the mechanised other Australian destroys his fellows on the roads. Aboriginal convictions and committals for traffic breaches will increase with affluence; they were about 6 per cent of these returns.

Crimes against the person might offer a further clue to tensions; and it may be significant that although those committed by Aborigines were consistently less than 3 per cent of the total, they were still consistently over twice the proportion for non-Aborigines. This might be seen in part as resulting from the historical background; in part (as with liquor offences) as a symptom of a general poverty of outlook and sophistication, which Aborigines may largely share with others living in similar conditions. For Aborigines, poverty is the norm: for other Australians, it characterises a minority.

As comparable statistics were not available from other States, an effort was made to obtain some basis for comparison. In this, this Project received very real help from the police departments of Victoria, New

South Wales, and South Australia (in addition to that already referred to from the Commissioner in Western Australia). The Commissioners of Police in each of the three States agreed to have certain police stations, in police districts which were known to have comparatively large Aboriginal populations, return separate statistics of Aborigines and others arrested and charged, and of the offences with which they were charged, for the six months from 1 July 1965 to 31 December 1965. The police stations selected in Victoria were Collingwood, Fitzroy, and St Kilda in Melbourne, and Echuca, Lakes Entrance, Mildura, Mooroopna, Robinvale, Shepparton, Swan Hill, and Warrnambool in the non-metropolitan area. A major problem with all figures collected in this way was that Aboriginal populations could not be established for police districts, and that where total figures for police districts were obtained, they were only approximate. Another factor preventing any valid conclusions being drawn for the State as a whole is that the selection of police stations had to be more or less arbitrary, the main gain being that in each case Aborigines and others had been arrested by the same police officers. Identification as Aboriginal or other had to be left to the police officer keeping the records, so that an 'Aboriginal' in these cases means one who by appearance or on the basis of local repute was identified as Aboriginal. As only one Aboriginal was listed as having been arrested in St Kilda, as against 1,530 others, it was clear that this police district should not have been included. Even in Fitzroy and Collingwood, and in the eight non-metropolitan police districts stated, Aborigines form a small minority.

What is possible is a comparison of the kinds of offences leading to arrests and charges, for Aborigines and for others. In the non-metropolitan police districts, 60 per cent of Aboriginal offences were stated as being 'drunk and disorderly'; the comparable figure for others was 34 per cent. In the two metropolitan police districts the difference was less marked—with 90 per cent of Aboriginal, and 77 per cent of others, charged for this offence. In view of the fact that in Victoria Aborigines form a tiny minority of at the most about 3,000 people, or about one person in a thousand, it may be worth a note in passing that during the six months over 20 per cent of all arrests in the non-metropolitan towns listed were of Aborigines and that in the same period 9 per cent of arrests in the Fitzroy police district were of Aborigines. Even if all the 3,000 were congregated in these police districts, this would have indicated some special stress. For all the stations listed, even if we include St Kilda, where there was only one Aboriginal arrested and charged as against 1,530 others, Aborigines accounted for nearly 8 per cent of the total.

The police stations selected in New South Wales were in Redfern, in the centre of the Sydney metropolitan area, and in the country towns of Condobolin, Kempsey, Moree, Nowra, Walgett, and Wilcannia. In South Australia the metropolitan stations were at Adelaide and Port Adelaide, and the others at Port Augusta, Meningie, Berri, Port Victoria, Oodnadatta, Port Lincoln, and Ceduna. Fifty per cent of all charges at all the New South Wales stations listed, and 21 per cent of all charges in those of South Australia, were against Aborigines in this 6-month period. The difference is mainly due to the fact that we included two metropolitan police stations in South Australia and only one in Sydney. Aborigines are more greatly outnumbered in the metropolitan cities. If we look at non-metropolitan police stations only, the figures are, respectively, 67·75 per cent for New South Wales and 66·94 per cent for the South Australian stations. These figures suggest, at least, that where a distinct Aboriginal community can be identified (as was done in order to select these police stations), police arrests of and charges against Aborigines will be distinctly higher than those of others as proportions of the respective populations. This seems to be a very conservative estimate of a quite marked situation of long standing. But where one has no figures of the two populations in each locality, one may only offer these as suggestive. It is, for instance, suggestive that for all the country towns listed, including Victoria where the Aboriginal groups are even less numerous, charges against Aborigines accounted for over 57 per cent of the total. In the metropolitan districts of Fitzroy (Melbourne), Redfern (Sydney), and Adelaide, Aborigines form a very small minority indeed, so that they are lost in the mass as it were; but 6 per cent of all charges over the six months were against Aborigines.

However, the really significant figures, which can be stated with some confidence, are those of the types of offence for which Aborigines and other persons were arrested and charged, as percentages of the total offences by members of each racial group—see Table 35.

Probably the selection was too arbitrary for the emergence of any clear pattern in the case of crimes against the person. The figures for 'drunk and disorderly' charges against Aborigines are, however, what one might expect from the Western Australian statistics. But the disparity between charges of this kind against Aborigines and against others is not so great. Separating the metropolitan figures from those from country town police stations showed that on the combined figures for Adelaide and Port Adelaide police stations, over the six months, non-Aborigines arrested were more likely to have been charged with drunkenness and disorderly conduct than were the Aborigines arrested. But this was the one exception.

**Table 35:** *Types of Offences for which Aborigines and Others Were Arrested and Charged, 1 July to 31 December 1965*

| Police Areas | Aboriginal | | | Non-Aboriginal | |
| | Drunk and disorderly, etc.* | Offences against the person* | Breaches of special 'Aboriginal' legislation* | Drunk and disorderly | Offences against the person* |
|---|---|---|---|---|---|
| Victorian metropolitan (Collingwood and Fitzroy) | 89·9 | 1·8 | Nil | 77·2 | 5·7 |
| Victorian non-metropolitan† | 59·8 | 4·6 | Nil | 34·1 | 7·1 |
| N.S.W. metropolitan Redfern† | 47·0 | 2·4 | Nil | 31·9 | 3·4 |
| N.S.W. non-metropolitan† | 67·9 | 1·7 | 10·6 | 37·0 | 5·6 |
| S.A. metropolitan Adelaide–Port Adelaide | 80·6 | 2·5 | Nil | 89·8 | 0·4 |
| S.A. non-metropolitan† | 60·9 | 7·8 | 11·5 | 55·3 | 5·6 |

\* % of total offences.
† See pp. 355-6.

The relationship of drunkenness to other offences need not be dwelt on here; nor is there any evidence that this relationship is any more marked for Aborigines than for others who for any reason are especially addicted to the use of alcohol. Even the figures for arrests and charges have to be used with caution, since they reflect other factors, such as the relationship between Aborigines and police in country towns. Too often, of course, addiction to alcohol is regarded as a special feature of Aboriginal personality, without asking the further question of why an Aboriginal is more likely to be drunk and to defy the law. Yet it is here that our look at the history of Aboriginal affairs may have indicated more deep-seated causes. A significant one must have been the long-standing restrictions on Aboriginal drinking. But this, I believe, has not been so significant as the other factors, operating right from the beginning of white settlement, which disintegrated Aboriginal society and which have prevented the emergence of any effective new framework of leadership or any social organisation capable of functioning at a level other than that of sporadic protest.[2] In brief, the situation has been that for generations there was nothing of real value which an Aboriginal community could decide for itself, except for periods when it was left unmolested in its own 'country'. A high incidence of addiction to alcohol, noted in the literature from the early contacts, can be easily enough accounted for as escape from the tragedy of a disintegrating society and world view; as a form of defiance of authority, and as a means of discharging those tensions and resentments which normally had to be hidden under the mask of apathy.

Aborigines obtained the right to drink in New South Wales (for the second time) with the adoption of the Aborigines Protection (Amendment) Act in March 1963. The Board at the end of June of that year reported 'no increase in unfavourable incidence', and commented on the 'restraint and common sense' of the majority of the Aborigines.[3] The prohibition was removed by the Queensland Act of 1965 and made effective with the regulations introduced in 1966. In South Australia and Western Australia the prohibition was being removed progressively by regions, commencing in the areas of closer settlement. In South Australia, by early 1965, the right had been extended to the areas north and west of Port Augusta, on the recommendations of both the Department of Aboriginal Affairs and the Commissioner of Police, who stated that there had been a decline in 'excess consumption' by Aborigines in the areas where the prohibition had already been lifted.[4]

In Western Australia, a start was made in 1964. The situation was that supplying or receiving liquor constituted the offence for Aborigines, under sections 150 and 151 of the Western Australian Licensing Act 1911-1964, but that this provision applied only in proclaimed areas. As from 1 July 1964 the prohibitions ceased to apply in the South West Land Division. No further deletion of areas was made until November 1966, partly no doubt because of the resistance of local government bodies. Thus a conference of the Eastern Goldfields local government authorities in September 1966 opposed further extensions of drinking rights.[5] But the November proclamation extended the rights into the Murchison, the

[2] See *The Destruction of Aboriginal Society.*
[3] *N.S.W.P.P.*, 1962-4, vol. 1, no. 241—A.W.B. Report, 1963, p. 3.
[4] The last restrictions were removed by an Executive Council proclamation which withdrew prohibitions imposed under sections 172 and 173 of the South Australian Licensing Act. See *Advertiser* (Adelaide), 2 April 1965.
[5] *West Australian*, 26 September 1966.

North West and the Southern Cross areas, which left out the Kimberleys and the Eastern Goldfields.[6] The last two and the Esperance Bay area still had prohibition of Aboriginal drinking at the beginning of 1968.

Prohibitions remained, within the areas where rights were given, in the Aboriginal institutions, including the reserves. The way out of the situation is probably to withdraw the managements along with all restrictive laws applying on these, so that here again Queensland appears to be caught with a dilemma which arises from an obsolete policy. The ostensible reason for political resistance in the remaining areas of Western Australia are the typical 'colonial' ones which so nicely fit the situations— that liquor is especially harmful to full-bloods. There is a moral problem, perhaps, in allowing free sale of liquor to a completely unsophisticated person. But the legal restriction has little to do with real restriction; it is based mainly on prejudice of the colonial type. Such unsophisticated persons would be extremely few: and one of the first signs of sophistication will be use of liquor, legally or otherwise. Within the settled areas being discussed here, drinking rights have been accorded everywhere.

Needless to say, there was much fuss in the press over such a grave step— to which there might have been more point if the prohibitions had ever, at any time, been effective. The real significance, in view of the fact that Aborigines could now drink openly, was that they could not legally be excluded, as Aborigines, from the hotel bar. Some hotelkeepers did exclude them by refusing service—an action which is legally an offence only in South Australia. Service in the bar has become something of a symbol of equality, partly as the result of a few protest actions. In South Australia there were grim predictions being made, towards the end of the first full year of full drinking rights, of a marked increase in Aboriginal crime, but reliable figures were not available in such a way as to show the effects of *legal* drinking; nor probably could they be. In July 1966 the Minister for Aboriginal Affairs commented on a police report, which stated that charges against Aborigines in the Far North Police Division had increased during the year from 556 to 1,002, by quoting other figures to show that there had been no significant difference.[7] In August the story appeared in the Adelaide and Canberra press that the Aboriginal 1 per cent of the population of South Australia was providing 20 per cent of criminals in the State's gaols (which left out of account that Adelaide gaols are used where security is required for Northern Territory criminals).[8]

[6] For discussion at the time see Ibid., 27 September and 2 November 1966.
[7] *Advertiser* (Adelaide), 27 July 1966.
[8] Ibid., 13 August 1966; *Canberra Times*, 18 August 1966.

But this figure was not inconsistent with figures we obtained from the police stations mentioned above.

It was possible to obtain figures for the South West Land Division of Western Australia for the period immediately before, and that immediately after, the withdrawal of drinking restrictions. They are shown in Table 36.

**Table 36:** *Charges against Aborigines, Before and After Obtaining Drinking Rights, in the South West Land Division of Western Australia*

| Period | Convictions against natives No. | State of Law |
|---|---|---|
| 1 January–30 June 1964 | 2,022 | Alcohol prohibited |
| 1 July–31 December 1964 | 2,242 | Alcohol not prohibited |
| 1 January–30 June 1965 | 2,181 | Alcohol not prohibited |

*Source:* Letter from Commissioner of Police, Perth, W.A., 22 October 1965—SSRC-AP file.

Thus the increase was of 10·88 per cent in the first six months after the change. In the second 6-month period the increase over the six months preceding the change was 7·86 per cent. But one has to allow for more public drinking than before, with greater likelihood of arrests: for the greater alertness of the police during what had been much publicised as a critical time; and of course for the first aggressive assertion of rights by the Aborigines.

Except for the evidence in Table 34 on crimes against the person, these statistics mainly suggest a mental health problem arising from social and economic frustration, and the poverty of outlook which is shared by others, as the statistics in Table 35 indicate. If there is a current increase of Aboriginal crimes of violence, this might well offer a political warning. Dr Fay Gale has attributed an apparent increase to the frustration arising from gaining legal equality and being refused acceptance.[9] Most of the evidence appears to come periodically from areas like that west from Ceduna, where Aborigines had in the past little opportunity to acquire alcohol.[10]

It appears then that the pattern of Aboriginal offences, with the emphasis

[9] Quoted in *Advertiser* (Adelaide), 13 August 1966.
[10] See *Advertiser* (Adelaide), 9 May 1967 (editorial) and *Canberra Times*, 16 May 1967, and replies discounting 'exaggerations' from the Minister, Mr D. Dunstan, and Professor A.A. Abbie, Chairman of the Board, *Advertiser* (Adelaide), 6 and 24 May 1967. Note that the complaints came just before the referendum of 27 May 1967.

on over-use of alcohol, is significant but that there is not yet evidence of offences which suggest a drift towards a general repudiation of the law. In 1967 this situation called for the kind of negotiation, and for support by central government, of Aboriginal aspirations, which presented major political difficulties in a prejudiced democracy. Yet the conditions for the emergence of responsible Aboriginal leadership were a major priority in the national interest. Here was an area of responsibility in which the national government must rule. The opportunity to do so was presented in the result of the 1967 referendum.

It is difficult to answer the question of whether Aborigines are becoming big city dwellers at the rate of the rest of the community. The census figures indicate that this is far from the case. Some intensive searches by the referral method, for people identifying as Aboriginal, were sponsored by this Project in several capital cities, where the numbers found were markedly greater than the available census figures. On the other hand, when the School of Public Health and Tropical Medicine undertook the same kind of work in one non-metropolitan area of New South Wales, the result was also a marked increase in the census figure, although less so than in capital cities. From other evidence, it seems that Aboriginal capital city dwellers, even in the settled areas, probably form a much lower proportion of total Aboriginal people who so identify than do total capital city dwellers of total population in the same areas. Evidence also suggests that this situation is changing somewhat rapidly but that the present time is marked by high mobility, in both directions, between city and country town or rural area, and between different parts of the capital city.

This high mobility seems partly the result of frustration of urban aspirations, partly the initial indecisiveness which marks any poor minority group which has not the resources to be almost independent of the family and of the physical environment.

Factors operating against permanent settlement in the new environment include the lack of housing in the city, attachment to family, the difficulty of breaking out of economic dependence on seasonal work for those lacking in skills and basic education, a real pleasure in the country environment shared by comparatively few non-Aborigines, and feelings of loyalty to communities which have long been frozen, as it were, on stations, settlements, and reserves. On the other hand, the Aboriginal is especially vulnerable to economic factors which stimulate urbanisation. One of these is the increasing mechanisation of farming and pastoral work, which places more emphasis on special skills and elementary education, and has already drastically reduced the demand for rural labour of the traditional kind—a process which has been emphasised by drought. The vulnerability of the Aboriginal is in his lack of rural property interests. He has hung suspended, as it were, in the rural economy, as economic flotsam and as a marginal labour supply.

So the movement in and out of the capital is something more than experiment in social change, though this is important. When a family can no longer make a living in the country, it must move to the city, and the move will be possible if there are relatives and friends there. The problem of reception is critical. In many cases it proves impossible to get a foothold, even at a very low level of welfare. Rents, too, are critical. One cannot build shacks adjacent to the place of work in the city; and the cost of the poor housing in the inner suburbs tends to be very high. In a comparatively small city like Brisbane, it may be possible to establish a shack on the outskirts within a reasonable distance of urban places of work. In Sydney or Melbourne, this is generally impossible. Otherwise one might find attempts to settle in low standard housing in a ring round the city. It is more feasible to crowd into the obsolete housing in the centre.

High mobility is a fact commonly noted wherever there has been an attempt to establish a capital city population. Working by the system of referral from one family to another (the only one possible where the census figure is known to be a considerable understatement) one must, by the end of the process, make some sensible allowance for those who have moved out between the beginning and end of the count, and especially for the single persons (generally the young) whose movements it is impossible to check.

Another factor in this process is the attraction of the city. The Aboriginal is not only pushed from the country areas by economic factors, and by local discrimination; he is attracted by the same vision of the greater excitement of metropolitan living as attracts other Australians. Part of the growing attraction must be the realisation that in the city money gives the entrée to entertainment and services which may still be restricted in a country town. But the Aboriginal has not yet become 'economic man' to the degree of other Australians. He is more likely to move in or out for family reasons and loyalties than others are.

Metropolitan urbanisation has generally, in the past, been frustrated by *de facto* and legal control on movements. To some extent the present situation seems to arise from relaxation of the special legislation, and perhaps a more reasonable use of vagrancy and other laws. In this case the assimilation policy has enabled some real advances to be made. This kind of urbanisation cannot be considered apart from that much older one which has resulted in the fringe settlements round country towns, where for so long the effort to become established in the cash economy of the nation has been arrested, except for the cosmetically favoured. I refer elsewhere to the limited range of movements after seasonal work in the settled regions, and to the economic factors which may or may not have operated to perpetuate much older patterns of hunting and gathering migrations—the fact that most workers had to stay with relatives while not welcome in hotels, the limiting effect of higher employment risk on speculative movements, lack of capital, and insecurity of the home base. The new kind of urbanisation seems to be an attempt to break out of these constricting circumstances. But the movement is not always successful, so that it remains experimental for many, who may come and go until assets in the metropolis, social and economic, will so far outweigh those in the areas of origin that the city becomes the home; then journeys to the old home are visits made for social reasons. In this respect the urbanisation of a part-indigenous or indigenous minority resembles that of the indigenous majority in a colonial situation.

During 1964 and 1965 the conditions of Aborigines in Sydney were subject to considerable publicity, partly because of the obvious hardships involved,[1] partly owing to the imaginative step taken by a few persons interested in Aboriginal welfare, in establishing the Foundation for Aboriginal Affairs, and the purchase, following a public appeal (which fell a good deal short of its target despite the hiring of an effective organisation specialising in 'door-knock' techniques) of an Aboriginal place of resort for help and advice in the centre of the city. It proved possible to secure from the management (without names of course) details of 160 consecutive requests made to the Centre, by 84 men and 49 women in the five months of February to June 1965. Requests were often multiple; and occasionally so was the action taken. What proportion of requests went to this Centre, and what to the head office of the Aborigines Welfare Board (which previously handled all requests directly) is not known. The following are the types of action taken:

[1] For a well-written and by no means exaggerated description of the situation in Sydney, see Fred Wells, 'Taste of a Bitter Utopia', *S.M.H.*, 24 February 1966.

| Type of Action Taken | Percentage (to nearest unit) |
|---|---|
| Employment sought | 28 |
| Immediate food relief | 16 |
| Financial help sought or given | 15 |
| Housing and accommodation sought | 13 |
| Assistance with rail transport | 8 |
| Legal advice obtained | 6 |
| Medical assistance obtained | 6 |
| Advice on family welfare matters given | 6 |
| Approach to Social Service authority | 1 |
| Furniture supplied | 1 |
| Advice on educational matter | 1 |

What is at once clear is that such a Centre plays an intermediary part between the person in need and various public authorities concerned with welfare. One imaginative step was to have an Aboriginal manager of the Centre from the beginning; and the effort to move towards Aboriginal management has been consistent. One result of this is probably to attract those in need who do not feel themselves equipped to deal directly with the government authority or who may feel that they will not receive the same attention from such authorities. A great deal of help appears to have been given by the office of the Aborigines Welfare Board and by other government agencies. The New South Wales government recognised the value of the Foundation by subsidising its funds.

The order of relative emphasis in requests and action indicates that there are Aborigines who move to the city, or who have established themselves, without permanent employment; employment, and immediate requirements for food and for shelter accounted for 57 per cent of the cases. By February 1968, formal interviews were averaging round 2,000 a year, with approximately an additional thousand where the applicant wanted mainly reassurance and discussion of his problems. The Centre was badly understaffed, so that no statistics could be abstracted. The problem of multiple family problems was such, for instance, that one interview could lead to action in three or four different areas of social administration. The Foundation appears to have had considerable success in establishing people in permanent employment. According to an estimate by Charles Perkins, then manager of the Centre, at least five hundred had been placed in the eighteen months up till the end of February 1968, and accommodation found in another three hundred cases.[2]

These figures suggest the important role of such a body, increasingly thought of by Aborigines as something of their own, in negotiation with the relevant government authorities and in the reception of innovators

[2] Information supplied on 4 March 1968.

moving in from country towns. The Foundation was from the beginning a body corporate; and in my opinion the best hope is that it will become, as the resources of Aboriginal leadership develop, an Aboriginal body, to which the specialist advice of those competent to give it will be available on request. The development has been both imaginative and careful. W.R. Geddes, Professor of Anthropology of the University of Sydney, and prime mover in this project, with his management committee, had to face in the early stages a good deal of opposition. Part came from ill-informed persons who regarded an *Aboriginal* Centre as an obstruction to 'assimilation'. Part came from those who had either their own recipes for Aboriginal advancement or who saw in the new organisation a threat to their own status or interests: the absence of unified Aboriginal leadership means that there are many opportunities for otherwise frustrated non-Aborigines to assume leadership roles. The initial success of the Foundation at least shows that this problem, of the micro-politics of Aboriginal organisations, is not insuperable.

The possibilities are important for the tactics of developing policy in which corporate bodies play a leading part, for sophisticated leadership requires urban experience. It was to the big cities that the innovators, and those who will increasingly turn to political action, were moving in the 1960s. In the kind of experience which the Foundation for Aboriginal Affairs is providing, the potential for leadership can be realised and Aboriginal hitting power within the law and within the framework of bureaucratic procedures can grow. Here is a growing point which governments could well subsidise further: similar organisations could well be founded in country towns, where one can envisage the growth of linked or separate Aboriginal companies as Aboriginal leadership acquires legitimacy among local groups and learns the techniques of negotiation and management. This seems to offer one alternative to other kinds of action arising from impatience and desperation.

One argument for this approach is that case-work with individual 'problem' families, Aboriginal or other, requires the framework of community organisation to be effective.

That the move into the cities has been mainly a development of the last two decades is, I think, to be largely explained by legislation and administrative practice before the war years. During the war, however, Aborigines found employment in the cities, partly because there was a general tendency to relax restrictions on movement. Policy on social service benefits was a factor, also, since for a time those on reserves could not get them; but the main attraction seems to have been permanent employment for higher wages for those who could establish themselves—a study of newspaper cuttings indicates that after the war ended the problem of the Aboriginal unemployed in the capital city increased.[3] At the same time, many had established homes in the central city areas; and these homes, poor as they often were, were no worse and no more overcrowded than those occupied by other slum-dwellers. While the crowding into limited facilities served to increase prejudice, non-Aborigines in similar case in the same areas, in a time of great housing shortages which have been maintained by the effects of the immigration policy (especially those who were themselves migrants adjusting to a new environment without the long tradition of prejudiced attitudes to persons of Aboriginal descent), would have no particular reason to reject the part-Aboriginal neighbour. These homes, once established in the centre of a city, often served as staging points for others coming in to try their fortunes.

## SYDNEY

The urban drift into Sydney seems to have become an item for press articles from about 1948, when the Superintendent of the Methodist Mission in South Sydney began to speak of the special problems being faced in the inner suburbs of Redfern and Surry Hills.[4] By 1950 the Redfern All Blacks football team was said to be drawing large crowds on Sunday afternoons, though a few years later this effort to express pride of the Aboriginal group was to be questioned as contrary to the requirements of assimilation! Another indicator of an incipient Aboriginal community feeling in the inner suburb was the increased membership of religious organisations which had welcomed Aborigines in the rural areas. Pentecostalism was being strengthened in the city. The Church of the Four Square Gospel, one of whose missionaries I was to meet at Condobolin during the field work for this book, was one of the rallying points for those who sought comfort and support. A trained social worker who was also a Congregational pastor in Redfern and working with Aboriginal people told me that a main attraction into the city was the hope of permanent employment; that those he met had seldom had permanent work in the areas from which they came.

[3] Press cuttings over several decades were maintained by a former secretary of the Victorian Aboriginal Group, mainly from the Victorian newspapers. These were lent to the Project through the good offices of P.E. Felton, Superintendent of Aborigines' Welfare, Melbourne. The extracts on urbanisation and other matters were made and summarised by Jennifer Atkins, Research Assistant in the SSRC-AP. All this material is in the SSRC-AP files.
[4] See Articles in *Smith's Weekly* (Sydney), for 22 May 1948, 7 January 1949, 8 April and 20 May 1950; *S.M.H.*, 12 July 1948, 11 February 1949; and *Sun* (Sydney), 11 February 1949.

Those who remained, he thought, generally obtained permanent work in the end. He estimated a period of hardship and adaptation to be commonly one or two years, at the end of which time those at least who received some help had generally obtained a house and employment. By inference, then, the inner city areas were serving to some extent as staging areas. There would now be few, if any, suburbs in Sydney which do not have families of Aboriginal descent.

Urbanisation was in full swing during the term of the research for this Project. One found that people in distant parts of New South Wales, for instance, would know certain addresses in Sydney where a person without a bed could always at least get a 'shake-down' on the floor. I remember well discussing the point with a typical motherly Aboriginal woman in a street in Redfern, whose response to my question was simple and humane, 'You can't let them sleep on the footpath, can you?'

By 1964 the effects of rationalisation in rural industries had begun to combine with those of the drought. There was a much publicised inspection by pressmen of inner city areas at the end of August.[5] Perhaps the migration pattern was illustrating the real weakness of a vague 'assimilation' policy; since if assimilation was the aim, it could be reasonably argued that the Aboriginal slum-dweller was living like some non-Aborigines. In an interesting statement on the 1963 debate which led to the removal of restrictions on alcohol in New South Wales, the Member for Armidale argued that, though the rates of increase were high, migration to the city was taking from the rural areas half the number of the annual increase (which could only have been a wild guess); that in the city they were being accepted as 'white'; that this was the story which should be told rather than that of old injustices.[6]

By 1964, however, distress was becoming more obvious in Sydney, and a matter for editorials and headlines, but nobody knew the size of the problem. When the Foundation for Aboriginal Affairs announced the purchase of a 3-storey building in July 1964, Geddes estimated that the numbers in the city were from 6,000 to 12,000;[7] but until a count is made, using a referral technique, an accurate estimate is impossible.

Mrs Pamela Beasley made at the beginning of 1964 an interim report on conditions in the Redfern-Chippendale area. She found over 500 persons willing to be interviewed as Aboriginal, in a small area including part of

[5] *The Australian*, 1 September 1964.
[6] *N.S.W.P.D.*, 1963, vol. 45 (L.A.), pp. 3339 *et seq.*—speech by Davis Hughes, Member for Armidale.
[7] See editorials in *S.M.H.* for 7 July and 3 September 1964.

Redfern and part of Chippendale, both run-down inner city areas where factories have been rapidly replacing dwellings. Over 46 per cent of her population were children under fifteen years—a figure well above the census average for the Australian community but well below the proportion established by sample surveys of Aboriginal families in rural areas. There were very few old people, for obvious reasons. Of the adults, only three were in employment which could be classed as skilled. Of 103 dependent on employment, fourteen were unemployed at the time of interview. On the average two persons lived in each room, including kitchens as living rooms. One family owned a house and two more were in the process of purchasing theirs. High rents were common by the rent standards of that time:

In spite of the hospitality of most of the Aboriginal people in the area, there were some who had great difficulty in solving their accommodation problems, and were without places to sleep for periods ranging from one day to a week or two. Some of these solved their problem in ways which could not be accepted by white authorities. Some 'squatted' in temporarily untenanted homes, leaving by the back door and over the fence if a knock came at the front door. Some walked around the streets for a few nights before being 'smuggled' into a residential where there were already one or two 'stowaways'. Some left luggage with friends and split up among different homes for the night, or nights, involved. Their difficulty would seem to be no reflection upon the willingness of their friends and relatives to help them, but rather upon the housing situation as it exists in the area.[8]

Reasons for coming into Sydney were stated as:

| A. | To find work | 99 |
| B. | To find accommodation | 65 |
| C. | Illness of self or relative | 81 |
| D. | Social | 15 |
| E. | Other reasons | 13 |

It was noted that fifty-one of a total of 208 children were 'not living with parents or with the one parent normally responsible for their care and up-bringing'. In forty-three cases, the reasons offered, in order of importance, were lack of accommodation, removal by the Child Welfare authority, and illness. Extended family arrangements accounted for only

[8] Pamela Beasley, Draft Preliminary Report on Redfern-Chippendale area of Sydney: seminar paper, February 1964. Mrs Beasley was subsequently assisted by the SSRC–AP to complete a study of 100 selected Aboriginal families in Sydney which she had begun while working for Professor W.R. Geddes. It was quite impossible with our limited resources to estimate the Aboriginal population of Sydney. We could only use a referral method. The census figures were useless for our purposes. See 'The Aboriginal Household in Sydney', in *Attitudes and Social Conditions*.

six such cases, where the child was stated to be residing with grand-mother.[9]

Just half the adults included in the survey had been living in this area for over three years. Other evidence indicates two directions of movement out from such areas—back to the country town or into the outer suburbs. This was a typical area for Aboriginal experiment in big city life.

Some later work by Mrs Pamela Beasley indicates that those families which do establish homes in the capital are likely, on the average, to be better off for living space than they were in the country area,[10] for it is simply not possible to live in a fringe-dweller's shack in the city. The only 'self-built' shacks seen were on the Aboriginal reserve (and just off it) at La Perouse, which is a fringe-dwellers' settlement now surrounded by the expanding city, and illustrating many of the social problems of such dwelling areas. For the city as a whole, Mrs Beasley found an average sized house of 5·5 rooms, somewhat below the urban average for New South Wales, but well above that for Aboriginal housing found in our rural survey. Yet there were 1·25 persons per room as compared with 0·67, the Australian average in 1961. (Our rural average was 1·63.) Even in the better conditions of Sydney there was a good deal of obvious over-crowding, with over 70 per cent of Aborigines subject to accommodation pressure of two or more persons per room. Here again, the situation was favourable when compared with our country town sample.

An interesting indication of the tendency for the household group to remain together was that these one hundred households averaged 7·03 persons, remarkably close to the 7·04 which was the average of the rural households surveyed. Both are about twice the Australian average. Just over half this metropolitan group were under fifteen years of age: somewhat less than in the rural areas, which might be accounted for by the fact that moves to the city are more difficult for people with families in certain age groupings. On the other hand, there was a high proportion of young people, in the 15-20, and 21-24 age groups, among those who had migrated to the city. Migrants accounted for about half the city group, even although the non-migrants would usually include their younger children; thus this population had more than doubled within living memory. Over 71 per cent of the migrants had been in Sydney for less than ten years; about 47 per cent for less than five.

In the country areas we found that some 9 per cent of homes were owned or being purchased along with the land on which they stood.

[9] Ibid.
[10] Ibid.

In the city, 24 per cent were owned or being purchased by occupiers. This was still well below the 67·5 per cent owned by occupants in Australia as a whole.

The main reason for movement to the city was stated by the informants to be the search for employment. Other reasons, in order of frequency, were the need for treatment of illness and a desire for better opportunities for the children. All three reasons suggest escape from restrictive situations and the effect of rising hopes. Of 138 employable men, seventy-three were in unskilled labour and factory work. Only nine were unemployed; for the unemployed would be forced back to the place of origin by high rents and other costs. Only two were skilled tradesmen with recognised qualifications.

Yet the situation, in spite of the considerable publicity given to living conditions in the central city areas, seemed to offer more hope than those of the country areas. If this is to be hope frustrated, it seems not impossible that some trouble lies ahead in the Australian metropolis, though possibly on such a small scale that there is danger of it being only sporadically a matter for political attention. The demonstration effect of the Foundation for Aboriginal Affairs seems especially valuable in this connection.

## BRISBANE

Other capitals shared the influx. In Brisbane the living conditions and health hazards were being publicised in 1945, along with the high room rents in South Brisbane.[11] Here was a city small enough for people to camp on the outskirts to find work or a stake in urban living. In 1949, at the prosecution of a woman who was living in an unauthorised tent, the Department of Native Affairs was reported as saying that she and others like her were not a departmental responsibility, as they were not 'under the Act'.[12]

In course of the next ten years, according to press reports, Aborigines were finding homes in considerable numbers in South Brisbane, where Negro troops had been quartered during the war years. The Central Executive of the Labor Party was told by the President of the Postal Workers' Union in 1959 that young Aborigines coming to Brisbane were being forced by the police to live in South Brisbane. The Commissioner of Police replied that there were no such zones or restrictions; that 'coloured people' had chosen to live on the south side and that the police

[11] See article by Cliff Stanaway in *Courier-Mail* (Brisbane), 19 April 1945.
[12] *Telegraph* (Brisbane), 7 December 1949.

were assisting them to do so.[13] There were press references to South Brisbane as a 'Little Rock'.

There was, however, another side to the picture one gets from press reports, here as elsewhere, since persons of Aboriginal descent had been moving into Brisbane for a long time. One of the earliest surveys of the Aboriginal urban situation was made in Brisbane in the Housing Commission settlements at Inala and Acacia Ridge, in 1961, by two medical students from the University of Queensland, A.J. McArthur and B.J. Ryan.[14] It established some useful facts. The survey included 160 families, of whom forty were 'coloured'—the term which seems to be favoured in Queensland. All were thought to be working or lower middle class.

The 'coloured' households averaged 5·9 persons (which appears to accord with statistics we have obtained from field work), the others, 4·1. There were more young children, but only six from all forty families were at secondary school, and four of these were of Torres Strait Islander descent. Whereas the white workers were about evenly distributed between skilled, semi-skilled, and unskilled employment, there were only three tradesmen in the 'coloured' group. It was the time of the short economic recession; 25·6 per cent of 'coloured' and 15·6 per cent of other workers were unemployed. The Aboriginal families had either come from less favoured suburbs or direct from the country—a situation which seems comparable with that in Sydney, where the poor city areas have been those for early reception, from which those who succeed in gaining permanent employment move out. Fewer 'coloured' people read newspapers, books, and magazines than others; 25 per cent of 'coloured' adults, and 50 per cent of others, were covered by life insurance. The 'coloured' paid lower medical benefit insurance.

Thus they were less well equipped than the whites they lived amongst for urban living. From the figures quoted they were less safe in the cash economy, yet one must allow for the other kinds of insurance, in possible resort to family and friends in bad times, though their option for change would inevitably weaken these ties.

The conclusion by the students is well worth quoting:

The coloureds in Inala and Acacia Ridge form a wedge who are determined to hold the conditions they have won . . . This wedge is a tough, proud, minority group with a common desire to prove that they are as good as the whites in every way. At

[13] Reported in *Herald* (Melbourne), 28 July 1959.
[14] A Comparative Survey of the Living Standards of Coloured and White Families in the Greater Brisbane area. A comprehensive study of the Brisbane situation was made for the Project by Hazel M. Smith and Ellen Biddle. See *Look Forward, Not Back* (forthcoming).

the moment it is a small group, relatively ineffective politically . . . It seems logical to assume that . . . shanty dwellers will pour in to avail themselves of better conditions. They will then be a much more powerful pressure group. . . .[15]

To the credit of the Queensland government, it appears to have anticipated that of New South Wales by a subsidy to the OPAL House hostel in South Brisbane, which has been maintained since 1963 and which, according to the report of OPAL for 1964, had provided short-term accommodation for round fifty adults and thirty children per day, with meals.[16] It arranged hospitalisation, took in neglected children referred by the police, distributed food, and found employment.

### ADELAIDE

In Adelaide there were press reports of Aboriginal violence from the beginning of 1946, with the men making Light Square their place of congregation; and reports that police had been 'clearing the streets'. Drunkenness was alleged, and demands with threats for money by groups which were increased in the week-ends by others from the nearby country areas. The Secretary of the Board stated that some had been removed from the city; that drink was obtained from those who were 'exempt', and that these should be dealt with by the police for 'consorting'. The basis for the unrest seems to have been the discharge of numbers of Aborigines from the wartime industries, a practice which seems to have been common to all capital cities. As usual, officials tended to ascribe violence and reports of disorder to alcohol, but there were others like the indefatigable Dr Duguid, who pointed out the predicament of people suddenly out of employment and who opposed moves to expel them from the city.[17] Some had been removed and 'found employment' in the country. But in 1948 there were still many unemployed in Adelaide, with Dr Duguid, and later the Aboriginal Advancement League, attempting to raise funds from a not very interested community or government to establish hostels for them.[18]

As in Brisbane and in other capitals, publicity went to the more sensational events and situations. Fortunately Mrs J. Inglis undertook a research project in 1960, and some of her findings were published in

[15] Ibid.

[16] OPAL—Third Annual General Report, April 1965, p. 7.

[17] See reports in *News* (Adelaide), 11, 12, 15, and 17 January 1946; *Sunday Mail* (Adelaide), 12 January 1946; *Advertiser* (Adelaide), 28 February 1946.

[18] *News* (Adelaide), 17 October 1948; *Advertiser* (Adelaide), 19 August 1949; *Sunday Mail* (Adelaide), 20 April 1951.

1961.[19] The families she studied tended, in spite of educational handicaps, to earn more than their neighbours. In the fifty non-Aboriginal households she found much the same situation as with the Aboriginal ones. Few of either had savings or cheque accounts.

In the urban areas, the logic of poverty is equally oppressive, irrespective of race. It is not easy to learn much of what was happening from the Board's Reports before that for 1963-4, which commented on the urban movement by Aborigines who ignored departmental advice. The South Australian Housing Trust had, however, established sixty-two families in Trust homes by June 1964, some of which were in Adelaide. In addition, the Department of Aboriginal Affairs was establishing some homes in the city. But Aborigines were continuing to move into poor accommodation at high rentals. The continued influx, claimed to have reached 2,000, and questions in parliament on the subject were reported in August 1966.[20]

PERTH

The policy of governments had been geared to deal with a 'problem' always conceived as a rural one, to such an extent that urbanisation even in the country town had not been really faced; and it was not until the government of New South Wales supported the Foundation for Aboriginal Affairs in Sydney that any real move was made to deal with the situation in any capital city as a whole, other than by use of pressures to have the Aborigines move back to the country regions. There had been the old Aboriginal station, later reserve, at La Perouse, but even in 1967 this remains a typical old reserve surrounded by the expanding city. There was a somewhat comparable case at South Guildford, Perth, where before the urban expansion there had been an Aboriginal reserve. This was taken over by the Commonwealth Department of Interior for war purposes. After the war the Kurra League, mainly of part-Aborigines, was encouraged by the Department of Native Welfare to establish an Aboriginal community here, at Allowah Grove, and there were over two hundred persons there by January 1958. The project met with problems arising from the absence of effective internal leadership, and of course prejudice which was further stimulated by the maintenance of patterns of conduct expressing frustra-

---

[19] Judy Inglis, 'Aborigines in Adelaide', *Journal of the Polynesian Society*, vol. 70, no. 2, June 1961, pp. 200-18.
[20] *Advertiser* (Adelaide), 11 August 1966. The facts were already being established by Dr Fay Gale, sponsored by this Project and by the University of Adelaide.

tions and resentment. In effect it seems to have become mainly a fringe settlement of Perth: comparable with La Perouse as an obsolete importation or retention in the urban area of the low grade services and amenities which have characterised fringe settlements and stations.

Perth had had problems both during and after the war. As it is a good example of the smaller capital city which grew rapidly, so that it could have fringe settlements which were overgrown by the expanding urban building, and as it is possible to trace this growth from press files, it may be useful to look back into this process in some detail.

Perth had been declared a 'prohibited area' for Aborigines not in lawful employment as far back as 1927.[21] That the proscription was a real one was illustrated by the airing in parliament of two cases of removals in November 1938. A married couple refused to get a permit to remain in Perth, and went to the press with their story. The wife, a part-Aboriginal married to an Aboriginal, had done so well at Moore River that she was brought into Perth by the Department of Native Affairs for further schooling. The other case was that of a woman who had been 'removed from sordid surroundings'; but in her case the department had lost a subsequent court case.[22]

During the war years there was conflict between the department and employers who required additional labour. The Commissioner was reported in February 1943 as stating that urban employers were trying to get 'native' labour, but that policy was that 'natives' should be employed on rural work, and that steps would be taken to prevent such urban employment, especially of domestic servants.[23] This seems to have been against the law, which provided only for areas being prohibited for those not in employment; but other powers could be used.

The issue came to a head with complaints from the Bayswater area, where there was a fringe camp. The Road Board held a meeting in 1944, at which some *native* ex-servicemen spoke. The meeting agreed that they should be allowed to settle on the outskirts of Perth suburbs. The Minister in reply stated that in cases where they lived in camps they had been ordered 'back to the country', in the national interest and to increase the food supply. He would not interfere if they lived even in condemned housing, as that was a matter for the local authority. But he also referred to a large group of 150 to 200 in the Guildford area: they were to be 'transferred' to the country because the Army wanted the site (which became Allowah

---

[21] *Courier-Mail* (Brisbane), 20 March 1927; and comment in *Our Aim*, published for the Aborigines Inland Mission, 26 April 1927.

[22] *W.A.P.D.*, 1938, vol. 2 (Council), pp. 2325-58.

[23] *West Australian*, 1 February 1943.

Grove). But his department had leased land at Bayswater for a camp site and he spoke of a possible church hostel there.[24]

In 1947, with the reduction of Aboriginal employment opportunities in the city, more Aborigines were establishing themselves with their problems on the outer fringes of the city area. In that year there was a meeting of the Guildford municipality with a representative of the adjacent Bassendean Road Board, attended by representatives of local religious bodies. The purpose was to make a combined approach to the Department of Native Affairs. There were the usual complaints of violence, insanitary conditions, and liquor. The Acting Commissioner spoke of the possibility of having Guildford included in the restricted area, but apparently the development at Allowah Grove was more in keeping with changing attitudes.[25] In November, the Minister for Native Affairs stated in parliament that it was intended to vary section 42 of the Act, which allowed the proclamation of a 'municipal district, town or any other place' to be restricted; that the earlier proclamation of Perth meant a blanket exclusion from the whole area; and that it was desired to enable 'natives' to come into East Perth. The words in the Act were altered to read 'place or area specified or defined', by amendment to the Act at the end of 1947.[26] Two years later, there were complaints about Aborigines living near the Bassendean sanitary depot. There was now a new broom in Native Affairs, and the new Commissioner, S.G. Middleton, reversing the usual order of priorities in this field of administration, told the Bassendean Road Board that the Aborigines concerned were land owners and ratepayers, and that they had every right to petition for the removal of the sanitary depot.[27]

Perth was extending to Bassendean. Land near the depot was still not valuable, but was increasing in value. The people in houses there were paying taxation, but only a few with citizen rights were eligible for social service benefits. They were working in and round Perth, and their children going to school. They seem to have gone there first in a genuine attempt to establish an Aboriginal community. A year later the conditions were still news. By this time there were several 'colonies' near Perth, including another near the Swanbourne rifle range. But at Bassendean the women went out washing and the men worked in the new local factories: other houses were being built in the area, in spite of the sanitation treatment plant. In August 1951 the Minister stated that this was only one aspect of the

[24] Ibid., 18, 26 May, 2 and 8 June 1944.
[25] Ibid., 28, 30 July, and 14 November 1947.
[26] Native Administration Act Amendment Act, 1947, section 2.
[27] *West Australian*, 13 and 17 August 1949.

desperate housing shortage for the part-Aborigines of the south-west; that about a thousand houses were required. He also stated that his department no longer had power to remove Aborigines from the city, nor should it have such power; that the common suggestion from local government bodies that this would be in the interests of those removed offered no solution to their personal problems.[28]

In November 1952 the Commissioner was outlining a plan for a properly built community centre at Success Hill. The Bassendean Road Board was opposing this as likely to spoil a beauty spot! Letters and telegrams of protest went to the Premier; and this first move for an Aboriginal Centre seems to have been frustrated.[29]

Another area with a similar history was the camp at Swanbourne, on swamp lands in the Nedlands area. The protests may be traced in the press from 1949 till 1951, with the Nedlands Road Board pressing the Department of Native Welfare to remove a typical shanty settlement from Swanbourne.[30] At the end of 1951, the Commissioner was in dispute with a recommendation of the Commissioner for Health that the Aborigines should be evicted because of health risks to the general community. The view that Aboriginal health is expendable in the national interest was of course by no means new. Yet it seems that public health risk has been a real factor in stimulating official interest in the Aboriginal predicament.

In the meantime, following the lifting of the restrictions on entry to East Perth, Aborigines had begun to establish themselves there and to frequent the centre of the city.

By 1950 there were stories in the press of the unemployed Aborigines and the 'native women' causing 'trouble' with prostitution and drink in the centre of the city.[31] At the end of the 1950s there were still press stories of 'natives spreading terror and squalor' in East Perth; and the government was thinking of reserves out of, but close to, the city.[32]

What was happening round Perth was a good example of how a problem which had very low priority might seem more urgent when imported from small rural communities to the centre of government. As elsewhere, the notion that the Aboriginal issues were mainly rural died hard. One can guess that, in Perth as elsewhere (where it is news for a week and then forgotten for months), Aboriginal resentments have

[28] Ibid., 12, 14, and 19 April and 17 June 1951; 9, 14, and 30 May 1951.

[29] Ibid., 8, 11, and 12 November 1952.

[30] Ibid., 21-3 September 1949; and 5 March, 18 April 1951.

[31] See, for instance, comments by the magistrate in Perth Police Court, in *Daily News* (Perth), 17 February 1950.

[32] *West Australian*, 20 January and 28 March 1958.

increased in the meantime. For instance, press reports in 1959 told of brawls in East Perth, of prostitution, hungry and ragged children; and of non-Aborigines who could not sell their houses and go because of depreciated values.[33] In 1960, five Protestant denominations stated that they had joined with the Roelands Mission Inc., to assist in reception of Aborigines, in matters of employment, accommodation, and entertainment.[34]

But in 1965 the prostitution of young Aboriginal girls in Perth at weekends was the topic of an editorial in the *West Australian*.[35] In 1967 the same paper published a leading article on the same topic, on drunkenness, and on similar circumstances at Allowah Grove, where a Swan-Guildford councillor was quoted as saying that problems arising from prostitution, begging, and drinking, especially by 'itinerant natives', had never been worse.[36] This is a very good example of how far conditions in the rural areas of origin dictate some of the patterns of urbanisation. The long neglected problems of the Western Australian Aborigines have come to town. And in the town, like colonial problems, they come to a head with the confrontation between white respectability and prosperity and indigenous desperation and recklessness. There have again been moves for a reception centre in Perth.

Yet all this 'trouble' indicated a very great change from the situation as it had been before the 1939-45 war. On the other hand, in the light of current United States experience, there were obvious, if distant, dangers in rebuffing or seeming to rebuff those who were in the forefront of social change and who were trying to break out of the old patterns of rural discrimination. On a very small scale the movement of the Aboriginal into the capital cities is reminiscent of that by the American Negro from the southern States into the big cities of the north.[37]

It seems fair to say that the various State authorities for Aboriginal affairs had not by 1967 organised their activities for this situation; that they were still largely preoccupied with country town and rural groups. The annual reports, with the amount of consideration offered on metropolitan urbanisation, bear out this statement. Yet of all the possible growing points, and in spite of the present hardships, the metropolis seems to offer

---

[33] *Weekend Mail* (W.A.), 28 March 1959.
[34] *West Australian*, 13 July 1960.
[35] Ibid., 7 January 1965.
[36] Ibid., 3 January 1967.
[37] It was partly for this reason that under this Project a number of studies of capital city situations were sponsored. Some of these will, it is hoped, be published as part of the Project series. At the time of writing I have had the benefit of access to some of the material only.

the best hope for a constructive integration, if only because this is the goal of those in the forefront of change. Official preoccupation with the rural scene has one advantage—that what has been done by governments in the metropolis has been largely through voluntary agencies. If more of these were developed with a view to full Aboriginal management, like the Foundation for Aboriginal Affairs in Sydney, there might be more immediate hope for proper reception, and for increased Aboriginal responsibility.

IV                              POLICIES

As the history of the United States Indian Bureau demonstrated prior to 1934, a policy of 'assimilation' may be consistent with exercise of rigid controls over the groups to be 'assimilated'.

## THE ASSIMILATION POLICY AND THE EMERGENCE OF AN ABORIGINAL POLITICAL ISSUE

In Aboriginal affairs, the same possibility had been demonstrated in the somewhat sporadic efforts to school the half-caste, even to regulate marriages, during the 1930s. As a particular branch of government does not easily change its methods, or its philosophy, a good deal of the policy and practice which had been relevant in the days of protection by segregation, and then in relation to the absorption of the part-Aboriginal, could be carried over into the post-war period, when whatever a particular government was accustomed to do could be described as promoting assimilation.

One can say this, I think, fairly; but it would not be fair to argue that all who support the assimilation policy believe in the necessity of tuition before the concession of equality. Much of the criticism of the assimilation policy has been criticism of the extreme position which predicates the disappearance of the Aboriginal. But many of those who had to administer Aboriginal affairs with no training or intellectual preparation (for what surely must be one of Australia's most complicated administrative tasks) certainly believed this, and said so; and so did many of the politicians who supported the policy. It is therefore somewhat difficult to argue that the quite spectacular amendments to legislation which have occurred in a little over a decade were the *result* of an assimilation policy. The most noted illustration of this is in the case of the Northern Territory, where a whole pattern of special legislation for programmed and schooled assimilation was suddenly withdrawn, with the Welfare Ordinance, in August 1964.

Both the policy and the relaxation of restrictive laws, with the advances in equality and civil rights, have resulted from a changing public opinion. Looking beyond attempts to state policies in terms of distant objectives, what appears now to be increasing is a genuine public concern with practical improvement in Aboriginal conditions in matters like housing, education, health, employment, and the like—pragmatic and attainable ends, with an increasing readiness to spend money on them. If this trend continues, the social climate should be propitious for the setting of particular goals in particular areas; though it might be too optimistic to assume that local resistances from those who feel that, while the 'problem' should be 'solved', the solution should begin in other streets and other municipalities than their own, will disappear. The result of the referendum of 1967, especially the granting by such an overwhelming majority of a concurrent power in Aboriginal affairs to the Commonwealth, probably indicates little more than a general view that something has been seriously wrong, that an issue of national importance has remained too long neglected, that it is up to the Commonwealth Government, with its control of taxation, to provide the solution. By establishing a Council of Aboriginal Affairs, and an Office to co-ordinate policies with the States, the Commonwealth has inevitably been committed to progressively increasing intervention. It has the power, and the time is propitious, for a definite lead.

There is little point in semantic arguments, of the kind which have been common over the last few years, and which at the present time have resulted in increased support for 'integration', as a more humane long-range aim than 'assimilation'. This has probably been mainly a reaction to those in politics and administration, and to others who have been active in the voluntary bodies or expressing their views in the mass media, who have interpreted 'assimilation' as involving the complete loss of Aboriginal identity, with the consequent disappearance of the 'problem' population.

The greatly increased interest in the issues, especially in the 1960s, has increasingly involved the expression of views by Aborigines. The Aboriginal voice is now continuous; and this in itself is indicative of a growing confidence, of a potential for leadership. But it seems fair to say that as yet these voices are not backed by effective *Aboriginal* pressure groups and organisations. This seems to be something of a transitional period. An interesting comparison could be made with the first groups of spokesmen either for the American Negro or for people living under colonial administration. One theme, however, has been continuously repeated— that the Aboriginal does not want to lose his Aboriginal identity. To some extent he is forced into this situation, since what he wants is equality of opportunity *now*. If he has been cosmetically favoured for 'passing', and has made that decision, the Aboriginal spokesman no longer represents him. The demand for immediate equality is often couched in terms of opposition to assimilation; and what is being opposed is, I think, the extreme assimilationist position.

The opposition has been a response mainly to practices and some legislation which has continued from the time when, to the legislators and many of the administrators, assimilation meant genetic absorption. Perhaps more important than this idea of eventual disappearance of regrettable features and objectional characteristics of a whole group of persons was the other concept of 'readiness' before rights and equality. This was expressed in practice in the efforts at tuition and exhortation on reserves, and among fringe groups, to make them 'ready' and acceptable to the townsfolk. The same idea of tuition before rights, in the cause of assimilation, was expressed in the idea of the 'transitional' (and cheap) houses, provided by the Aboriginal authority rather than by the housing authority. It was used to justify the restrictions which were maintained— the prohibitions on the use of alcohol, exclusion from the franchise, the provisions for exemption from the restrictions, with other provisions to reimpose them, in cases of those who were 'ready'; the limits on rights to social service benefits, which frequently were paid through the settlement, with the Aboriginal being paid pocket money only (and even, in outlying areas, a similar arrangement to pay through employers); and the powers vested in managers of stations and settlements.

Those Aborigines who began to protest have often gone for their extreme examples of these situations to the frontier areas, where they are seen more clearly in a less complicated situation. Here also they have been able to question both the delegation of government powers to particular religious missions and the development of new resources in a way which emphasises the legal situation with respect to land tenure rights at the expense of traditional claims. To some extent, then, objections to a view in which current restrictions or discriminations seem compatible with *eventual* equality, or even a means to reach it, have fused with the wider demands for equality now. Nor has it been uncommon for those who regard themselves as protecting their legitimate interests by the kind of discrimination which has been the daily irritant of resentment—in hotels and cafes and other places for service to the public, in hiring for employment, the letting of houses, in objections to integrated schooling, or in the local cinema—to argue that they are supporters of assimilation: that their current attitudes are justified because the Aboriginal is not yet 'ready'.

The current Aboriginal spokesmen have not yet coalesced into a coherent leadership; and from the background we have looked at, it would be a miracle if they had yet done so. Even their criticism of the vaguely defined assimilation policy tends to echo those by other persons, for few of the Aborigines yet have the education necessary to grasp the essentials of a complicated issue such as this. Obviously such a situation is ready-made for those who have their own political and personal axes to grind; and this has led some governments to suspect all Aboriginal protest as essentially the work of agitators. The growing interest in academic circles may offer some hope that Aboriginal leaders may find advice when they want it on particular issues, with no pressure to take it. Through this confusing maze of contradictory voices, the Aboriginal leadership must find its own way and face the task of identifying and isolating specifically Aboriginal interests. It is here that machinery for direct negotiation with government, and for the growth of an Aboriginal leadership with direct ties with local groups, seems essential. Only in some such way can the Aborigines be given the chance to work out their own destiny.

That they are quite capable of this, that they are on the way to finding a new adjustment, is perhaps best illustrated by the movement into the capital cities, which may have been the most significant of all the changes since World War II. But without the opportunity to work out adjustments and to present demands from their present places of residence, this could result in a long period of lop-sided change. Those who have been the outstanding spokesmen for assimilation, like Elkin and Hasluck, no matter to what extent they have had to compromise with an actual political situation, have not been advocates of racial absorption or of the disappearance of Aboriginal culture. What has tended to discredit the assimilation policy has been its espousal by governments, and the basing of practice on a very common fallacy about the processes of social change —that it can be imposed by intensive educational and administrative effort upon social groups whose standards deviate from those which are assumed to be met by the majority. Many academics, hoping for quick solutions, have found them in particular methods or emphases in education. This is psychologically inept, if only because it tends to emphasise the Australian of European descent as the tutor—and thus to stimulate further opposition.

Social changes occur as the result of decisions made by groups and individuals in response to new situations, those by the groups resulting from the complex interactions between families and between individuals —a process far too complex for administrative management. Its results will not conform to some administrative blueprint, as the result of passive reception of the government's message. The responses which produce the changes will be in accordance with the respondents' systems of belief. To those who do not understand the beliefs, they have in the past appeared strange, and indicative of limited intelligence. Because of past history, the groups will be deeply suspicious: great patience is the price which must be paid for past errors. In this sense, a social group will change in accordance with its own laws. Thus the concepts of 'social engineering' are irrelevant; and the attempts at management of deviant individuals, which have taken up so much administrative time and effort, miss the point that the assumed deviance is conditioned by the system of belief within the social group.

The main task of government is to provide for a constructive interaction with the groups which have to find their way to equality. The first task should be to 'get out of the way' of the Aborigines, as Felix Cohen once said in relation to American Indian policy and practice.[1] This involves the withdrawal of all restrictive legislation applying only to Aborigines; what still remains will be mentioned briefly below. It involves a particular refinement of the assimilation policy, which will make possible the emergence of practical projects on the basis of agreement with Aboriginal groups. If a slogan is needed, and it probably is, it might be *Aboriginal initiative and development, and assistance on request*. In this way governments may find a democratic 'solution' and adjustment between what Alexander Lesser called (in the case of the American Indians) 'the stubbornest non-conformists among us' and the rest of us.

If the history of all the Aboriginal policies in the past teaches anything, it is the fallacy of planning in such a situation for very distant goals. Whether Aborigines, or most Aborigines, will eventually be hard to find in the general community or whether they will remain distinct and contribute

---

[1] Quoted by Alexander Lesser, 'Education and the Future of Tribalism in the United States: The Case of the American Indian', *Social Service Review*, vol. 35, no. 2, June 1961.

something very special of their own is not something which can be decided now. Moreover, it is *their* business, not that of governments nor the rest of us. There seems good reason to phase out the habit of gearing what we do now to such distant goals, a habit which has had unfortunate effects in condemning almost anything Aborigines want to organise for themselves as segregation—to the absurd lengths of condemning Aboriginal football teams, centres for urban congregation and social activities, or the wish to have places of their own on the old reserves. The fallacy of the extreme assimilationist view may be compared with profit, perhaps, with that of White Australia.

Such an emphasis must involve abdication by special Aboriginal Boards and departments from the field of social services. The principles of self-determination and of respect for the individual demand that these must be the same for all. The special activities of government dealing with Aborigines would have to be (progressively, no doubt) confined to activities arising from Aboriginal requests and to policing the requirements of equality—for instance, to ensure that the Aboriginal has a place in the queue for housing or other government assistance in accordance with his needs and with the date of his application.

Yet there can be no doubt that the adoption by all governments of an assimilation policy for all persons of Aboriginal descent has been an important step both in mobilising public opinion and in clarifying the issues. Perhaps it is the main example, in the long history of Aboriginal affairs, of statesmanship giving a lead. What would have been difficult before the war was becoming increasingly essential, as a wealthy country contrasted more obviously with the spectacle of appalling Aboriginal poverty. What Australians often did not notice shocked some migrants and visitors. More was becoming known overseas; and criticism began to be made in awkward places. There could eventually be effects on external relations. The post-war generation of youth helped the rest of us to see these things with fresh minds: and to some extent the revolt against an un-thinking materialism was linked with concern for the Aboriginal condition. It was, to these young people, not so very different from the increasingly publicised accounts of Asian poverty. In New South Wales, Student Action for Aborigines confronted prejudice and discrimination in a few country towns. Possibly this was an important turning point. Once the Aboriginal situation became a matter for political action, and Aboriginal hopes began to stir, it became essential for governments to develop a national strategy and local practice which would avoid the sourness of frustrated aspirations.

## THE COMMONWEALTH AND THE STATES AGREE TO AN
## ASSIMILATION OBJECTIVE

The first meeting, in 1937, of the Commonwealth and State officials working in Aboriginal affairs had set a precedent in the decision to limit their discussions to members of the bureaucracies involved. Since the war, the principle has been extended to provide also for separate meetings of the Commonwealth and State ministers responsible. There has been no attempt to promote and support voluntary bodies such as those interested in the 'assimilation' of 'New Australians', and nothing to compare with what have now become annual meetings of representatives of the voluntary organisations interested in immigration—in itself another interesting example of the relative priorities. As the meetings of both officials and Ministers are closed to the public,[2] and as there are no arrangements for Aboriginal representation, these sessions would not be likely ones for the reappraisal of policies. That the terms of the assimilation policy were outlined and later adjusted by the Ministers is perhaps sufficient indication that they were not considered to commit governments to any immediate steps away from the kinds of administration they were currently managing. While changes in legislation were justified in the name of assimilation, when they came, it was only in the Northern Territory that very great efforts were begun and high priority given to an assimilation policy.

One reason for this was the Commonwealth's favourable financial situation; the other was the high priority given to Aboriginal welfare by Hasluck, the first Minister for Territories, who succeeded in committing the Commonwealth to a new order of priorities.

The matter of Commonwealth control had been broached, and rejected, at the Premiers' Conference in 1936. It had also been rejected, with other amendments to the Constitution, at a wartime referendum. In February 1948 a second Conference of Commonwealth and State Aboriginal Welfare Authorities (at which Victoria was not represented) dealt with a resolution referred from the Premiers' Conference earlier in that year: that it should consider the alternatives of a transfer of power in Aboriginal affairs to the Commonwealth or of Commonwealth assistance to the States for Aboriginal welfare. The first, of course, raised issues of State powers, and was opposed by the officers from Queensland, Western Australia, and New South Wales, though Elkin, Vice-Chairman of the Aborigines Welfare Board of New South Wales, stressed the need

[2] The Press has been admitted to some sessions of the Ministers' Conferences.

for a national policy, saw no difficulty arising from Commonwealth control, and supported a South Australian motion for it.[3] The State officials made various suggestions on Commonwealth assistance, and finally agreed that there should be a pound-for-pound subsidy on State expenditure. The Commonwealth Director-General of Social Services stated that by this time his Department was spending over £400,000 annually on social service benefits for Aborigines, more than half of it on child endowment, but only £3,000 on unemployment and sickness benefits. This indicated that the reserve and welfare measures by the Aboriginal welfare authorities still formed the main protections, as far as they went, against unemployment; it also raised the other issue of differences in the Aboriginal legislation, especially in the matter of exemptions from the various Acts.

The Commonwealth Social Services Act had by this time become a somewhat confusing document on the differing Aboriginal entitlements, the differences being linked to degrees of Aboriginal origin, mainly as a result of different amendments made during the war years; and confusion was increased by the different State laws on who was Aboriginal. A submission from South Australia, to the effect that any person who paid his taxes or who lived and worked under conditions where his earnings were assessable for taxation should be entitled to the benefits on the same basis as other citizens, made good sense; and there was a unanimous resolution that only 'full-blood Aboriginals living under primitive or nomadic conditions should be excluded'.[4] Such a discussion and such a recommendation would have been beyond all hope ten years earlier; and though such a move would leave unprovided for the needs of those who most needed help as they moved into the cash economy, there was a kind of logic here for which one looks in vain in the records of the 1937 Conference. Perhaps wartime experience in dealing with manpower and its needs had developed a greater sophistication, especially in the Commonwealth public service.

But this did nothing in one of the most vital areas, for Aborigines under the various Acts who were still being paid wages below those for others, especially in the pastoral industry: these wages could be so low that they fell well below the unemployment or sickness benefit. The conference did no more than recommend that money wages be paid and that they be uniform throughout the pastoral areas for employed

[3] Notes of a Conference of Commonwealth and State Aboriginal Welfare Authorities, Canberra, 3 and 4 February 1948—Department of the Interior (roneo).
[4] Ibid.

Aborigines. From this, the Western Australian representative dissociated his government. It is relevant here that unemployment benefits may not be paid to an Aboriginal who refuses to work for a wage well below the award wage, or to one who moves into a town or settled area and needs the benefit while seeking employment. (In 1967 it appeared that, when the latest decisions on the various pastoral awards were implemented in full, the anomaly should disappear.)

The recommendation on wages had been formulated a year earlier at a meeting of relevant State and Northern Territory representatives with the indefatigable Elkin, under the auspices of the North Australian Development Committee, and it is quite clear from the record of this earlier conference, attended by the authorities from Western Australia, Queensland, South Australia, and the Northern Territory, that there had been a change in official appraisal of the Aboriginal potential as a worker. Elkin, from the chair, had stressed how the armed forces had shown 'that these people could be hygienic, good workers, and could live in a cultured community group ... The Army had the money to do it, and they made a success of it.'[5] Both the conferences dealt with a series of practical problems, and the record of each is notable for the absence of the racist nonsense of 1937. The 1947 meeting had discussed the efficiency of Aboriginal workers in the pastoral and pearling industries, with a view to extending benefits under the Commonwealth Reconstruction Training Scheme to the northern areas affected by the war. There was no longer talk of isolating the half-caste from the full-blood, or of developing a special policy for the half-castes: though to be sure the legislation which expressed these intentions was still on the books. Settlements and stations were to be used for training for employment and as havens for the aged and infirm. In fact the whole emphasis had moved to economic matters. But the first inter-governmental discussion on citizenship status for Aborigines did not occur until the meeting of the Australian Council of Native Welfare, in September 1951.[6]

This meeting of the Ministers responsible and their advisers, and the establishment of the Council to make recommendations to governments, with the Commonwealth meeting the costs, had come from a Cabinet decision in June 1951. The invitations to join had been accepted by four governments, but rejected by Victoria on grounds already indicated and

[5] Commonwealth Archives: Department of the Interior file 46/1607: Northern Australian Development Committee—Welfare of Natives, 3 and 4 February, 1947.
[6] Recorded in Dept. of Territories file 55/857 (Commonwealth Archives). I am indebted to the Minister for Territories and the Secretary of the Department for access to it.

by the Premier of Tasmania on the grounds that his State had no
Aborigines of full descent and that the part-Aborigines on Cape Barren
Island Reserve would, under an Act of 1945, become ordinary citizens of
the State and free from any special laws by the end of 1951. The agenda
for this meeting are valuable historical documents. That on Citizenship
Status is a precise legal document, in the area of scholarship already
pioneered in *Black Australians* by the Minister for Territories. It sets out
in detail the tangle of definitions of who was then Aboriginal—some
strict and some loose. It points out that exemption meant nothing when it
could be withdrawn and when the only freedom which followed it
(except in South Australia) was from the particular Act under which
Aboriginal administration was carried on. It points out that, by State
Acts and Ordinances of the Northern Territory, special restrictions
remained on people who were legally British subjects (a theme Hasluck
had developed in *Black Australians*), and that, like all others born in
Australia, they had become Australian citizens under the Nationality and
Citizenship Act of 1948.

Speaking to this, Hasluck argued for uniform principles: that when
persons were brought under special laws, the reasons should relate to
special needs, not to racial origin; that the federal franchise depended on
the franchise in each State (which was not strictly correct); and that
eligibility for social service benefits depended on State Aboriginal
legislation (which was). Queensland opposed the idea of common
citizenship on the grounds that Aborigines would be entitled to full award
wages, which they were incapable of earning; and a South Australian
comment was that citizen rights would be dangerous where large numbers
lived together on reserves and would have access to liquor. This was just
after Clive Evatt, the Minister responsible in New South Wales, had
managed to institute a 'trial period' for Aboriginal drinking rights; he
was able to argue that no catastrophe had followed.

Under section 41 of the Commonwealth Constitution, Aborigines
who had the right to vote for 'the more numerous House of Parliament
of a State' were in the same situation as other citizens, in that they could
not be *prevented* by a Commonwealth law from voting at Commonwealth elections. The Commonwealth Electoral Act provided that only
those *Aborigines*, enrolled so to vote in the States or who had been
members of the defence forces could vote[7] (a restrictive provision). At
that time a *native* in Western Australia could not, as a matter of law, vote,
unless he held a Certificate of Citizenship under the Native (Citizenship

[7] Commonwealth Electoral Act 1918-61, section 39 (5).

Rights) Act passed in 1944. In Queensland, the Elections Acts from 1915 had excluded Aborigines, half-castes 'under the Act', and Pacific Islanders from the vote.[8] Though section 41 of the Commonwealth Constitution referred only to those who could vote at State elections, it was a positive provision in these cases, and not an excluding clause applicable to other cases.[9] The Commonwealth had power to extend the franchise for Commonwealth elections under other sections of the Constitution;[10] and as section 41 was not restrictive in its application, it also had the right to ensure that Aborigines were enrolled for Commonwealth electoral purposes.

In Queensland, many part-Aborigines who would fall outside the Commonwealth definition of *Aboriginal* (in that they did not have a 'preponderance' of Aboriginal descent) were not enrolled for the State elections (for all who came 'under the Act' would be treated as Aboriginal). The Government of Queensland would not be anxious for Commonwealth intrusion in a civil rights matter. A very significant indicator of changing official attitudes was a step taken in 1945, significant because it was taken not by an Aboriginal welfare authority but by the Commonwealth Electoral Office, which approached the superintendent of Cherbourg Aboriginal Settlement for information on the number of inmates who would be entitled to enrolment (as not having a 'preponderance' of Aboriginal descent) with a view to informing them of their rights as citizens of the Commonwealth. The matter was referred eventually to the Queensland Cabinet. Cabinet refused to supply the information. (The chances were that it was not possible to establish it in many cases, and that an Aboriginal administratively was a person who looked like one.) But the Commonwealth officer was allowed into the settlement. All he could do in the light of the refusal of information, which amounted to passive resistance to Commonwealth interference, was to ask the superintendent to distribute a circular setting out the information to all.[11]

The two things worthy of note here are the concern about rights, on the part of someone in the Electoral Office, and the farcical tangle of restrictive laws. The Queensland Government obviously wanted no 'trouble' or publicity; but at that time the Commonwealth was not prepared to take the matter further, nor to extend its own franchise.

---

[8] The Elections Acts 1915 to 1959, sections 9, 11, and 11A.
[9] For opinions on the point by the Solicitor-General and Professor Geoffrey Sawer, see *C.P.P.* (H. of R.), 1961, vol. II, pp. 1391 *et seq.*—Report from the Select Committee on Voting Rights of Aborigines, Part I, p. 7, paras. 64-7.
[10] For opinion by Sawer see ibid., para. 63.
[11] Ibid., p. 4, para. 35.

In fact, section 22 of the Northern Territory Electoral Regulations excluded 'Aboriginal natives' from enrolment and voting. In 1953 the Commonwealth, in pursuit of its special brand of assimilation in the Territory, had to find a way of placing Aborigines in the *ward* category without using 'Aboriginal' or other racial terms. It also had to avoid including any non-Aborigines in this group (supposed to have no relationship to racial origin), for the obvious reason that there would have been political protests. The Electoral Regulations provided the answer, and the *ward* was defined as a person who could not vote under the Electoral Regulations.

There were no special restrictions on the voting rights of Aborigines in New South Wales, Victoria, or South Australia.

Thus was the Aboriginal, at the time when official attention was moving from his physical and alleged mental attributes to his rights as a human being, entangled in a whole network of legislation for which there was no logical reason. Nor have these remnants of the history of race relations in Australia yet been swept out of the way of the Aboriginal. A complete legal conspectus would be a sobering document; but this must wait for the attention of some legal expert with a special concern with Aboriginal affairs.

The matter of voting rights may serve to illustrate why a conference of Aboriginal authorities is powerless in the most important areas of human rights, for the function of each authority is to discharge those responsibilities and make recommendations on those matters for which it has been set up: the authorities must operate within the system. Aboriginal legislation, in turn, depends for its effects often on other laws, as for instance in relation to the right to vote. Where this is withheld under the voting laws of three governments and a Territory administration, where the extent of the withholding differs, where the categories from which the vote is withheld have been differently defined and there has been no real attempt to adjust the Aboriginal Acts to the Electoral Acts, confusion is added to powerlessness. It is not surprising, then, that the 1951 Conference merely decided without much discussion to ask the States to review their electoral laws.

Since the 1939-45 war, which does seem to have marked a real change in overt attitudes, this tangle of interlocked uncertainties and restrictions has been whittled away; but the need has been for a clean sweep: for the kind of purge of racist laws which was undertaken in Papua and New Guinea. But this demands thought and effort, and a proper priority. In the meantime, much of the old law remains as a bolster to the *status quo*.

On the general issue of citizen rights, the conference expressed the curious view that the barriers were not legal but social. The implication was that there was no urgency for the removal of legal restrictions, since it was social restrictions which formed the main hindrances to equality. The public at large must co-operate with governments for the 'ultimate assimilation of our native people'. But surely such 'co-operation' would also be opposition, since it would involve agitation for the removal of the legal barriers, the significance of which was being discounted.

Another area illustrating confusion of a transitory situation was Social Services. In the then state of the Social Services Consolidation Act, age and invalid pensions, widows' pensions, and maternity allowances could be granted to those who had been exempted (except that the full-blood mother was excluded) or to those to whom the Director-General of Social Services was satisfied that the granting was desirable 'by reason of character . . . intelligence and social development'.[12] This, of course, meant that an attempt at some sensible adjustment within each State would have to be made. The rule of thumb would tend to place all who lived on managed stations among those who lagged in 'character, intelligence and social development' (whatever that meant); and there was also the belief that those who lived on stations did not need these benefits because they were receiving equivalent benefits from the State. Evatt, the New South Wales Minister, pointed out that an invalid would have to leave his home on the station and find another one, in order to qualify for a pension, irrespective of the fact that he might have paid taxes all his life.

Child endowment could be granted unless the family was nomadic or the child already being supported 'wholly or mainly' by the Commonwealth or a State. This particular benefit had already gone far to revolutionise the conditions of the Aborigines. With an exploding population, it meant that, where previously there was no certain cushion against family starvation, now, so long as there were children, no one would starve. There had of course been much ado among the officials of the Aboriginal authorities to ensure that the money was spent on the children. In fact, on the Queensland settlements, it was taken over and spent on them by the managements. That this money was spent by families for families as economic units throughout the community in general was irrelevant in this kind of administration. In some cases it was fortunate that the eager efforts of the officials could be frustrated by the Aborigines: in others, these efforts probably saved the lives of children whose parents

[12] Social Services Consolidation Act 1947-1950, sections 19 (2), 62 (2), and 86 (3).

had become completely demoralised. 'Nomadic' persons could not qualify, but there was no precise definition of 'nomadic'. It was also anomalous that while a full-blood mother could not receive a maternity allowance, she could receive child endowment after the child was born.

A principle of the social services system is that payment is made in cash to the individual recipient; but there have to be some exceptions, as when a sick person is being maintained within an institution, perhaps unable to manage his own affairs, and where he or his agent makes arrangements for payment to be made to the institution. Yet this is somewhat different from the provision that payment may be made, in the case of an Aboriginal inmate of a multi-purposed settlement (who in Queensland or the Northern Territory might then still be confined against his will) to the authority which controlled his affairs. This was the situation with age and invalid, and widows' pensions, and with maternity allowances. Even this might be justified where the recipient had no knowledge of money. But the practice had developed (and is only now being terminated) of paying the pensions to the institution for all inmates who qualify for it, irrespective of their capacity. This was especially a matter of discrimination where the institution was in a settled area and populated mainly by sophisticates, and from whence the men went out regularly into employment, as they did in the four large Queensland settlements.[13]

The Director-General had a wider discretion, and could regard other individuals as proper recipients of the money; and this in turn had led to the practice of making the payments to employers and others, a system open to obvious abuses. There had also developed the administrative habit of paying only the 'pocket money' component direct to the individual entitled—from the analogy with the poor person in hospital; and as a final result of a string of administratively determined analogies, even some employers on distant cattle stations paid the 'pocket money' (perhaps what many of them retained could be better so described) and were allowed to spend the remainder on items such as pensioners' housing or retain it until there was a capital sum sufficient for this.

Here was another whole area of almost nonsensical law and practice. A policy of assimilation should, one would think, have involved some practice in dealing with one's own money. The Council of Native Welfare showed no real initiative or grasp of the issues, although the carefully prepared documentation presented by the Commonwealth at least posed them.

The greatest discrimination at that time was in provisions for un-

[13] Ibid., sections 47, 76, and 91.

employment and sickness benefit, meant for the normally employed person out of work. In 1951 the Aboriginal was not qualified for either unless the Director-General considered that his 'character . . . intelligence and social development' made it 'desirable' that the discriminating section of the Act should not apply in his case.[14] Where there was legal entitlement established, the money could be paid to a person other than the one entitled to it;[15] but the risks here were so obvious, especially where the benefit was likely to be worth more than the wage, that payment was almost always avoided.

Equality was not yet an immediate concern, as the recommendation on civil rights indicated. The question was asked, but the answer not assumed, whether benefits should be extended to those who were legally Aboriginal, or whether they should be separately provided for. The Commonwealth expressed the view that proper *care* of people could be more important to them than money. Probably the answer to this is that one does not exclude the other; that government, once professing an aim of equality, must itself ensure that the under-privileged group has all the rights which others have; and having ensured this, provide what additional 'care' is necessary.

There was imaginative discussion of the housing situation and of health, with some foreshadowing of research; and the work done since on nutrition, and on general health in the northern and central areas (however easy it may be to contrast Aboriginal health there with the national norms), has been considerable. Planning to use local materials in building of homes came to little in the great housing shortage, which is still marked by the Aboriginal's place at the very end of the queue. This conference, like others, was marked by the trend for all general discussion to be dominated by the worst conditions, in the remoter regions; these, of course, have been a hindrance for the Aboriginal in the settled areas since the early days of settlement. The same thing happened in a somewhat inefficient discussion on education in which the talk about maintaining 'temporary segregation' where 'social and cultural development' made attendance at State schools 'impracticable' certainly had more point where the Aborigines did not speak English. Talk about temporary segregation could readily excuse the reluctance of departments of education to move against local prejudice by integrating the State schools. There was general comment on the tendency to leave school at puberty, which there still is.

[14] Ibid., section 111.
[15] Ibid., section 123 (1).

The same emphasis on conditions furthest from the all-Australian norms marked the discussion on employment. The Commonwealth agendum argued in effect against wage equality: that the Aboriginal worker should be paid 'what he has learned to need and use in an intelligent manner', and mentioned the gambling and 'profligate use of taxis' in Darwin. While rights in employment were emphasised, the rights were to be those considered *suitable*. Those with full citizenship, it was recommended, should have the wage rights of other Australians; this would refer to the few exempted, and to those who have avoided coming under the Aboriginal legislation. For those who did, there was to be careful inspection of employment situations, with a fair wage—which is different from an equal wage, since fairness is subjectively determined, and subject to ideas as to what is suitable.

The attitude was in keeping with the view that assimilation, now the main term for the promotion of equality, would be a long process requiring maintenance of controls. In this process the mission activities, like those on the stations and settlements, could be regarded as promoting readiness for equality. Mission needs should be reassessed from this point of view; and this hastened the trend for the missions to be placed in a position where many of them came to confuse the Christian message, which had produced such barren results for such a long time, with the assimilation message, which at least brought Caesar on side, and greatly increased the facilities over and above what church and other private sources of mission funds were willing to provide.

It is interesting that although Victoria and Tasmania were not represented at the 1951 conference of Ministers and officials, this meeting is generally assumed as beginning joint action in accordance with an assimilation policy. In fact each government seems to have gone on as before, with the exception of the Commonwealth in the Northern Territory. An official Commonwealth publicity statement in 1964 states that 'Assimilation of Aborigines has been the policy of all Australian governments since 1951. This policy was stated at the 1961 Conference of Commonwealth and State Ministers. . . .'[16] Obviously the assimilation policy was no more than a general term for what each government was doing anyway, up till 1961, since it was not until then that a common definition of assimilation was worked out and agreed to. Perhaps it had, in the ten years after 1951, little more political significance than as an assurance to a mildly concerned public opinion, which by 1961 had become a fairly consistent agitation through the mass media.

[16] Hon. C.E. Barnes, Minister for Territories, *Assimilation in Action: Progress* (Canberra, 1964).

The 1961 Native Welfare Conference was attended by the responsible Ministers and officials in charge from all Australian governments. The first task was to agree to the definition.

The policy of assimilation means that all Aborigines and part-Aborigines are expected eventually to attain the same manner of living as other Australians and to live as members of a single Australian community enjoying the same rights and privileges, accepting the same responsibilities, observing the same customs and influenced by the same beliefs, as other Australians.[17]

The statement could accommodate the extreme assimilationist view of eventual Aboriginal disappearance, which had always been present in Aboriginal administration. Or it could be explained by persons of liberal view as promising no more than a general equality, and even as compatible with rejecting as nonsense the idea of a monolithic society, of people all wanting the same things in the same way, because there will always be minority groups which will differ on a very wide range of issues from the majority.

I believe that on the whole the statement leans to the monolithic view of Australian society and that it represents the highest common factor of consensus in the minds of the politicians and officials who made it. At least it is free from the notion that those of a certain degree of Aboriginality have no hope of equality. If my assessment of the statement is correct, it does, on the other hand, envisage a price, in the loss of cultural and social autonomy, to be paid for an eventual equality. Both the price, which can be at least deduced, and the talk about deferment of rights were at that stage unfortunate, though one cannot guess just how politically necessary they were. The statement and the useless discussion to which it has given rise illustrate how foolish it is for a government to purport to plan the unplannable for the indeterminate future; to interfere in the course of so doing with business which does not belong to a government committed to democratic methods of decision making. If for some political reason this kind of statement had to be made, that was unfortunate, for such vague promise for the future defers the need to innovate now: either to think out difficult new objectives or to get advice as to new methods. Both kinds of innovation threaten the *status quo* in the branches of the public service concerned with Aboriginal affairs. Deferment of innovation is inevitable where the matter concerned has low priority; and Aboriginal affairs are still low in the scale of government priorities in most States, so that the main concern is to avoid 'trouble'.

---

[17] Native Welfare Conference, Commonwealth and State Authorities: Proceedings and Decisions, January 1961.

Those whose contacts with Aborigines stir it up will be condemned as 'agitators'.

The statement also excused the current situation in civil rights and controls as 'special measures', to be regarded as

temporary measures not based on colour but intended to meet their need for special care and assistance to protect them from any ill effects of sudden change, and to assist them to make the transition from one stage to another in such a way as will be favourable to their future social, economic and political advancement.

Whether the echo of United Nations Trusteeship Council jargon was intentional I do not know, but here was a new justification of the authoritarian management of Aborigines in the big settlements of Queensland and the Northern Territory. Rights could wait; readiness for them was the thing to worry about.

This assumption that an indefinite period of training for equality is necessary has probably done more than anything else to discredit the efforts which governments have made and which have increased considerably even since 1961, for it means also the acceptance of various degrees of inequality; and Aborigines need equality now. In 1961 the 'methods of advancing the policy' included extension of government settlements, as a first stage in the settlement and training of 'nomadic and semi-nomadic natives'; integrated schooling, but only 'to the extent possible'—otherwise separate schooling; removal of restrictive laws, but only 'as soon as the capacity and advancement of the individual makes this possible'—where it could well be argued that whatever 'advancement' meant it would be more likely to occur after than before the removal of the restrictions. Yet the fact remains that here was a whole list of areas for practical activity—health, education, housing and hygiene, vocational training, extension of Aboriginal welfare work to assist adjustment, and other welfare services (including social services); and attempts to have the local communities accept 'advanced Aborigines and part-Aborigines' without prejudice. In my own view it was unfortunate that the program was presented as though at some stage there would be assimilation, because it gave the popular impression that the Aboriginal, as his own man, and the Aboriginal group would disappear. The same range of areas for change could have been as well or better presented as a means to justice.

That the Welfare Conference was becoming in part an exercise in public relations is suggested by its concern to have what governments were doing appear in the best light. There was consideration of the growing public interest at home, and of the awkward international situation which could now arise from a bad reputation in race relations. It was decided that this situation was to be met by a series of publications. One result was a rather dreary series of pamphlets produced in the Department of Territories; they are nevertheless valuable sources of information.

As these pamphlets are aimed mainly at the popular level of appreciation of how social changes may be promoted, it is not fair to place too much emphasis on the somewhat schoolmasterly concepts, of the Aboriginal learning from others, in some of them. Hasluck, who was still Minister for Territories, had shown that he understood that social change is a complex and unpredictable process.

I do not share the self-confidence of modern administration that if you give enough public servants enough power or if you spend enough money you can do anything and I deplore the expectation of the present-day Australian community that politicians should perform a series of miracles while the nation sleeps.[18]

The greatest impediments in 'native welfare', he said, 'are the fixed and inflexible ideas and arrogant notions about our own power to direct the course of social change'.[19]

This would seem to question the value of restrictive laws applied to a racial minority; but there was a whole historic tradition to be offset. The 1961 Conference considered how this legislation applied to an Aboriginal 'assimilated' in one State, in the sense that he was free from restriction, but who, if he moved into another, would there be legally restricted. Of the five States and the Northern Territory, four authorities in 1961 exercised control of Aboriginal property; two required consent to marry; four exercised restrictions on freedom to move; two maintained special conditions of employment (and in two others there were *laissez-faire* conditions in the pastoral industry with the Aborigines excluded from the award); all but Victoria had laws against alcohol; four had laws to control cohabitation; three limited the franchise.[20]

In opening the Conference, Hasluck—perhaps more optimistic than he used to be about what administration can achieve in terms of social change, perhaps because the Minister has to play the politician—argued that the advancement and adjustment of 70,000 persons (the current census figure) was not really a problem of any magnitude. Already, he said, 'tens of thousands' of 'coloured people' were finding 'acceptance and usefulness in the general community'. He went so far as to deny the relevance of analogies 'with racial situations in other lands' (which of course was

---

[18] 'The Future of the Australian Aborigines', in *Native Welfare in Australia: Speeches and Addresses by the Hon. Paul Hasluck M.P.* (Perth, 1953), p. 57.
[19] Ibid., p. 59.
[20] Ibid., p. 19.

nonsense).[21] There was probably some irritation at the growing publicity
for alleged and real administrative shortcomings. But promises of
speedy solutions were hardly justified; the population at risk was rapidly
increasing; and the argument about coloured people having been accepted
in the general community might well have been qualified by some
examination of the kind of acceptance, and especially of the extent to
which only the cosmetically favoured were passing. On the other hand,
Hasluck on other occasions showed that he knew these things very well:
the politician who is also a scholar must theorise in different contexts.

Since the 1951 Conference, however, there had been advances in the
area of social services. Only the 'nomadic or primitive' were by now
excluded from pensions and maternity allowances; but missions, settlements, and pastoral properties were still being treated as pensioners'
institutions for these payments, and for child endowment. One effect of
this must have been to maintain and even increase the administrative
intervention between the Aboriginal and his pension, create a vested
interest in managing it, and emphasise controlled welfare at the expense of
free movement and of the chance, by making mistakes, to learn how
to manage one's own resources.

This conference considered the need for special training of teachers for
separate Aboriginal schools; the drinking laws; and the need for training
patrol and administrative officers. In none of these matters was innovation
recommended. It was agreed that to place officers from the States in the
course provided for Northern Territory officers, at the Australian School
of Pacific Administration, would be too expensive.

It was decided to recommend that the conferences should be held every
two years; and meetings, since 1961, have been held in 1963, 1965, and
1967. Meetings of State and Territory officials have become annual events.
Clearly these meetings were unlikely to produce new initiatives. One
feature is the increasing emphasis on public relations, which has led to a
small number of publications indicating that all is well and well-managed
in Aboriginal affairs.

In the meantime, initiatives, as is to be expected, have come from
pressures in parliament, significant especially in the Commonwealth and
in South Australia. There have been considerable relaxations in the
legislation since 1961. At the 1965 Conference, the Ministers agreed on
a new definition of assimilation. 'The policy of assimilation seeks that all
persons of Aboriginal descent will choose to attain a similar manner and

[21] Native Welfare Conference, Canberra, 25 January 1961: Opening Statement by the
Minister for Territories.

standard of living to that of other Australians and live as members of a single Australian community. . . .'[22] The eventual objective is less rigidly stated. The idea of choice is accepted, so long as the Aborigines 'choose' the objective defined. The explanation by the Minister for Territories did not seem to clarify the issues. Aborigines, he said, would 'choose' to become 'part of the general Australian community' (to which one might fairly ask whether in this 'general' sense they are not already); but governments would provide increased opportunities in education, housing, employment, 'or in any other way for Aborigines to attain full Australian standards'.[23]

Perhaps the important change was in the admission of choice by Aboriginal groups as the factor likely to be most decisive in change. By this time there had been important relaxations in the restrictive laws; and the application by the Northern Australian Workers Union for the removal of exclusion of Aborigines from the Northern Territory Cattle Station Industry Award was to create a new and wider debate on general issues of equality. One indication of the changes was an 'expression of interest' by the Ministers in 1965 in the possibility of State officers being trained for work in Aboriginal affairs. In 1967, officers from South Australia were attending courses at the Australian School of Pacific Administration.

THE SELECT COMMITTEE ON ABORIGINAL VOTING RIGHTS

In 1961, on the motion of the Minister for the Interior, the Commonwealth Parliament had established a Select Committee, of Government and Opposition members, to report on the need for changes in section 39 of the Commonwealth Electoral Act, the section dealing with Aboriginal enrolment and voting rights. The Committee travelled extensively in Western Australia, the Northern Territory, and Queensland, where the Aboriginal was not entitled to the Commonwealth vote because of the law linking this with enrolment for State or Territory elections. In stating integration as the only possible solution, the Committee Report may have implied criticism of the assimilation policy as still being defined. It stressed the need, in passing, for capital investment in education, industries, land tenure, and housing, and suggested that the Commonwealth should consider providing special assistance for Aboriginal

---

[22] Statement by C.E. Barnes, Minister for Territories, on Conference of Commonwealth and State Ministers on Aboriginal Welfare, July 1965.
[23] Ibid.

housing.[24] The Minutes of Evidence before this Committee form one of the most valuable documents on Aboriginal affairs, and attitudes to them, throughout the northern and central regions of Australia.[25]

It was recommended that in New South Wales and Victoria the provisions for compulsory voting should be enforced as for other citizens; that action be taken by the Commonwealth Electoral Office to inform Aborigines elsewhere, who were already entitled to vote, of their right to do so;[26] that the right to vote at Commonwealth elections 'be accorded to all aboriginal and Torres Strait Islander subjects of the Queen, of voting age, permanently residing within the limits of the Commonwealth'; that for the time being enrolment be voluntary outside New South Wales and Victoria (and of course Tasmania), but that a person who was enrolled must vote.[27] This was the compromise which had already been established in South Australia for elections for the House of Assembly. An important recommendation was that voting procedures and the structure of Parliament be the subjects of instruction on missions and settlements in the remote areas;[28] and with the adoption of the recommendations, this was attempted, in due course, by officers of the Electoral Office.

This breaching of the virtual monopoly of contact which had rested for so long in the hands of the special welfare authorities formed in itself an important new opportunity for confrontation with government in a new guise. The instruction could not have been so important as the other lesson implied, that the Aboriginal citizen had the right to consideration by other departments of government. When the Committee had considered who should advise Aborigines in this matter of enrolment, it excluded the welfare officers along with other vested interests—'private persons, organizations, or political parties'.[29]

The recommendations were made 'because any other basis of the franchise would either discriminate on the ground of race, or penalise for lack of opportunity'. It was 'better that a right be granted before there is a full capacity to exercise it on the part of some individuals, than that others should suffer the frustration of being denied a right that they can clearly exercise'. Tests of literacy, housing, employment, or wealth were

---

[24] *C.P.P.* (H. of R.), 1961, vol. II, pp. 1391 *et seq.*—Report from the Select Committee on Voting Rights of Aborigines, Part I, pp. 1-2 (paras. 10-16).
[25] Ibid., Part II.
[26] Ibid., Part I, p. 4 (para. 4).
[27] Ibid., p. 8 (para 77).
[28] Ibid., p. 9 (para. 85).
[29] Ibid. (para. 82).

dismissed as discriminatory; and the suggestions that the *wards* in the Northern Territory or those under special State legislation should not vote were also dismissed, 'because Australians of European origin are not usually disqualified from the franchise by their need for special public assistance'.[30]

It is too early to make an accurate assessment of the implications of this report. But the arguments used were possibly even more telling in their implications than the right to vote at Commonwealth elections, which followed, and the subsequent extensions of the franchise in the States and the Territory. They were certainly not really compatible with legal restrictions on rights, and therefore not with that deferment of rights during an indefinite period of tuition, upon which the administrative structure for a controlled assimilation had depended. In the background was the extension of the franchise for electors to the House of Assembly in Papua and New Guinea, which would have made restrictions on Aborigines a curious anomaly indeed.

The breach in the Welfare Branch-Aboriginal group relationship in the Northern Territory was made more explicit as a result of the petition received by the Commonwealth Parliament from the Aborigines of Yirrkala, in Arnhem Land, following a decision by Parliament to set up another Select Committee to investigate, in September 1963.[31] This led to the first confrontation and negotiation between Parliament and an Aboriginal group on Aboriginal initiative. The implications were profound. Suffice here to remark that this event was hardly consistent with the assumption on which special restrictive laws were based—that Aborigines were incapable of representing their own best interests; for it would have been difficult to find a more isolated group of people in the whole Commonwealth than the Yirrkala, who, when the barriers of language were removed by efficient interpretation, impressed the Select Committee with their very shrewd appreciation of just what was at stake in the proposal to lease what they considered to be their own land to a mining company.[32]

POLICIES RE-CONSIDERED: AND CHANGES IN LEGISLATION

Complex local pressures, represented in the Legislative Council, seem to have played some part in the withdrawal of the Welfare Ordinance

[30] Ibid. (paras. 88-92).
[31] *C.P.P.* (H. of R.), 1963, pp. 927 *et seq.*
[32] *C.P.P.* (H. of R.), 1962-3, vol. 4, pp. 949 *et seq.*—Report from the Select Committee on Grievances of Yirrkala Aborigines, Arnhem Land Reserve, 1963.

and the adoption of a new Social Welfare Ordinance in the Northern Territory, in August 1964. But the Council's ordinances are subject to disallowance by the Governor-General, on the advice of the Minister for Territories. It is perhaps too early to assess the implications of this withdrawal of the whole superstructure of quite rigid controls, through which the *ward* was to be assimilated. Once again, civil rights had been emphasised at the expense of official assimilation theory; and the legal foundations of a considerable administrative empire in the processing of settlement Aborigines had been removed. The restrictions which remain require permits to visit reserves, if one is not Aboriginal; and there are a few regulations, against fighting, riotous behaviour, drunkenness, and use of firearms, on the reserve. But there was a parallel equalising of the law in other respects, so that, for instance, the Territory Aboriginal has the right to drink alcohol.[33]

Why this happened in the Territory is not our main concern here, but the whole concept of a national plan for controlled assimilation had arisen from Commonwealth activity. That the Commonwealth should so quickly have offered a change of front in its own Territory must have had some influence in the States. The old certainties were being worn away; and it was becoming clearer that public opinion was ready for moves to legal equality. The strength of this growing opinion was illustrated in the Referendum of 1967, by which it was decided that Aborigines were to be counted in the census and that the Commonwealth should have a concurrent power in Aboriginal affairs.

The changes have been accompanied by unprecedented public interest; and if the debates echoed in the mass media have often been ill-informed, this has been inevitable because of the very great complexity in the state of the law and of long-established administrative procedures. Perhaps we are reaching a situation where the memory of past legal discrimination will form a greater barrier to equality than what remains of discrimination in the law itself. By the end of 1967 only the government of Queensland seemed to stand firmly committed to indefinite control of those still 'under the Act'.

In New South Wales, after the amendments to the old Aborigines Protection Act in 1963, the special controls remaining related mainly to Aboriginal child welfare and to the management of reserves, but with the progressive removal of managers from reserves and the development of an area welfare system, the regulation of conduct on reserves was

[33] See *Northern Territory Government Gazette*, 11 May 1965—Northern Territory: Social Welfare Ordinance 1964; and Social Welfare Regulations.

becoming a memory, although the Board remained still in the situation of landlord, with the question of rents still a matter for contention.

The provisions for separate custody and maintenance of Aboriginal children, and for control of Aboriginal wards of the State, along with the special provisions for apprenticeship, should obviously, in a move to legal equality, be handed over to departments of the State government which handle these matters for the community at large. This appeared to be the view of the New South Wales Aboriginal Welfare Board. The 1963 amendments withdrew special provisions relating to Aborigines, in Acts dealing with the supply of liquor, vagrancy, and police offences.[34] In 1967 a Select Committee of the Legislative Assembly submitted a rather undistinguished report, which is mainly of interest as a contrast with the reports by two Select Committees of the Commonwealth House of Representatives. This may be the last of a long string of reports which mainly echo the popular folklore of assimilation.

The progressive withdrawal of managers from the stations, so that they became like other reserves, leaves unanswered the question of eventual tenure of these reserves, where so many have established homes which are still the property of the Board. The questions of whether Aborigines should have the choice of living on reserves, and of government efforts to have them move off them, have been the most publicised cause of protest by Aboriginal organisations, and a matter of contention in Victorian Aboriginal politics, for some years. Since the Act of 1958, the main debate has been about what the Board should do to promote a greater equality of opportunity; and the main issue has been whether the Board should close down the old station at Lake Tyers and bring pressure on the last families there to re-locate their homes elsewhere.

Legal equality has not yet done much to solve the problem of fringe-dwellers in either New South Wales or Victoria; and the attempts to disperse the people from Lake Tyers came up against the typical resistances from local governments. On the other hand, there has been generous local support for the 'right' of Aboriginal families on the old reserve at Framlingham to remain where they are, from interested persons in the nearby town of Warrnambool. Perhaps Victoria, more than any of the States, illustrates the extent to which questions of Aboriginal rights present issues which are essentially political. With the old type of discriminatory legislation further into the past than elsewhere, Victoria is passing into the next stage in Aboriginal affairs. Much of the contention

[34] See Aborigines Protection Act, 1909-1963, and Schedule.

in that State has, I believe, been due to the absence of any institutional machinery for consultation with local groups of Aborigines directly affected by changes in policy.[35]

The Western Australian Native Welfare Act of 1963 retained the racial definitions of *native* already referred to, except for those qualified by war service for exemption and those already exempted under the Natives (Citizenship Rights) Act 1944-1958, the latest amendment to which removed the government power to revoke citizenship. The Act (section 20) restricted entry to reserves to Aborigines and approved persons. The Native Welfare Act Regulations 1944, establish drinking, gambling, insubordination, unseemly behaviour, threatening or abusive or indecent language, and trading without the consent of the manager as offences for those on reserves. The manager may exclude a 'native' and prohibit the bringing to the reserve of any livestock. He has the usual institutional powers, in that inmates must obey his 'reasonable' instructions (Regulations 38-44). But in the settled areas, most institutionalised Aborigines are children. Control of *natives* by mission organisations is envisaged; but the mission worker requires a personal permit from the Minister, in whom administrative control is vested (Regulations 41-6). The Commissioner of Native Welfare may administer the property of natives with their consent only, but may take over the property of a minor. There are special provisions for inspection of labour conditions, but in the main these relate to the conditions in the pastoral industry, which will be considered in *The Remote Aborigines*.

This legislation in 1967 was in that transitional stage which seems to await the emergence of a new principle. Theoretically, the restrictions on entry to reserves, and the requirements of discipline there, apply to the town reserves, and may be used for political purposes from time to time, as when it is not convenient for the government to allow a visit. But in general the regulations seem mainly an unnecessary irritant, especially as the right to drink has since been extended to all areas but the Kimberleys and the Eastern Goldfields. The area administration of the District officer and his staff involves responsibilities for reserves, in addition to that for natives elsewhere. The officer, therefore, hardly needs the powers of a manager of an institution. It appears logical to rely on the general law, and to repeal all special restrictive legislation. Obviously, innovation is called for to increase the chances of constructive negotiation between government and Aboriginal groups.

[35] I am indebted for an intensive study of Aboriginal affairs in Victoria to Diane Barwick, A Little More Than Kin (1965), ch. II.

## CONSTRUCTIVE INNOVATION IN SOUTH AUSTRALIA

South Australia, in 1966 and 1967, made the most daring and positive innovations of any Australian government so far. Many of the old restrictions had been cleared away in the Aboriginal Affairs Act, 1962, which repealed earlier legislation. The restrictions remaining in that Act relate mainly to management of reserves, health inspections, and the use of alcohol; and there is power to make special regulations for the care and education of Aboriginal children, and for their apprenticeship.[36] In accordance with the idea earlier shared with other governments that assimilation could be best promoted by administrative measures which cut the tie of the Aboriginal with his old reserve, 'depopulation of the reserves' had been equated with 'assimilation'. This did, I think, involve a misunderstanding of just how re-location of families from any community occurs, especially from old communities like Point Pearce and Point McLeay, where the venture into the outside world is one into an environment socially unsympathetic, so that there is a special need for reassurance and for that kind of security which springs from the belief that the innovator can always return 'home'. A good deal of the movement into Adelaide and other towns had been from reserves and stations, but it involved also considerable movement back on to reserves. Even where this is only for extended visits, the visitors present problems for station discipline and in accommodation, just at the time when policy is to bring station housing up to standards approved by local governments in the area.

The 1962 Act, liberal as it is in comparison with what had been earlier, provided for a somewhat heavy-handed push towards assimilation by the Minister, who under the Act held the executive power (which had the advantage of taking Aboriginal affairs into Cabinet, and was a recognition of their growing political implications). If a person had quit an 'institution' (which presumably included a mission station) he required Ministerial permission to return. If he stayed, he could be declared a trainee, and must stay on until he had completed his training to the satisfaction of the Minister (section 20). Under the Regulations, he required a permit to stay; and the permit could be cancelled. The duties stated for the superintendent were the usual ones, whether the emphasis was on segregation or controlled assimiliation. He, or a police officer, could enter any house at will. He fixed the wages and determined what was training—and in view of the resources of these places, training could not have been much more

[36] Sections are 20, 23, 25, 30, and 40.

than the old chores of keeping the institution going. There was a list of special offences on stations, from a failure in cleanliness to refusal to obey the superintendent or to attend a training course.[37]

A new range of possibilities for using the reserves was created with the Aboriginal Lands Trust Act of 1966. This establishes a Trust of three members, with provision for an additional nine to be recommended by Aborigines Reserve Councils. The consent of each particular Aborigines Reserve Council is necessary for the transfer of a reserve to the Trust. The reserve land is then to be vested, 'free of all encumbrances', in the Trust, except for reservation to the Crown of mineral rights. The Trust has the authority to sell, lease, or mortgage such land, or to develop it, subject to Ministerial approval; and, also subject to that approval, to grant technical or other assistance or to advance finance to Aboriginal individuals or groups (sections 6, 16, 18). The main value of the land and other assets for those living on reserves in the settled areas will be for homes, with some minor assets in farm lands.

Important provisions are that the Director of Aboriginal Affairs is Secretary to the Trust and that the Trust is not a department of government (sections 12, 14). Thus the government welfare authority has not a directing but an advisory role. On the question of rights to reserve lands, the way was thus cleared for discussion and negotiation, with a body on which the Aboriginal Reserve Councils would have a majority. This was an important step—from controlled welfare to negotiation with Aboriginal groups.

So long as Reserve Councils and other representative bodies had to operate without legally defined powers, they served mainly as instruments of control for the station superintendent. But in 1967 the Aboriginal Affairs Act was amended to provide for regulations under which the Reserve Councils could be legally constituted and established. It was specifically provided that the regulations should empower the Councils to control entry to the reserves, 'notwithstanding the powers of the Aboriginal Affairs Board'; and that entry without such permission should be an offence.[38] This could place the power to control visits and residence in the hands of those who live on the reserves. The problem has been that, with rising wages on the reserves and a policy to pay for the new construction work at rates which had been approaching the level of wages elsewhere, and with the improvements in accommodation and services, more people were being attracted back to them. It seems to be a wise move to have such

[37] Aboriginal Affairs Act, 1962, Regulations 5-10.
[38] Aboriginal Affairs Act Amendment Act, 1966-1967, section 3.

decisions as to who shall share in the use of the reserve in the hands of a properly constituted representative body. Here is where politics and leadership may have a beginning. While there must be difficulties in the retention of the other powers of superintendents, the aim seemed to be provision of buildings and services to allow the older stations in the settled areas to meet requirements of the adjacent local government bodies, so that they might become open villages.

Another provision was for the proper establishment and registration of societies to carry on business or trades on reserves, irrespective of the Industrial and Provident Societies Act 1923-1966 and the Companies Act 1962-1965.[39] In my own view the provision of the Companies Act could have been used for the establishment of an Aboriginal company on each reserve, to exercise the powers both of the councils and the societies; and it might have made for simpler administration. But there may be legal objections which I am not competent to discuss: and there are many ways of innovating when a new principle is being developed. The principles involved form perhaps the most constructive innovation in Aboriginal affairs.

The question of land 'rights' and reserves is only one of the 'neuralgic points' in race relations. If some measures like this can be generally adopted, reserves may continue to contribute to Aboriginal adjustment in so far as they offer a considerable psychological support and a small but possibly critical economic support for those groups which look to them as 'home'. For instance, the breadwinner who has some assured control of his home is less at the mercy of the seasons in the search for employment, and less at the mercy of the employer, since with a home and with social service benefits he does not have to make a private undertaking to work for less than the relevant award wage.

Most of these changes of the law either had recently been made or were in process of being made when this survey was being undertaken. A retrospect of the kind which I have attempted seemed necessary to indicate why they are not being received with enthusiastic co-operation by many Aborigines. Many of them are not widely known. Moreover, there is a great gulf between the changing intentions of central government and the situation in small localities which cumulatively make up the Aboriginal 'problem'. Probably, by 1967 public opinion had reached a point where it would accept innovation in general principle, but support for government is always likely to waver when the implications of the principle involve changes of personal and local habit. This leads us again

[39] Ibid.

to what seems the core of the situation, in the type of adjustment to be made at the level of local government and in the place and role of the Aboriginal group in the social life of the town. One may confidently look forward to the end of restrictive special laws. But the basic reason for these laws is in the daily habit of discrimination. Discrimination is the result of prejudice: and prejudice is supported by the situations which discrimination produces.

In local situations there are some things which a government can do. First, it can strengthen the economic and especially the *political* situation of the Aboriginal by promoting and negotiating with Aboriginal corporate bodies. Second, it can set standards of public behaviour, by making particular acts of discrimination either offences at law or matters for civil action by the injured party, or both. In addition, it may promote schemes of community education which involve Aborigines and other Australians; and particularly it may support such efforts sponsored by universities and other independent bodies, through extension and adult education techniques, to promote a constructive dialogue on particular local problems, such as access to local government facilities, Aboriginal housing in towns and cities, the discrimination by children against the dark child in the school, and equality of opportunity in employment.

This kind of educational effort has been attempted by many voluntary bodies, and there have been a few efforts in the 1960s by universities. But in the first place the effort needs support from governments, on the basis of the principle of continuing dialogue with Aborigines as a recognised group and as a group whose members face special social, economic, and health risks. The matter of equality raises political issues, in that Aboriginal advancement involves concessions on the part of those whose concept of their own 'rights' are partly founded on prejudice and the assumed 'right' to discriminate. So long as educational efforts of this broad nature are concerned only with a series of connected components of welfare, such as housing, education, health, and employment, without the integrating factor and the hope aroused by government commitment to a new principle, the lack of Aboriginal leadership and organisation for constructive change will continue. The educational effort will remain sporadic on their part. The promising seminars and local committees will, as in the past, become episodes in a long train of failures, continuing to lapse for lack of a defined purpose with government backing.

Briefly, the principle must be the recognition of the Aboriginal group as a body to be *negotiated* with, to be encouraged and helped to build its own organisation and to sort out its own leadership problems, so that it might have legitimate spokesmen. The long-range aim should, I believe, be to encourage incorporation of groups. This requires no new law; and a company is the ideal multi-purposed organisation. But government does not have to wait for incorporation to listen and to negotiate. The results of such moves must be to put pressure on the more unsympathetic local government bodies and to strengthen the hands of local persons and organisations working for changes.

It seemed, as this was written, that South Australia was moving in this direction. This of course involved the transition from managed welfare of more or less inarticulate people to politics and pressure groups. The transition was illustrated by the resistance in the Legislative Council to the Aboriginal Land Trust Bill; and by the success of the Opposition in having the provision for the transfer of mineral rights to the Lands Trust deleted from the Bill.

The South Australian Government has also pioneered with an attempt to set public standards in the matter of discrimination, with the Prohibition of Discrimination Act of 1966. This provides that refusal of admission to licensed premises, places of public entertainment, or shops, because of the race, country of origin, or skin colour of the person rejected, constitutes an offence. Refusals to supply a service, or, by a person catering for the public, to supply food, drink, or accommodation, for the same reasons, are also offences (sections 3-5). It is also an offence to refuse to let a house, or room in a boarding house, or to enter into an agreement which restricts the passing of land or buildings to a person because of his race, country of origin, or skin colour (sections 6, 8). Dismissal of an employee, or injury in his employment, for the same reasons, are offences (section 7).

As the experience of the last decade in the United States has shown, the difficulty of proving intent must form a major hindrance to prosecutions. This is probably why the Act does not also make the refusal of employment an offence. But, irrespective of this, the Act must create clear rights in practice, as well as set public standards. As an example, the Aboriginal who is refused entry to a public place has a clear recourse in that he can report the matter to the police; the police have a clear duty in a matter where no such duty was clear before the Act; and police intervention may result in assertion of the right to equality without the matter coming into court. The Act does not create a right of civil action by the Aboriginal or other person rejected, though there may be other grounds for such action. In effect the government is committed to bear the costs of prosecution and to impose the penalty of up to $200 in proven cases. Perhaps the difficulty of proving motivation for refusals was the reason why there is no cause for civil action—and perhaps a well enough founded assumption that few Aborigines will be in a position to go to the court. On the other hand, such a cause of action could enable some Aborigines with potential for leadership to gain the experience of using the law, by their own decision and in their own interest; and to be compensated for injury.

Yet this Act is of historic significance, in that at least one Australian government has committed itself to equality in the area of race relations. It might well set a precedent for the Commonwealth Government to undertake a similar commitment for all citizens of the nation, under the concurrent power voted at the Referendum of 1967.

### LEGISLATIVE CHANGES RELAX RESTRICTIONS

The South Australian legislation was especially significant as the most positive move up until 1967 towards the formulation of a new policy. The main trend in the sixties was seen in the more spectacular withdrawals of controls, over Aboriginal drinking for instance; and the much publicised fears of chaos, which did not come to much anyway, because Aborigines in the past had developed special ways of avoiding the law. The ban was removed finally in New South Wales (having been reimposed in 1952 after a 'trial period' of six years) in 1963. The effect was to raise civil rights issues with at least the neutrality of the law, in cases where Aborigines were excluded from what often amounted to the local 'club' in the hotel bar. This soon became a universal issue, with relaxations elsewhere—throughout the Northern Territory in 1964, progressively by regions in South Australia in 1964 and 1965; and progressively in Western Australia from 1964, commencing in the South West, but by the end of 1967 remaining short of the Kimberleys and Eastern Goldfields. Queensland followed in 1965. Liquor was still illegal on reserves, and other restrictions remained, such as bringing it to an Aboriginal camp on a pastoral property in the Territory. There were inevitable *de facto* restrictions involved, where Aborigines long under control of an official either did not know that he had lost his power to restrain or did not dare to assert rights he would not acknowledge.

In the extension of voting rights, the only delay of consequence was in Queensland, where amendments to the Elections Act were delayed for some time while the government gave serious consideration to whether the Aborigines should vote on a separate communal roll and have separate representation. Probably this was never really likely, especially as all other citizens of Australia and those in Papua and New Guinea voted on common rolls. But the extension of rights was again indicating that political interests must be involved; that such positive provisions bring Aboriginal affairs into the political arena, from which they have been long excluded, almost by bi-partisan consent, as objects only of welfare provisions under administrative controls and outside the mainstream of national affairs. The Bill to amend the Elections Act, in accordance with the previous recommendations of the Select Committee of the Commonwealth Parliament on Voting Rights, was finally introduced to the Queensland Parliament in December 1965.

As K.E. Beazley pointed out, this relaxation of controls was not in itself likely to solve the problem. Equal rights to drink and fornicate were important, and might have been granted because they cost little to the taxpayer, but the real issues demanded positive measures to deal with practical needs in health, housing, education, and employment.[40]

Perhaps we have now enough evidence of what has happened in the past to realise what Aboriginal resentments are all about; and why non-Aboriginal Australians for the most part share a folklore which assumes a feckless and undependable Aboriginal community and something less than average capacity in the Aboriginal individual.

[40] *Dispossession and Disease—or Dignity?* Provocative Pamphlet No. 115.

Members of Aboriginal groups in the 'settled' areas lack adequate education, incomes, housing, and employment. In the 'colonial' areas of Australia the needs are greater, and the position more obsolete: but possibly the issues are more clear cut. Aborigines everywhere suffer handicaps arising from prejudice which limits their social and spatial mobility and their economic opportunities. The establishment of boards and sub-departments to deal with a whole range of Aboriginal needs at least acknowledged that these needs were interrelated. But there were other reasons, such as the kind of help considered suitable, and the funds to be allocated, which were generally different from those available for non-Aborigines. This distinction is enough in itself to explain the existence of specialist *Aboriginal* relief organisations.

It seems that the individual, irrespective of his descent, will soon be legally entitled to equal access to the government sources of assistance in all States and in the Northern Territory, and that these will no longer be related to racial origin. The Aboriginal family or individual already has the right in most States to take his own case to the various specialist welfare authorities. Such a right is of course essential; and to this extent there can be no quarrel with the 'assimilation' policy.

I believe, however, that after all the history, and in view of the pattern of belief which is one ground for Aboriginal defiance and scepticism, removal of legal disqualifications does no more than clear away some of the obstacles for a national policy in Aboriginal affairs. Aborigines have special *group* needs, related to patterns of belief and to social penalties suffered by those of Aboriginal appearance in 'white Australia'. For a long time their defence has been stubborn adherence to a separate identity. In so far as this is no longer necessary (and legal equality will not make this difference), more than a few changes in the law will be required to convince them, even if group reactions in such cases could possibly be calm and rational ones. The aim of 'assimilation' has been to winkle out the deviant individual from the group, to persuade him to cut the ties which bind him and his family to it, and to set him up as a householder in the street of the country town. But policies which aim to change social habit by educating individuals, while ignoring the social context which has made him what he is, can have only limited success. A program involving social change must deal with the social group.

The welfare of an individual is worth while for its own sake, and properly regarded as an end in itself. Welfare means nothing except in terms of individual satisfactions. But national policies should utilise the most effective and the quickest means. The most effective methods will be found from analysis of the *whole* situation; and when we look at the situation of the Aboriginal as a whole, he is a member of a special group united at least in the beliefs held about the white majority. Moreover, the cause of the individual's special handicaps is related to his membership of the group. To ignore such a causal connection is to deal with the symptom while ignoring the cause. In this way also policy can be bogged down and lost in the welter of individual needs. To meet these is certainly the object of the whole effort; but to assume that they will be most effectively met only by dealing with individuals as 'ordinary Australians', while ignoring the effect on their attitudes and beliefs of membership of a special sub-group, is to concentrate on the part to the neglect of the whole.

### THE STRATEGY

The needs described in this volume arise directly from the inferior status of the group. Thus the relationship of government administration to Aborigines cannot be the impersonal relationship of the administration of welfare to 'ordinary' citizens, even if the officials are perfectly just. New educational gains, ease of access to the mass media, and knowledge of the changing power balance in the colonial world and among the Negro minority in the United States must increase awareness that the social and economic dominance of the whites can be challenged; and this process has begun. Welfare administration must be affected by more open expressions of resentment, cynicism, and disbelief in the good faith of government agencies.

A policy which appears to verify beliefs that government is concerned only to maintain white interests could soon lead to open dissidence. So policy has to be concerned with the system of beliefs. This means that there has to be some way of establishing contact between government and the groups themselves, even though at the present time they lack coherent leadership and acknowledged spokesmen. Policy must be concerned with *rapprochement*, reconciliation, and face-to-face discussion with Aboriginal representatives. If there are no representatives, policy must be concerned with their emergence and their legitimacy within the groups they represent. Therefore an objective must be such constructive social changes as will enable Aborigines to solve their problems of leadership. A policy concerned with social change has to be far more sophisticated than those in the past, which have proclaimed the faith in 'social engineering' seen as the progressive processing of the minds of individuals. It has to take into account how social change occurs; and it has to wait for Aboriginal groups to work out their own ways of responding to genuine opportunities.

The idea of negotiation may well be opposed by those who deplore any move to regard Aboriginal welfare as a political matter. Members of parliaments have been accusing one another of making 'political capital' from Aboriginal affairs. Some people assume that in some way welfare administration is not a political matter—although the age pensioners' organisations would probably disagree. Aboriginal affairs have only recently become political, because in the past they have been excluded from politics, sometimes by the most extreme of means—by physical removal to isolated reserves.

Aboriginal apathy and aggression are characteristic of people who are politically impotent; who believe that the sources of power and influence in the nation to which they belong, and the authorities which make up the government to which they are subject, cannot be influenced by their needs or anything they can do. Such reactions and beliefs have political meaning, because they are concerned with morality, with what should be the proper relationship between men; in other words, with their place in the political system and with what it should be. The Aboriginal shares with others the sentiment of egalitarianism. This, at least, is a most definite impression which I have gained from work in this Project and from the work of others. This is also what one would expect. If he did not, there would be no protest. Now that he has increased access to the sources of information, there must be increased concern with equal access to the opportunities of material wealth.

As an inmate of an institution, the Aboriginal could be regarded as the object of careful husbandry. But political man will demand the right to decide what he wants and the chance to work, through the available channels to the holders of power and influence, to get it. The basis of the Aboriginal 'problem' being political, government policy should take the fact into account by facilitating the growth of Aboriginal organisations and pressure groups. It should assist to make them more effective in competition with other special interests—both locally and nationally.

This involves an act of faith; but so does the attempt to establish and maintain democracy. It also involves a complete break with the ideas of 'training' for 'acceptance', of isolation in institutions, and of special legal or administrative controls. Measures based on these ideas, whatever the justifications in moralistic terms, were also attempts to get rid of problem groups round country towns. They involved political priorities to sustain the comfort and recognised interests of the white town dwellers. Aboriginal priorities were illustrated in fringe-dwellings, reserves, and settlements, illustrating the 'who gets what, when, and how' of politics. Such trends, taken to a logical conclusion, require the devotion of a totalitarian government to racist priorities. Thus the Nazis produced the perfection, for Nazi purposes, of the concentration camp. South Africa, with its apartheid laws, has established racist priorities, and no doubt deplores the efforts of those who would 'play politics' to interfere with its efforts to promote 'native welfare'. It can also use statistics of material welfare of Africans within its borders, to the detriment of poorer African states which have mainly subsistence and freedom. But this begs the real question, the priorities allocated by the same government. The issue, then, is equality; and this has to be recognised for what it is, a political *value*.

Australian governments (with the current continued hesitation of Queensland) having backed away from the implications of removing a class of citizens from participation in politics, have, as it were, only one direction in which to go. The progressive and accelerating withdrawal of restrictions is one aspect of the reintroduction of the Aboriginal interest into politics. It would be surprising if the period of tribulation had not sharpened the Aboriginal appreciation of special interests. At the same time, for reasons already stated, it has operated against the emergence of leadership, of effective political organisation within Aboriginal groups, to such an extent that only now are the main spokesmen for the Aborigines themselves persons of Aboriginal descent. In the settled areas, these are deeply divided.

This is far less true of the Aboriginal remnants of the north and centre of the continent, where some continuity of tribal organisation or of other bases for autonomous adaptation to changing circumstances has been maintained. Just after the war, Aboriginal leadership (with non-Aboriginal advice, to be sure) was a significant factor in the strikes and subsequent action which founded the Pindan movement, and which has maintained a separate organisation up till the present time; interestingly enough, using the western legal method of incorporation as a framework for autonomous decision making which had to be recognised by the government. The recent action of the Gurindji, sitting down on what they claim, after some centuries of prior occupation, to be their own 'country', could not have occurred without a considerable degree of coherence within the group. These events require analysis; but accounts do suggest the emergence of multi-purposed leadership among the Gurindji, vested in Vincent Lingiari—again, acting with non-Aboriginal advice.

A feature of the annual meetings of the Federal Council for the Advancement of Aborigines and Torres Strait Islanders has been the emphasis given to what the full-bloods in the north have done. Figures like Captain Major and Dexter Daniels are household words among the part-Aborigines of the south, who perhaps seek here a clearer identity. But the issues are, from a distance, simpler, because some of the original Aboriginal assets have been apparently less irrevocably alienated. The conflict of black and white is seen in clearer form. But it still remains true that in some places in these distant parts there has been maintained a more continuous tradition and a greater approach to that minimum degree of autonomy for decision making and adjustment to the intruder which makes consensus attainable when the opportunity for group action arrives.

Such remnants of political and social continuity and autonomy have gone from most of the part-Aboriginal groups in the settled areas. In most cases all there is in common is folklore and the tradition of camp or reserve, with common inmate-to-management reactions determining political attitudes. It is perhaps not much to build on, but it is all that their would-be leaders have. Moreover, the events I have referred to in the north have been exceptional. They might have come to very little without advice and help from non-Aboriginal sources. More recently in the Northern Territory the Council for Aboriginal Rights, an Aboriginal body, has accompanied political statements with action on the Gurindji's behalf.

Such exercises in the political sphere are inseparable from resurgence of the Aboriginal group. In fact, instead of deploring them as 'political', governments should provide means to facilitate them, regard them as signs of increasing participation, and show readiness to negotiate with those involved. This implies government interest in having, as soon as possible, defined leadership within Aboriginal groups. In order to participate in the conflict of interest groups for benefits allocated by government, Aboriginal society needs this internal discipline. Governments cannot develop it; in fact, it will probably be developed, like anti-colonial nationalism, as a method of opposition. But governments can provide incentive and opportunity for Aboriginal organisation.

There is probably not much choice for government in the long run. Aborigines will organise themselves as pressure groups in any case. In fact, the process is becoming clearer every year; and there is a growing body of sympathisers, especially among the students and other young white Australians. Either Aboriginal influence comes sooner or Aboriginal 'black power' comes later. As R.G. Menzies, after an experience of these trends elsewhere, and in the colonial rather than in the minority context, said in reference to New Guinea a few years ago, 'Better sooner than later'. For later there seems to be a point of no return, with the minority finally alienated.

But how much better for all concerned, says the supporter of an 'assimilation' policy (and these include some responsible Aboriginal leaders), if the Aboriginal groups would now disperse and share their interests with others, accepting the interests of others as their own. Why not 'merge' with other Australians and forget their Aboriginality? This has been an argument from the time of first European settlement. The assimilation assumption can be supported by the innumerable cases of the disappearance of Aborigines from Aboriginal groups. But it leaves out of account stubborn adherence by human groups to their own *mores* and to their separate identity; and their tendency to demand dignity and equality on the basis of what they are, and not for what they or their children become. It also leaves out of consideration the continuing effects of discrimination in social and economic matters, even after the legal discriminations have been withdrawn. This emphasises the in-group solidarity in separate traditions and *mores*. Such continuing discrimination is illustrated by the process of 'assimilation', whereby individual Aborigines disappear into the majority. For this happens mainly where physical appearance enables them to elude discrimination, and does not arouse prejudice.

Only South Australia has introduced anti-discrimination laws. Other States have based policies on hope of disappearing prejudice, for which there are no real grounds. In spite of some promising gestures following the 1967 Referendum, the Commonwealth has not yet applied its new powers to a national policy. A government which limits coloured immigration to avoid racial conflict has already assumed that racial antipathy is inevitable; so it is hardly consistent to base Aboriginal policy on measures which attack discrimination on principle.

In the meantime, an increasingly well-educated Aboriginal *élite* has already made contacts with Africa and the United States. At this stage it is hardly likely to accept as adequate vague foreshadowings of equality some generations from now, and would neither believe in nor be satisfied with such 'pie in the sky' for its descendants if they did.

In one way or another Aboriginal leaders will come to the fore and develop political pressures. Governments may negotiate with leaders willing to operate within the political system or face others who have rejected it. The Commonwealth Minister and Council for Aboriginal Affairs, by 1968, seemed to have ideas of negotiation. Reconciliation is difficult, because it involves the admission of injustices by government in the past.

A requirement for negotiation is representative spokesmen for the Aborigines. These in turn depend on accepted ways of making decisions which are binding on the group and on recognition of authority held by some individuals to express views based on consensus. Aboriginal society at present is marked by the dearth of such spokesmen and leaders. Those Aborigines who speak for their people have tenuous and vaguely defined authority; the groups for whom they speak are even more vaguely defined. Governments with policies of *rapprochement* with Aborigines must be concerned with the emergence of a *structure of authority* within Aboriginal groups. This in turn requires that the limits of the groups be defined, probably on the basis of location and common interests.

Such an objective involves both political and administrative innovation to capitalise on the initiative of the Aborigines themselves and the emergence of a new type of Aboriginal institution, the very reverse of those of the past, since it results from the initiative of the members.

The national strategy should be common to the whole country. Its main purpose should be to strengthen the political influence of the Aboriginal people, so that they may, within the law and within reason, choose how and where they live, and operate as pressure groups for change. These requirements demand the establishment of new Aboriginal institutions which can be entrusted with property, either in perpetuity in recognition of a claim arising from long or prior occupation or in the form of loans, user rights, or on a rental basis. They may also be entrusted to administer government property which is devoted to the requirements of Aborigines.

In addition the institutions must have an autonomy recognised in law, providing what Aboriginal society has not had since the days of the first occupation by Europeans—the carapace structure within which the members have comparative security from interference, to develop patterns of leadership. Here I am assuming that the groups institutionally defined on their own initiative could be counted on to react much as other groups in similar situations. They would not react at all, in most cases, unless there were decisions which had to be made. If one side of the strategy is to establish such local institutions, the other is that they are presented immediately with the need for decision making on issues of importance to themselves. This is possibly about as far as a government can go in planning for social change.

Where, as in Pacific Island villages, there has remained a degree of autonomy, the villagers have been able to adapt to rapidly changing circumstances because they have continued to some extent to make their own decisions in response to changes which affect them. Much of their decision-making traditions have remained intact. This has enabled them to conserve basic values in the face of imposed colonial controls, new goods, money, absence of young men for long periods, and so on. Villages have been able to adapt their old ways to new activities (like cash cropping) introduced by the village innovators. Each new decision has unforeseen consequences; about these also decisions have to be made. This is part of the process of social change. Whether or not the group retains its original coherence through all this depends on the weight of the impact of the new influences. If it does not, the continuity of auto-nomous adaptation breaks down into chaos or dependency on an outside authority, as happened to most Aboriginal groups and their part-Aboriginal successors.

The kind of institution I have in mind should provide an area of security for autonomous adjustment. This in turn involves emergence of authority structures. It is probable that in the settled areas the processes will be generally democratic. Among people with tribal traditions, leaders in traditional fields may find new tasks. Such varying adjustments can easily be made within a formally and legally uniform institutional model which meets the requirement of a single national strategy while offering the security of a familiar community membership.

This is part of the answer to the argument for racially integrated institutions. Would not Aboriginal institutions be divisive? Or (as the press had it when Aborigines in Redfern formed a football team of their own) is this not discrimination in reverse? Discrimination in what? One is not recommending the establishment of wealthy institutions to be endowed by government, but institutions for those suffering from the very special handicap of Aboriginal appearance and associations—a handicap in the sort of society we live in. I would not for a moment rule out government assistance to multi-racial institutions. They are obviously essential. What I am concerned with first is the kind of institution in which the Aboriginal can gain the confidence and knowledge which will enable him to claim his due in all kinds of multi-racial situations.

Moreover, the mixed group, of persons who are Aboriginal and of those who want to help, is not clearly articulated as an interest group. It certainly is an essential extension of political activity, as the civil rights movement in the United States has shown. But the lack of clearly defined interest for the Negro as minority group is illustrated by the split in the Negro movement, with Black Power hiving off from the moderate and educated Negro leaders and their non-Negro associates. Then, inevitably, the moderate leadership is either drawn after the majority of the Negroes or isolated from them. I am not suggesting that there should be some racial test for membership of an Aboriginal institution, but that the institution should be composed of members who consider themselves to be Aboriginal; that the association be voluntary; and that whether other persons are members or not might well be left to the decision of members.

I have on occasions in these volumes anticipated these recommendations, in references to Aboriginal bodies corporate. I see great advantages to be won from the formation of associations of all kinds, at the option of the people concerned, and for purposes they define, with government assistance and advice. In fact this could be the first large-scale community development operation in this country. Incorporation might come quickly in some cases where the point of it is clear. In the majority of cases it will probably never come. But it is essential, I believe, that the *Aboriginal company* be the *objective* of the national strategy in local organisation. I am thinking here not of new or special legislation but of institutions which are new mainly because they have only or pre-dominantly Aboriginal members, and because their objectives are different from those of other companies. But they could well, when the time comes in each case that there is a leadership which is trusted and which can provide members of a company board, be registered as proprietary companies, for proprietary companies have rather less tangled legislation to control them than others. The main difficulty about them is that the membership is limited; but this should require only a minor amendment in each State law.

I can hear the objections of those who know all about the limitations of the local Aboriginal group. I have seen the same reaction to the first plans for local government in New Guinea; and later when the idea of industrial organisations was new there. What seems impossible in one decade, in periods of rapid social change, is accepted as usual in the next. We have to remember that in ten years time there should be Aboriginal lawyers, medical and other graduates, and professional men. That times are changing, and incorporation of Aboriginal interests is quite feasible, is illustrated by the South Australian Aboriginal Land Trust. Yet the Aboriginal company is as important as an *objective* as for what it may achieve. Such an objective completely re-orients the whole approach of the government and the public service to Aboriginal affairs. Instead of a disappearing liability, as in 'assimilation', the Aboriginal group is re-sited in policy as an asset, to be endowed, by its own efforts, with enduring legal personality. The fringe group is the raw material for a corporation in perpetuity.

Administration could establish a series of stages in development of Aboriginal organisations, flexible enough for wide variations in local tactics. The first stage might be the formation of an Aboriginal association by those who elect (or appoint in some other way) representatives to express their wishes. In and round some towns, where there is tension between groups (as where those on the reserve look down on those off it), there could well be two or three associations. But at least the starting point for more formal politics has been established, and an initial problem of obtaining unity of interests is posed. Tactics may be worked out on the spot, perhaps by a multi-purpose field worker (almost unknown so far in Aboriginal affairs): he requires special educational preparation and training mainly in the techniques of community development. But at this stage something new has begun. The official has been withdrawn from the position of power, and the initiative in future relationships with government can henceforth be taken by the people's representatives. If no further step succeeded, the effort would not have been wasted, for the Aboriginal would have made his first move into politics, becoming again a full man and a 'political animal'.

In recommending that action to reverse the implicit politics of government-to-Aboriginal group relations come first, I do not mean to imply that any services or assistance now given be neglected. Material and servicing handicaps which must be overcome include especially employment, housing, education, health, and the relationship to both local and central government. What I am looking to is a way to make effort and money devoted to such ends as effective as possible: it will certainly not be effective without the co-operative involvement of the Aborigines. One might mention here the responses in some areas of government effort in the past: that families might take over a new house and refuse to pay rent for what they assume to be rightfully theirs, or simply as protest. There have been indifferent efforts at maintenance, or even deliberate destruction; off-handed responses to efforts for homework centres and pre-schools, from people who see no point in them because their children must lead the kind of life that they have known; and the reckless disregard of health by desperate persons. Without consultation, resulting in agreement as a basis for change, the most skilful techniques and the best material will probably be wasted, as they so often have been in the past.

Many field officers of course know this. A good deal must have been achieved in particular places on the basis of local *rapport*. But what has been achieved may depend for continuity on the chance that a subsequent official carries on the work. So there has to be a common background of training in Aboriginal affairs, related to a formally established series of steps from the first Aboriginal associations to bodies corporate. In addition there has to be an approved set of tactics based partly on the experience and knowledge to be gathered. Australia is specially deficient in persons trained for such work.

The community development philosophy and techniques will help to establish new forms of organisation which arise logically and naturally from the needs felt by the people themselves. They offer the best means of identifying needs. Although few Australians are familiar with these techniques, they have (with variable results) been widely applied in the 'developing' world. Here we have a 'developing' world in miniature under our noses; and such it will remain until some of us learn the techniques of getting people to think about their needs, to delineate their wants, and to plan to get what they want.

Obviously as many as possible of the field workers (and the policy makers), as soon as possible, must be Aborigines. Here too there is hope, since so many more Aboriginal children are receiving a full basic education. It seems reasonable to assume that this field work can become a special field of employment for Aboriginal men and women.

Another field of employment would be provided by the companies.

Such development would provide an important incentive for youths and girls to continue schooling. A series of cadetships might be established. As the new institutions develop towards incorporation, and are increasingly entrusted with the administration of government funds and with property, they must employ clerical and administrative staff. An important stage will have been reached when the Aboriginal company employs non-Aborigines.

For such measures there are more apparent advantages where some patterns of leadership have survived, in the 'colonial' areas. On the debit side, there are probably more political difficulties in such areas from the organised resistance of pastoral lessees, and more open discrimination by white town-dwellers. Yet the problems are basically the same as in 'settled' areas, though in an earlier stage: with the Aboriginal group merely *becoming* the fringe group typical of the southern regions. The principles I have outlined are equally applicable.

By developing a method of attack to deal with this type of problem, supported by a suitable organisation of staff and materials, the government could produce skills transferable to regions beyond Australia. Such skills, with the attitude of respect for other cultural and ethnic groups, are equally relevant in programs of overseas aid. In teams which provide such aid to Asian countries, there may well be a point in having Aboriginal Australians.

The corporate body can, under the various companies acts, be quite flexible. Its purposes can include anything which is wanted by members, reasonable in the circumstances, and agreed to by company (or association) and government. It is the kind of organisation which for commercial purposes has to be complex, because of the need to protect the interests of shareholders; but the complexities can be handled by legal advisers either made available by the government or employed by the organisation. It exists indefinitely; and it offers a permanent identity which does not really have to be expressed in racial terms. It has the advantages of a legal person, to sue or be sued without directly involving its members personally. It does not involve the introduction of further special legislation for Aborigines, though there may be advantages in amending the Commonwealth and State Companies Acts to simplify them, in cases of companies established for non-profit purposes and even for profit purposes where especially approved by government (as, for instance, in the management of reserve lands for tourism by an Aboriginal company).

It seems necessary to refer here to the co-operatives, reserve councils, and other organisations which have been established for Aboriginal groups in the past. In general, these have failed; and partly this has been a matter of motivation, for motivation must involve hope. There is no hope where there is no prospect of real change. There is no need to question here the good faith of the departments and the officers who have commenced projects of this kind. Often these men have established a *rapport* with Aborigines which has begun real re-thinking within departmental organisations, wearing away authoritarian patterns of administration from within. But neither the resources nor adequate freedom of decision could be made available. Thus there have been 'co-operatives' whose members own nothing as individuals, but who have farmed lands on reserves. Sometimes these have involved many more members than the limited assets could support.

Limiting factors have similarly doomed in advance the settlement councils set up in Queensland and in the Northern Territory. In Queensland these have been formally constituted; I have commented on them, and no further comment is necessary here, except to say that functions relating to law and order should obviously be discharged by the State courts and police. In so far as they are concerned with municipal government, there can hardly be separate kinds of municipal government, corresponding to the race of those governed, especially once Aborigines know that they are free to leave these places.

This brings us to the further development of policy which is necessary: that those assets now held for administration of Aboriginal welfare should be progressively handed over to Aboriginal associations to manage, and eventually handed over, on the basis of the most permanent tenure possible in the State or Territory, to the relevant Aboriginal company. This policy should be made known to the Aborigines concerned and offered as further incentive for successful transition to registration as a company.

At the present time there is no effective communication between governments and the Aboriginal communities. This can only be established in circumstances which enable the emergence of Aboriginal leadership recognised by Aborigines, government, and the general community. There are some hopeful signs. More Aborigines now have higher education, and this is obviously an accelerating process. The problem of leadership is clearly a more complicated matter than training in western techniques. To win Aboriginal followers, would-be leaders must command Aboriginal allegiance and confidence. Selection by government authority would probably be equivalent to what New Guinean politicians have referred to as 'the kiss of death' to ambition. Here is one of the main justifications for the planning of new Aboriginal institutions, presenting opportunity and challenge to organise for economic gains and to articulate the Aboriginal political interest.

Government policy based on the philosophy of tuition before rights seems bound to fail. Deferring equality indefinitely increases hostility and confirms suspicions well grounded in the history. So-called 'social engineering', even if it can produce predictable results to fit some policy of advancement (which is doubtful), would require subtleties which are beyond the resources or competence of governments. The people whom government sets out to help have to be *trusted*: and they must be offered hope. They will make their own adjustments, for reasons which make sense to them, in a process of accommodation and compromise. The changes they make will inevitably make other changes necessary.

I have suggested one kind of 'grass roots' institution which seems to me to offer some hope of restoring to Aboriginal groups, and of maintaining the necessary autonomy of the process of social change, behind the legal-administrative barricade, or under the carapace, of the Aboriginal company. I believe that efforts in this direction will face very great difficulties; that the results will be disappointing to those who believe in the possibility of rapid economic and social advances for the Aboriginal community. But this kind of effort has the best chance of winning Aboriginal support, of leading towards reconciliation and increased *rapport* between government and Aborigines.

The establishment of equal opportunity for Aborigines demands that it be planned as an integral part of national 'development', to the extent that no plans for economic advance exclude consideration of existing Aboriginal claims and needs, even at the cost of slowing down the rate of material development and profit. In some parts of Australia, cultural differences can still be used to justify special restrictive laws, different wage levels, denial of social service benefits, and administrative means to restrict Aboriginal mobility, spatial and social. In addition, there is *de facto* segregation in housing, schooling, and location of services. The direction and nature of Aboriginal and non-Aboriginal social change will continue to be influenced by such circumstances. Government has to be courageous enough to overcome this *vis inertia* and to confront prejudice at the local level, for instance by encouraging Aborigines to flock to the towns and other growing points, and by doing what it can to support their organisations and to strengthen the Aboriginal case.

Culture is largely the response to circumstances. There has to be a high priority given to changes in the basic circumstances. This has been important enough for the greatest of the democracies (and in many ways the most courageously democratic) to have taken a stand on the necessity of spatial integration, and of integration of services. The 'trouble' which has followed illustrates the difficulties facing a democracy marked by long-standing prejudices and perhaps the strength of resistances which have delayed or frustrated change. There is no easy way ahead in Australia either, yet the longer such measures are delayed the more trouble there will be.

We all tend to be entranced with the idea of inevitable 'progress'. But in a fast changing economy the distance between the Aboriginal and the other Australian could easily be increased; in fact, there is a real danger that it will be. Even if the lot of the Aboriginal improves, it is in the failure to decrease this distance, while at the same time the welfare and expectations of the Aboriginal are rising, that the possibility of effective dissidence lies. Here again we have the example of the situation in the United States, where the Negro is certainly far better off than he used to be. Whatever the chances are for a reconciliation in Australia, they can best be used by Aboriginal decision making and by provision of assistance on request.

The assimilation policy, at least as attempted in practice, has involved a too facile assumption that training and education of individuals will bring Aboriginal society quickly into equal participation in the national life and economy, making its members effective in the use of national institutions for their own purposes (or, as there is good evidence to show, the assumption has rather been that they will become effective in using these institutions in ways approved by the governments). But equal opportunity cannot come from programs which ignore the existence of a resentful, sceptical, Aboriginal community whose members widely share a conviction of government injustice and bad faith.

This is not to question the need for training and education, but rather to suggest a way of making efforts in this direction more effective. The facilities and the money are now well within the reach of a wealthy Australia. The questioning of Aboriginal capacity may be safely dismissed as racist nonsense. The real barrier in education (if we ignore for the moment the widespread prejudice which is the basic reason for concern with a 'problem') is not in the area of educational techniques, as some classroom educators are prone to assume, but in that of motivation. In this kind of background, 'motivation' and 'hope' are almost synonymous.

The basis for hope must be conviction that Aborigines can do something for themselves: that there is point in having spokesmen and defining what they want. Without a new basis for hope, attitudes must harden even more, with increasing populations in the economically marginal areas of the pastoral stations, missions, government settlements, and the 'fringe' non-suburbs of the towns; with the continued passing of the cosmetically favoured few out of frustrated Aboriginal communities; and with a probably increasing tendency to escape from rural poverty into the big cities. If we can do no better than this, the increased opportunities for education will mainly produce more articulate expressions of frustration and resentment.

Aboriginal companies could be flexible and multi-purposed, and could be so utilised that Aboriginal leaders and spokesmen could confront and negotiate with government at all levels—local, State, and Commonwealth. The very effort to promote them involves an attempt at reconciliation. They could provide the means of getting real property and financial resources into control of Aboriginal organisations and into individual Aboriginal hands. They could be used to increase the economic strength of Aboriginal communities, especially in the settled areas, where reparation by restoration of land taken long ago has been rendered irrelevant by economic and social changes. But reparation makes a direct appeal to Aborigines and others emotionally involved. A new Aboriginal body offers the best prospect of converting demands into realistic programs. Nothing seems to me so adaptable to different circumstances and therefore so suitable for a national policy. Innovation is obviously required; and there are few guides for one who has to propose it.

One advantage of a company organisation is that it contains within itself the basis for progressive amalgamation into more extensive corporate bodies. The total organisation can be loose or rigid, according to needs and possibilities, including big companies and small ones. It does not seem too much to hope that in time there could be two or three or even one large Aboriginal corporate body, made up of many others, to bring special pressures to bear on a State government.

I return to my assertion that this is a political problem, but one deeply rooted in Australian history. It cannot be solved by the offer of increased material welfare alone. If there is not to be continuing dialogue, the conflict of interests will be expressed in other, more uncomfortable, ways.

What the Aboriginal will demand as a 'right' will often conflict with what others regard as a 'right', in a whole range of situations. There is the conflict between a 'right' based on prior occupation, in the last frontier regions, and a 'right' based on the terms of an unexpired lease. There is conflict of 'rights' between the Aboriginal family claiming to live in town and the non-Aboriginal householder who assumes that he may use political pressure to keep that family out of his street. To deal with such political issues, Aboriginal organisations require strength in negotiation, for conflict between Aboriginal and other vested interests, and for support of the central against local government. Central government must win, and must be able to depend on Aboriginal support on major issues.

It is admittedly risky to generalise so widely. But policies have to be based on generalising that is as informed as possible. The safest principle is not necessarily that which requires detailed special studies of each Aboriginal group. A far safer basis for policy making is what is common to all men, not what is peculiar to certain groups, for basically the special attitudes and reactions are what one would expect from any human groups with similar histories and in similar circumstances. The studies most urgently required are inter-disciplinary, multi-focused, and regional —of the Aborigines, the whites, the economic potential, and the social and political factors which maintain the current adjustment. The delegation of decision making to formal procedures approved and organised by dissident and opposed groups, the readiness to maintain a running discussion, either to give help as requested or to refuse it with explanation, is by no means revolutionary policy. It is revolutionary only in the Aboriginal context. The safest political assumption in the end is that all citizens require certain basic 'goods' (material, social, or what have you); and that there cannot safely be people who cannot aspire to these 'goods' except in the deprived caricatures of the caste group. The Aboriginal association-to-company offers hope and establishes the means whereby the group may change according to its own laws. These are no less binding on members if they are mainly 'inmate' traditions or based on a habitual rejection of what the Australian establishment or officialdom appear to want of Aborigines. (There is no doubt that some groups have deliberately set out to scandalise the local community. I have seen first-hand evidence which, as far as my imagination could stretch, could be explained in no other way.)

What I have argued for is not a specially complex operation. It is concerned with social changes which are enormously complex, but it involves respect for the competence and motives of those whose decisions it is hoped to influence. In a sense, it is the simplest way towards equality, which would have seemed impossible two decades ago, but which to an increasing number of Australians, and especially to the young, is 'natural'.

There seems little doubt that Aborigines, like others living in, or in contact with, an egalitarian and materialistic society, have come to accept its standards for basic needs, that they will demand opportunities for equality and back the demand with increasing pressure, and that they will eventually organise in a realistic way to get them. It seems logical to assume that this is an inevitable development. What I have suggested is, I hope, a constructive clearing of the way for Aboriginal leadership and followers to organise within the law before other ways appear to be more realistic, and for government to establish a constructive *rapport*.

This rapidly increasing group of Australians is a largely undeveloped market and work force and, possibly, a source for unique cultural stimulus, which might enable the rest of us to see, in ways new to us, what this continent has to offer. Current changes in education, health, housing, wages, conditions of employment, and the like all indicate, even where they have only begun, a new honesty of purpose in governments. They will be more effective with Aboriginal decision making, participation in planning and administration, and responsibility. Without such participation, the trend may well be continually to draw off from the groups the potential leaders, leaving the same politically disorganised but numerically increasing communities behind. The kind of organisation I suggest seems to me essential to counteract and offset prejudice. Efficient operations by Aborigines, with government backing, will provide the best kind of education in race relations.

So the slogan for a national policy might well be 'Aboriginal initiative, and assistance on request'. Variations in local tactics and priorities should arise from expressed wants and needs. Priorities would be fixed by agreement with the association or company—not by accepting official estimates of what is required. Instead of being aimed at some abstract target like 'assimilation', programs may be relevant to actual needs. This avoids the exercise of outlining some comprehensive Utopian dream and seeking to adapt plans, conceived by assuming the end result, to very variable conditions. Those who work in technical assistance have learned this lesson. Why cannot it be applied within Australia?

The administrative approach, the philosophy, and the techniques will be worth nothing without a high priority, reflected both in the skills devoted to the work and the finance allocated to it. The reasons for high priority given to migration justify at least equal priority for measures to promote acceptance and effective citizenship of the Aboriginal. The same reasons, social and economic, would support the same priority both for the policy as a whole and for the essential prerequisites to its operation— health, housing, education, and the rest. Perhaps even higher priorities will be needed, for the hurt from decades of derogation will be as difficult to erase from Aboriginal memory as the habit of derision from the traditions of the majority. Here is a field for statesmanship, and for government to lead public opinion—not to defer to it. The initial cost will include political conflict.

The most serious criticism of this approach has come to me from those who maintain the need for very different priorities. One whose capacity I respect has maintained that the position of Aboriginal housing is so desperate that nothing else should be attempted until at least the worst-housed families are safely established in reasonable dwellings. If this were merely a matter of priorities, for building materials, finance, labour, and if necessary resumption of suitable land in or as extensions to established towns, I would agree. But there are many other matters which have to be settled in the process of getting people into housing; and they are essentially political matters. 'Who gets what, how, and when' remains the basic question. Who decides, in any one area, what people move into the new homes? Only some method of delegation of decisions like these to group organisation will avoid the new houses being treated like the houses made available in many areas in the past; for the protest will go on. In any case, the delegation of the decision is the quickest way to get firm decisions made, for the method of making them is likely to be *legitimate* from the point of view of the group and likely to appeal to the greatest number as the fairest. No time has to be lost at all. Housing becomes a multi-focused project, with the building authority pushing ahead with building, while the relevant agency of the central government acts well ahead of the building program, so that houses are allocated well ahead of completion. Here is an immediate task on which a new Aboriginal organisation may cut its teeth while the government agency learns the techniques of working with communities.

The change I have urged must be a decisive one, because it involves an abdication of power to interfere more deeply in Aboriginal lives than in others. It probably involves major re-staffing and re-training for government officers, since the previous types of experience, considered in themselves, would probably form a disqualification for the kind of work I have outlined. Without this, a new policy is in danger of becoming a new form of words which justify what is done; and what is done may be mainly what has always been done—which happened in many places with the assimilation policy.

### THE TACTICS

Such general principles may be applied in many different ways. We have already referred to the South Australian Aboriginal Lands Trust, the body corporate in which has been vested all Aboriginal reserves in the State, subject to the agreement of the Aboriginal Reserve Council in the case of each reserve. Especially where assets used for Aboriginal administration include very large areas, which are occupied by people who are not yet knowledgeable in the defence of rights, this approach of vesting all assets in one corporate body has definite advantages. Something like this will probably be used in the 'colonial' regions when governments decide to transfer these property rights to Aboriginal ownership. In my opinion, the plan would be more flexible if the Reserve Councils were also moving towards incorporation as companies. This would make it unnecessary to set up special additional organisations (such as co-operatives) for economic and other purposes and would limit the demand on leadership by limiting the number of organisations.

An excellent example of tactics applying these principles was set by the Commonwealth Department of the Interior, in the case of Wreck Bay Aboriginal Station. The department had not been committed to any methods of Aboriginal administration, and in default of tradition it followed the dictates of common sense. The station, a few miles from the Naval College at Jervis Bay, was in the Australian Capital Territory, but had been administered up until November 1965 (when it ceased to be a reserve) by the New South Wales Aborigines Welfare Board. The standard of housing was higher than on Board stations elsewhere, and the manager had more money to spend. The special status of Wreck Bay probably inhibited the Board from using it (as Wallaga Lake, farther south, was used) as a place to concentrate widows, deserted wives, and others in specially vulnerable situations.

In 1964 the Department of the Interior first broached the matter of making Wreck Bay an open village, proposing that homes which fell vacant might be used by its non-Aboriginal employees in the area. This led to protests from organisations working for Aboriginal advancement. In August the *Canberra Times* referred to rumours that the Aborigines were to be evicted. In April 1965, at a meeting of the Federal Council for Aboriginal Advancement, the suspicion was expressed that this beautiful coastal site, ideal for recreation, was to be thrown open to real estate interests.

But the department, probably unaware of the extent of the innovation, sent senior officers to ask the people what they wanted. This, and some other advice, induced some of the people to organise, to give answers, and to negotiate for their interests. By June 1965 there was a Progress Association, although the leadership pattern had by no means been firmly established. But the people had been assured that there would not be evictions to make way for other settlers. A special problem was arrears in rents, in the typical New South Wales pattern, and this was to be the subject of much discussion between the parties. Naturally those who had always paid, and those who had almost always paid, had different views from those who were years in arrears. But the discussion did move on to vital issues of how the houses might be purchased. An Aboriginal suggestion that rent arrears be forgotten was rejected.

The status of these people had been defined, as late as 1954, on the usual basis of degrees of descent, special restrictions applying to persons of half-Aboriginal descent or more domiciled in the A.C.T., or merely visiting there.[1] They could be expelled from the Territory or directed by a court to live on a reserve. (Perhaps this is why there are fringe-dwelling Aborigines in Yass, but none in Canberra.) But this ordinance was repealed in 1965, and since then there has been neither an Aboriginal category of persons nor reserves. So far no disaster has occurred to those deprived of the advantages of this legislation, which is a reminder that an obvious step in a new policy must be repeal of all laws of this type.

The Department of the Interior had two advantages—it had no tradition of Aboriginal administration, and it was not a welfare authority recognised by Aborigines. It also had local employment to offer, in its Parks and Gardens, and Forestry branches. These soon provided permanent work for a number of the men, which provided a new kind of security and must have had its effect on attitudes.

The earlier position had been especially absurd in that the ordinance had retained supply of liquor as an offence, after the drinking restrictions had been removed in New South Wales. Moreover, many of the residents did not fall within the racial categories as defined in the ordinance.

What more should be done? Is it enough to open up a way to comparative security as labourers, some of whom would purchase their houses? If it is enough to have a few more people secure in a rather out-of-the-way spot, and dependent mainly on labouring work in the vicinity, there was no need for further planning. Had there been a national policy of the kind I have advocated, here was a real opportunity to build a new Aboriginal organisation, by offering to vest houses and long leasehold tenure of the Wreck Bay land in a Wreck Bay Aboriginal company, with a period of years allowed for people to make up their minds. Discussion of conditions for loans, management, and the like might have resulted in a completely different plan. But some further advances could at least have been discussed. The need for this was probably disguised by the pleasantness of the location and the *comparative* comfort

[1] A.C.T. Aborigines Welfare Ordinance 1954, section 3.

of the families. (They were very well housed 'for Aborigines'.) Had this been closer to the town of Nowra, which must offer the main hope of additional employment, the need for some kind of permanent investment in this group would have been more obvious. Land and a plan for tourism, with the rights for certain kinds of development (for instance a motel and boat-house) might have made an important difference to hope. It would have meant the offer of something more than a safe retreat from a generally hostile majority.

A national strategy applied here on the lines I have suggested would have involved the possibility of specialist advice and financial assistance from government sources for development of the site if and when the people wanted it. Tourism in this area there will certainly be; so why not enable Aborigines already there to develop a resort like that which the Makah Indians now manage at Neah Bay, on the extreme north-western coast of the United States? The special interest in things Aboriginal could well make this place uniquely attractive to the increasing flow of tourists from Sydney and Canberra.

It may be that what I have suggested in this case is not economically feasible, thus indicating the need for regional and local surveys as an initial step. Needless to say, there is point in employing Aborigines as far as possible in any such surveys; and in smaller ones, there is good reason for an Aboriginal community to be helped to survey its own needs.

The common sense displayed at Wreck Bay may be contrasted with the many situations where a Welfare Board or State department is both involved in the assimilation effort and discharges the role of landlord. The quickest way out of this impossible situation is to transfer responsibility for the collection of rents to some organisation of the group; to force the group as a whole to work out logical arrangements, internalise conflicts within the group, and reduce the level of tension between it and the government agencies. Thus the initial tactics employed in establishing new institutions may well be concerned with rationalising the relationship of landlord and Aboriginal tenant.

A most instructive indication of where the present arrangements may lead is to be seen in the contrast between the old reserve at La Perouse, Sydney, and the areas adjacent to it. In 1965 even the garbage from the reserve seemed, from what remained, to be disposed of in some special way, the electric power to be specially arranged, and the houses to be comparable with many on country reserves. The conditions were then a startling indication of an increasing gulf between living standards within and outside Aboriginal communities. They also contrasted with those of

Aboriginal families who were being established in homes in suburbs all
over the metropolis, many of them through the assistance of the Housing
Commission. If no more were needed than to scatter the La Perouse
families through the community, the solution would be to liquidate the
reserve and offer the alternative house somewhere else—which is precisely
what has been tried for some time, with the disappointing result that
people so moved against their real wishes refuse to co-operate, will not
pay rent—and the whole unhappy business starts again.

There being no short cuts, then, the tactics must avoid any continuation of official assessments of who is 'suitable' to live where: no other
persons have to be so assessed. The government has to ignore the resistance
of local councils and of those who are concerned about real estate values,
and the best way to confront such objections is by strengthening the
hand of the Aborigines. Their own organisation might allot any priorities
as between members for housing, and at the same time give the support
needed to groups of families which are setting themselves up in towns.
The united pressure group can be effective where the dispersed families
divided among themselves are not.

The group organisation should eventually deal with the normal
providing authority directly—in this case, the Housing Commission. It
should in this have new strength from a new unity in organisation. But
the necessary financial guarantees could well be underwritten by a special
government-backed credit agency. The individual Aboriginal's lack of
credit is replaced by the institution with credit guaranteed. If the houses
are being purchased by the company, the company must collect the rents
or arrange the sales on terms, whichever it decides.

In the case of a more isolated station like Murrin Bridge, the disciplinary
functions which managers tried to execute would pass to the organisation.
People would have the option of establishing internal discipline or of living
with the consequences. Responsibility for the light, power, water, and other
services should of course rest with the shire; but the houses and land could
easily be vested in the company when organised, and in a trust in the
interim, so that the shire council would have a guaranteed body with which
to deal for rates. The interim association and the eventual company in such
a place would have a special function which in 1964 the manager was
trying to perform—establishing contacts with employers in the adjacent
towns and district and arranging for reception of those who wished to
try their luck in Sydney. The link with another corporate body like the
Foundation for Aboriginal Affairs in the metropolis would be of obvious
value. At this stage urbanisation into the metropolis is still somewhat

experimental, the unsuccessful returning to their areas of origin, and possibly trying again later. Aboriginal companies, and especially an organisation like the Foundation, could well be subsidised to establish hotels or other transient accommodation, for *all* persons who need cheap accommodation, but especially to bring pressure to bear on hotels which refuse to accept Aborigines.

Aboriginal companies in strategic areas like the capital cities, where all the frustrations of the rural areas come to a head, have an especially important part to play in helping persons in remote and economically hopeless situations to go elsewhere at will. Such a role tends towards linking up these organisations into State-wide and nation-wide pressure groups. Even if what is now spent by Aboriginal authorities on rail fares, administration involved with reception and accommodation, employment assistance, and other assistance to Aborigines on the move were to be transferred to Aboriginal corporate bodies, with the Aboriginal having the same recourse as others to the general welfare authorities, it is possible that at least as much would be achieved for the money; and the element of official control would be eliminated. This role of the company in facilitating mobility is especially relevant to the current situation in the 'colonial' areas, where the restrictions on movements have been removed (except for Queensland), but where probably many people do not yet realise any difference in their situations.

I can only suggest the range of tactical situations. It is possible to envisage a very early contract between a government agency and a company, perhaps formed for the purpose, for the company to attempt (with suitable assistance on request) to survey the needs and the problems of its members as the members see them. This might leave an administration less dependent on the occasional anthropological expert or on the informed or other guesses of its own officers. It would be a revolutionary step. Such a survey could begin with the basic things—age and sex of the population, housing and housing needs, earnings, crime and its causes, alcoholism, unemployment, qualifications for employment, youth and recreational needs—the list could easily be extended. Finance could be made available to pay for the survey; and if the women and children could be associated in such an effort, so much the more educational gain.

It is not impossible that we will see companies managing transit hostels, boarding houses, and hotels, clubs and sporting teams; acting as the repositories of interim property rights on old stations and settlements, as purchasing agencies and guarantors for both private firms and government stores; arranging transport for seasonal work, funerals, and social occasions; discussing with employers or contractors the rationalisation of movements and transport in seasonal work, where the relevant trade union is not interested; or acting as guarantors for the purchase of washing machines and furniture. They could operate as savings and loan societies, or in support of them, according to circumstances; establish and maintain, in the interests of members and others, liaison with the social service departments and agencies, the Commonwealth Employment Service, voluntary bodies interested in Aboriginal affairs, research workers and universities, schools and technical colleges. The involvement of mothers in pre-school training, perhaps on the model of the New Zealand scheme for Maori children, could be facilitated, along with parents' organisations interested in schooling. A company could financially guarantee a member in whom it had confidence; it could be the means whereby the Aboriginal members get the full benefit of hire purchase arrangements. A company could be, in most cases would have to be, guaranteed by government to some degree: it could then be a recipient for bank and other loans. A company could hire lawyers for criminal or civil cases in which a member became involved. That this is a real issue may be illustrated by the willingness to do so of some private persons concerned with civil rights and of some local organisations for Aboriginal advancement. It could enter into contracts of employment, as the Gurindji wished to do with neighbouring stations.

A most important field in which companies might become involved is political and legal action in those areas of decision making where Aborigines have long claimed and, in their commonly held view, been denied special rights; or where the rights, having been recognised earlier, may have been lost by some legal change. Have the people long constrained to live on stations or reserves acquired any special rights in equity or law to remain there? What political or legal action may be taken to advance claims based on prior occupation? Where a group has occupied shacks on *de facto* permissive occupancy on Crown land or town common, have its members acquired any rights of further occupancy? How may the law or political pressure be used to prevent the destruction of a shack under health regulations where there is no alternative accommodation? How may the rights of access to natural waters on pastoral leases be safeguarded through the changes which are now in train? Political and legal action both become possible. An organised group is stronger in efforts to get itself heard, as the Yirrkala group did.

The effort to make such companies work effectively involves adult education with immediate relevance and appeal for the people. The association-company offers scope for employment of young people who complete secondary and higher education; while the effort to develop it involves the most effective form of adult education, with an outlet in political and other action. Moreover, the company could supplement the remedial education to be undertaken by education departments. For youths and young adults who have few or no skills, there would be no point in establishing separate training facilities for courses already given elsewhere. But there would be point in having institutions in some areas organised like the folk high schools of Denmark, which made such a contribution to economic development by affecting motivation. This was achieved by concentrating not on technical processes but on the background of Danish culture and history. There is no reason why the same kind of approach should not affect Aboriginal motivation. This could well be the best use for the isolated stations and settlements with education as the main industry—not only for Aborigines but also for others who want to learn. Here would be a challenge to scholars to teach the history of this country without omitting the Aboriginal role and interest. There will inevitably come a demand for Aboriginal studies for Aborigines—which poses the problem of an Aboriginal political mythology. 'Learn and Earn' schemes on the United States pattern, with those formerly unemployed being paid for learning new types of work, would present many problems, especially in view of trade union attitudes to re-training schemes. But the Aboriginal association or company would play an essential part in local implementation.

One can only suggest what the local tactics might include. A company is a very flexible institution, adaptable to the requirements of local situations. Its functioning allows the part-Aboriginal with his problem of identity to develop the idea that he is a member of a special group, while offering both a career and human dignity. Those who feel that they are Aborigines may join; those who want to forget their Aboriginal descent will not. This will tend to solve the awkward problem of legal definition, of who is entitled to special help from governments.

Here too is an entity which can be dealt with by scholars, businessmen, and others who have special business with Aborigines. They may find out whether they are welcome from the people's spokesmen, where the community is still an isolated one, without anxious public servants hovering round the meeting. Members of Aboriginal companies will have increased chances of courteous and fair service from public bodies where the officer knows that there is an articulate organisation in the background.

## POLICY FORMULATION AND ADMINISTRATION

A national policy seems to require administrative organisation on the national scale. The acquisition by the Commonwealth, by Referendum in 1967, of a concurrent power to legislate in Aboriginal affairs appears to make it easier to work towards such organisation. Ideally, and regarded purely from the point of view of administrative simplicity and financing, this should, I think, be in the hands of the Commonwealth Government. The 1967 Referendum indicated how quickly constitutional barriers may be removed. Fears of misuse by the Commonwealth of its power to legislate 'for the people of any race . . . for whom it is deemed necessary to make special laws', in section 51 (xxvi) of the Constitution, if the words 'other than the Aboriginal race in any State' ceased to qualify the phrase 'people of any race', were typical legalistic ones. A government which would misuse deliberately a constitutional power would hardly respect a constitutional restriction.[2] Governments will generally find ways to do what they want, provided that what they want is politically possible. But while the Commonwealth now has a concurrent power, the political and administrative obstacles to complete Commonwealth control of Aboriginal affairs seem to make it unlikely for some time to come. There is the jealous defence of State rights; nor can Aboriginal affairs be separated out nicely from many other matters, which remain with the States. Among these, and of great importance in Aboriginal affairs, are education, housing, local government, and land tenure within the States. Politically, any move to override the State governments would serve mainly to

[2] The possible dangers in removing the phrase were stated by Sir Robert Menzies, then Prime Minister, in the House, in April 1965. He pointed out that in the historical context the phrase was meant to exclude Aboriginal citizens from action which might be taken in other cases. 'I have no doubt whatever that this provision in the Constitution was designed having regard to conditions that existed at that time and the possibility of having to make a special law dealing with, for example, kanaka labourers—perhaps a special law to deport them from the country or to confine them to some particular area . . . Therefore the framers of the Constitution inserted this provision, but they left out the aboriginal race because they did not want to discriminate against the people of the aboriginal race. All we have to do now is to cross out this reference "other than the aboriginal race" and we confer on this Parliament a power to make a special law which relates to Aborigines and to no other people . . . I wonder what limitations will be on that . . . power. Would this enable the Parliament to set up a separate body of industrial laws relating to Aborigines or some other kind of law—health laws, quarantine laws or laws under any of the other powers of the Parliament?' (C.P.D. (H. of R.), 1965, vol. 45, pp. 533-4.) The point is subtle and the doubt remains. But does it not simply mean that the Commonwealth now has concurrent powers in an area where the States have exercised sovereign powers, and exercised them to do all the things, except deportation, to which Sir Robert referred?

confuse the issues. Clearly, then, we have to plan for joint action by Commonwealth and States.

Arguments for a continuous dialogue between governments and Aboriginal communities, for incorporation of communities where possible, and for financial pump-priming of Aboriginal activities, along with necessary advisory services to them, if accepted, involve working out a special kind of administrative structure. Central to this would be the necessity to maintain a special interest in all the parliaments concerned. From time to time, and in response to political pressures of the moment, Select Committees have been established to make inquiries and reports. There is a long list of these reports, some of which have resulted in legislative changes.

The history of the Standing Committees in Australia has not been very encouraging. Nonetheless, in the first stage of working towards a new policy especially, there is a special need for continuous and public discussion of Aboriginal affairs. It would help to promote this if a Standing Committee of the Commonwealth Parliament invited evidence and recommendations from all over the nation, from individuals and from organisations. Publication of the resultant parliamentary papers, and the presence of the press at the discussions, would help to increase general knowledge of the issues and public awareness. If the State parliaments also established Standing Committees, so much the better, especially if they were to operate in the way suggested here—suggested in the full knowledge that this is far more in the United States tradition than in the Australian.

The essential function of such bodies, of course, is to seek continuously the best policy, and to frame legislation for consideration of the parties and parliaments. It is politically unreal to hope that in any such Standing Committee there could develop a genuine bi-partisan approach to policy and legislation. Suppose, for instance, there is a move to place the control of real assets in the hands of Aboriginal groups. There is no known important economic asset in the whole country in which nobody has an interest; and to protect those interests there will be political action of some kind. But at least the Standing Committee can provide an airing in public of issues involved. Another reason for Standing Committees in all parliaments (and the Legislative Council of the Northern Territory might well be included) is that there is much legislation not obviously concerned with Aboriginal affairs but affecting Aborigines in special ways. Standing Committees could look at all legislation with this special interest in mind.

In 1967 the Prime Minister announced that the Commonwealth had assumed a co-ordinating role and that he proposed to set up a new Office of Aboriginal Affairs in his own Department. Mr Holt's death may have been the reason for making Aboriginal affairs an additional responsibility of the Minister for Social Services. The Council for Aboriginal Affairs, established by Mr Holt, appeared still to be an advisory body with no precise channel for advice to the States. But a considerable gain was the removal of policy formation from the Department of Territories and into a more flexible type of organisation. Probably the Minister concerned with Aboriginal affairs should chair the Standing Committee in each parliament. The Council would seem to be well constituted to advise such a Committee of the House of Representatives, and the new Office of Aboriginal Affairs, whose Director is executive member of the Council, seems well constituted to service it.

There are important differences between the approach of other States and that of Queensland. There is agreement at the verbal level of proclaimed policy, but the implications of Queensland legislation are very different from those in any State, though vestiges of old restrictions remain in Western Australia. No doubt this will change in time; but in the meantime injustice is being maintained (as any careful study of the Queensland Aboriginal legislation will indicate). There would be a case for Commonwealth intervention on an issue which may yet have international repercussions, but it would be much better for a Standing Committee of the Queensland Parliament to make a comparative study of all Aboriginal legislation as a prelude to discussions with the Commonwealth. In fact, such studies would be necessary for all Standing Committees, as a means towards an agreed basis for a national policy.

One important function of the Office of Aboriginal Affairs should be the continuous collation of information for the Commonwealth Parliamentary Standing Committee. Perhaps an arrangement could be made for it to service all the parliaments in this way. To assist it, one tentative suggestion is a panel of expert advisers, including Aborigines who have come to prominence in Aboriginal affairs, not, perhaps, Aborigines only, as yet, but the time may soon come for that. The Office must employ Aborigines.

What should be the respective roles of Commonwealth and State governments? It seems clear that so long as the present Commonwealth-States financial arrangements are maintained, the main source of additional financial assistance to Aboriginal groups must be the Commonwealth. For administrative simplicity, and for the working out of detailed procedures, I think that requests for Commonwealth assistance from particular Aboriginal companies should pass from them, through such Aboriginal corporate bodies as might be formed, by combining companies, to the Office of Aboriginal Affairs. They could well be examined (with evidence, or through visits) by the members of the Commonwealth Parliamentary Standing Committee. To acknowledge the important role of the relevant State, its Parliament could be represented by the chairman, or all members, of its own Parliamentary Standing Committee. The Commonwealth, however, would be only one source of help. For better housing, health, and other services which the State provides for its citizens, the Aboriginal group naturally should go to the State government. This suggests a possible line of division as between Commonwealth and State governments. It is obviously preferable for Aborigines to share common services with others, and to share with others in the States such services as the State (or the Northern Territory) provides. Perhaps the formula could be that where the request from an Aboriginal group involves special additional costs, the source should be the Commonwealth. This could also well apply for any interim special assistance, such as temporary housing, to hold the situation until the normal State service can be provided.

Any new kind of service, special loan, grant, or other assistance which the State does not already provide to all citizens should probably be provided or refused by the Commonwealth (and provided or refused on request after discussion with the organisation which makes the request). This arrangement would make possible the working out of defined fields for Commonwealth and State in each case. The Aboriginal group would be advised as to the proper destination of its requests. Where there is doubt, reference can be made to the Standing Committee of the State Parliament through the State government's organisation for Aboriginal affairs, or to the responsible Minister.

Obviously such a scheme would involve very different roles for the State departments and boards concerned now with Aboriginal affairs, but these are roles towards which most of them are moving. Upon them must fall the tasks involved in the development of Aboriginal organisations. This will involve a considerable recruiting and re-training task, which the Commonwealth might well subsidise further than it does now. (At the present time it provides training for work in Aboriginal affairs at the Australian School of Pacific Administration, not only for officers of the Northern Territory but also for State officers sent by their governments. By 1967 South Australia was the only State to have sent officers, mainly it seems because of costs involved.) Techniques resembling those of community development will be necessary in the initial stages; and these involve many radical departures from past methods of field work.

Eventually, Aboriginal corporations should formulate requests to Standing Committees of the parliaments in sophisticated ways. They could be assisted, in requests to State Standing Committees, by the relevant departments or boards concerned with Aboriginal affairs; which hould, it is suggested, perform the same servicing function for the Standing Committee of the State Parliament as that proposed for the Commonwealth Office of Aboriginal Affairs in relation to the Standing Committee of the Commonwealth Parliament. It is unrealistic to expect that this kind of sophisticated action would develop quickly. There could be a long period during which many of the special services to individuals will have to be maintained, though as far as possible these should be provided by the departments which provide them for other citizens.

A Standing Committee cannot, of course, make a financial allocation, but policies may only be realistically constructed and related to changing needs by the continual involvement of policy makers in the facts to be dealt with. The Standing Committee might well make recommendations to the Minister who is its chairman, and who is responsible to Cabinet for the expenditure. It might recommend priorities within the financial allocation, although the Minister, who is responsible, must decide them.

There will be an interim period, which, to take the pessimistic view, will last indefinitely, with only a few Aboriginal companies really effective in presenting their requests. Until the Standing Committee in a State can have advice from representative bodies of Aborigines, it must depend on that of experts and others, including Aborigines, who play a prominent part in Aboriginal affairs. It may not be necessary to formalise the process by establishing consultative committees in the States. Perhaps the situation remains more flexible where consultation does not become the prerogative of the few recognised as expert at a particular stage and where the way is more obviously open for the representatives of the Aboriginal companies to come forward.

But there are many ways of dealing with the problems of consultation and policy making: and it is highly improbable that this indication of what might be done will prove prophetic. All I am concerned with here is to demonstrate that there will be no special hindrance to co-ordinated national policies arising from the kind of basic organisations I have been advocating. I argue only for the principles, not the outline of a super-structure; but also I argue that an effective superstructure is possible.

The basic principle should be *assistance on request*. The long-term objectives should include a nation-wide association of Aboriginal corporate bodies, to negotiate with the Commonwealth government.

CONCLUSION

The effect on attitudes and comparative status, and on the comparative political and economic situations of the races, of the methods by which control was extended, and of the failure to recognise any land areas or rights other than those which a British subject could claim, while hard to assess, must have been profound. There is the obvious effect on Aboriginal attitudes, especially where, as on cattle properties in Western Australia and the Northern Territory, the people may still be living in their own 'country'. In some such situations, the most recent cases of frontier violence will be within living memory. For all of them, violence inevitably forms part of the folklore, for such treatment will be part of the traditions of persons now living whose ancestors suffered several generations ago. I know from personal experience that this background of tradition remains in the minds of part-Aborigines even in the south of New South Wales, and is likely to come into discussion under the influence of strong emotion. There will be a continual renewal, both from the increasing contact with full-bloods in 'colonial' Australia as the part-Aborigines of the south seek there the identity they have been denied in white Australia and from the proliferating voluntary bodies, with non-Aborigines prominent in the discussion of old wrongs.

Perhaps the effect on the whites had been almost as profound and significant. How far the century and a half of contempt, and of treating Aborigines as members of a lower order, contributed to the unthinking assumptions in successive generations about the relationship of skin colour to status, and so to the foundations of the White Australia Policy, I am not competent to say. But it must have been significant. And the concept of White Australia in turn made it more certain that equality would be difficult even for the part-Aboriginal—in some ways especially for him, since it was so easily assumed from his often miserable condition that he had inherited the 'worst of both races'.

The frontier situations, as the story is becoming better known, provide a special kind of spur to the consciences of those who have concerned themselves in 'Aboriginal advancement' groups which in the last decade have proliferated all over the country. So much of what happened was not the work of 'bad men' like the bushrangers, who defied the government, but of the responsible agents of government, which long accorded a very low priority to Aboriginal life and welfare. There is an almost inexhaustible fund of injustices which can be used to attack current governments. One reaction, understandably enough, is to demand reparation, often including reparation to the descendants of people who were dispossessed over a century ago.

Emotional responses to this past often lead members of voluntary bodies and organisations for Aboriginal advancement so to distrust the official agencies, so far to read ill intent into everything attempted by government, as to see nothing good in any plan; and to read into current plans and decisions the worst motives of the past. This is inevitable for Aborigines; perhaps dangerously destructive for others. The Aboriginal is often led into the hopelessness of withdrawal and distrust by his traditions about government, tempted to refuse to commit himself to action for the betterment of himself and others, and to question Aboriginal leadership as the 'front' of a manipulating white man's establishment. A consequence of these types of reaction has been that Aboriginal affairs especially have offered the chance of expatiation for many non-Aborigines with psychological problems of their own. The Aboriginal members of 'advancement' organisations have remained sceptical and withdrawn, educationally handicapped and inarticulate. The non-Aboriginal members have often had an arena for their politics, for the discharge of their frustrations, or for their ambition to dominate.

The neglect of this aspect of Australian history suggests some deep unease. Almost certainly, generations of Australian schoolchildren have gained an impression, from their school lessons in Australian history, that Australia is a place where very little ever happened. When one takes the Aboriginal out of the story of exploration, little remains but the geography of the route and the struggle to get from point to point on the map. When he is ignored in the story of the struggle for 'freedom', there is a false ring about it, with one lot of Britishers demanding rights from those 'at home'. It is doubtful that this kind of omission is merely a matter of neglect; it is certainly not due to lack of sources; and earlier historians of note, like Rusden, made enough of it. But the effect of this reticence, of course, has been that public education has avoided issues of this kind. This must have contributed to the absence of any considerable public interest or concern for so long.

Memories of old violence in themselves would not make reconciliation impossible. Aborigines could claim if not to have done their share, at least to have maintained an unbeatable intransigence to the time of reconciliation. In the meantime, what has happened since, and what is currently happening, with the daily manifestations of race prejudice from country towns in the south to pastoral stations in the north, continually prompts the Aboriginal to dig into the memories of old wrongs. Until he wins, within new institutions, the strength to challenge prejudice, he will be driven back to dwell on the story of dispossession. Current attitudes will be confirmed, not weakened. The stories of the past will play a part resembling that played by the story of slavery among the American Negroes: and recently given its most virulent re-interpretations. Is it so unlikely that the Australian situation may produce a book like the *Autobiography of Malcolm X*?

The end of the period of frontier expansion came without any real advance having been made in dealing with Aborigines in social groups. From beginning to end the matter was a most difficult one. It may be that what happened was inevitable, since the continued emphasis in the welfare programs which were undertaken was on changing the individual, considered outside the context of his social group, to make him a more effective British subject and Christian. Indigenous groups, divorced progressively from their 'country', continued to be atomised. Little thought was given to the provision of new opportunities for group cohesion in the missions and government stations. Where this did happen and leadership did develop, it had to be, in the whole authoritarian situation of such institutions, leadership against authority; it was therefore discounted as subversive.

The Aboriginal minority in 'settled' Australia was left, at the end of all this, in a situation more comparable with that of the American Negro, or the Metis of Canada, than with that of the Amerindian or the Maori. Today mainly of part-Aboriginal descent, members of this minority lack any real opportunity of advancing their interests except as participants in the cash economy and as members of the general Australian society. To offset the effects of individual prejudice, there has to be the kind of Aboriginal organisation which produces strength and confidence. Like the American Negro, the Aboriginal will obtain hitting power within the law or develop it outside the law. Organisation within the law, educational advance, economic gains, and leadership are all inextricably intertwined in a causal cycle. We arrive therefore at the seeming contradiction that to become an effective member of the Australian society the Aboriginal individual must find strength to stand on his own feet; and that he can find this only by developing organisations with others in like case, i.e. with other Aborigines—with people who believe with him that they are members of a special in-group with common interests.

I have been concerned in these recommendations to present a possible basis for an integrated policy, rather than to set out a list of what should be done, for integrated policy and philosophy generate their own changes, arising from progressive consideration involving those most concerned. If, for instance, we think of the position in legislation, it is obvious that all restrictive laws would be questioned; the logic of the policy suggested would involve their repeal. In the field of education, the demand and the requirements of the policy would again be equality—of opportunity and of services, so that the separate schools would be integrated except where there are genuine geographical barriers. The school syllabi would certainly be examined to make certain of a fair balance in the treatment of the Aboriginal themes. Teaching of history and social studies may require a careful reappraisal. Aboriginal studies which are realistic should probably be included in all primary schooling. This would be a small part of a total educational effort against the prejudice which has long formed an almost unacknowledged challenge to adult education bodies.

Over two decades ago Gunnar Myrdal, towards the end of *An American Dilemma*, gave a prophetic view of what was to come from the contradiction between the American Creed and the situation of Negro citizens. He then pleaded for innovation through realistic 'social engineering', which is concerned with the re-shaping of institutions. Perhaps Australian governments have begun to realise that past efforts to change the life of the Aboriginal have been mainly futile because they have been attempts directly to reshape people; and that the best chance of equality for the Aboriginal will come by making it possible for him to make his own adjustments through the establishment and use of free institutions.

# REFERENCES

## I. GOVERNMENT AND OFFICIAL PUBLICATIONS

### AUSTRALIA

COMMONWEALTH

*Aboriginal Welfare: Conference of Commonwealth and State Authorities, July, 1963.* Darwin, 1963.

*Aboriginal Welfare: Initial Conference of Commonwealth and States Aboriginal Authorities, April 1937.* Canberra, 1937.

BARNES, Hon. C.E., Minister for Territories. *Assimilation in Action: Progress.* Canberra, 1964.

Bureau of Census and Statistics. *Census of the Commonwealth of Australia, 30th June, 1961.* Canberra, 1962-5.

——. Official Year Book of the Commonwealth of Australia. No. 1- , 1901/7- . Canberra.

——. *Statistical Register of Western Australia, 1962.* Canberra, 1962.

Department of the Interior. *The Northern Territory of Australia: Commonwealth Government's Policy with respect to Aboriginals.* Canberra, 1939.

*Parliamentary Papers*, 1961-3.

Report from the Select Committee on Grievances of Yirrkala Aborigines, Arnhem Land Reserve. *C.P.P.* (H. of R.), vol. 4, 1962-3.

Report from the Select Committee on Voting Rights of Aborigines. *C.P.P.* (H. of R.), vol. 2, 1961.

NEW SOUTH WALES

Aborigines Protection Board (after 1940, Aborigines Welfare Board).
  Annual Report, 1883, *N.S.W.V. & P.*, vol. 11, 1883-4.
  Annual Report, 1915, ibid., vol. 2, 1916.
  Annual Report, 1933, ibid., vol. 3, 1934-5.
  Annual Report, 1935, ibid., vol. 3, 1935-6.
  Annual Report, 1936, ibid., vol. 1, 1936-7.
  Annual Report, 1938, ibid., 1941-2.
  Annual Report, 1939, ibid., 1941-2.
  Annual Report, 1940, ibid.

Annual Report, 1941, ibid.
Annual Report, 1944, ibid., vol. 2, 1945-6.
Annual Report, 1945, ibid.
Annual Report, 1948, ibid., vol. 3, 1948-49-50.
Annual Report, 1961, ibid., vol. 1, 1961-2.
Annual Report, 1962, ibid., 1962-63-64.
Annual Report, 1963, ibid.
Annual Report, 1964, ibid., 1965.
*Parliamentary Debates*, 1883-1963.
*Parliamentary Papers*, 1934-65.

QUEENSLAND
Director of Native Affairs.
Annual Report, 1945, *Q.P.P.*, 1945-6.
Annual Report, 1946, ibid., vol. 2, 1946.
Annual Report, 1947, ibid., 1947.
Annual Report, 1948, ibid., 1948-9.
*Parliamentary Debates*, 1884-1929.
*Parliamentary Papers*, 1859-96.
Report of the Special Committee enquiring into Legislation for the Promotion of the Well-Being of Aborigines and Torres Strait Islanders in Queensland, 1964. *Q.P.P.*, vol. 2, 1964-5.
Report of the Sub-Department of Aboriginal Affairs, 1929. *Q.P.P.*, vol. 1, 1929.
Report on the Aboriginals of Queensland by Archibald Meston to Home Secretary H. Tozer, *Q.V. & P.* (L.A.), vol. 4, 1896.

VICTORIA
Report from the Select Committee upon Protection to the Aborigines. *V.P.P.*, vol. 2, 1859-60.

WESTERN AUSTRALIA
Aborigines Department.
Annual Report, 1901, *W.A.P.P.*, vol. 2, 1901-2.
Annual Report, 1902, ibid., 1902.
Annual Report, 1903, ibid., 1903-4.
Chief Protector of Aborigines.
Annual Report, 1918, *W.A.P.P.*, vol. 1, 1919.
Annual Report, 1919, ibid., vol. 2, 1919.
Annual Report, 1935, ibid., 1935.
Commissioner of Native Affairs.
Annual Report, 1937, *W.A.P.P.*, vol. 1, 1938.
Annual Report, 1945, ibid., vol. 2, 1947.
Annual Report, 1949, ibid., 1951.
Annual Report, 1950, ibid.
*Parliamentary Debates*, 1936-8.
*Parliamentary Papers*, 1901-51.
Report of the Royal Commissioner appointed to Investigate, Report, and Advise upon Matters in relation to the Condition and Treatment of Aborigines. *W.A.P.P.*, vol. 1, 1935.

CANADA

Lagassé, Jean. *The People of Indian Ancestry in Manitoba*. Social and Economic Research Office, Department of Agriculture and Immigration, Winnipeg, 1959.

UNITED STATES

Department of Labor, Office of Planning and Research. *The Negro Family: The Case for National Action*. Washington, 1965.

## II. BOOKS AND ARTICLES

BALDWIN, James. *The Fire Next Time*. Harmondsworth, 1968.
BEASLEY, Pamela. 'The Aboriginal Household in Sydney'. In *Attitudes and Social Conditions*. Canberra, 1970.
BEAZLEY, K.E. *Dispossession and Disease—or Dignity?—Some Thoughts on Aboriginal Policy*. A.L.P. Provocative Pamphlet no. 115. Sydney, 1964.
BECKETT, Jeremy. 'Aboriginal Balladeer'. *The Australian*, 3 July 1965.
——. 'Aborigines, Alcohol and Assimilation'. In *Aborigines Now* (ed. Marie Reay). Sydney, 1964.
——. 'Aborigines Make Music'. *Quadrant*, vol. 2, no. 4, Spring 1958.
——. 'Kinship, Mobility and Community among Part-Aborigines in Rural Australia'. *International Journal of Comparative Sociology*, vol. 6, no. 1, March 1965.
——. 'The Land where the Crow Flies Backwards'. *Quadrant*, vol. 9, no. 4, July-August 1965.
BLEAKLEY, J.W. *The Aborigines of Australia*. Brisbane, 1961.

CALLEY, Malcolm J.C. 'Pentecostalism among the Bandjalang'. In *Aborigines Now* (ed. Marie Reay). Sydney, 1964.
——. 'Race Relations on the North Coast of New South Wales'. *Oceania*, vol. 27, no. 3, March 1957.
CASE, Fred and Lynn CLARK. 'Property and Race'. In *Race and Property* (ed. John H. Denton). Berkeley, California, 1964.
CLARKE, Edith. *My Mother who Fathered Me*. London, 1957.

DENTON, John H. (ed.). *Race and Property*. Berkeley, California, 1964.
DEUTSCH, M. and M.C.E. COLLINS. *Inter-racial Housing: a Psychological Evaluation of a Social Experiment*. Minnesota, 1951.

ELKIN, A.P. 'Civilised Aborigines and Native Culture'. *Oceania*, vol. 6, no. 2, December 1935.
——. 'Reaction and Interaction: A food gathering people and European settlement in Australia'. *American Anthropologist*, vol. 53, no. 2, April-June 1951.

FINK, Ruth. 'The Caste Barrier—An Obstacle to the Assimilation of Part-Aborigines in the North-West of New South Wales'. *Oceania*, vol. 28, no. 2, December 1957.

GALE, Fay. *A Study of Assimilation: Part-Aborigines in South Australia*. Adelaide, 1964.
GOFFMAN, Erving. *Asylums. Essays on the Social Situation of Mental Patients and Other Inmates*. New York, 1961.
GOLDIE, Anne. 'Harmony in Black and White—There's No Colour Bar in Bourke'. *Woman's Day*. 12 April 1965.
GRIFFIN, John Howard. *Black Like Me*. London, 1962.

HANKS, L.M. and J.R. HANKS. *Tribe under Trust: a Study of the Blackfoot Reserve of Alberta*. Toronto, 1950.
HARRIS, W.K. *Outback in Australia or Three Australian Overlanders*. Letch City, 1913.
HASLUCK, P.M.C. *Black Australians: A Survey of Native Policy in Western Australia 1829-1897*. 2nd ed., Melbourne, 1970.
——. *Native Welfare in Australia; Speeches and Addresses by the Hon. Paul Hasluck M.P.* Perth, 1953.

INGLIS, Judy. 'One Hundred Years at Point McLeay, South Australia'. *Mankind*, vol. 5, no. 2, 1962.
——. 'Aborigines in Adelaide'. *Journal of the Polynesian Society*, vol. 70, no. 2, June 1961.

JONES, F. Lancaster. *The Structure and Growth of Australia's Aboriginal Population*. Canberra, 1970.

LESSER, Alexander. 'Education and the Future of Tribalism in the United States: The case of the American Indian'. *Social Science Review*, vol. 35, no. 2, June 1961.
LONG, J.P.M. *Aboriginal Settlements: A survey of institutional communities in eastern Australia*. Canberra, 1970.

McLEAN, Charles. *Report on the Operation of the Aborigines Act 1928 and the Regulations and Orders Made Thereunder*. Melbourne, 1957.
MEAD, Margaret. *The Changing Culture of an Indian Tribe*. New York, 1932.
MEREDITH, Heather. 'Tasmanian Racial Problem—Cape Barren Island'. *Honi Soit*, University of Sydney, 23 June 1964.
MYRDAL, Gunnar. *An American Dilemma*. New York, 1962.

QUILPER, Leo. 'Sociological Aspects of Housing Discrimination'. In John H. Denton (ed.) *Race and Property*. Berkeley, California, 1964.

REAY, Marie (ed.). *Aborigines Now: New perspectives in the study of Aboriginal communities.* Sydney, 1964.
——. 'Behavioural Responses to Discrimination. A Supplementary Note.' *Oceania,* vol. 28, no. 2, December 1957.
——. 'A Half-Caste Aboriginal Community in North Western New South Wales'. *Oceania,* vol. 15, no. 4, June 1945.
——. 'Native Thought in Rural New South Wales'. *Oceania,* vol. 20, no. 2, December 1949.
——, and Grace SITLINGTON. 'Class and Status in a Mixed-blood Community (Moree, New South Wales)'. *Oceania,* vol. 18, no. 3, March 1948.
ROWLEY, C.D. 'Aborigines and Other Australians'. *Oceania,* vol. 32, no. 4, June 1962.
——. *The Destruction of Aboriginal Society. (Aboriginal Policy and Practice,* Vol. I). Canberra, 1970.

SIMPSON, George E. and J. Milton YINGER. *Racial and Cultural Minorities: An Analysis of Prejudice and Discrimination.* New York, 1965.

TATZ, C.M. 'Queensland's Aborigines: Natural Justice and the Rule of Law'. *Australian Quarterly,* vol. 5, no. 3, September-December 1963.
TINDALE, Norman B. 'Growth of a People: Formation and development of a hybrid Aboriginal and white stock on the islands of Bass Strait, Tasmania, 1915-1949'. *Records of the Queen Victoria Museum, Launceston,* (N.S.) no. 2, 1 June 1953.
——. 'Survey of the Half-caste Problem in South Australia'. *Proceedings of the Royal Geographical Society of Australasia, South Australia,* vol. XLII, November 1941.

WELLS, Fred. 'Taste of a Bitter Utopia'. *Sydney Morning Herald,* 24 February 1966.

## III. NEWSPAPERS

*A.B.C. Weekly.* Sydney.
*Advertiser.* Adelaide.
*Age.* Melbourne.
*Argus.* Melbourne.
*Australian Women's Weekly.* Sydney.
*Barrier Daily Truth.* Broken Hill.
*Canberra Times.* Canberra.
*Courier-Mail.* Brisbane.
*Daily Mirror.* Sydney.
*Daily News.* Perth.
*Daily Telegraph.* Sydney.
*Examiner.* Launceston.
*Herald.* Melbourne.
*Illawarra Daily Mercury.* Wollongong.
*Labor Daily.* Sydney.

*News.* Adelaide.
*Northern Advertiser,* Moonee Ponds, Vic.
*Our Aim.* Aborigines Inland Mission, West Maitland.
*Smith's Weekly.* Sydney.
*Smoke Signals.* Journal of the Federal Council for the Advancement of Aborigines and Torres Strait Islanders, Ivanhoe.
*Sun.* Sydney.
*Sunday Mail.* Adelaide.
*Sunday Mail.* Brisbane.
*Sun-News Pictorial.* Melbourne.
*Sunday Telegraph.* Sydney.
*Sunday Times.* Perth.
*Sydney Morning Herald.* Sydney.
*Telegraph.* Brisbane.
*Weekend Mail (T.V.).* Perth.
*Wellington Times.* Wellington.
*West Australian.* Perth.
*Yass Tribune Courier.* Yass.

## IV. UNPUBLISHED MATERIAL

BARWICK, Diane. A Little More Than Kin: Regional affinity and group identity among Aboriginal migrants in Melbourne (Ph.D. thesis, Australian National University, 1963 and later versions 1964, 1965.).
——. Rebellion at Coranderrk (unpublished seminar paper, Department of Anthropology and Sociology, Australian National University, 1967).
BEASLEY, Pamela. The Aboriginal Household in Sydney. SSRC-AP.
——. Draft Preliminary Report on Redfern-Chippendale Area of Sydney, Seminar paper SSRC-AP, February 1964.
BECKETT, Jeremy. A Study of a Mixed-Blood Aboriginal Minority in the Pastoral West of New South Wales (M.A. thesis, Australian National University, 1958).
——. Politics in the Torres Strait Islands (Ph.D. thesis, Australian National University, 1963).
BISKUP, Peter. Native Administration and Welfare in Western Australia 1897-1954 (M.A. thesis, University of Western Australia, 1965).

CALLEY, M.J.C. Bandjalang Social Organisation (Ph.D. thesis, University of Sydney, 1959).

ELLIS, Catherine J. The History of Music is the History of Mankind. SSRC-AP.

FARRELL, K. Some Problems of Aboriginal Employment in Relation to Education (unpublished seminar paper, Centre for Research into Aboriginal Affairs, Monash University, August 1967).

FINK, Ruth. The Changing Status and Cultural Identity of Western Australian Aborigines. A Field Study of Aborigines in the Murchison District, Western Australia, 1955-1957 (Ph.D. thesis, Columbia University, 1960).

——. Social Stratification—a Sequel to the Assimilation Process in a Part-Aboriginal Community (M.A. thesis, University of Sydney, 1955).

HAUSFELD, R.G. Aspects of Aboriginal Station Management (M.A. thesis, University of Sydney, 1960).

HERCUS, L.A. Notes on People of Aboriginal Descent living at Balranald, N.S.W., and at Dareton (Coomealla), N.S.W. SSRC-AP.

IREDALE, Robyn R. The Enigma of Assimilation: The position of the part-Aboriginal in New South Wales (B.A. (hons.) thesis, University of Sydney, 1965).

JONES, F. Lancaster. Some Notes on the Demography of Australia's Aboriginal Population, with an Estimate of Population Growth to 1981. SSRC-AP.

LONG, J.P.M. Report on Supervised Aboriginal Communities in Eastern Australia. SSRC-AP.

MACARTHUR, A.J. and B.J. RYAN. A Comparative Survey of the Living Standard of Coloured and White Families in the Greater Brisbane Area (1961). SSRC-AP.

MAKIN, C. A Socio-Cultural Anthropological Survey of People of Aboriginal Descent in the Metropolitan Area of Perth. SSRC-AP.

SHINOFF, Paul and RODGERS, Burt. Selected attitudes of Murrin Bridge Aborigines.

WAGSTAFFE, P., J. GIBSON, and J. MANNING. Report on a Visit to Cape Barren Island, February 1966. SSRC-AP.

WILSON, John. Authority and Leadership in a 'New-style' Australian Aboriginal Community: Pindan, Western Australia (M.A. thesis, University of Western Australia, 1961).

——. Coonaradale (B.A. (hons.) thesis, University of Western Australia, 1958).

## INDEX

Aboriginal, definition, vii, 3-5, 44, 45, 46, 47, 157, 189, 192, 193, 207, 352, 355, 390, 392, 393, 397, 441

Aboriginal administration (general), vii, x, 4, 6, 24, 33, 34, 35, 41, 62, 134, 142, 149, 169, 181, 187, 233, 382-415, 435-7, 442-6; Aboriginal affairs departments, 8; Aboriginal Welfare Conference of Commonwealth and State Authorities 1937, 16, 18, 21, 25-9, 31, 35, 47, 72, 73-4, 89, 118, 383, 389-91 *passim*; (1947), 391; (1948), 270, 389-91; (1951), 89, 394-8, 402; (1961), 398-401; (1963), 402; (1965), 402-3; (1967), 402; 'colonial', 59, 64, 113, 116; cross-cultural, 14, 125, *see also* Absorption policy, Assimilation policy, Commonwealth Government, Governments, Institutionalisation, Legislation (Aboriginal)

Aboriginal administration (by States and Territories), 29, 322; A.C.T., 435-7; N.S.W., ix-x, 9-10, 12, 26, 32, 42, 45, 49-50, 57, 66-85, 117, 165, 198, 200, 203, 392, 406-7, 414; N.T., 14-15, 37, 83, 117, 394, 398, 406, 414; Qld, ix, 13, 15, 16, 22, 25, 28, 32, 42, 50, 54-6, 107-30, 371, 392-3, 406, 414, 444; S.A., 17-18, 26, 33, 42-3, 46, 47, 50, 55, 90-3, 265-6, 306, 316, 358, 374, 392, 409-14, 421, 434-5; Tas., viii, 36, 392; Vic., 5-6, 12-13, 20-1, 25, 43-5, 85-90, 407-8; W.A., 4, 6, 7, 23-5, 27, 32-3, 41, 46, 49, 50, 55-7, 93-106, 374-8, 392-3, 408-14

Aboriginal Advancement League (S.A.), 373

Aboriginal Affairs Act 1962 (S.A.), 46, 60n., 93, 409, 410

Aboriginal Affairs Act Amendment Act 1966-1967 (S.A.), 93n., 410

Aboriginal Affairs Board (S.A.), 410

Aboriginal Lands Trust (S.A.), 62, 93, 146, 413, 425, 434

Aboriginal Lands Trust Act 1966 (S.A.), 93n., 96, 410

Aboriginal Protection (Amendment) Act 1936 (N.S.W.), 45, 49, 56n., 58, 59n., 66, 67

Aboriginal Reserve Councils (S.A.), 410

Aboriginals Preservation and Protection Act 1939 (Qld), 22n., 39n., 47, 48n., 50, 55n., 56n., 108n., 110n., 113, 116n., 122n.; (1946), 108n., 124n.

Aboriginals Protection and Restriction of the Sale of Opium Act 1897 to 1934 (Qld), 13, 14, 21, 22, 42, 45

Aboriginals Regulations 1945 (Qld), 110n., 111n., 114, 116, 119, 123

Aborigines Act 1911 (S.A.), 18, 46, 55, 58, 90, 91

Aborigines Act 1934-1939 (S.A.), 18, 47, 50, 55, 56n., 58-9

Aborigines Act 1928 (Vic.), 43, 44, 85

Aborigines Act 1957 (Vic.), 88n.

Aborigines Act 1905 (W.A.), 6, 22-3, 46, 47, 50, 55n., 94, 95

Aborigines Act Amendment Act 1936 (W.A.), 23, 25, 27, 42, 46n., 48, 50, 55n., 56n., 59n.

Aborigines Advancement League (Vic.), 170-2

Aborigines' and Torres Strait Islanders' Affairs Act 1965 (Qld), 25, 43, 46, 50, 56n., 108, 109n., 114, 121, 122n., 358

Aborigines' and Torres Strait Islanders' Regulations 1966 (Qld), 54, 121-3, 125, 358

Aborigines Assimilation Organisation (Griffith), 142-4, 147, 148

Aborigines Department (W.A.), 6

*Designed by Philippa Walker*

*Text set in 11 pt Monotype Bembo, one point leaded
and printed on 85 gsm English Finish paper
at The Griffin Press, Adelaide, South Australia*

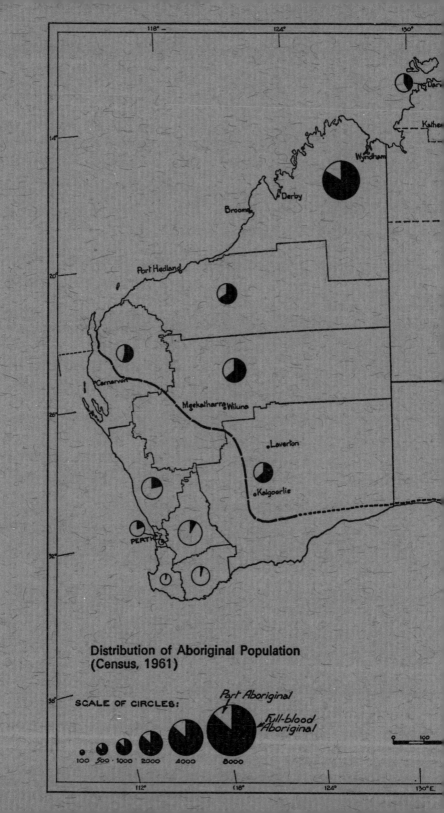

**Distribution of Aboriginal Population
(Census, 1961)**

SCALE OF CIRCLES:

*Part Aboriginal*

*Full-blood Aboriginal*

100   500  1000  2000   4000   8000